Big History

Big History

BETWEEN NOTHING AND EVERYTHING

David Christian
Macquarie University

Cynthia Stokes Brown
Dominican University of California

Craig Benjamin
Grand Valley State University

Mc
Graw
Hill
Education

BIG HISTORY: BETWEEN NOTHING AND EVERYTHING
Published by McGraw-Hill Education, 2 Penn Plaza, New York, NY 10121. Copyright © 2014 by
McGraw-Hill Education. All rights reserved. Printed in the United States of America. No part of this
publication may be reproduced or distributed in any form or by any means, or stored in a database or
retrieval system, without the prior written consent of McGraw-Hill Education, including, but not limited
to, in any network or other electronic storage or transmission, or broadcast for distance learning.

Some ancillaries, including electronic and print components, may not be available to customers outside
the United States.

This book is printed on acid-free paper.

2 3 4 5 6 7 8 9 0 DOW/DOW 1 0 9 8 7 6 5 4

ISBN   978-0-07-338561-7
MHID   0-07-338561-1

Senior Vice President, Products & Markets: Brand Coordinator: *Kaelyn Schulz*
  Kurt L. Strand   Marketing Specialist: *Alexandra Schultz*
Vice President, General Manager, Products &   Director, Content Production: *Terri Schiesl*
  Markets: *Michael J. Ryan*   Content Project Manager: *Jean R. Starr*
Vice President, Content Production & Technology   Buyer: *Nichole Birkenholz*
  Services: *Kimberly Meriwether David*   Design: *Lisa King*
Managing Director: *Gina Boedeker*   Cover Image: © *Stéphane Guisard/UNAM/INAH*
Director: *Matt Busbridge*   Content Licensing Specialist: *Shawntel Schmitt*
Director of Development: *Rhona Robbin*   Typeface: *10/12 Times LT Std*
Managing Development Editor: *Nancy Crochiere*   Compositor: *MPS Limited*
Freelance Development Editor: *Art Pomponio*   Printer: *R. R. Donnelley*

All credits appearing on page or at the end of the book are considered to be an extension of the
copyright page.

Library of Congress Cataloging-in-Publication Data
Christian, David, 1946- author.
  Big history : between nothing and everything / David Christian, Macquarie University, Cynthia
Stokes Brown, Dominican University of California, Craig Benjamin, Grand Valley State University.
      pages cm
  Includes bibliographical references and index.
  ISBN-13: 978-0-07-338561-7 (alk. paper)
  ISBN-10: 0-07-338561-1 (alk. paper)
  1. Civilization—Philosophy. 2. Cosmology. 3. Human evolution. 4. Biocomplexity. 5. World history.
  I. Brown, Cynthia Stokes, author. II. Benjamin, Craig, author. III. Title.
CB19.C476 2014
909—dc23
                                        2013013609

The Internet addresses listed in the text were accurate at the time of publication. The inclusion of a
website does not indicate an endorsement by the authors or McGraw-Hill Education, and McGraw-Hill
Education does not guarantee the accuracy of the information presented at these sites.

www.mhhe.com

About the cover photo: Orion over the Mayan Temple of Kukulkan
In this photo, Orion is rising over the Temple of Kukulkan, the feathered serpent god. The temple is the
central pyramid at Chichén Itzá, one of the great Mayan centers on the Yucatan Peninsula. Also known by
the Spanish name, El Castillo, the temple stands 33 yards (30 meters) tall and 60 yards (55 meters) wide
at the base. Built about 1000 CE, the structure is aligned so that at the equinoxes the light of the setting
sun casts triangular, undulating shadows down the sides, ending at the sculpted heads of serpents at the
base. The constellation currently called Orion the Hunter represented a turtle to the Maya.

Dedication

Big History describes human history as part of a much larger story that embraces the history of the entire universe; and it tells this grand story through a series of thresholds of increasing complexity. But *Big History* is about the future as well as the past, because it provides a wonderful framework for asking where it is all going. What can we say about the future of humanity, of the Earth, and of the universe as a whole? With this in mind, the authors would like to dedicate this book to our students and their entire generation throughout the world. It is they who will have to deal with the unprecedented global challenges we face in the Anthropocene epoch, and with the daunting, but also exciting, prospect that we may be on the verge of a new threshold. We hope that the broad, transdisciplinary perspectives of big history will prepare our students well for these challenges. We are optimists because we are teachers. As we work with our students every day to try to understand the past and the present, we feel reassured that, however great the challenges, the future is in very good hands.

Brief Contents

Contents

the first three thresholds — chapter 1

The Universe, Stars, and New Chemical Elements   11

the fourth threshold — chapter 2

The Emergence of the Sun, the Solar System, and the Earth   33

Preface

Big History: Between Nothing and Everything is the first textbook in the new interdisciplinary field called *big history.*

Big history surveys the past not just of humanity, or even of planet Earth, but of the entire universe. In reading this book, instructors and students will retrace a voyage that began 13.8 billion years ago with the big bang and the appearance of the universe. Big history incorporates findings from cosmology, Earth and life sciences, and human history, and assembles them into a single, universal historical narrative of our universe and of our place within it.

All societies have constructed universal stories that helped people understand their place in space and time. Only very recently, however, have scientists and scholars throughout the world begun to piece together a universal story that is based on scientific evidence. Some of the bits and pieces of that story—the idea, for example, that the Earth might be many millions of years old, or that modern life-forms might have evolved from earlier life-forms—were already familiar in the nineteenth century. But most of the story's details have been assembled only within the last hundred years. Those of us lucky enough to be alive today belong to the first generation able to understand scientifically how everything came to be as it is.

Goals of the Textbook

As students become more familiar with this story, they will start to see how all of its different pieces fit together. They will learn how atoms form the cells that make up our bodies, how atoms themselves were formed either in the big bang or in the interiors of exploding stars, how our Earth was assembled from chunks of orbiting ice and dust, and how life itself first appeared on Earth and then spread and diversified over the entire planet. They will also learn how humans first appeared on the Earth 200,000 years ago, and why we seem to be both so similar to and so different from all the other living organisms with which we share this beautiful planet. Finally, we will ask about the future: Where is the story going? What is the likely fate of humanity and of our Earth? And what will be the ultimate fate of our universe?

The features we have included in this textbook serve to enhance students' critical thinking skills to help them see and assess the many links that hold the historical narrative together.

Features of This First Edition

In addition to an engaging writing style, *Big History: Between Nothing and Everything* presents a number of features that bring the story of big history to life and that help students learn this exciting story. These include:

Introduction The book begins with a chapter-length presentation that defines big history, outlines the concepts of *complexity* and *emergence,* and presents the eight major *thresholds* of big history.

Seeing the Big Picture Asking questions is the best preparation for reading new material. Each chapter opens with several questions to pique readers' curiosity and to provoke them into thinking on the large scales of big history. Examples from Chapter 6 include:

- What is a city? What is a state? What is an agrarian civilization?
- What did people learn to increase agricultural production for themselves?
- What technological changes laid the foundation for the emergence of cities?

Chapter Questions

Just as each chapter begins with a set of questions to inspire reading, each ends with a set of questions to help students integrate and assess what they have read and learned:

- Why did people begin to congregate in cities?
- Where did the first cities appear around the world? How can you explain why they appeared where they did?
- Describe the differences in the evolution of cities and states in the four different world zones.
- Describe the kinds of evidence used to reconstruct early civilizations.
- This chapter focuses on similarities in Early Agrarian civilizations; what were some of the differences?

- What role did religion play in the emergence of cities and states?

Threshold Summaries To tell 13.8 billion years of history, the authors have identified eight major breakthroughs when something entirely new emerged. They call these breakthroughs *thresholds*. Each time the story reaches a new threshold, a summary box appears to provide a quick visual survey of the major components of that threshold. Here are examples from Chapters 1 and 11.

Threshold 1 Summary

THRESHOLD	INGREDIENTS ▶	STRUCTURE ▶	GOLDILOCKS CONDITIONS =	EMERGENT PROPERTIES
BIG BANG: ORIGIN OF UNIVERSE	Energy, matter, space, time (everything in our universe!).	Energy and matter within a rapidly expanding space–time continuum.	Uncertain: Possibly quantum fluctuations within the multiverse.	Potential to create everything around us.

Threshold 8 Summary

THRESHOLD	INGREDIENTS ▶	STRUCTURE ▶	GOLDILOCKS CONDITIONS =	EMERGENT PROPERTIES
MODERN WORLD/ ANTHROPOCENE	Globalization; rapid acceleration in Collective Learning; innovation; use of fossil fuels.	Globally connected human communities with rapidly accelerating capacity to manipulate the biosphere.	Acceleration in Collective Learning at global scales.	Vast increase in human use of resources → entirely new lifeways, social relationships → first single species in the history of Earth capable of transforming the biosphere.

Maps, Photographs, and Line Art

These visuals have been carefully chosen to illuminate the text and to imprint its meaning unforgettably.

Key Terms and Glossary

Highlighted in bold type, key terms are ideas, people, or places that readers will want to remember. The key terms are listed at the end of each chapter for easy studying. They are collected at the end of the book for ease in finding definitions when the terms show up in later chapters.

Additional Resources

Big history is growing rapidly so the number of relevant websites will undoubtedly grow. Meanwhile, here are three of the most important sites for students of big history:

- International Big History Association (IBHA) **http://ibhanet.org/**
- Big History Project (BHP) **www.bighistoryproject.com/Home**
- ChronoZoom (a big history timeline) **www.chronozoomproject.org/**

Acknowledgments

Many people have helped us write *Big History: Between Nothing and Everything*, and we would like to thank them. First of all, we extend a general thanks to all the many friends and colleagues who have discussed big history with us over the years. They include partners, friends, and colleagues from many different disciplines, but particularly from the large community of world historians and the rapidly growing community of big historians.

William McNeill, one of the great pioneers of world history, has been extraordinarily supportive of the idea of big history, seeing it (as we do) as a natural extension of many of the goals of world history. One friend we particularly want to thank by name is the late Jerry Bentley, founder and editor of the *Journal of World History*. Jerry was another one of the great pioneers of world history. He was extraordinarily generous with his ideas and his support, and was a great supporter of the idea of big history. Indeed, he commissioned one of the earliest articles on big history for his journal. We will all miss Jerry very much.

We have been very lucky with our editors at McGraw-Hill. Jon-David Hague, our initial editor, had enough faith in the idea of big history to commission this, the first text in the field, and his successor, Matthew Busbridge, has seen it through to completion with the efficient editorial support of Arthur Pomponio and Nancy Crochiere, Jean Starr (content project manager), Sharon O'Donnell (copyeditor), and Chet Gottfried (proofreader). Our thanks to all of our editors for their support and advice throughout the long and often complex process of producing a textbook.

In 2010, a preliminary version of our text was made available for use by teachers and students at Dominican University of California and Grand Valley State University. We would like to thank all involved in the trials for the extremely valuable feedback we received, which has shaped the final version of the text in many ways.

We owe special thanks to the instructors who formally reviewed earlier versions of our text (although we are ultimately responsible for accuracy). Hats off to:

Hope Benne, Salem State University

Todd Duncan, Portland State University

Kevin Fernlund, University of Missouri in St. Louis

Ursula Goodenough, Washington University in St. Louis

John Mears, Southern Methodist University

Alexander Mirkovic, Arkansas Tech University

Joel Primack, University of California, Santa Cruz

David Christian would like to thank Macquarie University for its generous support of big history over many years and specifically for supporting trips to the founding meeting of the International Big History Association in 2010 and to its first conference in 2012. He would also like to thank colleagues, friends, and students at San Diego State University, where he taught big history from 2002 to 2008, for their support in this new intellectual enterprise. Our thanks, too, to Bill Gates, who has been an enthusiastic and generous supporter of big history; he is supporting the construction of a free online course for high schools students and the general public through the Big History Project (**www.bighistoryproject.com/Home**). Students, both at Macquarie and San Diego State University, have played a much more important role in the evolution of big history than they may have realized, for they always raised the important questions and helped ensure that big history never got lost in the details. He would also like to thank Chardi, Joshua, and Emily for their patience as he buried himself away, once more, to work on one more book. Finally, he wants to thank his first teacher and inspirer, his mother, Carol, who taught him in Nigeria. The excitement of those very early lessons has never quite left him. Working with Cynthia Brown and Craig Benjamin has been pure delight; may all co-authors have such smart, supportive, and congenial colleagues!

Cynthia Stokes Brown would like to thank the students, administration, and highly creative faculty of Dominican University of California, especially Jim Cunningham and Phil Novak, who pioneered teaching big history with her; Dominican president, Mary Marcy, who has fully embraced big history; and, most of all, the director of the Big History Program at the university, Mojgan Behmand, who has led an amazing and effective collaboration. In addition, she is grateful to Russ and Cheryl Genet for organizing the Epic of Evolution conference in January 2008, where the three authors were able to discuss their first three chapters in person and meet many other big historians, and to her colleagues in the International Big History Association. Ursula Goodenough, Katherine Berry, and Larry Gonick offered special assistance. Finally, Cynthia wants to thank Jack Robbins and their large family for their constant support.

Craig Benjamin would like to thank the students, faculty, and administration of Grand Valley State University in Michigan for their generous support of big history over the past 10 years, particularly the president and provost of the university and the dean of the Brooks College of Interdisciplinary Studies for their encouragement and enthusiasm for the field, and for agreeing to house the Global Institute for Big History, the headquarters of the International Big History Association, within the Brooks College. He would also like to thank his children Zoe and Asher (both of whom coincidentally studied big history at Macquarie University in the 1990s); and his wife Pamela for her patience and unwavering support, and for her many contributions to the field through her role as chair of the IBHA Advisory Council. Craig would also like to thank his co-authors Cynthia and David for being not only such dynamic colleagues but also dear and close friends.

An Author Team That Sees the Big Picture

The three authors of *Big History: Between Nothing and Everything* are pioneers in the field of big history. David Christian, one of the founders of the discipline, coined the term *big history* to describe a course he created in 1989 in Sydney, Australia. Cynthia Brown learned of Christian's work and in 1993 began to offer such a course at the Dominican University of California. Craig Benjamin learned his big history from Christian by serving as his teaching assistant. Today, big history is taught in universities across the United States and around the world.

The authors are keen to encourage a critical reading of this book that questions its assumptions and notes its limitations. The brief biographies that follow will help the reader appreciate the particular types of expertise that each brings to this project.

DAVID CHRISTIAN (DPhil, Oxford University) is by training a historian of Russia and the Soviet Union. He has spent most of his career at Macquarie University in Sydney, Australia, apart from an eight-year period teaching at San Diego State University from 2001 to 2008. Christian has published histories of modern Russia and also a study of the role of the trade in vodka in nineteenth-century Russia. In 1998, he published *A History of Russia, Central Asia and Mongolia,* the first volume in the Blackwell History of the World Series. He began teaching courses on big history in 1989 at Macquarie University. He first used the phrase *big history* for such courses in an article published in the *Journal of World History* in 1991 titled "The Case for 'Big History.'" Additional publications include *Maps of Time: An Introduction to Big History* (2004) and *This Fleeting World: A Short History of Humanity* (2007). In the same year (2007), he recorded 48 lectures on big history for the Teaching Company. In 2010, with Bill Gates, he founded the "Big History Project," which is building a free online high school course in big history due for release in late 2013. Christian is a member of the Australian Academy of Humanities and the Royal Holland Society of Sciences and Humanities. He is the founding president of the International Big History Association.

CYNTHIA STOKES BROWN (PhD, Johns Hopkins University) spent most of her career directing the secondary teaching credential program at Dominican University of California. She taught selected courses in the history department and wrote books about civil rights history and teachers, including *Alexander Meiklejohn: Teacher of Freedom* (1981); *Ready from Within: Septima Clark and the Civil Rights Movement* (1986); *Connecting with the Past: History Workshop in Middle and High School* (1994); and *Refusing Racism: White Allies and the Struggle for Civil Rights* (2001). Brown's book *Big History: From the Big Bang to the Present* was published in 2007. Since then her interests have been consulting with the big history program at Dominican, serving on the board of the International Big History Association since its inception, and writing big history essays for high school students through the Big History Project funded by Bill Gates.

CRAIG BENJAMIN (PhD, Macquarie University) is an associate professor of history in the Meijer Honors College at Grand Valley State University in Michigan. Like both his co-authors, Benjamin is a frequent presenter of lectures at conferences worldwide, and the author of numerous publications including books, chapters, and essays on ancient Central Asian history, big history, and world history. In addition, Benjamin has recorded lectures for the History Channel, The Teaching Company, and the Big History Project. He is currently a member of both the Advanced Placement and SAT World History Test Development Committees, vice president (president elect) of the World History Association, and has been treasurer of the International Big History Association since its inception in January 2011.

What Is Big History and How Do We Study It?

Seeing the Big Picture

▶ Is it possible to tell a story about the whole of the past?

▶ Why is it important to try to understand the history of everything?

▶ Why are origin stories important in all societies?

▶ What is different about today's modern "origin story"?

▶ What is complexity and why does today's universe seem to be more complex than the universe at the moment of its appearance, 13.8 billion years ago?

▶ How would you place yourself within the big story told in this book?

"For, in fact, what is man in nature? A Nothing in comparison with the Infinite, an All in comparison with the Nothing, a mean between nothing and everything. Since he is infinitely removed from contemplating the extremes, the end of things and their beginnings are hopelessly hidden from him in an impenetrable secret; he is equally incapable of seeing the Nothing from which he was made, and the Infinite in which he is swallowed up."[1]

—BLAISE PASCAL

Seeing the Whole of the Past

In this book, we will introduce you to a new vision of the past that has been constructed very recently by scholars from many different scientific disciplines, ranging from history to geology, from biology to cosmology. Today, we can map out much more of the past than ever before, and we can do so with astonishing precision. So this is a revolutionary time for historical studies of all kinds.

These changes in our understanding of the past have occurred largely since the middle of the twentieth century, and partly as a result of what we will call the *chronometric revolution*.

History before the Chronometric Revolution

At the center of the chronometric revolution was a series of new techniques for dating past events.

Methods of dating past events are fundamental to our understanding of the past. In fact, you cannot really have "history" without dates. If we knew what had happened in the past but not the order in which it had happened, or when it happened, our idea of the past would be just a jumble of facts with no meaning, no depth, and no real shape. Dates help us make sense of the past because they allow us to "map" the past chronologically, to see its shape in time. And mapping our world like this can give us a powerful sense of meaning. However, until just a few decades ago, our ability to map the past was extremely limited. We could give absolute dates only to a tiny part of the past, to those parts that human beings could either remember, or those that happened to be mentioned in written records.

Before the middle of the twentieth century, written documents provided by far the most important and reliable way of dating past events. As a result, history came to mean something like "the past as seen through the evidence of written documents."

Unfortunately, though they provided us with many reliable dates, written documents also limited our understanding of the past to that tiny portion of the past that they happened to illuminate. As a result, "history" came to mean only "human history." Even worse, in practice history came to mean the history of the wealthy and powerful because those were the groups that could produce written documents (or pay scribes to produce them). The result was that, until the spread of mass literacy in recent centuries, history was mainly about kings and aristocrats, the wars they fought, the literature they wrote, and the gods they worshiped. Most of the past remained in darkness and most human beings left no record of their existence, their thoughts, and their lifeways. We could not discuss societies without writing, unless someone who could write (someone like the Greek historian Herodotus or the Chinese historian Sima Qian) happened to say something about them. Even then, what literate societies thought and said about their illiterate neighbors was often extremely distorted. We could say even less about eras before the invention of writing. And this is rather important, as we now know that these eras include at least 95 percent of the time that human beings have been on Earth. Finally, history excluded everything before humans appeared, though geologists, since the eighteenth century, were beginning to get a sense of the rough order in which geological events had occurred. All in all, the reliance of historians on written documents meant that history was mostly about those tiny groups of humans who could write. Not surprisingly, history came to mean, in practice, the history of governments, wars, religions, and nobles.

History after the Chronometric Revolution

In the middle of the twentieth century our understanding of the past was transformed by the appearance of new ways of dating past events. These made it possible to assign absolute dates to events not mentioned in any documents, events reaching back to the origin of life on Earth and even to the very origin of the universe.

The most important of these new techniques were based on *radiometric dating*. Radiometric dating techniques depend on the fact that radioactive materials break down at a very regular pace to form new *daughter* materials. This means that if you have a lump of material containing some radioactive material (such as uranium), and you can measure how many of the daughter materials have been formed (such as lead), you can estimate when the lump was formed.

Although the possibilities of using radioactive materials in this way were appreciated in the first decade of the twentieth century, radiometric dating techniques were not reliable or cheap enough to be widely used before the 1950s. The first radiometric technique to be used widely is known as carbon-14 dating because it was based on the breakdown of a particular form (or *isotope*) of carbon. (**Isotopes** are atoms of the same element that have different numbers of neutrons in their core, so they also have slightly different atomic weights.) Carbon-14 dating was developed by Willard F. Libby in the early 1950s. Libby had worked on the manufacture of nuclear weapons, which also required the ability to separate out and measure different isotopes of a particular element (uranium, in the case of nuclear weapons). Carbon-14 dating revolutionized archaeology by making it possible to date materials containing carbon (which includes most remains of living organisms) as far back as about 50,000 years. This was already 10 times further back in time than the oldest dates based on written evidence. Soon many other radiometric techniques were developed that extended our chronologies even further back in time. These used radioactive materials such as uranium that broke down much more slowly, making it possible to date materials that had formed millions or even billions of years ago. The age of the Earth itself was determined by Clair Paterson in 1953, by measuring the breakdown of uranium to lead in meteorites.

Other, nonradiometric dating techniques were also developed. One of the most important was *genetic* dating. After the discovery of how the genetic code works in 1953, it became possible to compare differences between the DNA of different species. (DNA is a molecule, present in all living cells, that contains the genetic information used to form and maintain the cell and pass that information to offspring cells. For more details see Chapter 3.) In 1967, Vincent Sarich and Alan Wilson pointed out that much DNA changed quite regularly over long periods of time. This meant that such changes could also be used as a type of clock. By comparing the DNA of two related species you could tell approximately when they had shared a common ancestor. Genetic dating has transformed our understanding of the evolution of our own and many other species. For example, genetic dating showed that chimps and humans had shared a common ancestor about 7 million years ago, a finding that revolutionized the study of human evolution. Meanwhile, astronomers and cosmologists developed new techniques for estimating the age of stars and, eventually, of the universe as a whole. For example, using data from the European Space Agency's Planck satellite, launched in 2009 to study the cosmic background radiation, astronomers have come up with a more precise origin date for the universe! It began 13,820,000,000 years ago; in the text we round this to 13.8 billion years.

These changes in our ability to date past events have transformed our understanding of the past. When H. G. Wells tried to write a "universal" history in 1919, he admitted that he could give no real dates for any events before the first Olympiad (776 BCE). Now, we can give reasonable dates for events reaching back to the very origin of our universe. Suddenly, for the first time in human history, we can construct a history of the whole of the past on the basis of solid, scientific evidence.

The Natural Sciences Join History in Studying the Past

Associated with the chronometric revolution were a series of scientific breakthroughs that made science itself more interested in the past. In the twentieth century, cosmology, geology, and biology all became historical disciplines.

Before the late eighteenth century, it was widely believed that the natural world had changed little since its creation. Astronomers assumed that the stars and galaxies were much as they had always been. Geologists assumed that, even if landscapes had changed in minor ways, the Earth as a whole had changed little. Most biologists—including Carl Linnaeus (1707–78), the founder of modern systems for classifying living species—assumed that today's living species were the same as those that had flourished when the Earth was first created.

As early as the late seventeenth century, however, doubts began to appear within geology and biology, largely because of increasing interest in fossils. Fossils of organisms such as trilobites that no longer existed suggested that the mix of species had changed over time. The discovery of fossils of marine organisms high up in mountain ranges such as the Alps also suggested that landscapes had changed quite dramatically over time. It became clear that in some sense both the Earth and the natural world had "histories." Yet without precise dates, it was impossible to reconstruct those histories with any precision. The result was that "history" continued to mean "human history," and "science" continued to be thought of as the study of those aspects of the world that did not change significantly over time.

In the nineteenth and early twentieth centuries, geologists, astronomers, and biologists began to appreciate that the past was very different from the present and that one of their central challenges was to explain how the world had become as it is today. Astronomy, geology, and biology all became historical disciplines. The chronometric revolution allowed the creation of precise timelines for the past of living organisms, of the Earth itself, and even of the universe. The discovery of the structure of DNA in 1953 (see Chapter 3) made it possible to track and explain changes in the natural world with greater precision than ever before. In geology, the new paradigm of **plate tectonics,** which emerged during the 1960s (see Chapter 2), showed that the Earth's surface had changed fundamentally over time and helped explain how and why it had changed. Finally, also in the 1960s, the discovery of the cosmic background radiation persuaded most astronomers that the universe itself had evolved over time, beginning in a huge "explosion" many billions of years ago (see Chapter 1).

Suddenly, we had to think of the past in new ways. Instead of studying only the last few thousand years of human history, we could study a past of many billions of years that included the history of the biosphere, the Earth, and the entire universe. We could start constructing the history of all of the past!

What Is Big History?

Reconstructing this past is the central challenge of "big history." **Big history** attempts to reconstruct the history of the whole of time, back to the very beginning of the universe. That is what we do in this book. We offer an account of the past from the very beginnings of time to the present day, based on the conclusions of modern scientific scholarship.

We will see that this offers a powerful way of understanding the place of our own species, *Homo sapiens,* within the universe. By doing so it helps us understand better what human history is about.

Thinking about the whole of the past is something that all human societies have tried to do. The results can be found in **origin stories** (stories about how everything was created), or in the major texts of all the great religions. As far as we know, origin stories have been told in all societies; they offer accounts of the origin of all things, of people, animals, landscapes, the Earth, stars, and the universe as a whole. And they are based on the best available knowledge in each society. So they provide a sort of road map for understanding the history of everything. These maps of the past are powerful because they help individuals understand how they fit into the whole story of the universe and of life on Earth.

Origin stories seem to have been central to education in most human societies. They were often told to younger members of society at the very beginning of their education. The result was that most people understood their own society's explanations of the origin of everything. Even the most ancient societies we know of, from Australia to France to the Americas, painted strange figures on cave walls or built sculptures that hint at the existence of origin stories.

Unfortunately, today our schools and universities no longer teach origin stories of any kind. That's one of the many reasons why big history is important: It can play the educational role that origin stories played in most earlier human societies. And, like other origin stories, big history too is based on the best knowledge available to us. Today that means knowledge derived from modern **science.** Modern science is the dominant form of knowledge in the modern world. Its roots go back to the seventeenth-century scientific revolution. Scientific knowledge is global in its reach, and is based on the rigorous use of carefully tested evidence.

So, it is helpful to think of big history as a modern, scientific origin story. It, too, offers a sort of map of the universe, within which you can find your own place. It is different from traditional origin stories, first because it is scientific. That is, it is based on the best findings of modern science. It is based on much more information than any previous origin story, and on information that has been tested with great rigor and in many different societies, so it is more reliable and precise than that available in traditional societies. Of course, that does not mean that a modern origin story will simply eclipse all other origin stories; but what we can claim for it is that it has a peculiar salience in today's globally interconnected world, transformed as it has been by modern technologies and modern science.

Big history also differs from traditional origin stories in that it is universal. Most origin stories were constructed by and for particular societies, so they tended to emphasize the differences between different human groups. Big history attempts to construct an origin story that is universal, that draws on scientific knowledge from all parts of the world, and expects to make as much sense in Delhi or Durban as in Dublin or Denver. Constructing a truly universal origin story is particularly important today, in a globalized world that faces challenges such as the threat of nuclear war or global warming, problems that cannot be solved by any community on its own, but will require the cooperation of humans across the entire world.

Yet curiously, universal histories are rarely taught in modern schools and universities. Instead, we learn different parts of the story in a disconnected way. In history courses we learn not about humanity, but about our own community; we learn the history of America, or Russia, or China, depending on where our school is. And we rarely learn how human histories are linked to the history of the natural world. We may learn a bit of chemistry, or a bit of geology, or even a bit of astronomy, but rarely are we helped to see the interconnections between these different forms of knowledge.

Now, at last, we are in a position to tell a new, scientifically based, universal history, a history that includes all human societies and places their histories within the larger histories of the Earth and the universe as a whole. As far as we know, this is the first modern text on big history. In it, we will survey what modern science can tell us about the past of the universe, of the stars, its largest single objects, of our solar system and Earth, of life on Earth, and finally, of our own species, *H. sapiens.*

The Basic Shape of the Story: Increasing Complexity

It may seem a daunting task to study the history of the whole universe. But, as we will show, it is in many ways no harder than telling the history of a huge nation such as the United States or Russia. The key is to begin with a clear sense of the overall shape of the story. Helping us is the fact that there is a single thread that runs through the whole story: the emergence, over the 13.8 billion years since the universe appeared, of more and more complex things. Complex things have many diverse components that are arranged in precise ways so that they generate new qualities. We call these new qualities **emergent properties.**

We will not pretend to describe all of the new things that emerged, or all the stages by which parts of the universe became more complex, but we will focus on some of the main stages in this process, look at some of the most interesting objects that appeared, and try to figure out how we fit into this large story.

The early universe was very simple. At its beginning, the universe was dominated by huge flows of energy in what cosmologists describe as the *radiation era.* The whole universe was a bit like the center of the sun, where the heat was too intense to allow the creation of complex chemical structures. There were no atoms, no stars, no planets, no living organisms. However, the universe cooled as it expanded, and almost 400,000 years after its origin, it was cool enough for atoms of hydrogen and helium (and a few other simple elements) to congeal out of this hot "plasma." Atoms were the first complex material structures to emerge. But even then, and for millions of years, the universe was very simple, consisting of little more than huge clouds of hydrogen and helium atoms, with lots of energy pouring through them. (There was also lots of so-called dark matter, but as that seems never to have formed complex entities we will largely ignore dark matter.)

Then, with atoms as their basic ingredients, more complex things began to appear. But they appeared only where the conditions were "just right." We call such conditions **Goldilocks conditions.** First, whole galaxies of stars appeared, perhaps from 200 million years after the universe itself appeared. Within galaxies, dying stars began to form new types of atoms, new chemical elements, such as carbon and oxygen and gold and silver, and scatter them into the space around them. Where conditions were right (not too hot, not too cold, not too empty, not too dense) the elements began to combine in complex ways to form new types of matter. Stars also poured energy into nearby space. So, while most of the universe remained very simple (and remains simple to this day), within galaxies things got more complex. As more and more chemical elements were scattered into the spaces between stars, new forms of matter—water and ice or dust and rocks—began to gather around newly formed stars, eventually forming the first planetary systems. On at least one planet (and probably on many more, though so far we have no direct evidence that this is true), chemical elements combined into more and more complex structures until eventually they formed simple living cells that could reproduce and multiply with great precision and slowly adapt to their environments, creating an increasing variety of different types of single-celled organisms. Slowly more complex cells began to evolve until, certainly by about 600 million years ago, some cells joined together to form multicelled organisms. Within the last few hundred thousand years, our own species evolved. As we will see, with human history, things got even more complex.

Before we go any further, we must look more deeply at the central idea of *complexity*. **Complexity** is the opposite of simplicity. But that's not very helpful. The difficulty is that no one is quite sure of the best way of defining what makes complex things complex. Here's a rough definition that will take us a long way.

First, complex entities contain diverse components.
Simple things such as atoms contain few elements: just one proton and one electron in the case of hydrogen. More complex things, like a molecule of DNA, may contain billions of atoms of different kinds. So, the first thing we can say is that complex things contain many diverse components.

Second, those components are arranged in very particular ways.
Take all the pieces of a modern airliner and rearrange them arbitrarily. You'll soon realize that you can't fly unless the parts are arranged in just the right way. The different parts must function as if they were part of a single team. Similarly, the atoms that make up a molecule of DNA can do nothing much unless they are arranged in a particular pattern so that the many genes making up the DNA molecule can work together. Even an atom of hydrogen is arranged in a very precise way with the proton at the center and an electron moving around it at some distance. The two particles are held together by electromagnetic forces, because the proton has a positive charge and the electron a negative charge. The atom is more complex than its unassembled constituents.

Third, complex things have new or emergent properties.
When complex things are arranged in the right patterns, in patterns that enable their parts to work together, they can do new things. New features "emerge." "Pound St. Paul's Church into atoms," said Samuel Johnson, "and consider any single atom; it is, to be sure, good for nothing: but, put all these atoms together, and you have St. Paul's Church."[2] A pile of bits and pieces of an aircraft cannot do anything interesting. But arrange them correctly and they can fly. Arrange a molecule of amoeba DNA correctly, and it provides all the information needed to assemble a living organism. (That's pretty impressive because, despite all the achievements of modern science, we still cannot do this in a research lab.) Even a hydrogen atom has new properties; for example, it is electrically neutral (because the negative and positive charges cancel each other out); and, if it crashes into another hydrogen atom at very high speeds and temperatures, it can fuse to form an atom of helium. These new features are examples of emergent properties. They often seem magical because they do not exist in the components from which a complex entity is made. They emerge only from the arrangement of those components into a precise pattern. They arise out of the pattern as much as out of the components themselves. It is the fact that the pattern strikes us as immaterial or abstract, whereas the components seem to be solid and material, that accounts for the magical quality of emergence.

Fourth, complex entities seem to emerge only where there exist the necessary Goldilocks conditions.
Most of the universe remains simple today. But in pockets there appear conditions that are just right, and it is here that we see the emergence of more complex entities. For example, the surface of our Earth is ideal for complex chemical reactions. There are lots of different chemical elements, there are solids, gases, and liquids, and temperatures are just right for chemical reactions.

Fifth, complex entities seem to be associated with flows of energy that help them maintain their structure.
If you let marbles flow into a hole at the bottom of a small hill, they will stay together because

that configuration requires the least energy. This is a static and not particularly interesting form of complexity. The forms of complexity that will interest us most are dynamic. They are more like the complex patterns created by a skillful juggler. Maintaining them requires a constant flow of energy. Furthermore, broadly speaking, it seems to be true that the more complicated these structures are the more energy it takes to hold them together. This is what the astronomer Eric Chaisson has argued. Chaisson shows that if you do the sums, it turns out, roughly speaking, that planets seem to be more complex than stars because there is more energy flowing each second through each gram of matter on the planet than is flowing through the same amount of mass in a star. Similarly, living things seem to be more complex than planets, and modern human society may be one of the most complex things we know! For human beings, and for historians, that's a pretty significant conclusion. And it will give shape to the story we tell in this text.

To summarize, here are the five key features of complex things:

1. **They consist of multiple diverse components:** Complex things are composed of many diverse components.
2. **They are arranged within a precise structure:** Their components are bound together in precisely specified ways.
3. **They have new or emergent properties:** The ways in which things are structured give them certain distinctive properties.
4. **They appear only where the conditions are just right:** They appear only where you find the perfect Goldilocks conditions for creating more complex things.
5. **They are held together by flows of energy:** The forms of complexity that will interest us most depend on flows of energy. Take away the energy flows and they lose the emergent properties that make them different. This is true whether they are stars, which cease to shine when deprived of fusion reactions at their center, or humans who die when deprived of energy from food, or cars that stop moving when they run out of gas.

A Framework: Eight Major Thresholds of Big History

Although many new forms of complexity have emerged in the history of our universe, we will focus on only those that are of most interest to us as human beings. The table lists eight **thresholds of increasing complexity,** points at which new and more complex entities emerged, with new properties, each adding something to the variety of the universe as a whole. The thresholds will provide a framework for this book. A threshold is, literally, a doorsill; it is the point at which you move from the outside to the inside of a house, so a threshold is the point at which you encounter something new (see the Eight Thresholds of Increasing Complexity table).

Eight Thresholds of Increasing Complexity

THRESHOLD	INGREDIENTS ▶	STRUCTURE ▶	GOLDILOCKS CONDITIONS =	EMERGENT PROPERTIES
1. BIG BANG: ORIGIN OF UNIVERSE	Energy, matter, space, time (everything in our universe!).	Energy and matter within a rapidly expanding space–time continuum.	Uncertain: Possibly quantum fluctuations within the multiverse.	Potential to create everything around us.
2. STARS	Atomic matter, in the form of hydrogen (H) and helium (He) atoms and/or their nuclei.	Inner core (fusion); outer layers with reserves of H and He + eventually other elements up to iron.	Gradients of density and temperature in early universe + gravity creating temperatures high enough for fusion.	New local energy flows; galaxies; potential to create new chemical elements through fusion.
3. HEAVIER CHEMICAL ELEMENTS	Hydrogen and helium nuclei (i.e., protons).	Increasing numbers of protons linked by strong nuclear force into increasingly large atomic nuclei.	Extremely high temperatures created in dying stars or (even more extreme) in supernovae + strong nuclear force.	Potential for chemical combination, mainly via electromagnetism, to create almost infinite range of new types of matter.

THRESHOLD	INGREDIENTS ▶	STRUCTURE ▶	GOLDILOCKS CONDITIONS =	EMERGENT PROPERTIES
4. PLANETS	New chemical elements and compounds in orbit around stars.	Diversity of materials bound together gravitationally and chemically into large balls of matter normally orbiting stars.	Increasing abundance of heavier elements in regions of star formation.	New astronomical objects with more physical and chemical complexity and potential to generate even greater chemical complexity.
5. LIFE	Complex chemicals + energy.	Complex molecules bound together chemically and physically in cells capable of reproduction.	Abundant complex chemicals + moderate energy flows + liquid medium such as water + suitable planet.	Metabolism (capacity to extract energy); reproduction (ability to copy themselves almost perfectly); adaptation (slow change and appearance of new forms through natural selection).
6. *HOMO SAPIENS*	Same as all life + highly developed manipulative, perceptive, and neurological capacity.	Highly specific biological structures governed by human DNA.	Long preceding period of evolution generating highly developed manipulative, perceptive, and neurological capacity.	Collective Learning, i.e., capacity to share information precisely and rapidly so that information accumulates at the level of the community and species giving rise to long-term historical change.
7. AGRICULTURE	Increasing Collective Learning → innovation increasing ability to manipulate and extract resources from environment and other organisms.	Human communities sharing information needed to manipulate their surroundings in new ways.	Long preceding period of Collective Learning; warmer climates; population pressure.	Increased capacity of humans to extract energy and food → larger, denser communities → increased social complexity → accelerating Collective Learning.
8. MODERN WORLD/ ANTHROPOCENE	Globalization; rapid acceleration in Collective Learning; innovation; use of fossil fuels.	Globally connected human communities with rapidly accelerating capacity to manipulate the biosphere.	Acceleration in Collective Learning at global scales.	Vast increase in human use of resources → entirely new lifeways, social relationships → first single species in the history of Earth capable of transforming the biosphere.

Armed with the ideas described in this introduction, we are ready to start telling the history of the universe. This is in many ways a thrilling story, the story of how everything around us came to be. It is an origin story for the twenty-first century, and it should help you better understand how you fit into the overall scheme of things.

A Note on Chronological Systems and Dates

In the early parts of this text, dates will be given as BP ("before the present"). This is a dating terminology used by paleontologists and archaeologists. Strictly, it means "before 1950," which was when radiometric dating techniques began to be used, but in practice, this makes no difference when dealing with dates thousands or millions of years before the present. From Chapter 5 on—that is, for the last 10,000 years or so (from ca. 10,000 BP)—we will shift to the dating system used by world historians, which gives dates as BCE ("before the Common Era") and CE ("Common Era"). The Common Era begins about 2,000 years ago, so this system gives the same dates as the older system using BC ("before Christ") and AD ("in the year of the Lord"), but its advantage is that it is less culturally specific.

To get a feeling for these systems, note that 5000 BP is the same date as 3000 BCE, whereas 500 BP is the same date as 1500 CE.

CHAPTER QUESTIONS

1. What is big history and how is it different from traditional forms of history?
2. Why is it easier to tell a scientifically based origin story today than it was in the early twentieth century?
3. What are the key themes in the story of big history?
4. Explain the ideas of complexity and emergence.
5. Why is it important to study the sciences, the social sciences, and the humanities together? And why is it difficult to do so?

KEY TERMS

big history
complexity
emergent properties

Goldilocks conditions
isotopes
origin stories

plate tectonics
science

thresholds of increasing
complexity

FURTHER READING

Big History

Bighistoryproject.com—a high school and independent learners' course in big history, expected to be online in 2013.

Brown, Cynthia Stokes. *Big History: From the Big Bang to the Present.* 2nd ed. New York: New Press, 2012. First published in 2007.

Chaisson, Eric J. *Cosmic Evolution: The Rise of Complexity in Nature.* Cambridge, MA: Harvard University Press, 2001.

Christian, David. *Maps of Time: An Introduction to Big History.* 2nd ed. Berkeley: University of California Press, 2011.

Christian, David. "Big History: The Big Bang, Life on Earth, and the Rise of Humanity." *The Teaching Company,* Course No.

8050 (2008). **www.thegreatcourses.com/tgc/courses/course_detail.aspx?cid=8050** [April 4, 2012].

Spier, Fred. *Big History and the Future of Humanity.* Chichester, West Sussex, UK; Malden, MA: Wiley-Blackwell, 2010.

General Science

Angier, Natalie. *The Canon: A Whirligig Tour of the Beautiful Basics of Science.* New York: Houghton Mifflin, 2007.

Hazen, Robert M., and James Trefil. *Science Matters: Achieving Scientific Literacy.* 2nd ed. New York: Anchor Books, 2009.

General World History

Christian, David. *This Fleeting World: A Short History of Humanity.* Great Barrington, MA: Berkshire Publishing Group, 2008.

McNeill, William H., and J. R. McNeill. *The Human Web: A Bird's-Eye View of World History.* New York: Norton, 2003.

ENDNOTES

1. From Blaise Pascal, *Pensées* (1670), No. 72.
2. James Boswell, *Life of Johnson* . . . , with additions and notes by J. W. Croker, 1831, vol. 1, 453 [originally published 1763].

the first three thresholds

chapter 1

The Universe, Stars, and New Chemical Elements

Seeing the Big Picture

13.8 to 4.6 Billion Years Ago

▶ What do we mean by "thresholds" in big history? And why are these turning points so important?

▶ Why does the appearance of the universe count as the first threshold? What existed after that threshold that did not exist before?

▶ If you wanted to persuade someone that the big bang was a true story of the origin of the universe, what evidence would you give?

▶ Why does the emergence of stars count as the second threshold of increasing complexity?

▶ Why does the emergence of new elements in dying stars count as the third threshold of increasing complexity?

Threshold 1: Big Bang Cosmology and the Origin of the Universe

The formation of the universe counts as our first threshold because, as far as we know, that moment saw the origin of everything around us. It is the beginning of the history of everything (Threshold 1 Summary).

So, our first question is: How did history begin? This is one of the deepest and the most important questions we can possibly ask. Whatever society you live in, it is important to know the best available answers, whether or not you agree with them.

Threshold 1 Summary

THRESHOLD	INGREDIENTS ▶	STRUCTURE ▶	GOLDILOCKS CONDITIONS =	EMERGENT PROPERTIES
BIG BANG: ORIGIN OF UNIVERSE	Energy, matter, space, time (everything in our universe!).	Energy and matter within a rapidly expanding space–time continuum.	Uncertain: Possibly quantum fluctuations within the multiverse.	Potential to create everything around us.

Traditional Origin Stories

For most of human history, accounts of the origin of everything depended on little more than imaginative guesses, or intuition, or what many experienced as "revelation," the whispered words of divine beings or inner voices (Figures 1.1 and 1.2). Nevertheless, the question of how our universe came to exist is so important that people seem to have asked it in all human societies. And, having asked the question, humans came up with a huge variety of answers.

Table 1.1 shows some brief extracts from the beginnings of a number of traditional origin stories. Note that despite their differences these accounts of the origin of everything share important features.

First, note that from outside, the origin stories of other societies usually seem naive and simplistic. They also lack emotional power for those who did not grow up with them. But we should not forget that within the societies that told them, such stories could have great, almost magical power, like the story of the birth of Christ in Christian societies, or accounts of the Buddha's *nirvana* or *enlightenment* within Buddhist societies.

Second, all the extracts we have cited are poetic. Whenever humans try to describe the indescribable, they must resort to metaphors, stories, parables, to language that tries to convey more than can be conveyed in simple, direct prose. So it is usually a mistake to take origin stories too literally, and it is probable that those who told them did not always treat them as the literal truth. Origin stories are attempts to describe things that words never fully convey, to "point a finger at the moon" in the Buddhist metaphor. Notice how this phrase invites curiosity. It's mysterious like the cosmos itself because, though we can understand a lot, we can never fully understand everything. That's why people always use complex, poetic, and metaphorical language when they try to explain things as mysterious as the origin of the universe.

Third, at the center of all these stories is a paradox, the paradox of beginnings. All these stories begin by trying to describe a time when what we know did not exist.

FIGURE 1.1 Some cave paintings, such as this Australian painting of a "rainbow serpent" from Arnhem Land in northern Australia, hint at the origin stories that all human societies seem to have told.

FIGURE 1.2 *God Grants Adam Life,* **Sistine Chapel, the Vatican.** This famous artwork conveys a powerful origin story from the West. In it, God is depicted imparting life to Adam, that is, to humankind.

Then they explain how something appeared out of nothing. Many of them insist that a creator made the world, but always there is the nagging problem: How was the creator created? Or, to put it more generally, how did something come out of nothing

We will see that the account of origin contained within modern **big bang cosmology** (the modern, scientific explanation of the origin of the universe) shares all these features. Viewed from outside, it may seem quite crazy. It also has poetic or metaphorical qualities because even modern

TABLE 1.1 Accounts of the Origin of Everything from Origin Stories

From the Hopi of northeastern Arizona	"The first world was Tokpela [endless space]. But first, they say, there was only the Creator, Taiowa. All else was endless space. There was no beginning and no end, no time, no shape, no life. Just an immeasurable void that had its beginning and end, time, shape, and life in the mind of Taiowa the Creator."
From southern China, one of many versions of the story of Pangu	"At first there was nothing. Time passed and nothing became something. Time passed and something split in two: the two were male and female. These two produced two more, and these two produced Pangu, the first being, the Great Man, the Creator."
From another version of the story of Pangu	"First there was the great cosmic egg. Inside the egg was Chaos, and floating in Chaos was Pangu, the Undeveloped, the divine Embryo. And Pangu burst out of the egg, four times larger than any man today, with an adze in his hand . . . with which he fashioned the world."
From the Indian cycle of hymns, the Rig-Veda, which dates to ca. 1200 BCE	"When neither Being nor Not-being was Nor atmosphere, nor firmament, nor what is beyond. What did it encompass? Where? In whose protection? What was water, the deep unfathomable? Neither death nor immortality was there then, No sign of night or day. That One breathed, windless, by its own energy: Nought else existed then."
An Islamic origin story from Somalia	"Before the beginning of time there was God. He was never born nor will He ever die. If He wishes a thing, He merely says to it: 'Be!' and it exists."
From the Old Testament, Genesis 1:1	"In the beginning, God created the heavens and the Earth. The Earth was without form and void, and darkness was upon the face of the deep; and the Spirit of God was moving over the face of the waters."

science must sometimes use poetic language when it tries to describe the indescribable. The phrase "big bang," for example, is a metaphor; no modern cosmologist really thinks there was a "bang" when the universe appeared!

Finally, even modern **cosmology** (the study of the evolution of the universe) cannot solve the paradox of beginnings. Although cosmologists are often keen to speculate about what was there before the big bang, the truth is that at present we have no idea why a universe should have appeared out of nothingness. We don't even know if there was nothing there before the big bang. One speculation, which was taken quite seriously until recently, is that there was a previous universe that shriveled to nothing, then exploded again to form a new universe (see Chapter 13). Another speculation, which is now taken more seriously, is that there is a vast multidimensional "multiverse" within which universes keep appearing, each with its own distinctive features, so that our universe may be one of countless billions of universes.

The modern origin story is also different from other origin stories in important ways. Above all, it offers a literal account of the origin of everything. It expects to be taken seriously as a description of what actually happened beginning about 13.8 billion years ago. It is not simply a poetic attempt to make up for ignorance. It claims to offer an accurate account of the very beginnings of history because it is based on a huge amount of evidence, generated through numerous measurements over several centuries, and based on rigorous and carefully tested scientific theories. It is the only origin story accepted by scientists throughout the world. But because it is based on evidence, and new evidence can always turn up, the same scientists also know that many of its details will change in coming years. It is not a fixed or absolute story and does not claim to be perfect.

The Origin of Big Bang Cosmology

It is easier to understand modern big bang cosmology if you understand how it evolved over many centuries. The cosmological ideas that are shared today by scientists throughout the world evolved within the modern European scientific tradition. However, the roots of those ideas can be traced back to mathematical, scientific, and religious ideas that originated in ancient Mesopotamia, Egypt, and India; in classical Greece and Rome; and in the Muslim world. Modern cosmology draws on ideas, techniques, and traditions from much of Afro-Eurasia.

Early Cosmologies   In medieval Europe, explanations of the origin of the universe were based on two main traditions. The first was Christian theology. Christianity, like Judaism, is a monotheistic religion. It posits the existence of a single, supreme God, and it explains the appearance of the universe as God's work. By the third century CE, as Christianity spread within the Roman Empire, a number of Christian theologians attempted to *date* the moment of creation. Their attempts were "scientific" insofar as they were based on evidence from the most authoritative written source they knew: the Bible. Using this source, a number of early Christian scholars tried to estimate the moment of creation by counting the generations recorded in the Old Testament. These estimates suggested that God had made the Earth and the universe in about 4000 BCE. That meant that the universe was just over 4,000 years old at the height of the Roman Empire. (See the section "Shaping of Earth's Surface" in Chapter 2 for more on this.)

The second tradition on which medieval Christian cosmologies were built was the work of the Roman-Egyptian astronomer Ptolemy of Alexandria (ca. 90–168 CE). Ptolemy was a geographer, mathematician, and astronomer. His greatest work on astronomy was written in Greek, but when Muslim scholars translated it into Arabic, they called it *al-Majisti,* or "The Great Work." Medieval Christian translators referred to it as the *Almagest,* and in the Christian world it became the foundation for ideas about astronomy and the universe (Figure 1.3). Ptolemy rejected earlier Greek models of the universe, which suggested that the Earth and planets orbited the sun. Instead, he argued that the Earth lay at the center of the universe and all the other heavenly bodies orbited around it. Christian theologians argued that the Earth was a realm of sin and imperfection; but surrounding it, in Ptolemy's model, was a realm of perfection. This upper world consisted of several perfect, flawless, transparent crystalline spheres that carried the stars, the sun, the planets, and other heavenly bodies. The spheres rotated at different rates, and their rotations explained the movements of the heavenly bodies as seen from Earth.

In the Christian world, most scholars accepted Ptolemy's model for more than 1,500 years. This was partly because it enjoyed the backing of the Catholic Church. But it also did a pretty good job of explaining the movements of the heavenly bodies. And it fit well with our strong intuitive sense that Earth is not moving. After all, if Earth were moving, wouldn't you expect to feel the movement?

Scientific Challenges   However, in the sixteenth century, Ptolemy's model of the universe came under attack from several directions. The Protestant Reformation undermined the authority of the Catholic Church. Even more significant were the scientific criticisms directed at Ptolemy's cosmology. Nicolaus Copernicus (1473–1543), a Polish-born astronomer, revived the ancient idea that the sun, not the Earth, lay at the center of the universe. And he was able to show that such an idea could solve some important anomalies in the Ptolemaic system. For example, Ptolemy's cosmology offered somewhat contrived explanations for the "retrograde" movement of the planets, the fact that each year their orbits seem briefly to go into reverse. Copernicus showed that if Earth were orbiting the sun, along with all the other planets, this is exactly what you would expect to see.

FIGURE 1.3 Ptolemy's universe. In medieval Europe, most scholars accepted the view of the universe proposed by the ancient Egyptian astronomer Ptolemy in which the Earth was at the center of the universe and surrounded by revolving transparent spheres that carried the heavenly bodies.

Furthermore, a German astronomer, Johannes Kepler (1571–1630), demonstrated that the planets did not orbit in the perfect circles required by Ptolemy's cosmology, but in ellipses, or squashed-up circles.

Finally, Galileo Galilei (1564–1642), an Italian scholar, put to rest the idea that the sublunar and heavenly regions were completely distinct. Galileo was one of the first astronomers to view the heavens through a telescope. By doing so he was able to show that the sun's face, far from being flawless, was covered with spots, while Jupiter had moons. Both facts contradicted Ptolemy's model. Galileo also explained why we don't feel the Earth moving. He pointed out that if everything on Earth is moving in the same direction, it *feels* as if nothing is moving. After all, if you are sitting on a plane and you throw a ball in the air it doesn't shoot backward at 500 miles per hour (800 kilometers per hour); it falls back into your hand because it shares with you the plane's forward movement. That's why, although the Earth is moving through space at a speed of almost 70,000 mph (112,000 kph), we don't feel it moving.

Toward the end of the seventeenth century, the English physicist and mathematician Isaac Newton (1642–1727) showed that to understand astronomy you didn't need Ptolemy's complicated system of imaginary spheres. Instead, you could explain the movements of objects in heaven and Earth, both the movements of planets and the falling of apples, with just a few simple equations. He suggested that there was a universal force, which he called gravity. This force pulled all physical objects toward each other, and its strength increased as the mass of the objects increased, but decreased as they moved farther apart. Newton's laws of motion were one of the greatest of all scientific breakthroughs, for they provided an extremely simple way of explaining movements in general. To many they seemed to provide the key to understanding the universe.

By 1700, few scientists took Ptolemy's model of the universe seriously. They accepted that the Earth orbited the sun. They also came to believe that the universe as a whole could be explained through simple scientific laws such as those formulated by Newton.

Mapping the Universe Now astronomers faced new challenges. Understanding the universe better meant mapping it. Could you map the universe as geographers were beginning to map the Earth? To do this you would have to determine the exact position and movements of the stars. And that was not easy. Not until the nineteenth century did astronomers develop more reliable ways of measuring the distances to nearby stars and tracking their motion through space. Modern ideas about the universe and its origin would emerge from these attempts to map the universe. We will take each of these two questions—the position and the motion of stars—in turn.

How can you tell the distance to the stars? It's worth going out one evening to look at the stars and try to figure out whether you could do it. It's a subtle and complex problem. The ancient Greeks already knew in principle how to do it. You use **parallax:** the change in the apparent relationship between two fixed objects caused by the movement of the observer (Figure 1.4).

To get a sense of how parallax works, hold up your finger in front of you, close to your nose. Now keep your finger still, but waggle your head from side to side. Your finger will seem to move against the background; and how far it moves will depend on how far away it is from your eyes. (Move it away from your nose and wag your head to check this.) The Greeks saw that this simple principle should allow you to measure the distance to the nearest stars. As the Earth orbits the sun each year (remember, some ancient Greek astronomers accepted a sun-centered model of the

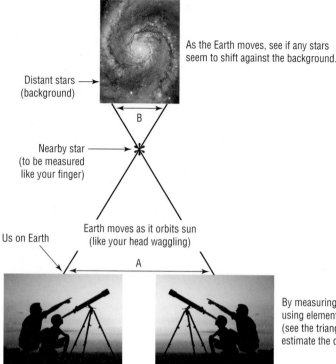

Distant stars (background) →

As the Earth moves, see if any stars seem to shift against the background.

B

Nearby star → (to be measured like your finger)

Earth moves as it orbits sun (like your head waggling)

Us on Earth

A

By measuring the shift and using elementary trigonometry (see the triangles?) you can estimate the distance to the star.

FIGURE 1.4 How parallax works, showing the triangles that allow trigonometrical calculations. Parallax depends on the fact that as you move, objects in the middle distance (such as a nearby star) seem to move against objects that are farther away (such as more remote stars or galaxies). In principle, it should be possible to determine the extent of the motion and then use trigonometry (note the triangles in the diagram) to determine the real distance to the nearby star. In practice, the movements even of the nearest stars are so small that it was not possible to use this method to determine the distance to nearby stars until the nineteenth century.

universe), some of the nearest stars ought to move against a background of more distant stars, just as your finger seems to move across the background when you wag your head. By measuring how far nearby stars seem to move against the background of more distant stars, and using simple trigonometry combined with rough estimates of the size of the Earth's orbit and the distance to the sun, you should be able to estimate how far away the stars are.

The Greeks had the right idea. Unfortunately, even the nearest stars are so remote that you cannot detect any movement with the naked eye. Not until the mid-nineteenth century were telescopes and measuring instruments precise enough to detect and measure tiny changes in the position of some of the nearest stars. But these were enough to allow astronomers to estimate the distance to some of these stars. And when they did so they began to realize that the universe was far larger than most of them had supposed. We now know that even the nearest star, Proxima Centauri, is more than 4 light-years away. That's about 25 trillion miles (40 trillion kilometers) away. If you tried to fly there in a commercial jet cruising at about 550 mph (880 kph), it would take you about 5 million years! And remember that there are hundreds of billions of stars out there, and this is the closest of them all; in astronomical terms Proxima Centauri is our next-door neighbor.

Measuring more distant stars required different techniques. One was developed by an American astronomer, Henrietta Leavitt (1868–1921). At the end of the nineteenth century she studied a special type of star whose brightness seems to vary in a regular pattern. These were known as **Cepheid variables,** after the constellation of Cepheus in which they were first detected. She realized that the rate

at which their brightness varied depended on their size, and that meant you could calculate how big they were. Because the size of stars correlates closely with their brightness, this meant you could estimate their true (or "intrinsic") brightness—that is, how bright they would be if you could observe them from close up. By calculating how bright they appeared to be when seen from Earth, you could estimate how far away they were because the amount of starlight that reaches a distant object diminishes in a mathematically precise way as the light is spread through a larger and larger volume of space. In this roundabout way, Leavitt realized you could estimate the real distance of Cepheid variables.

In 1924, Edwin Hubble (whom we will return to later) showed that some Cepheid variables were outside our own galaxy, the Milky Way. This proved for the first time that there were many different galaxies in the universe, which showed once again that the universe was much bigger than most astronomers had supposed.

Astronomers also wanted to know whether stars and galaxies were moving through space. Remarkably, techniques emerged in the nineteenth century for doing just this. And these would eventually lead to some even more momentous discoveries.

Early in the nineteenth century, a German glassmaker, Joseph von Fraunhofer (1787–1826), created a device called a **spectroscope.** Spectroscopes (or spectrographs) allowed observers to split the light from stars into its different frequencies. Simple glass prisms do exactly the same thing. They split light into different frequencies, which we see as different colors, which is why prisms seem to create artificial rainbows, with colors running from red (which has a lower frequency) at one extreme to blue (with a higher frequency) at the other. But in the spectra (the "rainbows of light") that Fraunhofer's spectroscopes created from starlight, he saw something odd. He found dark lines with reduced energy, which are now

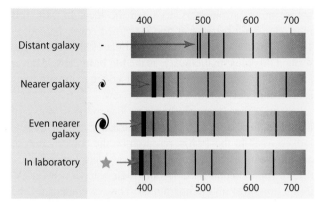

FIGURE 1.5 The Doppler effect and absorption lines. Absorption lines, the dark lines that appear on the spectra of light from stars, show the presence of particular elements at particular frequencies. Often, however, the absorption lines are slightly shifted from their expected position (i.e., their frequency). This is due to the Doppler effect. Light waves from the star are either stretched or compressed because it is either moving away from us (when the frequency is *red-shifted*) or toward us (when the frequency is *blue-shifted*). Hubble used such measurements to discover that all distant objects in the universe seem to be moving away from us, and the farther away they are, the faster they are moving away.

known as **absorption lines** (Figure 1.5). Experiments in laboratories showed that these lines were due to the presence of specific elements, each of which tended to absorb light energy at different frequencies. If you knew those frequencies, you could tell from the absorption lines what elements were present in the stars from which the light had come. This idea would prove crucial later when astronomers began to figure out how stars were formed and what was in them.

At the end of the nineteenth century, Vesto Slipher, working at the Lowell observatory in Flagstaff, Arizona, found another curious feature of absorption lines. Occasionally, in the spectra of distant objects absorption lines seemed to have shifted away from their expected positions. Thus, the absorption lines for hydrogen

might be blue-shifted (shifted toward higher frequencies at the blue end of the spectrum) or red-shifted (shifted toward lower frequencies at the red end). Slipher argued that these shifts were caused by the movements of the stars either toward us (the blue shifts) or away from us (the red shifts). They were caused by the **Doppler effect,** the same effect that seems to cause the sound from a siren to rise in pitch as it comes toward us, and drop in pitch as it moves away from us. The effect is caused by the fact that we experience sound waves as being bunched up if the object emitting them is moving toward us, but stretched out if it is moving away from us. If Slipher was right (and we now know he was), this meant that we could determine whether distant objects such as remote galaxies were moving toward us or away from us. We could even calculate how fast they were moving. This was a remarkable technical breakthrough.

We have discussed these techniques for measuring the distance and movements of stars in some detail because they laid the foundation for modern big bang cosmology.

Big Bang Cosmology

The work that put all these findings together was done by American astronomer Edwin Hubble (1889–1953) in the 1920s. Working at the Mount Wilson observatory in Pasadena, California, one of the largest telescopes in the world at the time, he used the techniques we have been describing to try to map the overall shape of the universe. The picture that emerged was completely unexpected. The first oddity was that the universe seemed to be unstable. Most remote objects in the universe seemed to be **red-shifted.** In other words, they seemed to be moving away from the Earth. No one expected that because since Newton's time, most astronomers assumed the universe was stable. When Hubble combined estimates of these movements with estimates of the distances to these objects, he found something even more curious: The farther away the object was, the larger the red shift; in other words, the faster it seemed to be moving away from us (Figure 1.6).

FIGURE 1.6 Hubble's graph of the distance and movements of remote galaxies. Hubble used the Mount Wilson telescope in Pasadena, California, to study remote galaxies. He found that the farther away an object was, the faster it seemed to be moving away. This was the fundamental discovery that showed that our universe is expanding.

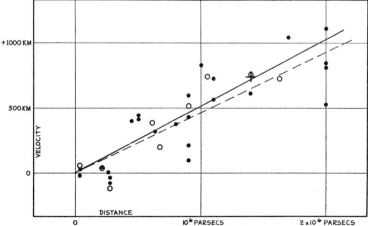

Velocity-Distance Relation among Extra-Galactic Nebulae

What did this mean? It appeared to mean that when seen at very large scales different parts of the universe were moving away from each other. We now know that gravity is powerful enough to hold groups of galaxies together. This is true, for example, of the group of galaxies that includes the Milky Way and the Andromeda galaxy, so the Andromeda galaxy is *not* moving away from us. But Hubble was observing objects at much greater distances, and at these huge scales, whole groups of galaxies seemed to be moving apart from each other. It seemed as if the entire universe was expanding. It was as if different parts of the universe were like separate fragments from an exploding grenade.

No astronomer had expected this. Indeed, Einstein—whose theory of relativity had appeared a few years before Hubble published his results—was so shocked by Hubble's results that he insisted for a time that there must be an error. He even modified his own theory of relativity to avoid the possibility of an unstable universe by suggesting the existence of a new type of force that balanced gravity. (He later accepted Hubble's results, calling his attempts to avoid it one of his greatest blunders. Curiously, recent developments may have partly vindicated Einstein, for, as we will see later, his quick fix seemed to point to the existence of a new force that we now call *dark energy*. Dark energy is a form of energy that seems to push space itself apart, and that pervades the entire universe.)

Whereas Ptolemy's universe had been small and stable, and Newton's universe had seemed to be vast and stable, the universe Hubble described was very *un*stable. Hubble's universe began tiny and kept expanding until it became very large indeed. But we now know it wasn't really expanding *into* anything because it was creating the dimensions of time and space as it expanded. And that makes it hard to imagine its shape. Don't try to think of the universe as having a center or an edge. It doesn't, just as the surface of the Earth doesn't have an edge or a center.

Had Hubble come up with a realistic description of the universe? Or were his results due to a sort of optical illusion? At first no one was sure. But if his description was realistic it had important consequences for our understanding of the history of the universe. In 1927, Belgian astronomer and Catholic priest Georges Lemaitre (1894–1966) pointed out that if the universe was expanding, this meant that it had a history. Cosmology was not a static description of the universe; it was a historical discipline, like human history. He added that it was possible to say some significant things about the shape of that history. If the universe was expanding now, then in the past it must have been smaller than today. And at some time in an inconceivably remote past, everything in the universe must have been packed into a tiny space as small as an atom. Lemaitre called this the *primeval atom.*

For astronomers, this was an astonishing conclusion. Lemaitre had described how the entire universe must have begun in an unimaginably small bundle of energy. And if the universe really was expanding, he had to be right.

Although Hubble's research laid the foundations for modern big bang cosmology, it would take several decades before most astronomers accepted the idea. In part, this may have been because at first it seemed crazy. Indeed, in 1950 a British astronomer, Fred Hoyle (1915–2001), described this idea, maliciously, as the **big bang.** Hoyle never accepted big bang cosmology, and used the name *big bang* as a term of derision in a radio interview.

At first, few scientists had any idea what to make of Hubble's findings. What would the early universe have looked like? In the 1940s, research on the construction of atomic weapons began to generate new ideas about the nature of fundamental particles and their behavior under extreme pressures and temperatures. These were exactly the conditions that must have existed early in the history of the universe if Hubble's and Lemaitre's model was correct.

The Large Hadron Collider

Today, cosmologists research the origin of the universe using huge, expensive machines that smash particles together at extremely high speeds to see what they are made of. In the Large Hadron Collider (LHC; Figure 1.7), a huge circular tube under the airport in Geneva, Switzerland,

FIGURE 1.7 The Large Hadron Collider, Cern. The Large Hadron Collider is the largest and most expensive scientific experiment ever created. It consists of a huge underground tunnel beneath Geneva airport, in which subatomic particles are smashed together at close to the speed of light in order to discover what they consist of. This is a bit like smashing cars together to find out what is inside them, but it is our only way of determining the nature of the basic components that make up our universe. The white circle marks the position of the LHC. In the foreground is the Geneva airport. The red line marks the border between France and Switzerland.

particles are being smashed together so violently that scientists are in effect re-creating conditions similar to those in the first second of the universe's existence. This is a bit like smashing two Ferraris together to see what they are made of! And it makes for very exciting science! Indeed, on July 4, 2012, scientists at the LHC announced that they had found evidence for the existence of a particle known as the "Higgs boson." This is the particle that explains why all matter has mass. The idea that there must be such a particle was first proposed in 1964 by the British physicist Peter Higgs, and subsequently by several other physicists. The discovery that there really is a particle that corresponds to Higgs's original idea counts as one of the great turning points in modern science.

In the 1940s, a number of scientists, including Fred Hoyle and the Russian American physicist George Gamow (1904–68), began to work out what the early universe might have looked like and how it might have behaved if Hubble's results were correct. Remarkably, they found that it was possible to construct a reasonably sensible story. In the decades since then, it has proved possible to explain in great detail the various stages that led from the moment when the universe first appeared to the sort of universe that exists today.

The Origin of Everything according to Big Bang Cosmology

What existed before our universe appeared remains unknown. We simply have no evidence, so we cannot say anything scientific about the moment when our universe appeared. Indeed, the very idea of a "before" may be meaningless, as it is possible that time itself was created in the big bang along with space, matter, and energy. In the future, astronomers may find a way of tackling this ultimate question, but at the moment big bang cosmology makes no attempt to explain the precise moment at which the universe appeared. However, from a tiny fraction of a second after the appearance of our universe, big bang cosmology can tell a detailed story based on large amounts of evidence. What follows is a brief, nontechnical account of parts of that story.

About 13.8 billion years ago, something appeared, and as it appeared it began to create space, time, **matter,** and **energy** (*matter* consists of entities that have mass and occupy space; *energy* consists of the forces that move and shape matter). At first, space itself may have been no larger than an atom. It was also inconceivably hot. This is hardly surprising. After all, this atom-sized space contained all the energy of today's universe. It was so hot that matter and energy were interchangeable. Energy constantly congealed into particles of matter, and these kept transforming back into energy. As Einstein's theory of relativity had proved, matter and energy are really different forms of the same underlying substance; loosely, we can think of matter as energy at rest. At extreme temperatures, such as those in a hydrogen bomb, or the center of a star, matter can be transformed back into energy. So at the very beginning, the universe consisted of a sort of soup of energy and matter. As it expanded, however, it cooled rapidly. And as it cooled this soup began to differentiate into different types of forces and different types of matter. Scientists called these changes *phase changes*. They are a bit like what happens when steam cools; suddenly, at about 212 degrees Fahrenheit (about 100 degrees Celsius) it undergoes a phase change and turns into liquid water.

For a moment (we are still within a billionth of a billionth of a billionth of a second after the appearance of the universe), the early universe expanded extremely fast. At the end of this period of "inflation," as the astronomers call it, the universe may have been the size of an entire galaxy in today's universe.

Within a fraction of a second more, four basic forms of energy appeared as a result of phase changes. They were gravity, electromagnetism, and the "strong" and "weak" nuclear forces. (We will come back to gravity and electromagnetism later; they are familiar forces and will play a major role in our story. We will spend less time with the other forces. They act only over distances smaller than an atom and help control the behavior of atoms and subatomic particles such as protons and electrons. So they are of interest mainly to nuclear physicists.) Along with these four forces, the basic constituents of matter also appeared, including dark matter (which we don't really understand), and also the sort of matter we are made from, **atomic matter.**

Within the first 20 minutes, matter and energy began to take on more stable forms. Protons, the positively charged nuclei of hydrogen atoms, had already appeared, and about 25 percent of them fused together and joined up with neutrons (which have a similar mass to protons but no charge) to form the nuclei of helium atoms. A tiny number of protons fused to form lithium nuclei, but the universe was cooling so fast that no more fusion could occur. Matter now existed in the form of a **plasma,** a hot, gaslike state in which protons and electrons (which have negative charges) were not yet bound together within atoms. Similar conditions (plasma) exist today at the center of stars. Because protons and electrons carry electric charges, most of the atomic matter in the universe would have been crackling with electricity and constantly buffeted by intense electromagnetic energy. Photons, which we can think of as small packages of electromagnetic energy, would have been entangled with these charged particles.

The plasma existed for almost 380,000 years. (That's about twice as long as humans have lived on Earth.) Then, at about 380,000 years after the big bang, there was an important new phase change. As the universe cooled to a temperature close to that on the surface of our sun, photons of light began to lose energy, and subatomic particles began to jiggle around less frantically. Eventually, in a cooler and more subdued universe, the electric charges between positively charged protons and negatively charged electrons were powerful enough to bind them together. Suddenly, as a critical temperature threshold was crossed, protons and electrons throughout the universe linked up to form atoms that were electrically neutral because the opposite charges of protons and electrons canceled each other out. It was as if the entire universe suddenly lost its electric charge. The networks of charges in which electromagnetic radiation had been entangled vanished, and photons of light could now move freely through the universe.

In the late 1940s, George Gamow suggested that at this point in the story there would have been something like a huge flash of energy as photons disentangled themselves from matter. Perhaps, he suggested, it still might be possible to detect that flash. It is a sign of how skeptical most cosmologists still were about the idea of a big bang that at the time no one seems to have seriously looked for the remnants of this ancient flash of energy.

More Evidence in Support of Big Bang Cosmology

As late as the early 1960s, the idea that the universe had been created in a big bang remained little more than an intriguing hypothesis. (A *hypothesis* is a scientific idea that does not yet have enough supporting evidence to be widely accepted. A *theory* is a scientific idea that does have enough evidence to be widely accepted.) Most astronomers doubted that it was a real description of what had actually happened. An alternative hypothesis, known at the time as the *steady state theory* (it was described as a theory because at the time it was widely accepted), was first proposed in the 1920s and subsequently modified and improved. It gained the support, among others, of Fred Hoyle, who would remain a critic of big bang cosmology throughout his life. The steady state theory argued that though the universe was indeed expanding, new matter and energy were being constantly created at a rate that balanced the rate of expansion. The result, according to the steady state theory, was that on very large scales the universe had always looked much the same as it does today.

How could you test these two hypotheses, both of which claimed to explain the red shift that Hubble had found? Which was right?

The answer arrived, suddenly and unexpectedly, in 1964. Arno Penzias (b. 1933) and Robert Wilson (b. 1936), two astronomers working at the Bell Telephone laboratories in New Jersey, were trying to create an extremely sensitive receiver for satellite communication (Figure 1.8). To refine the hornlike antenna they were building, they tried to eliminate all background signals. They found a tiny, but persistent and uniform background hum of energy that they could not get rid of. Remarkably, it seemed to be present in whatever direction the antenna was pointed, so it did not seem to come from any particular object in space. They began to suspect problems with their own equipment and at one point removed pigeon droppings from the antenna, fearing that the tiny amounts of heat emitted by the droppings might be the source of the hum. Eventually, they contacted Robert Dicke (1916–97), a professor of physics at nearby Princeton University. Dicke knew of predictions

FIGURE 1.8 Cosmic background radiation. The radio antenna with which Penzias and Wilson first detected the cosmic background radiation in 1964.

that the big bang should have released a huge flash of energy and was in the process of trying to build a radio telescope that could detect this background energy. He immediately concluded that Penzias and Wilson had detected the ancient flash of energy predicted by Gamow and others.

Penzias and Wilson had found a very weak signal, whose energy levels were equivalent to approximately –455 degrees Fahrenheit (–270 degrees Celsius), just a few degrees above absolute zero. (Absolute zero is the lowest temperature that is possible.) This was very close to the energy level that cosmologists such as Gamow and Dicke had predicted. What was most remarkable was the uniformity of the background radiation. It came from everywhere in the universe. In short, even though the signal was very weak, it represented a colossal amount of energy, and it seemed to be at almost exactly the same intensity everywhere. The steady state theory had no way of explaining the source of this **cosmic background radiation (CBR).** But, as we have seen, the big bang theory predicted it.

Making strange predictions that turn out to be true is one of the most powerful tests of any scientific hypothesis. And that is why, since the discovery of CBR, most cosmologists and astronomers have come to accept that the big bang hypothesis offers a correct account of the origin of the universe. That is why we can now describe the big bang as an established theory, and why we will start describing the steady state theory as a hypothesis. Furthermore, since its discovery, CBR has been studied very closely because it can tell us a lot about the nature of the universe at the time it was emitted, about 380,000 years after the big bang.

Even More Evidence for Big Bang Cosmology Although CBR and the red shift are perhaps the most powerful pieces of evidence in support of big bang cosmology, there are plenty of other forms of evidence in its support. Here, we list just three more important pieces of evidence, all of which are relatively easy to understand.

First, no object in the universe appears to be older than about 13 billion years. We will see later in this chapter that astronomers now have a reasonably good understanding of how stars evolve from their infancy to their old age and final collapse. This means that, just as we can approximately tell a person's age by posture, skin tone, and movements, astronomers can estimate a star's age by measuring features such as its temperature, its chemical composition, and its mass. None of these calculations are easy, but none suggest that any stars are older than about 13 billion years. If the universe was in fact hundreds of billions of years old, or if it were infinitely old (as the steady state hypothesis assumed), the absence of older stars would be very strange. However, if the big bang theory is correct, this age distribution is just what you would expect.

Second, unlike the steady state hypothesis, the big bang theory implies that the universe has a history, so that, like human societies, it has changed over time. Just as we expect that human societies 10,000 years ago were very different from societies today (see Chapter 4 to get some idea of *how* different they were), cosmologists expect that the universe 10 billion years ago was very different from what it is today. And that is just what they find. The most powerful modern telescopes can detect objects billions of light-years from Earth. (A **light-year** is the distance that light can travel in a year, or about 6 trillion miles [9.6 trillion kilometers].) By doing so they are, in effect, looking at those objects as they were billions of years ago because it has taken the light they emit billions of years to reach Earth. Powerful telescopes are like time-travelers, and some of the most powerful can show us the universe as it was not long after the big bang. These telescopes show that the early universe was indeed different from today's universe. It was more crowded, and it contained objects such as quasars that are very rare in today's universe. (*Quasar* stands for "quasi-stellar radio source"; quasars form as stars are sucked into the huge black holes that seem to lie at the center of all galaxies.) Such research supports the conclusion of big bang cosmology that the universe, like human society, has a history of change over time, and refutes the conclusion of the steady state hypothesis, that there was little change over time.

Third, the early theorists of the big bang theory argued that, as the universe cooled rapidly in the first few seconds, there would be time for only the simplest of all chemical nuclei to form. The simplest elements are hydrogen (with just one proton at its center and one orbiting electron) and helium (which has two protons and two electrons). Each chemical element has a characteristic number of protons in its nucleus, all the way up to uranium (with 92 protons and 92 electrons). So, for elements larger than hydrogen or helium to form, atomic nuclei must be fused together to form larger nuclei with more protons. Very high temperatures are needed to overcome the repulsion between protons, all of which have positive electric changes, but by the time the first atoms had formed, temperatures were nowhere high enough to do this. This meant that most of the universe ought to consist of hydrogen and helium. That itself was an unexpected prediction because both are rare on the Earth's surface. However, as astronomers used spectrographs to find out what elements were present in stars and in the space between stars, they found that about 75 percent of the atomic matter in the universe consists of hydrogen, and most of the rest consists of helium. Once again, big bang cosmology had generated a strange prediction that turned out to be true.

Problems with Big Bang Cosmology

Today, most astronomers and cosmologists accept that the big bang theory offers a reasonably accurate account of the origin of the universe. But it is far from perfect. One of the most striking anomalies, and the one that is most likely to generate revisions in the near future, is the existence of dark matter and dark energy. These, as we have already seen, are forms of matter and energy that we can detect but do not yet understand.

Astronomers first realized that there must be much more matter than we can see when studying the movements of stars in galaxies. Using the laws of gravity, it is possible to estimate how fast stars should be orbiting large galaxies. The actual movements of stars suggest that there must be perhaps 20 times as much mass as astronomers can actually detect. Some of that mass consists of **dark matter.** In addition, in the late 1990s it became apparent that the rate of expansion of the universe is accelerating, and most cosmologists believe that this acceleration is driven by a new form of energy, known as **dark energy,** which acts as a sort of antigravity, driving things apart rather than pulling them together.

Dark energy makes up about 70 percent of the mass of the universe. Because dark energy is linked to the amount of space that exists, this is a form of energy whose importance will increase as the universe expands. Indeed, it seems that the rate of expansion of the universe began to accelerate, due to the increasing power of dark energy, about 9 billion years after the big bang, at about the time our Earth was formed. Dark matter accounts for another 25 percent of the mass of the universe. The remaining 4 to 5 percent is made up of atomic matter. Most atomic matter is in the form of hydrogen and helium and only about 1 to 2 percent consists of heavier chemical elements from carbon to uranium. But even most atomic matter is invisible, so we can actually detect less than 1 percent of the matter in the universe. The fact that we don't really understand most of the matter and energy in the universe is deeply troubling to many astronomers. Until the true nature of dark matter and energy is explained, a question mark will continue to hover over the entire big bang theory.

However, astronomers and cosmologists are optimistic that experiments such as the Large Hadron Collider may soon offer some answers. We have already seen that the LHC has discovered what appears to be the Higgs boson. As it begins to operate at even higher energy levels, many hope it will discover other forms of energy and matter that can help explain what dark energy and matter really consist of. These are exciting times to be a physicist or a cosmologist!

Meanwhile, despite such difficulties, there is no theory that seriously rivals big bang cosmology, and it manages to explain a colossal amount of information about the universe. It is by far the most powerful and convincing answer available today to the fundamental question: How did the universe begin?

Threshold 2: The Origin of Galaxies and Stars

A few hundred thousand years after the big bang, the universe was simple by today's standards. Most atomic matter existed in the form of vast clouds of hydrogen and helium atoms embedded within and shaped by the gravitational tug of even vaster clouds of dark matter. There were no galaxies, no stars, no planets, and certainly no living organisms. The universe was dark, apart from a dim glow from the cosmic background radiation. There was hardly any variation from region to region: Indeed the wonderful surveys of CBR taken by the Wilkinson Microwave Anisotropy Probe (WMAP) satellite have shown that temperatures varied by less than 0.0006 of a degree Fahrenheit (0.0003 of a degree Celsius) over the whole universe. Everywhere, the universe seemed to be exactly the same, with no variety, no diversity, nothing, really, to make it at all interesting.

Yet a few hundred million years later, the universe contained huge smudges of light, the first galaxies. Each was made up of billions of points of light: the first stars. The evolution of galaxies and stars was the first step toward the evolution of more complex things, including planets, bacteria, and eventually, ourselves. So, to understand the appearance of more complex things in the universe, we must begin with the evolution of stars and galaxies. The appearance of the first stars counts as the second major threshold in our course because their presence made the universe brighter, more complex, and more varied. In a sense, though, this is a threshold that keeps being crossed, even today, because stars have been appearing ever since (Threshold 2 Summary).

Threshold 2 Summary

THRESHOLD	INGREDIENTS ▶	STRUCTURE ▶	GOLDILOCKS CONDITIONS =	EMERGENT PROPERTIES
STARS	Atomic matter, in the form of hydrogen (H) and helium (He) atoms and/or their nuclei.	Inner core (fusion); outer layers with reserves of H and He + eventually other elements up to iron.	Gradients of density and temperature in early universe + gravity creating temperatures high enough for fusion.	New local energy flows; galaxies; potential to create new chemical elements through fusion.

How Were the First Galaxies and Stars Formed?

To explain how the first stars appeared, we must return to gravity, one of the four fundamental forces created in the big bang. Gravity was the force identified by Isaac Newton in the seventeenth century. He realized that the same force that pulled a falling apple to Earth could also explain the movements of the planets around the sun. Gravity was a force of attraction that operated between all forms of matter.

Early in the twentieth century, Einstein showed that gravity also affects energy. As we have seen, Einstein proved that matter and energy were different forms of the same underlying "stuff." At extremely high temperatures, matter can change into energy, and vice versa. So it should not surprise us that gravity affects energy as well as mass. This was demonstrated in 1919, just after the end of World War I, by an English astronomer, Arthur Eddington (1882–1944), who was also a well-known pacifist and a conscientious objector. Eddington decided that you could test Einstein's idea by seeing if the gravitational pull of the sun could bend light rays. He realized you could do this by watching the position of a star as the sun moved in front of it. If the gravity of the sun was bending light rays from the star, then you ought to be able to see the star for a moment just after the sun moved in front of it because its light beams would be slightly curved by the sun's gravity. Unfortunately, the sun is so bright that you cannot normally watch stars near the sun. But you *can* do this during a total eclipse of the sun, and that's why Eddington had to wait until 1919. What he found when he studied an eclipse from the African island of Principe was exactly what Einstein had predicted. As they approached the edge of the sun, the stars seemed to hover momentarily and then vanish quite quickly. The hovering effect was caused by the fact that light from them was bent enough that they remained visible for a moment even after they had passed behind the sun. Here is another example of good science (Einstein's in this case) generating strange predictions that turn out to be true when they are tested.

Gravity, CBR, and Temperature

Gravity plays a central role in our story because it had the ability to change a simple universe into something more interesting. The power of gravity increases where there is more mass, and it decreases as the distance between masses increases. This means that its effect varies from area to area depending on the mass of the objects involved and the distances between them. Clearly if the universe had been perfectly homogeneous (i.e., if every atom in the universe had been exactly the same distance from every other atom), the result would have been a sort of log-jam, with everything exerting exactly the same pull on everything else. But if there were even tiny differences in the density of the early universe, then gravity would pull more strongly in areas with slightly more mass, and by doing so it could start creating clumps of matter with areas of relative emptiness in between them. This was the first step toward new forms of complexity because the gathering of matter into dense clouds would eventually lead to the formation of galaxies and stars. So it was vital for astronomers to find out whether the early universe was homogeneous or not.

Fortunately, CBR provided exactly the information astronomers needed because it offers a sort of snapshot of differences in density and temperature in the early universe. When astronomers first studied it, in the 1960s, they were struck by how homogeneous it was. There seemed to be no significant differences. But later and more precise studies showed that there were, in fact, tiny differences in its temperature. In 1992, an American astronomer, George Smoot, studied these differences using a satellite specially designed to study CBR. It turned out that the differences he found were enough to explain how galaxies of stars could have formed. When the cosmologist Joseph Silk saw Smoot's diagram of the early universe, he exclaimed, "We are viewing the birth of the universe!"

Where there happened to be slightly more matter, gravity pulled more strongly, drawing those areas in on themselves. As huge clouds of dark matter and atomic matter collapsed in on themselves they began to heat up. This is a general principle: Pack more energy into a smaller space and the temperature rises. (*Smaller* is a relative term here. We are talking of regions the size of galaxies!) So, in these areas of increasing density, the temperature began to rise. This was a novel phenomenon in the life of the young universe because, so far, the universe had been cooling down. Now we can imagine vast clouds of dark matter throughout the early universe slowly collapsing in on themselves. Embedded within were smaller clouds of atomic matter that were heating up as they collapsed. Heat energized the atoms within these clouds, and they began to move more rapidly, colliding with each other more frequently and more violently. Eventually, the heat was so intense that electrons were once again stripped from their protons, re-creating the plasma of the early universe, which was full of isolated, charged protons and electrons.

Then, at about 18 million degrees Fahrenheit (about 10 million degrees Celsius), a critical threshold was crossed. Protons began to collide so violently that they fused together.

Protons are positively charged, so normally they repel each other. However, if the collision is violent enough it may overcome the force of repulsion, and once two protons get close enough to each other, they can be bound together by the strong nuclear force, which operates only over tiny, sub-atomic distances. The result is the appearance of new helium nuclei, which consist of two protons and two neutrons bound tightly together. The process by which protons smash together to form helium nuclei is known as **fusion.** As protons fuse, a tiny amount of their matter is converted into a lot of energy. (We know this because the four particles of a helium nucleus have slightly less mass than four isolated protons.) This is what happens in the center of a hydrogen bomb. Einstein's famous equation, $E = mc^2$, says that the amount of energy released in such a process (E) is equivalent to the amount of mass (m) converted to energy, times the speed of light (c) squared! Light travels at about 186,000 miles per second (300,000 kilometers per second), so this is a colossal number. And that explains why hydrogen bombs are so powerful. The first H-bomb, tested on the Pacific atoll of Enewetak in 1952, was almost 500 times as powerful as the atomic bomb dropped on Nagasaki on August 9, 1945.

As new helium atoms are formed by fusion, a huge amount of heat is generated at the center of the collapsing cloud of atoms. This furnace at the center of each cloud stops it collapsing any further and stabilizes it. As this process was repeated throughout the huge, collapsing clouds of matter in the early universe, the first galaxies appeared, composed of billions of individual stars, and the universe began to light up.

"And There Was Light!"

Stars are essentially huge stores of hydrogen (and some helium), with a center so hot that as hydrogen nuclei (i.e., protons) fall into the core they fuse to form nuclei of helium. This furnace at the center of each star generates heat and light that slowly works its way through the star until eventually it escapes into empty space. Each star can keep generating heat and light as long as it has enough hydrogen to keep fusion reactions going. Our own sun formed in the same way, about 4.5 billion years ago, and it will probably exist for 8 or 9 billion years (Figure 1.9). Today, it is about halfway through its life.

So we can imagine the dark universe lighting up as galaxies appeared, with billions of tiny lights switching on as new stars were formed. The young stars formed hot spots, from which energy poured into the extreme cold of empty space. These energy flows from stars into surrounding space would eventually be used to create new and more complex entities, including human beings. Galaxies represent a new level of complexity. They are objects formed by the gravitational links between billions of stars, and they are relatively stable, most having existed almost as long as the universe. Each star, in turn, has its own structure, with a hot core in which fusion occurs, and outer layers whose pressure maintains the heat of the core and supplies it with more hydrogen. Stars are relatively stable; some last for just a few million years, while others will last for many billions of years. Like all complex

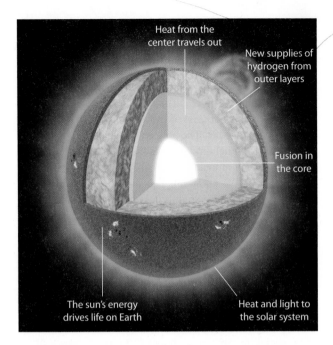

FIGURE 1.9 **The structure of our sun.** The sun has a simple structure, with fusion taking place in the center, and stores of hydrogen in the upper layers. But it is a more complex object than anything that had existed previously, and the energy produced in stars created new local energy flows that would help create more complex entities such as planets and, eventually, living organisms.

things, stars display emergent properties such as the ability to generate energy from fusion in their cores, and they are sustained and stabilized by these same energy flows.

Galaxies and stars also lay the foundations for new forms of complexity. Within galaxies there is a sweet spot, perfect for complexity. It is not too close to the center with its multiple "supernova" explosions (discussed later in the chapter), nor at the edge where there is much less energy, but in the regions in between. Similarly, it is unlikely that very complex things can be created *inside* stars, where there is so much energy that anything complex is likely to be destroyed as soon as it forms. Where we should expect to find greater complexity is not in the center of stars, nor in empty space where there is not enough energy, but in the regions around stars. And that is where most of the story of big history will take place: close to stars.

From about 200 million years after the big bang, then, we can imagine billions of clouds of matter collapsing to form billions of new stars held together in billions of new galaxies. Gravity herded galaxies into large clusters to form the huge, weblike structures that are the largest organized structures in our universe. At scales larger than clusters of galaxies, the power of gravity diminishes and we begin to see less structure as the force of expansion takes over. At these very large scales, different parts of the universe move away from one another. That was the expansion that Hubble had observed in the 1920s.

Threshold 3: The Creation of New Chemical Elements

Stars not only generate huge flows of energy in the regions close to them; they also create new forms of matter, new chemical *elements*. These chemical elements are the key to the next levels of complexity. That's why the forging of new chemical elements in dying stars counts as the third major threshold. With new chemical elements it was possible to make new types of matter by assembling atoms in new and more complex ways. After the crossing of threshold 3, the universe became more chemically complex (Threshold 3 Summary).

Threshold 3 Summary

THRESHOLD	INGREDIENTS ▶	STRUCTURE ▶	GOLDILOCKS CONDITIONS =	EMERGENT PROPERTIES
HEAVIER CHEMICAL ELEMENTS	Hydrogen and helium nuclei (i.e., protons).	Increasing numbers of protons linked by strong nuclear force into increasingly large atomic nuclei.	Extremely high temperatures created in dying stars or (even more extreme) in supernovae + strong nuclear force.	Potential for chemical combination, mainly via electromagnetism, to create almost infinite range of new types of matter.

We have seen that in the early universe atomic matter consisted, essentially, of hydrogen and helium. It is impossible to imagine a world as complex as ours created from just these two elements. This is partly because helium is inert; it does not react with any other elements. For planets, bacteria, and humans to emerge, a much more diverse palette of chemical elements is needed. Today, instead of just 2 elements, we have 92 different stable elements, as well as a few more that break up rapidly because their huge nuclei disintegrate as a result of the repulsive forces between their numerous protons.

Creating new elements was the dream of medieval alchemists. Many hoped that, by forging new elements, or by turning lead into gold, they could create elixirs of life, drugs that could cheat death. We now know that new elements were being formed throughout the universe within the hot furnaces of dying stars. By creating these elements, stars bequeathed to the universe not elixirs, but the possibility of life itself.

Chemical Elements

Today, atoms appear in 92 distinct forms, or elements (as well as a few more elements, such as plutonium, that are so unstable that we don't normally encounter them). As we have seen, atoms consist of a nucleus at their center that contains positively charged protons. Most nuclei also contain particles called neutrons that are similar to protons but have no electrical charge. Negatively charged electrons buzz around the nucleus at a great distance; indeed, according to Natalie Angier, "If the nucleus of an atom were a basketball located at the center of Earth, the electrons would be cherry pits whizzing about in the outermost layer of Earth's atmosphere."[1] Electrons have only 1/1,800th as much mass as protons, but their negative charges are the same as those of the protons so that the charges normally cancel each other out, making most atoms electrically neutral. All the different types of matter around us are made by combining these 92 types of atoms into more complicated structures known as molecules or compounds, structures that form as the electrons at the edges of atoms link up with neighboring atoms. Explaining in detail how elements combine to make more complicated materials is the central challenge of chemistry.

One of the great achievements of nineteenth-century chemists was to distinguish clearly between the chemical elements, the fundamental building blocks of chemistry, and the countless materials formed by assembling the elements into different types of compounds. The modern list of chemical elements and their properties is based on the pioneering work of the Russian chemist Dmitrii Mendeleev (1834–1907), who compiled the first, albeit incomplete, list of elements in 1869. Nowadays, the list of elements is called the **periodic table** because, as Mendeleev discovered, similar chemical properties seem to recur regularly as the number of protons increases (Figure 1.10). For example, some extremely unreactive gases—such as helium,

FIGURE 1.10 The periodic table. The elements present today in the periodic table were forged in three stages. Hydrogen and helium appeared soon after the big bang. Elements up to iron were formed by fusion in dying large stars and elements up to lead were formed by *neutron capture* in dying large stars. Finally, all other elements were formed in supernovae.

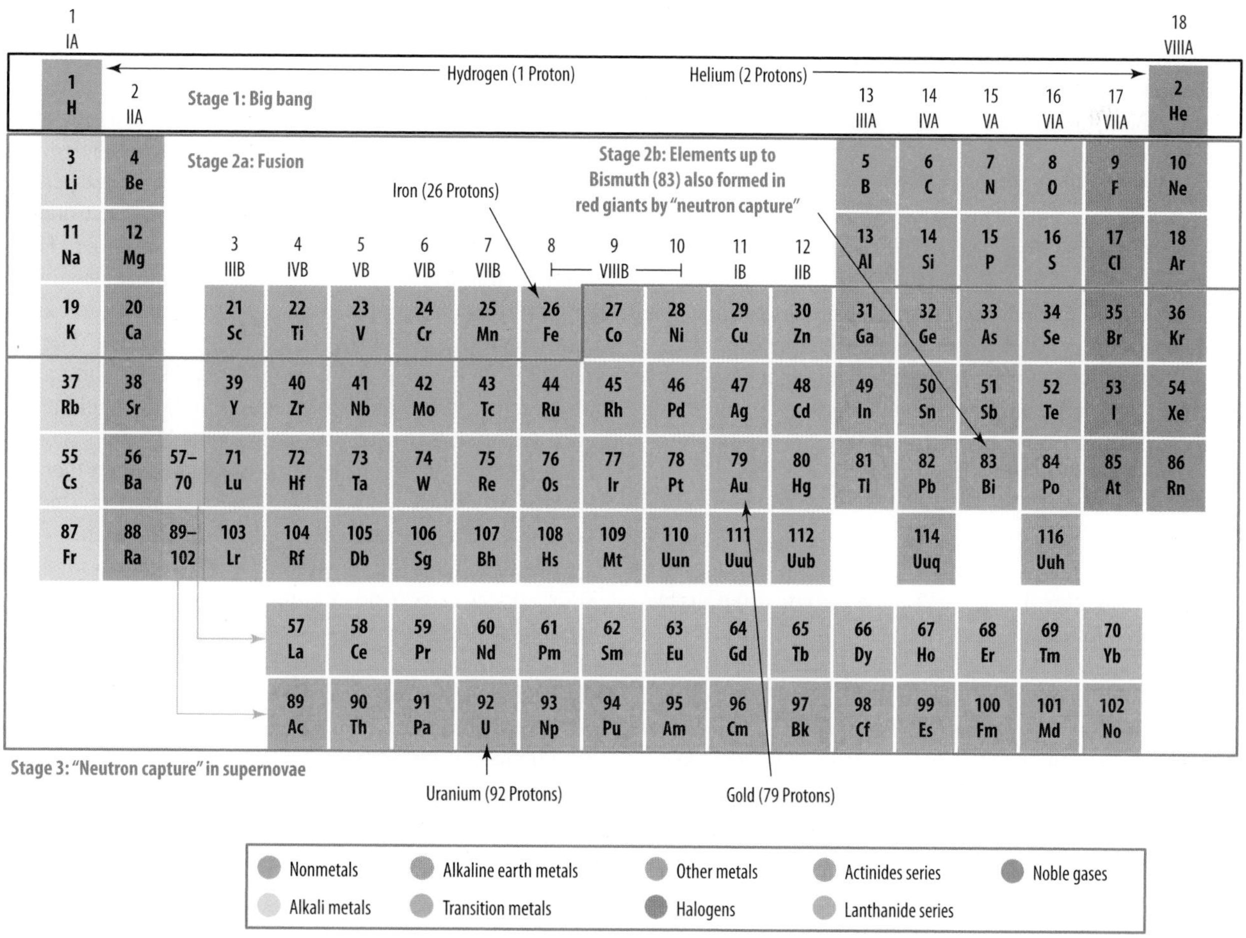

Nonmetals • Alkaline earth metals • Other metals • Actinides series • Noble gases
Alkali metals • Transition metals • Halogens • Lanthanide series

neon, argon, krypton, xenon, and radon—are grouped together at the right side of the periodic table. They are known as the *noble* gases. They are grouped together partly because they have similar chemical qualities and partly because the number of protons they contain increases in a reasonably regular pattern (helium has 2 protons, neon 10, argon 18, krypton 36, xenon 54, and radon 86).

To explain the forging of new chemical elements we must return to the hydrogen atoms that still make up most of the atoms in the universe, and we need to review some very elementary chemistry. Because hydrogen has just one proton in its nucleus, it is given the atomic number of 1 and appears as the first element in the periodic table. A tiny number of hydrogen atoms (roughly 0.02 percent) also have a neutron in their nucleus. We call this form of hydrogen deuterium. It weighs about twice as much as a normal atom of hydrogen because neutrons have about the same mass as a proton. Chemists call such deviant forms of atoms *isotopes*. As we will see, most elements come in standard forms, but can also exist as isotopes, or atoms that contain more or less neutrons than the element's standard form. (Carbon-14, which we met in the introduction, is an isotope of carbon with 6 protons and 8 neutrons; the most common form of carbon is carbon-12, with 6 protons and 6 neutrons.)

Helium, the next element on the periodic table, consists of two protons and two electrons. It is rare on Earth and was not discovered until the middle of the nineteenth century, when astronomers using spectroscopes detected huge amounts of it in the sun. The most common form of helium contains two neutrons as well as the two protons, but there also exists an isotope with just one neutron, which is, of course, about three-fourths of the weight of a normal helium atom.

So the defining feature of each element is the number of protons in its nucleus. This determines its atomic number. But each element may also exist in a number of slightly different forms, or isotopes, depending on the number of neutrons in the nucleus, so different isotopes of the same element may have slightly different *atomic weights*. Other important elements are carbon (atomic number 6), oxygen (8), iron (26), and uranium (92), the largest of all the stable elements. All elements heavier than lithium (atomic number 3) were made inside dying stars.

The Life and Death of Stars

The atomic matter in the early universe consisted, as we have seen, almost entirely of hydrogen and helium. To create new elements it was necessary to smash protons together so violently that they fused to form larger nuclei with larger atomic numbers. Where in the universe could you find temperatures hot enough to do this? In dying stars. So, to understand how elements were created in dying stars, we need to understand the life cycle of stars.

Even the shortest-lived stars keep burning for millions of years. So from Earth we can never watch the life cycle of a single star as it is born, matures, and dies. Instead, astronomers have studied millions of stars, each at a different stage in its life cycle. Slowly and painstakingly, they have used this vast database, accumulated since the nineteenth century, to build up a collective portrait of how stars live and die.

For a long time, the most important instrument for studying stars was the spectroscope. We saw earlier that the absorption lines on the spectra from starlight can tell you what elements a star contains, and their intensity makes it possible to estimate roughly how much of each element it contains. (More of a given element absorbs more light at particular frequencies so that the absorption lines are darker.)

The surface temperature of a star can be estimated from its color. As a general rule, red stars have lower surface temperatures than blue stars. The *real* (or intrinsic) brightness of a star, or the total energy it emits, depends on the amount of matter it contains. This is because stars with greater mass generally have denser and hotter cores so they generate more energy. We will see that, in general, large stars have higher surface temperatures and also larger masses, but there are some exceptions and they turn out to be rather interesting.

Using spectroscopes and powerful telescopes, astronomers can tell a lot about the mass, the temperature, and the chemical composition of stars. Using this information, astronomers have built up a general account of the life and death of stars.

As so often in science, understanding came when someone found a simple way of making sense of complicated information. This is what Newton had done with the huge amount of data available in his time about the movements of the stars. He had distilled that information into a few simple statements about the workings of gravity. Mendeleev had done something similar when he created the first periodic table of chemical elements. In 1910, a Danish astronomer, Ejnar Hertzsprung, and an American astronomer, Henry Russell, found a way of distilling the rapidly accumulating information about stars in a way that began to explain a lot about the life cycles of stars (Figure 1.11). They assembled information about many different stars into a simple graph. On one axis they plotted the real brightness of each star (which, as we have seen, can tell you its mass, or the amount of material it contains); and on the other they showed its surface temperature. The graph they produced is known as a **Hertzsprung–Russell (H–R) diagram.**

The first thing to note on the H–R diagram is that most stars appear in a band running from the bottom right to the upper left. In the bottom right corner we find stars that are reddish, which means they have lower surface temperatures, emit less energy, and are smaller. In the upper left corner we find stars that are blue, which means their surface temperatures are very high, they emit more energy in total, and have a lot of mass. Rigel, at one of the corners of the constellation of Orion, is an example of a blue star. This band of stars running diagonally from the top left to the bottom right corners of the diagram is known to astronomers as the *main sequence*. All the stars on the main

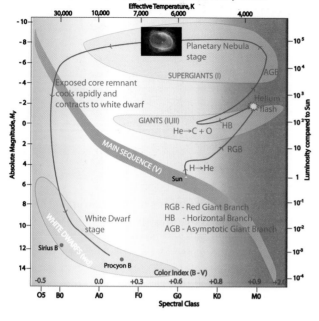

Sun's Post-Main Sequence Evolutionary Track

FIGURE 1.11 Simplified version of the Hertzprung–Russell diagram. The Hertzsprung–Russell diagram graphs the position of stars according to basic qualities such as their surface temperature and their absolute brightness. By graphing the position of many stars, astronomers slowly built up a picture of the life cycles of stars of different sizes. The main sequence, running from the bottom right to the top left, shows where most stars can be found during the phase in which they are converting hydrogen to helium, with larger and brighter stars to the left. The sun is approximately in the middle of the main sequence. Red giants can be found in the top right, and white dwarfs at the bottom left of the diagram.

sequence are mature stars, doing what most stars do most of the time: fusing protons into helium nuclei in their cores. Their position on the sequence depends on one thing: how much mass they contain, because more mass means higher densities at their cores and hotter temperatures. So, as you move leftward and upward along the main sequence you find stars that are more massive, as well as hotter and brighter. Those with high surface temperatures appear hot because they *are* hot, and they are hot because they have a lot of mass so they create a lot of pressure in their cores. Within the main sequence, surface temperature and real brightness are correlated because they both depend on the star's mass. Our sun appears roughly in the middle of the sequence; it is a medium-sized star, perhaps just slightly larger than average.

But not all stars appear on the main sequence. In the upper right corner there are stars that are emitting a huge amount of energy, which means they are very large. Yet their surface temperatures are relatively low, so they appear as red stars. These are known as **red giants.** A famous example is Betelgeuse, the large red star at one corner of the constellation of Orion. It can easily be seen on a clear night with the naked eye. At the bottom of the graph, on the other hand, are stars that have hot surfaces even though they seem quite small. These are known as white dwarfs. Sirius B, the companion star to Sirius, the brightest star in the night sky, is a white dwarf. Both red giants and white dwarfs are behaving oddly because they are at the end of their lives. They have begun to run out of hydrogen nuclei, the protons that sustain stars throughout most of their lives.

Inside Dying Stars

What happens when a star has turned so much hydrogen into helium that it begins to run out of fuel? Deprive a human of food and the human will die. Deprive a star of fuel and the results may be even more spectacular.

You will remember that stars form within huge clouds of atoms that are collapsing in on themselves as gravity pulls them together. But once fusion starts in the star's core, the heat at the center stops the collapse. A balance is achieved between gravity (which tends to collapse the star in on itself) and the heat at the center (which checks the collapse). At that point, the star settles down into a long life on the main sequence, usually lasting many billions of years. If the heat at the center falls slightly, the star may shrink slightly; if the heat increases, the star may expand slightly. Such tiny variations explain why stars such as Cepheid variables vary slightly in brightness and size.

As a star burns, it slowly uses up its stocks of hydrogen nuclei and creates more and more helium in its core. Eventually, the core will fill up with helium, the star will run out of hydrogen, and fusion will cease. The core will then collapse. If the star is small, it will shed its outer layers into nearby space. Its core will contract until it may be no larger than Earth, and its center will heat up. It is now a white dwarf, much smaller than the original star, but shining very brightly because of the intense heat in its core. It has now moved off the main sequence of the H–R diagram and to the lower part of the diagram. Its heat now comes from the energy generated when it was a real star. But slowly this heat will dissipate and it will cool, turning eventually into a cold, inert, cinder of a star. Astronomers call these burnt-out stars black dwarfs. It will simply sit there, invisible, and doing nothing for countless billions of years, side by side with an increasing number of other dead stars, in a vast and constantly growing star cemetery that will keep growing until the end of time.

However, if the star is large enough, its death agonies will be more complicated, more prolonged, and, for us at least, more interesting. As the core of a large star collapses because the star no longer has enough hydrogen to burn, temperatures may rise high enough in its outer layers for hydrogen fusion to continue. As a result, the star will expand, turning into a red giant. Meanwhile, the shrinking of its core raises the temperature at the center. If the star is large enough, the core may reach such a high temperature that helium atoms begin to fuse. These processes move the star off the main sequence, but in the opposite direction of a white dwarf. Its surface temperature may fall as it expands, but the total amount of light being emitted will increase as the temperature rises in its core. In another 4 or 5 billion years, our sun will turn into a red giant. When it does so, it will expand until it includes (and obliterates!) the inner planets of Mercury, Venus, and Earth.

In very large stars the collapse of the center creates temperatures so high that helium begins to fuse to form carbon, one of the more abundant elements in the universe, and the critical element in the evolution of life itself. However, helium burns at higher temperatures, and much faster than hydrogen, so the star will run out of helium much faster than it ran out of hydrogen. When that happens, the core will collapse once again.

What happens next? When our sun reaches this point it will shed its outer layers, scattering carbon through nearby space. Then it will collapse on itself, and turn into a white dwarf. It will move from the upper right part of the H–R diagram to join the other white dwarfs at the bottom of the graph. And, like all white dwarfs, it will eventually cool down and turn into a black dwarf, after which it will do nothing more.

However, stars that are larger than our sun have a few more tricks up their sleeves. When they run out of helium, their cores collapse, but there is still enough mass so that the collapse builds up much higher temperatures, temperatures high enough for carbon to start fusing, creating other elements such as oxygen and silicon in a series of violent burns. This pattern repeats. As each new fuel is used up, the core collapses once more, temperatures rise to even higher levels, and the dying star starts burning new fuels. The process becomes more and more frenetic, with different fuels being used in different layers of the star. Eventually, when their cores reach about 7 billion degrees Fahrenheit (about 4 billion degrees Celsius), stars start producing large amounts of iron (atomic number 26). Here is Cesare Emiliani's description of the violent final years of a very large star: "A star 25 times more massive than the sun will exhaust the hydrogen in its core in a few million years, will burn helium for half a million years, and—as the core continues to contract and the temperature continues to rise—will burn carbon for 600 years, oxygen for 6 months, and silicon for 1 day."[2] (See Figure 1.12.)

This process of creating new elements through fusion ends with iron. However, a second process, known as neutron capture, can form significant amounts of even heavier elements in dying massive stars. In this process, nuclei capture stray neutrons, which then decay to form protons. More protons increase the "atomic number" of the nucleus, transforming it into a heavier element. Step by step, this process can form nuclei as heavy as those of bismuth (83).

Once the center of a massive star has filled up with iron, fusion will cease and the star will collapse one last time in a colossal explosion known as a supernova. Briefly the star will shine as brightly as an entire galaxy, and most of its mass will be blown into outer space, while its center will collapse into a tight dense mass to form a neutron star or even a *black hole.* A neutron star is a form of matter as

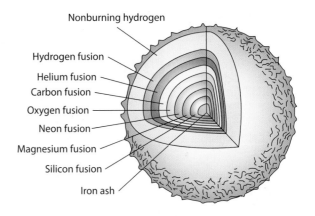

FIGURE 1.12 Illustrations of the buildup of the new elements in dying large stars. In the final stages of their existence, large stars start burning helium and other elements. Gradually, they develop a layered structure until finally, they start creating iron in their core. After that, they will either collapse or, if they are large enough, explode in a supernova.

dense as the nucleus of an atom; it is so dense that a mass the size of a small mountain might weigh as much as the whole Earth, and the whole thing may spin several times a second to form what astronomers call a *pulsar,* a body that emits regular flashes of light. If the original star is large enough, it will collapse to form a **black hole,** a region of space so dense that nothing can escape its gravitational pull, not even light. Black holes are very strange objects, and they will make one more brief appearance at the very end of this book.

In the explosion of a supernova one more thing happens: In just a few seconds all the remaining elements in the periodic table, from iron (26) up to uranium (92), are created by neutron capture and blown into space. (Some elements beyond uranium are also created but they are so unstable that they decay within fractions of a second.) We can see the results of such an explosion in the Crab Nebula, which represents the remnants of a supernova explosion observed by Chinese astronomers in 1054 (Figure 1.13).

So, the elements of the periodic table, the basic constituents of the matter from which we are made, were manufactured in three main stages. Most of the universe consists of hydrogen (almost 75 percent) and helium (about 23 percent), which were created in the big bang. That's the first stage. The second stage happens inside stars. Here, a lot of hydrogen is turned into helium by fusion, and in bigger stars some of the helium is then turned into carbon, oxygen, silicon, and several other elements up to iron (atomic number 26). In red giants, neutron capture can create even heavier elements, up to bismuth. As these stars die, the new elements they have manufactured are scattered into surrounding space. The third stage occurs in supernovae, the huge explosions that accompany the final seconds of the life of the very biggest stars. In the intense heat of a

FIGURE 1.13 Remnants of Crab Nebula. The Crab Nebula consists of the remains of a supernova that was observed by Chinese astronomers in 1054.

supernova so many neutrons are generated that all the other elements of the periodic table are manufactured by neutron capture in just a few seconds. Then these new elements are scattered into space.

Today, hydrogen and helium still make up about 98 percent of all atoms. Among the remaining 2 percent, the most common are those elements, up to iron, that were manufactured by fusion within dying stars. They include oxygen, carbon, nitrogen, iron, and silicon, all of which play crucial roles in the chemistry of the Earth and of life on Earth. The remaining elements were all manufactured by neutron capture either in dying stars or in supernovae; they exist in much smaller quantities.

The Importance of Chemistry

The first large stars probably died or exploded as supernovae 200 to 300 million years after the big bang. Ever since then, the number of new elements floating in clouds between the stars has been slowly increasing. At first there were no higher elements, but today, as we have seen, they may make up about 2 percent of all the atomic matter in the universe. Their presence increased the diversity of the universe because each element has a different number of protons and electrons and, as a result it behaves in slightly different ways from all other elements.

In much of the universe, the new elements made little difference, but in some places, higher elements appeared in greater abundance and played a much more important role. The young sun blasted most hydrogen and helium away from the orbit of our early Earth, so the Earth's crust is dominated by heavier elements such as oxygen and silicon, and many other elements, including iron, carbon, aluminum, and nitrogen are only slightly less common. That's why the chemical composition of Earth is very different from the average composition of the universe.

Atoms can combine in many different ways to form new types of materials with entirely new emergent properties. For example, if you combine two hydrogen atoms with one oxygen atom you get something entirely different from both of these colorless gases: you get water (Figure 1.14)! And water, as we will see, is vital for life.

Atoms bond together in various ways to form **molecules,** some with just a few atoms, some with millions or even billions of atoms. All chemical bonds between atoms depend on the behavior of the outermost electrons orbiting each atom. In *covalent* bonds, such as those that form molecules of water, two or more atoms can share the electrons in their outer shells. The electrons are attracted to the positive charges in several nuclei and this electromagnetic bond holds the atoms together. In *ionic* bonds, such as those that

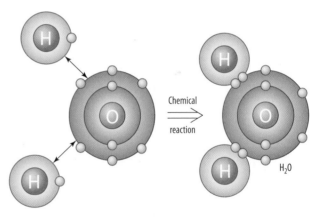

(a) Covalent Bond

(b) Water Molecule

FIGURE 1.14 Illustration of covalent bond and a water molecule. (*a*) A covalent bond, in which electrons are shared and (*b*) a water molecule, in which two atoms of hydrogen and one atom of oxygen are linked by a covalent bond.

form salt (sodium chloride, or NaCl), electrons migrate from one atom to the other. This gives one atom a negative charge and the other a positive charge, and it is these charges that bind the atoms together. In *metallic* bonds, the bonds that hold most metals together, almost all atoms lose electrons from their outer shells, and hordes of unattached electrons flow through and between the individual atoms. Because each atom has lost an electron, it has a slight positive charge, so it is attracted to the sea of electrons flowing around it.

Chemistry is the study of how atoms combine to form new materials, from rocks to diamonds, to DNA, and of course to you and me. This is why the formation of new elements inside stars counts as one of the fundamental thresholds in this course. It made possible a vast range of new materials with entirely new properties. Nowadays, we can study the clouds of matter around distant stars, and identify many different molecules, including simple materials such as water, and also some of the basic ingredients of life. But space is a tough environment; it's very cold and there is limited energy, so few of the molecules we find in space contain more than 100 atoms.

The surface of Earth was a much more promising environment for interesting chemistry because it contained many elements that could combine in different ways to produce entirely new materials. It was a Goldilocks environment for chemistry. In each of the Threshold Summaries that appear throughout this book, the Goldilocks factors are those that permitted the threshold to occur and be crossed. The next chapter will describe the creation of Earth and the Goldilocks conditions that would eventually make it possible for life to appear.

SUMMARY

In this chapter we described how modern science explains three crucial thresholds in the appearance and evolution of our universe. We saw how big bang cosmology explains the beginnings of our universe; how, in the simple early universe, the first galaxies and stars appeared; and how, in their death throes, large stars created the chemical elements that provided the raw materials that would eventually make it possible to build new types of materials and new objects such as planets and life itself.

In our own part of the universe, a supernova explosion occurred just over 4.5 billion years ago, scattering new chemical elements into nearby space. Shock waves from this explosion, like the vibrating skin of a drum, rippled through the clouds of matter near the supernova and triggered the beginnings of a slow, gravitational collapse. Slowly, in a pattern that should by now be familiar, a cloud of matter consisting mostly of hydrogen and helium, but also containing tiny amounts of all the other chemical elements, began to collapse in the early stages of star formation. Out of this collapse our own sun and solar system eventually formed. That story leads us to a new threshold of complexity, and we will tell it in the next chapter.

CHAPTER QUESTIONS

1. What do you think are the main differences between traditional origin stories and the accounts of origin contained in modern science?
2. What new forms of evidence persuaded Edwin Hubble that the universe was expanding? How convincing is that evidence?
3. What were the most important events that happened in the first three minutes after the big bang?
4. What is cosmic background radiation and why was its discovery so important for modern cosmology?
5. How were stars created?
6. How were new elements created inside dying stars?
7. In what ways can we say that the emergence of stars and the death of stars make the universe more complex than it was just after the big bang?

KEY TERMS

absorption lines	cosmic background	fusion	parallax
atomic matter	radiation (CBR)	Hertzsprung–Russell (H–R)	periodic table
big bang	cosmology	diagram	plasma
big bang cosmology	dark matter and dark energy	light-year	red giants
black hole	Doppler effect	matter	red shift
Cepheid variables	energy	molecules	spectroscope

FURTHER READING

Angier, Natalie. *The Canon: A Whirligig Tour of the Beautiful Basics of Science.* New York: Houghton Mifflin, 2007 (particularly the chapters on calibration, physics, and astronomy).

Bryson, Bill. *A Short History of Nearly Everything.* New York: Broadway Books, 2003.

Delsemme, Armande. *Our Cosmic Origins: From the Big Bang to the Emergence of Life and Intelligence.* Cambridge, UK: Cambridge University Press, 1998.

Duncan, Todd, and Craig Tyler. *Your Cosmic Context: An Introduction to Modern Cosmology.* San Francisco: Pearson Addison-Wesley, 2007.

Emiliani, Cesare. *The Scientific Companion: Exploring the Physical World with Facts, Figures, and Formulas.* 2nd ed. New York: Wiley, 1995.

Greene, Brian. *The Fabric of the Cosmos: Space, Time and the Texture of Reality.* London: Penguin Books, 2005.

Primack, Joel, and Nancy Abrams. *The View from the Center of the Universe: Discovering Our Extraordinary Place in the Cosmos.* New York: Penguin, 2006.

Sproul, Barbara. *Primal Myths: Creation Myths around the World.* San Francisco: Harper, 1991.

ENDNOTES

1. Natalie Angier, *Canon: A Whirligig Tour of the Beautiful Basics of Science* (New York: Houghton Mifflin, 2007), 86.
2. Cesare Emiliani, *The Scientific Companion: Exploring the Physical World with Facts, Figures, and Formulas,* 2nd ed. (New York: Wiley, 1995), 61.

the fourth threshold

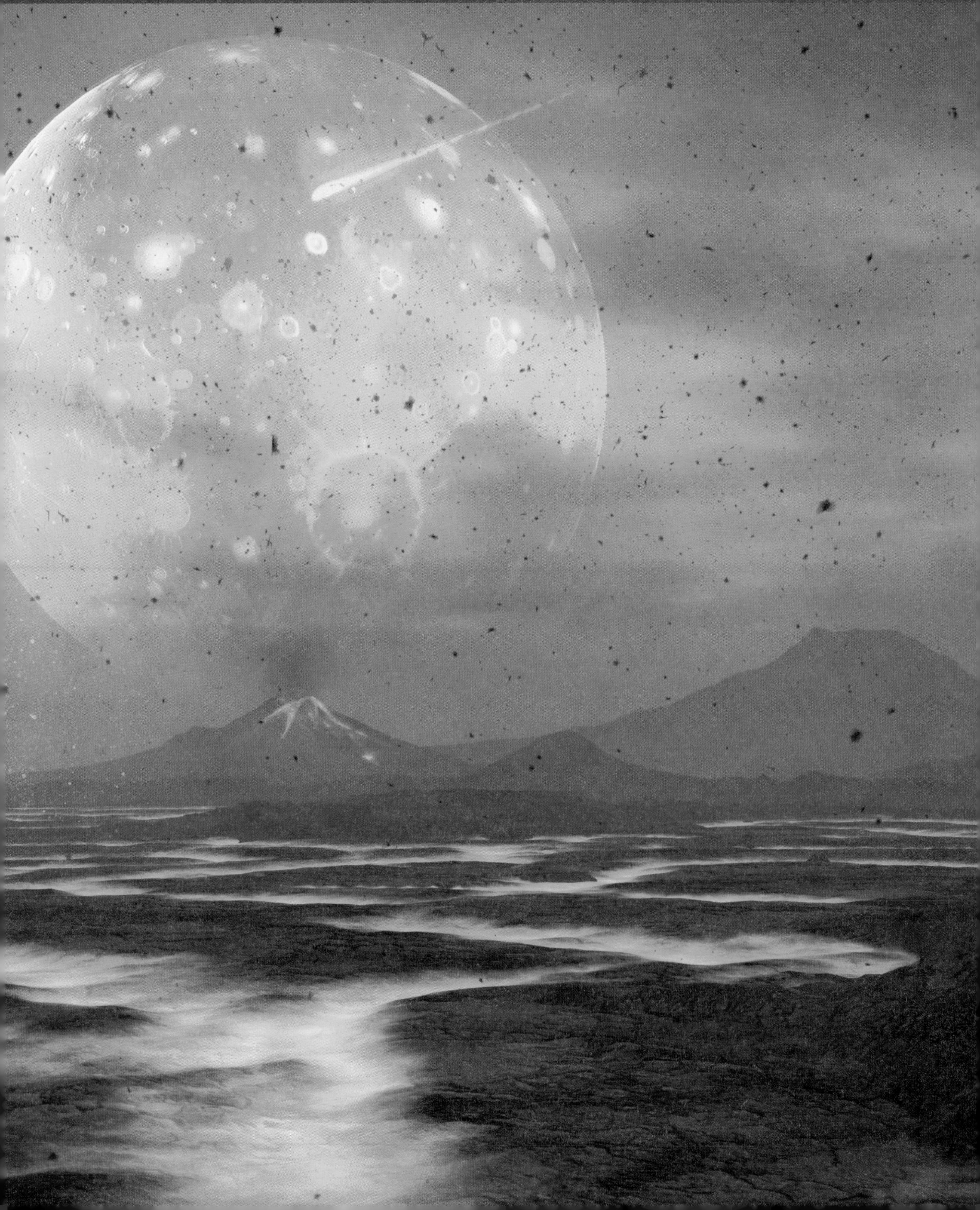

The Emergence of the Sun, the Solar System, and the Earth

Seeing the Big Picture

4.6 to 3.8 Billion Years Ago

▶ In what way did the birth of our sun and solar system lead us across a new threshold of complexity?

▶ How does the solar nebula theory explain the formation of solar systems, and of Earth?

▶ What were conditions like during the first billion years of Earth's history—that is, during the Hadean eon?

▶ What is the theory of plate tectonics, and why has it become one of the core paradigms of modern science?

With the birth of our own star, the sun, and the solar system that includes planet Earth, cosmic history crossed a new threshold of complexity in one small part of the universe (Threshold 4 Summary). The solar system, which consists of the sun and the collection of planets and other celestial bodies that revolve around it, is the cosmic context in which Earth was formed and shaped in a location and manner that made it possible for life to appear on a hitherto lifeless object. The sun is located about two-thirds of the distance from the center to the edge of the Milky Way, and is just one of perhaps 400 billion other stars in the galaxy. A range of scientists, including astronomers, physicists, chemists, and geologists, have contributed to the construction of a coherent and convincing account of the emergence of the sun, the solar system, Earth itself, and the forces linked back to the birth of the universe that allowed Earth to assume its particular structure and appearance. This chapter will summarize those scientific accounts, and the evidence that supports them, and conclude with Earth on the verge of crossing the fifth threshold of complexity by giving birth to its first living organisms.

Threshold 4 Summary

THRESHOLD	INGREDIENTS ▶	STRUCTURE ▶	GOLDILOCKS CONDITIONS =	EMERGENT PROPERTIES
PLANETS	New chemical elements and compounds in orbit around stars.	Diversity of materials bound together gravitationally and chemically into large balls of matter normally orbiting stars.	Increasing abundance of heavier elements in regions of star formation.	New astronomical objects with more physical and chemical complexity and potential to generate even greater chemical complexity.

Threshold 4: The Emergence of the Sun and Solar System

From the beginning of human history our species has demonstrated an extraordinary degree of curiosity about our environment. This interest in our surroundings has inspired countless adventurers to explore the mountains, jungles, deserts, and oceans of planet Earth. Early humans also exhibited an intense interest in the night sky, and especially in the stars and planets that occupy our particular tiny corner of the cosmos. Ancient civilizations developed elaborate explanatory schemes about our cosmic neighborhood and constructed sophisticated and often surprisingly accurate models to explain its workings.

With the invention of the telescope in Europe during the first decade of the seventeenth century, observation with the naked eye (which responds only to a very restricted set of light and color wavelengths) was replaced by magnification tools that allowed early astronomers to study nearby celestial objects in more detail, and to discover many more distant objects that had not even been suspected to this point. Seventeenth-century observers, beginning with Galileo, soon became aware of the moons of Jupiter and Saturn, for example. With the development of more powerful telescopes in the eighteenth and nineteenth centuries, astronomers were able to observe Uranus directly for the first time in 1781, and Neptune in 1846.

By the late nineteenth century, the new technology of photography was being applied to astronomy. Film could accumulate light from objects through long time exposures, often of several hours' duration, and its use allowed for the permanent recording of stars and *nebulae* (glowing clouds of gas or dust reflecting the light of nearby stars) much fainter than anything the human eye could have seen, even with the aid of a telescope. As we saw in Chapter 1, astronomers also learned to use a spectroscope, which was able to sort light from distant sources, such as a star, into constituent colors or "frequencies."

It is hardly surprising that our solar system has been of great interest to humans of all cultures and times, because it is literally our cosmic neighborhood. Despite its apparent obscurity in the overall scheme of the expanding universe, our cosmic neighborhood is of considerable interest to those of us who live in it, in the same way that we are fascinated by the physical environment of our region, continents, and planet. And in our ongoing attempts to answer important questions about our neighborhood—such as how and when the sun and planets arose—scientists have developed an increasingly sophisticated array of technology, which has provided the evidence needed to construct the account outlined in this chapter.

Evidence for the Origin of the Solar System

Three observational tools in particular have helped scientists accumulate a substantial body of evidence to support the current theory of planetary formation. These are land-based and orbiting telescopes, and unpiloted spacecraft. In addition, radiometric dating has allowed researchers to date precisely many of the events in the history of the solar system and planet Earth.

Land-Based Telescopes From the early seventeenth century until quite recently, scientists have largely depended on land-based telescopes in their quest to construct a convincing account of the origin of the solar system. However, despite their reliability and ever-increasing sophistication, land-based telescopes struggle to overcome problems such as light pollution, which is excess and obtrusive light created by humans.

Orbiting Telescopes In the second half of the twentieth century, new technology was developed that allowed astronomers to penetrate the most distant corners of the universe. Rocket technology, which, like so many technological advancements of the century was developed to provide a military advantage during World War II, allowed humans direct access to space for the first time. By the 1960s rockets were being used to fire telescopes into space. These "mobile observatories" were sent up in satellites that orbit Earth. By escaping the light and other atmospheric pollutants above the surface of the planet, flying telescopes have allowed us to observe the entire spectrum of electromagnetic radiation, from the longest radio wavelengths to the shortest gamma rays. Highly sophisticated sensing materials (particularly silicon, a heat-resistant inert compound) have then been used to detect radiation at the widest range of wavelengths. Attaching giant silicon cameras to large orbiting telescopes has made direct observation of much of the universe a reality for the first time in human history.

One of the most important early satellites to penetrate the universe's darkest corners was the Uhuru X-ray satellite, launched in 1970. By mapping the X-ray sky (i.e., by showing what the sky looked like at X-ray frequencies), remnants of hundreds of massive stars that had exploded in the past were discovered, along with the first direct evidence for black holes. Astronomers today use information from the Chandra X-ray Observatory and the European Space Agency's (ESA) multimirrored XMM-Newton to obtain extraordinary high-resolution X-ray images of the cosmos.

The most remarkable of all orbiting telescopes is the National Aeronautics and Space Administration's (NASA) Hubble Space Telescope (HST), which was launched from a space shuttle on April 25, 1990. About the size of a school bus, it orbits Earth every 97 minutes. Within days of its launch, however, the HST began sending back images that were badly out of focus. NASA scientists

FIGURE 2.1 The Hubble Space Telescope.
Satellite astronomy has transformed our knowledge of space. The extraordinary Hubble Space Telescope has contributed an enormous amount of data about the history of our solar system and the universe.

quickly discovered the reason—a major flaw in the giant mirror, which was too flat on one edge by one-fiftieth of the width of a human hair! In December 1993 the space shuttle *Endeavour* was able to capture the HST and add a camera to rectify the problem with the mirror. The Hubble was refurbished again in February 1997, when it was equipped with an infrared spectrograph (Figure 2.1). As it orbits above Earth's atmosphere, the HST records images of startling clarity that have revolutionized our knowledge of space. The HST can deliver images to astronomers with about 0.1 arc second resolution (a tiny fraction of a degree and the standard unit for measuring resolution), but scientists believe that during the next few decades, giant orbiting interferometers may push resolution into the range of one-billionth of an arc second!

Unpiloted Spacecraft Over the past four decades a number of unpiloted spacecraft have been sent out into space, in most cases never to return. The data sent back by these spacecraft have allowed scientists to study our solar system in even greater detail. Information provided by unpiloted spacecraft has been able both to debunk old theories and help create new ones.

For example, a number of visiting unpiloted spacecraft refuted long-standing theories that the surface of Mars was covered in artificial canals, by proving that these were in fact natural features. The exploration of Mars by spacecraft began in 1965 with NASA's Mariner 4 probe. In 1971,

the fourth threshold

Mariner 9 was placed into permanent orbit around Mars, and within one year it had effectively photographed the entire surface of the planet. This photographic survey discovered Olympus Mons, the largest volcano known in the solar system, and what appeared to be a significant number of dried-up riverbeds. In 1976, as part of the search for any evidence that life had once existed on Mars, NASA landed two modules on the surface of Mars at different locations, but they found no trace of any organic material.

Just over 20 years later the Mars Pathfinder also landed on the surface, followed soon after by the Mars Global Surveyor, which was maneuvered into orbit around the planet and has been sending back detailed images for the past decade. More recently the Mars rovers Spirit and Opportunity were landed on the surface. These hardy all-terrain vehicles have been transmitting images from, and conducting geological experiments on, the surface of the planet since 2003. So far, they have been unsuccessful in finding any traces of residual water on Mars. There is evidence of erosion on the surface, however, including signs of large floods and small river systems, which suggests that at some time in the past there must have been some form of liquid on the planet. Although liquid water is the obvious candidate, there are other possible explanations, including cold, dry eruptions of gas, dust, and rock fueled by exploding liquid carbon dioxide.

On May 25, 2008, the Phoenix explorer landed in the Martian northern polar region and began a search for microbial life and evidence of water on the planet. Data collected by Phoenix suggested that liquid water had interacted with the Martian surface throughout the planet's history into modern times and also that volcanic activity had continued on the planet until relatively recent geological times, several million years ago. The latest NASA mission to Mars successfully landed the probe Curiosity inside the massive Gale Crater on August 6, 2012. Curiosity is double the size and five times the weight of Spirit and Opportunity, and it has the overall objective of determining just how habitable Mars was and is. It has begun its study of the climate and geology of the planet, particularly evidence that rivers once flowed on the surface, and is also collecting data that might assist in the planning of a possible piloted mission to Mars in the future.

Venus, the planet whose size is closest to Earth's, has also been the target of space probes. The first of these, NASA's Mariner 2, flew over the planet as early as 1962 and recorded temperatures radiating from the surface of approximately 570 degrees Fahrenheit (300 degrees Celsius). Between 1965 and 1975 the Soviet Union launched 15 different Venera space probes, most of which missed their target or crashed on the surface. However, five did land smoothly, despite the extreme heat (using asbestos parachutes), and recorded surface temperatures of an astonishing 860 degrees Fahrenheit (460 degrees Celsius)! The NASA Magellan probe observed two complete rotations of Venus (each lasting 243 days) between 1990 and 1992 and created a detailed topographic map of the entire surface at the same time, which revealed numerous craters and volcanic systems.

Two of the most significant journeys made by unpiloted spacecraft were those undertaken by NASA's Voyagers 1 and 2. The vessels were launched in 1977, to take advantage of a rare alignment of four of the giant gas planets of our solar system—Jupiter, Saturn, Uranus, and Neptune—an alignment that would occur only once every 175 years. This allowed the two spacecraft to gain velocity assistance from the gravitational fields of each planet, which effectively meant that they were flung from one planet to the next at speeds of up to 35,000 miles per hour (56,000 kilometers per hour)! Even so, it took Voyager 2 nine years to reach Uranus, and twelve to reach Neptune. By 2010 the Voyagers had reached the edge of the solar system, from where they are expected to keep sending data back to Earth to beyond 2020.

The use of unpiloted spacecraft continues to provide information about our solar system neighbors far beyond that available from Earth-based observation technology. In December 2007, for example, data from the Cassini unpiloted spacecraft orbiting Saturn demonstrated that the rings of the planet were as old as the solar system itself, about 4.5 billion years. This debunked earlier theories, based partly on data gathered by the Voyager spacecraft, that the rings might have formed as recently as 100 million years ago out of debris thrown up from a violent meteoric collision with Earth's moon.

Determining the Age of the Solar System

As we noted in the introductory chapter, since the mid-1950s astronomers have also used radiometric dating in their attempts to understand the solar system. **Radiometric dating** is a technique used to date materials such as rocks by measuring the rate of radioactive decay. This technology has provided scientists with reliable absolute numerical dates about the past and has been central to what we are calling the chronometric revolution. Radiometric dating has shown, for example, that Earth is about 4.5 billion years old, and other significant dates in our planet's history from formation to the present are now chronologically fixed. It turns out that most objects in our solar system were formed at about the same time as Earth.

The principles of radiometric dating emerged as scientists began to understand more about the spontaneous breakdown, or decay, of atomic nuclei in isotopes, a process known as **radioactivity.** As we saw in Chapter 1, the nucleus of an atom is formed of protons and neutrons; in isotopes the nucleus loses neutrons, but not protons or the electrons that surround the nucleus. Scientists refer to the unstable radioactive isotope as the *parent,* and the isotopes that are formed as a result of decay are called the *daughter products.* When the radioactive parent, uranium-238, decays, for example, it passes through a number of steps before finally becoming the stable daughter product, lead-206.

This decay process is regular and statistically measurable. Scientists in the 1950s realized that radioactivity provided a reliable means of measuring the age of rocks and minerals that contained radioactive isotopes. Radiometric dating is possible because the rates of decay for many isotopes have been precisely measured and apparently do not vary under normal conditions.

Scientists express the rate of radioactive decay in a unit known as a **half-life,** which is the time required for an entity to fall to half its value as measured from the beginning of a time period. Essentially, when the quantities of both parent and daughter products are equal, one half-life has transpired. When one-quarter of the parent atoms remain, but three-quarters have decayed into the daughter product, the parent–daughter ratio of 1:3 tells us that two half-lives have passed. By the time parent–daughter ratios have reached 1:15 in a sample, four half-lives have passed. So if the half-life of any particular isotope is, for example, 1 million years, a 1:15 ratio tells us that four half-lives have passed, and the sample must be 4 million years old. Many radioactive isotopes exist in nature, but five have proved particularly useful for dating events associated with the history of Earth. Uranium-238 decays to form the daughter product of lead-206, with a half-life of 4.5 billion years. Uranium-235 decays to form the daughter lead-207, with a half-life of 713 million years. Thorium-232 decays to form lead-208, with a half-life of 14.1 billion years. Rubidium-87 decays to form strontium-87, with an enormous half-life of 47 billion years. Finally, potassium-40 decays to form the daughter product argon-40, with a half-life of 1.3 billion years.

Despite its half-life of 1.3 billion years, the potassium-40 to argon-40 decay clock has proved the most versatile of the five radioactive isotopes and has even been useful in dating materials that are younger than 100,000 years. There are problems associated with its use, however, in that a correct date cannot be obtained unless the mineral has remained in a closed system during the entire period since it first formed. If the rock is subject to high temperatures during its life, for example, it will lose argon gas and a correct date will be unobtainable. Scientists try to counter this source of error by working with only fresh, unweathered samples.

The most useful isotope for dating recent events is carbon-14, which is the radioactive isotope of carbon. The half-life for carbon-14 is short—only 5,730 years—which makes it particularly useful for dating human history and the recent geologic past. Carbon-14 is present in the upper atmosphere, and the isotope is incorporated into carbon dioxide, which in turn is absorbed by living organisms. When a plant or animal dies, carbon-14 gradually decays and converts to nitrogen-14 at a rate that is statistically measurable. Although carbon-14 is useful only in dating organic materials, including wood, bones, and cotton fibers, it has provided such a reliable chronological framework for archaeologists, anthropologists, historians, and geologists that the chemist who discovered its use, Willard F. Libby, received a Nobel Prize in 1960.

These generally reliable principles and techniques have produced an extraordinary number of dates, and radiometric dating has become an indispensable tool for a wide range of scientists. Astronomers, cosmologists, and geologists have used the technique to date materials like the moon rocks, asteroids, and the rocks of our own planet, and in so doing have provided an accurate chronology of the history of our solar system and planet.

The Sun—the Energy That Drives Our World

Although of great significance to us, our sun is a fairly ordinary specimen of star. The most massive stars astronomers have observed are about 100 times larger in mass than the sun, and these tend to consume all their available fuel in just a few million years before dying a cataclysmic death in supernovae (see Chapter 13). In contrast, the sun will live for about 10 billion years in total. This relative "normalcy" might have implications for the existence of other planets capable of supporting life. That is, if the processes involved in forming our particular star and orbiting planets are nothing special, such processes might be very common and apply to billions of other stars and solar systems.

We know that the sun, like all stars, was formed from the collapse of a giant molecular cloud. The cloud that formed the solar system appeared some 5 billion years ago and was probably quite similar to another cloud astronomers have been observing that has appeared much more recently in the Orion constellation, within our Milky Way galaxy (Figure 2.2). This cloud is some 1,600 light-years from Earth and measures several hundred light-years across, making it easily visible to modern astronomers. Analysis of the Orion Cloud suggests it consists of some 70 percent hydrogen, 27 percent helium, 1 percent oxygen, 0.3 percent carbon, and 0.1 percent nitrogen. Astronomers

FIGURE 2.2 The Orion Cloud. The Orion Cloud as observed by the Hubble Space Telescope. Is this the way our solar system began?

believe that the cloud contains some 92 natural chemical elements in total, in a mixture very similar to the blend of elements found in our sun and planets. Several hundred stars in the process of formation have been discovered in the cloud since 1993, most of them surrounded by rings of dust in accretion disks that might form planets. The Orion Cloud offers an extraordinary insight into the sort of processes that probably led to the emergence of our own solar system.

Our planet is spinning around our sun and is made of the same material that formed it, although the balance of elements in the sun is very different from that of Earth. The light from the sun has to travel 93 million miles (150 million kilometers) to reach us, taking about eight minutes to do so, and yet it warms the planet and makes liquid water and living organisms possible. If there were no sun, the temperature on Earth would be 400 degrees Fahrenheit below zero (240 degrees Celsius below zero), and life would not exist. It is Earth's proximity to the sun that is thus critical, and also the massive size of the sun— one million times larger than Earth. Cosmologist Brian Swimme puts it like this:

> It's just this vast fire that enables all of life to take place here. And what I find really fascinating is the way in which the sun produces this light. Right at its core it is transforming hydrogen into helium. And in that transformation it's converting some of its mass into energy. Every second, four million tons of the sun [are] being transformed into this light.[1]

Formation of the Solar System: Early Stages

Scientists attempted for centuries to explain the origin of the solar system. In the eighteenth century, German philosopher Immanuel Kant (1724–1804) and French mathematician Pierre Simon Laplace (1749–1827) independently argued that a *solar nebula* (a flattened and rotating disk of gas and dust such as has been observed in the Orion Cloud) must have coalesced around the sun, and from this the planets were created. This theory has survived the centuries and is the most widely accepted explanation, although a number of unanswered questions still remain concerning the process of planetary formation.

The theory suggests that the solar nebula formed from a dense core in a molecular cloud that collapsed under the pressure of gravity, a process that may have also been triggered by a shock wave from a supernova. As it collapsed, the cloud began to heat up, rotate, and spin, and matter fell into a disk that formed around the developing *proto-sun*. The rotating disk released enormous amounts of energy (produced by colliding atoms), and temperatures in the inner disk may have reached more than 3,092 degrees Fahrenheit (1,700 degrees Celsius)! This would have vaporized dust grains close to the center, but in the outer regions of the nebula interstellar molecules, grains, and ices survived. Eventually the nebula began to cool, allowing molecules and solid particles to re-form, although the spinning

disk would still have consisted of about 98.5 percent gas and only 1.5 percent dust. However, recent analysis of the composition of several meteorites known to have formed within the first 3 million years of the solar system's formation has indicated that between 1 and 2 million years after the formation of the sun, the solar system received an influx of iron produced by a supernova in its immediate vicinity.

The distribution of the solid particles and gases was important in the subsequent story of the solar nebula. The inner nebula contained silicates and iron compounds, while the outer regions included large quantities of carbon dioxide, water, and other interstellar grains inherited from the original molecular cloud. This distribution is reflected in the makeup and location of the planets today, with the inner terrestrial planets consisting mainly of rocky materials such as silicates and metals, and the outer planets (from Jupiter and beyond) consisting mainly of hydrogen, helium, and water.

Eventually the matter in the inner zones began to spin more slowly, and as it slowed was drawn in a spiral nearer to the central mass of the proto-sun. This drift toward the center was accentuated for fractions of an inch- to yard-sized (centimeter- to meter-sized) solids, which may have drifted toward the proto-sun at a rate of 600,000 miles (1 million kilometers) per year. Some material may have fallen into the sun, but much of it survived to form the rocky terrestrial planets. Why all of the material did not fall into the sun remains one of the unanswered questions of the solar nebular theory, although it may have something to do with centrifugal force in the spinning disk, which would have tended to drive matter away from the center.

By 100,000 years after the start of the process, the sun probably reached its final mass, at which time collapsing would have finished and turbulence within the disk subsided. This moment becomes *age zero* for the solar system, and a precise date for this has been determined by the radiometric dating of *chondrites* (primitive stony materials from the asteroid belts). In December 2007, researchers at the University of California–Davis analyzed material from a carbonaceous chondrite to propose that the solar system is precisely 4.568 billion years old.

A large number of young stars with relatively low mass have been discovered in other regions of the Milky Way galaxy over the past decade or so, still with dust rings around them (remnants of the original accretion disk). Astronomers have observed violent winds escaping from many of these stars, much more intense than the solar winds that currently escape from the sun. Scientists now realize that stars not only emit radiation, but also release particles in a steady stream, probably caused by pressure expansion in the star; and it is these particle emissions that are called stellar winds. The first star discovered emitting this powerful wind was the T star of the Taurus constellation, and these winds have been known ever since as the T Tauri. The winds seem to emerge at the time that the accretion disk stops directly feeding the star; they are so powerful that in a few million years they disperse a huge amount of the stellar cloud. As the winds collided with the inner edge of the disk, the growth process of the sun was stopped. Only the heaviest objects in the disk were unaffected by the T Tauri, because their mass was large enough to resist the winds.

The T Tauri wind also influenced the fact that there is so little hydrogen and helium in the Earth's crust and so much in the orbits of the gas giants. This intense solar wind drove the lighter elements (such as H and He) away out toward the orbits of Jupiter and Saturn. This explains both the domination of heavier elements in the Earth's crust, and also the great size of the gas giants.

By the time the growth process of the sun was ended by the T Tauri, the sun had absorbed almost all of the material in the original solar nebula. Only a very small amount was left over, perhaps as little as 0.1 percent. It is this tiny surviving remnant that concerns us next, because the leftovers were used to make all the rest of the objects in our solar system, including planet Earth.

Formation of the Planets: Accretion

How do astronomers explain how the remaining debris trapped in the solar nebula formed into planets? The larger objects (up to 6.2 miles [10 kilometers] in diameter) that somehow managed to avoid spiraling into the sun are called *planetesimals*. The force of gravitational attraction between these objects caused many of them to assume elliptical orbits, which led to regular violent collisions between them. Although the extreme violence of many of these collisions resulted in the disintegration of many planetesimals, others began to coalesce together through gravity in a process known as **accretion,** a word that describes the process in which stellar objects grow in size through the collision and sticking together of particles. Astronomers do not yet have a complete understanding of the accretion processes that led to the formation of planetesimals. The main problem is that particles measured in centimeters tend to shatter or bounce off when they collide, which means that some other mechanism must be involved in allowing these colliding particles to stick together. Latest research is focused on whether turbulence in the solar nebula actually creates areas of higher density that increase gravitational attraction, or whether drag created by slower moving gases causes a pileup of materials that can coalesce into stable planetesimals.

The largest objects acquired stronger gravitational fields and swept up more and more of the debris in their orbit, and rather like a snowball effect, the size of these entities kept increasing (or accreting). Computer models have shown that after some 10,000 years, out of millions of smaller objects, growth through continuing collisions led to the emergence of hundreds of planetesimals, some of which were nearly as large as our moon. These planetesimals would have orbited the sun in thin giant rings not unlike the rings of Saturn, surrounded by clouds of thick nebular gas.

Over the next 10 to 100 million years, continuing planetesimal collisions and accretion led to the emergence of a much smaller number of proto-planets, similar in size to the terrestrial planets of our solar system today, each

following its own orbiting plane. In that way, 100 million years of violence eventually resulted in the sort of gravitational and orbital calm that characterizes the solar system today. However, we have evidence from the moon that suggests that between 4.1 and 3.8 billion years ago, the moon and inner planets may have been subject to a late cataclysmic bombardment by rogue asteroids or comets that had been diverted from their orbits.

While this model explains the formation of the inner terrestrial planets, it is less successful in accounting for the gas giants of the outer solar system. In the outer regions temperatures were so low that the planetesimals, which consisted of mostly hydrogen and helium, also contained large amounts of water snow. Somehow the planetesimals that became the giant outer planets were able to scoop up large quantities of additional material from the nebula, which included light gas and solids.

The standard explanation for this action is that the core of these giants probably formed through collision growth like the terrestrial planets, and as these cores grew larger they accreted gas and ices from the surrounding nebula. The increasing mass of these giants led to *runaway accretion,* which meant that growth did not stop until all the gas in each planet's orbit was swept up. An alternative theory—the gravitational instability model—suggests that the giant planets may have formed directly from the disk in a few thousand years, where regions simply collapsed due to the pressure of gravity.

Formation of Moons

As early as 1610, Galileo used his newly invented telescope to discover four moons orbiting Jupiter. Modern telescopes reveal that Jupiter actually has dozens of small moons surrounding it, constituting a mini planetary system that resembles that of the solar system. While the inner planets have only a handful of moons between them, the giant planets all have ring systems. The rings of Saturn (also observed by Galileo) are by far the largest and best known. The rings consist of solid particles ranging in size from dust grains to boulders to moonlets. (Figure 2.3)

The formation of Earth's moon remained a mystery until the 1970s, when scientists began proposing various explanations. The standard theory today is that Earth collided with a Mars-sized object around 4.45 billion years ago. The impact was so violent that a vast plume of vapor and molten rock was ejected, some of which was then trapped in orbit around Earth. The process of accretion explains the coalescence of this material into the shape of the moon. At first the orbit of the moon would have been very close to Earth, but that distance has extended outward from Earth to where it is today. The moon continues to move away from Earth at the rate of 2 inches (5 centimeters) per year because of its very slowly increasing orbital velocity.

The moon does not have an atmosphere, which means its surface is far less susceptible to erosion than that of Earth. As a result, the scars caused by collisions with

FIGURE 2.3 Voyager 2 and the rings of Saturn.
Astronomers gained a very good idea of what the early solar nebula was like when they tried to send the unpiloted spacecraft Voyager 2 through the rings of Saturn. They had assumed that the rings consisted only of gas, but when the tiny unpiloted spacecraft got close enough they realized that the main rings are tightly packed with frequently colliding objects that range in size from dust grains to objects the size of moonlets, similar to the state of the early solar system during the accretion phase. At the last minute they were able to divert the course of Voyager and save it from destruction in what would have been a cosmic demolition derby!

(perhaps the same collision that led to the formation of the moon) during the formation of the planet. The presence of the orbiting moon has prevented this tilt from becoming more pronounced. This tilt is responsible for the relatively stable seasons we enjoy on the planet. If there were no tilt, the temperature variations between temperate and tropical regions would be greater, and the seasons much harsher; but if we tilted too much, climatic conditions would be chaotic. It was the moon's influence that allowed us to tilt to precisely the degree required for life to emerge.

The moon also causes the ocean tides, which formed alternating wet and dry zones in which ancient tetrapods, or vertebrate animals having four limbs, like *Acanthostega* and *Ichthyostega* first began to make the transition from living in the sea to living on land some 380 million years ago, as will be explored in Chapter 3. The pull of the tides was also responsible for slowing the rapid spin of the early Earth, which lengthened the day from 12 to 24 hours. In so many ways the moon and our planet have been locked together in a relationship that has profoundly and (from the point of view of humans) positively influenced conditions on Earth.

The Planetary System Today

The planetary system consists of the four terrestrial planets (Mercury, Venus, Earth, and Mars); four giant outer planets (Jupiter, Saturn, Uranus, and Neptune); and a number of smaller objects such as moons and innumerable asteroids (Figure 2.4).

Pluto, for a long time regarded as the most distant planet from the sun, lost its planetary designation in August 2006 when the International Astronomical Union (IAU) downgraded it to "dwarf planet" status. According to new IAU rules, planets must meet the following three criteria: A "planet" is a celestial body that (a) is in orbit around the sun, (b) has sufficient mass for its self-gravity to overcome rigid body forces so that it assumes a hydrostatic equilibrium (nearly round) shape, and (c) has cleared the neighborhood around its orbit. The third criteria demoted Pluto, which orbits among many other objects in the Kuiper Belt, a ring of comets beyond Neptune that is the remnant of an accretion disk where no planet was formed. In the late 1990s, millions of very small, icy planetesimals were discovered within the Kuiper Belt.

The satellite systems around the giant outer planets are the result of the formation of minor accretion disks, a process similar to that which produced the solar system. The terrestrial inner planets are composed mainly of silicates covering an inner core of mostly iron. Approximately 90 percent of Earth's crust, for example, consists of *silicates,* which are rock-forming minerals consisting of silicon and oxygen. (The process that led to Earth's acquiring its current structure will be explained in the next section.) Venus and Earth are remarkably similar in mass, although Venus retained a much thicker atmosphere and was not subject to the sort of violent collision that formed Earth's moon. Mars is much smaller, with a mass just over 10 percent of Earth's, and Mercury is less than half the mass of Mars (Figure 2.5).

other objects have remained virtually unchanged since the moon's crust solidified, in the form of craters. Moon rocks brought back to Earth by astronauts have been radiometrically dated to around 4.45 billion years. The crater-covered lunar surface is evidence of the violence of the last stage of the formation of the solar system. Remaining debris and leftover planetesimals battered the surfaces of the planets and their satellites until most of the material had been absorbed into the planetary system we see today.

Recently, NASA and a number of global governments (including the Chinese, European, and Russian) have announced the possibility of launching more piloted missions to the moon, in what might be a prelude to establishing some permanent human presence there. The lunar south pole would be the preferred landing target, not only because of the possible presence of ice there, but also because it is the likeliest part of the surface to have permanent sunlight.

The moon has had, and continues to have, a major impact on Earth. Early in its formation Earth developed a tilt along its axis because of collisions with large bodies

FIGURE 2.4 The planets of our solar system. The planets of the solar system formed in the various orbiting rings of the original solar nebula around the sun. Earth is the third planet out from the sun (the left side of the photo). Not to scale.

The Search for Other Solar Systems and Planets

Before the 1990s astronomers had a hunch that solar systems probably formed quite commonly around new stars, but they had no way of observing the process directly. Over the past two decades this hunch has proved correct, and they have been able to directly observe large numbers of stars surrounded by rings of dust and material, with solar systems of their own. The first discovery of a planet beyond our solar system, called an *exoplanet,* was made in 1995 by professional astronomers in Switzerland. Amateur astronomers have also made significant contributions to the search: In 2002 alone, some 31 new exoplanets were discovered by backyard astronomers looking outside our own solar system. However, it is the work of large space agencies like NASA that have contributed most to these discoveries.

FIGURE 2.5 The relative sizes of the planets. Compare the size of Earth with Saturn, or the giant Jupiter!

NASA's Hubble Space Telescope has found evidence of a rich bounty of planets circling stars a great distance from Earth, and NASA's planet-hunting Kepler probe, which was sent aloft in 2009, is certain to add many more to the tally. Kepler's mission is to look continuously at more than 150,000 stars in a region of sky near the constellation Cygnus, seeking evidence of planetary transits. So far more than 1,000 exoplanets had been found, most of them giants closer to the size of Jupiter. These worlds are light-years away, so it is impossible for scientists to view surface details; at best they can detect indirect evidence of the planet's existence, its mass, and the width of its orbit. But by combining this observational evidence with theoretical models and knowledge of our own solar system, more complex portraits of these far distant planets are emerging. Some of the latest research suggests that many of these planets might be geophysically active and possess atmospheres and climates that could support life.

Exoplanet-hunting astronomers have also been using land-based telescopes in California (notably the Lick Observatory near San Jose), Hawaii, Chile, and Australia in a concerted effort to closely monitor some 2,000 stars. These researchers are responsible for the discovery of many exoplanets, but finding planets from Earth-based observatories is just the beginning. Long-term plans include equipping more small robotic spacecraft (like Kepler) with digital cameras and sending them on incredibly long-range expeditions to photograph the surface of planets orbiting distant stars. Realistically, however, the technology required to send a spacecraft over distances of 10 to 12 light-years will probably take centuries to develop. Until then the painstaking search to discover solar systems and planets similar to our own will continue to be carried out by professional and amateur astronomers here on Earth, and with robotic spacecraft.

The Early Earth—a Short History

When Apollo astronauts in the 1960s first beamed back grainy black and white photos of Earth, and even more so when the first color photographs of our planet taken from space were published in *Time* magazine in January 1970, two facts were immediately apparent to astonished humans. First, Earth is extraordinarily beautiful, a magnificent cosmic object upon which the dark blue of the great global oceans interacts with brown and green landmasses under swirling white cloud systems. And second, the planet seemed startlingly solitary and fragile, a tiny self-contained entity swarming with life that contrasted dramatically with the vast "emptiness" of space surrounding it (Figure 2.6). As will be explored later in this book, many scientists now view Earth as an interconnected system in which all components, organic and inorganic, work in harmony to sustain the planet and biosphere. This section and the next will explore current scientific explanations of how Earth came to assume the shape and form that so captivated the astronauts and awestruck humans who first gazed upon those images in the 1960s.

FIGURE 2.6 Earthrise from space. Beautiful "Lifeboat Earth" as photographed by astronauts on Apollo 8 in 1969.

Formation of Earth's Structure: Differentiation

The first process we need to explain is the shaping of the early Earth—the "third rock from the sun"—before we consider the various stages of the planet's history. We know that early Earth was incredibly hot because of continuing violent collisions with nebular debris, the decay of internal radioactive materials, and increasing internal pressure caused by the crushing effect of gravity. As a result of this intense heating, iron and nickel trapped within began to melt, allowing a process called **chemical differentiation** to occur. Because of gravity, liquid blobs of heavy metals sank toward the center of the planet, quite quickly (on the scale of geologic time) producing a dense iron core.

At the same time, the melting of the planet caused lighter masses of molten rock to rise toward the surface, where they began to solidify into a form of primitive crust, the eggshell-thin layer at the surface of the planet. The rocky materials of the crust contained substantial amounts of silicon and aluminum; lesser quantities of calcium, sodium, potassium, magnesium, and iron; and some heavy metals including gold, lead, and uranium. In the time since differentiation occurred, the primitive crust has been lost or radically altered by erosion, so that we have little direct evidence of its original makeup. Even with radiometric dating, the precise date at which the earliest continental crust was formed is a matter of continuing research by geologists. However, because the oldest rocks so far discovered have radiometric dates of around 4 billion years, the assumption is that the primitive crust must also have formed by at least 4 billion years ago.

The Structure of Earth

Geologists use two criteria to describe the structure of the planet. The layers of Earth can be defined by their chemical composition and by their physical properties. Earth consists of a crust, mantle, and core. The *crust* is divided into oceanic and continental crust. The thin oceanic crust consists mostly of dark igneous rocks, which are rocks formed by the solidification of molten materials. It is approximately 5 miles (8 kilometers) thick. The thicker continental crust averages 25 miles (40 kilometers) thick, but can be greater than 40 miles (64 kilometers) in mountainous regions. The continental crust contains many different rock types. In general, the upper continental crust is composed of granites, and the lower of basalts.

By far the greatest percentage of the planet's volume (over 80 percent) is found in the *mantle*. This is an area of solid rock that extends to depths of 1,800 miles (2,900 kilometers). In the region where the crust and mantle meet, geologists have identified a major change in chemical composition. The upper mantle consists of peridotite, which is a coarse-grained igneous rock rich in magnesium. It is compressed at greater depth into a denser crystalline structure. The chemical composition of the *core* is assumed to be an iron-nickel alloy, along with lesser amounts of other elements that form compounds with iron. Under the extreme pressure of the core, the density of these elements is approximately 14 times the density of water.

The *physical properties* of Earth's structure are affected by this increasing density at greater depths and also by dramatically increasing temperatures toward the center. Although no data have been directly collected, best estimates are that the temperature of Earth at a depth of 60 miles (96 kilometers) is approximately 2,190 to 2,550 degrees Fahrenheit (1,200 to 1,400 degrees Celsius), while the temperature in the core is higher than 12,000 degrees Fahrenheit (6,700 degrees Celsius). The exceptionally high temperature at the core is an indication that Earth has retained much of the heat energy it acquired during its formation by accretion. The planet is divided into five principal layers as defined by physical properties: the lithosphere (crust and small portion of the upper mantle), asthenosphere (deeper and hotter part of the mantle), mesosphere (the region below the asthenosphere but above the outer core), outer core, and inner core.

The *lithosphere* and *asthenosphere* are the outermost layers of the planet, forming the crust and upper mantle. These layers function as a unit that is cool and very strong. The lithosphere averages 60 miles (96 kilometers) in thickness (much thicker under the older continents), while the asthenosphere beneath descends through the upper mantle to a depth of some 400 miles (640 kilometers). The top of the asthenosphere has a region of relatively high temperatures where some melting occurs, which allows the lithosphere above to move independently. This fact is of critical importance in plate tectonics, as will be shown later in this chapter.

The *mesosphere* is the layer of the lower mantle, where increasing pressure strengthens the rocks below the weaker and more fluid asthenosphere, although temperatures are still very hot. The more rigid mesosphere exists between depths of about 410 and 1,800 miles (660 and 2,900 kilometers). Deeper yet are the *outer* and *inner core*, each of which possesses very different mechanical properties. The outer core is a liquid layer about 1,410 miles (2,260 kilometers) thick. It is the flow of metallic iron in convective currents within the outer core that generates the planet's magnetic field. The spherical inner core (with a radius of 754 miles [1,206 kilometers]) is subject to very high temperatures, but because of immense pressure behaves more like a solid (Figure 2.7).

How Do Scientists Know about Earth's Structure?

For many it might seem difficult to understand how scientists can know what the interior of Earth looks like. They certainly can't dig deep enough to have a direct look; in fact, the deepest mine in the world (in South Africa) has penetrated to a depth of only 2.5 miles (4 kilometers). The deepest hole ever drilled is actually in the Kola Peninsula of Russia, which in 1992 reached a depth of some 7.5 miles (12 kilometers). More recently, scientists in California have

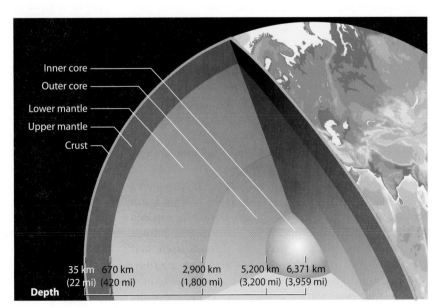

FIGURE 2.7 The structure of Earth. The structure of Earth includes the inner core, outer core, lower mantle, upper mantle, and crust.

Inner core
Outer core
Lower mantle
Upper mantle
Crust

35 km 670 km   2,900 km   5,200 km 6,371 km
(22 mi) (420 mi)   (1,800 mi) (3,200 mi) (3,959 mi)
Depth

dug about halfway down to a proposed depth of 2 miles (3.2 kilometers) in an attempt to create the world's first underground observatory of the active San Andreas Fault.

With no directly observed and tested data, our current understanding of Earth's structure is a result of inferences based on indirect evidence. What scientists have been able to measure are the waves from earthquakes as they pass through Earth. These *seismic waves* penetrate the interior of the planet, and they change speed or are bent as they move through zones of different chemical and physical properties. By using *seismographs,* instruments developed in 1880 to measure waves of energy transmitted through Earth (which have now been set up in a worldwide grid), computers are able to analyze seismic waves and construct images of the planet's layered structure.

Geologists also use rocks collected on the surface of the planet that originated in the mantle as evidence of Earth's internal composition. Rock samples that bear diamonds have been analyzed in laboratories to show that they can form only in the sort of high-pressure environments found at depths greater than 124 miles (190 kilometers). Pieces of mantle have also been thrust to the surface above sea level in various parts of the world, including Cyprus, Newfoundland, and Oman. No sample from the core has ever reached the surface, but all indirect evidence (particularly the principles of magnetism) indicates that it must consist mainly of iron. Additional evidence comes from meteorites, because they are examples of the material that formed the terrestrial planets. Meteorites are composed of iron, nickel, and silicates, remnants of the solar nebula that formed around the sun. Because meteorites contain a lot more iron than is found in Earth's crust or mantle, the only possible conclusion is that most of this iron sank into the core during differentiation.

The First Billion Years

Geologists have divided the vast 4.5-billion-year span of geologic history into various temporal units. *Eons* cover the greatest expanses and are subdivided into *eras.* In turn, eras are divided into shorter units known as *periods,* and periods into smaller units again known as *epochs.* However, the detailed geologic time scale begins only with the start of the *Cambrian* period some 540 million years ago, which marks the date of the appearance of multicellular life-forms (see the next chapter). The 4 billion years before that are divided into three eons—the Hadean, Archean, and Proterozoic.

The **Hadean eon** lasted from 4.5 to 3.8 billion years ago. It is named after the underworld of the ancient Greeks, the realm where departed spirits dwelt. Geologists refer to this earliest stage of our planet's history as the Hadean Earth because it was such a "hellish" place. During the Hadean eon the principal components of the planet were all formed and put in place, but they were very different from their appearance today. With no direct observation possible, this first billion years of the planet's history is something of a "lost interval" for Earth scientists, and much of the reconstruction science offers of the Hadean eon is based on assumption and extrapolation.

Even so, science is able to offer a compelling portrait of the planet approximately 4 billion years ago, roughly 500 million years after its formation. The sky would have appeared red in color because of the vast amounts of carbon dioxide in the atmosphere. The sun was dim, the moon was a lot closer to Earth, days were only 15 hours in length, and the surface of the planet was still being bombarded regularly by meteorites and comets that plunged out of the red sky.

The atmosphere above the Hadean Earth was very different from the atmosphere today. It would have been cloudy and much thicker, thus protecting the ground and preventing rapid cooling. There was no free oxygen, but instead many gases that would be poisonous to life-forms today. These probably included carbon dioxide (80 percent), methane (10 percent), carbon monoxide (5 percent), and nitrogen (5 percent). The planet was also probably subject to a *greenhouse effect* because the large quantities of carbon dioxide in the atmosphere trapped the heat of the sun on the planet's surface, leading to constant global warming. The sea did not exist during the early Hadean eon. Temperatures on and above the surface were so hot that surface water evaporated—it was all trapped in dense clouds in the atmosphere—and the land itself was volcanic and molten. The prospects of life appearing in this environment would have seemed slim indeed to any observers!

The presence of so much continuing volcanic activity showed, however, that the planet was geologically alive, and therefore capable of changing. During the first billion years physical and chemical aspects of the Hadean Earth did indeed stabilize. As the planet cooled and the ground temperature dropped below the boiling point of water, the water vapor stored in clouds in the atmosphere was released, and it rained down onto the surface in storms that literally lasted for millions of years. The first seas were formed as this released water filled up hollows on the surface. These incessant torrential rainstorms of water, acidified with large quantities of carbon dioxide, would have attacked and dissolved many of the silicates that formed the primitive crust, another reason for the lack of direct evidence available to geologists from the Hadean eon.

The origin of the primeval source of water that makes up the oceans is still a source of speculation by astrophysicists and geologists. The standard explanation that all the gases and water vapor that formed the primitive atmosphere outgassed from the interior of Earth through volcanoes is by no means universally accepted. An alternative theory is that much of this material was brought to the planet by the frequent cometary bombardments that characterized the first half-billion years. The craters on the moon are direct evidence of the intensity of this bombardment, to which Earth would also have been subject. On both the moon and Earth, the heat generated by these strikes from comets between 3 and 300 miles (5 and 500 kilometers) in diameter would have melted the surface silicates, destroying the fossil evidence of the Hadean eon.

Although collisions among the larger proto-planets diminished within the first 200 million years of the solar system's history, the rate of cometary bombardment may have taken 500 million years to decline to near zero. It took that long for most of the lose debris in the neighborhood to become trapped in the planets and other stable objects of the solar system. As noted earlier, radiometric ages of impact melt rocks found on the moon by Apollo astronauts in the 1960s indicate that the moon, and by implication Earth and other terrestrial planets, were subject to a late heavy bombardment by asteroids and comets some 4.1 to 3.8 billion years ago. If these comets contained large quantities of water and gases, the planet (unlike the moon) had sufficient mass to retain them in the primeval atmosphere.

Not everything had stabilized by late in the Hadean eon, however. The atmosphere still contained large quantities of carbon dioxide and other gases that are poisonous to us, and had no oxygen whatsoever. There was no ozone layer to protect the surface from ultraviolet radiation from the sun, because ozone (a molecule consisting of three oxygen atoms) is a by-product of oxygen (see Chapter 3 and the glossary). By the Late Hadean eon, Earth was cooler, largely covered in surface water, being bombarded far less often, and was ready for living organisms to emerge and thrive during the Achaean and Proterozoic eons, as will be described in Chapter 3.

Acquiring an Atmosphere

Planet Earth is surrounded today by a gassy envelope called the **atmosphere.** Half of the atmosphere lies below an altitude of 3.5 miles (5.6 kilometers), and 90 percent is found below an altitude of 10 miles (16 kilometers). This thin blanket of gas provides the air that we breathe and protects us from the sun's heat and dangerous radiation. Scientists are able to identify four stages in the history of Earth's atmosphere:

Stage 1: No Atmosphere. During the earliest stages of the formation of Earth, the planet was too small to have a strong gravitational field. Any free (that is, not chemically bound) gases in the region would not be held around the planet and would have drifted off into space.

Stage 2: Early Atmosphere—Outgassing or Comets? The gases that formed the planet's first atmosphere may have bubbled up from volcanoes or been brought to Earth by comets. Proponents of the former process, known as *outgassing,* offer a precise chemical description of Earth's first atmosphere by analyzing the sort of gases still emitted by volcanoes today (mainly carbon dioxide and nitrogen). Proponents of the cometary gassing and water vapor theory suggest that comets may have brought to Earth 10 times more water than is now present in the oceans, and 1,000 times more gas than is found in today's atmosphere. (The collision that formed the moon must have produced an extraordinary amount of heat, which may have resulted in the complete loss of gas and water vapor amassed on the planet up to that time.)

Stage 3: The Oxygen Revolution. As we will show in the next chapter, for a period of over 3 billion years, single-cell organisms floating in the oceans evolved to acquire the ability to *photosynthesize,* a word that denotes the conversion of sunlight, water, and carbon dioxide into oxygen and energy-rich carbohydrates. As photosynthesis took place, these living organisms absorbed much of the carbon dioxide (CO_2) in the atmosphere and converted it to oxygen instead, which slowly changed the chemical composition of the atmosphere. At first, oxygen combined with iron to form bands of red, rusted rock; only when most of the exposed iron had been turned to rust did free oxygen begin to accumulate in the atmosphere.

Stage 4: The Atmosphere Today. Photosynthesis was thus responsible for creating the atmosphere of today, which consists of 78 percent nitrogen; 21 percent oxygen; and 1 percent argon, carbon dioxide, and other gases. This provides a wonderful example of the power of living organisms to shape Earth's surface. The atmospheres of planets without life are very different because they lack processes such as photosynthesis that can continually alter the chemical composition of the surface, so they are shaped purely by physical and chemical processes. The atmosphere of Mars has only 1 percent of the density of Earth and consists mainly of carbon dioxide and a tiny amount of water vapor. Jupiter's atmosphere is dominated by alternating bands of light cloud regions (where gases are rising and cooling) and dark cloud regions (where gases are sinking). This generates high-speed winds and massive storms, like the Great Red Spot observed from only 26,000 miles (42,000 kilometers) above the surface by Pioneer 11 in 1974. Earth's atmosphere has come under sustained chemical assault since the Industrial Revolution, and particularly since the second half of the twentieth century, creating the potential for disastrous global warming that will be explored toward the end of the book. The impact of humans on today's atmosphere is one more reminder of how life has shaped our planet.

It is clear then that living organisms have played a critical role in the processes that have shaped the physical Earth, which means that geological and organic processes are closely intertwined. Although we are aware of their close relationship, however, in this chapter we have focused on geological processes, and on a few organic processes, such as the sedimentation of living organisms, which help create the sedimentary rock layers that are so important to Earth's history.

Shaping of Earth's Surface

Until the eighteenth century, Earth was widely believed to be only a few thousand years old and not to have changed much in that time. This was the view of most religions, including Christianity. In the 1650s the Irish archbishop of Armagh, James Ussher (1581–1656), declared in *The Annals of the World* that Earth had been created on Sunday,

October 23, 4004 BCE—at 9:00 a.m. Ussher was a leading scholar and church leader of his day: his date was not mere guesswork, but was based on a careful and intricate calculation of the correlation between Islamic, Mediterranean, and biblical histories. It was incorporated into an authorized version of the Bible in 1701.

Yet soon there were to be problems with the date of 4004 BCE, no matter how carefully Ussher had calculated it. Processes like mountain building were incredibly slow, which meant that Earth had to be very old. In the early nineteenth century mountaineers in the European Alps began to discover fossils of marine creatures near the summits of high mountains, which suggested that these mountains must once have been under sea. (More recently, fossilized forms of marine life have been found at elevations of 18,000 feet [5,500 meters] in the Himalayas, demonstrating that even the highest mountains on Earth had once been the floor of some primeval sea.) By the mid-nineteenth century, geologists like Charles Lyell (1797–1875) were arguing that Earth must be much older than had been suspected and that its appearance had changed greatly.

Early observers were also intrigued by the way in which the continents seemed to fit together like pieces of a jigsaw puzzle. As early as 1596, the Dutch mapmaker Abraham Ortelius (1527–98) had commented in his book on geography that the American continents must have been "torn away" from Europe and Africa by earthquakes and floods. English philosopher Francis Bacon (1561–1626) argued in 1620 that the close fit of coastlines on either side of the Atlantic could not be a coincidence, although he had no explanation as to the cause. French naturalist George de Buffon (1707–88) stated in 1750 that South America and Africa must once have fit together; and in 1858 another French geographer, Antonio Snider-Pellegrini (1802–85), drew the first ever series of "before and after" maps of the world, showing that the Americas had once been joined to Europe and Africa.

Other pieces of evidence supported these arguments. The German geographer Alexander von Humboldt (1769–1859) demonstrated in the early nineteenth century that the rocks of Brazil were very similar to those of the Congo and argued that these lands were joined together in the past until a massive tidal wave carved out the Atlantic. During the same century, naturalists traveling to distant continents began to note that the same species of marine life and reptiles existed in both South America and Africa. Fossil discoveries deepened these connections by revealing many similarities between fossilized plant and animal species in Europe and North America. But naturalists were also at a loss to explain this evidence, even speculating that perhaps vast land bridges had once connected the continents before falling into the Atlantic.

The first fully articulated theory of continental drift was published in 1885 by Austrian geologist Edward Seuss (1831–1914). In *The Face of the Earth*, Seuss proposed that in the distant past (he actually dated this to 180 million years ago) all the continents on the face of the planet had been condensed into two giant supercontinents. He named the southern mass *Gondwanaland* (which gave birth to

Australia, Antarctica, Africa, and South America) and the northern conglomeration *Laurasia* (which contained Europe, Asia, and North America). During the first decade of the twentieth century, two American geologists, Frank Taylor and Howard Baker, independently began to argue that the continents had moved. But none of these scientists could offer any evidence to support such an extraordinary theory, and their proposals were dismissed by the geological community. Such also was to be the fate of the hypotheses of a German meteorologist known today as the "father" of continental drift theory, Alfred Wegener (1880–1930), although his ideas are now at the heart of the major paradigm of modern Earth science, *plate tectonics.*

Alfred Wegener and Continental Drift

A meteorologist who made several important contributions to weather science, Wegener is best remembered for his theory of **continental drift,** a phrase that describes the movement, formation, and reformation of continents. In 1911 Wegener happened upon a paper about fossilized discoveries of identical plants and animals on either side of the Atlantic Ocean. He was particularly intrigued by fossils of the *Mesosaurus,* an aquatic reptile whose remains are found only in black shales of the Permian age in eastern South America and southern Africa. If the reptile had been capable of crossing the oceans, Wegener argued, its remains would be found more widely; and as this was not the case, these two regions must once have been joined together. Wegener rejected the popular land-bridge theory and focused instead on the jigsaw-like fit of the coastlines of South America and Africa, although Wegener himself realized that this fit was rather crude (Map 2.1).

It wasn't until the 1960s that Edward Bullard (1907–80) and his associates were able to demonstrate a truly remarkable fit between continents if this was attempted at the true outer boundary of a continent, the seaward edge of its continental shelf. With this sort of observational precision unavailable to Wegener, Bullard began to assemble other evidence to "prove" that the continents had once been joined. He noted that very old igneous rocks in Brazil closely resembled similarly aged rocks in South Africa. Bullard also argued that the Appalachian Mountains in North America are of similar age and structure to the mountains of Greenland, the Scottish Highlands, and the higher elevations of Scandinavia. When these landmasses were reassembled in a mental model, he noted, the various chains formed a nearly continuous range.

As a meteorologist Wegener was also able to use *paleoclimatic,* or ancient climate, evidence. Scouring fossil data he found evidence of dramatic climate change in the geologic past. He pointed to fossils of tropical plants in the rocks of arctic Spitzbergen, for example, and to glacial moraine deposits now found in tropical Australia and Africa, suggesting that these landmasses had moved to their current locations from different (and colder!) latitudes. Wegener rejected an explanation of global climate cooling by pointing to the contemporaneous existence of

MAP 2.1 The Earth's continental shelves. Alfred Wegener focused on the jigsaw-like fit of the coastlines of South America and Africa to help support his argument about continental drift, although he realized that this fit was still crude. Later geologists realized that the fit was much closer if measured at the edge of continental shelves, which are the true edge of continents.

tropical swamps in the Northern Hemisphere. The idea that the southern continents had once been joined together and located near the South Pole was a far more plausible explanation for the spread of ice over many of these previously glaciated regions than global cooling.

Armed with this array of compelling evidence, Wegener published this radical hypothesis of continental drift in his 1915 book, *The Origin of Continents and Oceans.* He argued that the only way this evidence could be explained was if all the landmasses on Earth had once coexisted hundreds of millions of years ago in a single supercontinent he called *Pangaea* (which is Greek for "all the Earth" and comes from the name of the ancient Greek goddess of the Earth, Gaia). During the Mesozoic era (ca. 200 million years ago), Pangaea had begun to break up into smaller continents, which all then slowly drifted into their current positions.

At first his proposal attracted little attention, but in 1924 his book was translated into English, French, Spanish, and Russian, and from that year until his death in 1930, the theory of continental drift was greeted with near-universal hostile dismissal. The American geologist R. T. Chamberlain attacked the theory because it took "considerable liberty with our globe," and the former president of the American Philosophical Society W. B. Scott declared it "utter damned rot"! Most of this criticism stemmed from Wegener's inability to identify a force that could move entire continents

across the face of the globe. Wegener's attempts to identify such a mechanism were confounded. One suggestion, that perhaps tidal forces might detach continents from the interior, was dismissed by the physicist Harold Jeffries who correctly countered that tidal forces of such magnitude would also halt the rotation of Earth! But Wegener did not abandon his theory and in 1929 published a fourth edition of his book that added new supporting evidence.

On his final expedition to Greenland, Wegener attempted to use longitude determinations to prove Greenland's drift to the west, but Danish workers who took measurements in 1927, 1936, 1938, and 1948 found no such evidence, adding further weight to the arguments of those opposed to the theory. Of course, modern Global Positioning Systems (GPSes) are used today to demonstrate indisputable evidence of continental drift, but again such technology was not available to Alfred Wegener, who died on a Greenland glacier, attempting a rescue, from heart failure in November 1930. His theory, however, clearly ahead of its time, did not die with him.

Not every geologist rejected Wegener's theory. Scottish geologist Arthur Holmes (1890–1965) proposed in his 1928 book *Our Wandering Continents* that landmasses might be moving because of flowing currents of hot, semi-molten rock in the mantle below, which is remarkably close to current theories that explain continental drift. Then, late in the 1930s, American geologist David Griggs (1911–74) demonstrated that solid rock can flow if it is subjected to enough pressure and high enough temperatures. The Swiss geologist Emile Argand (1879–1940) proposed that the folded pattern of strata in the Swiss Alps might be explained by a collision between continents. During the three decades following Wegener's death, scientists such as these and the South African geologist Alexander Du Toit (1878–1948) formed a small but committed band of supporters of continental drift theory. But it took dramatic discoveries in the 1950s and 1960s to convince the majority of scientists that Wegener had been correct all along.

The Modern Story of Plate Tectonics

Two new lines of evidence began to bear fruit in the mid-1950s—*paleomagnetism* and the exploration of the seafloor. **Paleomagnetism** is a science that uses magnetic minerals to study the history of Earth's magnetic field, which, as we saw earlier, we now know is a product of the planet's iron core flowing in currents. Attempting to explain the functioning of the magnetic compass in the sixteenth century, English scientist William Gilbert (1544–1603) had proposed that Earth functioned like a huge magnet, although he had no explanation for how or why. We know today that invisible lines of magnetic force pass through the planet from one pole to another, and that a freely floating compass needle (which is itself a small magnet) aligns itself with these lines of force and points to the magnetic pole. Similarly, some molten rocks that contain minerals gradually become magnetized in the direction of the prevailing magnetic force lines, and as they solidify they become frozen in position, pointing toward the magnetic poles at the date of their composition. Such rocks thus become records of the direction of the magnetic poles at various times in Earth's history. These magnetic records also indicate the latitude of the rocks at the time they became magnetized and thus provide a record of their distance from the poles at the time of magnetization.

Studies of rock magnetism in Europe in the 1950s by S. K. Runcorn (1922–95) showed that many different paleomagnetic poles had existed throughout the planet's history. Over the past 500 million years, the north magnetic pole seemed to have slowly "wandered" from Hawaii to Siberia to its present location near the North Pole. This meant that either the magnetic poles had moved, or the landmasses themselves had somehow drifted, which sent geologists back to Wegener's hypothesis for another look. By the end of the 1950s, paleomagnetists were also able to demonstrate that North America and Europe must have been joined in the past. When a polar wandering path was plotted for North America, it had a remarkably similar shape to Europe's path, but the two were separated by about 30 degrees of latitude. This can best be explained if the two landmasses were once joined and had moved relative to the poles as part of the same great continental landmass.

A second line of evidence was pursued by oceanographers in the decades following the end of World War II, using new marine technologies such as sonar that had been funded by the U.S. Office of Naval Research to develop

a means of detecting enemy submarines. By employing sonar and deep-sea submersibles, a "map" of the seafloor was painstakingly assembled, which eventually revealed a vast oceanic ridge system of volcanic mountains winding across the world's seafloors. The long Mid-Atlantic Range was found first, and the discovery of other mountain ranges eventually produced a mapped underwater ridge system some 36,000 miles (58,000 kilometers) long.

Oceanographers also discovered astonishingly deep undersea trenches, some descending steeply to depths approaching 6 miles (9.6 kilometers). The initial discovery of a massive rift valley was made in the mid-Atlantic, extending (and paralleling) the length of the Mid-Atlantic Range. More and more trenches were subsequently found in most of Earth's major oceans, including the Pacific and Indian. These rifts suggested to researchers that the planet's crust was actively pulled apart at great depths and that high heat flows and volcanic activity were occurring deep under the oceans as they did on the surface. These discoveries were totally unexpected and difficult to fit into existing theories about the shaping of the planet. In 1960, Princeton University geologist Harry Hess (1906–69) tried to offer a unified account of these intriguing phenomena when he published a hypothesis later called **seafloor spreading,** which Hess described as the process whereby new ocean floor is created as molten material from Earth's mantle rises in margins between plates and spreads out.

In essence Hess argued that upwelling material from the mantle spreads sideways, carrying seafloor material away from the great suboceanic ridge crests. The associated forces fracture the oceanic crust, allowing for magma to intrude and create new crust, so that as the old seafloor is carried away from the ranges, new crust replaces it. In other regions, oceanic crust is drawn back into the interior of the planet. In this way the oceanic crust is constantly being renewed by material from the mantle, which explained why dredging of the seafloor had not found any oceanic crust older than 180 million years. In contrast, the continental crust, which is generally lighter than the seafloor crust, is much older, as it has mostly stayed at the surface, some of it for billions of years.

Hess supplied the crucial element that Wegener's original hypothesis lacked—a plausible explanation of how continents might move. Hess's idea that the continents were passive passengers being carried along by the movement of semimolten rock just below the crust was considerably more compelling than Wegener's implication of vast continents somehow plowing through the seafloor. But despite Hess's logic and the testability of his hypothesis, seafloor spreading remained controversial. Cambridge student Fred Vine (1939–) and his supervisor D. H. Matthews (1931–97) provided the conclusive evidence some years later from the field of paleomagnetic studies.

By the early 1960s geophysicists were becoming more and more convinced that Earth's magnetic field had reversed polarity on several occasions. Researchers, measuring the magnetism of lavas and sedimentary rocks of different ages at a variety of places around the world, found that that rocks of the same age, wherever they were found, demonstrated the same direction of polarity. Moreover, this polarity was often reversed. Accumulating data established a magnetic time scale for the last several million years. Within each million-year period (called a *chron*), several short reversals had taken place, each lasting less than 200,000 years. Because seafloor crust took on the magnetic polarity prevalent at the time it was created, these reversals left evidence under the sea in the form of alternating strips of high- and low-intensity magnetism.

In 1963, Vives and Matthews attempted to tie this evidence back to Hess's theory of seafloor spreading. As the seafloor spread, they proposed, polarity reversals would build up a pattern of normal and reverse polarity stripes radiating away from either side of the under-ocean trench systems. If this were true, then polarity stripes on either side of the ridges should mirror each other. In the mid-1960s, surveys on either side of the Mid-Atlantic Ridge south of Iceland did indeed reveal a remarkably symmetrical pattern of alternative polarity stripes. The final piece of the puzzle of plate tectonics was provided by Canadian physicist-geologist J. Tuzo Wilson (1908–93) in 1965. Wilson proposed that the surface of the planet was divided into several rigid plates divided by different types of margins, three of which he identified. Wilson's hypothesis provided a unified explanation for a wide range of seemingly unrelated observations in the fields of oceanography, geophysics, geology, and paleontology, and by 1968 his hypothesis had become the theory known today as *plate tectonics,* the core paradigm of Earth science and the key to understanding most basic geological processes, from mountain formation to tectonic drift.

Earth's Tectonic Plates

The plate tectonics model understands the lithosphere as a rigid layer consisting of the uppermost crust. Like an eggshell, the lithosphere is brittle and has fractured into segments called plates, which "float" on a weaker section in the mantle called the asthenosphere. As we saw previously, the temperature and pressure in the upper asthenosphere keeps the rocks close to their melting point, which allows the lithosphere to be detached from the layers below and in essence float upon them.

The segmented plates of the lithosphere are in constant motion and are continually changing their shape and size (Map 2.2). The seven major lithospheric plates are the

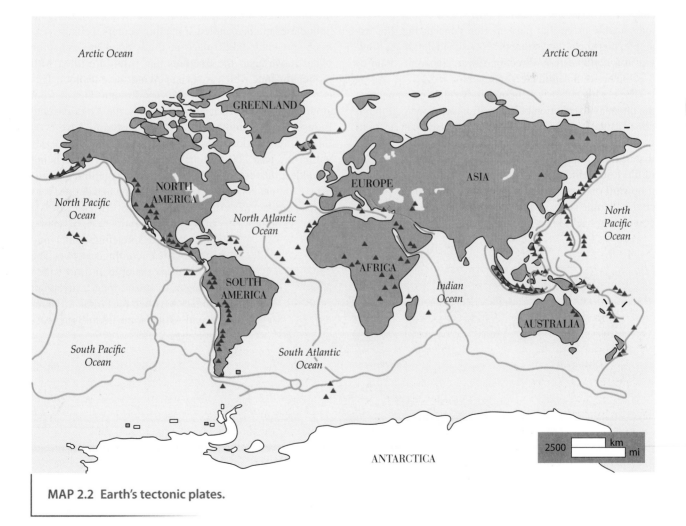

MAP 2.2 Earth's tectonic plates.

Antarctic, Australian-Indian, Eurasian, African, Pacific, South American, and North American plates. The largest of these is the Pacific Plate, which encompasses most of the Pacific Ocean basin. A number of intermediate-sized plates have also been identified, including the Juan de le Fuca, Scotia, Cocos, Arabian, Philippine, Nazca, and Caribbean Plates. These lithospheric plates are moving relative to each other at an average rate of 2 inches (5 centimeters) per year.

Plate velocities are measured with a high degree of accuracy by using space-age technology. Two methods are used in making these calculations. The *Very Long Baseline Interferometry (VLBI)* system uses radio telescopes to record signals from distant quasars, which provide fixed reference points. By having two widely spaced radio telescopes observe a dozen quasars 5 to 10 times each, the distance between these observatories can be measured to an accuracy of 0.787 of an inch (2 centimeters). Repeating the experiment at later dates establishes the relative velocities (and directional movements) of these observatories as the plates move beneath them.

The *Global Positioning System (GPS)* uses numerous satellites to measure accurately the location of various sites on Earth. GPS receivers are particularly useful in measuring small crustal movements that take place along tectonically active faults. The data from these methods provide indisputable proof that plate motion is occurring. For example, they have shown that the Hawaiian Islands are moving in a northwesterly direction toward Japan at a rate of 3.26 inches (8.3 centimeters) per year.

The engine that drives these massive plate movements is the unequal distribution of heat within the planet, although none of the specific models so far proposed can account for all plate tectonic activity. There is general agreement that heat from the center of Earth constantly melts sections of the 1,800-mile (2,900-kilometer) -thick mantle, moving it upward on internal convection currents. In other places, cooler, denser slabs of lithosphere (under the oceans) are descending back down into the mantle. These movements cause the great crustal plates of the lithosphere to move, generating earthquakes, volcanic activity, and mountain building.

This internal heat comes from a combination of forces: from the meteoric collisions that pounded the surface of the early Earth; from radioactivity; and from pressure caused by accretion and gravity when the planet was being formed. So the heat inside our planet that drives plate movements is a result of the way stars are formed, of the evolution of our solar system, and of the effects of gravity. The heat is thus a direct product of the energy that was generated in the birth and evolution of the entire universe!

Tectonic Margins (Plate Boundaries)

Because lithospheric plates move as coherent units, most of the activity and deformations caused by plate tectonics occur along the boundaries. Geologists have identified three different types of boundaries, differentiated by the types of movement they exhibit, and the geological phenomena they produce—*divergent, convergent,* and *transform* fault boundaries. Often the plates are bounded by a combination of these types (Figure 2.8).

Divergent boundaries are found where two plates move away from each other, which allows material from the mantle to rise up and create new seafloor. Divergent boundaries are also called spreading centers, because seafloor spreading takes place at these boundaries. As the plates move apart the fractures that result are filled with molten magma, which cools and creates new seafloor. This is the process that created the vast Atlantic Ocean from a narrow inlet between what are today the Americas and Eurasia. In fact, most of Earth's ocean basins have been formed by seafloor spreading along divergent boundaries within the past 200 million years, with the Pacific being the oldest. Divergent plates can also form within a continent. Continents begin to split along elongated depressions called *continental rifts,* of which the East African Rift is a perfect example. This rift has the potential to develop into a fully fledged spreading center and split the African continent in two. The Red Sea is an example of a rift valley that began to open along a divergent boundary between the Arabian Peninsula and Africa some 20 million years ago (Figure 2.9).

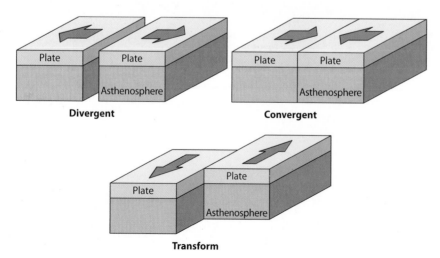

Divergent

Convergent

Transform

FIGURE 2.8 **Tectonic margins.**
The three types of tectonic margins are divergent, convergent, and transform.

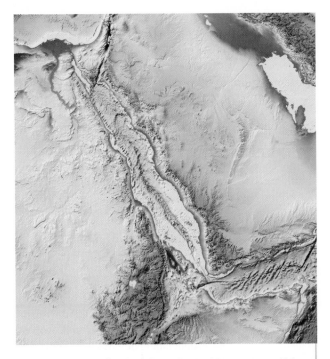

FIGURE 2.9 The Red Sea. The Red Sea, an incredibly important waterway in human history, is actually a rift valley located above a divergent boundary between Arabia and Africa.

Convergent boundaries are found where two plates move together, forcing oceanic lithosphere either to descend beneath an overriding plate and be recycled back into the mantle, or to rise up and create a new mountain system. This sort of collision is very slow, and the result will depend on the properties of the plates involved. Boundaries where the denser oceanic crust slips under the lighter continental crust are known as *subduction zones.* The Andes Mountains of South America were formed by the subduction of the Nazca Plate beneath the South American continent, along the Peru–Chile oceanic trench. The volcanic mountains of Washington, Oregon, and California are also a product of the subduction of oceanic lithosphere.

Where two oceanic plates converge, one is generally subducted under another. The world's deepest trench—the Marianas Trench in the Pacific—was created by a collision between the faster-moving Pacific Plate and the slower Philippine Plate. If subduction is sustained, a chain of volcanic islands generally will emerge. The Aleutian, Mariana, and Tonga Islands are all examples of this volcanic arc building, and each is located between 60 to 180 miles (96 to 290 kilometers) from a deep ocean trench.

Where two continental plates converge, the results are spectacular. The lithosphere of each continental plate is buoyant, which prevents subduction to any great depths, so the edges of both plates buckle up or sideways to produce great mountain ranges. The highest mountain range on Earth, the Himalayas, was produced when the subcontinent of India collided with Asia some 50 million years ago (Figure 2.10). Other major ranges produced by convergent continental boundaries include the European Alps, the Appalachians, and the Urals, which explains why marine fossils have been found on many of their summits.

Transform plate boundaries are found where two plates grind past each other without either producing or destroying lithospheric crust. Most transform boundaries form faults between two segments of oceanic crust, where they are known as *fracture zones.* Here the seafloor at the edges of two plates moves in opposite directions as the adjacent slabs grind past each other. Some significant examples of transform plate boundaries are found cutting through continental crust. The most famous (and potentially devastating) of these is the San Andreas Fault of California, where the Pacific Plate is grinding in a northwesterly direction against the edge of the North American Plate (Figure 2.11). This activity has been ongoing for about 10 million years, and if it continues

FIGURE 2.10 The Himalayas. The highest mountain range on Earth was produced by a slow-motion collision between the Indian subcontinent and Eurasia that began some 50 million years ago.

FIGURE 2.11 The San Andreas Fault. The earthquake-prone San Andreas Fault of California lies on a fracture zone where the Pacific Plate is grinding in a northwesterly direction against the edge of the North American Plate.

the regions of California west of the fault line (including the Baja Peninsula) will eventually become an island. Another active example of a transform plate boundary is the Alpine Fault of New Zealand.

Plate Tectonics—the Core Paradigm of Earth Science

Plate tectonics has become one of the most significant paradigms of modern science. Just as the big bang theory explains the origin of the universe, and evolution by natural selection explains the way life changes and evolves, plate tectonics helps us understand how Earth has changed. Because they explain change over time, these three great scientific theories are also *historical* paradigms, which is why they must be included in a textbook on big history. The plate tectonics paradigm explains many phenomena of central interest to humans and has linked many geological processes that were previously considered unrelated. Plate tectonics explains how mountains are created; why volcanoes and earthquakes happen; how the continents move; how the oceans were created; how different minerals were formed; and the shape of the modern world. Despite the fact that, like all major scientific paradigms, it is a constantly evolving model, plate tectonics is the core paradigm of modern Earth science.

SUMMARY

In this chapter we have explored the solar nebula theory of the origin of the solar system, which argues that planets and other objects of the solar system were formed out of a flattened disk of gas and debris that formed around the embryonic sun. Evidence that supports this theory comes from land-based and orbiting telescopes, unpiloted spacecraft, and radiometric dating. We also considered the processes that helped form and shape Earth, including differentiation, which gave the planet its layered structure. Evidence for our knowledge of the internal structure of the planet comes mainly from seismographs. We also offered a portrait of the planet during the first billion years of its history, during the Hadean and early Archean eons, focusing particularly on how Earth acquired its water and atmosphere. Finally we examined the core paradigm of modern Earth science—plate tectonics—which offers a unifying model that explains many of the geological processes that occur on the surface of the planet. The next chapter will pick up the story some 3.8 billion years ago, where in the inhospitable and chaotic oceans of the Hadean eon an astonishing phenomenon was taking place: life was emerging on planet Earth!

CHAPTER QUESTIONS

1. What are the key observational tools scientists have used to understand the birth of our sun and solar system?

2. How do we know the age of the solar system and Earth?

3. What is accretion, and how does it explain the way planets are formed?

4. Why does the International Astronomical Union no longer consider Pluto to be a planet?

5. How do Earth scientists know what the inside of the planet looks like?

6. How did Earth acquire an atmosphere?

7. Why is the theory of plate tectonics one of the core paradigms of modern science?

8. What evidence do scientists have that continents are moving across the face of the planet?

9. How was the highest mountain range on Earth—the Himalayas—formed?

KEY TERMS

accretion	continental drift	paleomagnetism	radiometric dating
atmosphere	Hadean eon	radioactivity	seafloor spreading
chemical differentiation	half-life		

FURTHER READING

Bally, J., and B. Reipurth. *The Birth of Stars and Planets.* Cambridge, UK: Cambridge University Press, 2006.

Bryson, Bill. *A Short History of Nearly Everything.* New York: Broadway Books, 2003.

Cloud, P. *Oasis in Space: Earth History from the Beginning.* New York: Norton, 1988.

Condie, K. C. *Earth: An Evolving System.* Amsterdam: Elsevier, 2005.

Delsemme, Armande. *Our Cosmic Origins. From the Big Bang to the Emergence of Life and Intelligence.* Cambridge, UK: Cambridge University Press, 1998.

Fortey, R. A. *Earth: An Intimate History.* New York: Knopf, 2004.

Hazen, Robert M. *The Story of Earth: The First 4.5 Billion Years, from Stardust to Living Planet.* New York: Viking, 2012.

Lunine, J. I. *Earth: Evolution of a Habitable World.* Cambridge, UK: Cambridge University Press, 1999.

McSween, H. Y. *Stardust to Planets.* New York: St. Martin's Press, 1993.

Morrison, D., and T. Owen. *The Planetary System.* New York: Addison-Wesley, 1988.

Sasselov, D. M., and D. Valencia. "Planets We Could Call Home." *Scientific American,* August 2010, 8–45.

Swimme, B. "The Fire of Creation." From *The Sacred Balance* (TV documentary series), 2002. www.sacredbalance.com/web/portal/.

Tarbuck, E. J., and F. K. Lutgens. *Earth: An Introduction to Physical Geology.* Upper Saddle River, NJ: Pearson Prentice Hall, 2005.

Taylor, S. R. *Solar System Evolution.* Cambridge, UK: Cambridge University Press, 1992.

Ussher, J. *The Annals of the World.* London: E. Tyler, for F. Crook and G. Bedell, 1658.

Ward, P., and D. Brownlee. *The Life and Death of Planet Earth.* New York: Henry Holt, 2002.

ENDNOTE

1. Brian Swimme, "The Fire of Creation," from *The Sacred Balance* (TV documentary series), 2002.

the fourth threshold

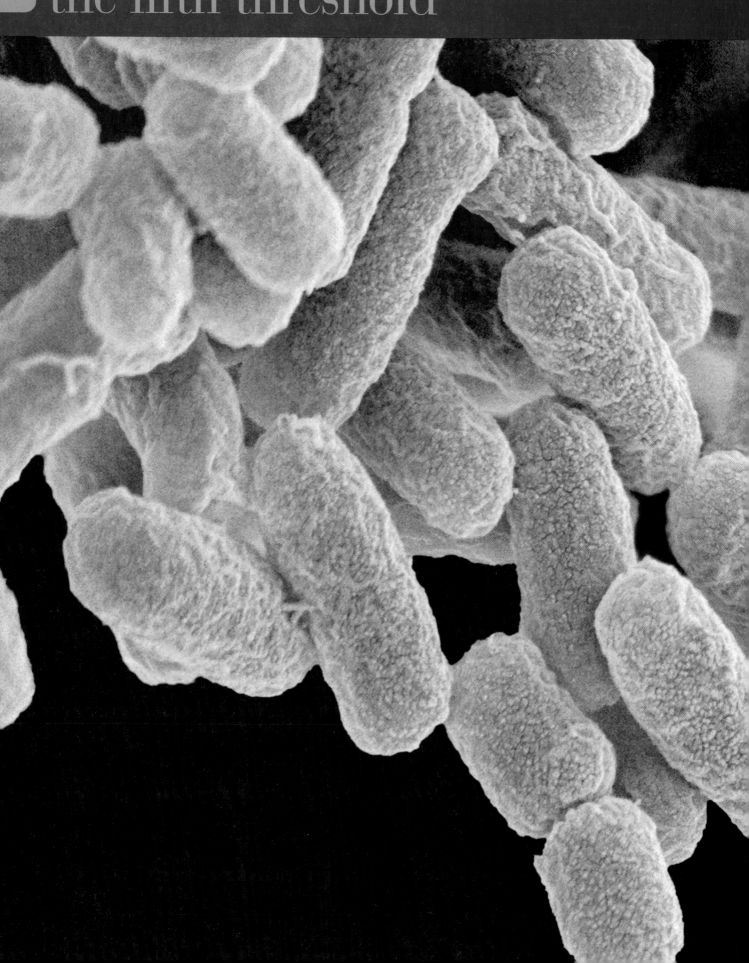

chapter 3

The Emergence of Life

Seeing the Big Picture

3.8 Billion to 8 Million Years Ago

▶ How do scientists define life? How does this fit with your view of life?

▶ What kind of man was Charles Darwin and how did he figure out the central tenet of contemporary biology?

▶ How does the emergence of life qualify as a new threshold?

▶ How did the first living cells emerge?

▶ How do bacteria figure in the history of life?

▶ What is the role of extinctions in the evolution of life?

Somehow, sometime during the first billion or two years after the formation of Earth, some chemicals in the seas came alive. We are calling this emergence of life the fifth threshold of complexity, the move from the relative simplicity of atoms and molecules in the brew of the early planet to the greatly increased complexity of living cells, in which membranes enclosed a dynamic system of interdependent molecules that was capable of reproducing itself and adapting over time and through which energy flowed as metabolism took place.

At the outset it must be stated that scientists still do not understand exactly how life began. They have not yet been able to recreate life in a lab, although some think they are on the verge of doing so. If they succeed, it will be a feat of modern chemistry and genetic engineering, not the emergence of life under primordial conditions.

Yet scientists have learned to create the building blocks of life in a lab, and we can now put together the framework of the amazing story of how inert matter turned into living organisms. In previous chapters we used the knowledge laboriously built up over time in the disciplines of astronomy, cosmology, physics, chemistry, and geology to describe the origins of the universe and the solar system. In this chapter we still need physics, chemistry, and geology, but to those we will add biology, the study of life.

We will start by discussing two basic questions: What is life? And how does it change over time? Only by describing how life changes over time by natural selection (evolution) can we then describe how life emerged, for that depended on the evolution of nonliving chemicals by a form of natural selection. Finally, we give a brief account of how life evolved from bacteria through a process of diversification, up to the great apes, leaving to the next chapter the story of evolution in the last 8 million years.

How Life Changes through Natural Selection

Life seems miraculous because of its astonishing variety, its many unexpected, original, interdependent species. Viewed over the whole span of Earth's history, these emerging life-forms seem to generate ever more varied and more complex forms, in the sense that they assemble ever more intricate parts in increasingly elaborate structures and command ever larger flows of energy. Life plays, dances, mutates, merges, morphs, competes, cooperates, and keeps emerging into spectacular new forms, as old species go extinct over time.

What Is Life?

To define life we must distinguish it from nonlife, which is not easy to do because in fact there is a continuum. Thinkers have been trying to define life for a long time. Some traditional answers include (1) living things are made from different material than nonliving things and were created separately, and (2) living things have a life force or soul that nonliving things do not have.

The modern scientific answer says that both living and nonliving things are made from the same elements of matter, whose atoms bond chemically into molecules. One basic characteristic of living matter is that chemically it is not in equilibrium; that is, it is not in a stable, balanced condition with reciprocal reactions going on. Instead, in living cells energy flows take place as membranes let some chemicals in and keep others out.

Other attributes of life are more ambiguous. For example, one characteristic usually attributed to life is the ability to reproduce. Yet living beings exist—mules, for example—that cannot reproduce. (Mules are a cross between two different species, donkeys and horses, which succeed in producing offspring, but the offspring are infertile.) On the other hand, stars, which are considered nonliving, do reproduce in the sense of recreating other stars by exploding into particles, which re-form as new stars.

Without going further into the nuances and exceptions, we will use three commonly accepted attributes of **life:** (1) it uses energy from the environment by eating or breathing or photosynthesizing (metabolism); (2) it makes copies of itself (reproduction); and (3) over many generations it can change characteristics to adapt to its changing environment (adaptation).

Life is an extension of the complexities of matter; single atoms joined together to form molecules consisting of thousands or millions of atoms, and molecules joined together to form cells consisting of billions of atoms: the first living organisms. These single-celled organisms arose spontaneously from nonliving things through a gradual increase of molecular complexity over vast periods of time. Metabolism, reproduction, and adaptation began to operate in a feedback cycle, each reinforcing the other. Living organisms were able to find more ways to extract energy from their environment, to reproduce themselves more bountifully, and to adapt to their environment.

The continuum between life and nonlife is neatly illustrated by viruses, which occupy the boundary between the two. Viruses (such as the flu virus) are much smaller than a typical modern cell; they contain proteins (the building blocks of most forms of life) and either DNA or RNA (the molecule in each virus that carries the chemical instructions for how to maintain itself and to duplicate other viruses) and not much else—no extra molecules to use for energy, reproduction, or repairs. When alone, a virus does not have the characteristics of life. But when it inserts itself into a living organism by injecting its genetic material (DNA or RNA), a virus acquires all the properties of life. The DNA or RNA of the virus seizes control of the cells of the organism it has infected, growing and reproducing by using the cellular apparatus to make its own proteins. Some viruses reproduce rapidly and eventually kill the invaded organisms, while others exist passively within a host, posing no immediate threat. Thus, the living or nonliving status of a virus depends on its environmental circumstances.

How we think about the whole arena of life has undergone a sea change in recent decades. During the previous several centuries, European people spoke of "the great chain of being." They imagined life as a hierarchy of separate forms, from what they considered the least perfect to the most nearly perfect, from rocks to the topmost superior form on Earth—man (a term formerly used for humanity). In the great chain of being, each form was distinct from its neighbors, rising vertically into the heavens, where angels and God completed the hierarchy.

More recently, biologists have begun to think of life as consisting of organisms nesting within larger contexts. No organism is separate from other organisms and the environment; more complex forms arise from the combination and recombination of the parts, which produce new, emergent forms. Seen as a whole, then, life seems more like a collection that interacts than a chain of separate beings, with all living organisms nested within the biosphere of planet Earth.

Biologists have also revised their system of how the different forms of life are arranged, called a **taxonomy,** or a system of naming and classifying based on shared characteristics. The previous *tree of life* showed five major kingdoms: cells without a nucleus were called *monera,* single cells with a nucleus were called *protists,* while plants, fungi, and animals (multicellular organisms, each cell of which has a nucleus) were considered most of life.

Since the late 1970s the tree of life has been reconstructed, showing that life's deeper history is microbial; most life-forms cannot be seen with the naked eye. All the main branches are now microbial, each leading out from the **last universal common ancestor (LUCA),** defined as the most recent organism or populations of organisms from which all organisms now living on Earth descended. The three main branches are Bacteria, Archaea, and Eukaryota. (Bacteria and Archaea are each a group of single-celled microorganisms without a nucleus, but with different genes and enzymes. The first Eukaryota were single-celled microorganisms, but with a nucleus and more complex chemistry than the other two groups.) Plants, fungi, and animals emerged from the single-celled Eukaryota and now count as a tiny part of that huge group of organisms that today still contain single-celled organisms such as Baker's yeast (Figure 3.1).

The Bacteria and Archaea have not died out. They constitute perhaps 50 percent of the Earth's biomass, the combined weight of living and recently dead material. Not only was life in the past overwhelmingly microbial, it still is. A human body contains about 10 times more microbial cells than animal cells. Each human intestine has about 1,000 species of microbes with about 3 million genes, compared to about 18,000 human genes. All human cells have incorporated a bacterial partner permanently into them in the form of mitochondria, which generate most of a cell's energy. We, and the life around us, consist mostly of single-celled microorganisms.

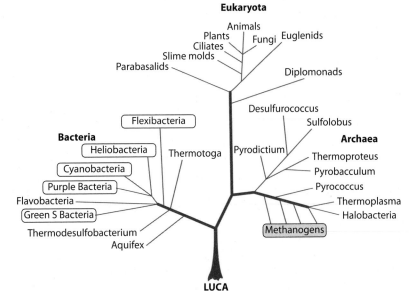

FIGURE 3.1 **The tree of life.** This is one version of the modern tree of life based on genetic analysis. Researchers have not agreed about exactly how to arrange the lines off the last universal common ancestor (LUCA), since evidence from billions of years ago is hard to find. For example, they disagree about whether Eukaryota should be shown coming directly off the LUCA or should be a line off Archaea. Some researchers suggest that, instead of a tree, this should be a network since bacteria exchange genetic material.

Darwinian Theory

We experience life in myriad forms. Consider the variety in the eyes of the spider, the fruit fly, and the human. How did this amazing multiplicity of eyesight come about? The theories of British naturalist Charles Darwin provided the foundation for our modern understanding of this diversity.

Background to Darwin's Ideas
The first European to catalog living organisms, Carl Linnaeus (1701–78), classified by the outward appearance of organisms. Following Aristotle, whose ideas had been assimilated into Christian thought by Thomas Aquinas, Linnaeus believed that organisms do not change, that God the creator made creatures adapted to their environment, and that they hadn't changed since their creation.

What's wrong with this idea of Aristotle and Linnaeus? Why did it not hold up under scientific scrutiny? The fact is that species (but not individual specimens) do change over time. Two unassailable pieces of evidence prove it: fossils and the results of animal breeding.

Over the centuries, people have found **fossils,** the mineralized remains of dead organisms. As long as people believed that animals did not change, however, they could not make sense out of the fossils. Europeans invented legends of ogres and griffins; early Chinese may have created the idea of dragons from their discovery of dinosaur bones, not realizing what they were.

By the nineteenth century, biologists in Europe became aware that fossils represented earlier forms of life. They had in their collections evidence of many organisms that no longer existed—dinosaur bones (first named in 1842), *trilobites* (a large group of invertebrate animals extinct since about 250 million years ago, whose fossils constitute nearly 50 percent of all known fossils), fossilized leaves of plants long gone, and midge flies preserved in amber, the fossilized resin found on plants. Biologists still had no way of knowing how old these relics were, but they proved that life-forms change through time.

Meanwhile, people were busy improving their domesticated plants and animals. Domesticated plants had been changed by agriculturists through the centuries, as will be described in Chapter 5. Herders, by choosing which animals would reproduce, changed the size and behavior of domesticated animals over time. Dramatically, in the nineteenth century, animal breeders produced many distinct breeds of dogs. All domestic dogs originated from Asian gray wolves about 15,000 years ago, and all are still genetically close enough to be able to breed with each other, meaning that they still form one species. But people can control their breeding; breeders choose which pups from a litter they allow to mate in order to create the characteristics they want. For instance, breeders created long, skinny dachshunds to use for hunting badgers, just as they created other breeds for other purposes. This is called artificial selection, in which people artificially select which organisms are allowed to reproduce.

By the nineteenth century, European scientists had to confront the fact that populations of living organisms do change and adapt to their environments. How organisms do this became the fundamental question of modern scientific biology. How do changes occur in groups of individuals of a given species living in a certain place? How can fixed features lead to adaptation in the future? European scientists could not solve this puzzle in part because they continued to think that God's creation of Earth and its inhabitants was quite recent.

Darwin and the Theory of Evolution
The individual who answered this question was an English naturalist, Charles Darwin (1809–82). His father was a wealthy physician and his mother the daughter of Josiah Wedgwood, whose pottery business was an early success story of the Industrial Revolution.

When Darwin was only 22, he set sail on the H.M.S. *Beagle* for a scientific voyage to survey the coasts of South America. The voyage was intended to last for three years but stretched to almost five. When Darwin returned, he published his travel report, married his cousin, Emma Wedgwood, and was set up by his father as a country gentleman 16 miles (26 kilometers) south of London in Down, Kent (you can still visit his house today), where he conducted his studies and wrote books for the remainder of his life.

Darwin's voyage provided the observations that enabled him to develop his theory of evolution, particularly what he saw on the isolated Galapagos Islands, located on the equator some 525 miles (840 kilometers) out from the South American continent (Map 3.1).

MAP 3.1 Galapagos Islands. These are geologically young volcanic islands located around the equator, now belonging to Ecuador. They had English names when Darwin visited, but now have Spanish names. Why do you think Darwin was so determined to go on this trip?

On this string of some 14 volcanic islands, Darwin saw many strange species new to him; he collected specimens and filled notebooks with descriptions. He noticed especially that there were at least a dozen nearly identical finches, but the heads and beaks differed slightly from one island to another. When he left the Galapagos, Darwin still thought he was seeing varieties of birds, not new species.

After Darwin returned to London and consulted with respected ornithologists, he realized that the finches were indeed different species. He had another important insight after reading a passage from the work of the English pioneer of population studies, the Reverend Thomas Malthus (1766–1834), whom we will meet again in later chapters. Malthus argued that the populations of all species tend to grow faster than available food supplies, meaning that in every generation large numbers of offspring die before reproducing. This gave Darwin the clue he needed to formulate his theory of natural selection. He concluded (1) that tiny random variations among individuals mean that some do better than others, (2) that those lucky enough to be well adapted to conditions on a particular island flourish and have more descendants, (3) that gradually populations change and diverge on different islands, and (4) that eventually the differences between birds on different islands became great enough that individuals can no longer interbreed, which is the usual definition of a new species.

Darwin took with him to the Galapagos an early copy of *The Principles of Geology* by Charles Lyell (1797–1875). This three-volume book went through 12 editions in Lyell's lifetime and influenced geological thinking into the 1980s. Lyell legitimized the idea that geological, and hence biological, processes took place over long spans of time. He also argued against *catastrophism,* the theory that the Earth is shaped by abrupt, cataclysmic events, and for *uniformitarianism,* the idea that changes on Earth are gradual and happen over immense stretches of time. Darwin's findings on the Galapagos supported Lyell's uniformitarianism.

Darwin wrote down a comprehensive outline of his theory in 1842, six years after he returned from his voyage in 1836; he delayed going public with his ideas until 1859, when he permitted their publication as *The Origin of Species.* Knowing the dismay and opposition that his ideas would arouse, Darwin waited until he had established his reputation among fellow scientists. He was provoked into publishing by receiving the draft of a paper from Alfred Russel Wallace (1833–1913), a young naturalist traveling in Malaysia and Indonesia. Wallace had reached the same conclusions about the origin of species, independently of Darwin. The dilemma of who would claim the ideas was solved by having papers by both Wallace and Darwin presented to the public on July 1, 1858, at a meeting of the Linnaean Society.

In *The Origin of Species,* Darwin called his ideas the theory of "natural selection," contrasting it to artificial selection, which he thought would be familiar to people through the breeding of animals (now called "selective breeding"). **Natural selection** he defined as "preservation of favorable variations and rejection of injurious variations," with

nature making the selection over time. Darwin named his theory with the positive word *selection*; he could just as well have called it "natural elimination." These were his central tenets:

1. A species is a collection of individuals (a population) similar enough to breed with one another; species adapt while individuals do not.
2. Within a species chance variations occur; individuals differ some but not too much.
3. Variations within a species are likely to be inherited by an individual's offspring. (Darwin observed this but did not know how it occurred.)
4. Some variants prove to be better adapted to, or fitter for, their particular environment; hence, they get more resources and have more offspring.
5. Because the more adapted, or fitter, individuals live to have more offspring, later populations will look more like them and will inherit their adaptive characteristics.
6. Individuals who possess traits that are sexually attractive are also likely to have more offspring (sexual selection).
7. This process of evolution produces endless change because the environment changes continually.

Darwin's theory of natural selection explained the variations among the Galapagos finches. On each island, individuals with beaks best suited to the local food sources got slightly more food and had more offspring whose beaks resembled the parental beaks; over hundreds or thousands of years, a new species evolved on each island, too different to interbreed with birds from other islands.

In artificial selection, change occurs rapidly as breeders choose which individuals will be allowed to breed to achieve the traits the breeders want. In natural selection, the number of years it takes to sort out the fittest individuals and create a new species varies. For fast-breeding species like viruses, only a few months or years are needed, but for slow-breeding species, such as primates, tens of thousands of years are required.

Since the long-term environment (including food sources, moisture, and landscape) changes, oscillating between ice ages and warm periods for example, the definition of fitness changes in tandem with it. Natural selection in response to the changing environment is the source of biodiversity, argued Darwin, the explanation for the huge variety of organisms that have inhabited Earth over what we now know to be almost 4 billion years.

As Darwin predicted, the implications of his theory aroused passionate opposition, despite the fact that most knowledgeable biologists and geologists accepted it rather quickly. For starters, his theory implies that all living creatures are related, descending from the primordial forms, which means that humans are closely related to apes; we now know that we share a common ancestor quite recently in biological terms. Worse yet for traditional Christian believers, Darwin's theory clearly implies that if repeated over millions of years, blind processes alone are able to

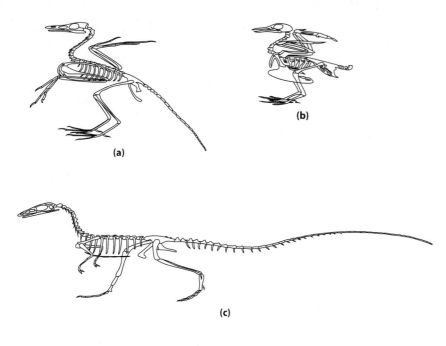

produce exquisitely complex organisms; a creator God is not necessary to explain the huge variety on Earth. To offset this implication, Darwin concluded his book by suggesting that his theory could be reconciled with traditional belief by viewing natural selection as the best way for God to ensure progress in such a complex world; just what Darwin himself believed by then he never made clear.

·Darwin's theory of natural selection rested on three kinds of evidence: (1) *fossils,* which showed that species have changed; (2) *geographic distribution,* like the data he collected on the Galapagos Islands, which showed that species are descended from local ancestors, not products of deliberate engineering by a creator; and on (3) *homologies,* or unexpected similarities between species. Each of these forms of evidence provided an argument in the debate Darwin was conducting with his opponents, who supported the idea of a creator God who designed each species individually.

1. Fossils: As mentioned previously, by the early nineteenth century biologists in Europe realized that fossils represented earlier forms of life. Darwin knew the principle of faunal (animal) succession, named by an English canal engineer, William Smith (1769–1839), who noticed that rocks of different ages preserve different assemblages of fossils and that these assemblages succeeded each other in regular order. Smith could not explain this, but Darwin used this evidence to support his theory of natural selection, which explains the findings: As organisms evolve, change, and go extinct, they leave behind fossils in layers representing time elapsed. This demonstration proves that organisms change over time, rather than being created in a form that does not change.

In Darwin's day, the fossil record was tantalizingly incomplete; today some fossil lineages are remarkably complete, such as that from the ancestral horse to the modern horse or that from the land-living ancestors of whales to

their aquatic descendants. Darwin explained that not finding transitional species must be expected, since fossilization of any organism is extremely rare. Organisms decompose quickly after death, and to become fossils they must be covered in sediment, frozen, dried out, or deposited in an oxygen-free environment, as soon as possible. Only those organisms with hard body parts and with wide territories could have a chance to be recorded as fossils.

Two years after the publication of *The Origin of Species,* an important fossil was discovered in southern Germany— the skeleton of a creature called *Archaeopteryx.* With features intermediate between living birds and ancient reptiles, it seemed a kind of missing link, although this term is now considered outmoded and has been replaced by the term *intermediate form.* About the size of a crow, *Archaeopteryx* had birdlike feathers, wings, and large eyes, with reptilian teeth, clawed hands, and a long tail (Figure 3.2). This fossil confirmed Darwin's theory in the strongest possible way, showing that reptiles and birds shared a common ancestor. Several more of these fossils have since been found. Fossils of feathered dinosaurs have also been found, mostly in China.

2. Geographic Distribution: In considering the geographic distribution of plants and animals, Darwin observed that climate and environment alone do not account for similarity or dissimilarity of inhabitants. For example, Australia, South America, and South Africa between latitudes 25 and 35 degrees all contain similar conditions but utterly dissimilar plants and animals. From this and other observations Darwin concluded that each species is produced in one area and then migrates from out of that area as far as it can adapt to conditions.

3. Homologies: Homologies are similarities of form seen in plants and animals. In evolutionary biology, *homology* has come to mean any similarity that is due to shared ancestry. For instance, cats, whales, bats, and humans all have fingers, suggesting that these species are all related despite the huge differences (Figure 3.3). We know now that whales (and dolphins) are probably descendants of hippopotamus-like creatures that returned to the sea to cool off during a particularly warm period around 50 million years

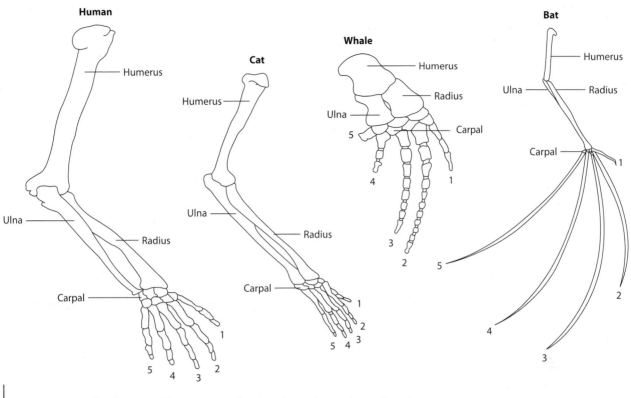

FIGURE 3.3 The fingers of four mammals. These homologous bones have been modified by natural selection in response to environment and function. We humans are closely related, not only to cats, but also to bats and whales. How does the theory of natural selection explain the differences and similarities of these bones?

ago and stayed, continuing to breathe air. The finger bones of whales and bats are useless relics that have been retained as parts of fins or wings. Such relics make no sense if one imagines a designer God starting from scratch with each species, but the relics do make sense if each species has evolved from another species.

Unexpected similarities between species at the level of embryos are even more astonishing. In its early stages, a human embryo has traits found in fish, amphibians, and reptiles before developing its mammalian characteristics. Darwin explained that adaptive modifications generally are produced in later stages of growth, leaving the early pattern of development unchanged and revealing the natural relationships. Since Darwin, biologists have learned that these ancestral structures serve as organizers in the ensuing steps of development.

Darwin was aware of another kind of similarity of form, which he called **convergent evolution,** or the acquisition of the same biological trait in unrelated lineages. This occurs when animals come to resemble each other, not because they are related genetically, but because they evolve similar equipment in response to a similar environment, which may be in unconnected regions or at widely different times. For example, four animals that evolved in areas rich in ants resemble one another without being closely related: the giant anteater in South America, the aardvark in

Africa, the pangolin in Asia and Africa, and the echidna in Australia. Darwin's theory expects different lineages to appear in different regions, even if they eventually converge on similar solutions.

Solutions to Darwin's Problems

In addition to religious objections, real gaps in the knowledge of his day hindered Darwin as he defended his theory. His problems were that (1) he believed natural selection moved too slowly ever to be observed in one lifetime, (2) he did not understand how characteristics are inherited, (3) he could not prove that species were related, and (4) he did not know how old Earth is. In the first edition of *The Origin of Species* Darwin estimated the age of the Earth at some 300 million years, while his learned contemporaries were calculating much less than that.

Modern science has resolved these problems of Darwin with powerful evidence supporting his theory of natural selection. Biologists have found that they can actually see evolution happen. They have seen that, within decades, most houseflies have become resistant to DDT. Some bacteria, like gold staphylococcus (*Staphylococcus aureus*), whose ancestors in the 1940s were killed by penicillin, now are able to resist it. Biologist Jonathan Weiner has even studied the finches on the Galapagos Islands and found that the average size of their beaks changes a millimeter or two within periods of wetter or dryer weather, much faster than expected. They do not become a new species this fast, but rather a new variety with a small change in the genetic makeup of the population.

Darwin's second problem was that he did not know how heredity, or inheritance, worked; no one in his day understood the specific way in which traits are passed from parents to their offspring. Darwin adopted a theory called pangenesis, a group of ideas that had been circulating since the time of Hippocrates, an ancient Greek physician. Darwin believed that each part of an animal body buds off minute particles he called "gemmules"; each gemmule has the capacity to grow into the appropriate organ. Darwin thought that gemmules circulate in the bloodstream and collect in the sexual organs. Gemmules from each parent are mixed together in fertilized eggs, and embryos grow from the developmental power of the gemmules. This theory implied that parental traits are combined, rather than being transmitted as separate units, which would dilute the potentially successful mutations of one individual and undermine the whole theory of natural selection. Gregor Mendel (1822–84), an Austrian Augustinian monk, demonstrated in his studies of peas, published only two years after *The Origin of Species,* that for many traits the offspring show either the characteristics of mother or father, not a blend of the two. Mendel's work, however, received little attention for many years, when it eventually became clear that it was the basis for a whole new theory of heredity.

How heredity works was not solved until 1953, when an American and an Englishman, James Watson (b. 1928) and Francis Crick (1916–2004), figured out the structure of the DNA macromolecule (Figure 3.4). **DNA,** which stands for *deoxyribonucleic acid,* is the large molecule in every cell that carries the chemical instructions for how to build and maintain cells and that passes that information to off-spring cells. The structure of DNA is a double helix: two complementary strands twist around each other and form connections. In reproduction, the strands untwist and form new copies of themselves or, in sexual reproduction, find partner strands to join. DNA is present in all living cells, providing evidence that all life originated from the chemistry of a common single-celled ancestor, the LUCA. (See the next section for details about DNA.)

Knowledge about DNA unambiguously supports Darwin's theory of natural selection. For natural selection to work, individuals must reproduce almost perfectly to preserve the basic structure of their species, but not with complete perfection. A few differences must creep in to provide the variation from which nature selects as the environment changes. This is precisely what happens when the DNA molecule splits; enzymes usually make identical copies of each double strand, but occasional errors, called mutations, occur.

Knowledge of DNA and genetics also solves Darwin's third problem—how to prove that species are related. Biologists can now create molecular clocks based on the

FIGURE 3.4 Watson and Crick with their stick model of DNA. Notice how young Watson and Crick were; Watson was a postdoctorate student, and Crick was still working on his doctorate. To make their leap they used some data from another young researcher, Rosalind Franklin, who died of cancer before she could share with Watson and Crick the Nobel Prize in Medicine/Physiology, awarded in 1962.

fact that genetic mutations occur at a regular average rate for each species. By measuring how many mutations have occurred between two species, they can estimate how long ago the two species diverged. This has shown, for example, that bananas and humans had a common ancestor more than a billion years ago, ants and humans about 600 million, chimpanzees and humans about 5 to 8 million years ago.

Darwin's fourth problem, too, has been solved by modern science with an answer that supports his theory. Now we know, through radiometric dating, that our planet formed about 4.5 billion years ago. This is 15 times longer than Darwin thought Earth had existed, and it provides plenty of time for natural selection to have produced the wonders of life around Darwin and us.

In summary, the evidence for natural selection in Darwin's time consisted of fossils, geographic distribution, and homologies. The evidence since his time has supported his theory unequivocally; biologists have watched species change in relation to their environment, have discovered and explained the structure and function of DNA, have shown via genetic studies that all species are related, and have used radiometric dating to prove that Earth is much older than Darwin realized.

Just as we now have new evidence for Darwin's theory, so, too, some aspects of his theory are now interpreted differently. For example, Stephen Jay Gould (1941–2002) and Niles Eldredge have argued persuasively that the pace of evolutionary change can vary greatly, while Darwin assumed it was always gradual and slow. In addition, some contemporary thinkers (Margulis, Goodenough) believe that Darwin and/or his popularizers emphasized too much the competition needed for survival, without stressing enough that often the most effective strategy for competing lies in cooperation within the population and interdependence with other populations. Partnership seems to these thinkers an essential aspect to all living forms that survive. (More follows about Margulis's ideas.) The sociobiologist E. O. Wilson asserts that human groups with more altruistic, cooperative behavior prevail over those with less. But none of these modifications undermine Darwin's core idea, which remains today at the heart of biological thinking.

Darwin's idea has become the central tenet of contemporary biology—that species of living organisms change in relation to their changing environment by natural selection. This idea is as fundamental to biology as the big bang theory is to astronomy or the theory of plate tectonics is to Earth science. By the time of Darwin's death in 1882,

scientists and Parliament in England recognized the significance of his contribution; they managed to have him buried in Westminster Abby near the tomb of Isaac Newton. Scientists still refer to the theory of evolution, because in science a theory is an idea with enough evidence to be widely supported, and today almost all professional biologists accept the theory of evolution.

Threshold 5: The Emergence of Life on Earth

Life is the marvel of our planet and perhaps on planets elsewhere that we don't know about yet. Life presents such a new level of complexity that we are characterizing the leap to life as the fifth threshold of increasing complexity in the history of the universe. Life is the extension of the complexities of matter, the leap from inert chemicals to living organisms that, organized in a more complex way, are able to take energy from the environment, reproduce, and adapt to generate stunning new forms of complexity, including ourselves (Threshold 5 Summary).

Threshold 5 Summary

THRESHOLD	INGREDIENTS ▶	STRUCTURE ▶	GOLDILOCKS CONDITIONS =	EMERGENT PROPERTIES
LIFE	Complex chemicals + energy.	Complex molecules bound together chemically and physically in cells capable of reproduction.	Abundant complex chemicals + moderate energy flows + liquid medium such as water + suitable planet.	Metabolism (capacity to extract energy); reproduction (ability to copy themselves almost perfectly); adaptation (slow change and appearance of new forms through natural selection).

Darwin's theory of natural selection explains how living organisms adapt over time, but how did life itself emerge from nonlife? How did a living organism, able to metabolize, reproduce, and adapt, arise out of inert chemicals? Darwin did not even try to answer this question, but in a charming letter to a friend in 1871, he outlined the idea that has guided scientific thinking ever since: Conditions on the early Earth may have been more favorable to the creation of simple forms of life than they are today:

> It is often said that all the conditions for the first production of a living organism are now present, which could ever have been present. But if (and oh! What a big if!) we could conceive in some warm little pond, with all sorts of ammonia and phosphoric salts, light, heat, electricity, [etc.] present,

that a proteine [sic] compound was chemically formed ready to undergo still more complex changes, at the present day such matter would be instantly devoured or absorbed, which would not have been the case before living creatures were formed.[1]

Before we discuss current scientific ideas about the origin of life, we want to set the context by summarizing some traditional ideas.

Traditional Ideas about the Origin of Life

Many cultures and societies over time have postulated that the gods, or a single God, created living beings and humans by supernaturally intervening in nature. In the

Judeo-Christian tradition this view found high expression in the masterpiece by Michelangelo on the ceiling of the Sistine Chapel in Rome, Italy, which shows the hand of God reaching from the heavens to touch the hand of man (humanity). Since there is no objectively verifiable evidence to date for this view, and no way of testing it, scientists regard this idea as a matter of belief or as a metaphor. Instead they look for naturalistic explanations that can be supported by objective evidence.

Even up to the mid-nineteenth century, naturalists clung to an old idea called spontaneous generation. It posited that new life could emerge suddenly and spontaneously from the decayed remnants of old life. For instance, worms or maggots were seen to appear suddenly on garbage. People accepted as evidence what their eyes could see, not yet realizing that an entire world of microbial organisms existed that could be perceived only by microscopes.

Darwin's contemporary, the Parisian chemist and bacteriologist Louis Pasteur (1822–95), proved the idea of spontaneous generation of life to be false. Pasteur did this by conducting experiments under sterilized conditions. He showed that air contains microorganisms that, if brought into contact with sterile water, give the illusion that life has arisen spontaneously. Pasteur devised ways to heat the air enough to kill the microorganisms; he showed that air, once it is sterilized and isolated, remains free of life indefinitely, proving that life does not appear spontaneously from nonlife. Life comes only from life, or *omnevivum ex viva* as Pasteur put it in Latin.

A third theory of the origin of life is called panspermia, or "germs everywhere." This ancient idea, going back to the Greek scientist Anaxagoras, is still held by some today. The cosmologist Fred Hoyle (1915–2001) was one of the most famous supporters of panspermia. This theory posits that life came to Earth from space, carried by meteorites and comets that bombarded Earth in the early days. It can easily be embroidered to include exciting stories about aliens bringing life here. Most space scientists argue that life would not be able to survive conditions in outer space or the fiery trip through the Earth's atmosphere; on the other hand, microscopic life might survive if it were protected deep inside the incoming rocks. The theory of panspermia suffers from the basic problem that it does not explain the origin of life; it simply moves the location elsewhere.

Some current scientists accept a weak version of panspermia, the idea that some of the building blocks or constituents of life probably arrived on Earth carried by comets (balls of dirty ice) or meteorites (meteors, or rocks, that strike Earth) without burning up in the atmosphere. As we saw in Chapter 2, comets are thought to have provided much of the water on Earth; it is easy to suppose this water contained constituent chemicals for life. It is known that some meteorites, like the one that fell near Murchison, Australia, in 1969, contain some of the chemicals needed to produce living cells. Other meteorites, like the one that fell in Canada's Yukon Territory a few days into 2000, contain bubble-like organic globules. These finds confirm at least that the molecules needed for life exist in space; they spur on the search for extraterrestrial life and pose the basic question of how widespread life is in the universe.

Modern Ideas about the Origin of Life

If life can arise only from life, as Pasteur demonstrated, then how did life originally arise from nonlife? The assumption held by most scientists is that life evolved from nonlife through a gradual increase in molecular complexity over immense periods of time. The most primitive forms of life now living are single-celled microorganisms so small that nearly a thousand of them would fit on the period at the end of this sentence. These suggest what the earliest and simplest forms of life on Earth looked like.

The date for the beginning of life is understandably murky. Some biologists consider the oldest fossils of living organisms to be embedded in rocks dated at nearly 3.5 billion years old, rocks found in Kruger Park in South Africa and in northwestern Australia. Others—for example, Nick Lane, a researcher at University College, London—believe that those supposed microfossils are really natural artifacts and that the earliest reliable fossil of a living organism is about 2.4 billion years old. If he is right, life may have taken longer to get underway (2 billion instead of 1 billion years) than we once thought. Others suggest that the 3.5-billion-year-old fossils were living organisms but not yet photosynthesizers. This debate continues.

So how did the first living cell, similar to the simplest cells that still exist, come to life? The hypothesis favored by biologists today, called the **theory of chemical evolution,** holds that molecules slowly evolved by natural selection into long chains of amino acids (the building blocks of proteins) and nucleotides (the building blocks of nucleic acid). Just like natural selection in the world of living organisms, the chemical chains that worked in their environment survived, while others vanished, eventually giving rise to the first populations of living organisms. The details of this process remain uncertain, but lab experiments have produced some suggestions.

In the 1920s and early 1930s a biochemist and a physicist operating independently conceived the hypothesis of chemical evolution. Alexander Oparin (1894–1980) in Moscow and J. B. S. Haldane (1892–1964) in London proposed similar scenarios for the origin of life, in which the early atmosphere, rich in hydrogen compounds (methane and ammonia) with little free oxygen, allowed the synthesis of increasingly complex organic molecules. Haldane stressed the point that developing life must have arisen in an oxygen-free environment because oxygen is highly reactive (fire is an example of oxygen reacting) and would probably have destroyed any simple forms of life that evolved on the early Earth. As we saw in Chapter 2, oxygen did not form a significant part of the atmosphere until the rise of photosynthetic bacteria about 2.5 billion years ago.

Since the atmosphere and surface of Earth today differ greatly from those of early Earth, the problem of how early life arose must be studied in a lab, where early conditions can be simulated. One significant experiment took place at the University of Chicago in 1952, when graduate student Stanley Miller worked in the lab of Nobel Laureate Harold Urey. Miller wondered if lightning could have synthesized the raw materials of life as it moved through the early atmosphere in a world without free oxygen. Miller filled tubes with gases he thought approximated the early atmosphere, set them over a flask of sterilized water, and bombarded the gases with an electrical discharge, more than he estimated present in early Earth to speed up the process. Within a week the tubes turned reddish brown, tinted by a sludgy film on its inner surface. When analyzed, the sludge proved to be composed of a variety of organic molecules (those containing carbon–hydrogen bonds and found in living organisms). Included in these molecules were at least half a dozen amino acids, from which proteins are made (Figure 3.5).

After these lab experiments showed that simple amino acids and nucleotides could easily form in an atmosphere free of oxygen, the next step was to show that these simple compounds could assemble themselves into more complex proteins and nucleic acids. Further lab experiments have shown that under the right conditions simple amino acids do form long chains of thousands or millions of atoms. Many biologists assume that for life to emerge one of these proto-cells happened on a chemical evolution that gradually, over at least half a billion years, led it to a fully living cell. But this has not been demonstrated in a laboratory and remains one of the great unknowns of this story.

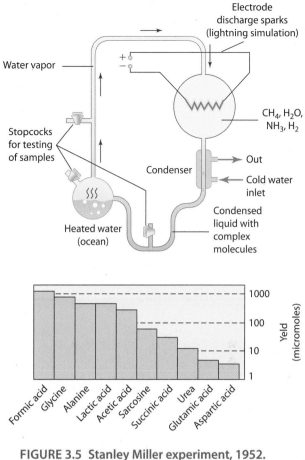

FIGURE 3.5 Stanley Miller experiment, 1952. Miller was a graduate student of the Nobel Prize–winning chemist Harold C. Urey, when he tried to simulate in the laboratory the early conditions on Earth. Darwin was 22 when he set off for the Galapagos; young people seem to be crucial to the advance of science.

The Chemistry of Cells

To understand the chemical evolution that took place as life emerged, it helps to be familiar with the components of the simplest living cell, based on the most basic physics and chemistry. An atom is the smallest unit of an element, never broken down into smaller particles in chemical reactions, even though atoms are formed from even smaller particles. On Earth, as explained in Chapter 1, 92 elements, or distinct kinds of atoms, occur naturally.

The chemistry of life is based on the unique structure of the carbon atom, whose most common isotope has 6 protons, 6 electrons, and 6 neutrons. It is able to form long chains with other carbon atoms, while still having two sites per carbon atom where other atoms may attach, causing the carbon chain to fold into stable structures of great diversity and complexity. Carbon atoms combine with the atoms of five other elements that form the common proteins of

life: hydrogen (1 proton, 1 electron), nitrogen (7 protons, 7 electrons), oxygen (8 protons, 8 electrons), phosphorus (15 protons, 15 electrons), and sulfur (16 protons, 16 electrons).

Here is the big picture of a cell; more details will follow. The simplest living cell is called a **prokaryote** (pro-CARRY-oat), which means a cell without a nucleus (Figure 3.6). Even though it has no nucleus, a prokaryote is already highly complex. A membrane encloses all of its contents and regulates molecular traffic in and out. The content of the cell, except for the genetic material, is called cytoplasm; it is made up primarily of proteins, which are long chains of amino acids folded into a three-dimensional (3-D) shape. New proteins are constructed at special structures in the cell's cytoplasm called ribosomes. In prokaryotes the genetic material, the DNA molecule, floats around not enclosed in a membrane that would form a nucleus.

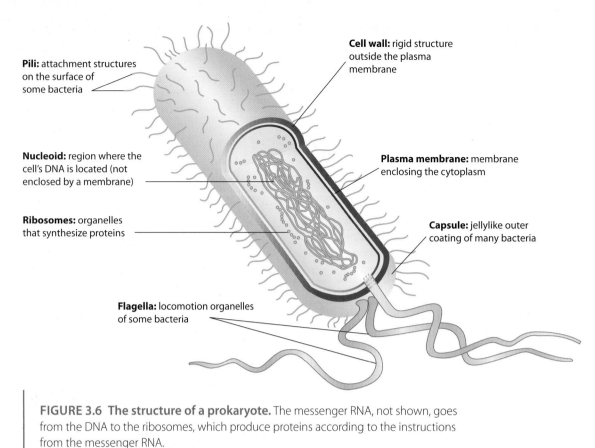

FIGURE 3.6 The structure of a prokaryote. The messenger RNA, not shown, goes from the DNA to the ribosomes, which produce proteins according to the instructions from the messenger RNA.

Labels in figure:

Pili: attachment structures on the surface of some bacteria

Cell wall: rigid structure outside the plasma membrane

Nucleoid: region where the cell's DNA is located (not enclosed by a membrane)

Plasma membrane: membrane enclosing the cytoplasm

Ribosomes: organelles that synthesize proteins

Capsule: jellylike outer coating of many bacteria

Flagella: locomotion organelles of some bacteria

Where and How Did the First Cells Emerge?

Where on Earth were conditions right for that original cell to emerge? Water seems the most likely site. Darwin already thought it would happen in a "warm little pond." Water in liquid form seems vital for life because in gases the atoms move rapidly and come into contact only fleetingly, while in solids the atoms hardly move at all. In liquids the movement is just right; the atoms contact each other slowly enough to link up or bond into more complex molecules. Water remains in liquid form at a wide range of temperatures, from just above freezing (32 degrees Fahrenheit [0 degrees Celsius]) to just under boiling (212 degrees Fahrenheit [100 degrees Celsius]). Water is formed of two abundant atoms, hydrogen and oxygen, and water does not affect the bonds that carbon makes with other atoms.

Modern biologists have often considered the shallow edges of oceans as the most likely site where conditions would be right for the emergence of life. More recent deep exploration of oceans suggests that another likely site lies in vents, called "black smokers," near deep-sea volcanoes at the edges of moving tectonic plates, where there is liquid water, lots of heat, energy, and chemicals, and not much oxygen. Heat-loving bacteria that are not dependent on oxygen or sunlight have been found in these vents. Among them are the *archaea,* the domain of life discovered in 1977 that goes back to some of the most ancient life-forms. Some biologists believe that the heat at these vents is too great for the survival of the original cells or that the constituents of life are too dilute; agreement has not yet been reached about the most likely site for the origin of life.

In thinking about how living cells began, scientists imagine complex molecules, made of the same elements as living cells, joined together into cell-like balls with a protective membrane, getting energy by absorbing other atoms and molecules, and breaking apart to replicate. But how could these proto-cells reproduce with enough precision to preserve the useful adaptations they acquired and evolve into life? This is the question that has yet to be answered fully, the gap in our understanding of the emergence of life.

Breakthroughs, however, have been made, the first in 1944 when the genetic material was found to consist of nucleic acids, not proteins. Then, in 1953 Watson and Crick explained the structure of the DNA molecule, as described earlier.

DNA masterminds the building and maintenance of cells and passes that information to offspring cells. Present in every cell of every living organism, DNA is a long chain of nucleotides, which are different from the amino acids that form proteins and the phospholipids that form cell membranes.

DNA molecules are the largest and most complex molecules in living cells; in humans about 6 feet

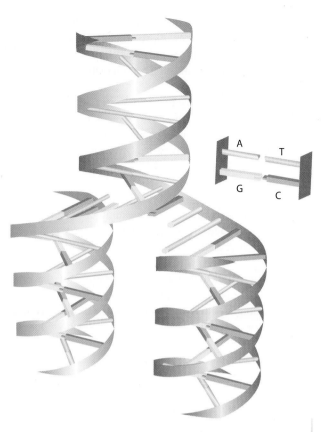

FIGURE 3.7 The double helix of DNA. DNA takes the shape of two strands twisted into a helix, or spiral, in every cell, except in the reproductive sex cells, where DNA splits into a single strand waiting to match up with a partner sex cell.

(2 meters) of DNA (stretched out) is squeezed into every cell. DNA is grouped into chromosomes, each with a section of DNA called a gene. Each gene encodes the sequence of amino acids in a single protein. A molecule called messenger RNA carries the gene's instructions to the ribosomes, where a protein is produced out of amino acids in the cytoplasm, in accordance with the gene's instructions.

The DNA is structured like a long, twisted ladder (Figure 3.7). The vertical supports in the ladder are chains of alternating phosphate and sugar molecules. The rungs consist of complementary pairs of molecules called bases—cytosine (C), paired with guanine (G) and adenine (A) paired with thymine (T).

When DNA makes a copy of itself, the two complementary strands split down the middle. Each of the bases bonds with only one other type, so each strand is predictable from the other. Each strand collects free molecules from its surroundings until a new exact copy of itself results, with an occasional error, or mutation, for variety. (There are other sources of errors as well, caused by radiation or chemicals, by movement of genes, and other changes.) For visualizations of DNA see www.apod.nasa.gov/apod/ap120821.html.

DNA's close relative, **RNA,** or ribonucleic acid, has a slightly different sugar in its backbone and generally exists as a single strand of molecules. As described two paragraphs earlier, in modern cells a strand of messenger RNA is copied from a portion of the DNA, then moves out into the cytoplasm to give the instructions to the ribosomes of how to produce new proteins. RNA may have earlier had shapes that early cells could use to make the proteins themselves, as well as passing on the instructions to offspring cells. If so, then RNA might have been a precursor to DNA.

The idea that RNA preceded DNA has become the current dominant hypothesis of biologists; they call it RNA World theory. It postulates that ancient RNA stored genetic information instead of DNA, that ancient RNA replicated like modern DNA, and that ancient RNA carried out the same catalytic roles as modern protein enzymes do. If this hypothesis proves correct, then the first life-form would have used a self-replicating strand of RNA, perhaps enclosed in a protective membrane; metabolism would emerge later.

For life to emerge, two different sets of molecules had to evolve: nucleic acids for coding reproduction and amino acids as protein precursors for metabolism and maintenance. The questions to be answered are: How did they interact to ensure the survival of each other? What is the sequence in which they developed?

Just for the fun of thinking about it, here are a few possible hypotheses. Perhaps both proteins (metabolism) and DNA developed simultaneously and cooperatively. Or perhaps RNA developed first, with proteins coming later; or vice versa. Perhaps RNA and proteins each arose in separate proto-cells, then merged to form an alliance. In any case, the origin of the genetic code, in all of its astonishing complexity, is still a mystery. Most biochemists believe that the chemistry involved in the first life would seem probable and expected, if they could only figure out what it was.

Although the question of how life emerged remains a mystery, we know from genetic evidence that all life has evolved from one original group of cells, LUCA, that developed the chemistry to metabolize and to reproduce accurately the chemical advantages it pioneered. We humans are connected to every living organism on Earth because we share with each one the same genetic code that has been maintaining and reproducing life since the first living cell emerged. This may be the most extraordinary fact known about life on Earth.

We also know that conditions on Earth had to be just right for life to be able to emerge and continue. From its early molten state, Earth cooled down and evolved ways to dissipate its internal heat. Since the oceans formed about 4.3 to 2 billion years ago, Earth has never been so cold that the entire planet completely froze or so hot that all the water has evaporated. In contrast, on Venus and Mars, our nearest neighbors, life may have emerged, but circumstances changed too drastically for it to continue. Venus became too hot, as the sun gradually increased its heat output about 30 percent since its inception and as CO_2 in Venus's atmosphere raised its temperatures further. Mars is too small to retain its atmosphere and surface liquid water; these losses would have killed any life that might have emerged there.

A Brief History of Life on Earth

Now the background is in place for us to consider a new question: How did life evolve over approximately 3.8 billion years to form the diversity of living organisms that we know today? If we were chickens or praying mantises, we would pose this question to focus on the pathways that led to chickens or praying mantises. Since we are humans, we will follow those turns through the maze of diversity that led to humans.

By focusing on complex life-forms, we do not mean to imply that greater complexity is necessarily more important or better than less complexity. All life-forms are interdependent; more complex entities depend on less complex ones. Bacteria still mediate all the important cycles of elements on Earth. We humans have expanded our population so dramatically since the mid-twentieth century that we are inclined to think that we are in charge or have pulled off some kind of a coup d'etat over the rest of life. Yet we still remain dependent on less complex forms of life. In this text we are focusing on humans not just because humans seem dominant at the moment, but also because we, who are human, are writing for other humans, who presumably are most interested in the story of their own species.

In describing the evolution of life it is difficult to tell the two strands of the story—the biological strand and the geological strand—simultaneously. At every moment that living organisms are changing, Earth is also changing; each is affecting the other. As we focus on the biological changes, we also provide some examples of the reciprocal effects of living organisms on the composition of Earth and its effect on organisms.

To simplify the history of life on Earth, we are dividing it into eight stages, which can be seen in Figure 3.8. The first four stages will concern the development of single-celled organisms over a period of 3 billion years. These stages are:

1. The emergence of prokaryotes
2. Photosynthesis or energy from sunlight
3. Respiration and the emergence of eukaryotes
4. Sexual reproduction

These first four stages cover six-sevenths of the time elapsed in our story. Throughout this period, life consisted of single-celled microorganisms. If humans find life anywhere else than on Earth, this is probably what we will find.

The next four stages cover the final one-seventh of time, or only about 600 million years. They include:

5. The emergence of multicelled organisms
6. The vertebrates, or animals with backbones
7. Life coming on land
8. Dinosaurs and mammals, up to 8 million years ago

FIGURE 3.8 Timeline of life on Earth. Notice how long it took for the percentage of oxygen to increase in the atmosphere. What does thinking on this time scale contribute to your understanding of humans?

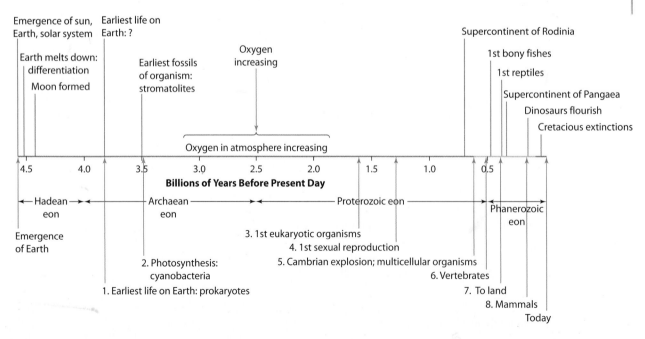

The Earliest Four Stages (3.8 Billion to 600 Million Years Ago)

The first four stages of life involved only single-celled microorganisms, which developed the basic processes of life: fermentation, photosynthesis, respiration and the emergence of eukaryotes, and sexual reproduction. This took about 3 billion years.

Stage 1: The First Life (ca. 3.8 Billion Years Ago) The first living organisms were probably similar to prokaryotes: single-celled microorganisms with no nucleus, as described previously. The smallest bacteria and archaea have a diameter a thousand times that of an atom of hydrogen; a thousand fit into the dot made by a pencil. In this tiny space are packed millions and millions of molecules; bacteria and archaea are masters of nanotechnology.

The simplest microorganisms replicate by dividing in half; hence, they normally do not die. They can be killed by starvation, heat, salt, drying out, or antibiotics, but unless these conditions occur they just keep halving and multiplying.

Early organisms, both archaea in deep-sea vents and bacteria everywhere else, ate simple molecules in their vicinity for their energy and food. Early bacteria made use of fermentation, a form of metabolism without oxygen. (Oxygen would eventually become an important part of metabolism, but not until it became a prominent part of the atmosphere some billion years later.) The bacteria excreted acids and alcohols that contain less energy than the food ingested. Some of them continue to this day to act as fermenters—for example, the bacteria that metabolize dairy products to make cheese. Archaea were more adept than bacteria at inhabiting extreme environments, such as very warm or very salty water. Whereas bacteria typically need to eat organic compounds (molecules that contain carbon), such as amino acids or sugars, as food, archaea evolved as ability to use extremely simple inorganic compounds in their metabolism, such as the sulfur released by deep-sea vents.

Stage 2: Photosynthesis (ca. 3.4 to 2.5 Billion Years Ago) In the early days of life microorganisms eventually began to run out of amino acids and proteins in their surroundings and had to find other ways to obtain their energy. Some of them evolved the capacity to make their food from sunlight via **photosynthesis,** a process in which some cells found a way to use the carbon dioxide that was expelled into the air as a waste product of the fermentation of other cells. These photosynthesizers could literally eat air, although they still had to get elements like nitrogen and sulfur from someplace else.

In photosynthesis, the chlorophyll molecule has atoms arranged in such a way, like tiny solar panels, that sunlight, when it hits the surface, is captured within the molecule. The sun's energy knocks the hydrogen atom off the oxygen atom in water. The hydrogen atoms, plus the attached solar energy, bond with carbon atoms from the carbon dioxide in the air to produce carbohydrate (sugar), at the same time releasing oxygen into the atmosphere. The sugar stores chemical energy from the sun.

The chlorophyll molecule is green. It first appeared in prokaryotes called blue-green bacteria, or *cyanobacteria.* They were formerly called blue-green algae, but algae are formed from the more complex cells known as *eukaryotes,* those with nuclei.

Photosynthesis represents perhaps the major metabolic development in history. It meant that photosynthetic bacteria could live directly off the energy of the sun, as do all their descendants, the plants. Plants have direct access to the energy of the sun, storing it for animals, which live by eating plants. Photosynthesis also meant that these bacteria expelled oxygen into the atmosphere as a waste product. Over time, from about 3 to 2 billion years ago, this would change the proportion of oxygen in the atmosphere from about 1 percent to its present 20 to 21 percent (see Chapter 2).

Humans are greatly indebted to photosynthetic bacteria, not only in the past but also in the present. Every day about 400 million tons (about 363 million metric tons) of carbon dioxide mix with some 200 million tons (181 million metric tons) of water to make about 300 million tons (272 million metric tons) of organic matter and another 300 million tons of oxygen. Half of each day's photosynthesis is still done by single-celled marine plankton living in the top layer of the ocean where enough light penetrates to support their growth.

Why have photosynthetic bacteria persisted so long with so little change? No one knows; perhaps because they are essential to the functioning of life and/or because they are so well adapted that they don't need to change, which is to say there has not been much selective pressure on them.

The early cyanobacteria spread across shallow areas of water to form mats, large colonies of bacteria up to half a yard or meter tall, called *stromatolites.* The surface of these mats trapped fine particles of sand or mud, while deep in the mat the bacteria consumed dead cells, causing carbonate crystals to form, resulting in accretions of limestone. Each cell in these mats functioned on its own; there is no evidence of more complex cells or any intercellular interaction. Many fossil stromatolites have been found, and a few are still forming today in the Bahama Banks and in Shark Bay in Western Australia, places where no grazing animals are present to eat them (Figure 3.9).

Cyanobacteria, having solved one crisis by developing photosynthesis, over time brought on another crisis—they emitted oxygen, which changed the composition of the atmosphere and the oceans. At first oxygen combined with iron to form huge bands of red rock. Much oxygen was also dissolved in the oceans. Gradually, by about 2.5 billion years ago, the oxygenation of the air and the water assumed global importance. Since the first bacteria were not

FIGURE 3.9 Stromatolites. These are structures generated by bacterial mats, the most ancient community of individual prokaryotic cells. This photo shows recent stromatolites forming in Shark Bay, Western Australia. These organisms have been reproducing themselves without dying for 3.5 billion years—how's that for longevity?

chemically organized to use oxygen, many of those gradually died out, supplanted by those that evolved a way to use oxygen. This transition was not a total holocaust; some non-oxygen-using (anaerobic) bacteria retain their function in the ecosystem today. But oxygen-using (aerobic) cells now dominate the world.

Stage 3: Respiration and Eukaryotes (ca. 2.5 to 1.5 Billion Years Ago) Somewhere along the way, between about 2.5 and 1.5 billion years ago, a third major step in the development of life occurred. Some bacteria developed a way to use oxygen, which is called **respiration,** the reverse process of photosynthesis. In respiration, oxygen (O_2) is ingested and used by the cell to digest carbohydrates, releasing energy used by the cell and giving off carbon dioxide (CO_2) and water as waste. Photosynthesis uses CO_2 and gives off O_2; respiration uses O_2 and gives off CO_2—*voila!* Bacteria had devised a recycling system that keeps the biosphere in balance, a textbook case of equilibrium, or balanced levels of gains and losses.

At about the same time, 2.5 to 1.5 billion years ago, partly as a consequence of developing respiration, a new kind of cell emerged among the mats of stromatolites. The earliest evidence for this new kind of cell comes from about 1.8 billion years ago. It may have appeared much earlier, but the earlier history of life is controversial due to gene transfer among the three domains and the sheer difficulty of finding evidence. This new cell proved to be a momentous increase of complexity, and no other cell innovation has appeared since.

This new cell, called a **eukaryote** (you-CARRY-oat), differs from a prokaryote in about 30 ways, but for our purposes 3 or 4 will suffice (Figure 3.10). Eukaryotes are much larger than prokaryotes, 10 to 1,000 times larger. Their DNA is enclosed in a protective membrane that constitutes a well-developed nucleus. The cell is large enough

that the cytoplasm has developed a cytoskeleton, which is a network of protein fibers that support the cell, allow it to move, and allow its contents to move around within the cell. In addition, these new cells contain organelles, which are separate functioning structures like organs in a body. The two most important organelles are mitochondria, the site of aerobic respiration that provides the cell's metabolism, and chloroplasts (in plants) that conduct photosynthesis.

Modern analysis of the genome of eukaryotes suggests that they may have developed from a symbiosis of archaea and bacteria. Subsequently these eukaryotic cells acquired other bacteria, the mitochondria, an oxygen-respiring bacterium, and, in plants, the chloroplasts, a cyanobacterium.

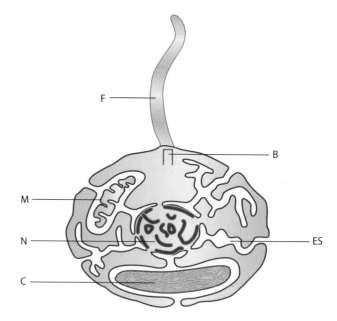

FIGURE 3.10 The structure of a eukaryotic cell. This diagram shows clearly the increase of complexity from a prokaryotic cell. The shaded area is the cytoplasm. There are both external membranes and internal ones (ES), which define the space that contains the nucleus (N) and the cytoplasm. The chloroplasts (C) and mitochondria (M) lie outside this space. (F) is the eukaryotic flagellum anchored by a basal body (B).

The larger cells apparently ingested the mitochrondria and chloroplasts but did not digest them. This aspect of eukaryotes was not understood until biologist Lynn Margulis proposed it in 1967, strongly indicating that evolution proceeds by cooperation as well as by competition. Biologists now largely accept her idea, in part because mitochondria carry their own DNA.

Some eukaryotes are single-celled—for example, diatoms or microscopic algae. Others are multicellular—for example, all the eukaryotic cells in human bodies. One science writer, Bill Bryson, describes a eukaryotic cell like this:

> If you could visit a cell, you wouldn't like it. Blown up to a scale at which atoms were about the size of peas, a cell itself would be a sphere roughly half a mile across, and supported by a complex framework of girders called the cytoskeleton. Within it, millions upon millions of objects—some the size of basketballs, others the size of cars—would whiz about like bullets. There wouldn't be a place you could stand without being pummeled and ripped thousands of times every second from every direction. Even for its full-time occupants the inside of a cell is a hazardous place. Each strand of DNA is on average attacked or damaged once every 8.4 seconds—a thousand times a day—by chemicals and other agents that whack into or carelessly slice through it, and each of these wounds must be swiftly stitched up if the cell is not to perish.
>
> The proteins are especially lively, spinning, pulsating, and flying into each other up to a billion times a second. Enzymes, themselves a type of protein, dash everywhere, performing up to a thousand tasks a second. Like greatly speeded up worker ants, they busily build and rebuild molecules, hauling a piece off this one, adding a piece to that one.[2]

Stage 4: Sexual Reproduction (ca. 1 Billion Plus Years Ago)

So far in our story all life-forms, both prokaryotes and eukaryotes, reproduced themselves by splitting in two parts, each part forming a clone of the original cell, genetically the same except for any mutations in the DNA.

Some billion or more years ago a fourth major step was taken by early eukaryotes like algae, amoebas, and slime molds. These eukaryotes developed a new way of reproduction, called sexual reproduction, in which the cells responsible for reproduction divide without doubling their DNA. The offspring cells are ready to find their other half in fertilization, by combining with offspring cells from another "parent" organism. All the other cells go on to eventual death, unlike asexual reproduction in which all the cells go on living. In the earliest forms of sexual reproduction eukaryotes are thought to have eaten each other whole in times of scarcity; sometimes their nuclei would have merged, sometimes producing DNA formed half from each; sexual reproduction may have originated in cannibalism. The price for sexual reproduction is the death of all the cells except the ones that manage to produce a new body.

No one knows exactly what advantage sexual reproduction had that caused it to proliferate. Whatever else, it added a major source of variation for natural selection to act on. When half the genes of each parent are recombined in sexual reproduction, a much greater variety of new genetic combinations is produced in the offspring than mutations alone can accomplish. None of us is a clone of one of our parents; we are a mixture of both. The greater variety of offspring began to accelerate evolution.

Meanwhile, of course, the environment on Earth continued to change as life evolved. As described, after bacteria developed photosynthesis, more oxygen began to accumulate in the atmosphere. It took some 2 billion years to reach the current level of 21 percent, about 600 million years ago.

Before much oxygen had accumulated in the atmosphere, ultraviolet rays from the sun hit Earth with full force. Since these rays broke up oxygen molecules, formed of two oxygen atoms, the free oxygen atoms recombined high in the atmosphere into **ozone,** with three oxygen atoms. This ozone gradually built up to form a thin shell completely surrounding Earth about 30 miles (48 kilometers) above the surface, protecting the surface and its life from harmful ultraviolet radiation. More oxygen meant more ozone and better survival for life. Ozone probably started to build up about 2.5 billion years ago and may have become a fully effective shield only about 500 million years ago.

Meanwhile, other major events happened in Earth's environment. About 2.5 billion years ago, some kind of unusual disturbance, not known precisely, seems to have occurred in the carbon cycle, the biochemical cycle in which carbon is recycled through the biosphere and all its organisms. Two billion years later, a bit more than 600 million years ago, an unusually severe ice age took place, with ice covering much of the planet's oceans and most of its continental shelves. These changes produced increased extinctions of plant and animal life and a marked acceleration of change in living forms in the following period. Living organisms were transforming the biosphere, in tandem with the environment transforming life.

The Next Four Stages (ca. 600 to 8 Million Years Ago)

Only in the last 600 million years have multicelled organisms in all their diversity evolved.

Stage 5: Multicelled Organisms (ca. 700 to 600 Million Years Ago)

Some eukaryotic cells gathered together to live in colonies or societies, at first still as separate cells. A slime mold is an example of a colony of millions of amoebas that did not develop into a single organism.

In some groups the cells gradually became more specialized, and extra molecules developed to hold the cells together. Cells found ways to communicate among themselves and developed genetic programs to control cell differentiation so that different cells could play different roles. This took place in the seas about 840 million years ago, possibly earlier. The first multicellular creatures began to emerge, similar to, but less complex than, a tube sponge. (The simplest form of multicellular animal life known today is *trichoplax,* a headless, tailless creature first found in 1965 in Philadelphia crawling on the side of a marine aquarium. It resembles a giant amoeba, except that it has a sex life and an embryo that starts as a hollow ball of cells.)

Between 600 and 550 million years ago almost all multicelled organisms had soft, mushy, gelatinous bodies. They were the first living organisms large enough to be visible to the naked eye. They lived in the sea feeding on microscopic plants and each other, some anchored to undersea slopes, some floating around. Because of their soft bodies, only a few fossils from this period have remained. The first discovered were sandstone imprints of tubular worms found at Ediacara (edi-YAK-ara), north of Adelaide in southeastern Australia. Now any such fossils found around the world from this period are called Ediacaran.

Suddenly, as geologic time goes, animal life developed an astonishing diversity of structural forms, or morphologies. Biologists call this the **Cambrian explosion,** a period of up to 15 to 20 million years about 542 million years ago. Cambria is an old name for Wales in southwest Great Britain, where some of these fossils were first located. By now these fossils have been found worldwide: in the Burgess Shale collection exposed on a high mountain in British Columbia, Canada; at Chengjiang in China's Yunnan province; at Sirius Point in northern Greenland; at the Grand Canyon in Arizona. No one can explain this apparently drastic change in the rate of evolution, except to observe that perhaps more fossils are found from this time since this is the period when already-existing animals formed hard skeletons that left imprints, or that it was a response to a sudden warming spell after a severe ice age.

Nearly half of all fossils found in the world are those of trilobites, an early group of invertebrates widespread some 500 million years ago. They appear suddenly in the fossil record with no trace of earlier forms and disappear in a mass extinction of 75 to 95 percent of species that occurred about 242 million years ago (see the following text for more details). Modern lobsters and horseshoe crabs are among their descendants.

Among the fossils found in the Burgess Shale is *Pikaia,* the first known member of the chordate group, to which belong humans and all other animals with backbones. *Pikaia* was a wormlike, swimming creature with a solid rod made of cartilage running down its back; it may have been the ancestor of all fish, amphibians, reptiles, birds, and mammals, as well as all of us.

Stage 6: The First Vertebrates (Chordates) (ca. 500 to 400 Million Years Ago)

The first vertebrate animals developed from those creatures, like *Pikaia,* with spinal columns of cartilage but no bones. Vertebrates, or animals with a spinal column made of bone, gradually added central backbones, jaws, a front and a backside, and a brain case shielding a nervous system. The early jawless fish, about 12 inches (30 centimeters) long, ate by sucking in water and whatever it contained. By 400 million years ago a sharklike creature had developed with jaws more powerful than any marine creature alive today. A fossilized claw was recently found in Germany of a sea scorpion 8 feet (2.4 meters) long, eventually wiped out by large fish with teeth and jaws.

Vertebrates developed similar eye structures. Since current controversies often focus on how the highly complex structure of the mammalian eye could develop by natural selection, a brief description of that evolution seems in order. In living organisms, as Darwin knew, there exists a spectrum of photosensitive organs, from the simplest eyespot (a concentration of pigment in a single cell) to the complex eye with muscles, lenses, and optic nerves. Every intermediate step in the development of the eye met the functional needs of its bearer. Even among mollusks one can see the development from a simple optic cup in the abalone to the complex-lensed eye of the octopus and marine snail. All eyes have one pigment, rhodopsin, which is vital to capturing light radiation. Molecular biologists now think that all creatures with eyes are descendants of some sea-dwelling worm living half a billion years ago that developed the gene for the original pigment. But the lenses and other components of eyes seem to have evolved quite separately in many different lineages in a spectacular example of convergent evolution.

In our story so far all living creatures inhabited the seas. Life could not survive on land; all life's chemistry had developed in water. Leaving the water would be like humans moving into space; elaborate support systems would be needed—portable supplies of water, tough skins to prevent drying out, protection for eggs and offspring, internal load-bearing support systems. Even after developing these systems, all present land-living organisms must still begin their development in a watery place, as humans do in placental fluid.

Stage 7: Life Comes on Land (ca. 475 to 360 Million Years Ago)

About 400 million years ago, some living creatures undertook the perilous journey from sea to land. Plants and fungi probably went first; insects likely were the first animals to venture onto land.

Fungi are often left out of the story of life, but they form a crucial group separate from plants and animals. Fungi live off the soil, not the sun, sometimes in utter darkness. A toadstool is the tip of an underground web of living threads that lack discrete borders. (One area near Crystal Falls, Michigan, has an underground fungus some 37 acres [150,000 square meters] large; it has been growing for about 1,500 years.) Some 60,000 species of fungi are known; 1.5 million are estimated to exist. Fungi reproduce by airborne spores, some of which land on bread to produce bread mold. Fungi recycle the dead by turning corpses into fertilizer. They also produce blue cheese mold, mushrooms, and penicillin. Coal was formed from the compression of seed ferns and tree ferns before fungi evolved a way of decomposing them. Fungi need to be in the story.

As the tides went in and out almost half a billion years ago, two different groups of eukaryotes got stuck on shore. One group ate sunlight, the other soil; they found each other and developed together into the first land plants and fungi. The ancestors of modern plants could not have colonized land without fungi, which are still symbiotically intertwined in the roots of more than 95 percent of plant species. They provide the plants with elements from the soil.

The earliest plants were upright stems, with no roots or seeds, but with spores for reproducing. By about 410 million years ago, a period of unusual warmth, these stems had developed into horsetails, plants with hollow, jointed stems, up to 46 feet (14 meters) high. By 345 million years ago they had become tropical seed ferns, which looked like overgrown pineapples rather than ferns. They did not survive the mass extinction of about 245 million years ago, but at least one of them gave rise to conifers, plants that could withstand freezing temperatures. This is the first time that the surface of the continents turned green. Before then it was either rock gray or rock red.

The earliest animals out of the sea may have been amphibians and nonflying insects. By means of natural selection, the fins of some fish changed into stubby, weblike feet. The lungfish was a transitional species; it could survive on land for brief periods if necessary. Today its ancestors still survive, but only in Australia.

Amphibians are defined by their ability to live both on land and in the water. The earliest known amphibian fossil, found in 1948, is that of *Ichthyostega*, which lived about 370 million years ago and may have gotten onto land, but needed to return to water to lay its eggs. By then trees were growing 60 feet (18 meters) high.

Reptiles emerged about 350 to 310 million years ago. They were even better adapted to land than amphibians; they had dry skin to seal in the moisture, and their eggs were encased in leathery shells to protect them on land. To reproduce away from the water, reptiles had to develop penetrative sex; the males added an appendage with which to fertilize the female's eggs inside her body, rather than outside in water. Reptiles made a great leap forward, from the human point of view. The earliest ones may have resembled turtles or crocodiles, not the sexiest creatures imaginable, except to other turtles and crocodiles.

One of the likely reasons that living organisms moved onto land is that moving continents squeezed them onto it. Remember, from Chapter 2, that over geologic time the Earth's mantle moves, carrying the continents around with it. In the years when plants, fungi, and animals crept onto land, all the continental pieces were converging into one giant world continent named **Pangaea** (Map 3.2). Dating

MAP 3.2 Pangaea. This supercontinent began forming about 300 million years ago and began rifting by 200 million years ago. Its name is derived from Greek—*pan* means "entire" and *gaia* means "Earth." The name was coined in 1927 during a symposium discussion of Alfred Wegener's theory of continental drift (see Chapter 2). He was a German meteorologist who hypothesized in 1915 that at one time all the continents formed a single supercontinent that he called the *Urkontinent*. What landmass lay adjacent to the present location of New York City?

techniques suggest that Pangaea was fused into a single landmass about 250 million years ago. During the millions of years preceding the fusion, the available shallow sea and coastline was shrinking, and the competition for food was fierce.

Darwin thought that life evolves slowly and gradually; with better dating techniques we know that occasionally life experiences a wipeout, a mass extinction that brings gradual evolution to a halt. After these mass die-offs, evolution responds with a creative outpouring of new species to fill the vacant environmental niches.

Since the Cambrian period began about 542 million years ago, five major extinctions have occurred, along with many minor ones (Figure 3.11). About 440 and again about 365 million years ago, living organisms saw their species reduced by 70 to 80 percent. The extinction of 365 million years ago may have been a factor in living organisms moving onto land. No one knows whether the deaths occurred over millions, or thousands, of years, or in a single day.

About 245 million years ago came the mother of all extinctions, the end-Permian extinction, which almost put life out of business. It resulted in the death of about 95 percent of marine species, 75 percent of land species. (Remember, since no one knows exactly how many species exist now, or then, these are estimates.) Trilobites vanished in this extinction, and about a third of insect species. Cockroaches made it through.

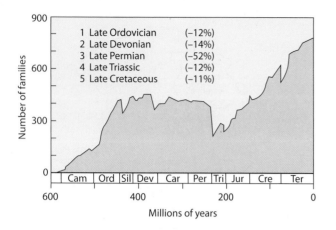

FIGURE 3.11 Graph of the number of families of vertebrates and invertebrates over time. This graph shows the five major extinctions, among others, that have occurred since the Cambrian explosion about 542 million years ago by showing the loss of families. The loss of species was much higher, since families include genera and species. Each major extinction was followed by a rapid development of new species, usually with different dominant groups.

So did our ancestors, a kind of small reptile that had evolved into small proto-mammals. Ginkgo trees and horseshoe crabs survived; they haven't changed much in the last hundred million years.

No one knows for certain what causes these massive extinctions, but they are part of life. At least two dozen theories have been proposed, among them global warming, global cooling, massive volcanism, impacts by meteors and comets, changing position of continents, huge variations in solar flares, plagues of bacteria, magnetic field reversals, changing sea levels, oxygen depletion of the seas, leaks of methane from ocean floors, and/or changes in the Earth's tilt, wobble, and orbit (Milankovitch cycles—see Chapter 4 and the glossary). Extinctions have formed an integral part of the epic of evolution, periodically clearing the way for a prolific outburst of new organisms.

Stage 8: Dinosaurs and Mammals (ca. 245 Million Years Ago)

In the vacuum left by the extinction of 245 million years ago, small reptiles evolved into dinosaurs, the largest land creatures that have ever lived. (Blue whales in the sea are much larger.) Pangaea began to break up by 200 million years ago, and by that time dinosaurs had occupied every part of it. They ruled the world for 150 million years, until the next extinction wiped out every one of them.

Dinosaurs take their name from the Greek words *deinos* (terrible) and *sauros* (lizard). They were mostly land creatures, some weighing as much as 25 tons (22 metric tons). They developed mating patterns and early parenting skills. Some paleontologists believe they may have had four-chambered hearts large enough to pump sufficient blood to qualify them as warm-blooded animals. Before dinosaurs went extinct, one line of them morphed into birds, as mentioned earlier with the fossil, *Archaeopteryx*.

A cousin reptile to the one that developed into dinosaurs morphed into a different sort of creature, called mammals, those who suckle their young on mammary glands, which evolved from sweat glands. The earliest mammals probably appeared about 200 million years ago, as a transitional species that was furry and warm-blooded, but laid eggs like a reptile. The duck-billed platypus survives today as an example of this primeval type of mammal (monotremes).

Later another sort of mammal evolved that dispensed with eggs, instead bearing its young alive, but the offspring were so immature that they had to crawl back into a pouch under their mother's belly for an extended incubation until they could survive in the world. Called marsupials, modern kangaroos and koala bears are their descendants.

A third group of mammals, the placentals, appeared; they could nourish their offspring internally in their mother's womb until they were large enough to survive without a pouch. The oldest known fossil of a placental mammal is *Eomaiascansoria*, found near Beijing, dated about 125 million years ago. The nearest modern relative is probably a tree shrew; modern humans are placental mammals.

As long as the dinosaurs lived, these early mammals remained small and close to the ground. They foraged at night, while dinosaurs rested, and developed their sense of smell and their brains. As warm-blooded creatures, these little mammals developed areas of their brains to keep internal temperature consistent in any external environment. They also developed early mechanisms for regulating the emotional responses that are common to all mammals.

Then one day 65 million years ago, a 6-mile-wide (9.6-kilometer-wide) asteroid roared out of the sky. (Researchers don't know whether it was a meteor, a rocky piece of debris, or a comet, an icy piece of debris.) The asteroid hit Earth head-on, striking the northern coast of the Yucatan Peninsula, near the village of Chicxulub (Map 3.3). The impact had the unimaginable force of a hundred million hydrogen bombs, as if Mount Everest fell from the sky, making a hole the size of Belgium. The debris from the impact and the smoke from fires rose up above the atmosphere, where it encircled the planet, probably obscuring the sun's energy for at least several years, shutting down photosynthesis, killing many plants. The impact may have set off eruptions by volcanoes around the world, adding more smoke and debris to the atmosphere. Earth went into a deep chill. (This theory has been recently confirmed, but a few researchers still argue that volcanic eruptions alone shut down the dinosaurs.)

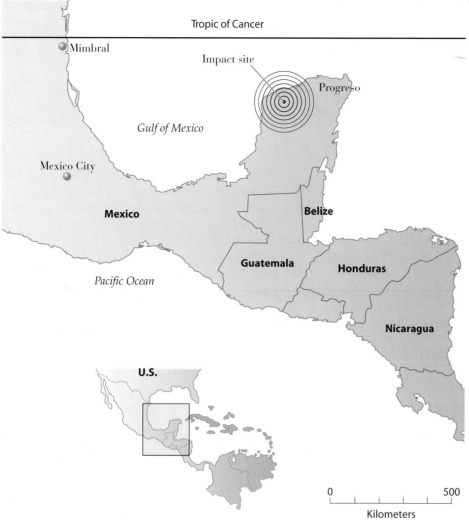

Tropic of Cancer

Mimbral

Impact site

Progreso

Gulf of Mexico

Mexico City

Mexico

Belize

Guatemala

Honduras

Pacific Ocean

Nicaragua

U.S.

0   500
Kilometers

MAP 3.3 Site of asteroid impact. This map shows the asteroid hitting on land, but the crater it formed now lies underwater. This delayed its being located until geologists, led by Walter Alvarez, followed clues to its location in the early 1990s.

mammals to occupy. Fossils show that by 50 million years ago most mammals still had small brains, large jaws, and clumsy, inefficient feet and teeth. But in the next 10 or so million years, an amazing array of mammals appeared—the ancestors of horses, whales, camels, elephants, and the common ancestor of cats and dogs: the tree-climbing, weasel-like *Miacis*.

About 60 million years ago some small ground mammals began looking for the fruit of flowering trees. Generation after generation, some adjusted to life aloft and flourished in their new environment. Gradually, as nature selected the most useful genes, their paws turned into hands, their claws became fingers, with opposable thumbs for grasping branches with one hand, while the other picked fruit. Their eyes shifted toward the front, so that their range of vision overlapped, providing the 3-D vision needed for swinging through tree branches. These little mammals became monkey-like, a new evolutionary path.

Eventually some of these monkey species ventured back to the ground looking for food, but now much better equipped with binocular vision and manual dexterity. Although they foraged for food on the ground, they retreated to trees at night for nesting and sleeping. They grew to the size of large cats, developing the larger brains and the rudimentary two-legged walking (knuckle-walking) of the great apes.

To review the evolution of mammals, they appeared soon after the mass extinction of 245 million years ago, as small, shrewlike creatures, and stayed on the ground until the dinosaurs' demise 65 million years ago. Soon afterward

The impact of the asteroid is an example of contingency, or things happening by chance, in the history of Earth. There seems to have been only a seven-minute window of opportunity for the asteroid to hit Earth, since Earth was in its path for only that long. (We have already seen other examples of contingency: Earth happened to be the right size to have plate tectonics and an atmosphere. It happened to have been hit so hard by an early meteor the size of Mars that it tilted on its axis, which resulted in seasons. The universe happened to have physical laws that permit it to exist, and so on.)

As a consequence of the impact 65 million years ago, an estimated 90 percent of land-based species were wiped out, 50 percent of all plant species. Every dinosaur disappeared; birds are their only descendants still alive. Animals larger than 50 pounds (23 kilograms) died. Only minimammals and cockroaches were left to dine on frozen dinosaur carcasses. "Had our evolution been more advanced, we would probably have been wiped out," says Bill Bryson in *A Short History of Nearly Everything*.[3]

The asteroid opened the way for mammals; it removed the terrible predators and provided ecological space for some climbed into trees to look for fruit, until food got scarce again, when some climbed down again to forage on the ground, remaining nested in trees. These tens of millions of years of refinements—fingers, thumbs, 3-D vision, bigger brains—we are heir to.

Here we leave our ancestors as great apes nesting in trees, foraging both in trees and on the ground. In the next chapter we will cross the sixth major threshold of complexity when one group of these great apes evolves into *Homo sapiens,* or modern humans.

SUMMARY

In this chapter life was defined as being capable of metabolism, reproduction, and adaptation. Life changes, or adapts, by natural selection, in which the changing environment selects those genetic mutations that are beneficial to the survival and reproduction of organisms. Living organisms first emerged through chemical evolution that produced a single cell capable of metabolism, reproduction, and adaptation. Using this cell's chemical system of proteins and nucleic acids surrounded by membranes, more single cells evolved. Over some 2 billion years they created the underlying systems of current life: fermentation, photosynthesis, oxygen respiration, eukaryotic cells,

and sexual reproduction. In the last half billion years, living organisms proliferated gloriously into a wild profusion of forms, from multicellular to vertebrates, to plants, fungi, and animals coming ashore, to dinosaurs and mammals, to the great apes. The evolution of the last half billion years occurred in waves following five major extinctions. The last of these extinction events removed the dinosaurs, clearing the way for the mammals to flourish. Among them were our ancestors, the tree-dwelling primates. Extinctions wiped out the more complex life-forms, but after each major extinction life rebounded with ever greater complexity.

CHAPTER QUESTIONS

1. What was Darwin's theory of natural selection?
2. What evidence since Darwin's day confirms his theory?
3. What are the components of the simplest living cell, the prokaryote?
4. What are the main stages in the evolution of single-celled organisms?
5. How do eukaryotes differ from prokaryotes?
6. Trace the big events in the development of multi-celled organisms.

KEY TERMS

Cambrian explosion
convergent evolution
DNA
eukaryotes
fossils

last universal common
  ancestor (LUCA)
life
natural selection
ozone

Pangaea
photosynthesis
prokaryotes
respiration
RNA

taxonomy
theory of chemical
  evolution

FURTHER READING

Alvarez, Walter. *T. rex and the Crater of Doom.* Princeton, NJ: Princeton University Press, 1997.

Browne, Janet. *Charles Darwin: The Power of Place.* Vol. 2. New York: Knopf, 2002.

Bryson, Bill. *A Short History of Nearly Everything.* New York: Broadway Books, 2003.

Chaisson, Eric. *Epic of Evolution: Seven Ages of the Cosmos.* New York: Columbia University Press, 2006.

Dawkins, Richard. *The Greatest Show on Earth: The Evidence for Evolution.* New York: Free Press, 2009.

Erwin, Douglas H. *Extinction: How Life on Earth Nearly Ended 250 Million Years Ago.* Princeton and Oxford: Princeton University Press, 2006.

Goodenough, Ursula. *The Sacred Depths of Nature.* New York and Oxford: Oxford University Press, 1998.

Hazen, Robert M. *Genesis: The Scientific Quest for Life's Origin.* Washington, DC: Joseph Henry Press, 2005.

Margulis, Lynn, and Dorion Sagan. *Microcosmos: Four Billion Years of Evolution from Our Microbial Ancestors.* Berkeley: University of California Press, 1986.

Smith, Cameron M., and Charles Sullivan. *The Top Ten Myths about Evolution.* Amherst, NY: Prometheus Books, 2007.

Weiner, Jonathan. *The Beak of the Finch: A Story of Evolution for Our Time.* New York: Knopf, 1994.

Wilson, Edward O. *The Social Conquest of Earth.* New York and London: Liveright Publishing (division of Norton), 2012.

ENDNOTES

1. Janet Browne, *Charles Darwin: The Power of Place,* vol. 2 (New York: Knopf, 2002), 392.
2. Bill Bryson, *A Short History of Nearly Everything* (New York: Broadway Books, 2003), 377–78.
3. Ibid., 347.

the fifth threshold

the sixth threshold

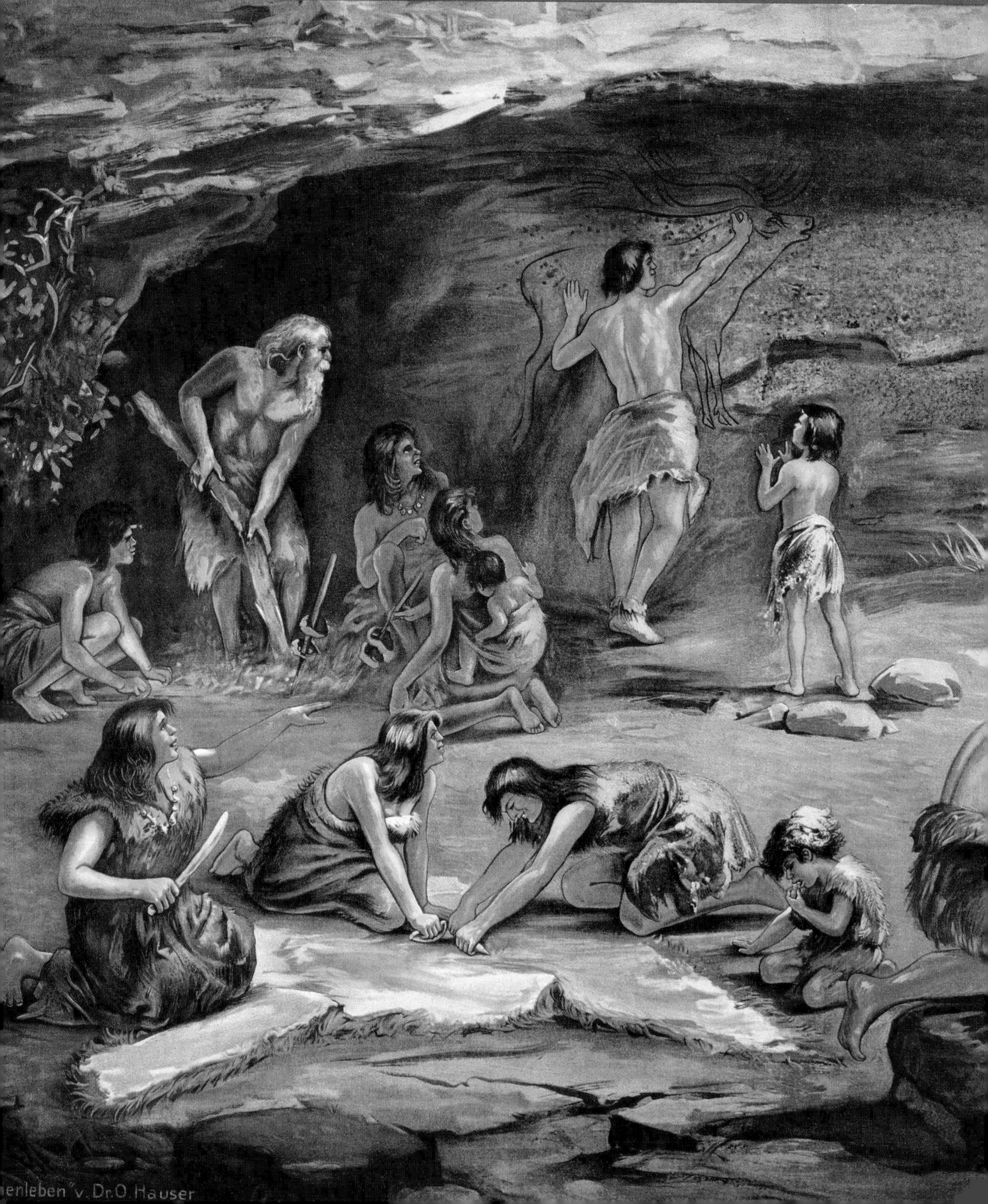

chapter 4

Hominines, Humans, and the Paleolithic Era

Seeing the Big Picture

8 Million to 10,000 Years Ago

▶ In what ways were early hominines like us? In what ways were they different?

▶ How do you feel about having a common ancestor with chimpanzees?

▶ What makes our own species so different from other species?

▶ What evidence can we use to tell when members of our species first appeared?

▶ What is Collective Learning and how important is it?

▶ What would life have been like if you had lived in the Paleolithic era?

▶ In what ways did the societies of the Paleolithic era lay the foundations for later human history up to the present day?

▶ What evidence is there of Collective Learning in the Paleolithic era?

In this chapter, we will guide you through one more threshold: the appearance of our own species, *Homo sapiens.*

We will describe the crossing of this momentous threshold in three stages. The first part of the chapter will describe how a group of great apes known as the *hominines* evolved over the last 8 million years and how, within that group, some species became more and more like us. These were our ancestors, and we now know a lot more about them than we did even 30 years ago. What has become increasingly clear in that period is that, though they look more and more like us—walking upright, developing larger and larger brains, and starting to manufacture stone tools, for example—nevertheless there was nothing really revolutionary about them. Of none of them is it tempting to say: the appearance of this species marks a new threshold in the Earth's history.

Then, from about 250,000 to 200,000 years ago, we find evidence for the appearance of a new species, **Homo sapiens,** of which we *can* say that its arrival *does* count as a revolution in the history of the biosphere. We are *H. sapiens,* the biological name for modern humans. The second part of this chapter describes this momentous change. If we are going to claim that our arrival marks a revolution, we need to be very clear *why* this is so. In some senses, we were merely one more hominine species, not that different from other hominines or even from the other great apes. On the other hand, if we started listing differences, we could find quite a lot. But then there are also many differences between chimps and gorillas. So what is it that makes *H. sapiens* so revolutionary? We will argue that we can see the revolutionary nature of this species only when we contemplate its history. Over the time this species has been on Earth, it has kept generating new ways of relating to the environment until, eventually, it generated revolutionary changes that have affected its own members, the environments they inhabited, and,

eventually, the entire biosphere. The profound impact of *H. sapiens* on its environment is what is so revolutionary.

What was it about this species that set it off on a history so different from that of all other large species on Earth? We will argue that the key change was linguistic. Members of our species could communicate with each other with much more precision and much greater "bandwidth" than any other species. That meant that individuals could exchange the information they had learned, so that information began to accumulate within each human community, increasing from generation to generation. It is this slow but accelerating accumulation of new information that shaped human history. We will describe this process of information sharing as Collective Learning. **Collective Learning** means that human beings, unlike all other species, can adapt to their environments through cultural change as well as through genetic change. And, as cultures can change much faster than genomes, this helps explain why the pace of change has accelerated within the last 200,000 years of human history. Having identified Collective Learning as the key to human history, we need to ask: When can we know that we are dealing with a species capable of Collective Learning? When can we be sure we are dealing with our own species? That, we will see, is a tricky question, and paleontologists remain divided on the best answers.

Once humans appeared, equipped with with a new and more powerful form of language that gave them a capacity for Collective Learning, human history could begin. The third part of this chapter will describe the oldest and longest era of human history, the way humans lived during this era, and some of the major changes the era embraced. We will describe this as the Paleolithic era of human history. It lasted from the appearance of the first humans, until the appearance of agriculture, about 11,000 to 10,000 years ago. The appearance of agriculture marks one more threshold that we will discuss in Chapter 5.

Hominine Evolution: 8 Million to 200,000 Years Ago

In the last chapter we left the great apes nesting in trees in equatorial Africa. By about 8 million years ago, the early great apes had become extinct elsewhere in the world, except for orangutans in Asia.

Humans evolved from one branch of the great apes, but whether it was gorillas or chimpanzees was not clear until genetic research revealed that humans are more closely related to chimpanzees; 98.5 percent of our genes are the same as those of chimpanzees, making them our closest relatives. Modern chimpanzees and modern humans have both evolved from a common ancestor from whom we split

TABLE 4.1 Classification of Hominines

The following classification of our species shows schematically how the features that make us human slowly accumulated. Humans belong to the

- Superkingdom of eukaryota (made of eukaryotic cells)
- Kingdom of animalia (not plants or fungi)
- Phylum of chordata (animals with backbones)
- Class of mammalia (chordates that suckle their young)
- Order of primata (large, tree-dwelling mammals)
- Superfamily of Hominoidae (humans and all apes—chimps, bonobos, gorillas, gibbons, and orangutans)
- Family of Hominidae (includes gorillas, chimps, bonobos, and humans)
- Subfamily of Homininae (bipedal apes [upright, two-footed posture]—every species on the human side since the split from the chimpanzee line)
- Genus of *Homo* (bipedal apes with brains larger than 800 cubic centimeters)
- Species of *sapiens* (anatomically modern humans—only remaining species of Homininae)

between 8 and 5 million years ago. This conclusion was reached by calculating the time it took to acquire the differences in genes between these species, based on an estimated rate of genetic change.

We use the term **hominine** to name all the species on the branch, including humans, since the split from a common ancestor with chimpanzees. This word may be confusing because until recently the term *hominid* was used. Genetic research, however, has showed that chimpanzees and bonobos (a second species of chimpanzee) are closer to humans than they are to gorillas, as was formerly believed. Therefore, the classification system needs to be rearranged, but scientists have not yet agreed about how to do it. What *hominid* now means depends on what classification system is used. All biological taxonomies use the same general levels, such as kingdom, class, and family (see the glossary), but biologists disagree about what belongs in subgroups. We are following the system shown in Table 4.1, which has all the great apes in the superfamily; hominoids—with gorillas, chimps, bonobos, and humans—in one family called hominids; and all descendants in the human line in a subfamily called homininae, or hominines. Debate continues about how exactly these classifications should be arranged.

Types of Evidence of Human Evolution

Tremendous advances have been made in the last 60 years in understanding human evolution because dating techniques have improved dramatically, as have other kinds of evidence. Here we will briefly describe evidence from four fields: paleoarchaeology (the study of fossil bones and stone tools), primatology (the study of modern primates), genetics (the study of genes), and climatology (the study of climate change).

Fossil Bones and Stone Tools

European scientists began to study hominine bones and stone tools by the mid-nineteenth century. Drawings of stone tools found in Sicily and in northern France were published in 1850. The first fossils of Neandertals were found in the Neander valley in Germany in 1857, while the first ancient but anatomically modern human bones, found in 1868, were named after Cro-Magnon, a shelter in the cliffs near Les Eyzies in France.

In the early twentieth century most European scientists believed that *H. sapiens* evolved in Europe only about 60,000 years ago. After World War II paleoarchaeologists began looking for bones in Africa; preeminent among them were Louis Leakey (1903–72), his wife, Mary Leakey (1913–96), and their son Richard (1944–), who worked in the Olduvai Gorge of Tanzania in the East African Rift valley (Map 4.1 and Chapter 2). Richard Leakey branched out to find, in Ethiopia, in 1967, what Louis claimed were the first *H. sapiens* bones in Africa. By the early 1990s many archaeologists agreed that *H. sapiens* must have evolved in Africa. Darwin had already deduced this in his book *The Descent of Man* (1863) because of the presence in Africa of our close relatives, gorillas and chimpanzees.

African evidence from species earlier than *H. sapiens* was also found. In 1960–63, the Leakeys found some remains that they called *H. habilis* (meaning "handy man" because they appeared to have made stone tools). They dated from about 2.5 to 1.75 million years ago. In 1974 Donald Johanson (1943–) found in the Afar Triangle in Ethiopia even older bones, the well-known partial skeleton that he named Lucy, that dated about 3.2 million years ago. Two years later Mary Leakey found hominine footprints in volcanic ash at Laetoli in Tanzania, dated about 3.5 million years ago. From 1994 to 2004 eight new early hominine species were discovered, making this decade one of the most fruitful periods ever in human paleontology.

Fossil remains can tell us a huge amount about our ancestors. They can tell us not just the shape of their bodies and how they walked and moved, but also the size of their brains, what sort of environments they lived in, and even, if we study their teeth carefully, whether they were vegetarians or meat-eaters.

Modern Primates

Studying modern primates provides indirect evidence about how our ancestors may have lived, though how much that evidence can tell us about our own species remains controversial. Until the mid-1960s little was known about any primates in the wild; most specialists studied primates in zoos. In the following 20 years the field of primatology blossomed, under difficult constraints. Tropical forests were disappearing, together with their populations of monkeys and apes. Researchers often found themselves working as hard to protect their subjects as to study them.

Jane Goodall (1934–), who began her career working with the Leakeys, pioneered the study of chimpanzees in the wild by going in 1960 to Gombe Stream Game Reserve (now a national park), on the shores of Lake Tanganyika

the sixth threshold

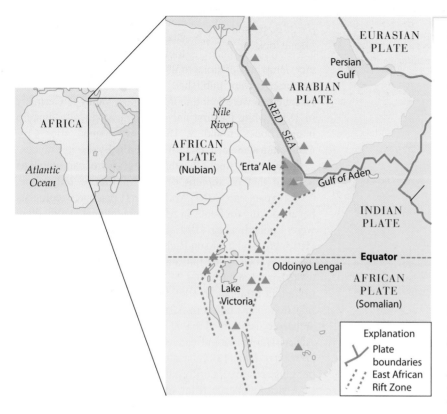

The East African Rift is formed by a rift in the African continental plate; the eastern piece is splitting off and will someday drift away in the Indian Ocean. The Afar Triangle (shaded, center) is a triple junction where three plates are pulling away from one another: the Arabian Plate and the two parts of the African Plate (the Nubian and the Somalian). The historically active volcanoes (triangles) produced by the rift spread ash that buried bodies and preserved bones.

When genetic dating was first used in 1967 to estimate that humans and African apes shared a common ancestor only about 7 million years ago, most paleoanthropologists strongly disagreed, believing that a date of 20 to 15 million years ago was more likely. Further research, however, has consistently pointed to the split occurring 8 to 5 million years ago, dates now accepted by most paleoanthropologists.

in Tanzania, to live among chimps. Her reports shocked the public, for she found that chimpanzees used tools—sticks to collect termites from their nests, stones to crack open fruit, and leaves to wipe after defecation. Goodall was amazed that medical researchers had been able to recognize the close physiological similarities between chimpanzees and humans—for instance, that we can exchange blood transfusions—but had ignored the close emotional and social similarities. Goodall created a shift in attitudes by revealing how much of human behavior fits into that of the animal world. In 1965 Toshisada Nishida began studying chimpanzees in the Mahale Mountains of Tanzania, also making important contributions.

Gene Comparisons

Since the 1960s a new form of evidence has become available as scientists have learned to compare the genes of distinct species. As we saw in Chapter 3, when two species separate from each other, neutral mutations accumulate in each line. Neutral mutations are changes in the noncoding DNA of a gene, the parts of DNA that do not provide instruction for making a protein and are not eliminated by natural selection. The function of the noncoding, neutral or silent, parts of the genome is not yet understood. Because the rate of accumulation of neutral mutations is fairly constant in each species, the number of neutral mutations can reveal how old the species is. Also, researchers can calculate the differences between the DNA sequences of two modern species to estimate when the two lines diverged from a common ancestor, or they can count the number of neutral mutations in a single gene to estimate when that gene became prevalent.

Climate Change

Early in the twentieth century, scientists thought that global climate could change only gradually over thousands of years. In the 1950s a few scientists found evidence, using carbon-14 dating, that some climate changes in the past had taken only a few thousand years. In the 1980s and 1990s evidence came in that global climate could shift within a century, or even within a decade. This evidence consisted primarily of studies of ice core drillings into massive ice sheets to depths of up to 2 miles (3.2 kilometers). A typical cylinder of ice is about 4 inches (10 centimeters) in diameter, brought to the surface in lengths of about 12 inches (30.5 centimeters), so that the annual layers of ice can be analyzed with powerful microscopes. Each layer contains tiny bubbles of air from the time it formed, and these can be analyzed to determine the composition of the atmosphere at the time and the average temperature at the Earth's surface.

Evidence of climate change comes both from ice core samples and from samples of sediment on the ocean floor. Floor samples tell a longer story, up to a million years ago, while ice core samples give a more detailed, year-by-year picture. Climatologists can plot climate change by decade for almost the past 800,000 years and monthly for the past 3,000 years using high-resolution evidence from Greenland ice cores. Studies of pollen, plentiful and hardy, also contribute to our understanding of climate change. Since different plant species have distinctive pollen, whole floral ecosystems can be reconstructed.

FIGURE 4.1 Global temperatures 20,000 BCE to present. This graph is based on changes in the chemical composition of an ice core taken from Greenland. What is being measured is the relative presence of two isotopes of oxygen, ^{16}O and ^{18}O. Notice how much warmer and more stable the temperature has been during the last 10,000 years compared with the previous 10,000 years.

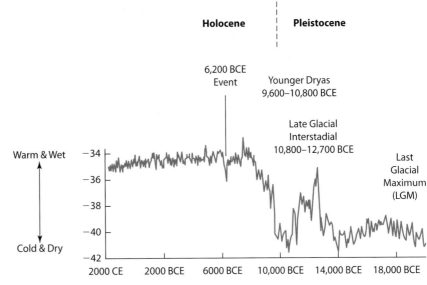

For the last 700,000 years Earth's climate has fluctuated with ice ages occurring about every 100,000 years and with short warm spells, or "inter-glacials," of about 10,000 years between them. The ice core evidence reveals that in the final thousand years of the last ice age, there were frequent warm–cold oscillations, with dramatic changes taking place within a matter of years or decades (Figure 4.1). If the pattern were holding today, the current warm spell of 10,000 years would typically be ending, and we would be entering a new ice age. These patterns suggest that humans evolved during a period of great climatic instability, which may have favored the evolution of highly adaptable species.

Within the past generation scientists have learned to correlate climate changes with variations in Earth's orbit around the sun. These variations affect the amount of solar radiation striking Earth at different times of the year. They occur in regular cycles, called **Milankovitch cycles,** named for the Serbian astronomer Milutin Milankovitch (1879–1958) who discovered them. There are three different changes in Earth's orbit. One is the direction in which the axis points, the wobble; it varies on a cycle of about 21,000 years. The second is the degree of tilt of Earth's axis, from 22.1 to 24.5 degrees; this cycles every 41,000 years. The third is the deviation of Earth's orbit from a perfect circle due to the gravitational pull of nearby planets; this varies about every 100,000 years and also every 400,000 years. These Milankovitch cycles have formed our planetary clock since about 35 million years ago; their effects can still be seen in the layers of rock.

Periods in Hominine Development

Is it difficult to think about humans evolving from an ancestor common to chimpanzees? Many people find it so; perhaps they have trouble factoring in the estimated 7 million years that it took, approximately 280,000 human generations.

Table 4.2 summarizes some of the main differences between modern chimpanzees and modern humans. We will discuss these changes as they occurred over millions of years in three periods—the rain forest, the tree savanna, and the bush savanna—each marked by changes in the environment.

The Rain Forest

Modern chimpanzees live in equatorial rain forest, formerly known as jungle (Hindi for *forest*). It is hot, moist, and filled with quick-growing plants. There chimpanzees live on a diet of fruit, nuts, seeds and leaves, ants, caterpillars, honey, and eggs, with the meat of monkeys, bush piglets, and bush buck fawns added when possible.

TABLE 4.2 Some Differences in Modern Chimps and Modern Humans: What Changed over 7 Million Years

Chimpanzees	Humans
Knuckle walking	Bipedalism
Smaller brain size (about 3 times smaller)	Larger brain size
Large teeth, jaws, and mouth	Smaller teeth, jaws, and mouth
Dark fur, light skin	Little hair, dark skin (now variable)
Sociable	More sociable
High larynx	Lower larynx
Unassisted solitary childbirth	Assisted social childbirth
Males 25–30% larger than females	Males 15–20% larger than females
Male and female hierarchies	Pair bonding
Solitary eating	Social eating
No use of fire (raw food)	Use of fire (cooked food)
Simple tools	Complex tools
Vocalizations and gestures	Full speech with syntax
48 chromosomes	46 chromosomes

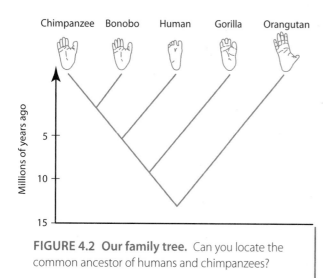

FIGURE 4.2 **Our family tree.** Can you locate the common ancestor of humans and chimpanzees?

Are we humans descended from these modern-day chimpanzees? No, clearly not, since no time has elapsed over which we could have evolved from them. This is a common misperception. Instead, both modern humans and modern chimps have evolved over about 7 million years from a common ancestor who was probably more like a chimpanzee than a human because during this time chimps seem to have changed only a little, while humans and our ancestors have changed a great deal.

In the 7 million years since the chimp and the human lines diverged from a creature common to both, the chimpanzee line evolved into two surviving species: the common chimp (*Pan troglodytes*) and the bonobos (*P. panicus*). On the human side at least 18 different species appeared, several of which may have existed just 50,000 years ago, although only one (*H. sapiens*) has survived to the present day (Figure 4.2).

The two species of chimpanzees differ from each other, possibly dramatically, as described in the following text. Primatologists argue passionately about which one is more likely to resemble the common ancestor, but they agree that both kinds of chimpanzees are more likely to resemble the common ancestor than humans are. The evidence for this is that the earliest fossils on the human side are hard to distinguish from those of modern chimps, and neither chimps nor bonobos have changed much in the last million and a half years. One likely reason is that both kinds of chimpanzees stayed in the rain forest, while the human line adapted to a new environment, the open savanna, produced by the cooling, drying climate. Studying our chimp relatives is a way to imagine what the last common ancestor of chimps and humans may have been like, as long as we remember that they, too, have changed in some ways.

Common chimpanzees live in communities of 15 to 80, around a group of related males, each having many mates. The males establish boundaries to their territory, set up border patrols, and defend their territory aggressively. The females usually leave their group of origin soon after puberty and move to a nearby group; this prevents inbreeding. Anthropologists call this *patrilocality* as contrasted with *matrilocality*, in which males move to another group. Patrilocality gives males the advantage of being kin-bonded, while females have no network of kin support.

Each sex has its own hierarchy, with all females lower than every male. Chimps have promiscuous sex, with no permanent attachments around mating and childrearing, which the females carry out mainly on their own. Multiple matings seem advantageous for the females because the practice confuses paternity; this is desirable to females because chimpanzee males will sometimes kill male infants that they know are not their own.

Before 1960 humans were believed to be the only tool-using animals. But in that year Jane Goodall observed a chimp strip the leaves from a twig and use it to poke into a termite mound so that the termites clung to it when it was withdrawn. Since then researchers have observed chimpanzees making and/or using more than a half-dozen kinds of tools for numerous purposes. Each community has its own subset of tools, with juveniles learning how to use them by observing adults. Chimpanzee societies vary across Africa in their use of tools. (Many other species are now known to use tools, including some birds and dolphins.)

After 10 years of research Goodall believed that chimps, though very like humans in behavior, were rather nicer on the whole. In 1971, however, researchers at Gombe observed behavior not seen before—a brutal, aggressive attack on a lone female from a neighboring community. They also observed multiple infant killings in their own community by a high-ranking female and her daughter who were currently childless. In the mid-1970s a group of chimps split off from the initial community to claim a portion of territory as its own; over four years the initial group attacked and killed every member of the breakaway group except three young females, reclaiming their territory. Goodall had to accept the conclusion that chimps have a strong predisposition to act aggressively in certain contexts—competition for food, sex, or territory, or under strong emotions of jealousy, fear, and revenge.

Yet among chimps one sees frequent expressions of sharing, helping, compassion, and altruism. Deep, often lifelong, ties develop between mothers and children and siblings. Brothers become close friends as they mature and often allies in social conflicts. Older siblings adopt younger ones when a mother dies. Nonsiblings even adopt orphans who have no older sibling to protect them. Chimpanzees cannot swim; when they are kept in zoo enclosures surrounded by water, death by drowning is a common mishap. Usually when a chimp falls in water, other chimps rush to attempt a rescue.

Chimpanzees, each with a recognizable voice, have a rich repertoire of sounds, postures, and facial expressions that facilitate the exchange of information. Their gestures include extending a hand to ask for food and raising both arms to be picked up and carried, both of which are used by human infants 9 to 15 months old. Chimp greeting gestures include embracing, hand holding, kissing, and back patting. Goodall listed 34 different vocalizations, which are variations of grunts, barks, screams, and hoots.

In chimps the larynx, a structure of muscle and cartilage, is located high in their throat; it prevents the esophagus, carrying food, from crossing the trachea, carrying air. Because the tubes don't cross, chimps can't choke on their food. In humans the larynx has lowered, giving us an air chamber from which to resonate sound; we have traded language for a small risk of choking. Chimps lack a resonating chamber, plus our flexible tongues. However, in captivity and with the help of human trainers, they have been able to learn rudimentary sign language, some signing up to 150 words by age seven, with one, Washoe, signing some 200 to 300 words. Chimps can create correct two- or three-word sentences, but their longer ones are usually grammatically incorrect. (By contrast, a human child by age six has a vocabulary of about 10,000 words and speaks in long sentences.) Chimps in the wild vocalize frequently at night, from their nests in the treetops, as if to affirm that everyone is safe. Chimps cannot synchronize their vocalizations or keep a beat, even with training.

The second species of chimpanzee, the bonobos, split off several million years ago when a group of them were cut off from the others by the Congo River (called the Zaire River from 1971 to 1997). By breeding only within their group, these chimps developed enough distinctive traits to become a separate species. Their area today is about the size of England, in the present-day Democratic Republic of the Congo, formerly Zaire.

Bonobos are slightly lighter in weight than common chimpanzees, with a slim upper body, narrow shoulders, and smaller heads in contrast with chimps' large chests, shoulders, and heads. Bonobos' legs are longer, resulting in more upright posture when standing; they are also more arboreal and more gymnastic than chimps, since their area is dense, humid swamp forest with no trace of savanna. The humid forest supports huge trees producing abundant fruit year-round. This abundance of food permits bonobos to feed in larger groups than chimps do, which enables females to form strong, secure bonds, even though they had left their original group as adolescents. Some researchers theorize that this is why bonobos seem to exhibit less male violence and aggression—no forced matings, infanticides, border patrols, or aggression to neighbors have been observed by humans (Figure 4.3)

Some hunting goes on among bonobos; females dominate by solidarity, preventing most outbreaks of aggression by encouraging frequent and varied sexual activities, both heterosexual and homosexual, among all members of the group. Studies of bonobos in the wild have been difficult due to human civil wars in the Democratic Republic of the Congo; researchers hope to learn more while bonobos still exist in the wild.

Both bonobos and chimpanzees share the pursuit of power and sex as central concerns. Both groups show exquisite awareness of social status and of the emotional reactions of others, constantly calculating who is allied with whom. Their behavior mirrors that of humans in so many ways that our common ancestor must have been quite similar to all three species in these respects.

FIGURE 4.3 Female bonobo (*P. panicus*). It is estimated that fewer than 10,000 bonobos remain in the wild.

The Tree Savanna The climate in East Africa changed dramatically in the period 15 to 5 million years ago. Tectonic plates were, and continue to be, separating in a long fault running from Mozambique to Ethiopia, as in Map 4.1. Eventually this eastern part of Africa will disconnect from the continent and float off. In the meantime, this tectonic activity raised highlands, which blocked rain patterns, creating a patchwork of different habitats in East Africa. The high mountains and deep valleys along the fault may actually have separated the hominine chimps from their rain forest cousins.

The global climate during the period 10 to 5 million years ago was in a cooling period, with 6.5 to 5 million years ago a particularly harsh time. So much water froze into glaciers that the Mediterranean Sea drained repeatedly. As the climate became colder and drier, the equatorial forest shrank, and the periphery fragmented into woodlands. This climate change over several million years reinforced the first characteristic of hominines, bipedalism.

In 1994 a breakthrough discovery occurred in Ethiopia in the Afar Triangle—the bones of the earliest species of hominine ever found, dated at 4.4 million years. These bones were not the last common ancestor, but the closest to it yet found, a million years earlier than the bones of Lucy, found in 1974, only 46 miles (74 kilometers) away. The newly found species is called *Ardipithecus ramidus,* from words in the Afar language meaning "ground floor" and "root." More informally, the individual whose bones were found is nicknamed "Ardi."

The bones of Ardi are those of a female, 110 pounds (50 kilograms) in weight and 4 feet (122 centimeters) tall. She lived in woodlands and could walk upright, as well as climb on all fours along branches. Bones of 36 other individuals were found nearby, showing small canine teeth in both males and females. Scientists have concluded from the study of Ardi that the last common ancestor was not as chimplike as they had supposed, that bipedalism developed for some reason other than having no available trees, and that small canine teeth indicate reduced male conflict over females, with more pair bonding, earlier than formerly supposed.

The famous Lucy belonged to the species *Australopithecus afarensis,* which includes most fossils dated from 3.5 to 1.8 million years ago. With only one exception, **australopithecine** fossils are from southern or eastern Africa, volcanic areas where bones fossilize more easily than elsewhere and are more easily dated by the volcanic ash above and below them. But paleoarchaeologists believe that australopithecines probably lived throughout Africa. They are characterized by brains only slightly larger than those of chimpanzees (about 400 to 500 cubic centimeters), by sexual dimorphism (a difference in size between males and females, with males 50 percent larger than females), and by bipedalism.

Why was bipedalism the first trait to develop in human evolution? Current explanations vary. Bipedalism used to be seen as an adaptation to savannas, where trees were scarce and walking a necessity. Since 1994, however, a number of early bipedal fossils of hominines have been found in woodland environments, thus discrediting the hypothesis that bipedalism is solely an adaptation to savannas. Current theories abound that chimps developed upright posture as a more efficient way to walk from one wooded area to another, that it permitted males to carry food back to females, or that it arose as males displayed their penises to attract mates. Whatever function it originally filled, bipedalism gave a reproductive edge as several species of hominines developed in a diversity of habitats in eastern and southern Africa.

Along with bipedalism probably came the gradual loss of body hair, although there is no direct evidence of this. Loss of hair is considered an adaptation for keeping cool on the savanna; hominines maintained their hair on the top where the sun beat down directly, but gradually lost their long hair on their bodies and developed other cooling systems, both of which enabled them to forage during the daytime. Another possible interpretation: females selected males with little hair because they could feel certain that such males had fewer parasites. Of course, modern humans are not completely hairless; we retain vestiges of body hair

and the goose bumps that used to enable our hair to stand on end for increased insulation or as a threatening gesture.

Life on the open ground proved challenging for early hominines, even while there were still some scattered trees up which to escape from terrestrial predators. Bipedalism was the first adaptation of these early hominines, with rapidly expanding brains not yet in the picture.

The Bush Savanna Another period of dramatic cooling began about 2.5 million years ago, when early forms of the **genus *Homo*** appear. (These names are given by anthropologists; *Homo* was given by Louis Leakey who still thought that tool making defined human beings.) These fossils were from creatures with larger brains, shorter arms, and smaller guts and teeth, indicating that they ate more meat and less vegetation. Among these early forms were *H. rudolfensis, H. habilis,* and *H. ergaster.* Still apelike in many aspects, these early *Homo* bones are found with the earliest stone tools, simple chopping tools made by knocking a few edges off a core. The sharp edges may have been used as blades. Because these stone tools were found in the Olduvai Gorge, they are called Olduwan; they remained in use unchanged over at least a million years. Species called *Homo* are characterized by tool use, independence from trees, and rapid brain growth, from the volume of an apple to that of a full grapefruit in the next million years.

By 2 million years ago australopithecines and various *Homo* species were living in open landscapes in larger groups than earlier and eating some meat, mostly scavenged. The vocalizations and gestures of the several *Homo* species probably remained similar to those of apes, with complete messages rather than individual words used to influence the behavior of others.

Out of the various *Homo* species emerged a new species, ***H. erectus,*** about 1.8 to 1.7 million years ago, with an appearance decidedly more human than apelike. About 75 individual skeletons of *H. erectus* have been located all over the world, except for the Americas. Whether this species arose in Africa or in Asia has not been conclusively settled. Some experts prefer to call early *H. erectus* skeletons *H. ergaster.*

Skeletons from *H. erectus* were almost as tall as modern humans, with a brain size about 70 percent of ours. They showed full bipedalism, with shorter arms no longer useful for swinging in trees. They had acquired the three semicircular canals of the inner ear that provide balance for jumping, running, and dancing. The pelvis of both males and females had considerably narrowed and flattened as compared with that of chimpanzees, providing the base required for full standing and running, but also reducing the diameter of the birth canal, the space inside the pelvic bones.

Birthing is so easy for both kinds of chimps that the females go off alone to have their babies. In *H. erectus,* with the birth canal becoming smaller and the infant's brain becoming larger, giving birth became more problematic. Infants had to emerge earlier, actually prematurely, to get out before their heads grew too large. A modern human infant's brain at birth is only 23 percent of adult size, while that of a chimpanzee's is 45 percent. Pelvic bones of *H. erectus* indicate that females could not have given birth to infants with 45 percent of their adult brain size; hence, the pattern of rapid brain growth after birth had begun.

More helpless newborns required longer and more intense care; females needed male assistance in feeding infants and in protecting both mothers and infants from other males and from predators. Somehow hominines changed the chimp pattern of no permanent male–female attachment into one of at least temporary pair bonding between parents of offspring. Perhaps females gave up their sexual freedom for protection and assistance in child care; males gave it up to increase the chances that their offspring survived. However it happened, *H. erectus* developed persistent patterns of cooperation and mutual assistance.

Indirect evidence for pair bonding is the fact that male skeletons of this period are about 25 percent larger than female ones, reduced from the 50 percent difference in *Australopithecus*. This reduction in sexual dimorphism indicates less competition among males for females. (Modern human males are only 15 to 20 percent larger than modern females on average.)

Along with pair bonding, *H. erectus* people probably tamed fire, using it to cook or to preserve their food, which now probably included a higher proportion of meat and some tubers, or roots. Cooking food would have reduced the time spent eating and chewing and allowed a shortening of the intestine, which may have been a precondition for brain expansion, as argued by Richard Wrangham in his book *Catching Fire: How Cooking Made Us Human* (2009).

The use of fire is among the most significant steps that hominines ever took; it is one trait that distinguishes us from other animals, and it laid the basis for many further developments. The social scene around fires may have contributed to language development and to a new level of skill in tool making, called the *Acheulian*, characterized by larger, more precisely flaked, bifacial hand axes that persisted for at least a million years, until about 250,000 years ago. The use of fire increased the flow of energy through hominine communities.

Homo erectus distinguished itself as well by being the first hominine species to venture out of the African continent, although recent discoveries have indicated it may have been an earlier relative, *H. ergaster,* who did this. Some groups of *H. erectus* reached Georgia in the Caucasus region on the edge of Europe at least 1.8 million years ago. There, during glacial conditions, they evolved into **Neandertals** (*H. neanderthalensis*), near relatives of *H. sapiens* that lived until about 30,000 to 20,000 years ago. How much communication was going on? No one knows; the majority view is that *H. erectus* spoke a protolanguage, using simple nouns and verbs, which gradually increased in speed, vocabulary, and complexity.

Another change that likely occurred during the time of *H. erectus* was the darkening skin color. Chimpanzees have light skin under their dark fur. As early hominines lost their hair, their pale skin made them vulnerable to ultraviolet radiation, which causes skin cancer and destroys an essential nutrient, folic acid, which reduces fertility. Geneticists think that a gene mutation for dark skin probably swept Africa by 1.2 million years ago. Outside of Africa early humans became lighter-skinned again to help them synthesize enough vitamin D, which is partially blocked by dark skin. In every current population in the world, women's skin is 3 to 4 percent lighter than men's; no one knows why. Is it sexual selection, a greater need for vitamin D, or something else?

Two recent discoveries have been made of offshoots of *H. erectus*. One are bones called *H. floresiensis,* found in 2003 on an island east of Java. These nine partial skeletons were from a hominine standing only a bit more than 3 feet (1 meter) high, popularly known as "hobbits." They may or may not have been *H. erectus.* The other discovery are finger and toe bones found in 2010 in Denisova Cave in the Altai Mountains where Russia, Mongolia, China, and Kazakhstan come together. Dated at 41,000 years, these Denisovans are distinct from Neandertals and modern humans.

This short survey of hominine evolution has described how the characteristics of the common ancestors of chimpanzees and humans evolved into the characteristics of modern humans. Over about 7 million years spines got straighter, pelvises got narrower, brains got bigger, arms got shorter, pairs bonded, communication and cooperation increased, fires got built, and hand axes got shaped—all in the context of dramatic climate changes.

The descendants of *H. erectus* spread out over Afro-Eurasia and evolved in several different ways. In Asia they changed so little that they remained the same species; in Europe they adapted to glacial conditions and became Neandertals, while in Africa they evolved into modern humans (*H. sapiens*). Whether Neandertals are a separate species from *H. sapiens* and to what extent they are ancestors to *H. sapiens* continues to be debated. Since Neandertals lived in Europe and the Middle East during the same period of time that *H. sapiens* was evolving in Africa, we will consider them in the following section.

Threshold 6: The Appearance of *Homo sapiens*

How can we tell when our own species has arrived? The middle section of this chapter will step aside from the larger narrative and ask what it is that makes us not just *different* from other great apes (Table 4.2 lists some of these features), but what it is that makes us so *extraordinarily* different from all other large animals. Once we have an answer to that question we will have a better idea of what features to look for to tell when our own species appeared, and when human history really began. We will see that, though this is one of the most important questions we can ask about human history, it is also subtle. We must approach it with delicacy.

What Makes Us Different?

In our body plans and even our genes, we are so close to the chimps, and even closer to our ancestors, such as *H. erectus* or *H. neanderthalensis,* that it seems arbitrary to draw a sharp line between us and them. Yet we have already seen that it is easy to construct a long list of things that distinguish us radically from our closest relatives, and indeed from all other large animals on Earth.

We judge that a threshold has been crossed when minor changes generate a cascade of further changes that yield new emergent properties. If the appearance of our species really does count as a significant threshold in big history, we should be able to identify small but profound changes that set the history of our species off on new pathways. We can sidestep some of the philosophical complexities of this question by approaching the issue as historians, by looking not at individual humans, but at the species as a whole, and how our species has changed during its time on Earth. This historical question reveals profound differences between humans and all other large species of animals, including our hominine relatives.

You can see the differences clearly by comparing modern human societies with the societies of chimps today, or any other large species you care to name. The differences are enormous. The most important differences can be found in our unusual relationship to the environment. Most species have distinctive behaviors that do not change much during the species' existence on Earth. There may be changes in detail as different communities adapt in slightly different ways to environmental changes. But we should not expect to find fundamental changes. For example, we know that different communities of chimps live in slightly different ways, but we have no evidence for fundamental changes in chimp behavior over hundreds or thousands of years. None of them seem to have a "history" in the way that our species has a history.

In contrast, human behaviors *have* changed since our species first appeared, and they have changed radically. When the first humans appeared, sometime within the last quarter of a million years, their populations cannot have been much larger than those of chimps today. They undoubtedly lived as foragers. And they probably evolved in savanna environments. That these communities were the founders of a new species would not have been obvious at the time; to an imaginary Jane Goodall, watching them 250,000 years ago, they would have seemed to differ only in minor ways from their close relatives. But viewed from today, we can see the differences very clearly. Humans have learned how to exploit many new environments, from woodlands to coasts and eventually from tropical jungles to arctic tundra. By 13,000 years ago, humans could be found on all the continents apart from Antarctica. Each of these migrations required new behaviors and new ways of dealing with the environment. No other large organism has ever adapted so effectively to so many different environments or migrated over such large areas. With many different environments at their disposal, our ancestors multiplied perhaps to a few million.

After 10,000 years ago, the pace of change accelerated. Humans started reshaping their environments to increase the production of those plant and animal species they could eat or use in other ways (such as corn or wheat or sheep and cattle) and eliminate those they could not use (such as weeds and rats). We call this change *agriculture,* and it will be the main theme of Chapter 5. With the emergence of agriculture, human communities grew in size and complexity; so did the amount of energy and resources they used; and so did the total number of humans, until today there are almost 7 billion humans, and we are rearranging the biosphere and transforming the atmosphere. In less than 250,000 years we have become the dominant large organisms on Earth and the first species in the history of the planet to exercise such control over the biosphere. Indeed, one modern scientist, Paul Crutzen, has argued that our impact is now so great that the Earth has entered a new geological epoch, the **Anthropocene,** or the epoch in which human beings have come to dominate the biosphere (see Chapter 12).

What made these unprecedented changes possible? If we can answer that question, we will have defined the threshold marked by the appearance of *H. sapiens.*

What is distinctive about our ancestors is that, unlike all other species, whose technologies were limited, our ancestors kept finding *new* ways of adapting to their environments. As a result, they began to control more and more energy and resources. While most species have a more or less fixed suite of technologies and ways of adapting to their environments, humans seem to have an endless repertoire of ecological tricks, and the repertoire seems to keep expanding. Even our hominine ancestors, such as *H. erectus* or *H. ergaster,* despite their intelligence and their many skills, including the ability to use fire, had a limited range of technologies; their Acheulian stone axes hardly changed in 1 million years. It is the astonishing ability of humans to keep adapting to environments in new ways that is so striking and so potent. Our capacity to keep finding new ways of relating to our environment and to each other is the foundation of human history and the source of our power as a species.

Teamwork What is the source of this astonishing ecological and social creativity? The short answer is teamwork. Humans are remarkably good at working together. This is not just a matter of males and females sharing in the task of child-rearing (though that is already a significant difference between humans and chimps). Humans can collaborate, deliberately and unconsciously between communities and across generations, and they can do so better than any other large organism.

You may remember that we have seen something a bit like this before in this book. Indeed, collaboration of some kind is apparent in all forms of complexity. Over and over again, we have seen that new levels of complexity arise when entities that once existed separately are linked in new ways that generate new emergent properties. Chemistry arises when atoms join together in new combinations. Life emerges when complex chemicals begin to work together, under the control of DNA, so as to mold themselves to their environments through natural selection. Eukaryotic cells evolved when individual prokaryotic cells merged to form larger and more complex cells. Multicelled organisms evolved when eukaryotic cells combined to form vast biological leviathans unified by the fact that each cell contained the same DNA. Social insects such as termites and ants show that superorganisms can even arise whose components are individual organisms. Something similar seems to have happened with our own species. Human history began when our ancestors began to collaborate in new ways.

In what sense is our species uniquely good at teamwork? After all, it might seem that we are equally good at conflict and that the two abilities must cancel out. Yet even a brief comparison between modern human society—with its systems of government, trade, production, and information exchange extending over the entire globe—and the largest and most complex of chimpanzee communities, is enough to make the point. We can collaborate in fantastically complex teams. Within these teams there is, to be sure, plenty of jostling, much of it brutal and painful for individuals, and no single individual controls more than a small part of the teamwork. Nevertheless, the end result of such collaboration, even if it is painful to individuals and often takes place beyond their conscious will, is an astonishing collective ability to manipulate our environment in our own interests. Even warfare depends on elaborate teamwork!

Symbolic Language

Why can humans collaborate so much more effectively than their closest biological relatives? At present, there are many reasons for thinking that the transformative event for our species was the appearance of new and more powerful forms of language that allow humans to share information and ideas more efficiently than any other species on Earth. As a result, humans can collaborate by sharing learned information. It is worth noting how unusual this is. Many species can communicate; owls do it, and so do chimps. But there are significant limits to how much they can communicate. In particular, it seems clear that no other species can communicate so efficiently that shared information begins to accumulate and increase from generation to generation. A good illustration of these limits can be found in a study by an American primatologist, Shirley Strum, of a group of baboons that she called the Pumphouse Gang. This group was unusual because they were very good at hunting, so it was tempting to think that information about hunting was being shared within the group. However, Strum also noted that the leader in the hunt was an individual who was particularly good at hunting. And when he died, the group's ability to hunt effectively died with him. The information they had once had simply leaked away again.[1]

We can be reasonably sure that this cultural leakiness is characteristic of all other species, because if a species had existed that could lock in information more efficiently, its members would surely have accumulated more and more information, including new information about how

to control their environments; their numbers would have grown and eventually they would have had such an impact that they would have shown up in the archaeological record. In short, they would have behaved a bit like our own species.

In contrast, modern humans can communicate with such precision, speed, and complexity that information contributed by individual members is held more firmly within the group memory. We can even communicate about things that are not right in front of us. We can discuss the past and future; we can describe the tiger that sometimes visits the creek beyond the large rock (and warn you when not to go there); we can even discuss things that may not exist, such as pink elephants or arrow-tailed goat-horned devils. This is because we possess what Terrence Deacon has called **symbolic language.** Rather than using sounds or gestures to refer to one particular thing, we can use sounds as conceptual parcels that refer to whole categories of ideas and things. Furthermore, through syntax, or the careful arrangement of words according to grammatical rules, we can convey multiple possible relationships between different people, things, and ideas. (We can tell the difference between "I kicked you" and "I was kicked by you.") The result is that we share so much information that the amount of shared information in each community begins to accumulate from generation to generation. That sustained increase in shared knowledge is the foundation of human history because it ensures that, as a general rule, later generations will have more knowledge than earlier generations so that their behaviors will slowly change over time. These slow behavioral changes are what we call "history."

Symbolic language accounts for our remarkable ability to collaborate through Collective Learning, or the ability to share in great detail and precision what each individual learns through symbolic language. The difference between us and species without such an efficient form of communication is a bit like the difference between stand-alone computers, which rely entirely on whatever information they can store in their memory, and networked computers, which can use the information stored in millions of other computers. As Steven Pinker puts it, in a species that can share information efficiently

> a group can pool the hard-won discoveries of members, present and past, and end up far smarter than a race of hermits. Hunter-gatherers accumulate the know-how to make tools, control fire, outsmart prey, and detoxify plants, and can live by this collective ingenuity even if no member could re-create it all from scratch. Also, by co-coordinating their behavior (say, in driving game or taking turns watching children while others forage), they can act like a big multi-headed, multi-limbed beast and accomplish feats that a die-hard individualist could not. And an array of interconnected eyes, ears, and heads is more robust than a single set with all its shortcomings and idiosyncrasies.[2]

This process of accumulation, extended over perhaps 200,000 years, is what human history is all about. That is why we regard Collective Learning as the key to understanding threshold 6 (see the Threshold 6 Summary).

THRESHOLD	INGREDIENTS ▶	STRUCTURE ▶	GOLDILOCKS CONDITIONS =	EMERGENT PROPERTIES
HOMO SAPIENS	Same as all life and highly developed manipulative, perceptive, and neurological capacity.	Highly specific biological structures governed by human DNA.	Long preceding period of evolution generating highly developed manipulative, perceptive, and neurological capacity.	Collective Learning, i.e., capacity to share information precisely and rapidly so that information accumulates at the level of the community and species giving rise to long-term historical change.

When and Where Did *Homo sapiens* Appear?

When did our species first appear? All the evidence available at present suggests our species emerged in what archaeologists refer to as the Middle Paleolithic, sometime between 250,000 years ago (the start of the Middle Paleolithic) and 50,000 years ago (the start of the Upper Paleolithic).

Can We Be More Precise about When Human History Began? One way of answering this question might be to determine when symbolic language and Collective Learning first appeared. But that is not easy because spoken language leaves no direct trace. Are there, perhaps, indirect traces of humans using symbolic language to talk with each other? After all, many different skills are required for human language. You need a lot of brain power; you need rapid and efficient ways of managing how you produce and hear sounds; you need the ability to intuit what is going on inside the mind of those you are talking with. Unfortunately, these skills, too, leave little direct evidence. Many of these abilities may have been present, in limited forms, in our close relatives, the hominines; and practical experiments have shown that some are present in the great apes, some of whom have been taught to speak in very limited ways. But clearly, something happened to bring all these abilities together into a single, exceptionally powerful form of communication. And the relative suddenness with which things began to change in the last 200,000 years suggests that the package came together quite swiftly in evolutionary terms, over perhaps a few tens of thousands of years.

We have some intriguing hints about how the door to language may have been opened. Studies of a family living in England, many of whose members seemed incapable of using grammar properly, showed that the family shared a single mutation on a single gene, known as FOXP2. The particular form of this gene present in human beings is different from that present in our relatives, the great apes. Indeed, it is estimated that the human form of the FOXP2 gene appeared within the last 200,000 years. All this is highly suggestive and hints that symbolic language may

have appeared quite suddenly on evolutionary time scales. Yet few would argue that this one gene is enough to explain our unique capacity for symbolic language, particularly as there is evidence that Neandertals shared the same form of the FOXP2 gene as humans. This is a story whose details still need to be teased out.

If we cannot detect the presence of human language directly, can we use less direct methods? There are two promising candidates: fossil evidence and genetic evidence. Unfortunately, the archaeological record remains patchy, particularly in Africa, where far less archaeological research into this period has been conducted than in Europe. Indeed, we will see that this is one reason why there remains so much room for different interpretations.

Where Did Our Species Evolve? In the last million years, we have evidence of the appearance of many different species of hominines, all apparently descended from *H. erectus.* But when did our species, *H. sapiens,* split off from these other species? At present, there are two broad interpretations of the evolution of *H. sapiens;* the first is often described as the Out of Africa hypothesis and the second is referred to as the multiregional hypothesis. From the 1960s, a number of scholars argued, mainly on the basis of fossil remains from the whole of Eurasia, that various forms of *H. erectus* or *H. ergaster* evolved slowly into our own species over much of Afro-Eurasia and over many hundreds of thousands of years. This is the *multiregional hypothesis.* It presumes that there was enough contact between hominine groups over this entire area that they remained, genetically speaking, a single species.

However, since the 1980s, new evidence, both from archaeology and genetic studies, has tended to support an alternative theory, the *Out of Africa hypothesis.* This theory asserts that modern humans evolved in Africa within the last 250,000 to 200,000 years. In the late 1990s, it became possible to extract enough DNA from Neandertal remains to show that Neandertals are not a variant of our own species, but are a distinct species, and that our two species must have diverged about half a million years ago from later forms of *H. erectus,* though more recent studies suggest

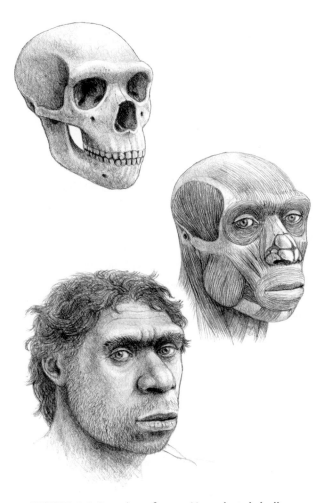

FIGURE 4.4 Drawings from a Neandertal skull.
Neandertals were physically different from modern humans in several ways. In the skull, these included more prominent brow ridges, a broader, flatter nose, and a projecting mid-face with little or no chin. Neandertals lived across Europe and western and central Asia for some 200,000 years. Genetic research shows that the DNA of people with European and Asian ancestry is 1 to 4 percent Neandertal. Interbreeding likely took place 80,000 to 50,000 years ago when modern humans moved into Europe from Africa. Neandertals died out 35,000 to 30,000 years ago.

there may have been a small amount of interbreeding (Figure 4.4). Genetic studies also point to two other important conclusions. First, all modern humans are remarkably similar genetically speaking, so similar that they probably had a common ancestor within the last 200,000 years or so. Second, the greatest genetic variety can be found within Africa. This suggests strongly that this is where our species first appeared, because this is where minor genetic differences have had the most time to accumulate.

Recent fossil discoveries reinforce the genetic evidence that supports the Out of Africa hypothesis. For example, skulls from Omo in Ethiopia, found in the mid-twentieth century, and essentially the same as modern human skulls,

have recently been dated to almost 200,000 years ago, which is much earlier than was once supposed. We now have many skeletal remains from Africa dating from about 125,000 years ago that clearly belong to our own species. That is, they fit a checklist of skeletal features associated with our species. Here, to give some idea of how this works, are some of the main features that paleontologists look for in the skulls of modern humans:

Cranial capacity usually in excess of 1,350 cc (though admittedly this is variable)

Relatively vertical frontal bone (forehead)

High and parallel-walled cranial vault

Rounded occipital region (the back of the head) lacking a prominent horizontal bulge (the occipital torus) and with a relatively flat angle of the cranial base (basicranial angle)

Non-continuous brow ridge expressed more clearly in males

Relatively flat, non-projecting face "tucked in" below the expanded frontal region of the braincase

Distinct chin[3]

As a result of these new forms of evidence, most scholars now accept that our species evolved in Africa sometime within the last 250,000 years. But there remains debate about exactly how and when. The major difficulty is that the skeletal evidence and genetic evidence seem to point one way, while the evidence of human artifacts seems to point in another, so that human *behaviors* seem to appear later than human *bodies*.

From about 50,000 years ago, at the start of the Upper Paleolithic, archaeological sites in both Eurasia and Africa show very clear evidence of technological innovation. The range of tools diversifies, with the appearance of delicate implements such as needles and harpoons, made sometimes according to standard patterns; tools are made from new materials such as ivory and bone; art objects appear, including carved shells, bones, and cave paintings; there is growing evidence of objects, including useful types of stone, being exchanged over large areas; evidence appears of the exploitation of an increasing range of animal and plant species; humans begin to enter more difficult or more inaccessible regions, including Australia and Siberia; and human populations start to increase.

These are exactly the types of evidence we should expect from a species capable of Collective Learning. It seems that, quite suddenly, technologies became more diverse; groups began to exchange goods (and presumably also genes and information) over large areas; innovation accelerated; and human numbers increased as humans learned to manage a greater variety of environments. Equally significant is the appearance of art objects, for artistic activity suggests that these humans were *thinking* symbolically, and presumably that means that they were *talking* in symbolic language as well. This suite of changes occurring from about 50,000 years ago is described by archaeologists as the "Revolution of the Upper Paleolithic." Many archaeologists, such as Richard Klein, have argued that even if creatures that *looked* a lot like us had evolved well over 100,000 years ago, the Upper Paleolithic provides the earliest evidence for creatures that also *behaved* like us.

But that's not quite the end of the story. In a lengthy article (it took up the entire space of the *Journal of Human Evolution* in 2000), Sally McBrearty and Alison Brooks argued that the appearance of distinctively human behaviors was a more gradual process, beginning perhaps 200,000 years ago and originating in Africa.[4] The delicate evidence they present suggests that our species did in fact appear between 300,000 and 200,000 years ago, but that it took a long time before more powerful evidence of their distinctiveness showed up in the archaeological record. (That is why their article is called "The Revolution That Wasn't.") The problem, they argued, was that so much less archaeology has been done in Africa that the evidence for distinctively human behaviors has been either missed or ignored. Accordingly, McBrearty and Brooks's article consists of a very detailed review of the archaeological evidence, and they conclude that almost all the changes found in the Revolution of the Upper Paleolithic can be found much earlier in the African record. Their evidence is summarized in Figure 4.5.

As Figure 4.5 shows, there are hints that humans may have been using ocher pigment, a yellowish or reddish earth containing iron oxide, as early as 280,000 years ago. As such pigments have often been used for body painting, and body painting is a form of art, they conclude that here we have indirect evidence for the presence of symbolic thinking, and perhaps of symbolic language, almost 300,000

years ago, and in Africa. The figure also shows evidence for the early appearance of a wider range of stone tools, a wider range of foodstuffs, evidence for interregional exchanges, and so on. Important African archaeological sites such as Blombos cave in South Africa lend powerful support to the idea that our species developed much earlier, during the Middle Paleolithic, rather than 50,000 years ago, at the beginning of the Upper Paleolithic.

Meanwhile, we can summarize what we know at present. First, what makes us unique as a species is our capacity to keep developing new forms of behavior and new ways of relating to our environment. This ecological, technological, and artistic creativity explains why we alone have a history of long-term change. Second, the source of this creativity seems to be the peculiar efficiency of human language, the fact that we can share ideas so well that they get locked within the collective memory, and begin to accumulate. This is what we call Collective Learning. Third, most paleontologists argue that our species evolved within the last 250,000 years, probably somewhere in Africa. From about 100,000 years ago, the evidence that our ancestors not only *looked* like modern humans, but also *behaved* like them (in other words, that they were adapting through Collective Learning), becomes increasingly powerful; and from about 50,000 years ago, it is indisputable.

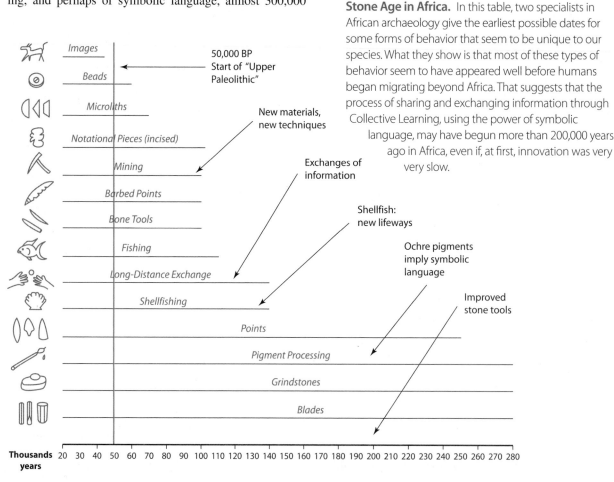

FIGURE 4.5 Behavioral innovations of the Middle Stone Age in Africa. In this table, two specialists in African archaeology give the earliest possible dates for some forms of behavior that seem to be unique to our species. What they show is that most of these types of behavior seem to have appeared well before humans began migrating beyond Africa. That suggests that the process of sharing and exchanging information through Collective Learning, using the power of symbolic language, may have begun more than 200,000 years ago in Africa, even if, at first, innovation was very very slow.

Images
Beads — 50,000 BP Start of "Upper Paleolithic"
Microliths
Notational Pieces (incised)
Mining — New materials, new techniques
Barbed Points
Bone Tools — Exchanges of information
Fishing
Long-Distance Exchange — Shellfish: new lifeways
Shellfishing
Points — Ochre pigments imply symbolic language
Pigment Processing — Improved stone tools
Grindstones
Blades

Thousands years 20 30 40 50 60 70 80 90 100 110 120 130 140 150 160 170 180 190 200 210 220 230 240 250 260 270 280

The Paleolithic Era: 200,000 to 10,000 Years Ago

This final section of the chapter takes us definitively into human history. Yet the era of human history we are looking at here is not one that looms large in most mainstream history courses or textbooks. This is a pity, because most of human history has taken place in this Paleolithic era, and we hope to remind everyone of its fundamental significance.

Definition and Significance of the Paleolithic Era of Human History

The word *Paleolithic* comes from two ancient Greek words, and means "the Old Stone Age." This label derives from the three-age system of historical periodization, which divides all of human history into three consecutive chronological periods, each named for the predominant material used for tools and weapons (stone, bronze, and iron). The term *Paleolithic era* was first used by archaeologist John Lubbock in 1865 and applied to that era of history distinguished by stone tools. If we include our hominine ancestors who, as we have seen, also used stone tools, the Paleolithic extends from about 2.5 million years ago to around 12,000 years ago. However, in this textbook we are defining the term **Paleolithic era** more specifically as the first age of distinctly human history, from the appearance of *H. sapiens* roughly 200,000 years ago, to the beginning of agriculture about 12,000 years ago (Figure 4.6).

The inclusion of the Paleolithic within the world history narrative is critically important for at least two significant reasons. First, it is the period during which we became who we are and began to realize our species' potential physically, socially, technologically, and linguistically. Examining this period helps provide answers to the fundamental question of what it means to be human. Second, since the Paleolithic era is the foundation of all subsequent world history, the most recent 5 percent of human history, which includes the Agrarian and Modern eras, makes little sense at all if the preceding 95 percent is ignored.

Of course, the argument that something is significant just because it lasted a long time can be disingenuous. The Paleolithic may be the longest era by far, but there were far fewer humans around in the Paleolithic. If we assume, as modern demographers do, that a total of about 80 billion humans have lived on Earth since the first modern human emerged, 20 percent of that total has lived in the last 250 years alone, while about 68 percent lived in the Agrarian era. The Paleolithic accounted for only about 12 percent of all the humans who have ever lived. When measured by population, the Agrarian and Modern eras are much more important, which might partly explain the neglect of the Paleolithic in most history books and courses.

Two Main Events of the Paleolithic Era

We will be considering two major Paleolithic "events" here. The first is climate change, specifically the impact of the last ice age on human history. The second is *extensification,* a term that describes the spread of humans around the world, as a result of new technologies they developed to cope with a range of different environments.

Climatic Changes: Survival in the Ice Ages By the early twentieth century, geologists were able to map accurately the extent of ice age glaciation and to prove that there had been not just one ice age, but many. Paleolithic humans lived through two distinct ice ages. Around 200,000 years ago the climate was relatively mild and conditions benign. Beginning about 195,000 years ago, however, conditions began to deteriorate and the planet entered a long glacial stage that lasted until approximately 123,000 years ago. The second period of cooling—which represents the most recent ice age episode in the history of Earth—began roughly 110,000 years ago, and the last interglacial began around 11,500 years ago. This means that human lifeways in the Paleolithic largely evolved under ice age conditions.

FIGURE 4.6 Timeline of the past 200,000 years.

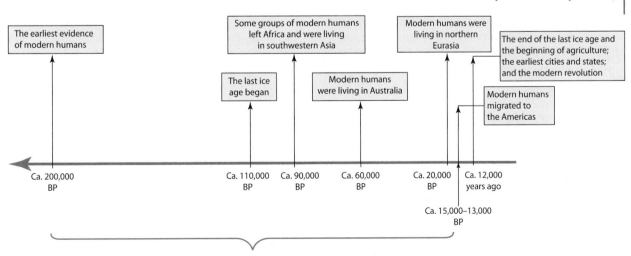

The Paleolithic Era (95 percent of all human history)

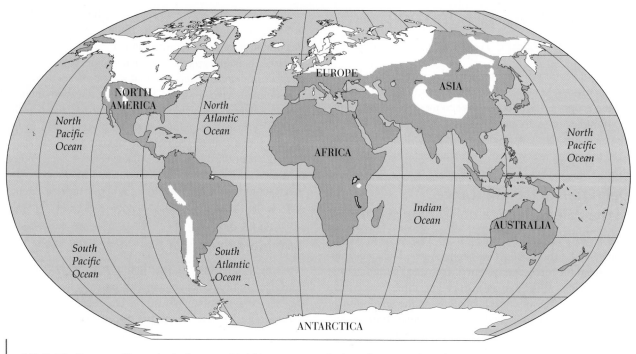

MAP 4.2 Extent of last glaciation, ca. 21,000 years ago during the Last Glacial Maximum.

Between about 123,000 and 110,000 years ago (during the last interglacial), Earth's temperatures were similar to those of today. Beginning around 110,000 years ago, sediment samples from around the globe show a long-term and relatively sudden shift to considerably colder climates. Recent high-resolution Atlantic sediment analysis indicates that the change from warm interglacial to glacial conditions may have happened over a period of fewer than 400 years. The northern forests quickly fragmented and retreated, the winters grew longer and colder, and great ice sheets began to spread across the landscape in high latitudes. Since glaciers leave a lot of evidence of where they have been, we have a clear geographic picture of the extent of glaciation. Geologists now estimate that during the most recent ice age, glacial ice affected perhaps 30 percent of Earth's land area, including some 3.8 million square miles (10 million square kilometers) of North America, 1.9 million square miles (5 million square kilometers) of Europe, and 1.54 million square miles (4 million square kilometers) of Siberia. The glaciation in the Northern Hemisphere was approximately twice that of the Southern Hemisphere, because the southern oceans prevented the ice sheets from spreading too far from Antarctica.

Even in those regions of the globe not directly affected by ice, the increasing cold caused Earth's climate to become dryer because, with lower temperatures, there was less evaporation and less rainfall. Forests died out extensively, to be replaced by dry grasslands that turned into widespread deserts by about 70,000 years ago. Temperatures warmed up again between 60,000 and 55,000 years ago, but around 30,000 BP ("before the present") Earth was once again plunged into the grip of an intense, dry cold that reached its most extreme temperatures between 21,000 and 17,000 years ago (see

Map 4.2). These dates mark the point at which global ice reached its greatest extent, and humans trying to survive in this harsh environment would have faced shrunken forests and desert or semidesert conditions across huge areas of the continents that were not actually under ice.

Then, around 14,000 years ago, Earth experienced a rapid global warming and moistening. The ice sheets began to retreat, and the forests to grow back. After a couple of thousand years or so of recovery, the planet was plunged back into a new, though short-lived, glacial event known as the *Younger Dryas.* This may have come on over a period as brief as 100 years before disappearing again even more quickly about 11,500 years ago, in just a few decades, or even faster. This marks the start of what geologists call the **Holocene epoch.** From 11,500 BP Earth became warmer and wetter, the ice sheets gradually melted (although it took them 2,000 years to do so), and vegetation became lusher over much of Afro-Eurasia. The period between 9,000 and 5,000 years ago is known to geologists as the Holocene Optimum, and as we will see in the next chapter, these conditions were crucial in facilitating the domestication of various plant and animal species during the agricultural revolution.

Collective Learning generated the knowledge and technologies that allowed humans to migrate out of Africa and into an increasingly cold and inhospitable world. The use and control of fire, for example, was crucial to survival in cold climates. Humans living in ice age climates also improved hunting techniques, made warm clothing with stitched seams, built sturdy dwellings (often made of animal products or ice), and developed sophisticated techniques to hunt the large herbivores of the steppes such as mammoth. Specific examples of sites that have provided evidence of these adaptive strategies will be considered in the "Paleolithic Lifeways" section that follows, but collectively they provide clear early evidence of the astonishing adaptability of humans when faced with devastating climate change. Is there a lesson here for the future?

Extensification: The Spread of Humans	

There is indisputable archaeological and genetic evidence that small groups of modern humans began to migrate out of Africa from about 90,000 years ago. These migrations were slow and piecemeal affairs, as groups moved into new lands adjacent to those they had been occupying. Small populations of *H. sapiens* moved out of Africa, then settled in a new home until their population increased, at which point a subgroup broke off and moved away. Through this process humans colonized the entire planet (with the exception of Antarctica), although the size of the human global population remained small.

David Christian has used the term *extensification* to describe the process of global colonization. Christian defines **extensification** as a form of innovation that allows "an increase in the range of humans without any parallel increase in the average size or density of human communities."[5] This term suggests that during these Paleolithic migrations, there was little increase in the size or social complexity of human societies. However, human communities during the Paleolithic were far from primitive because Collective Learning is clearly evident in the creation of new tools, technologies, and sophisticated art; in migrations into inhospitable glacial regions; and in the application of new technologies that allowed humans to settle in this diversity of environmental niches.

The chronology for these global migrations suggests that humans had left Africa and migrated into West Asia and the Mediterranean regions by about 100,000 to 90,000 BP; had made it to East Asia and Australia by 60,000 BP; were occupying cold regions of the Ukraine and Russia by about 35,000 BP; Siberia by about 20,000 BP; and the Americas by at least 13,000 BP (possibly considerably earlier). A correlation of these dates with the chronology of various climate episodes during the last ice age provides further evidence of human adaptability and also possible explanations for these migrations. The movement out of Africa began soon after the onset of glacial conditions. A global warming that began between 60,000 and 55,000 years ago apparently corresponds with human settlement of East Asia and Australia. Extraordinarily, some groups of humans seem to have chosen the very moment of the Last Glacial Maximum approximately 20,000 years ago to move into the inhospitable cold of Siberia! But the same conditions also made it easier to migrate to the Americas because low sea levels left a land bridge from Sibera to Alaska. Finally, as global warming commenced some 14,000 years ago, other human groups of East Asian genetic origin found themselves trapped in the Americas by rising sea levels.

During the Paleolithic, then, humans peopled much of Earth; until 10,000 BP only lions came close to human distribution. At the same time, although the human population grew somewhat, the size and complexity of human communities did not significantly increase.

Paleolithic Lifeways: How Did People Live?

Since we have no written evidence for 95 percent of human history, anthropologists and historians interested in reconstructing Paleolithic lifeways have to rely on other forms of evidence. These consist mainly of the study of archaeological remains (including bones, tools, and living sites) and analogies with modern societies most like Paleolithic societies. We have to be careful how we interpret this evidence, because both forms can be misleading.

Foraging as a Way of Living	

Foraging, a term virtually interchangeable with *hunter-gathering,* involves the gathering of foodstuffs and other needed materials from the environment to survive. It might seem at first glance that this is how many other large animals also live, so what is special about foraging lifeways? The answer lies in the level of teamwork. Some animals do hunt in packs, of course. What makes humans different is that as they gather or hunt the resources they need, they do so armed with the information accumulated over many generations. This makes human foraging more precise, more varied, and more information-dependent than that of other species. And of course, that makes it far more efficient and more creative. Once again we come back to the crucial distinguishing characteristic of our species: that we exploit our environment with vastly more information and therefore with more effectiveness than any other species. This difference also explains why, over time, the impact of our species has inexorably increased.

Foraging can take many different forms. Some foragers specialize in particular species, for example, while others are "generalists." Some move around a great deal, while others stay close to their main camp all year. Yet certain fundamentals are common to all foragers. For example, anthropological studies of modern foragers demonstrate that every foraging community needs a large territory to support itself, which means that populations must remain small. In early Holocene Europe, for example, foraging lifeways required an estimated 3.85 square miles (10 square kilometers) of land to support an individual, whereas early farming communities could support densities of 50 to 100 people from the same area.

Because they have to gather food over large areas, foragers are mostly nomadic, moving through their lands according to the seasonal availability of foods. To succeed in a nomadic lifeway, human communities needed to keep populations small because it is impossible for migrating bands to support too many feeding infants or elderly members of the group who have reduced mobility. Survival in the Paleolithic thus demanded the use of practices such as natural birth control, infanticide, and senilicide (allowing infants or older people to die or deliberately killing them). One researcher has argued for an infanticide rate of up to 50 percent among prehistoric communities. Other comparative anthropologists suggest that 50 percent of all female newborn babies were killed by their parents in the

Paleolithic. As a result of these practices, populations of nomadic foragers grew very slowly.

The diet of modern foragers consists mainly of gathered foods—plants, roots, nuts, small animals, and insects—supplemented by scavenging or hunting. Evidence from the Klaises River Mouth in South Africa shows that some 100,000 years ago, humans were hunting elands by driving them into traps. At the La Quinta site in France, early hunters may have driven herds of horses and reindeer over cliffs. These examples suggest that more confrontational big-game hunting was something that developed only late in the Paleolithic. Scavenging, on the other hand, was opportunistic, less dangerous, and easier, and early Paleolithic humans probably gained most of their meat by stealing carcasses that had been killed by large carnivores, dragging them to a safe place, then using tools to butcher the meat and marrow.

Archaeological evidence of plant gathering is a lot more difficult to find than that of hunting, because bones and tools last while plant remains generally do not. One important exception to this is the Kalambo Falls site in Zambia, which has yielded evidence of gathered leaves, nuts, fruits, seeds, and wooden tools dated to 180,000 BP. Anthropological studies of modern foraging lifeways show that the food obtained through gathering is far more important to survival than meat. Indeed, the general impression held by most prehistorians today is that hunting was of a hit-or-miss strategy during the Paleolithic and that in any tropical or temperate environment most calories were supplied through the gathering and consumption of plants and small animals.

Examples of Diverse Foraging Technologies To modern eyes the various foraging technologies employed by humans during the Paleolithic might at first glance appear simple. Yet to survive, Paleolithic foragers needed an immensely detailed knowledge of their environment, along with the ability to apply the most appropriate and efficient technologies and skills to a particular environmental niche. Although all Paleolithic humans pursued the foraging lifeway, their techniques and technologies varied greatly as humans migrated into a widely varied range of environments. As already noted, living in cold climates required a particularly specialized range of skills, which the Inuit of Alaska and northern Canada have been demonstrating for millennia. With their fur clothing, canoes, and other hunting and fishing equipment (all made from stone, bone, tusk, and antlers), the Inuit have managed to prosper in regions where few other members of our species could live.

Further evidence of human Paleolithic adaptations to cold climate environments comes from the site of Mezherich, near Kiev in the Ukraine. In 1965, a farmer digging in his cellar struck the lower jaw bone of a mammoth, which further excavation revealed to be part of an entire, semipermanent dwelling that had been constructed entirely out of mammoth bones. Three dozen huge, curving tusks had been used as arch supports for the roof, other bones had been knitted together to create a framework for the walls, and even the "tent pegs" used to tie down the

mammoth skin external membrane were made of bone. It has been estimated that the bones from perhaps 95 mammoths had been used in the construction, which has been dated to roughly 20,000 BP. The interior of the dwelling contained amber ornaments, fossilized shells, a mammoth-head "drum" that appears to have been beaten by bone drumsticks, and tiny slivers of mammoth bones used to make needles, presumably to stitch garments together.

Two other examples of deceptively simple techniques and materials will suffice here to demonstrate the ingenuity of Paleolithic hunter-gatherers. In North America, the sharp and hard-chipped stone Clovis points (so named because the first examples were discovered near Clovis, New Mexico) were used by North American native peoples between about 11,500 and 11,000 BP. These points are thin, fluted projectile points that were once fastened (or hafted) to wooden spears. The spear could then have been thrown by hand or by a spear thrower (like the Australian aboriginal woomera). From around 10,000 BCE the Clovis points were replaced by Folsom points, which were used widely across North America until about 8000 BCE. Both Clovis and Folsom points have often been discovered in the vicinity of mammoth skeletons, and it is probable that these deadly efficient projectile points contributed to the extinction of the mammoth and other megafauna in North America.

The San Bush people of the Kalahari Desert in South Africa may have followed traditional hunter-gatherer lifeways since the early Paleolithic, although since the 1990s many have adopted or been forced to adopt farming. Genetic and anthropological studies of San lifeways have provided invaluable insight into the Paleolithic. Their traditional hunting and gathering tools appear simple, yet they have ensured San survival for many millennia. Gathering equipment used mainly by San women includes a blanket, a hide sling, a type of cloak used to carry foods and firewood, some smaller carry bags, and a digging stick. San men use a simple bow and (poison-tipped) arrow, plus a spear, to hunt the small animals of the Kalahari. With this basic toolkit, plus an immense knowledge of their environment, the San demonstrate the range of survival possibilities that Paleolithic humans devised.

Paleolithic Standards of Living Prehistorians have debated vigorously the standards of physical and mental health enjoyed by Paleolithic foragers, a debate in which the San have played a crucial role. Until the 1960s, the modern conception of early humans held that they lived lives that were "nasty, brutish and short." However, fieldwork done in the 1960s among the San, who were at the time seen as a relatively pristine, untouched foraging people, caused anthropologists to revise this view substantially. A new conception emerged of foragers who enjoyed an almost idyllic lifeway with plenty of free time for interests beyond food gathering and a diet that ensured good nutritional health. Studies of other Stone Age societies assumed to have been living in untouched isolation, including Australian aboriginals, strengthened this interpretation.

By 1972, anthropologist Marshall Sahlins was prepared to describe Paleolithic communities as "the original affluent society," characterized by adequate and varied food supplies, high levels of health and fitness because of a balanced diet and frequent exercise, freedom from the sort of disease epidemics that would later decimate sedentary communities, and even ample "leisure" time. However, Sahlins's conclusion, perhaps deliberately and provocatively overstated, has been increasingly challenged since the 1980s. A new generation of anthropologists working in the Kalahari Desert have noted that the San often live on the verge of starvation; that they did not choose to continue pursuing this lifeway but had no other option; and that none of the so-called pristine societies studied by anthropologists had in fact been untouched by the modern world. While the jury is still out on the Paleolithic standard of living, the debate reminds us of the difficulties of using modern hunter-gatherer societies to understand the Paleolithic past, while reminding us of the dangers of viewing human history as a story of continuing "progress."

Living in Small Groups: A Do-It-Yourself Approach to Life
Foragers generally live in small groups of perhaps 10 to 20 people. The family is the basic social unit, and kinship the fundamental organizing principle that bound all human communities together before the emergence of agriculture. Studies of modern foraging societies show that the core community would split into even smaller groups to carry out specialized tasks when necessary and also that regular meetings with other nomadic communities would take place—for a few days only—in large-group gatherings. These events (the Australian *corroboree* is a good example) had to be held where resources were plentiful, such as in the foothills of the Australian Alps when the large Bogong moth swarmed between September and November. Feasting on the moths, the aboriginal people of the region held large gatherings at which they exchanged gifts, ideas, and information; made marriages; moved as individuals from group to group; conducted rituals; and played games. Gift giving was a particularly important way of cementing social relations within these larger networks, using the principle of *reciprocity* (or mutual exchanges) to maintain good relations. Paleolithic people living in other regions of the world enjoyed similar gatherings and also ensured ongoing communal relationships through exchanges of material goods and ideas. Despite the significance of these larger intergroup gatherings, the opportunities for large-scale Collective Learning remained limited; anthropologists estimate that most Paleolithic humans would have met fewer than 500 other humans during their lifetimes!

Living in small groups demanded a "do-it-yourself" approach to all aspects of life. There were neither government nor police or courts during the Paleolithic; everything had to be done "within the family." The administration of justice and punishment, when necessary, was a particularly personal process. Anthropologist Richard Lee offers the following observation of do-it-yourself justice among the San people of the Kalahari, giving us a glimpse into capital punishment during the Paleolithic:

> Twi had killed three other people, when the community, in a rare move of unanimity, ambushed and fatally wounded him in full daylight. As he lay dying, all the men fired at him with poisoned arrows until, in the words of one informant, "he looked like a porcupine." Then, after he was dead, all the women as well as the men approached his body and stabbed him with spears, symbolically sharing the responsibility for his death.[6]

Gender Relations in the Paleolithic
The traditional view of gender relations in the Paleolithic is that man was the hunter, and woman the gatherer. However, recent scholarship has begun to challenge this model. Primatologists in particular have pointed out that female chimpanzees can be responsible for hunting up to 35 percent of the food needed by the group and that primate females are perfectly capable of providing for themselves and their children without male assistance. Anthropologists have also discovered examples of modern Stone Age cultures in which the men gather plants (the San of the Kalahari), and the women hunt and fish (in the Agta culture of Luzon in the Philippines). The more accepted model today is that these behaviors were flexible and that the selection of who would hunt and who would gather was often based on abilities, knowledge, necessity, and the reproductive cycles of females, rather than on gender stereotypes.

Paleolithic Ideas about the World?
Given the scarcity and ambiguous nature of evidence about Paleolithic lifeways, our comments about the ideology and belief systems of Paleolithic humans must be viewed as exceptionally speculative. Studies of modern small-scale societies do strongly suggest that foragers probably thought of themselves as part of the natural world. Many believed that their spirits would return in the form of other animals or natural features of the landscape. They believed in a world full of spirits of many different kinds and also that it was possible to enter that world under certain conditions. Yet Paleolithic views on this spirit world were specific and localized, tied to a particular place rather than to any sense of a universal divinity. Paleolithic "religious" beliefs are illustrated through three different examples, although prehistorians do not agree on precisely what these examples mean.

San Cave Art: Some 15,000 rock art sites of the San Bush people have been discovered in South Africa, the oldest dated to as early as 70,000 BP. The art does not appear to have been painted simply to decorate the walls of a rock shelter or to depict everyday hunting scenes and animals, but rather seems to have a powerful ritual significance that might be associated with the shamanistic religious practices of the San. These shamans, perhaps under the influence of drug-induced altered states of consciousness, would enter the spirit world by somehow activating a supernatural force in the animals of the region and then later paint these spiritual experiences. The most

FIGURE 4.8 Venus figurine. What is the meaning and purpose of this small female figurine?

FIGURE 4.7 San cave art, East Zimbabwe. Scenes from the daily life of the San.

commonly depicted animals are the eland and the kudu. Not all San art is supernatural or magical in character; much of it depicts daily life and the skills needed to cope with survival in the harsh environment (see Figure 4.7).

Venus Figurines: Beginning from around 25,000 BP, small clay figurines of heavily pregnant women began to appear widely across Eurasia, from the Pyrenees to the River Don. These figures are the oldest sculptures depicting the human image to have been discovered thus far, and their meaning and purpose has been variously interpreted. Some historians have argued that the statues of powerful, fertile women are evidence of ancient religious practices based on the worship of a mother goddess, who was associated with the fertility of the Earth. Others believe they might have been manufactured by men as almost pornographic objects to be touched and fondled. Yet others believe they might have been toys or female self-portraits (see Figure 4.8).

Australian Aboriginal Cave Art: Australian aboriginal rock art dates back to at least 40,000 BP, and perhaps earlier. Recent research suggests that artistic technique did not evolve gradually, but rather appeared suddenly and explosively. Although specialists have been able to chronologically sequence the thousands of known examples, aboriginal rock art sites tend to be dynamic and represent images accumulated over thousands of years. In Western

Arnhem Land, local environmental and climatic changes are clearly represented in the art. A dry era is represented by depictions of extinct thylacines (a wolflike carnivorous marsupial); the subsequent wetter Estuarine era art shows rising river levels, barramundi, saltwater crocodiles, and the extraordinary Rainbow Serpent; and the later Freshwater period features geese and goose feather decorative motifs. Within the last 3,000 years, aboriginals painted X-ray images of freshwater fauna, revealing the internal anatomy of various birds and reptiles.

The aboriginal people of Western Arnhem have their own sequence for the rock art, one much more imbued with spirituality. They attribute the oldest images to the Mimi people, who they believe inhabited the land during the Dreaming, before the Rainbow Serpent created the aboriginals. The Mimi taught the aboriginals how to survive in the region, then became spirit beings. The more recent art was all created by the aboriginals themselves. The Wandjina paintings of the Kimberley depict the powerful creator spirits, who control the elemental forces of nature such as the wind, storms, and floods. These gods are shown in human form, but with large bodies outlined in red; huge, dark eyes; and no mouths—wearing halos of cloud and lightning (see Figure 4.9).

Paleolithic Impacts on the Planet

Did Paleolithic foragers have much of an impact on the environment? The traditional view suggested that they lived in harmony with nature, yet modern evidence indicates that, despite their relatively low numbers, Paleolithic humans did have a significant environmental impact.

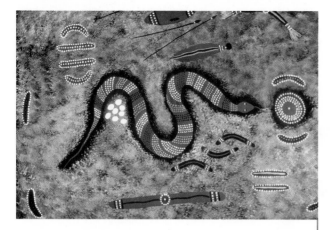

FIGURE 4.9 Aboriginal cave art. This image celebrates the snake and the witchetty grub, and must have spiritual significance.

Estimates of human populations are extremely tentative, but most calculations give a number of 5 to 10 million humans living at the end of the last ice age, with a high estimate of 15 million. The Italian demographer Massimo Livi-Bacci is more conservative and suggests: 10,000 at the beginning of the first ice age; 500,000 in the early Paleolithic; and only 6 million by the end of the last ice age around 10,000 years ago. These figures allow for a general sense of population densities: roughly 1 person per 10 square miles (25 square kilometers) in 10,000 BP. Despite these low overall figures and densities, a range of evidence supports the hypothesis that early humans dramatically affected the biosphere through the practice of fire-stick farming and the extinction of other large animals.

Fire-Stick Farming We have already considered the critical importance of the controlled use of fire in the Paleolithic, the first energy revolution in human history. Although one of our hominine ancestors, *H. erectus,* probably "invented" the use of fire, such use reached a significant level of exploitation in the Paleolithic. Although providing an obvious advantage in cooking (by predigesting food) and the provision of warmth, fire was also put to large-scale hunting use through the practice of **fire-stick farming** (which was not strictly a form of farming).

For tens of thousands of years, Australian aboriginals set fire to huge tracts of bushland, both to drive game out for hunting and to promote the growth of new vegetation for gathering and hunting. Australian archaeologist Rhys Jones coined the term *fire-stick farming* in 1969 to describe this practice, which had the long-term effect of turning scrubland into grassland and suppressing the succession of certain species. Although some researchers argue that aboriginal use of fire had little impact on the environment, it is clear that in many areas the practice transformed natural ecosystems by altering the vegetation (for example by encouraging an increase in fire-loving Eucalypts) to maximize productivity in terms of aboriginal food requirements. Fire-stick farming was also practiced in parts of Eurasia, New Zealand, and North America and has been implicated in the other significant impact of Paleolithic humans on the environment, megafaunal extinctions.

Megafaunal Extinctions As early humans spread across the globe in waves of migration, they entered continents that had no earlier hominine colonization, particularly Australia and the Americas. By the 1960s, paleontologists like Paul S. Martin were beginning to amass evidence of the dramatic impact of these migrations. To put it bluntly, humans demonstrated their adaptive abilities and technological prowess by initiating a wave of **extinctions,** among the **megafaunal** (that is, large-sized animal) inhabitants of these continents, who had had no previous experience with this introduced predator. In the Americas nearly 75 percent of all animals weighing more than 100 pounds (45 kilograms) disappeared after humans arrived. In Australia the figure is 86.4 percent.

The largest species were the most threatened because they moved and reproduced very slowly. The mammoth, woolly rhinoceros, and giant elk disappeared in Eurasia; the horse, elephant, giant armadillo, and sloth vanished in North America (Figure 4.10); and in Australia dozens

FIGURE 4.10 Procoptodon, the world's tallest marsupial. Measuring up to 10 feet (3 meters) in height, this short faced kangaroo had two extra long clawed fingers that were probably used to reach the leaves of high branches. The Procoptodon also went extinct around the time that humans arrived in Australia.

FIGURE 4.11 Extinct Australian megafauna. This chart illustrates species of Australian megafauna that became extinct around the time of human migration to Australia. This extinction was partly the result of climate change and partly the result of the activity of human hunters. Human stone hunting tools and evidence of other human activity were found near the remains of several of these animals.

of large marsupials disappeared, some before and others soon after the arrival of humans (Figure 4.11). Although climate change clearly played a role, most scientists are in no doubt that, both through opportunistic hunting and fire-stick farming, colonizing humans were at least partly responsible for these extinctions. In the Americas and Australia the elimination of large animals that might have been domesticable played a significant role in the possibilities and timing of the adoption of agriculture, as will be considered in the next chapter.

SUMMARY

After tracing the evolution of hominines over 7 to 6 million years from our common ancestor with chimpanzees, we crossed the sixth threshold in our story of the universe, the appearance of the human species, *H. sapiens*. We claimed that the revolutionary human trait is linguistic and that our ability to communicate with precision has resulted in Collective Learning, greatly accelerating the pace of change in human history and affecting change in planetary history. The chapter concluded by describing some of the extraordinary lifeways developed during the longest era of human history, the approximately quarter of a million years from the appearance of *H. sapiens* to the next threshold, the beginning of agriculture about 10,000 years ago.

CHAPTER QUESTIONS

1. How did our ancestors, the bipedal hominines, evolve over several million years?
2. What evidence do we use to tell the history of hominines?
3. What is symbolic language and how did it ensure that humans alone would be capable of Collective Learning?
4. How does the idea of Collective Learning explain why humans alone of all species have a history of long-term change?
5. How can we tell when and where our species, *H. sapiens*, first appeared?
6. What were two of the most important events of the Paleolithic era?
7. What do we mean by a foraging lifeway?
8. What evidence do we have about Paleolithic humans' ideas about the world?
9. What impacts did Paleolithic humans have on the environment?

KEY TERMS

Anthropocene

Australopithecines

Collective Learning

extensification

fire-stick farming

foraging

genus *Homo*

Holocene epoch

hominines

Homo erectus or *Homo ergaster*

Homo sapiens

megafaunal extinction

Milankovitch cycles

Neandertal

Paleolithic era

symbolic language

FURTHER READING

Brantingham, P. J., S. L. Kuhn, and K. W. Kerry. *The Early Upper Paleolithic beyond Western Europe.* Berkeley: University of California Press, 2004.

Deacon, Terrence W. *The Symbolic Species: The Co-evolution of Language and the Brain.* Harmondsworth, UK: Penguin, 1997; New York: Norton, 1998.

Dunbar, Robin. *The Human Story: A New History of Mankind's Evolution.* London: Faber and Faber, 2004.

Gazzaniga, Michael S. *Human: The Science behind What Makes Us Unique.* New York: Ecco/HarperCollins, 2008.

Goodall, Jane. *Through a Window: My Thirty Years with the Chimpanzees of Gombe.* Boston: Houghton Mifflin, 1990.

Green, R. E., et al. "A Draft Sequence of the Neandertal Genome." *Science* 328, no. 5979 (May 2010):710–22.

Hardy, Sarah Blaffer. *Mother Nature: A History of Mothers, Infants and Natural Selection.* New York: Pantheon, 1999.

Klein, Richard. *The Dawn of Human Culture.* New York: Wiley, 2002.

Lewis-Williams, D. *The Mind in the Cave: Consciousness and the Origin of Art.* London: Thames & Hudson, 2002.

Lee, Richard. *The Dobe !Kung.* New York: Holt, Rinehart and Winston, 1984.

Markale, Jean. *The Great Goddess: Reverence of the Divine Feminine from the Paleolithic to the Present.* Rochester, VT: Inner Traditions, 1999.

McBrearty, Sally, and Alison S. Brooks. "The Revolution That Wasn't: A New Interpretation of the Origin of Modern Human Behavior." *Journal of Human Evolution* 39 (2000):453–563.

Pinker, Steven. *The Blank Slate: The Modern Denial of Human Nature.* New York: Penguin, 2003.

Ristvet, Lauren. *In the Beginning: World History from Human Evolution to the First States.* New York: McGraw-Hill, 2007.

Scarre, Chris, ed. *The Human Past: World Prehistory and the Development of Human Societies.* London: Thames & Hudson, 2005.

Stix, Gary. "Human Origins. Traces of a Distant Past." *Scientific American,* July 2008, 56–63.

Tattersall, Ian. *Becoming Human: Evolution and Human Uniqueness.* New York: Harcourt Brace, 1998.

Wrangham, Richard. *Catching Fire: How Cooking Made Us Human.* New York: Basic Books, 2009.

ENDNOTES

1. Cited from David Christian, *Maps of Time: An Introduction to Big History,* 2nd ed. (Berkeley: University of California Press, 2011), 146.
2. Steven Pinker, *The Blank Slate: The Modern Denial of Human Nature* (New York: Penguin, 2003), 63.
3. Chris Scarre, ed., *The Human Past: World Prehistory and the Development of Human Societies* (London: Thames & Hudson, 2005), 132.
4. Sally McBrearty and Alison S. Brooks, "The Revolution That Wasn't: A New Interpretation of the Origin of Modern Human Behaviour," *Journal of Human Evolution* 39 (2000):453–563.
5. Cited from Christian, *Maps of Time,* 190.
6. Richard Lee, *The Dobe !Kung* (New York: Holt, Rinehart and Winston, 1984), 75.

chapter 5

Origins of Agriculture and the Early Agrarian Era

Seeing the Big Picture

10,000 BCE to 3500 BCE

▶ Why did humans make the transition from foraging to farming?

▶ What distinguishes a farming from a foraging lifeway?

▶ What was the Early Agrarian era?

▶ How did humans live during the thousands of years that followed the transition to agriculture?

▶ Why did power first emerge during the Early Agrarian era?

▶ What was the impact of the transition to agriculture on the environment?

After our discussion in the last chapter of our hominine ancestors, the origins of modern humans, and the Paleolithic era, this chapter focuses on arguably the most significant revolution in all human history—the emergence of **agriculture,** or increasing the productivity of those plant and animal species most beneficial for human beings. As small groups of humans across scattered regions of the globe gradually made the transition from nomadic foraging to sedentary farming, the pace of historical change began to speed up. This revolution proved so significant on the global scale that it constitutes the crossing of a seventh threshold of complexity (Threshold 7 Summary). To portray the magnitude of the agricultural revolution, this chapter discusses some fundamental questions about the nature of agriculture, why some human communities adopted it, how it profoundly impacted the biosphere, and how new forms of power emerged.

Threshold 7 Summary

THRESHOLD	INGREDIENTS ▶	STRUCTURE ▶	GOLDILOCKS CONDITIONS =	EMERGENT PROPERTIES
AGRICULTURE	Increasing Collective Learning → innovation increasing ability to manipulate and extract resources from environment and other organisms.	Human communities sharing information needed to manipulate their surroundings in new ways.	Long preceding period of Collective Learning; warmer climates; population pressure.	Increased capacity of humans to extract energy and food → larger, denser communities → increased social complexity → accelerating Collective Learning.

Threshold 7: Agriculture

Let's start with a brief survey of the situation 12,000 years ago. Geographically, humans were living on all continents of the globe, with the exception of Antarctica. Every person on the planet, no matter where they lived, pursued a foraging lifeway, although there were many different ways of doing this. As we saw in the previous chapter, human communities had invented a huge range of foraging technologies specifically adapted to different environments, ranging from African savannas to the deserts of Australia to the arctic ice. In this astonishing diversity of adaptations our species was clearly demonstrating its unique ability to learn collectively. But the small size of most human groups, and the fact that limited exchanges took place between them, meant that, by comparison with later eras of human history, the pace of Collective Learning was relatively slow during the Paleolithic era.

Then something changed. The archaeological record shows that from 12,000 to 10,000 years ago, new technologies began to appear in certain regions of the planet. These technologies gave humans access to more energy and resources. With more food and energy available, humans began to multiply more rapidly and to live in larger and denser communities like agrarian villages and even more complex communities called towns. These processes led to a new level of complexity in human societies. The adoption of agriculture was thus the first step in an economic and cultural revolution that utterly transformed human societies.

One way of demonstrating this is by considering changes to population densities. Table 5.1 shows roughly how many humans could be supported per square mile (square kilometer) by particular food production technologies.

Not all human communities adopted agriculture at the same time, and some never adopted it until later invaders

TABLE 5.1 Population Densities by Lifeway (Number of Persons per Square Mile [Square Kilometer])

Foragers	0.004–0.02/sq mi (0.01–0.05/sq km)
Pastoralists	0.077–0.38/sq mi (0.2–1.0/sq km)
Subsistence farming	0.077–4.6/sq mi (0.2–12/sq km)
Preindustrial	15.4–23/sq mi (40–60/sq km)
Modern United States	11.5/sq mi (30/sq km)
India	115/sq mi (300/sq km)
Bangladesh	347/sq mi (900/sq km)

and migrants forced it on them. This variety of experience meant that for the first time in human history the pace of change began to vary significantly from region to region. Where agriculture was adopted and denser populations appeared, the pace of change was generally faster. Where foraging remained the dominant lifeway and populations remained small and scattered, change generally occurred more slowly, although this is not to downplay the creative strategies foraging peoples continued to invent as they strove to manage wild resources. These different conditions did mean, however, that different regions of the globe began to follow different historical trajectories.

One way of understanding this is to think of the world of 10,000 years ago as being divided into four different spatial regions or "world zones"—Afro-Eurasia, the Americas, Australasia, and the Pacific. Agriculture was adopted early in parts of Afro-Eurasia and a small region of Australasia, considerably later in some regions of the Americas and the Pacific, and hardly at all in most of Australasia. The impact of the timing and geography of the agricultural revolution on subsequent human history is one of the major questions this book considers. (See Chapter 6 and the glossary for more on world zones.)

Where denser farming communities appeared, the pace of Collective Learning began to accelerate. Some regions and their populations began to change in fundamental ways, and a historical "gear shift" to a faster pace took place. The agricultural revolution put humans on a path that led directly toward the astonishing complexity of the modern world.

Explaining the Agricultural Revolution

As we saw in the previous chapter, foragers are good at finding new energy sources by spreading into new niches and environments, a process that we termed *extensification*. Farmers, on the other hand, find ways to extract more energy from a given area, a process that we call **intensification**. Foragers "harvest" and live off a wide variety of different animals and plants that are provided by natural selection. Farmers harvest a much smaller number of animals and plants, whose output they have learned to increase artificially. Both foragers and farmers have the ability to manipulate nature in significant ways, but farmers do so on an entirely unprecedented scale.

What Is Agriculture?

Defining agriculture is not as easy as it may seem. It might be best to think of it as a series of methods to increase the energy and resources available to humans by manipulating the plants, animals, and landscapes around them. Agriculture thus hinges on the establishment of a mutual interaction between plants and animals (including the human animal). This mutual interaction can evolve into a form of

symbiosis, which is a biological term to describe species' codependence. In the natural world, many organisms come to rely on each other for food or protection. Over time, this relationship begins to affect the way in which each species evolves. Some species evolve to become more and more dependent on each other until eventually they can no longer survive alone. This is symbiosis, and there are many examples in the nonhuman world.

One example is the African cultivator ant, which carefully tends and harvests fields of fungus, as an important part of its diet. Without the ant's interference, the fungus would die, and vice versa. Honeypot ants have also learned to domesticate another species, the aphid. They protect them, herd them, help them reproduce, and then milk them for honeydew. Over many generations both species have evolved to fit this symbiotic niche.

Like cultivator ants and honeypot ants, human farmers have learned to herd and otherwise manipulate useful species, such as corn and cattle, and to increase production of their domesticates. It is not just humans who benefit from this arrangement of **domestication.** Domesticated species also benefit because farmers protect them from predators and help them reproduce, ensuring their survival. (That's why there are so many sheep, cows, and dogs, and so much rice and wheat in the world today.) Over time, both humans and domesticates have come to depend on the relationship, so much so that the survival of each might be seriously endangered if the other were to disappear.

The long-term impact of this symbiotic relationship on the species involved has been different for each partner in the relationship. Humans have changed culturally as a product of domestication, leading to the discovery of new technologies and lifeways. Human communities, for example, grew from small foraging bands 10,000 years ago to complex, interdependent cities and states by around 5,000 years ago. Domesticated species have changed genetically, resulting in the evolution of new species. Teosinte, the ancestor of modern corn, is an excellent example of the evolution of domesticated plants. In its natural form, teosinte is a small, weedy, and not very nutritious plant, although it does have the ability to survive in the wild without human assistance. Modern varieties of corn are much larger and more nutritious, but have lost the ability to survive in the wild; they can no longer reproduce without active human intervention. These differing reactions to domestication illustrate the fundamental difference between human history, which is driven mainly by cultural change, and biological history, which is driven mainly by genetic change.

A Slow Revolution

The agricultural revolution took place at first in a few widely separated areas of the globe and then gradually spread to other regions in a process that has continued up to the present day (Map 5.1). Until the late twentieth century, most archaeologists imagined the advent of agriculture as a quite rapid process and an abrupt break from foraging. However, over the past decade researchers have

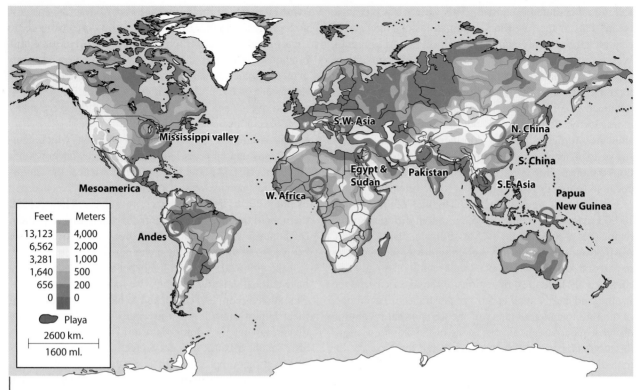

MAP 5.1 Early agricultural sites.

argued that fully developed domestication probably took many thousands of years to occur, rather than the few centuries previously envisaged. New data suggest that the road from gathering plants in the wild, then cultivating and finally domesticating them, was long and convoluted. Part of this chronological revision is the product of work on plant genomes, looking for genetic evidence of physical changes as a product of domestication. It appears, for example, that humans were using wild cereals for thousands of years before full-blown domestication resulted in the emergence of telltale genetic changes in these same plants.

Evidence of just how long humans were gathering and utilizing wild cereal crops comes from the archaeological site of Ohalo II, a village with huts, hearths, and burial chambers located on the southwestern shore of the Sea of Galilee in Israel. The settlement has been dated to 23,000 BCE (10,000 years before plant domestication occurred). Excavators found evidence of more than 90,000 individual plants that had been eaten by the inhabitants, including wild olives, pistachios, acorns, and a large quantity of wild wheat and barley. Although there is no genetic evidence of any attempted domestication of these plants, researchers did discover remains of wheat and barley on stone implements, suggesting that the residents were grinding grains to make flour and probably baking dough in the hearths. This shows that humans were harvesting and using wild cereals for many millennia before any attempt was made to domesticate them.

The earliest sites and dates for the emergence of agriculture are still open to interpretation, and there is considerable disagreement among specialists. Table 5.2 provides the approximate dates where archaeologists have found evidence of the earliest attempts at domestication in various regions of the world. Of course, foraging peoples initiated the first successful domestication long before the first farmers—the domestication of the dog. Although the oldest known remains of a domesticated dog date to a little over 10,000 years ago, DNA evidence indicates an initial domestication of at least 15,000 years ago.

The Transition to Agriculture

Many theories have been proposed over the past several decades to explain the transition to agriculture. An initial

TABLE 5.2 Sites and Dates for the Emergence of Agriculture (BCE)

Southwest Asia (Fertile Crescent) 9000
Egypt and the Sudan (Nile valley) 8000
China (Yangtze and Huang He valleys) 7000
Australasia (New Guinea Highlands) 7000–4000
Sub-Saharan Africa 3000–2000
Indus valley 2200
Mesoamerica (Central Mexico) 3000–2000
South America (Andes and Amazonia) 3000–2000
North America (Eastern United States) 2000–1000

argument was that some creative individual must have "invented" it, and everyone else subsequently copied it. Although this seems logical at first, a problem quickly emerged with this theory. Archaeology shows unequivocally that agriculture emerged separately in different parts of the world within a few millennia. Many of these early farming regions had no contact with each other, so copying could not have occurred. This is most probably true of China and New Guinea, and certainly the case in the Americas, a world zone that was geographically isolated from Afro-Eurasia, but where very similar processes of domestication occurred.

Archaeology also indicates that foragers did not always see agriculture as a more attractive lifeway. Foraging persisted for centuries or even millennia in close proximity to early farming communities. For example, foraging communities in both the Kalahari Desert of southern Africa and the Cape York area of northern Australia knew about farming and even lived in close proximity to agricultural communities, but apparently chose not to adopt it. Along with the fact that many Australian and Kalahari environments were less conducive to agriculture, it also appears that not everyone wanted to be a farmer, perhaps because an agricultural lifeway was often a lot more physically demanding, less healthy, and more stressful than foraging. (Remember our discussion of the original affluent society in the previous chapter?) Analysis of skeletal remains shows that early farmers were also subject to new diseases, many of which spread from domesticated animals to humans, as well as greater levels of stress. There is even evidence of decreased human life spans and increased infant mortality rates among early farming communities. Life was tough for the first farmers!

Although much bigger than Tasmania, the Australian mainland was also largely isolated from other human populations and agriculture never developed. It is a reasonable presumption that here there were simply no regions where farming was clearly more beneficial than foraging. In general, Australian soils were poor and population densities low. The total population of the continent was probably no more than a few hundred thousand when Europeans arrived at the end of the eighteenth century, though there were certainly areas, particularly along the coasts, where populations were much denser than inland. There is also the largely contingent fact that Australia, unlike Mesopotamia, did not evolve easily domesticable plant species. The macadamia nut is the only indigenous plant to have been domesticated in modern times, although there were some potential domesticates, including types of yam and taro that were farmed in Papua New Guinea and gathered by Australians.

This evidence suggests that the "brilliant idea" theory—the appearance of some Paleolithic Einstein—to explain the emergence of agriculture simply does not work. An alternative approach, more widely accepted today, explains the agricultural revolution as a step-by-step process in which conscious human planning played a limited role. This "evolutionary, not revolutionary" account focuses on climate change and the emergence of environmental conditions that facilitated the transition from foraging to farming, coupled with demographic pressure as a result of increasing population densities in some regions.

The Role of Climate

The last cycle of the most recent ice age began around 110,000 years ago, and as the ice sheets spread and sea levels fell, global temperatures dropped to their coldest level between 21,000 and 16,000 years ago (see Chapter 4). During the so-called glacial maximum, conditions were so cold that forests disappeared and frigid tundra covered much of the planet. These harsh conditions, along with wildly fluctuating variability, meant that agriculture could not possibly have been established during most of the Pleistocene (a geological epoch lasting from 1.8 million to 13,000 years ago). Indeed, with animal migration paths so often altered, and with different plant species emerging and disappearing, hunter-gathering was a much better survival strategy for human communities in the Pleistocene.

With the beginning of a new geological epoch—the **Holocene epoch,** which commenced some 13,000 years ago (see Chapter 4)—Earth experienced a rapid global warming and the last ice age came to an end, although not without a final sting in the shape of a brief global cold snap during the Younger Dryas (from about 12,800 BP to 11,500 BP). Recent excavations at the site of Abu Hureyra in Syria's Euphrates valley have suggested that the Younger Dryas may have decimated wild cereal crops and caused people to domesticate rye to cope with food shortages. Other archaeologists argue convincingly that only after the Younger Dryas had been replaced by the more stable Holocene does farming begin to appear in the archaeological record at most sites.

With the advent of the Holocene, not only did conditions become warmer, more stable, and generally more benign, but entire landscapes were transformed as rainfall became more reliable. Rainfall increased because higher global temperatures meant more evaporation from the oceans, a factor that modern climate change scientists take into account in their forecasts of the potential impact of global warming in the future. Because of this increased rainfall early in the Holocene, forests spread into regions that had previously been cold steppes, and this in turn displaced many of the large steppe species like mammoths and bison that had grazed there. As the herds of large animals that humans had depended on during the Paleolithic migrated northward or were hunted to extinction, communities were forced to become dependent on smaller game like boar, deer, and rabbit, as well as new root and seed plants. Upper Paleolithic foraging communities were able to experiment with a wide suite of plant and animal species and to eat a "broad-spectrum" diet. This experimentation led eventually to the emergence of full-blown agriculture.

A Cultural and Biological Adaptation Model

American archaeologist Peter Richerson and his colleagues believe that the adoption of agriculture during the Holocene not only became possible but in the long run compulsory. As different groups experimented with domestication they increased in size relative to foraging bands. Richerson contends that subsequent intergroup competition more or less forced communities to adopt farming, leading to its inevitable diffusion.

Attempts by researchers like Richerson to combine environmental with sociological factors offer a more convincing explanation of the origins of agriculture than those that rely on single factors. We follow a multicausal theoretical model of both cultural and biological adaptation, at the heart of which remains the critical role of climate, fundamental to any explanation. The five steps we use to describe this process can be summarized as follows:

Step 1 (Precondition 1): Humans already possessed a lot of the necessary knowledge and skills for agriculture.

Step 2 (Precondition 2): Some plant and animal species were "preadapted" as potential "domesticates."

Step 3: Humans in certain key regions of the globe were already adopting less nomadic lifestyles and becoming at least "part-time" sedentary.

Step 4: As a result of climate change and population pressure, these communities found themselves caught in the "trap of **sedentism.**" Their sedentary lifeway, or living in one place for most of the year, made further intensification absolutely necessary to avoid starvation among increased populations. This in turn led to step 5.

Step 5: Agriculture, the only remaining option.

Step 1 (Precondition 1): Humans Already Possessed Much of the Necessary Knowledge and Skills for Agriculture

Agriculture depends on the process of domestication, which applies not only to individual plant and animal species, but also to entire landscapes. In a desire to feed, protect, and propagate our species, humans have domesticated vast areas of the planet and entire ecosystems. Today, some 50 percent of the world's surface area has been domesticated to suit grazing and land cultivation, and more than half of the world's forests have been lost in that transformation.[1] This is not a new phenomenon; since our appearance on the planet more than 200,000 years ago, humans have been manipulating species and landscapes to enhance their food supply and reduce their exposure to predators. We can say that foragers were "preadapted" culturally to understanding plants and animals and to manipulating the natural environment. Foragers had also demonstrated their ability to radically transform their environments through practices like fire-stick farming and the hunting strategies that led to megafaunal extinctions (see Chapter 4). But the scale of that manipulation increased dramatically with the appearance of agriculture.

Step 2 (Precondition 2): Some Plant and Animal Species Were Preadapted as Potential Domesticates

At the same time, purely by chance, some plant and animal species had evolved in a way that made them more suitable for domestication than others. Not all plants and animals are open to domestication. Only about 100 plants have become valuable domesticates. Farmers have been able to domesticate only 14 of the 148 species of land mammals on the planet because potential animal domesticates have to meet demanding criteria, including rapid growth, regular birthrates, a herd mentality, and a good disposition.

Of the hundred or so plant domesticates, wheat is a prime example of a species genetically preadapted for domestication. The domestication in Southwest Asia of three cereals in particular—einkorn and emmer wheat and barley—effectively marks the beginning of the transition from foraging to agriculture (Figure 5.1). Plant geneticists have used genetic relationships between wild and domesticated einkorn and emmer to contend that the region west of Diyarbakir in southeastern Turkey is the most likely site of their initial domestication. If this is correct, domesticated einkorn and emmer spread from this site across Afro-Eurasia, and eventually to the rest of the world. Today our planet produces over 620 million tons (562.45 metric tons) of wheat each year, which provides roughly one-fifth of the calories consumed by the 6.7 billion members of the human community.

FIGURE 5.1 Early wheat domesticates. The domestication in Southwest Asia of emmer wheat and barley was critical to the transition from foraging to agriculture.

There were many such promising potential domesticate species. In Southwest Asia, a region called the Fertile Crescent had just the right climate, fertility, and soils for agriculture, as well as a wide suite of wild species growing and grazing. The Fertile Crescent is an arc of high ground that stretches north up the eastern Mediterranean, east through the mountains of eastern Turkey and northern Iraq, then south along high ground to the east of the Tigris and Euphrates river valleys. The abundant potential of the Fertile Crescent is one obvious reason why agriculture began there, an argument proffered by environmental world historian Jared Diamond in his book *Guns, Germs, and Steel.*

Conversely, the Americas lacked an easily domesticable cereal species. As we have seen, teosinte, the ancestor to corn, did not have large ears of grain like emmer and einkorn wheat. Instead teosinte had small, nutlike kernels distributed in small, feathery knobs over numerous tertiary branches. It took early American farmers many generations of selective breeding of teosinte to produce genetic changes that resulted in larger ears, more rows of kernels, and softer casings. This delayed the widespread availability of a nutritious and successful grain crop in the American world zone.

Step 3: Humans in Certain Key Regions of the Globe Were Already Adopting Less Nomadic Lifestyles and Becoming at Least "Part-Time" Sedentary

Archaeological evidence demonstrates that sedentism increased in some parts of the world from about 15,000 years ago. Climate change and population pressure accounted for this. As climates became warmer and wetter at the end of the last ice age, large numbers of humans settled in areas of natural abundance. It is no coincidence that the biblical "Garden of Eden" was located in Southwest Asia. The people who settled in these regions were not farming at first, just living off the abundant natural fruits of the land. Their sedentism eventually led to overpopulation because sedentary peoples do not have the same constraints on population growth that nomadic peoples do.

Migration contributed to the pressures of overpopulation. Many of these same regions of abundance were also natural funnels for human migration. Southwest Asia is a clear example because it is a principal conduit for people moving between Africa and Eurasia. Similarly, migrants moving between the two large American continents had to pass through Mesoamerica, which may help explain the dense populations that eventually settled there. Certainly by about 10,000 years ago there is evidence in the form of an increasing number of archaeological sites that these interregional migrations had led to localized population pressure.

Human communities that, as a result of climate change, were able to abandon nomadism and adopt sedentism while still pursuing hunter-gathering lifeways have been described as "affluent foragers"—foragers who have access to sufficient resources that they can settle down and become "sedentarized." In Australia, for example, some groups of aboriginals abandoned full-time nomadism, built

fish weirs, and settled in villages nearby. The Gunditjmara people of southeastern Australia may have "farmed" eels for thousands of years. They were not nomadic but lived in large, permanent villages and had powerful chiefs. In other words, even though they were not farmers, they had adopted many of the social and political features of agrarian society. Archaeologists have found evidence of the remains of hundreds of permanent huts, 45 square miles (116 square kilometers) of artificial channels and ponds for farming the eels, and trees used for smoking the product to facilitate its transportation to other parts of southeastern Australia.

Yet, despite this affluent foraging lifeway, and the relative proximity of northern Australia to agriculturalists in New Guinea and nearby islands, indigenous Australians never moved beyond affluent foraging and took up agriculture. A range of geographic, climatic, and social theories, none of them wholly convincing, have been promoted to try to explain the fact that when European explorers arrived in Australia, the continent was populated entirely by humans pursuing foraging lifeways. The most likely explanation would be that indigenous Australians, particularly in coastal regions, lived in a land of relative plenty, and that with such an abundance of resources there was simply no attraction in abandoning a successful nomadic lifeway for a more demanding and stressful lifeway based on the cultivation of yams and taro. To this day some traditional aboriginal groups enjoy foraging and prefer the taste of "bush tucker" to commercial, processed foods.

Evidence of affluent foraging lifeways has also been discovered in Mesoamerica, the Baltic coasts, Egypt and the Sudan, and the eastern Mediterranean. Humans living along both the Gulf and Pacific coasts of Mesoamerica enjoyed such an abundance of marine resources that they had become sedentarized by 5,000 years ago. Mostly sedentary communities of affluent foragers also emerged along the shores of the Baltic Sea, where they developed an extraordinary array of fishing, hunting, and gathering technologies at sites that were occupied continuously between 1500 and 300 BCE. Much earlier evidence of affluent foragers has been discovered along the Nile valley near Aswan, where settlements dated to 15,000 BP have yielded fishing, hunting, and grain-harvesting tools.[2]

Significant affluent foraging communities developed in West Asia, in the western Fertile Crescent (present-day Israel, Jordan, Lebanon, and Syria) from about 14,000 years ago. The first evidence for this came to light in 1928, with discoveries made by Dorothy Garrod at Wadi en-Natuf in northern Israel. Hence the culture is called "Natufian." These people lived in villages, harvested wild grains, and hunted gazelles. The Natufian toolkit is not necessarily any more sophisticated than that of their predecessors, although their more intense use of sickle blades is evidence of a widespread change in food-gathering practices (Figure 5.2). Their grain was also subject to far higher levels of processing than before. Standard mortars and grinding stones were supplemented by higher-volume bedrock mortars, which are depressions in rock outcrops or slabs used for the communal grinding of grain.

FIGURE 5.2 Natufians. Artist's impression of Natufian affluent foragers harvesting wild grain in the western Fertile Crescent.

The construction of regular cemeteries further distinguishes the Natufians, providing evidence of complex communities with leaders and possible social hierarchies. A number of individuals were buried wearing a range of personal adornments—caps, bracelets, garters—that could be indicators of status. Although there might be little direct evidence of hierarchies, archaeologists have not been able to account for the fact that only a tiny minority of the population was apparently "selected" for ceremonial burial within or beside Natufian settlements.[3]

Evidence that the Natufian diet consisted mainly of harvested and prepared cereal grains was discovered at Ain Mallaha in Syria. Skeletal remains showed that most individuals had suffered from rotten teeth as a result of eating too much barley gruel and wheat flatbread. Ain Mallaha, like all the Natufian sites, also provides clear evidence of sedentary lifeways and increased population densities as a result of Natufian intensification of affluent foraging lifeways. Although Ain Mallaha's estimated year-round population of 200 to 300 might seem tiny by today's standards, this may have been one of the largest human communities that had ever existed up to that time.[4] Natufians were probably also the founders of the world's oldest city, Jericho, excavated by Kathleen Kenyon in the late 1950s. After digging her way down to prepottery levels of occupation, radiocarbon dates proved that Jericho had been continuously occupied since 9600 BCE. Even more significantly, evidence of an earlier Natufian occupation of the site was discovered, stretching back to 12,000 BCE. We will return to the story of Jericho later in the chapter.

Eventually population pressures resulting from sedentism, local population growth, and continuing migration into the region forced human communities into smaller and smaller territories. By 10,000 BCE foragers had migrated to most parts of the world, and in some areas there was not enough room for them all to settle. With each group having to survive off smaller and smaller parcels of land, and with no more room for further migration, these communities found themselves caught in what we call the *trap of sedentism*.

Step 4: Human Communities Were Caught in the Trap of Sedentism

Once human groups were able to remain in one place through the pursuit of affluent foraging lifeways, there were no longer the same mobility constraints on population. Older members of the community did not have to be abandoned; communities were able to support more children. Larger populations also provided more labor resources. As a result of sedentism populations grew among affluent foraging groups (as Natufian villages demonstrate), leading eventually to the problem of overpopulation.

All the Natufian sites provide evidence of sedentism and increasingly dense local populations, suggesting that there may eventually have been too many people to support by affluent foraging practices. Excavations at the site of Ain Ghazal on the outskirts of Amman, Jordan, show that around 7000 BCE the settlement experienced a rapid fourfold increase in population, as a result of both natural population growth and migration from other nearby settlements. This put so much pressure on the settlement that increasingly desperate and environmentally unsustainable attempts were made to intensify crop harvests, including overtilling and forest clearing (which increased soil erosion), as well as overgrazing of goats (which prevented tree regeneration). At Ain Ghazal some groups of people left the settlement to pursue pastoralist and agricultural lifeways in the moist steppes of the region.

Faced with increasing populations, affluent foragers were left with few alternative survival strategies. A return to a nomadic, foraging lifeway was impossible because of continuing climate change and a lack of space, and after many generations of affluent foraging, the skills of the nomadic hunter-gatherer may well have been lost. The alternative was to concentrate on increasing the productivity of the crops and animals available to the community by removing unwanted trees or plants (weeding and deforestation); planting, tending, and harvesting desirable plant species (domestication); and tending and manipulating desirable and useful animal species (herding). In other words, the only viable option available for affluent foragers faced with overpopulation pressure and climate change was to intensify cultivation and adopt farming.

Step 5: Farming: The Only Remaining Option

One way of testing the general process outlined in this five-step account is to compare the transition to farming in West Asia, where the model seems to work very well, with what happened in other parts of the world, such as in China and the Americas. In central China the arrival of warmer, wetter weather following the end of the Younger Dryas gave hunter-gatherers access to herds of wild cattle and sheep and to a range of wild grasses that appeared in great profusion, particularly green foxtail millet. Sites such as Xueguan and Shizitan, excavated in the Fen River valley, provide clear evidence that the residents were pursuing affluent foraging lifeways, still surviving through hunting and gathering, but adopting sedentism. Although no transitional site has yet been unearthed, evidence of numerous sedentary Early Agrarian era farming villages begins appearing in the region from 6000 BCE, notably Cishan and Peiligang, suggesting that these communities were largely surviving through the domestication of millet 8,000 years ago.

In southern China, along the middle reaches of the Yangtze River, a warming climate soon after 8000 BCE led to an expansion of lakes along the river valley, which facilitated the spread of wild rice. Two sites in particular have provided evidence of the transition from foraging to farming. A cave at Diaotonghuan has yielded stratigraphic rice phytolith finds from wild, intermediate, and domesticated rice species. (A *phytolith,* which means "plant stone," is a rigid microscopic body that is found in many plants. Because inorganic phytoliths don't decay with the rest of the plant's organic material, they provide important evidence for bioarchaeologists.) Radiometric dating of phytoliths indicates that rice was probably being collected in the wild by foragers soon after 11,200 BCE, but that it disappeared from the site during the Younger Dryas cold snap, when the plant itself may have retreated south. Wild rice then returned to the valley as the climate warmed again and was apparently being domesticated by the residents by at least 6000 BCE. Diaotonghuan provides indisputable evidence of the increasing availability of a domesticable crop species because of climate change, and of the adoption of sedentary lifeways by affluent foragers, which led inevitably to population increases and the eventual domestication of rice.[5]

In North, Central, and South America the same trend is reflected in the archaeological record. A climate-related increase in the availability of different food sources led to increased sedentism and subsequent population pressure, which in turn trapped humans into having to adopt more labor-intensive cultivation practices and, eventually, full-scale agriculture. In Mexico, for example, the period ca. 9500 to 2500 BCE is characterized by high foraging mobility until, certainly by 2500 BCE and perhaps

earlier, humans were living in numerous agricultural villages that have been discovered and dated by archaeologists. The earliest crop species was squash, followed later by common beans and the chili pepper. The Mexican sites of Zohapilco and San Andreas appear to have been occupied long term by affluent foragers who eventually made the transition to farming, although the dates for this transition and for the first evidence of domestication remain difficult to pin down.

In North America, a conservative date for the domestication of corn in the Mogollon highlands of New Mexico is about 1500 BCE. The Phillips Spring site in Missouri suggests that the transition from gathering wild gourds to cultivation and eventual domestication of the species had started by as early as about 2500 BCE. In South America, the Tres Ventanas caves in the central highlands of Peru provide the earliest evidence of potato, gourd, and sweet potato in the diets of affluent foragers living there. The potato has been dated to about 5500 BCE, although its domestication status is unclear because these species were also growing in the wild in this beneficial environmental niche. Once the shift from affluent foraging to full-scale agriculture was made, virtually every South American site indicates the rapid development of complex, sedentary societies, and increased population densities, particularly along the Pacific Coast.[6]

Contemporary semiagricultural communities offer a glimpse back to the early stages of the process we have been describing in this chapter. The Yanomami of the Amazon basin, for example, have long practiced a simple form of swidden (or slash-and-burn) agriculture. They "weed out" excessive trees and undergrowth to provide more sunlight and nutrition for their fields and crops. The Yanomami dwelt in relative isolation in the Amazon rain forest along the Brazilian–Venezuelan border, but since their "discovery" in the twentieth century they have become one of the most studied groups in modern anthropology. Their shifting agricultural practice is based on the cultivation of the plantain and cassava (Figure 5.3), but they also fish, hunt,

FIGURE 5.3 Yanomami. A Yanomami "farm" in the Amazon basin. Using slash-and-burn agriculture, the Yanomami "weed out" excessive trees and undergrowth to provide more sunlight and nutrition for their fields and crops.

and gather forest foods. They live in villages of anywhere between 50 and 400 people, which are abandoned every year or two as the group moves on to a new area of the forest. These larger population densities led to an increasingly complex society. Although many marriages are monogamous, large polygamous families are common, based on one man and several women's family units. Domestic violence and warfare are common among the Yanomami, as males compete for women, status, and even slaves. The Yanomami pursue a hybrid lifeway somewhere between nomadic foraging and sedentary agriculture. Although we must realize that they have been affected by the modern world, the Yanomami provide a sort of living snapshot of the dramatic changes in human lifeways and societies that emerged as a product of the transition from foraging to farming.

The Early Agrarian Era

With the emergence of agriculture, human history entered a new stage in those regions where farming was being practiced. We call this stage the **Early Agrarian era.** This era is largely ignored in world history books, where there is often an implied assumption that the adoption of agriculture led directly to cities, states, and civilizations. This section of the chapter reminds us that these large power structures did not appear until several thousand years later. In fact, the Early Agrarian era was almost as long as the entire period from the first appearance of cities to today! How did early farmers live then? What were the earliest agricultural communities like? How did agriculture continue to spread, until increased population densities more or less demanded the concentration of large numbers of humans in complex cities and states?

When we use the term *Early Agrarian era* we are discussing societies that were clearly based on agriculture (i.e., everyone was being fed by agriculture). Yet these societies functioned without cities, states, or what is often referred to as "civilization." Early Agrarian societies still exist today in some parts of the world (the Yanomami and in the highlands of Papua New Guinea, for example) but they are marginal in the extreme. For 5,000 of the last 10,000 years, however, such societies dominated human lifeways and were the largest and most complex of all human communities.

Dates for the era globally vary substantially from region to region. In some parts of the world (Southwest Asia, for example), the era began roughly 11,000 years ago (i.e., about 9000 BCE) and continued there until the first appearance of cities and states some 5,200 years ago. But in other parts of the world, agriculture, and cities and states, appeared much later, while in yet other regions cities and states never appeared. In this chapter we are looking at roughly 6,000 years of human history, between about 9000 and 3000 BCE—that is, from the earliest evidence of agriculture to the appearance of the first cities and states.

The adoption of agriculture in certain regions meant that human history began to follow a very different trajectory in those world zones. Since agriculture first appeared in Afro-Eurasia, it subsequently housed the largest populations and had the greatest variety of domesticated plants and animals. The Americas, where agriculture appeared later, had the next largest populations and also considerable ecological variety, although its potential domesticable plants were not as nutritious as the wild grasses of Afro-Eurasia, and it had few potential animal domesticates, probably because early human hunters had driven them to extinction.

In Australasia, agriculture appeared early, but remained very limited in scope. Populations remained small, partly because farmers were faced with limited ecological variety and the absence of potential animal domesticates. True agriculture occurred only in Papua New Guinea, where the main crop was the taro plant. Farming never took hold in Australia, where aboriginals continued to pursue their successful foraging lifeways until the arrival of Europeans just over two centuries ago. In the Pacific world zone, farming spread much later through successful long-range canoe migrations, although the similarity of ecological environments limited the range of potential domesticates, and the fragility of many island environments limited population densities.

Technologies and Productivity in the Early Agrarian Era

Early farmers faced limitations on the amount of food they could produce. These included a shortage of energy and labor; a shortage of fertilizer and/or nutrients; and a shortage of water.

In the Early Agrarian era most energy and labor came from humans, so children became increasingly important as potential farm laborers. Apparently people had no understanding of the potential benefits of animal fertilizer for thousands of years, until the so-called secondary products revolution that we describe in the next chapter. For much of the era there was very limited use of irrigation. The coercive power of states was probably needed to carry it out on any large scale, which became increasingly necessary with continuing climate change and increasing populations.

The three main early farming technologies (or methods) that early farmers adopted reflected these limitations. The technologies were horticulture; swidden, or slash-and-burn agriculture; and chinampa agriculture. **Horticulture** resembles the sort of market gardening that many subsistence and community gardeners continued to pursue in the twentieth century. It used traditional techniques and implements such as stone axes hafted onto wooden handles for clearing the land; foot plows and hoes for planting; bone or stone sickles hafted onto wooden handles for harvesting; and stones for grinding grain. Since human labor supplied all the energy, the effectiveness of these tools and implements was critical (Figure 5.4). These same tools have provided important evidence for archaeologists as they attempt to understand and date human lifeways during the Early Agrarian era.

TRAVAXOS
PAPAALLAIMITAPA

Foot plow

Hoe

FIGURE 5.4 Horticulture. Harvesting potatoes in seventeenth-century Peru using horticultural tools (a foot plow and hoe) and techniques. Human labor is the basic source of energy.

One Chinese site provides an example of the technological innovation going on within horticultural communities during the Early Agrarian era. At Cishan in the Yellow River valley, Early Agrarian layers have been excavated and dated to between 6000 and 5700 BCE. Hundreds of pits were discovered, apparently built to store grain to provide sustenance for residents during the winter months. Stone spades and stone mortars and pestles were also found, used for the cultivation of millet, which was eaten from round bowls and three-legged platters.

Swidden agriculture, also known as slash-and-burn agriculture, is still practiced by the Yanomami people of the Amazon basin today. Faced with extensive forests, early swidden farmers "weeded out" excessive trees and undergrowth to provide more sunlight and nutrition for their fields, crops, and grazing animals. They selected an area of forest, cut the vegetation with hand axes or cleared through burning, and cultivated the plots for a limited period of one to five years. Once the fertility of a particular piece of land was exhausted, the community simply moved on to a new region of forest and began the slash-and-burn process all over again. In temperate regions of North America and Europe, farmers have largely abandoned swidden agriculture, but it persists in tropical rain forests today as the Yanomami demonstrate.

Chinampa agriculture, devised by Mesoamerican farmers, means growing crops on human-made floating fields of timber and soil, anchored in the middle of lakes (Figure 5.5). Since the use of chinampa agriculture is associated with Aztec urbanization, it is described in more detail in Chapter 9.

These early Agrarian technologies were much less productive than later farming technologies. Yet they were much more productive than those of the Paleolithic, and as they slowly improved in efficiency and productivity, human populations began to increase faster. Demographers estimate that by the end of the Paleolithic era, human populations may have reached at most 10 million; they estimate that during the Early Agrarian era the global human population increased to around 50 million, a fivefold increase in 6,000 years.

The Spread of Agriculture

Remember, agriculture developed independently in a few geographically isolated regions, based on the availability of suitable potential domesticates. Once established in these "centers of origin," farming began to spread inexorably around the globe. In some regions this spread was rapid, particularly across Afro-Eurasia, where the general east–west orientation of the world zone facilitated the transfer of domestic species across climatically similar environments. In other regions the spread was slowed by the need to adjust to climates at different latitudes.

Farming spread either because hunter-gathers adopted it or because hunter-gatherers were displaced by expanding agricultural communities, although archaeological evidence makes it difficult to distinguish which of these factors was most responsible in different regions. Certainly farming offers a demographic advantage over foraging, but as populations gradually increased, agricultural

FIGURE 5.5 Chinampa. Devised by Mesoamerican farmers, chinampa agriculture involves growing crops on human-made floating fields of timber and soil, anchored in the middle of lakes.

communities were faced with continuing sustainability problems. With more and more mouths to feed from limited numbers of crops and animals, families were forced to move on and clear new land. Not only did this mean that existing communities grew in size, but also that new farming communities were continuously being created. Researchers Ammerman and Cavalli-Sforza borrowed from the field of population biology to argue for a **wave of advance model.** They argue that population growth at the periphery of farming communities, in combination with local migration patterns, inevitably resulted in an increase in the range of agricultural populations as farmers moved steadily outward in all environmentally suitable directions.

Because the archaeological evidence on the causes and rate of this expansion can be ambiguous, two new approaches have emerged to help historians trace the spread of agriculture: the distribution of languages and genetic studies. Linguistic evidence has been used to show that in the Pacific world zone, speakers of Austronesian languages carried the cultivation of rice from China to Taiwan in about 3000 BCE, then to the Philippines by a thousand years later. Here they domesticated new crop species and then carried these to remote island groups of the Pacific in a series of stunning canoe migrations over the next 2,000 years. (See Chapter 9 for more on these migrations.) The displacement by migrant farmers of native hunter-gatherer populations living in Southeast Asia is demonstrated by the spread of languages, particularly by evidence of the movement of cognate words for "rice" as farmers migrated into new regions.

In sub-Saharan Africa, migrations by people speaking Bantu languages during the first millennium BCE helped spread cattle herding and sorghum and millet farming throughout the continent. The original homeland of these Bantu-speaking peoples may have been the savanna of modern-day Cameroon. From here, migrants spread south following savanna corridors through the forest, perhaps during a dry climate phase. Language evidence helps support the idea that it was the migration of these Bantu-speakers that facilitated the spread of farming throughout Africa.

Genetic researchers believe that farming communities probably carried a distinct genetic imprint of some sort as they moved and that this might be traceable in modern populations. However, the results of this work are ambiguous, and studies of mitochondrial-DNA (mtDNA), Y-chromosome DNA, and nuclear DNA have differed in their conclusions as to how much, for example, early Southwest Asian farmers contributed to the European gene pool. Some mtDNA studies indicate a contribution of West Asian farmers to the European gene pool of roughly 20 percent, but Y-chromosome studies have yielded results of up to 65 percent. The difference between the mtDNA percentages (which are inherited through the female line) and Y-chromosome DNA percentages (which are passed on by males) could be interpreted as evidence of a migration into Europe by male farmers who married indigenous foraging women. Recent work using mtDNA, Y-chromosome DNA, and other autosomal markers suggests that the Early Agrarian era contribution to the European gene pool is much higher than 20 percent in some regions and that it decreases from east to west (from as high as 85 percent in Greece to 15 percent in France) as would be expected in an expansion generating in West Asia.

A 2010 study comparing Early Agrarian era settlements in Turkey and northern Europe offers further support for the wave of advance model. Genetic analysis of domesticated animals and the skeletons of early farmers suggest that around 8000 BCE a mass migration of farmers began from Southwest Asia into Europe. These agriculturalists brought their domesticated cattle and pigs with them. Because of a genetic mutation, the farmers were able to drink and digest large quantities of raw cow's milk (something that the early *Homo sapiens* was originally unable to do), and this allowed for significant population growth. There are indications of conflict at some sites between the native foraging communities and the migrating farmers (the remains of 34 bodies that had been beaten to death with clubs were found near the German town of Talheim, for example), but also of occasional bartering and trade. The settlers advanced across the Balkans, then north into present-day Austria, Hungary, Germany, and Slovakia, and this relentless wave of migration led eventually to the demise of foraging populations across northern Europe.[7]

An even more recent 2010 study of mtDNA extracted from the bones of 8,000-year-old individuals found in a graveyard in Derenberg, Germany, also supports the wave of advance model, but offers evidence of interbreeding between farmers and foragers, rather than of conflict and displacement. The extracted mtDNA is a very close match to that of people living in modern Turkey and Iraq, further demonstrating that farming was most probably brought to Europe by migrants, rather than adopted by existing foragers. Unlike the archaeological study noted in the previous paragraph, however, the Derenberg mtDNA evidence suggests that foragers did not "die out" as a result of the migration of farmers, but rather mingled together to produce offspring of mixed genetic ancestry.[8]

Whatever the prime movers driving the expansion of agriculture, the indisputable result was that the number of farming communities increased during the Early Agrarian era until, by about 5,000 years ago, most people on Earth were farming for a living. Around 10,000 years ago agriculture was practiced only in Southwest Asia and perhaps Papua New Guinea. By 7,000 years ago farming had emerged in the hilly regions above the Indus valley in present-day Pakistan and along the Huang He and Yangtze river valleys in China. By the end of the Early Agrarian era some 5,000 years ago, agriculture had become the dominant lifeway in Europe, the Balkans, sub-Saharan Africa, and probably parts of Central and South America as well. Since increased population densities in all these regions enhanced the opportunities for Collective Learning, the Early Agrarian era introduced a new social dynamism into human history.

Increasing Social Complexity in the Early Agrarian Era

Farmers lived in permanent dwellings clustered together in a variety of villages. There were no cities and no states, and villagers dwelt in communities ranging in size from a dozen or so households to several thousands. For humans in the Early Agrarian era, the village was your world! This did not mean, however, that the Early Agrarian was an era of uniformity, because there was no single template for what a village should be. Because the villages differed substantially, so too did the lives of the people who lived in them.

Living permanently in the same settlement had major consequences for human societies; living in large, dense communities revolutionized the daily lives of residents. The tensions and conflicts that inevitably arose in these settlements required mechanisms to defuse conflicts, because families were now basically trapped into having to get on with their neighbors. Anthropologists describe this as the tension between *centrifugal* tendencies (the good of the community) and *centripetal* tendencies (the good of the individual family). The origins of government and legal institutions that subsequently appeared late in the Agrarian era can be traced back to these early village tensions. These relationships also led to an increase in social complexity, because larger group sizes and the emergence of private property created emerging issues of authority, gender differences, and questions of status for the first time in human history. Basic anthropological theory states that the larger the group, the more explicitly power and authority will be exercised; and gradually throughout the Early Agrarian era, the egalitarianism of Paleolithic kinship groups was replaced by steep hierarchies of wealth and power, evidenced by burials around the world with great differences in the abundance and value of burial goods.

The Early Agrarian Village

Although all farming communities display evidence of increasing complexity, the actual day-to-day experience of village life differed substantially, depending on the conditions and environmental location of the settlement. The emergence of the village was itself an evolutionary process, because simply settling in one place is not the same as creating a well-organized village. The earliest dwellings at Abu Hureya in the Euphrates valley were small, round, thatch-roofed houses sunk into the mud, which were apparently occupied by affluent foragers. The community was abandoned in about 9600 BCE, but was reoccupied by early farmers in about 8800 BCE. The settlement then grew rapidly to become a large village, with rectangular mud-brick buildings (which, unlike the circular structures, could more easily have rooms added on to them); they contained storage rooms on the ground floor and dwellings above.

An important early South Asian farming village was uncovered in the 1970s at the site of Mehrgarh in western Pakistan. Mehrgarh was occupied continuously from 6500 to 2800 BCE and is the earliest known Agrarian era community so far discovered in South Asia. It was situated not far from the Bolan River, but also adjacent to the Bolan Pass, a major passage connecting the highlands of the Indo–Iranian plateau with the plains of the Indus River. In the earliest layers of habitation, the houses consisted of rectangular mud-brick buildings divided into rooms and small compartments (which probably served as grain stores). Barley and wheat were the principal crops grown, augmented with dates and the hunting of wild gazelle and zebu cattle. In the prepottery phase, tombs yielded both practical and exotic artifacts, including sickles, baskets lined with bitumen, marine shells, and turquoise. After 6000 BCE, pottery appears in tombs; there is also genetic evidence of the domestication of the zebu cattle and possibly the earliest evidence known of domesticated cotton. Mehrgarh is a particularly significant discovery because it provides rare evidence of the long transition from affluent foraging to eventual urbanization in South Asia.

In southern China, the village at Bashidang was situated on a low-lying, water-logged plain in Hunan Province, between the Chang Jiang River and a nearby lake. The oldest layers excavated by archaeologists (dating to roughly 7000 BCE) reveal evidence of postholes dug into the peat that might have been used as foundations for village dwellings that needed to be raised above the floodplain. Bashidang is one of the oldest dated examples of a farming village in China and demonstrates the need for buildings to be constructed in a manner and location that facilitated successful agriculture, in this case based on the domestication of rice.

In northern China, evidence of the Early Agrarian era Yangshao culture has been unearthed at a number of sites in the Huang He valley. The Yangshao was a sophisticated sedentary agrarian culture that lasted for more than 2,000 years, between approximately 5200 and 3000 BCE. The most significant Yangshao site is Banpo, an impressive village that was surrounded by a deep defensive ditch. The dwellings were arranged within the defenses, while the village cemeteries were outside (see Figure 5.6). Several Chinese sites give us a tantalizing glimpse into the evolution of increasingly complex village life and the role played by specific environments during the unfolding of the Early Agrarian era in East Asia.

Archaeologists working in the Americas have also uncovered evidence of Early Agrarian village life across that vast world zone. The North American site of Koster, situated at the base of a bluff on the edge of the lower Illinois River floodplain, began life as a series of temporary camps for foragers, but then evolved into a complex suitable for long-term occupation, although the residents were probably affluent foragers rather than farmers. Houses were rectangular, built on platforms measuring 16 by 14 feet (4.8 by 4.25 meters), and contained fireplaces. Food was stored in pits, and basins were used for mussel steaming and meat roasting. The dead were buried in what appear to have been specific cemetery sites, and the remains of five interred dogs (dated to 6500 BCE) were also found.

The major South American village site of La Paloma was built on the Peruvian coast and was occupied continuously

FIGURE 5.6 Banpo. Excavations at the important Yangshao site of Banpo in northern China. The houses inside this early agricultural village were surrounded by a deep defensive ditch.

villages. The village of Skara Brae was situated on the west coast of the island of Orkney, north of Scotland. The village was completely covered over with soil and sand until a huge storm in 1850 revealed the outlines of several stone dwellings. Archaeologist Gordon Childe began excavations of the site in 1928 and uncovered seven houses; three more have since been discovered. Radiometric dating has shown that the village was continuously occupied between 3100 and 2500 BCE, and the site is the most complete Early Agrarian era village so far discovered in Europe.

The village was originally set some way back from the sea and was occupied by people who were farmers, but who also hunted and fished. The Orkneys suffer from a scarcity of timber, so its early inhabitants had to use other construction materials like stone. The residents needed these substantial stone-built dwellings to protect them from the fierce weather of the region, so they sank the foundations of their houses into mounds of preexisting domestic waste (which archaeologists call middens). The walls were constructed using large flagstones that were naturally shaped by sea erosion, and then quantities of timber, peat, earth, and grass were layered on the sides and roof to cover and weatherproof the dwelling. Not only were the dwellings made of stone, but so too were the contents. Stone beds, dressers, and storage spaces, along with pots, bone pins, necklace beads, enigmatic carved stone balls, and containers holding red ochre were all found on the site (Figure 5.7). One of the buildings may have functioned as some sort of workshop, because it was subdivided into small cubicles and fragments of bone, stone, and antler were found, perhaps by-products of tool making. We know tantalizingly little about the social structure of the village, but we do know that deteriorating weather around 2500 BCE may have made even this sturdiest of all Early Agrarian villages no longer habitable, because it appears to have been completely abandoned by residents.

Gender Relations in the Early Agrarian Era

Archaeology has also revealed something about gender relations in Early Agrarian era communities, but this evidence is ambiguous and provides at best only a partial answer to the question of what impact agriculture and the emergence of sedentary village life had on the status of women. This transition clearly changed the relative positions of men and women, but there is no standard model as to exactly how the change was manifested. Part of the problem is that it is often difficult to isolate male from female remains in the archaeological record, and many of the artifacts discovered do not explicitly show that they were used exclusively by either sex. Anthropologists and gender historians often try to reconstruct what might have been going on during this transition by making comparisons with modern-day early farming societies. One assumption, for example, is that because men generally make the stone tools used by twentieth-century horticultural societies, they probably did so in the Early Agrarian era as well, but this is hardly conclusive.

between about 6800 and 3700 BCE. At its peak the village housed 50 circular, dome-shaped dwellings that were built into flat-bottom pits. Cane provided a superstructure for the walls, and the roofs were thatched. Artifacts recovered demonstrate that the residents survived by gathering marine resources and also by domesticating gourds, squash, and beans from as early as 6000 BCE. Bodies of the dead were preserved in sea salts and wrapped in reed mats, and fires were built over the graves to help dry out and thus preserve the corpses. The distribution of artifacts, including pigments, fish hooks, obsidian, and exotic shells, suggest that this was a relatively egalitarian society without the steep hierarchies of power and wealth found at other Early Agrarian sites.

One last example, this time from the northern British Isles, will conclude this brief survey of Early Agrarian

to support such a model in observations of Sudanese affluent foragers.[9] On the other hand, analysis of skeletons from Abu Hureya in Syria shows that farming was probably even more physically demanding than foraging for women. Many of the female skeletons analyzed had deformed toe bones and powerful upper arms, probably from grinding grain all day, whereas the male skeletons did not have these deformities.

These ambiguous interpretations are complicated by evidence suggesting that living standards initially declined in Early Agrarian villages for residents of both sexes, compared to the lifeways of foragers. This may have been because farmers relied on fewer foodstuffs than foragers, so their diets were less varied and less nutritious, which explains why the remains of some early farmers appear physically shorter than individuals in neighboring foraging communities. Famine was a real possibility and constant threat if staple crops failed, and farmers probably worked harder and longer hours and suffered higher levels of stress (we can tell this from study of bones) than foragers as they attempted to stave off the myriad threats to survival faced by Early Agrarian communities. Within these communities, however, it is probably safe to say that men's and women's roles (and consequently status) were increasingly clearly defined.

Studies of San foragers in southern Africa led some researchers to argue that sedentism reduced the status of women. Nomadic groups tended to be more egalitarian, with men's and women's roles equally important for group survival. Sedentism changed all this, the argument suggests, by confining women to the relative isolation of the home and freeing up men to play more public roles, including cattle herding and "politics." Eventually this transition meant that certain women's jobs were designated as being of lower status, including drawing water from the well and other household chores.

Another interpretation of Early Agrarian gender roles is that women may have taken the lead in persuading the community to abandon nomadism and settle down through actively and intentionally experimenting with plant cultivation, because survival as a nomadic forager was particularly hard work for women. Anthropologists find evidence

Why Did Some Villages Become Towns?

Not all villages grew to become towns and cities. Here we focus on the particular reason that some villages did grow larger until they became towns. In Chapter 6 we take this analysis to the next stage by considering how some of these early towns grew to become cities and eventually states.

Archaeological evidence provides striking examples of certain villages that grew especially large, until they were the size of towns. The reason for the growth of these particular centers is far from clear, however. Some may have been important ritual centers that had spiritual significance for the surrounding villages. Others clearly had access to a valued resource, such as a reliable water supply. Yet others became important commercial centers perhaps because they controlled the trade in valuable goods or occupied a strategic site on important trade and migration routes. To conclude this section of the chapter we will consider two different examples from the Early Agrarian era, Jericho and Catalhoyuk. A third important example from the Americas, Chaco Canyon, is explored in Chapter 9.

Jericho, the Oldest Town in the World? The present-day city of Jericho is located in the Jordan River valley in modern Palestine, about 10 miles (16 kilometers) north of the Dead Sea. At an elevation of 864 feet (263 meters) below sea level, Jericho is the lowest permanently inhabited settlement in the world. Archaeological investigation of the site began in 1868 and continued sporadically during the first half of the twentieth century. Kathleen Kenyon (whom we met earlier in the chapter) began extensive investigation using modern archaeological techniques between 1952 and 1958. Kenyon was particularly interested in discovering the ancient city named in the Hebrew Bible as the "City of Palm Trees" and also revered in the Judeo-Christian tradition as the place the Israelites returned to from their enslavement in Egypt. Her excavations, however, soon revealed evidence of

occupation many millennia before the biblical period, and eventually her trenches reached the remains of an Early Agrarian era settlement about 6 acres (2.4 hectares) in area, dated to about 9600 BCE. An even earlier layer was subsequently discovered, which indicated that Natufian affluent foragers occupied Jericho as early as about 12,000 BCE, making it the oldest continuously inhabited settlement in human history.

The critical resource that helps explain Jericho's origins and longevity is water, which is absolutely essential to enable settlement in this harsh desert environment. The city is located in an oasis in Wadi Qelt, sustained by an astonishingly reliable underground water supply known as the Ein es-Sultan spring that has apparently not dried up during 14,000 years of continuous human residency. This natural water source is called Elisha's Spring in the Bible, after a story in II Kings (2:19–22) in which the prophet Elisha made the water at Jericho healthy. More than 1,000 gallons (3,800 liters) of freshwater bubble up from under this spring each minute, which a sophisticated system of irrigation canals disburses to about 2,500 acres (1,011 hectares) of farmland. The soil itself is alluvial and fertile, and the combination of soil, sunshine, and water has made this an attractive place for affluent foragers and farmers since the beginning of the transition to agriculture (Figure 5.8).

FIGURE 5.8 Jericho. Jericho, located in the Jordan River valley in modern Palestine, is the oldest town in the world. It has been continuously occupied for some 14,000 years.

After the original Natufian settlement, the earliest agrarian occupants domesticated emmer wheat and barley and demonstrated impressive cooperative behavior by constructing a stone wall around their village, surrounded by a rock-cut ditch. Between about 8350 and 7350 BCE the village evolved into a town that may have been home to as many as 3,000 farmers who lived in round, mud-brick houses arranged without any obvious evidence of town planning. Subsequent residents learned to domesticate sheep and also apparently developed a cult of preserving human skulls, which included placing shells in the eye sockets.

Later settlement layers display ambiguous evidence of increasing social complexity, indicating that Jericho had transitioned from a large village to a town. Archaeologists working in these pre–Bronze Age layers have discovered hunting and farming implements like arrowheads, sickle blades, axes, and grindstones; eating vessels including limestone dishes and bowls; spinning whorls and loom weights; and almost full-sized anthropomorphic plaster figures that must have been associated with some sort of religious or ritual practice. After millennia of continuous occupation, Jericho reached its most impressive size between 1700 and 1550 BCE, when a chariot-riding elite class organized substantial defenses during an age of widespread urbanization and intercity conflict across much of the region.

Catalhoyuk, Obsidian, and the Great Mother Goddess

Catalhoyuk, an Early Agrarian era settlement on the Konya plain in modern Turkey, was founded around 7300 BCE. The site, discovered and excavated by British archaeologist James Mellaart in the early 1960s, occupies 32 acres (13 hectares) and is divided into 12 "horizons," or levels of development. Although the Konya plain has one of the lowest rainfalls in Turkey, braided streams flowed here in the Early Agrarian era, and the combination of water, alluvial soil, and reed marshes made this an environmentally promising area for farming. Archaeologists believe the Catalhoyuk site represents the consolidation of a number of smaller, pre-existing villages in the region into a densely populated community that probably housed up to 8,000 people by about 6200 BCE.

The town was tightly packed with housing. Each dwelling was essentially a rectangular box built adjoining others on all sides, with no lanes or roads between. The rooftops were flat and access into the homes was via a trapdoor in the roof, accessed by a wooden ladder. Archaeologists estimate that each mud-brick home may have had a life of around 70 years, and they were regularly replaced by allowing the roof to collapse in, then rebuilding on the same foundations (Figure 5.9). Residents supported themselves through the domestication of cereal and vegetable crops and the herding of sheep. The occupants of Catalhoyuk also traded the volcanic glass known as obsidian that was found in the mountains of Cappadocia, about 80 miles (128 kilometers) away. This useful resource could be fractured in such a way that it produced hard, sharp edges that were invaluable in the manufacture of effective hunting and farming tools. Almost all the tools found in Catalhoyuk are made of obsidian.

At Catalhoyuk a series of dramatic, red-colored artistic images were painted onto the white mud-washed walls and floors of the houses. Both realistic figures and abstract geometric designs were unearthed. One motif depicts human figures engaged in a range of activities centered on a huge wild bull. The significance of wild bulls was reinforced by the recent discovery (2008) of several groups of wild bull horns set into pillars, which are arranged in such a way that they seem to be protecting the humans buried below. Another painting shows headless humans surrounded by vultures. Most intriguing are depictions of human figures all represented in stylized female form and also a number of carved female figurines. Mellaart originally believed that Catalhoyuk may have been an important cult center for the worship of a great mother goddess, but whatever the object of veneration, the extraordinary painted images, burial practices, and female iconography provide evidence of a rich and symbolic religious belief and of a possible reason why this agrarian village grew so large. As these examples demonstrate, we need to recognize that a combination of variables—including access to reliable water, fertile soil, valuable natural resources, and sacred or symbolic significance—were responsible for the evolutionary growth from village to town.

Despite the evidence of population densities, impressive architecture, and increasingly sophisticated sacred belief systems, the residents of these and most Early Agrarian era societies still coexisted in a relatively egalitarian social world. The houses in Catalhoyuk and Jericho are all essentially the same in size and possessions, indicating the absence of class hierarchies. Although men's and women's graves sometimes contained gender-specific artifacts, the objects themselves are not any more or less valuable, and women appear to have received the same amount of food, suggesting that the establishment of cultural distinctions between men and women in the Early Agrarian did not result in the economic subordination of women. Finally, even in these most impressive of all Early Agrarian era towns, there is no real evidence of the emergence of a religious or leadership elite. The final question this chapter needs to address, then, is how early forms of **consensual power** (where leaders ruled with the consent of their communities) emerged late in the Early Agrarian era. Chapter 6 will take up this discussion and consider how consensual power was converted to **coercive power** (where leaders ruled through the threat of force) late in the era, leading to the emergence of rich and poor, elites and peasants, and kings and emperors.

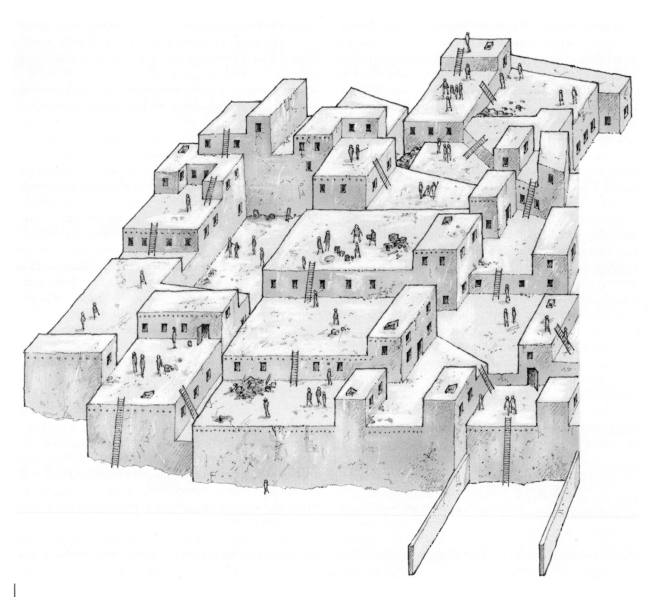

FIGURE 5.9 Catalhoyuk. An artist's impression of Catalhoyuk, modern Turkey. Founded in ca. 7300 BCE, the residents of this densely populated town supported themselves through farming and trading the important natural resource of obsidian, a valuable volcanic glass.

The Emergence of Consensual Power

In this final section of the chapter we will consider the early forms of power that emerged within those communities. Both this chapter and the next will suggest answers to two difficult yet crucial questions: How did some people get to rule over others in this relatively egalitarian world? How were rulers able to expand their power until, by the beginning of the later Agrarian era, large numbers of humans found themselves under the control of extremely powerful rulers like kings and emperors? Clearly, like the agricultural revolution with which this is closely linked,

the appearance of power in the world marks another fundamental transition in human history.

What Is Power?

A quick search through the dictionary will reveal a bewildering array of definitions of **power.** What they all have in common, though, are notions of *control* by individuals or groups over people and resources, and of *authority,* which is the capacity to exercise that control. The assumption in all these definitions is that control will be exercised by the few over the many, over *considerable* human and material resources. You can see, then, that until substantial resources of people and goods began to accumulate late in the Early Agrarian era, power was relatively unimportant. In the long Paleolithic and most of the Early Agrarian, there were simply too few people and resources for power to matter. Individuals who might have sought power would have gained control over few people and not much in the way of material possessions. Furthermore, in small foraging bands, and all but the largest villages and towns we have examined in this chapter, most activities could take place without the need for leaders. Administration and justice meant that family politics dominated, that matters were sorted out within the extended family, or communally in the case of the village.

How can archaeologists and historians tell whether particular communities had individuals exercising control and authority, whether power structures had emerged? They can look for differences in burial structures, evidence that some individuals within a community were buried in much more lavish tombs than the majority and with substantially more possessions than others. Archaeologists also look for differences in the quality and quantity of personal possessions in individual homes and compare the size and location of particular homes within the community. Finally, wherever they find evidence of monumental architecture—massive tombs like pyramids, or temples like Ziggurats, or statues such as those found on Rapa Nui (Easter Island)—they can say with a great deal of confidence that such structures demonstrate that someone or some group within that community had the ability and the authority to exercise considerable power over others.

Explaining the Appearance of Power

Anthropologists offer two different but overlapping types of theories to explain why humans eventually allowed a few people within their society to gain the sort of power over them that was needed to construct these tombs, buildings, and monuments. The first identifies what is called "bottom-up power." The focus here is on notions of *consent,* on the idea that power initially comes from below. The process identified with bottom-up power is that people living in larger and more complex societies eventually wanted or needed some mechanism of coordinated management, so they *agreed* to obey rulers. The question this theory addresses is: Why, after millennia of few or no leaders, did humans agree to let others rule them? The second group of theories focuses on notions of coercion, on the idea that power comes from above, or "top-down power." The argument here is that individuals or groups learned how to *impose* their will on others. The questions this explanation addresses are: How were rulers able to impose their will on their communities? And why did people put up with it?

Power from below might usefully be described as power based on consent, as *consensual* power. This label seems appropriate because it describes a process whereby humans willingly gave up some personal and family autonomy and allowed leaders to gain control over their lives and resources. Power from above might be understood as power based on force, as *coercive* power. In this model, leaders acquired the ability to control people and resources, if necessary by force.

The world of social insects offers an insight into the emergence of power. Termites, like ants and some bees and wasps, are genuinely social animals. Large termite mounds are organized in a way that resembles human communities. Up to a million individual termites live in large tropical savanna mounds, which function as home, reproduction chamber, and fungal garden. Constructed of soil, mud, chewed wood, saliva, and termite feces, some African mounds are as high as 30 feet (9.1 meters) and use columns of hot air rising out of the ground to ensure the circulation of clean air throughout the colony. The social structure of the nests is equally complex. In a typical colony the entire population is organized into castes, ranging from nymphs (semimature individuals), through workers and soldiers, up to reproductive individuals of both genders, dominated by egg-laying queens.

Clearly some members of termite society have more power than others—the soldiers for example—and one is the most powerful of all, the queen! This looks like bottom-up power, because all termites benefit from the organization of the termite mound, in that all would die if it were badly run. The queen also ensures hive cohesion through her ability to create and spread pheromones (secreted or excreted chemical factors that trigger a social reaction), which are distributed through shared feeding throughout the colony to enhance social integration. Yet this is also top-down power because the queens and other "elite" groups get more resources than their "subjects," and they use the self-sacrificing soldiers to control how the others behave, often by force. Everyone benefits from this arrangement, but some more than others. So rather than describing this social structure as either top-down or bottom-up power, in reality it is both!

In both the insect and human worlds, power is a combination of top-down and bottom-up. Power is essentially a relationship in which both sides gain something. Because of this it is usually supported from below, although one side generally gains more than the other. This means that those at the top might sometimes have to use force to maintain their power. In all power relationships, then, top-down and bottom-up power are mingled together.

There is a close parallel between the social world of termites and evolving human societies in the Early Agrarian era. As human communities grew larger and more complex, tasks needed to be divided up, individuals had to learn to become more dependent on others, and the entire structure needed more effective forms of management and control. In the same way that social insects adapted genetically to living in large colonies, humans adapted culturally to the new realities of sedentary, communal, interdependent living that emerged following the transition to agriculture.

This discussion suggests that we need a two-part explanation for the origins of power in human societies. The first and simplest forms of power that emerged were based on consent (bottom-up); but once leaders emerged in this way, they eventually acquired the resources needed to impose their will from above (top-down). To support this theoretical explanation, historians, anthropologists, and particularly archaeologists have sought evidence to show that power from below emerged first sometime in the Early Agrarian era, to be replaced later by power from above. The remainder of this chapter will focus on the emergence of bottom-up (or consensual) power. The next chapter will look at the transition to top-down (or coercive) power in early cities and states.

The Emergence of Consensual Power in the Early Agrarian Era

As populations grew in the Early Agrarian era, the need to coordinate activities must have become more apparent. A small community of just a few families can sort out its own problems and coordinate its communal tasks face-to-face, but a village of several hundred people, let alone a town of several thousand, can't do this without leaders of some kind. We have already seen that as farming spread from its centers of origin and more and more villages began to appear, some of them grew large enough to be described as towns. These towns in turn began to exert control over the smaller villages. Later we will see that once really big communities appeared—the cities—they in turn began to quickly tax and dominate the towns and villages.

What tasks would people in burgeoning agrarian communities need leaders to take care of? They needed leaders for defense (to lead them in conflicts against neighboring communities); for religion (to mediate with the gods, particularly when the community was so dependent on successful harvests); for legal matters (such as the settling of disputes); and for administration (for example, to maintain increasingly complex irrigation systems). In other words, leaders were needed for the first time in human history to take care of those tasks that the community could no longer manage without a coordinating mechanism. Which particular individuals should be selected? What attributes did one need to become a leader? The most obvious answer was individuals who possess particular talent as a priest or shaman, a warrior or diplomat, or an organizer of group projects. But often the selection seems to have had little to do with talent and more to do with birth, particularly in the selection of a chief.

The form of government adopted by many Early Agrarian villages was a chiefdom, a complex human society, led by a chief, in which the chief or an elite noble group is selected to make decisions for the community. As farmers got better at their jobs, the community was able to produce agricultural surpluses, which freed up the leaders from food production and allowed for the emergence of just such an elite group within the community. Generally chiefs were the oldest sons of the senior lineages within these communities, which still thought of themselves in terms of family, so that an accident of birth determined commoner and noble, and the possible futures open to each.

What remains unclear in this process is how agricultural surpluses began to accumulate in the first place, particularly when anthropologists are able to show that many farmers in simple villages today regard the notion of growing more than they need to survive as somewhat ridiculous. The need to store grain to survive through the winter is often undermined by archaeological evidence that these surpluses were often destroyed by rot or vermin.

An alternative explanation is that chiefs arose by giving away surplus food or other goods to create a sense of obligation from the recipients. As we saw in Chapter 4, gift giving was an essential means of maintaining intergroup harmony in the Paleolithic, and it remained significant in the Early Agrarian. This opened up a route to power through the display of extravagant generosity to potential supporters, a method practiced by the so-called Big Men of Polynesian societies. Generosity (through gift giving) is highly valued in all small-scale societies. The Big Men used this deeply ingrained sense of reciprocity engendered by gift giving to gain power. Modern anthropological studies have shown how the potential Big Man gradually accumulates and stores away significant resources (pigs, blankets, other valuable or useful objects), then redistributes them in times of communal need. The Big Man gains considerable social leverage through the accumulation of reciprocal IOUs, until eventually the beneficiaries of the Big Man's largesse have no option but to support him. An Eskimo proverb vividly illustrates this path to power: "Gifts make slaves, as whips make dogs."[10]

Evidence of Power in the Early Agrarian Era

This brief theoretical discussion of the origins of power suggests that the biological principle of convergent evolution (see Chapter 3) might also be applied to the process, in that growing communities faced with similar problems and needs came up with remarkably similar solutions through the creation of chiefdoms even when there was no contact between them. Yet this original form of government, based on agricultural surpluses, rank and lineages, and rules of reciprocity, took many different localized forms, as seen in the following three examples.

At Varna on the Black Sea coast of modern-day Bulgaria, archaeologists have investigated an extensive mid-fifth-millennium BCE cemetery. Their discoveries have been cited as an example of how cemetery burial might have been used as a means of promoting social integration by taking the rituals surrounding death out of individual households and making burial a public, communal enterprise. The archaeologists uncovered 211 tombs, which reveal considerable differences in the apparent wealth and status of the interred: 170 of the graves contained a cache of up to 10 items buried with the body; 18 contained a much larger assemblage of more valuable artifacts; and one grave of a 40- to 50-year-old male contained more than

1,000 objects, of which 980 were made of gold. The obvious assumption is that this is the grave of a high-status individual who probably wielded considerable power within his community.

In China, the Longshan culture (which followed the Early Agrarian Yangshao discussed earlier) had gained control of much of the central plains region of China by about 3000 BCE. Major Longshan cemeteries have been excavated at Changzi and Taosi, revealing increasing social complexity and dramatic differences in funerary objects. The great majority of graves at Taosi are clearly of poorer individuals with few accompanying offerings; about 80 contain jade axes and rings; and a handful of wealthy graves contain up to 200 valuable objects. Among these are jade rings and axes, but intriguingly also two wooden drums with skins made of crocodile skins. Ancient Chinese texts refer to drums as symbols of royalty!

Finally to Polynesia, where anthropologists have conducted extensive investigations into chiefdoms and other early forms of power. Polynesian societies cover a range of sociopolitical structures, from the warring, fragmented, tribal politics of the Marquesas and Easter Island, through the loosely ranked tribal societies of New Zealand, to the rigidly stratified chiefdoms of Tonga, Samoa, and Hawaii. Although the size, fertility, and degree of isolation of the various island groups play a role in determining social complexity, anthropologists argue that all Polynesian societies share notions of ancestral genealogical rank, and therefore of rights of status inheritance passed through the male line. The chiefs who emerged were thus genealogically sanctioned and were responsible for food production, community constructions, and for supervising religious rites because it was believed they had inherited supernatural power.

As the most important "laboratory" for the evolution of social complexity that anthropologists have available, Polynesia provides tantalizing glimpses of the factors that were probably at play in most early farming communities as notions of power and status slowly emerged. Clearly a range of prime movers has to be included in any nuanced model, including the role of the environment, inherited status, reciprocity, intragroup competition and consensus, and religion.

This brief survey has shown examples of the emergence of power in the Early Agrarian era and also the ambiguities and complexities associated with its evolution. As we leave the Early Agrarian era, it is worth noting that there were limitations to these early power structures. The leaders were mostly male, ruled largely with the consent of their populations, and were able to achieve significant levels of control over considerable human and material resources. At the same time, they could also be overthrown quite easily because their power was still based on consent. Early leaders had not yet learned to impose their will by force in a sustained way. The next chapter will show that, beginning a little over 5,000 years ago, in some regions these often fragile and limited forms of power were replaced by much more durable forms of power firmly based on the sustained exercise of coercion.

Farming and the Environment

One of the important themes this big history textbook addresses is the relationship between humans and the biosphere. As we saw in Chapter 4, even during the Paleolithic, when populations were small and diffused and human groups essentially pursued sustainable lifeways, the impact of our species through fire-stick farming and megafaunal extinctions was profound.

As humans moved from nomadic foraging to sedentary farming, the demands of feeding larger and denser populations placed inevitable strains on often fragile local environments. Villages and towns, and the croplands and pastures that sustained them, are constructed, artificial, domesticated, anthropocentric environments in which all elements are directed toward human survival. Without any intention or perhaps even awareness of doing so, early farmers often pursued unsustainable agricultural practices. These included the overfarming and overgrazing of poor soils (which led to desertification); excessive dependence on irrigation (which led to salinization); and widespread forest and jungle clearing (which led to serious erosion problems). In addition, the genetic modification of plant and animal species through domestication often led to the creation of new hybrids that were susceptible to a range of diseases and pests. Add to these the problems of continuing climate change and regular natural disasters, and it is easy to see why, as Chris Scarre puts it, "the problem of achieving long term environmental sustainability is one that has haunted complex societies for over 4000 years," and, as this chapter has shown, throughout the previous 4,000 years as well.[11]

Scholars have not much considered environmental degradation during the Early Agrarian era, but recently William Ruddiman, a U.S. paleoclimatologist, has argued that the impact of intensification in the Early Agrarian era was significant. Across the wide expanse of Afro-Eurasia initially, and later in the Americas, vast areas of forest were cleared to facilitate farming and herding. The result was a measurable increase in carbon dioxide and atmospheric methane levels over the past several thousand years that was significant enough to cause a steady rise in global temperatures, which in turn may have staved off any return to cooler or even glacial conditions.[12] Ruddiman's thesis is contentious, but the more stable, warmer conditions that have prevailed globally since the end of the last ice age have certainly facilitated large-scale intensive agriculture and dramatic increases in human population. We will return to this theme of human impact on the environment often in later chapters, but as we leave the Early Agrarian era behind, it is important to remember not just the social and political consequences of the transition to agriculture, but also the environmental.

SUMMARY

This chapter described the crossing of the seventh threshold of complexity—the adoption of agriculture—as a five-step process. Early agricultural villages were portrayed, as well as two, Jericho and Catalhoyuk, that became larger towns. Gender and environmental changes were considered. The chapter ended with an analysis of how new forms of power relationships emerged within the chiefdoms of some of the larger villages.

CHAPTER QUESTIONS

1. What is domestication?
2. Why might the relationship between farmers and domesticated species be termed symbiotic?
3. Where and when did agriculture first emerge?
4. Briefly outline the five-step model to explain the emergence of agriculture.
5. How did agriculture spread, and what evidence do we have to show this?
6. Compare and contrast horticulture, swidden agriculture, and chinampa agriculture.
7. What does archaeological evidence from the Early Agrarian era tell us about evolving social and gender relations?
8. Why did some villages become towns?
9. What tasks would consensual leaders have been needed for during the Early Agrarian era?

KEY TERMS

agriculture

chinampa agriculture

coercive power

consensual power

domestication

Early Agrarian era

Holocene epoch

horticulture

intensification

power

sedentism

swidden agriculture

symbiosis

wave of advance model

FURTHER READING

Ammerman, A. J., and L. L. Cavalli-Sforza. *The Neolithic Transition and the Genetics of Populations in Europe.* Princeton, NJ: Princeton University Press, 1984.

Bellwood, Peter. *First Farmers: The Origins of Agricultural Societies.* Oxford/Malden (MA): Blackwell, 2005.

Bellwood, Peter, and Colin Renfrew. *Examining the Language/Farming Dispersal Hypothesis.* Cambridge, UK: McDonald Institute for Archaeological Research, 2002.

Carneiro, R. L. "A Theory on the Origin of the State." *Science* 169 (1970):733–38.

Catalhoyuk Research Project, Institute of Archaeology, University College London (2008). www.catalhoyuk.com/.

Diamond, Jared. *Guns, Germs, and Steel: The Fates of Human Societies.* New York: Norton, 1997.

Hodder, I. "Women and Men at Catalhoyuk." *Scientific American* 290, no. 1 (2004):76–83.

Johnson, A. W., and T. Earle. *The Evolution of Human Societies: From Foraging Group to Agrarian State.* 2nd ed. Stanford, CA: Stanford University Press, 2000.

Kenyon, Kathleen M. *Digging up Jericho.* London: Ernest Benn, 1957.

Kitch, Patrick V. *The Evolution of the Polynesian Chiefdoms.* Cambridge, UK: Cambridge University Press, 1984.

Lewis-Williams, D. "Constructing a Cosmos—Architecture, Power, and Domestication at Catalhoyuk." *Journal of Social Archaeology* 4, no. 1 (2004):28–59.

Richerson, P., R. Boyd, and R. L. Bettinger. "Was Agriculture Impossible during the Pleistocene but Mandatory during the Holocene? A Climate Change Hypothesis." *American Antiquity* 66, no. 3 (July 2001):387–411.

Ristvet, Lauren. *In the Beginning: World History from Human Evolution to the First States.* New York: McGraw-Hill, 2007.

Robinson, R. "Ancient DNA Indicates Farmers, Not Just Farming, Spread West." *PLoS Biology* 8, no. 11 (2010):e1000535. doi:10.1371/journal.pbio.1000535.

Ruddiman, William. *Plows, Plagues, and Petroleum: How Humans Took Control of Climate.* Princeton, NJ: Princeton University Press, 2005.

Scarre, Chris, ed. *The Human Past: World Prehistory and the Development of Human Societies.* London: Thames & Hudson, 2005.

Smith, Bruce D. *The Emergence of Agriculture.* New York: Scientific American Library, 1995.

ENDNOTES

1. Peter Kareiva, Sean Watts, Robert McDonald, and Tim Boucher, "Domesticated Nature: Shaping Landscapes and Ecosystems for Human Welfare," *Science* 29 (June 2007):1866–69. doi:10.1126/science.1140170.

2. David Christian, *Maps of Time: An Introduction to Big History,* 2nd ed. (Berkeley: University of California Press, 2011), 229.

3. Chris Scarre, ed., *The Human Past: World Prehistory and the Development of Human Societies* (London: Thames & Hudson, 2005), 209.

4. Lauren Ristvet, *In the Beginning: World History from Human Evolution to the First States* (New York: McGraw-Hill, 2007), 41.

5. Scarre, *The Human Past,* 235–43.

6. Ibid., 313–47.

7. Matthias Schulz, "Neolithic Immigration: How Middle Eastern Milk Drinkers Conquered Europe," *Spiegel Online International,* October 15, 2010.

8. R. Robinson, "Ancient DNA Indicates Farmers, Not Just Farming, Spread West," *PLoS Biology* 8, no. 11 (2010):e1000535, doi:10.1371/journal.pbio.1000535.

9. Randi Haaland, "Sedentism, Cultivation, and Plant Domestication in the Holocene Middle Nile Region," *Journal of Field Archaeology* 22, no. 2 (Summer 1995):157–174.

10. Ristvet, *In the Beginning,* 78.

11. Scarre, *The Human Past,* 718.

12. William Ruddiman, *Plows, Plagues, and Petroleum: How Humans Took Control of Climate* (Princeton, NJ: Princeton University Press, 2005).

crossing a mini-threshold

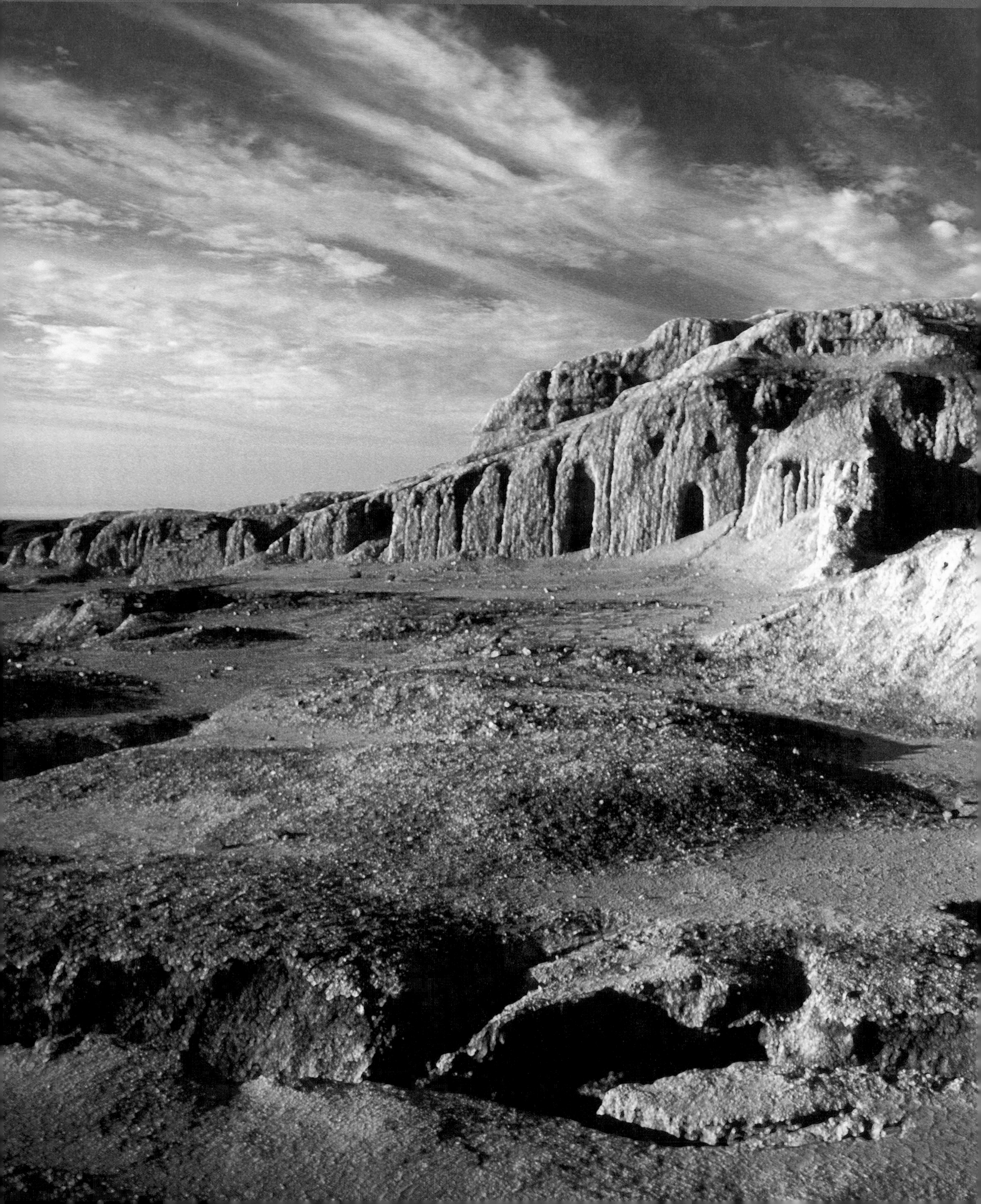

chapter 6

The Appearance of Cities, States, and Agrarian Civilizations

Seeing the Big Picture

Starting about 3500 BCE

▶ What is a city? What is a state? What is an agrarian civilization?

▶ Why does the emergence of cities and states qualify as a mini-threshold?

▶ What did people learn to increase agricultural production for themselves?

▶ What technological changes laid the foundation for the emergence of cities?

▶ How did states acquire enough power to be able to coerce people? Why did people allow this to happen?

▶ Why did cities appear about the same time in many parts of the world?

Today, almost everyone lives within a "state" of some kind. In addition, more than half the world's population currently lives in cities or urban areas. This benchmark, reached in 2008, is an extension of a process that began only about 5,000 years ago, probably in Mesopotamia, in the valley of the Tigris and Euphrates Rivers, now modern Iraq. With the first cities and states, human history entered a new era, the *Era of Agrarian Civilizations*. This chapter explores its early stages, from ca. 3500 to 2000 BCE, while Chapters 7, 8, and 9 cover from ca. 2000 BCE to ca. 1000 CE.

Defining Cities, States, and Agrarian Civilizations

Although we think the first city and state emerged in Mesopotamia about 3200 BCE, the significant fact is that cities and states emerged, probably independently, in at least seven other places around the world at nearly the same time, when viewed on a large time scale. In Egypt and Nubia, along the Nile River, there were states by about 3100 BCE. Northern India had a state and China had evidence of states by about 2000 BCE, with Mesoamerica and Peru in the Americas having them by approximately 1000 BCE.

To think about what a city is, imagine a person moving from a town to a city in 3000 BCE. Such a person would find herself or himself among many more people in the city—say, tens of thousands, instead of thousands in towns or hundreds in villages. Cities, however, were not simply larger; they had a complex internal division of labor, with most people working full time in some specialized occupation such as metalworker, brewer, potter, weaver, priest, stone mason, musician, artist, or soldier.

With the emergence of cities, the basic struggle, as always, was to provide enough food for everyone, but in a city the forms of cooperation became much more complex. Using the products of specialized artisans like potters and metalworkers, farmers in the outlying areas of cities were able to produce enough surplus food to feed the people in the cities. As a rough rule of thumb, it took about nine farmers to support one city dweller until the Modern era.

If a **city** is a dense collection of tens of thousands of people, with specialized occupations, what is a state? A **state** is a regionally organized society of a city and its nearby towns and farms, or of several cities and their environs, with a population of tens of thousands to hundreds of thousands or even millions. A state has political, social, and economic hierarchies, or power structures, that rest on systematic and institutionalized coercion, as well as on popular consent. *State* is not a synonym for *government;* government is only one aspect of a state. Cities and states arose at about the same time because the increased population density of cities required leadership and multiplied the resources available to those taking charge.

As cities and states traded with each other, some absorbed each other, and the scale of state systems expanded, eventually to be called empires, or imperial systems, when a single ruler controlled a large territory of many cities and states. Possibly the first imperial system was established about 3100 BCE by Menes, or Narmer, in the Nile River valley. Sargon of Akkad, who ruled from about 2334 to 2279 BCE, set up an imperial system in the Tigris–Euphrates valley. By about 1500 BCE the Shang Dynasty may have established an imperial system in northern China.

States and empires are embedded in large regions that share cultural characteristics and include the tribute-paying farmers on whom the states depend. We define **tribute** following the work of the influential American anthropologist, Eric Wolf (1923–99), as resources, which could include goods, labor, cash, or even people, controlled by the state largely through the threat of coercion. Slavery is the most obvious form of tribute, but a tribute-taking society is one in which many flows of resources are controlled by the threat of force and in which physical violence is regarded as admirable in many situations.

These complex arrangements are sometimes called civilizations, based on the Latin, *civilis*, the genitive form of *civis*, meaning "belonging to a city." The term *civilization* is used with many different meanings and often implies stages of progress, or the superiority of more "advanced" societies over other forms. To avoid implying progress archaeologists frequently substitute *complex society* for the term *civilization*. We use the term **agrarian civilization** to refer to large state and imperial systems; we include *agrarian* to remind ourselves that civilizations always depend on their agricultural surroundings. We do not mean to suggest that agrarian civilizations are superior, or more "advanced," than earlier kinds of societies; they are, however, more complex and controlled far more human and material resources.

The process of more complex social arrangements emerging out of less complex ones is similar to other instances of increasing complexity that we have seen throughout this book. It seems particularly similar to the evolution of multicellular organisms: entities that were once independent become linked into larger unities.

The Buildup of Resources and Collective Learning

In this section we summarize the slow buildup that resulted in the emergence of cities, states, and civilizations. This buildup included an increase in productivity and population density and a changing climate.

Increased Agricultural Productivity

People had a lot to learn after they settled down to farming. For the first several thousand years farmers apparently ate the animals they had domesticated as soon as they reached their adult size; why continue to feed them after that? (Archaeologists can tell from the bones an animal's age at slaughter.)

Gradually farmers realized that they could use their animals in more ways than for meat and skins. If they kept their animals alive longer, they could use their milk for food, their wool for clothes, their waste for fertilizer, and their muscle power for pulling plows and carrying loads.

An archaeologist at the University of Oxford in England, Andrew Sherratt, has called this extended use of domesticated animals the "secondary products revolution." He suggested that from about 4000 BCE farmers in Afro-Eurasia began making more efficient use of the secondary products of their livestock, those products you could use without slaughtering the animals. This hypothesis is contested, however; possibly milking was the first reason for domesticating some animals, such as goats.

Although goat's milk may have been used early on, cow's milk posed problems to humans. Even today the majority of the world's people are intolerant of the lactose, or sugar, in cow's milk; as adults many people cannot digest milk without generating uncomfortable flatulence and diarrhea. To use cow's milk for food, early farmers (probably their wives) had to figure out how to process the milk to make it more digestible and storable; in doing so they created yogurt and aged cheese, which contain much less lactose. The descendants of cattle herders eventually evolved a genetic ability to digest lactose.

To create desirable wool, not too stiff or too soft, people had to select which sheep to breed and nurture, discovering in the process that elderly castrated males provided the best fleece. Before using wool, people used plant fibers for clothing—flax for linen in the Mediterranean and Near East, hemp in China, cactus in Mesoamerica, cotton in India. Wool proved warmer and took dyes easily; it became a valuable commodity.

The development of secondary products helped change the nature of women's work. It seems clear from modern evidence of farming communities that the work of processing yogurt and cheese and of knitting and weaving usually fell to women. Why did women get these jobs? Judith K. Brown, an anthropologist, gave a persuasive answer in 1970; she argued that whether a community relies on women as the chief providers of a certain job depends on its compatibility with child care. She pointed out that women's jobs have the following characteristics: they are easily interrupted and easily resumed once interrupted, do not place the child in potential danger, and do not require the worker to range far from home.

In Afro-Eurasia plows and wheels emerged about 5000 BCE, as people began to realize they could hitch up their animals for more muscle power. Oxen, which are castrated bulls, could pull large plows that turned over four times the soil workable by a human pushing a plow. By about 4000 BCE people had domesticated horses, probably in the Ukraine, and donkeys in Egypt, using them for plowing and transport.

In the Americas, there were no large animals to domesticate other than llamas, vicunas, and guanacos in Peru. Other large animals that might have been domesticated—horses, elephants, camels—had previously been hunted to extinction or died from climate change (see Chapter 5). The different way that history developed in the Americas may have depended largely on this fact. Other animals that did survive—bison, elk, moose, deer, puma—could not be domesticated.

In these ways farmers in Afro-Eurasia gradually increased the efficiency with which they used their domesticated animals. At the same time, other people generated the new lifeway of pastoralism, in which they lived almost entirely off the products of their animals. This allowed people to inhabit areas too dry for farming, since these areas produced enough grass for their animals if they moved regularly. Such areas included the steppes of Eurasia, the deserts of southwestern Asia, and the savannas of eastern Africa. Once people learned to live mainly off the products of their animals, they could move into these dry areas. Nomadic pastoralists could survive on products of their herds, but always they wanted grains and other goods from settled farmers, which they acquired either by raiding or trading. They became a major force in history, connecting settled areas of Afro-Eurasia, for example, by bringing wheeled vehicles, horses, and bronze metallurgy to China.

Irrigation and Other Techniques

Another new technology that people developed from 5000 to 3000 BCE was irrigation, or water management for farming. This probably started as farmers learned to divert small steams onto their fields at the right time for watering their crops. Irrigation involved the work of digging channels, keeping them clear, and opening and closing them at the appropriate time. Over time large-scale systems of canals, dams, and water-dipping paddle wheels developed. These had the highest impact in dry areas with unusually fertile soil. There agriculture could become highly productive with irrigation, followed by rapid population increase.

Irrigation, however, had unsustainable long-term side effects. It involved changing the unmanaged ecosystem into a managed system, as all agriculture does. Irrigation raises the water table under the soil, often resulting in waterlogged soil that cannot drain. Irrigation also raises, by evaporation, the salt content in the soil. Water moving down from mountainous areas carries mineral salts acquired from the rocks it moves through. When this water is used for irrigation, it evaporates rather than draining away, leaving behind the mineral salts in the soil. Over hundreds of years this increasing salinization reduces crop output.

Other technological innovations prepared the way for cities to emerge. The invention of pottery solved problems of storage, transportation of liquids, and cooking. It may have been created first by hunting and gathering groups in Japan, called the Jomon culture; the earliest pottery shards there are radiocarbon-dated to about 14,000 BCE. Pottery was used in Mesopotamia by about 6500 BCE. Mesopotamians worked soft metals (gold, silver, and copper) by about 5500 BCE; harder metals (bronze and iron) came later because they required more efficient ovens to produce higher temperatures. Bronze is 10:1 copper mixed with tin; since tin was scarce, the need for it greatly increased trading. Bronze work appeared in Mesopotamia about 4000 BCE and in China by 2000 BCE. With the inventions of pottery and metallurgy, individuals who specialized in these skills may have been supported even in villages and small towns; it seems unlikely that every family would make its own pots or melt its own bronze.

Population Increase, Hierarchy, and Climate Change

Over time the human population increased, due the spread of agriculture to new regions and to technological advances that raised productivity. As we saw in Chapter 5, this increased density of population created a need for leadership; in larger communities decisions could no longer be reached with everyone participating. (Three hundred individuals is the maximum number considered manageable by an egalitarian system.) Large communities that depended on grain crops had to store surpluses, since grains ripen all at once, and they had to devise ways to distribute the stored crops; money had not yet been invented. Storage increased conflicts over control; leaders emerged who could manage conflicts and store surplus for emergencies. These leaders could also use the extra resources to increase their power. Hierarchies of power and wealth began to develop as population increased. Once underway, urbanization was a self-reinforcing process; cities attract people, who generate more resources, which attract more people.

The hierarchy of power between men and women may have been one of the earliest to emerge. The success of every farming household depended on rearing as many children as possible, because labor was a resource over which peasant families had some control. As described earlier, women could be relied on for other work only if it combined well with child care. Within the household they could share the work and power, depending on personal qualities; but once a denser population required political and economic activity in a public place, most women were too occupied at home with the crucial work of rearing children to assume power in the civic sphere.

Meanwhile, the climate, the ever-varying context to life on Earth, was changing. Generally stable warmth was reached about 8000 BCE, after the sudden cold spell from 10,800 to 9500 BCE called the Younger Dryas. After about 6000 BCE another sudden cool, dry spell occurred, followed by a return of wetness and humidity in the Northern Hemisphere. Yet a general trend toward increased aridity began, associated with the weakening and southward retreat of the Northern Hemisphere monsoon belt, probably driven by changes in the orbit of Earth (see Milankovitch cycles in the glossary). Within this general trend short periods of marked increased aridity occurred, from decades to centuries long. Around 4000 BCE such a period of accelerated aridity took place, possibly associated with cooling in the North Atlantic, with another such period occurring around 3000 BCE.

On the basis of recent data about climate change, many experts now argue that environmental desiccation provides at least the context for the emergence of some cities, states, and civilizations. Some have begun to argue that increasing aridity was the principal driving force behind their emergence, that at its core civilization is a form of adaptation to climate change—at high cost, with its increased inequality and disease, but also with high benefits.

Knowing that the climate in Afro-Eurasia was becoming drier in the years 4000 to 3000 BCE, we can easily imagine people flocking down from the highland areas, which were losing the rainfall needed for crops to grow, to the lowland areas where rivers provided water for irrigation farming. This may have accounted for some of the rapid increase of population in river valleys, in addition to the increase due to the agricultural productivity of the riverbed soil.

Many factors contributed to the emergence of cities and states. From the large-sale point of view, cities and states emerged from increases in population density after long, slow increases in productivity, after the power of Collective Learning generated new technologies, and after people responded to the changing climate.

The next section will describe the world's first city, Uruk, and possibly its first state, Sumer, in enough detail to provide a basis for thinking about the processes involved in their emergence. Subsequent sections will describe in less detail the emergence of cities and states in the Nile valley, the Indus valley, and two river valleys in China, as well as in the Americas, sub-Saharan Africa, and the Pacific Islands. The numerous dates are not to be memorized, but rather are to be used to understand the sequence in which events unfolded.

Uruk, the First City, in Sumer, the First State

To enter the time machine of our imagination, let's set the dial for 3600 BCE and zoom in on southern Mesopotamia, a Greek word meaning "the land between the rivers." In this case, the rivers are the Euphrates on the west and the Tigris on the east, both flowing from their origins in the Kurdesh Mountains of Turkey and the Taurus Mountains of Turkey and Armenia, respectively, down to the Persian Gulf, through what is present-day Iraq (Map 6.1).

In 3600 BCE southern Mesopotamia, or Sumer, presented an environment seemingly inauspicious for producing the world's first agrarian civilization. Both rivers spread into deltas as they reached the Persian Gulf, creating flat, waterlogged land that produced date palms and poplar trees

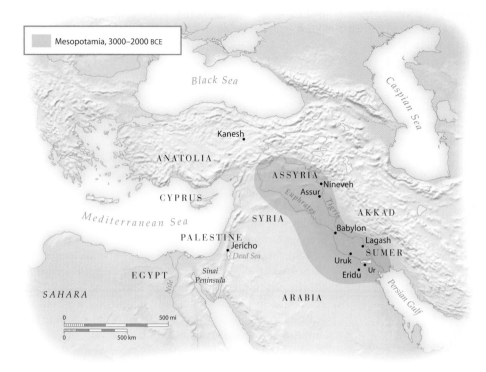

MAP 6.1 **Early Mesopotamia, 3000 to 2000 BCE.** The terminology about this region tends to be confusing because the names and centers of power have changed over time. *Mesopotamia* refers to the fertile valleys of the two rivers, including all of Iraq and neighboring parts of southeastern Turkey and eastern Syria. *Sumer,* containing about 12 city-states, refers to the area between and near the two rivers south of present-day Baghdad to the Persian Gulf. Southern Mesopotamia is another name for Sumer. *Uruk* (Ereck in the Bible, Warka today) was an important city-state in Sumer, about 150 miles (240 kilometers) south of present-day Baghdad. The *Fertile Crescent,* as described in the previous chapter, refers to the arch of high ground that stretches north up the eastern Mediterranean, east through the mountains of Turkey and northern Iraq, then south along the high ground that lies east of the Tigris and Euphrates valleys. *Akkad* refers to the region united under Sargon (ruled about 2334–2279 BCE); it lay in northern Mesopotamia, but its capital city, Akkad, has never been located. The city of *Babylon* lay near present-day Baghdad; Babylonia refers to the union of Akkad and Sumer, northern and southern Mesopotamia, accomplished by Hammurabi (about 1792–1750 BCE), among others. The later empire of *Assyria* was centered in the upper Tigris valley around the capital city of Nineveh, now Mosul.

and marshes filled with fish and fowl. Otherwise, the flatland grew no trees, had almost no stones and no minerals.

With irrigation, however, the rich soil deposited over centuries could produce abundant harvests of wheat, barley, and flax, a flowering plant that could be made into linen. Beyond the land that could be irrigated lay semidesert,

which could sustain sheep and goats. Beyond the subdesert lay full desert and mountains. From 4000 to 3000 BCE the climate was becoming ever drier, with annual rainfalls averaging less than 10 inches (25 centimeters), with no rain at all between May and October. The resources of Sumer included mud, reeds, grain, sheep, date and poplar trees, and people.

Precisely because deserts constricted this area, settlements with irrigation systems grew; people could not move nearby, especially not with the increasing aridity. The need for additional resources—wood, stone, metal, precious stone— motivated the development of trading networks; the Sumerians could offer linen and rugs, grain, and pottery for trade, receiving items such as copper from Oman or Elam, lapis lazuli from Afghanistan, hard stone for grinding grain from Arabia, and timber from Syria.

The City of Uruk

Uruk was the first of several cities that emerged in Sumer before 3000 BCE. It was located on the bank of the Euphrates River, although today the river flows about 10 miles (16 kilometers) to the west of its original site. Uruk is the Babylonian version of the Sumerian name, Unug. Most archaeologists agree that it is fair to claim Uruk as the world's first genuine city.

The ruins of Uruk at its height cover about 1,375 acres (556.5 hectares); about 250 acres (101 hectares) remain unexcavated, after excavations were suspended in 1990 by a United Nations sanction on Iraq. In 3500 BCE Uruk covered a site comparable to Athens in the fifth century BCE and half the area of Rome in 100 CE, with a population estimated at 10,000. This made it by far the densest human community that had ever existed until that date.

Excavations have revealed two ceremonial centers built around 3500 to 3200 BCE. The initial purpose of the centers is unknown; possibly they were used for storage, receptions, rituals, processions, or decision-making assemblies. They are characterized by free-flowing accessibility to terraces and courtyards. Archaeologists usually conclude that these centers are temples. The smaller one, called the White Temple, in time became associated with the sky god, An, the father of all gods, representing patriarchal authority. The larger one, called the Eanna Complex and containing many buildings, was associated with An's daughter, Inanna, originally the divinity of the storehouse, later seen

FIGURE 6.1 Ziggurat of Ur, ca. 2100 BCE. This elevated temple is an excellent example of monumental architecture; in the flatlands of Mesopotamia it would have been visible for many distances around. Why would kings build such structures?

as the Queen of Heaven and goddess of lovemaking and identified with the Babylonian goddess, Ishtar. The White Temple is set on a platform 42.7 feet (13 meters) high, a prototype of the ziggurats (stepped pyramids surmounted by small temples) characteristic of Sumerian culture in centuries to come. These temples are early examples of **monumental architecture.** As we saw in Chapter 5, large architectural structures seem to appear wherever powerful leaders emerge, and they are a feature of all agrarian civilizations (Figure 6.1).

The building of ceremonial centers suggests that some leadership must have been directing an organized skilled labor force. Scholars calculate that 1,500 laborers must have worked 10 hours per day for 5 years to construct the Eanna Complex. No buildings that suggest royal palaces appear until after 3000 BCE; we are left to imagine that priests associated with the early "temples" were in charge of building them, storing grain when it was harvested, overseeing ritual sacrifices to the gods, distributing the grain equitably, and storing some for periods of emergency use. As long as harvests were bountiful, the efficacy of the priests' appeals to the gods was confirmed. Religious, political, economic, and even military power may, for a brief time, have been in the hands of the priests.

Early Mesopotamians felt in awe of the forces of nature, which are known to us through their earliest myths and were kept alive orally until they could be written down. (This is the first time we get a whiff of what was inside people's minds, as the Mesopotamians were the first to write down their oral myths.) Mesopotamians regarded storms, rivers, mountains, the sun, wind, and fire as living beings, filled with spirits or energy. Gradually they personified the forces of nature into named gods who behaved as humans, except

that the gods were immortal; perhaps Mesopotamians did this as a way to establish meaningful relationships with their gods. As human society began to acquire different strata, ranks, or classes, Mesopotamians began to treat their gods as the most powerful, uppermost stratum of their society.

Fittingly, Mesopotamians respected water as the source of life. They believed that the world was created out of the mingling of sweet freshwater and salty ocean water. They named gods for each of these kinds of water, one female and one male. These original gods evolved into An, the sky god, who with the goddess Nammu, produced Enki, the god of water. (An older tradition has Nammu as self-generative primeval matter, with no male needed.) A list of deities was already established by 3500 to 3000 BCE, as seen in later writing.

Each Mesopotamian city set up its special temple, or household, to attract its chosen god to take up residence in the city, to protect it and bring it prosperity. As if the god or goddess were a human resident, its huge image was housed, fed, and clothed by a retinue of workers. The gods were believed to have created humans to be their servants, to care for them. The gods were believed to have also created the *me,* a Sumerian term for the institutions, forms of social behavior, emotions, and signs of office, which as a whole were seen as indispensable for the smooth operation of the world.

Evidence for these ideas has been derived from hymns and epics written during 2500 to 2000 BCE. For evidence of the earlier period there is an alabaster vase from the Eanna Complex in Uruk, called the Warka vase, dated about 3200 to 3000 BCE (see Figure 6.2). Religion seems to have served to foster social cohesion and to legitimate the ruler's authority in this early state, with local religions giving way to the **state religion** accepted and propagated by the rulers.

The agricultural productivity of early Uruk may have been based on the natural fertility of the soil, with the flooding coming between crops, or it may have been based on some form of irrigation. The evidence indicates that large-scale state-managed irrigation did not develop until the third millennium (2999–2000) BCE. By then individuals and small groups could no longer manage water systems; only government authorities had the clout to draft workers, distribute the water, and resolve disputes.

By about 3000 BCE the city of Uruk had a population of 40,000 to 50,000 people, as estimated by the size of its archaeological footprint. It had grown rapidly from about 10,000 in 3500 BCE to 20,000 in 3300 BCE; by its height in 2500 BCE Uruk may have had between 80,000 and 100,000 inhabitants. By this time 80 percent of all Sumerians were living in urban centers larger than 25 acres (10 hectares). Around 3000 BCE many people with Semitic names began arriving in Sumer from the Arabian Peninsula, probably unable to survive the increasingly arid conditions there, adding to the population in Sumer.

Uruk contained three areas: the walled section that included temples, palaces (after 3000 BCE), and residences of citizens; the outer area with farms, cattle fields, and gardens; and a commercial area with the stores of foreign a tablet found in Uruk enumerating 100 different professions, the first version dating from the end of the fourth millenium BCE.

Social distinctions in Uruk gradually became exaggerated from what they had been in villages or towns. Ruling and priestly elites emerged. Most people were either free commoners, who worked in occupations or farmed their own land, or were dependent clients, who owned no property but worked for those who did. Both free commoners and dependent clients paid tribute and provided labor when required by authorities. Some people were not free, but slaves; they were prisoners of war, convicted criminals, or heavily indebted individuals. Most slaves worked as domestic servants in wealthy households. This complex economic structure, with its specialization of occupations and the resultant removal of some forms of labor from individual families, defined the first city, a far cry from the village lifeways described in Chapter 5.

Palaces

In Uruk it seems that people gave increasing power to priests, in exchange for having someone in authority to take charge of distributing grain, to organize surplus crops for emergencies, and to intercede with the gods for good harvests. Or perhaps people gave over this power because they owned no land and were dependent on priests or others for employment. As they collected surplus grain, priests began to increase their power, levying tributes, enlarging their land holdings, and establishing state enterprises like weaving workshops and mass-produced pottery. How did kings ever come onto this scene?

As refugees from aridity crowded into Sumer, a city like Uruk needed to protect its stored grain from raiders, marauders, and nearby cities. Citizens needed walls around their land and residences to feel secure. Security called for leadership in defense; warrior leaders emerged.

Yet there is no evidence for kings in the early years of Uruk. One hypothesis suggests that early kings began as generals, chosen by the temple establishment to serve temporarily in emergencies. Eventually they came to serve permanently and then to arrange for their sons to follow them. They continued their influence at the temple households by appointing relatives as priests and priestesses. The ruler and his family may have come to own the temple estates. A strata of nobles emerged, mostly members of royal families. The first extravagant nonreligious residences, or palaces, in Uruk date from 2800 to 2600 BCE, about when the kingship became hereditary.

An alternative hypothesis about the emergence of kings in Sumer posits a more democratic model. Some early myths suggest that a council ruled each city, and the myths portray the gods and goddesses as governing themselves by councils, perhaps modeled on how early Sumerians governed themselves. In this scenario the early councils would have chosen the priest as administrator or the general for military operations, until gradually some individuals learned to retain these positions for themselves

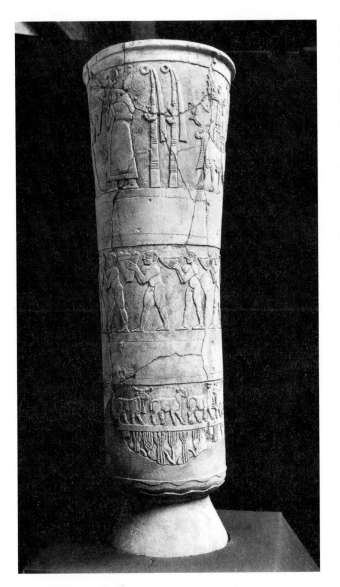

FIGURE 6.2 Warka vase. The vase is a carved alabaster stone vessel found in the temple complex of Inanna in the ruins of Uruk, dated about 3200 to 3000 BCE. It is 39 inches (100 centimeters) high and decorated with four bands of shallow relief carvings. The lowest band of carving is incised with a regular wavy line, probably symbolizing water. The next band shows ears of barley and date palms below, male and female sheep above. The third band portrays clean-shaven, bald, naked men walking in procession, each carrying a jug or vessel. The uppermost band, partially damaged, reveals a female figure, identified as Inanna, receiving tribute, overseen by the male priest-ruler, marked with the sign *EN*, the word for the highest male official. The vase presents a well-ordered, well-managed world, confidently meeting the challenges of collective life. The vase was looted from the National Museum of Iraq during the U.S. invasion of Iraq in 2003 and was later returned.

merchants. People inside the city walls did something other than farm; they had occupations such as scribes, priests, officials, bakers, cooks, potters, silversmiths, and snake charmers, as is known from the Standard Professions List, permanently. The question of how early leaders moved from consensual power to coercive power remains tantalizing and unclear.

The world's first written literature, the ***Epic of Gilgamesh,*** presents the story of Gilgamesh, said to be the fifth king of Uruk. The Sumerian king list of about 2000 BCE provides evidence that a king named Gilgamesh did actually rule over Uruk about 2750 BCE and successfully led the city in conflicts with Kish, a nearby city. The story of his rule was kept alive by oral retelling; the earliest texts that survive date from about 2100 BCE. In the epic the superhero, Gilgamesh, is portrayed as two-thirds divine, one-third human—the son of the goddess, Ninsun, and a high priest-ruler of Uruk. Gilgamesh has a male friend, Enkidu, who is transformed from a wild hunter into a city dweller. Together the two go on adventures, challenge the gods, seek immortality, and mourn their mortality. This first written account of a hero's journey portrays Gilgamesh finally returning to Uruk much wiser and appreciating it as never before.

Clothing

Before the invention of textiles, people wore animal skins if needed for warmth. After the domestication of sheep and goats in Mesopotamia, people there wore sheep- and goatskins; men used a belted skin as a kind of skirt, while women wore skins like a robe.

As part of the earliest development of agriculture, farmers around the eastern end of the Mediterranean Sea domesticated a tall, slender plant with dark leaves and bright blue flowers called flax. From the stem fibers of this plant, which grows about 4 feet (1.2 meters) tall, people learned to make the fabric called linen. The plant had to be watered, weeded, harvested, and dried. The dried stalks were dampened to rot the fleshy part of the stem off the fibers, which then had to be spliced together by wetting them with saliva, which contains an enzyme that decomposes the cellulose slightly. Finally, the fibers had to be spun into thread and woven into cloth, all of which took roughly 57 days of work to clothe one person for a year!

Since turning flax into linen proved laborious, in Uruk linen was reserved for priests and statues of gods. Sheep's fleece could be turned into wool more easily, first by spinning the fleece and then by weaving or knitting it into fabric. A hundred sheep could clothe 40 people a year after selective breeding produced fleecier sheep. Designs from Uruk show men wearing woolen skirts below their knees, probably not too comfortable in summer. The development of the state took the control of flax and wool away from women in their households. Paying tribute (see the glossary) may have forced poor families to sell women into debt slavery to work in urban textile workshops that employed thousands.

Writing

The earliest writing in the world, dated about 3500 BCE, comes from the Eanna Complex in Uruk; it is found slightly later in an area extending from Syria to Iran. Luckily for us, the

FIGURE 6.3 Cuneiform tablet from between 2900 and 2600 BCE. Found in Ur, a city in Sumer, this tablet records deliveries of barley to a temple.

Sumerians wrote with reed sticks on wet clay, which hardened into tablets that have survived the passage of time. Since other early people wrote on more perishable materials—Egyptians on papyrus, Chinese on bamboo, others on bark or wood—we cannot trace the long-term development of any other writing as clearly as we can that of Sumerian **cuneiform,** or wedge-shaped writing (the Latin term *cuneus* means "wedge"; see Figure 6.3).

Writing in Uruk was triggered by the need to keep track of the grain, sheep, and cattle that entered and left the warehouses and farms belonging to the city's rulers. Indeed, 85 percent of the earliest tablets found at Uruk recorded goods, food, and animals delivered by people or temples; the other 15 percent were lists of officials, commodities, and animals.

Writing evolved slowly over a long period. As early as 7500 BCE farmers near Uruk were using clay tokens the size of marbles to represent specific items: a cone meant one basket of grain, a cylinder meant one sheep. Gradually the tokens became more complex, with inscribed lines and drawings, including animal heads. Excavators have found tokens representing oil, honey, beer, cloth, and grain.

At the same time, round cylinder seals were used to guarantee that packages of goods were not broken into. The clay or stone seal, carved with a person's distinctive design, was rolled over wet clay applied to the packaging, which would harden and be broken if anyone not authorized tried to open the goods.

The initial signs on the clay tokens and on the cylinder seals pictured objects (pictographs); they did not represent spoken words, only the object itself. Hence, they could be read in both languages used in Sumer—Sumerian, not related to any other language living or dead, and Akkadian, a Semitic language related to Hebrew and Aramaic. The early Uruk tablets contain about 1,200 different signs.

Eventually, as states developed, administrators enclosed a group of tokens in round envelopes of clay, to organize them and to ensure that no one interfered with them. At first administrators made a picture of each token on the envelope to represent the tokens inside, because abstract numerals had not yet been conceptualized. Eventually someone realized that the tokens themselves were not needed, and the envelopes were flattened into tablets incised with pictures of items.

By 3100 BCE abstract numerals had appeared for the first time in history, stamped alongside the pictographs representing the commodity. The earliest numerical symbols were as follows: a small wedge stood for 1; a small circle meant 10. A large wedge stood for 60, a large wedge with a circle inside stood for 600, while a large circle meant 3,600. Hence, three small wedges plus three small circles meant 33, instead of drawing the item 33 times. Meanwhile, ordinary people dealing with small numbers went right on using the original tokens to keep track of their sheep and grain, with the latest set ever found dating about 1600 BCE, nearly 2,000 years after the invention of writing.

The early pictographs developed into symbols for ideas. For example, the picture for foot could also represent the idea "to stand" or "to walk." The Sumerian language contained many words of only one syllable, with quite a few of a single vowel sound. For example, the letter *a* (pronounced "a" as in *glass*) meant water. Hence, the picture for water could represent the sound of "a," the beginning of phonetic representation, especially needed to write the names of people.

Instruments for writing also evolved, beginning with simple stalks of reeds cut from marshes. The tip of the reed, or *stylus,* was cut obliquely into various shapes, eventually taking a wedge-shaped form, which is why Sumerian writing is called cuneiform, or wedge-shaped.

The transition from methods of accounting to true writing, with a complex combination of symbols representing sounds, syllables, ideas, and physical objects, may have happened quite rapidly as scribes in Uruk worked together about 3300 to 3200 BCE. Or this transition may have been more gradual, until about 2500 BCE, when texts began to appear that could be called full literature in the modern sense. Among the first literary pieces were incantations, hymns, superhero epics, and funeral songs. Recorded history is usually considered to have begun about 2700 BCE.

The invention of writing accelerated the elaboration of every aspect of human society. Collective Learning began to accelerate as the knowledge created by a whole society was recorded and preserved. In Mesopotamia, literacy led to the rapid expansion of knowledge, especially in astronomy (calendars) and mathematics (surveying). Sumerians used a mixed counting system based partly on 10 and partly on 60. (They counted animals and other discrete objects by 10 and grain by 60, perhaps because 60 is divisible 11 different ways.) They devised a calendar based on 12 months and divided the 24 hours of the day into 60 minutes with 60 seconds each. They divided a circle into 360 degrees. Does this sound familiar? Greek mathematicians used Sumerian ideas via Babylonia, transmitting this successful cultural convention to Western civilization and eventually to the entire modern world.

People used Sumerian cuneiform writing for recording several languages over a wide area from Syria to Elam in southwestern Iran. Even after Sumer declined in power, cuneiform script continued to be used for region-wide diplomacy; Aramaic superseded it in the seventh and sixth centuries BCE; conservative priests and scholars still used it into the first centuries of the Common Era.

Uruk in the Context of Sumer

In 500 years, between about 3600 and 3100 BCE, the people of Uruk led the development in Sumer of the city and the state, with their specialized occupations, institutions of coercion and protection, monumental temples and palaces, state religion, and writing as a form of accounting. As long as Uruk was the only large city in the vicinity, its artifacts spread throughout Mesopotamia and over sites from northern Syria, Lebanon, Palestine, and Oman to Anatolia (Turkey) to Iran, evidence of Uruk's extensive commercial relations.

This amazing period of invention came to an end about 3100 BCE, as revealed by the disappearance of Uruk cultural artifacts from the widespread sites. Apparently Uruk's burgeoning institutions of bureaucracy were scaled back to a more local level as new city centers developed throughout Sumer. Each of the new cities controlled its own territory and water, and each adopted Uruk's social institutions but became home to a different god or goddess in the pantheon.

By 3000 BCE Uruk had become just one of a dozen cities in southern Mesopotamia; others included Eridu, Ur, Lash, Nippur, Umma, and Kish, each ruled by a king who claimed absolute authority in his realm without, however, claiming to be divine, until Naram-sin, who ruled Akkad from 2254 to 2218 BCE, so claimed. It is estimated that in each city the temple owned about one-third of the arable land; nothing is known about how much land the ruling family owned, perhaps another third.

Warfare   **Warfare** had been present in Sumer since at least 4000 BCE; the earliest recovered cylinder seals depict battles and prisoners of war. After Gilgamesh, much fighting took place and seven kings reigned before the king of Ur overthrew the king of Uruk in 2560 BCE. For the next 200 years people in Sumerian cities engaged in almost constant warfare. Conflicts usually arose over land and over access to water and its control. During this time Sumerian kings controlled professional armies equipped with metal helmets, specialized weapons, and uniforms. Some soldiers fought in four-wheeled carts pulled by donkeys, but most, armed with long spears, served on foot. Constant military conflict justified military leaders increasing their landholdings and dominating political life. Professional soldiers were given land to support themselves and their families.

As described by Karen Nemet-Nejat in *Daily Life in Ancient Mesopotamia,* the standard of living in Sumerian cities often fell to just above subsistence level. Prosperity arrived only when the king and his army conquered other cities and distributed the booty and tribute among the soldiers and the bureaucracy. Then temples and palaces grew rich; imported luxuries became possible. But prosperity lasted for only short periods. Afterward people lived among the ruins of their city, prey to invading enemies and raids from people in open country.

The walls of Uruk were destroyed once again when Sargon of Akkad (ruled 2334–2279 BCE) conquered all of Sumer and beyond to the headwaters of the Euphrates to establish the first empire in the Tigris–Euphrates valley. Sargon's empire lasted less than 100 years. What caused the end? We know only that about 2250 BCE an unprecedented dry episode occurred, evidenced by soil samples from Tell Leilan, a site in northern Mesopotamia, which showed windblown dust and much-reduced rainfall. This site, abandoned suddenly, was not reoccupied for 300 years.

Along with drought, the Sumerians faced declining agricultural productivity from the increasing salinity of their soil. As soil becomes waterlogged from irrigation, salt rises to the surface. Wheat can tolerate a salt level of 0.5 percent, while barley can grow in twice this amount of salt. Scholars can deduce salinization by noting the declining proportions of wheat growth. In 3500 BCE half of the grain crop in Sumer was wheat; by 2500 BCE wheat constituted only 15 percent. Total crop yields fell by 40 percent between 2400 and 2100 BCE and had fallen by 66 percent by 1700 BCE, after which Sumer declined into insignificance as an impoverished backwater of other empires. Mesopotamian records of 2400 to 2000 BCE refer to salinization and loss of fertility caused by excessive irrigation; people were aware of what was happening. The problem of long-term sustainability, of not overexploiting the environment, has haunted complex societies for over 4,000 years.

The people of Uruk and Sumer invented technologies such as irrigation and writing that greatly increased their food supply and their offspring. Yet these innovations, up against the limits of soil and climate, could not prevent a decline in population, which decreased quite rapidly after its period of expansion. Such cycles, frequent in human history, are called **Malthusian cycles;** they are named for Thomas Malthus (1766–1834), an English pastor and economist who, in the early nineteenth century, argued that human populations will always rise faster than the supply of food, leading to times of famine and rapid decline. Malthus influenced Darwin's thinking, as described in Chapter 3, and he will appear again later in our story.

Cities and States in Other Regions

The people of Uruk may have been first to invent a city, but they were not alone. The forces at play—the drying climate driving people to river valleys, the increasing productivity from plows and irrigation, the extraordinary fertility of soil on floodplains, the density of population that occurred from successful reproduction and immigration—resulted in other cities arising independently at approximately the same latitude, namely in the Nile River valley and in the Indus River valley. Most modern scholars argue that these other cities arose independently rather than by diffusion, as earlier believed. Yet some new finding may at any time reverse this theory.

Egypt and Nubia in the Nile River Valley

In Egypt a dynasty of kings began its rule about 3100 BCE, only a few hundred years after people in Uruk invented the state. Until recently ancient Egypt was thought to be a "civilization without cities," but now it appears, from more excavations, that significant urban centers may have already existed there by the time Uruk became a city. Were these centers as large as those in Mesopotamia? Archaeologists simply aren't sure.

In about 9000 BCE, the Sahara Desert had lower temperatures and higher rainfall than at present. Grasslands with lakes, rivers, and streams were able to produce wild grains that supported humans and wild cattle. Within the next 4,000 years people in this grassland region domesticated cattle and began the independent cultivation of sorghum, gourds, watermelons, and cotton. Sheep and goats arrived from Mesopotamia, possibly replacing smaller ones already domesticated in Egypt. By about 5000 BCE chiefdoms had developed across the grasslands, based, not on cities, but on prosperous villages headed by hereditary chief-kings, already considered divine or semidivine.

As the climate became drier, the Sahara turned into a desert, driving humans and animals away, either southward to the area around Lake Chad or into the valley of the Nile River, flowing north from its source in Lake Victoria. Two prosperous regions grew along the Nile River, which is broken by six cataracts, or nonnavigable sections of rapids and waterfalls (Map 6.2). One region, called Egypt, reached 700 miles from the Mediterranean Sea to the first cataract near Aswan; the other stretched from the first to the sixth cataract, encompassing what is today the northern part of Sudan. It was called **Nubia** after the fourth century CE; earlier it was called Kush.

When people first began moving into the Nile River valley, they found extremely fertile soil, with annual flooding at the right season for watering their crops. At first irrigation probably proved unnecessary, but rapid population growth spurred a spread beyond the immediate floodplain; catchment basins to store water for irrigation had to be built, and canals for irrigation. By 4000 BCE agricultural villages flourished along the shores of the Nile from the Mediterranean to the fourth cataract, trading with each other regularly and cooperating in irrigation networks.

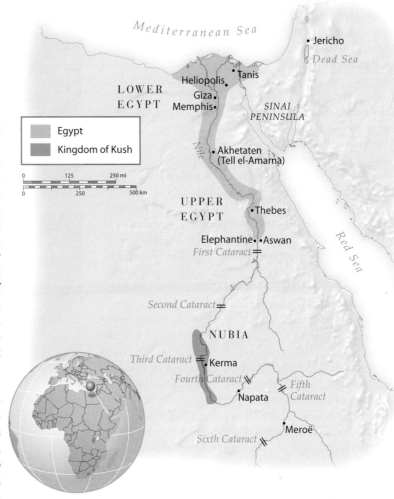

MAP 6.2 The Nile valley, 3000 to 2000 BCE. Notice how much larger Egypt is than Kush. What geographic advantages did the state of Egypt have?

Egypt was spared salinization of its soil, as the annual flooding of the Nile flushed out any accumulated salts.

About 3500 BCE a sudden decline in rainfall occurred across the Sahara region, and villages throughout Egypt and Nubia morphed into small chiefdoms with a somewhat larger-scale organization and administration but still without large central cities. Local kings organized their region by using a tradition that included sacrificing their servants in the burial of kings. Recent excavations at settlements on the Upper Nile (Koptos, Naqada, Abydos), however, have revealed larger populations than were formerly known, suggesting that some large cities may have existed.

Unification

Political and economic competition also intensified after 3500 BCE, perhaps in response to the drier conditions. A Nubian dynasty, the Ta-Seti, ruled from 3400 to 3200 BCE and extended its domain north of the first cataract. The Egyptians, on more fertile land than the Nubians, fought back; three centers in Upper Egypt were unified first: Naqada, Hierakonopolis, and Abydos. Tradition holds that about 3100 to 3000 BCE a leader named Menes, sometimes known as Narmer, united both parts of Egypt, Lower Egypt at the delta and Upper Egypt from the delta to the first cataract. The evidence for state control consists of the names of the first dynasty kings on pots, sealings, and labels, suggesting that a state system of tribute was in place.

Egypt's largest city at this time was Hierakonopolis, with a population of about 10,000, in Upper (southern) Egypt. To expedite unification, Menes founded the city of Memphis, near present-day Cairo at the head of the delta. By this time Egypt had developed extreme polarization of wealth, as revealed by grave goods, and a standardized material culture stretching from the delta to the first cataract. One could sail with the current down the Nile as it flowed to the Mediterranean Sea in a week, or back up it, since the prevailing winds blew southward.

Religious Beliefs

Egypt established a divine kingship from the earliest times, based on the traditions of early agricultural societies in this area. In the official ideology, the king was considered a god living on Earth; he was associated with Horus, or "the One on High," and with the golden falcon or hawk, the symbol of Horus. The king's role was to preserve the equilibrium of creation and to allow the world to function as it should. Egyptian ideology stressed the continuity of the past and the stability and prosperity achieved by the government of wise and pious kings.

Egyptian morality was based on respect for universal equilibrium as personified by the goddess, Ma'at, a naked adolescent girl who represented balance, order, and truth, the antithesis of chaos. The annual flooding of the Nile apparently gave a sense of assurance and security to Egyptians that the gods would provide stability.

Unlike the Mesopotamians, who thought that after death one persists only as a pale, faint approximation of life in a place of perpetual darkness (the House of Dust), the Egyptians believed in a vivid life after death that continued one's full earthly existence. Egyptians created the art of mummification, workable in a hot, dry climate, as part of this belief. Their kings, known as *pharaohs*, developed a passion for elaborate tombs to protect their bodies and ensure their afterlife. The first pharaoh of the Third Dynasty, Djoser (ca. 2650 BCE), built the step pyramid at Saqqara, the oldest stone building of its size in the world. Three generations of pharaohs built the largest pyramids, starting about 75 years later. These tombs stand today at Giza, near Cairo. The largest, known as Khufu, or Cheops, contains 2.3 million blocks of limestone, averaging 2.5 tons (2.3 metric tons)

crossing a mini-threshold

Cities and States in Other Regions   **137**

each, although the largest weigh 15 tons (13.6 metric tons). Building these pyramids required a state administration; an estimated 84,000 men must have labored 80 days a year for 20 years, and that is not counting the engineers, supervisors, cooks, and their families.

Egyptians used a 365-day calendar, consisting of twelve 30-day months, each divided into three 10-day weeks. They devoted the extra 5 days of the year to honoring their most important gods.

Writing

Tombs assumed such importance in early Egypt that one of the first pieces of recovered writing from this civilization is a label from a tomb, dating sometime before 3100 BCE. Much of the impetus for writing had come from the demands of accounting, as in Mesopotamia. By the time of Menes (about 3100 BCE) the distinctive Egyptian script was in full use. Little is known yet about the gradual development of the script; recent discoveries at Abydos may have revealed writing beginning even earlier than in Mesopotamia.

The Egyptians, like the Mesopotamians, began with simple pictographs, but they soon supplemented them with symbols representing sounds and ideas, resulting eventually in several thousand signs. Egyptians decorated their buildings, including temples, with written symbols, leading Greek visitors to call them "holy inscriptions," or hieroglyphs. These symbols were also drawn on papyrus, a writing material formed by gluing together the insides of papyrus reeds that flourished along the Nile River; papyrus records have survived because of the hot, dry climate in Egypt.

About 2800 to 2600 BCE a simplified and cursive form of **hieroglyphics** for use on papyrus appeared, called "hieratic"; later a simpler vernacular script, called "demotic," developed. Egyptian scribes enjoyed a privileged life, which we know from a short piece called "The Satire of Trades," in which a scribe-father exhorts his son to study diligently to become a scribe, since all other trades involve misery of some sort (see Chapter 7). Yet even privileged Egyptian scribes did not generate literary traditions as rich or varied as those found in Mesopotamia.

Hieroglyphics were used into the fourth century CE, when Arabic superseded them. Their meaning was lost until 1824, when a Frenchman, Jean-François Champollion, published his decipherment of the Rosetta Stone (Figure 6.4).

Nubians also used hieroglyphics, but eventually they transformed the symbols into an alphabetic script for their own language, Meroetic, named after their capital, Meroe (modern Begrawiya in Sudan). Their inscriptions survive, but scholars do not understand the language, which is completely different from any other.

Trade and Connections

Did the Egyptians borrow their writing in any way from the Sumerians? Since there is little similarity in language or script, scholars believe that Egyptian writing likely developed independently. Yet Egyptians had early connections to Sumer. Cylinder seals and Mesopotamian styles of

FIGURE 6.4 Rosetta Stone. The Rosetta Stone is an irregularly shaped stone of black basalt found in 1799 near the town of Rosetta (Rashid), near Alexandria, by Napoleon's soldiers. The inscription is a priestly decree affirming the royal cult of the 13-year-old Ptolemy V. It is written in hieroglyphs, demotic, and Greek, which enabled Champollion to decipher the hieroglyphs. The stone is kept in the British Museum in London.

architectural decoration, dated from about 3500 to 3000 BCE, have been found in the Delta region of Egypt, though the exact trade routes are not known.

Trade to the south is easier to trace. Since gold, ivory, ebony, and precious stones were available only in Nubia, Egyptians tried to control that trade. Their kings organized at least five military campaigns against Nubia between 3100 and 2600 BCE; they conquered the land between the first and second cataracts from 3000 to 2400 BCE. Nubian leaders established the powerful kingdom of Kush by 2500 BCE, with its capital, Kerma, at the third cataract. Interchange went on, with Nubian men figuring prominently in Egyptian armies and assimilating into Egyptian society by marrying Egyptian women.

Decline

About 2200 BCE, Egypt experienced some two centuries of drier conditions and low flood levels, which brought famine to the Nile valley. The central power of the kings diminished, with regional chiefs becoming more powerful. Trade through Syria declined; neighbors invaded; unity was not restored until about 2020 BCE. This Malthusian cycle interrupted briefly the celebrated stability of Egyptian civilization. Afterward, an independent Egyptian civilization

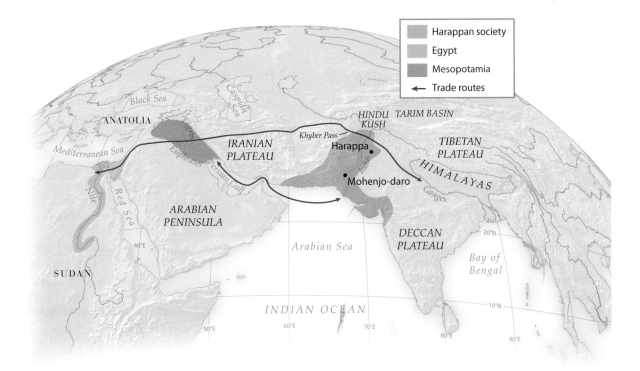

persisted until its conquest by Alexander the Great in 332 BCE.

A question of recent interest about ancient Egypt has been, what color was the skin of its people? In the United States, Egypt's population has often been portrayed as being primarily Semitic—from Palestine and Syria—rather than as being a black-skinned African population. In the mid-1980s claims were made that Egyptians were mostly black Africans, a needed corrective but an equal exaggeration, although for one century during the early first millennium BCE the Egyptian pharaohs were all black Nubians.

After much examination of this issue, scholars have concluded that Egypt's position at the bridge between Africa and Asia gave it a unique character. Its people were a mixture with a wide range of skin color and hair type. Studies of how Egyptians depicted themselves suggest that they saw themselves as midway between black Africans and paler Asians. No barriers to immigration into Egypt have been found in its earliest laws; Semitic people came, as well as Nubians. Egyptians, aware and tolerant of ethnic differences, seemed more concerned that immigrants behaved culturally as Egyptians.

The Indus River Valley

The Indus River begins high in the Hindu Kush and Himalayan mountain ranges, spilling down over a large floodplain, sometimes leaving its channel altogether and carving new courses to the sea. Another river, the Sarasvati or Ghaggar-Hakra, used to flow alongside the Indus, but eventually it dried up when earthquakes in the mountains caused its tributaries to flow into the Indus. The ancient floodplain of the two rivers covers much of modern Pakistan and a large part of northern India, an area larger than Mesopotamia and Egypt combined. As in those regions, the

MAP 6.3 Indus valley civilization, ca. 2000 BCE.
Compare the size of Indus valley civilization to that of Mesopotamia and Egypt. What conditions and technologies permitted trade to flow between the Indus River valley and Mesopotamia?

floodplain of the Indus River created rich agricultural land bounded by highlands, desert, and ocean (Map 6.3).

Less is known about the early rise of cities and civilization in the Indus valley than about others because the earliest physical remains there are now covered by water. Silt deposits have raised the level of the land, and the water table has risen along with it. The earliest accessible remains date to about 2500 BCE; by then, urban structures had already been established, but there seems no way to learn about the earlier time in which they developed.

Another problem lies in the fact that the Indus valley writing has not been deciphered. Thousands of clay seals, copper tablets, and other artifacts with inscriptions using about 400 signs have been found, some dating to 3000 BCE, but the language has vanished. No one agrees what the language was; no inscription is longer than 26 characters; no bilingual text like the Rosetta Stone has been found. For these reasons many scholars believe that the script is likely to remain undeciphered, despite continued attempts.

By 7000 BCE grain cultivation had taken root in the Indus valley, probably as a result of Mesopotamian influences, although all the early domesticates except wheat are also found wild in Pakistani Baluchistan and the nearby highlands. Wheat, barley, lentils, and millet were sown in the fall, after the floodwaters had subsided, and were harvested in the spring. Indus farmers cared for domestic cattle, water buffalo, sheep, goats, and chickens. They were growing cotton before 5000 BCE, the earliest evidence in the world.

By 3200 BCE the earliest cities were forming, at Harappa in northern India near the Himalayan foothills and at Mohenjo-Daro 250 miles to the south. There is evidence to indicate increasing aridity during the fourth millennium (3999–3000 BCE), suggesting that people on the Indian subcontinent may have flocked to the river valleys in response to climate change, just as people in Mesopotamia and Egypt probably did. A rapid transition to urbanization seems to have occurred; the population of the area is estimated to have tripled between 3000 and 2600 BCE.

At its height, about 2500 to 1900 BCE, Mohenjo-Daro was home to about 35,000 to 40,000 people, with Harappa slightly smaller. Each city had walls, a fortified citadel, a large granary, and a site for collecting and redistributing taxes paid in grain. The city streets were laid out on grids, indicating city planning, with marketplaces, small temples, and public buildings. Residences varied from one room in barrack-like buildings to houses with dozens of rooms and several interior courtyards. Indoor bathing facilities were found in almost all the houses, with a Great Bath in Mohenjo-Daro, and pipes under the streets to carry away wastewater, a significant investment of community resources. Standardization was evident throughout the Indus valley in weights, measures, architectural styles, and sizes of bricks. Specialized occupations included goldsmiths, potters, weavers, architects, jewelers, and merchants.

The people of the Indus valley carried on a lively trade with their neighbors. From what is now Iran they received gold, silver, copper, and semiprecious stones. With Sumer they traded carnelian (red stone) beads, ivory from elephants, and timber, in exchange for wool, leather, and olive oil. By 2300 BCE, if not before, Indus valley ships were anchoring in Sumerian ports. By 2000 BCE Harappans were trading with early cities in Central Asia, whose people were not fully literate despite their contacts with northern India, Sumer, and China. By the early second millennium, Indus people were trading with the southern coast of Arabia and the eastern coast of Africa, bringing home incense, sorghum, and millet.

Not much is known about the religious ideas of the people of the Indus valley because their writing has not been deciphered. From imagery it seems that Indus people especially venerated gods and goddesses associated with creation and procreation; many scholars believe, because of similarities between Indus valley and Hindu deities of fertility, that some of their deities found a place in the later Hindu pantheon. The ancient practice of yoga may go back to the days of the Indus valley civilization, as suggested by several yogi images among Harappan artifacts.

What was different about the rise of cities in the Indus valley? Have you noticed there has been no mention of weapons and warfare, kings, palaces, or large temples? Political hierarchy, or central administration, seems not to have existed. The Indus valley appears to have been a land without large-scale conflict. There are no depictions of soldiers or warfare in its art; some arrowheads, spears, and daggers have been found but no swords, maces, battle-axes, helmets, shields, or chariots, although recent excavations show more military fortification and economic stratification than previously thought.

No one knows what held Indus valley society together. Some scholars doubt that it qualifies as a state. Some imagine that decentralized councils must have governed. Others conjecture that the caste system that characterized later India must have developed as early as the third millennium (2999–2000 BCE). A **caste system,** in which people are rigidly organized in hierarchical groups determined by heredity, could explain how the Indus culture spread without warfare over such a large area. People had to marry within their own caste, but because the local pool was often too small, those arranging the marriage had to look to other communities, thus uniting distant towns.

Whatever held the Indus valley civilization together, it failed eventually. Sometime after 1900 BCE the valley entered a period of decline; by 1700 BCE people in Harappa and Mohenjo-Daro had abandoned those cities for smaller ones; by 1500 cities everywhere in the Indus valley had almost entirely devolved with a loss of urban traits and a reversion to local traditions.

A number of possible factors interacted to produce this result. Climate change about 2200 BCE brought prolonged droughts, although they seem to have been over by 1900 to 1700 BCE. Deforestation for land clearance and firewood seems to have resulted in erosion and reduced rainfall, although some scholars contest this. The Sarasvati River dried up between 2000 and 1000 BCE, as mentioned earlier, after earthquakes in the Himalayas diverted its tributaries to the Indus River. Malaria and cholera may have hit the urban areas, as sewerage may have contaminated the drinking water. Farmers from the Indus valley may have moved elsewhere as the use of rice and millet arrived, since these crops are grown in summer rather than in winter and are not suited to areas flooded in summer.

The most notable aspect of Indus valley civilization may lie in its absence of violence and military activity and in its more equitable distribution of wealth than in Egypt and Mesopotamia. Nonviolence and respect for life have been major themes in Indian religion and philosophy throughout recorded history; is it going too far to see this as a legacy of the first cities in the Indus valley? One scholar of this agrarian civilization (McIntosh) feels there must be a grain of truth in this suggestion. Others (Coningham) conclude that Indus people experienced as much violence as Sumerians, but did not celebrate or ritualize it in the same way.

China: Two River Valleys

Since scientific archaeology is only a few decades old in China, only the broad outlines of early state formation there have come to light. We can expect much more to be unearthed in the decades to come.

For a long time archaeologists and historians believed that the earliest Chinese cities arose in the valley of the Huang He, or Yellow River, because that is where excavations were carried out. Only recently have excavations on the Chang Jiang, or Yangtze, River been undertaken. These

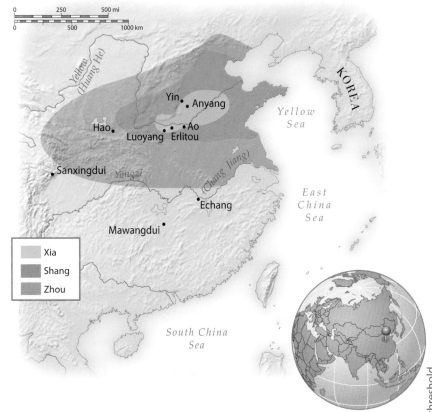

MAP 6.4 The Xia, Shang, and Zhou Dynasties, 2200 to 256 BCE. Notice how each dynasty gradually increased the size of its territory over time. What could explain the increasing size of these early Chinese states?

excavations have revealed large cities and such splendid grave goods that now archaeologists say that agrarian civilization arose independently and simultaneously in China in both of its great river valleys.

Huang He Valley

Huang means "yellow" in Chinese; *he* means "river." The river is so named because the water is colored yellow by a powder-like soil, called loess, suspended in it. The Huang He rises in the mountains bordering the high plateau of Tibet and flows 2,920 miles (4,700 kilometers) to the Yellow Sea. Like the Indus River, originating nearby, the Huang He is not consistent, periodically unleashing horrendous flooding and even changing course, causing enough destruction to earn the nickname, "China's sorrow" (see Map 6.4).

Loess soil was deposited on the plains of China after the retreat of glaciers, which ground rocks into dust about 15,000 to 12,000 years ago; winds from the Gobi Desert blow the soil over the Huang He valley. Loess soil has many advantages: organically rich, it requires little plowing and retains moisture from sparse rainfall.

In the previous chapter we saw that by 7000 BCE, people in the valley of the Huang He had domesticated millet, a drought-resistant and highly nutritious grain, with more protein than durum wheat. By 5000 BCE villages flourished in the valley, based on the cultivation of millet, supplemented by 2000 BCE with wheat and barley, which may have come from Mesopotamia. In addition to millet, people in the Huang He valley cultivated hemp for clothing, rapeseed and soybeans for edible oil, and pigs, which subsisted in part on human waste, for meat.

The period known as the Longshan culture (3000–2000 BCE), witnessed some momentous steps toward city life in the Huang He valley. By 2700 BCE there is evidence that people had learned to unwind silk from the cocoon of a particular species of silk moth caterpillar, which they domesticated, and had learned to spin the silk into fiber for weaving cloth. By 2500 BCE walled settlements and wheel-thrown pottery appear in the archaeological remains. Apparently in most years there was sufficient rainfall for crops to grow without the need for complex irrigation systems, but people dredged the river and built canals to control flooding. Metallurgy appeared during this period, as well as sophisticated pottery and jade ornaments,

suggesting specialized craftspeople. Sharp social distinctions arose, and warfare increased.

During these years the climate was changing from a warm, humid climate to a cooler, more arid condition. Evidence shows that maximum aridity occurred about 2500 to 1500 BCE. Population in the Huang He valley multiplied threefold over the years from 3000 to 2000 BCE as people migrated into the valley from adjacent areas as the climate became drier.

By about 1700 to 1500 BCE a dynasty called the Xia had arisen in the Huang He valley. The study of the Xia is still in its early stages. Recent excavations of Erlitou, near Luoyang, suggest to Chinese archaeologists that it may have been the capital of the Xia Dynasty. Findings include a palace-type structure, more modest homes, a pottery workshop, and a bronze foundry. Its discovery confirmed the accuracy of the accounts of early Chinese history by China's great historian, Sima Qian (ca. 145–86 BCE).

Chinese urban life and culture developed rapidly with the advent of the Shang Dynasty in about 1500 BCE, extending the area of the Xia in the valley of the Huang He. The Shang Dynasty ruled a large portion of northeast China, centered on the modern province of Henan, until about 1045 BCE and provided the foundation for the further development of Chinese civilization.

During the period of the Shang Dynasty the full characteristics of agrarian civilization emerged in northern China. Hereditary kings claiming divine descent ruled, supported by an elite aristocracy. No law codes have been found; kings apparently issued proclamations or decrees. Peasants, not owning their land, provided services in exchange for plots to cultivate, security, and a portion of the harvest. They were subject to conscription for military service and public works. A sizable class of slaves existed, mostly warriors captured in battle; hundreds of them were sacrificed during funerary and civil rituals.

The Shang rulers monopolized bronze production in the Huang He valley; they employed craftspeople to expand production of bronze axes, spears, knives, and arrowheads; and bronze fittings for horse-drawn chariots appeared. The chariots had been brought into the westernmost province of China, Xingiang, by Indo-European immigrants, which we know because the ancient Chinese words for wheel, spoke, axle, and chariot all derive from Indo-European roots.

The Shang kings moved their capital city five or six times. During their last few centuries they made Yin, near Anyang, their ritual capital. Incessant warfare occurred between numerous city-states; records mention armies up to 13,000, the capture of 30,000 soldiers, probably an inflated report. Unlike in Mesopotamia and Egypt, there is little indication of large-scale irrigation systems or of state religions.

Excavations at Yin have revealed a complex of royal palaces, archives of written records, residential neighborhoods, two large bronze foundries, craft workshops, and 11 lavish tombs, including one in which 300 people were sacrificed to join the king in death. One tomb, discovered in 1976, escaped previous notice by thieves because it lay in the palace rather than in the cemetery. It contained the bones of Fu Hao, a consort of the Shang king Wu Ding (d. 1189 BCE). Documents from the tomb showed that Fu Hao supervised her own domain, presided over sacrificial ceremonies, and could mobilize 3,000 warriors at her personal command. (Read more about Fu Hao's tomb in Chapter 8.)

In the Shang Dynasty men had public authority, but until the late dynasty years they received their right to it through their mother's family; Chinese elite society was matrilineal. Women seem to have exercised power more often than in other early civilizations, but by later Shang times society had lost its matrilineal character as the patriarchal family emerged as the dominant institution.

In China the extended family became particularly influential because families venerated their ancestors. They believed that the spirits of ancestors passed to another realm from which they could protect their surviving family members, if the descendants showed the proper respect. The ethic of family solidarity included a sense of the living and the dead working together. No organized religion or official priesthood existed; the eldest male of each family presided at rituals in honor of the ancestors' spirits. During the Shang Dynasty texts and inscriptions tell us that Shang nobles felt in constant communication with their ancestors, but they imagined no personal deity who intervened in human affairs.

Chinese merchants of the Shang period traded widely, although what they exported is not clear. They imported tin from the Malay Peninsula in Southeast Asia and cowry shells, which they used as a proto-money, from Burma and the Maldive Islands in the Indian Ocean. They had large,

oar-propelled ships by 2000 BCE; during Shang times ships went to Korea. Whether or not they had sails is not clear.

The heaviest trade went along routes to Central Asia from where the Chinese fetched their treasured jade. About 2000 BCE a cluster of trading cities appeared in Central Asia, called *Oxus* culture, with links to Sumer, China, and northern India, as well as to the pastoralists of inner Asia. Could this be called, already by 2000 BCE, a single Afro-Eurasian world system—that is, a systematically interrelated network driven by capital accumulation? That question is much debated by historians.

Chinese writing came into extensive use during the Shang Dynasty, in the early sixteenth century BCE. The roots of writing must have appeared much earlier, but evidence is scarce. Single characters used as identification have been found on pottery pieces dating back to the third millennium BCE, but most U.S. scholars consider these isolated characters, not part of a multicharacter system of writing. We know that the Shang Dynasty, and possibly earlier rulers, recorded important events on strips of bamboo and pieces of silk, all of which biodegraded in time.

In China, unlike in Mesopotamia and India, the earliest writing of which we have records served the interests of the rulers rather than the accountants. We know because one writing medium has survived—the so-called oracle bones, the shoulder blades from oxen or sheep or the under shells of turtles, supplied to royal courts by tribute. Most of the recovered oracle bones have come from royal archives, yet it is possible that Chinese script may have been invented for economic or administrative purposes, but those transactions have vanished on perishable materials.

In the last years of the nineteenth century CE, peasants working in fields near Anyang found bones they called "dragon bones." They sold them to druggists, who ground them into medicinal powders, until they soon came to the attention of historians and literary scholars. Since then, more than 100,000 such bones have been found. At an auction in China in 2008 twenty oracle bone fragments sold for 48 million Chinese yuan, or about $7 million.

In the second millennium (1999–1000) BCE Chinese diviners inscribed the bones with questions, mostly ones of concern to the court: Will the harvests be bountiful? Will the queen's child be a boy? Should the king attack his neighbors? Will there be any disasters in the next 10 days? After inscribing the bone or shell with the question, the diviner would heat it until it split into a network of cracks, which the diviner interpreted as the answer, often recording it on the bone.

Of the approximately 2,000 characters used on oracle bones, most have a modern recognizable counterpart. Unlike cuneiform or hieroglyphics, early Chinese writing has been in use continuously about 4,000 years. It began as pictures (pictographs); later, pictures were combined to represent complex or abstract ideas as, for example, the picture for mother and for child combined meaning "good." Unlike most other languages, Chinese writing never has adopted alphabetic or phonetic components. Evidence of writing being expanded into literature begins with the early Zhou Dynasty, starting in 1045 BCE.

Chang Jiang (Yangtze) River Valley

A river even longer than the Huang He flows through what is present-day southern China—the Yangtze River, or Chang Jiang (Long River), as it is known in China. With origins in the Qinghai Mountains of Tibet, the Chang Jiang wends 3,915 miles (6,300 kilometers) to the East China Sea. With a subtropical climate more humid and warmer than in the north, the southern areas could produce two rice crops a year. The Chang Jiang does not flood like the Huang He, but irrigation is needed to release its waters at the time crops need them. Rice was brought under cultivation in the middle Chang Jiang lake-lands by about 8000 BCE, providing a stable food supply on which large populations could depend.

Excavations in the 1990s at Chengtoushan revealed a walled town from about 4000 BCE with some elite goods that suggest social stratification. The most dramatic discovery, however, occurred in 1986 in Sichuan province at Sanxingdui, a city with walls built in 1400 BCE. Two pits there were filled with spectacular jade, gold, and bronze pieces of art, contemporary with Shang Dynasty artifacts, yet distinctive in style. No royal tombs have yet been found at Sanxingdui, but its discovery has convinced archaeologists that southern China produced a civilization that rivaled that at Anyang; it has been newly named the Changjiang culture.

The Qin and the Han Dynasties brought China under unified rule in the third century BCE, and since then the political centralization and agricultural productivity of China has consistently supported about 20 percent of the world's population. Farmers have farmed the same land for over 40 centuries. China today seems to many people a culture recognizably descended from one that began some 4,000 years ago, a continuity unlike any other contemporary culture.

Agrarian Civilization in the Americas

Agrarian civilizations began in the Americas later than in Afro-Eurasia, mostly for geographic reasons. None ever emerged in North America, but only in Mesoamerica and the Andes. These civilizations are of great interest because their evolution was very similar to that of civilizations in Afro-Eurasia, though they evolved a bit later, so they were still developing when Afro-Eurasians began to arrive in the Americas at the end of the fifteenth century.

Up to now we have focused most of our discussion on Afro-Eurasia. But remember from Chapter 5 that beginning about 10,000 years ago, the world was divided by the rising seas at the end of the last ice age into four nonconnected geographic zones. These four **world zones** were:

1. Afro-Eurasia (Africa and the Eurasian landmass, plus offshore islands like Britain and Japan).
2. The Americas (North, Central and South America, plus offshore islands).
3. Australasia (Australia, the island of Papua New Guinea, plus neighboring islands).
4. The island societies of the Pacific (New Zealand, Micronesia, Melanesia, and Hawaii).

In these four separate world zones, people developed distinctive lifeways and conducted their own experiments in human culture until the world became interconnected by the voyages of European sailors in the early sixteenth century.

Experiments in Mesoamerica

Mesoamerica is a cultural area that encompasses central Mexico to Panama, all of Guatemala, Belize, and El Salvador, and parts of Honduras, Costa Rica, and Nicaragua (Map 6.5). There sedentary farming

MAP 6.5 Early Mesoamerican societies, 1200 BCE to 1100 CE.
Describe the different geographic settings of these early Mesoamerican societies. How did the geographic and environmental conditions influence the development of these societies?

communities had formed by about 2000 BCE, based on growing corn, beans, and squash, with no domestic animals other than dogs and turkeys. Increasing social complexity followed rapidly in certain productive areas, with the buildup of productivity, Collective Learning, and population growth again the primary motors of social change.

By about 1200 BCE, a burgeoning society, known as the Olmecs, emerged in the lowlands of the Gulf region of modern Mexico, near the present city of Veracruz. The Olmecs created monumental architecture and extraordinary art; they organized warfare, trading and tribute networks, ceremonial centers, and pyramids up to 36 yards (33 meters) high for use as tombs, providing an apt symbol of hierarchy. (Why did nearly all Early Agrarian civilizations produce pyramids? Probably because they are the easiest to build of the possible shapes for a monumental structure capable of bearing its own weight. Or was it that they all attempted to get closer to the gods by building artificial mountains?) Archaeologists find hints in Olmec remains of an early writing system different from the Mayan and possibly the dating system subsequently adopted by Mesoamericans.

The Olmecs left nearly imperishable representations of themselves: huge heads carved from hunks of basalt, some weighing more than 20 tons (18 metric tons), hauled from quarries 37 miles (59 kilometers) away. Seventeen of these heads have been found, dated uncertainly at 1400 to 400 BCE (Figure 6.5).

The large heads provide indisputable evidence of the exercise of power by Olmec chiefs. Was this power consensual, indicating a chiefdom, or was it coercive, marking an agrarian civilization with state structures? By 800 BCE Olmec leaders were able to coordinate the construction of a spectacular ceremonial project at La Venta on an island in a coastal swamp. The discovery of a throne, as well as an elaborate tomb with rich burial goods at La Venta, gives evidence of an Olmec leader of inherited rank commanding people and resources.

Some see the Olmec society as a chiefdom rather than a state; some see it as the "mother culture" of Mesoamerica; others see it as one of many regional societies in Mexico rapidly evolving into more complex social and economic institutions. By 300 BCE Olmec culture was in decline, with Mayan culture burgeoning in the coastal lowlands into what would become an agrarian civilization by any standards (see Chapter 9).

Experiments in the Andes Mountains The unique geography of the Andean region presented a major challenge to any experiments in civilization there. Created by the Nazca tectonic plate at the bottom of the Pacific Ocean sliding eastward under the South American plate, two parallel mountain ranges run north and south only 60 miles (96 kilometers) east of the coast (Map 6.6). The mountains rise to some 22,000 feet (6,705 meters); they prevent the prevailing winds from the east from reaching the narrow coastland, which is a desert

FIGURE 6.5 Olmec head. This one was carved from basalt rock between 1000 and 600 BCE. These heads have inspired much speculation: The close-fitting helmets of some may have been caps worn by ballplayers; many faces have wide lips and flat noses, leading an Africanist historian like Ivan Van Septima to claim the Olmecs were visited by Africans or originated in Africa, views not widely held. Probably the heads represent rulers or shaman-rulers; no one knows.

most of the time, with an annual coastal precipitation of about 2 inches (5 centimeters), mostly from fog. East of the mountains lies the tropical rain forest, completing a mosaic of microclimates from the coast to the onset of the rain forest. Earthquakes caused by the moving tectonic plates rock the region frequently. People faced, in addition, the instability of warming–cooling episodes in the ocean's surface temperature, now called El Niño/La Niña events, which bring torrential rains and kill or divert the supply of fish.

Just south of Peru, on the Chilean coast, lies the driest place on Earth, the Atacama Desert. In some places no rainfall has ever been recorded, although many rivers run through the desert. Here the Chinchorro people created the world's first known mummies, some 2,000 years before the Egyptian ones. Two hundred and fifty mummies have been found, dating from about 5800 BCE. Even though the hot, dry sand could naturally mummify bodies, the Chinchorros dried the interior with fire, stiffened the spine and limbs with wooden shafts, and coated the body with painted clay, using the body ritually for extended periods.

Most of the early Andean heartland—contemporary Peru and Bolivia—came under cultivation between 2500 and 2000 BCE. Farmers near the coast relied on beans, peanuts, and sweet potatoes as their main crops, also cultivating cotton for textiles and fishnets. Marine life from the ocean supplemented food supplies, enabling an increasingly complex society. By at least 2000 BCE coastal communities had built up several technologies indicating developing states—canals and irrigation systems, pottery,

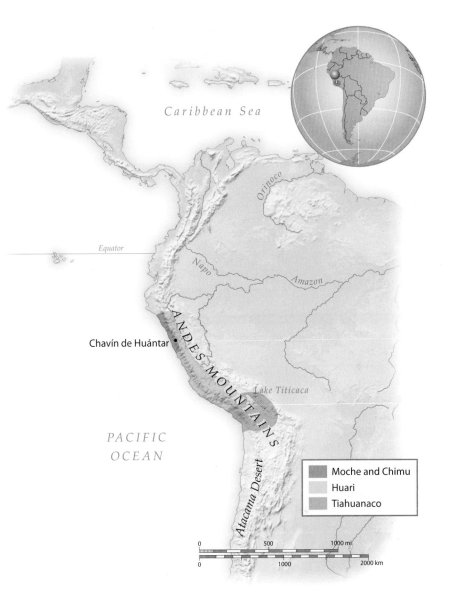

MAP 6.6 **Early societies of Andean south, 1000 BCE to 700 CE.** Notice the difficulties of contact with Mesoamerica. Why did these mountain societies not expand to the east?

Caribbean Sea

Orinoco

Equator

Napo

Amazon

Chavín de Huántar

ANDES MOUNTAINS

Lake Titicaca

PACIFIC
OCEAN

Atacama Desert

- Moche and Chimu
- Huari
- Tiahuanaco

0   500   1000 mi
0   1000   2000 km

temples, and stone pyramids. After 2000 BCE agricultural communities also subsisted in the highlands, where people cultivated tobacco and many varieties of potatoes. They herded llamas for meat, alpacas for wool. Potatoes, if eaten in sufficient quantities, can provide all the nutrition that humans need.

Early Andean societies arose contemporaneously with early Mesoamerican ones, raising the question of contact between them. Apparently the difficult geography between them discouraged travel and contact; neither society possessed abundant pack animals or a sailing technology. (Even today the Pan American Highway is unfinished at the Panama–Colombian border; bulldozers can't make it through the swamps and mountains.) Yet some contact happened, for slowly the cultivation of corn and squashes diffused from Mesoamerica to the Andes, while gold, silver, and copper metallurgy and tobacco spread north to Mesoamerica.

In about 1000 BCE a town called Chavín de Huántar began to emerge about 3,000 feet (914 meters) high in the Andes, on the Mosna River; it faded by 300 BCE. In its heyday some 2,000 to 3,000 people lived here. It seems to have been a religious ritual center, with ceremonial spaces, storehouses, and sculptures showing humans half transformed as jaguars and other animals. Chavín served as a distribution center for trade from the rain forest and influenced other Andean sites, but seems too small to be considered a state. Soon after its demise, several towns of about 10,000 people emerged in the Andes, with large public buildings, ceremonial plazas, and extensive residential districts.

Along with the large towns, regional states emerged, organized in the valleys of the mountains from the coast up through the midlands to the highlands. The coastal areas provided fish, cotton, and sweet potatoes; the midlands corn, beans, and squash; while the highlands produced potatoes, llama meat, and alpaca wool. This diversity of ecosystems provided enough to sustain growing populations and complexity of social organization.

Other Experiments in Early States

In a few places in the world, like sub-Saharan Africa and the Pacific Islands, only small states emerged. These are interesting as counterexamples to agrarian civilizations that give clues about what elements were necessary for the emergence of full-scale civilizations.

Sub-Saharan Africa   Like the people of the Andes, the people of sub-Saharan Africa had to deal with an unusually challenging environment. A harsh desert separated the sub-Saharan from the northern coast of Africa. Half the river drainage of Africa did not reach the coast or else the rivers cascaded from the highlands to the sea in a series of nonnavigable cataracts. Winds blew toward the shore along many coastlines, making sailing difficult. Dense forests and malarial rain forests covered much of the land; other tropical diseases abounded.

As mentioned in Chapter 5, agriculture spread slowly throughout sub-Saharan Africa by the gradual migration of Bantu people, starting from the eastern part of modern

crossing a mini-threshold

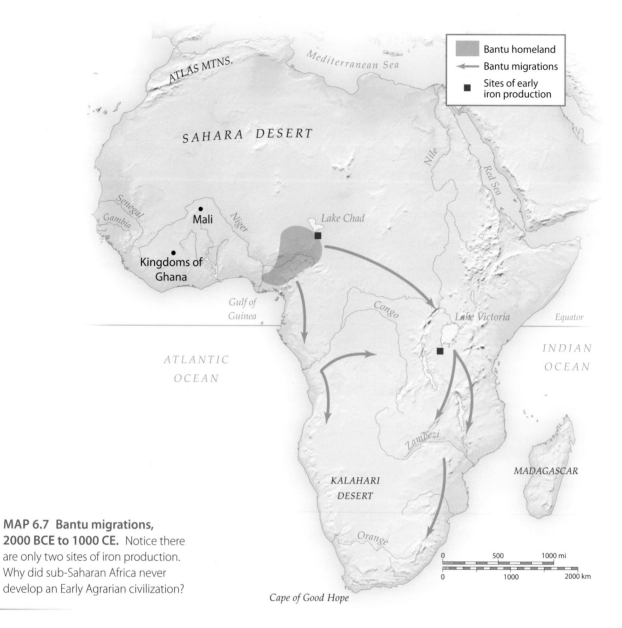

MAP 6.7 Bantu migrations, 2000 BCE to 1000 CE. Notice there are only two sites of iron production. Why did sub-Saharan Africa never develop an Early Agrarian civilization?

Nigeria and the southern part of modern Cameroon. The Bantu cultivated yams and oil palms, later adding millet and sorghum, and they herded cattle. About 1000 BCE they added the skill of making iron tools and weapons. By the last centuries BCE agriculture had reached all of sub-Saharan Africa except for densely forested areas and deserts. In the forested areas the Batwa people, commonly called Pygmies, remained as forest specialists, trading their forest products to Bantu groups (Map 6.7).

After 300 CE camels replaced horses and donkeys for travel across the Sahara Desert, providing some trade and communication and empowering some nomadic groups. Caravans crossing the desert could contain as many as 5,000 camels and hundreds of people. Traveling mostly at night to avoid the heat, the caravans took up to 70 days, covering 15 to 25 miles (24 to 40 kilometers) a day.

By the fourth or fifth century CE a small state appeared in western Africa, the kingdom of Ghana. This kingdom, not related to modern Ghana, was situated between the Senegal and Niger Rivers, straddling the border of modern Mali and Mauritania. Ghana developed into a state apparently when agriculturists sought protection from camel-riding nomads of the Sahara.

The only real axis of transcontinental communication in Africa stretched across the belt of grassland known as the Sahel, below the Sahara, from eastern Africa to the Niger River in western Africa. By this route Muslim merchants arrived in Ghana about 800 CE, enabling it to become a trading center, controlling and taxing gold (from further south) and providing ivory and slaves. In this way Ghana thrived in the ninth through the twelfth centuries, but even so its capital, Koumbi-Saleh, sheltered only some 15,000 to 20,000 inhabitants. Raiders from the

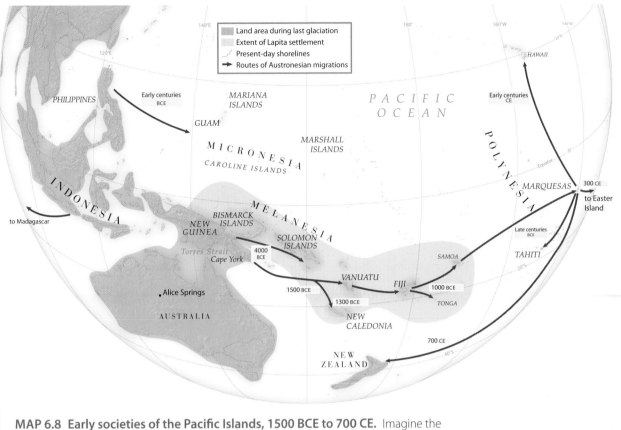

MAP 6.8 Early societies of the Pacific Islands, 1500 BCE to 700 CE. Imagine the navigational skill required to make these voyages (see Chapter 9). Why were the Pacific Islands the last inhabitable place to be settled by humans?

north weakened Ghana, and in the early thirteenth century it collapsed.

From the dissolution of Ghana emerged the Mali Empire, which controlled and taxed most of the trade going through West Africa from the thirteenth to late fifteenth centuries. In general, however, small regional states and large and small kingdoms continued to characterize sub-Saharan Africa after 1000 CE. It never became the seat of a major agrarian civilization.

The Pacific Islands Humans reached the Pacific Islands later than any other inhabitable place on Earth; the easternmost island, **Rapa Nui** (Easter Island), was settled about 900 CE. (For further discussion of Polynesian migrations, see Chapter 9.) Polynesian sailors may have managed to reach the western coast of South America, not regularly, but enough to bring back to Polynesia the cultivation of sweet potatoes. (Chicken bones from Polynesia found in Chile have now been dated between 1304 and 1424 CE, proving that Polynesians reached South America before the Europeans.) Sweet potatoes proved especially important to the people who sailed about 1200 CE to New Zealand, the last large inhabitable region to receive humans. These migrants found that, of the staple crops of the tropical Pacific (taro, bananas, coconut, breadfruit, sweet potatoes), only sweet potatoes could survive in the cooler climate of New Zealand, forcing them to remain primarily foragers (Map 6.8).

By the twelfth and thirteenth centuries CE, the Pacific Islands were experiencing rapid population growth as their people learned to exploit the ecosystems of their islands. Rapa Nui experienced dramatic problems from overpopulation that its people could not solve. By 1500 CE they had divided into hostile, warring camps as their society descended into cannibalism (Figure 6.6).

Other Pacific islands fared better, organizing their societies in the same patterns we have seen emerge elsewhere. Specialized workers developed, along with ruling elites and commoners, plus a strong ruling chief. The chiefs of Tonga and Hawaii mobilized labor, organized military forces, worked closely with priests, and tried to add additional islands by force, usually unsuccessfully.

Islands, by virtue of their small size, scarce resources, and isolation, simply did not have the range of resources that people could build up to create full-scale agrarian civilizations. Even so, their inhabitants created productive agricultural economies and well-organized societies with the same basic features that were present in other states around the world. Whenever the environment and human ingenuity produce sufficient surplus food to support a growing population, the amazing fact is that similar patterns of organization have emerged everywhere on our planet.

FIGURE 6.6 Moai of Rapa Nui.
Moai are human figures carved from rock on the island of Rapa Nui (Easter Island) between 1250 and 1500 CE. The tallest one erected was almost 33 feet (10 meters) high and weighed 82 tons (74 metric tons). How they were transported is still uncertain; perhaps people on Rapa Nui cut down their trees to roll these figures into place. This photo shows 6 of the 15 restored by a Chilean archaeologist in the 1990s at Ahu Tonariki. The figures are looking inland over their land.

SUMMARY

In this chapter we began by defining cities and states and agrarian civilizations. We described in some detail the emergence of the world's first state in Uruk, Mesopotamia, followed by briefer descriptions of the emergence of agrarian civilizations in Egypt, Nubia, the Indus valley, and two valleys in China. Then we examined two emerging states in Mesoamerica, two along the Peruvian coast, and a few attempts at states in sub-Saharan Africa and the Pacific Islands, even though these examples occurred later than in Afro-Eurasia. We conclude that around the world a similar process of increasing complexity occurs, no matter what the environment, whenever the human population reaches a certain density. In the next chapter we follow the evolution of these increasingly complex states into an era of human history dominated by vast agrarian civilizations.

CHAPTER QUESTIONS

1. What are the defining characteristics of cities and states?
2. Why did people begin to congregate in cities?
3. Where did the first cities appear around the world? How can you explain why they appeared where they did?
4. Describe the differences in the evolution of cities and states in the four different world zones.
5. Describe the kinds of evidence used to reconstruct early civilizations.
6. This chapter focuses on similarities in Early Agrarian civilizations; what were some of the differences?
7. What role did religion play in the emergence of cities and states?

KEY TERMS

agrarian civilizations
caste system
city
cuneiform
Epic of Gilgamesh

hieroglyphics
Malthusian cycles
Mesoamerica
monumental architecture
Nubia

Rapa Nui
state
state religion
tribute
Uruk

warfare
world zones

FURTHER READING

Barber, Elizabeth Wayland. *Women's Work: The First 20,000 Years: Women, Cloth and Society in Early Times.* New York: Norton, 1994.

Brown, Judith K. "Note on the Division of Labor by Sex." *American Anthropologist* 72 (1970):1075–76.

Burroughs, William James. *Climate Change in Prehistory: The End of the Reign of Chaos.* Cambridge, UK: Cambridge University Press, 2005.

Coningham, Robin. "South Asia: From Early Villages to Buddhism." In Chris Scarre, ed., *The Human Past: World Prehistory and the Development of Human Societies.* London: Thames & Hudson, 2005.

Johnson, Allen W., and Timothy Earle. *The Evolution of Human Societies.* 2nd ed. Stanford, CA: Stanford University Press, 2000.

Kemp, Barry J. *Ancient Egypt: Anatomy of a Civilization.* 2nd ed. London and New York: Routledge, 2006.

Leick, Gwendolyn. *Mesopotamia: The Invention of the City.* London: Penguin, 2001.

McIntosh, Jane R. *A Peaceful Realm: The Rise and Fall of Indus Civilization.* New York: Westview, 2002.

Mitchell, Stephen. *Gilgamesh: A New English Version.* New York: Free Press, 2004.

Nemet-Nejat, Karen Rhea. *Daily Life in Ancient Mesopotamia.* Westport, CT: Greenwood Press, 1998.

Ristvet, Lauren. *In the Beginning: World History from Human Evolution to the First States.* New York: McGraw-Hill, 2007.

Schmandt-Besserat, Denise. *How Writing Came About: Handbook to Life in Ancient Mesopotamia.* Austin: University of Texas Press, 1996.

Sherratt, Andrew. *Economy and Society in Prehistoric Europe: Changing Perspectives.* Princeton, NJ: Princeton University Press, 1997.

Wolf, Eric. *Europe and the People without History.* Berkeley: University of California Press, 1982.

chapter 7

Afro-Eurasia during the Era of Agrarian Civilizations

Seeing the Big Picture

3000 BCE to 1000 CE

▶ Why did humans start living in huge, interconnected communities known as agrarian civilizations?

▶ What were the main features that distinguished agrarian civilizations from the communities humans had lived in before?

▶ What were the most important long-term changes in agrarian civilizations as they evolved over several thousand years?

▶ What were the key phases of expansion of Afro-American agrarian civilizations between ca. 3000 BCE and ca. 1000 CE?

A New Type of Human Community

The changes described in the previous chapter marked the emergence of a new type of human community: agrarian civilizations. This chapter and the following two will describe the evolution of agrarian civilizations over several thousand years, after the era of early states considered in Chapter 6 through to the beginning of the early modern period considered in Chapter 10. Human history becomes so complex in this era that it will be necessary to depart from a strictly chronological presentation of world history. However, we will also see some remarkably similar trends throughout the world, as different communities tried to cope with many of the same problems in a manner very similar to a process we discussed in the previous chapter, something biologists call convergent evolution.

This chapter and the next will focus on the major trends and patterns that characterize agrarian civilizations throughout the Era of Agrarian Civilizations, but with a particular focus on the Afro-Eurasian world zone. It will treat agrarian civilizations as a distinctive type of human community, with features that recurred over and over again. It will use historical developments within Afro-Eurasia to illustrate these large trends evident in the world as a whole, building on the superb scholarship generated by a century of research in world history. This focus on the largest world zone of all, Afro-Eurasia, will allow us to describe both the agrarian civilizations of that region and the many human communities that remained beyond their control (though not always beyond their *influence*).

Chapter 9 will then consider the history of the other major world zones during the era. Separating the world zones makes some sense in this era because, although the histories of the different zones shared many important features, the chronologies of these histories differed in significant ways during the many millennia before the world zones were joined together in the last 500 years. Discussing the different world zones separately will help us see both the very large trends that seem to have driven human history in all parts of the world, and the many local variations generated by differences in the environments and the cultural and social structures of different regions.

What Were Agrarian Civilizations? A Taxonomy of Human Communities

Now that we have seen how the first agrarian civilizations emerged, we can stand back and study them as a new type of human community. Of course, all models of types of community are artificial, but as human history becomes more complex, it may help us if we use a simple taxonomy of human societies to highlight the major differences. You may remember that in biology, a *taxonomy* is a way of classifying different species and showing the links between them. Here, we try to classify the main types of human societies. However, unlike species of animals, human communities do not have well-defined boundaries and can merge almost imperceptibly into each other (Table 7.1).

Kin-Ordered Societies Chapter 4 described the small, kin-ordered communities of foraging societies, the only type of community that existed during the Paleolithic, which is to say, for most of human history. These were the first type of human community, and they have been present throughout all of human history. Today they have all but vanished, but in a sense they survive, like prokaryotic cells within eukaryotes, in the form of the families that continue to make up all modern societies.

TABLE 7.1 A Simple Taxonomy of the Major Types of Human Community

Type of Community	Main Features	When?
1. Kin-ordered societies	Small (less than 50), nomadic, links to neighbors	Paleolithic era, but some survived to the twenty-first century
2. Early Agrarian villages	Independent communities of farmers, with hundreds of individuals, loose links to neighbors	First appear with beginning of agriculture, from ca. 11,000 BP; spread to many parts of the world, and all four world zones, and survive to the present day in some regions
3. Pastoralist societies	Independent communities of pastoralists, with loose links to neighbors, capable occasionally of linking up to form large armies	First appear with secondary products revolution, from ca. 4000 BCE, which increases efficiency of exploitation of large livestock; only in arid zones of Afro-Eurasia, not suitable for farming
4. Agrarian civilizations	Huge communities of many millions, linking villages and cities together over large areas, with states, tax systems, literacy, and monumental architecture	First appear in the centuries before ca. 3000 BCE in Sumer and Egypt; also appear in other regions where farming is widespread, including in American world zone; dominant type of society until nineteenth century
5. Modern global society	Interlinked global communities, based on modern, industrial technologies	The type of society that appeared only in the Modern era of the Anthropocene

Early Agrarian Villages The second type of community, which we first encountered in Chapter 5, consisted of the village communities of the Early Agrarian era. By the end of the Agrarian era these were probably the most common types of community on Earth, and most people probably lived in villages. However, most villages by then had also been incorporated within the larger structures created by agrarian civilizations.

Pastoralist Societies A third type of community is worth mentioning here, one that—as we saw in the previous chapter—emerged as a result of the secondary products revolution. In some ways, pastoralists were like mobile farmers. They never included as many people as villages, but sometimes they exerted a disproportionate influence in the one world zone in which they flourished, Afro-Eurasia.

Agrarian Civilizations Within this simple taxonomy we can think of agrarian civilizations as a fourth type of community. The appearance of agrarian civilizations led to a new level of complexity. Agrarian civilizations were not just larger; they were much, much larger than all previous human communities. They linked hundreds of thousands and often many millions of people within relatively coherent communities of vast size. They were also extraordinarily diverse, incorporating many smaller communities, from villages to scattered diasporas of merchants to the great cities that were the hearts of all agrarian civilizations. Although agrarian civilizations were based on the productivity of large numbers of agriculturalists, they were much more diverse than any earlier communities. They contained farmers and pastoralists, priests and brewers, merchants and artists, snake charmers and wet-nurses, scribes and warriors.

In agrarian civilizations you can see many of the features we expect in all complex entities. Like all complex entities, agrarian civilizations were fragile. Their components were arranged in precise ways; for example, cities could not function if peasants stopped sending them produce, and if normal relations between groups broke down, that could lead quickly to the collapse of whole civilizations. Despite their great diversity, agrarian civilizations shared many important features. Just as the DNA of modern humans produces individuals who are very similar to each other despite some interesting differences, so too agrarian civilizations seemed to be generated by a sort of social and historical DNA that ensured they were quite alike. With the appearance of agrarian civilizations we see new emergent properties, from huge cities to royal palaces to vast armies to written literatures. Finally, like all complex things, agrarian civilizations required huge energy flows. Holding together these vast, complex social structures took the efforts of millions of people, who extracted these rapidly increasing flows of energy from the animals, plants, rivers, and winds of their environment.

The Era of Agrarian Civilizations

The emergence of the first cities, states, and agrarian civilizations introduced so many changes that it makes sense to think of it as the start of a new era of human history. We call this the *Era of Agrarian Civilizations*. This era lasted from approximately 3000 BCE to just a thousand years ago. During this period of almost 4,000 years, cities and states and agrarian civilizations spread and evolved in many different parts of the world, until they became the most important types of human community. The **Era of Agrarian Civilizations** can be defined as the era of human history in which agrarian civilizations were the largest, the most complex, and the most powerful of all human communities.

Defining Features of Agrarian Civilizations

Wherever agrarian civilizations appeared, they displayed similar features, and these are the features we use to define and identify this type of human community. Just as earlier we found that paleontologists have checklists of the features of human skeletons, so here we offer short checklists of the types of things we expect to find when we encounter an agrarian civilization. Here is a brief shortlist:

Agriculture Agrarian civilizations were based on the productivity of large numbers of peasants or agriculturalists (which is why we call them agrarian). Their basic technology was agriculture, just as the basic technology of the Paleolithic era was foraging.

Cities They also contained cities, regions of very dense settlement and with a greater variety of jobs and specializations than villages. The cities drew in the wealth and resources of their rural hinterlands, so it was in the cities that most wealth was found.

States It was also in the cities that power was concentrated. Here was where rulers spent most of their time and where the largest buildings, the highest walls, and the most beautiful temples were usually to be found. The cities and their leaders were at the heart of these large coercive power structures, which we have identified in the previous chapter as "states."

Specialization and a Division of Labor Agrarian civilizations were characterized by a much greater variety of human occupations and roles than all earlier types of societies. This was one measure of their greater complexity, but also a major explanation for the huge increase in the diversity of ideas and therefore in the synergy of Collective Learning in this era.

Armies
Rulers and states also concentrated power, and the most obvious form this concentration took was the creation of armies, large disciplined bodies of fighters who could be used to conquer neighbors or suppress internal opposition.

Writing
As we saw in the previous chapter, all agrarian civilizations developed writing in some form, because writing was itself a powerful way of controlling resources (in the form of accounting) or ideas (in the form of laws or religious pronouncements, or even in the form of auguries announced by rulers often with the help of soothsayers or astronomers).

Tributes
In agrarian civilizations, flows of wealth commonly took the form of tributes. As we saw in Chapter 6, tributes are very different from trade: they are flows of wealth and goods and labor that are controlled mainly through the threat or reality of coercion. Slavery is the most obvious form of tribute, but a tribute-taking society is one in which many flows of resources are controlled by the threat of force, in which physical violence is regarded as admirable in many contexts (so that elites are warriors), and is regarded as acceptable in the household not just in relations with slaves but also within the family.

Energy Flows and Interconnections between These Features

We can get some sense of what cities meant to early civilizations from the final verses of the *Epic of Gilgamesh,* about a semilegendary ruler of the city of Uruk, whose history was described in Chapter 6. Gilgamesh returns to his city after a long journey and as they approach he says to his companion:

> This is the wall of Uruk, which no city on earth can equal.
> See how its ramparts gleam like copper in the sun.
> Climb the stone staircase, more ancient than the mind can
>   imagine,
> Approach the Eanna Temple, sacred to Ishtar,
> A temple that no king has equaled in size or beauty,
> Walk on the wall of Uruk, follow its course
> Around the city, inspect its mighty foundations,
> Examine its brickwork, how masterfully it is built,
> Observe the land it encloses; the palm trees, the gardens,
> The orchards, the glorious palaces and temples, the shops
> And marketplaces, the houses, the public squares.[1]

If the cities—like Uruk, Chang'an, Pataliputra, Tenochtitlan, and Rome—were the centers of prestige and power, it was in the towns and villages that most resources were generated. Peasant farmers, sometimes working under powerful landlords in plantation-like conditions, provided the bulk of the foods and other produce used in the towns and cities. In all agrarian civilizations we find flows of wealth from the population at large to the wealthier sections of the population who dominate the states. These energy flows sustained the complex structures of agrarian civilizations.

Getting a feeling for how these flows of energy worked is important if we are to understand the evolution and internal workings of agrarian civilizations. Some of these flows were undoubtedly commercial. That is, like purchases in modern society, they took the form of relatively equal exchanges of goods in markets. Whenever a peasant exchanged some wheat for some pottery, beer, or clothing, it was a form of market exchange. But in all agrarian civilizations it seems that significant flows of wealth took the form of tributes. A book of exercises for scribes from Egypt, dating from the time of the New Kingdom late in the second millennium BCE, gives a vivid sense of what it really meant to have tributes exacted (Figure 7.1). This, the author explains, is why you don't want to end up as a peasant:

> By day he cuts his farming tools; by night he twists rope. Even his midday hour he spends on farm labor. . . . Now the scribe lands on the shore. He surveys the harvest. Attendants are behind him with staffs, Nubians [mercenaries from lands to the south of Egypt] with clubs. One says [to him]: "Give grain." "There is none [, he says]." He is beaten savagely. He is bound, thrown in the well, submerged head down. His wife is bound in his presence. His children are in fetters. His neighbors abandon them and flee.[2]

Though this is a satire, the point it makes is clear enough. To those who paid them, tributes normally felt like pure extortion.

Understanding how tributes worked may help you understand better the nature of government in most agrarian civilizations. Rulers were above all people capable of exercising force of some kind—coercive power—and often that meant controlling armies. The *Narmer Palette,* which can be seen in the Egyptian Museum in Cairo, is typical of the political propaganda of early states in showing a ruler (probably Narmer, the first ruler of a unified Egypt) holding a captive and threatening to beat or kill him. Such images can be found in all Early Agrarian civilizations, and they suggest that the role of coercer was one of the most important roles played by rulers. Much of the coercive power of states was used to maintain flows of wealth (of labor, of goods, and even of people) from the population at large to states. If you happened to be a wealthy member of the ruling class, of course, things tended to look rather different, and the fact that wealth flowed toward you must have seemed part of the natural order of things. The famous *Standard of Ur,* a mosaic excavated from the royal cemetery at Ur, and dating from approximately 2500 BCE, has two sides, one depicting peacetime activities, the other depicting war (Figure 7.2). The "peace" side shows wealthy people banqueting while in the panel below we see peasants bringing the foodstuffs they are eating.

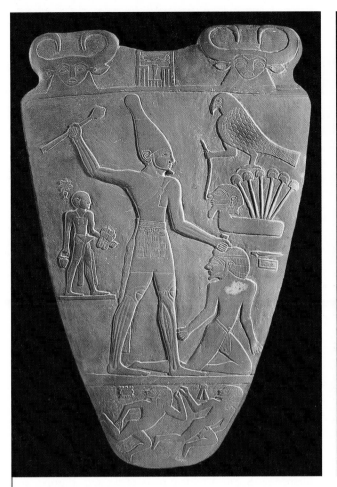

FIGURE 7.1 The Narmer Palette. This ceremonial object from the Old Kingdom period of Egypt might symbolically represent the unification of Upper and Lower Egypt by the pharaoh. In the left panel, the king is holding a mace that he is apparently about to use to crush the skull of of a captive.

The Coexistence of Different Types of Communities during the Era

Although we have talked thus far as if agrarian civilizations were single entities, in fact they were never as coherent as living organisms. Like all human communities, they had boundaries of a sort, boundaries that were often well understood by contemporaries who grasped perfectly well the difference between an insider and an outsider, between "one of us" and "one of them." But as we will see in this chapter and the following two, the boundaries were never absolute, so that different agrarian civilizations could interpenetrate each other and eventually merge to form larger and more unified civilizations or divide to form several distinct civilizations. Agrarian civilizations were so complex that they contained many distinct communities within themselves—separate cities, sometimes even separate states as in Sumer, and certainly different ethnic and language communities.

FIGURE 7.2 The Standard of Ur. These standards, from the royal cemetery at Ur, depict peacetime activities on one side (*right*), and war on the other (*left*).

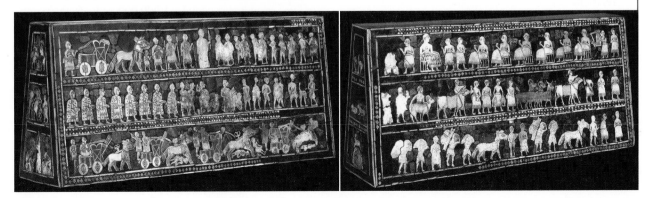

Furthermore, their borders were porous because agrarian civilizations had very good reasons to seek out relations with communities far away from their heartlands, whether through trade or through conquest.

Beyond their borders, you could find communities that were not organized as agrarian civilizations. Indeed, the coexistence of all the major types of communities listed earlier in our taxonomy of human societies is one of the main distinguishing features of the Era of Agrarian Civilizations. Never before had there existed such a diversity of different types of human societies. Even at the end of the era, huge regions in Siberia, the Americas, and Australia had barely any contact with agrarian civilizations. At the beginning of the era, most of the world was still occupied by communities living in smaller and older types of communities: foraging bands, pastoral nomadic groups, and villages, often linked into larger communities.

Long Trends in the Era of Agrarian Civilizations

The remainder of this chapter, and all of the next, considers the most important long-term trends of the Era of Agrarian Civilizations, with specific examples drawn from the rich history of Afro-Eurasia. What matters most to big historians is a consideration of the following questions: How did this complex new world, consisting of so many different types of communities intertwined in so many different ways, evolve over time? And how did it lay the foundations for today's world?

To attempt to answer these questions, we initially need to identify the very large changes that occurred in Afro-Eurasia over the 4,000 or so years during which human history was dominated by large agrarian civilizations. We will argue that four trends in particular need to be explored to help make sense of the era and its significance:

1. The expansion and increasing size, power, and effectiveness of agrarian civilizations and their administrations.
2. The establishment of significant networks of exchange between them, notably in Afro-Eurasia via the **Silk Roads,** which led to increasing interconnections between civilizations and the establishment of a trans-Afro-Eurasian world system, or "web."
3. The increasing complexity of social and gender relations.
4. The generally slow pace of change, tied to rates of innovation, growth, and Malthusian cycles.

The rest of this chapter will explore the first of these trends, the expansion of agrarian civilizations in the Afro-Eurasian world zone. Chapter 8 will be devoted to a discussion of the remaining three, also in the context of Afro-Eurasia. In each of these chapters on the Era of Agrarian Civilizations we will try to strike a balance between exploring the kaleidoscope of different cultural adaptations we can see at the regional scale, and the story of shared patterns and trends that we can discern at the interregional and global scales.

First Trend: The Expansion, Power, and Effectiveness of Agrarian Civilizations and Their Administrations

As we saw in Chapter 6, by 5,000 years ago—that is, by ca. 3000 BCE—agrarian civilizations had appeared in Mesopotamia and Egypt, but nowhere else on Earth. A new and extremely rare type of human community at that stage, they included large, densely settled populations and embraced substantial areas, so that even in 3000 BCE Sumerian and Egyptian civilization included many millions of people in a world whose population, according to the estimate of J. R. Biraben, totaled about 50 million.[3]

By 2000 BCE agrarian civilizations had also appeared in Central Asia, in the north of the Indian subcontinent, and in stretches along the Huang He valley in northern China. In Northeast Africa, agrarian civilizations were spreading south along the Nile to Sudan, and in West Asia Mesopotamian civilization was spreading north along the Tigris and Euphrates valleys and out toward the shores of the Mediterranean Sea.

By 1000 BCE civilizations had spread even further, to include many lands around the Mediterranean basin, Central Asia, and extensively in China along the valleys of the Huang He and also the Yangtze River in the south. Embryonic agrarian civilizations were also appearing in Mesoamerica, South America, parts of western Europe, and parts of western Africa.

By 1000 CE agrarian civilizations had expanded to include large areas of Mesoamerica, much of the Mediterranean shoreline, and most of Europe, as well as large areas of western Africa. In old established regions, such as Mesopotamia and Persia or India and China, they had spread to many new regions. Some periods of contraction could also be noted, such as late in the third millennium, when the population of Sumer contracted significantly, but the long-term trend was clearly expansionist.

An Estonian American scholar, Rein Taagepera, has tried to statistically measure this process (Table 7.2). His estimates are very approximate, but it is, after all, the general trend we are trying to grasp rather than the details.[4]

Taagepera has tried to estimate the area of land included within agrarian civilizations in square megameters. One square megameter equals 1,000,000 square kilometers (about 386,000 square miles), or about the size of modern Egypt. As there were few formal borders until the Modern era, Taagepera's estimates involve a lot of guesswork. Nevertheless, his figures can help us get a sense of the scale of these processes.

Five thousand years ago, the states of Egypt and Mesopotamia (and remember that agrarian civilizations are organized by states) controlled approximately 0.2 square megameter of the land of Afro-Eurasia, which is equivalent to about 0.2 percent of the total landmass of the world. These were tiny areas. Most people even in Afro-Eurasia

TABLE 7.2 Area within Agrarian Civilizations (Square Megameters)

Era	Date (BCE/CE)	Area Controlled (Square Megameters)	Area as % of Modern Area Controlled by State Structures
Era of Agrarian Civilizations 1	Early 3rd millennium BCE	0.15 (all in Southwest Asia)	0.2
	2nd millennium to mid-1st millennium BCE	0.36–1.61	0.75–2.0
Era of Agrarian Civilizations 2	1 BCE	8	6.0
	1000 CE	16	13.0
Transition to Modern era	13th century CE	33 (mainly Mongol Empire)	25.0
	17th century CE	44 (now includes the Americas)	33.0
Modern era	20th century CE	130 (approximately)	100.0

still lived in villages, following early agrarian lifeways, and the regions of agrarian civilization were rare, spectacular, and exotic. Two thousand years later, in about 1000 BCE, agrarian civilizations controlled about 10 times this area, or about 1.6 square megameters, which is equivalent to about 2 percent of the total area of of the globe. This is a significant expansion in the areas within agrarian civilizations, but a reminder that 98 percent of Afro-Eurasia (and all the rest of the world) still lay *outside* the world's agrarian civilizations. However, given the extraordinary density of populations within agrarian civilizations, by 1000 BCE they surely accounted for a significant proportion of the world's population, perhaps a quarter or even a half.

Two thousand years ago agrarian civilizations embraced 8 square megameters, or about 6 percent of the land area of the globe, roughly 40 times the area they had covered 5,000 years ago. By this date agrarian civilizations were also beginning to appear in the Americas. By 1,000 years ago, agrarian civilizations covered twice as much land again, or about 16 square megameters, or about 13 percent of the land of the globe. It is a reasonable assumption that by 1,000 years ago, and quite probably as early as 2,000 years ago, agrarian civilizations also included the great majority of the human population, despite the relatively small proportions of the Earth's surface that they embraced.

If these estimates are not wildly inaccurate, they indicate a remarkable transformation in the lifeways of most human beings. They suggest that agrarian civilizations had expanded within just a few thousand years from being an exotic new type of human community to one embracing most humans on Earth. Whereas 5,000 years ago independent agricultural villages were probably the home communities for a majority of human beings, 3,000 years later most humans lived within agrarian civilizations. True, most still lived within villages, but now they lived within villages that were *within* agrarian civilizations, and that meant that their lives were shaped to a considerable extent by the remote forces of distant empires and cities and in particular by the demands those communities and their local agents made for labor and tributes. At the same time, a large and increasing number of people (perhaps a tenth of all those within agrarian civilizations) lived in cities. In other words, the lifeways of the majority of humans had

been transformed within a mere 3,000 or so years. Between 5,000 and 2,000 years ago then, agrarian civilizations, from being a rare and exotic type of community, became the norm for most human beings. Given the extraordinarily slow pace of change during the 200,000 years of the Paleolithic era, this is evidence of a remarkable acceleration in the pace of historical change.

Meanwhile, the total numbers of humans had grown from approximately 50 million (5,000 years ago) to about 120 million (3,000 years ago) and 250 million (2,000 years ago). If we assume that at least half of all humans lived within agrarian civilizations by 2,000 years ago, this means that by then the number of humans within such communities (about 125 million) was more than twice as large as the total number of people in the world as a whole just 5,000 years ago (approximately 50 million). These changes are signs of a historical dynamism utterly different from that of the Paleolithic or Early Agrarian eras.

With this overview of the expansionary trend of agrarian civilizations in mind, it is time to consider in more detail how this historical growth played out at the interregional and regional levels in Afro-Eurasia. In Chapter 6 we traced the history of Mesopotamian civilization from about 3600 to about 2000 BCE; Egyptian civilization from about 3100 to 2020 BCE; Indus civilization from about 3200 to about 1700 BCE; Chinese civilization from the Early Agrarian era through to the end of the Shang Dynasty in approximately 1045 BCE; and sub-Saharan African states through to about 1000 CE. Now we pick up the histories of most of these regions (and some new ones) where we left off in the previous chapter, and trace their continuing evolution in three cycles of expansion—and also periodic contraction—over the ensuing millennia.

First Cycle of Expansion and Contraction: ca. 2000 to ca. 500 BCE

Mesopotamia and Egypt

We begin in Mesopotamia, the so-called cradle of civilization, where the empire constructed by Sargon of Akkad collapsed by 2150 BCE, leading to a period of instability. A Babylonian conqueror named Hammurabi (r. 1792–1770 BCE) reestablished control of the region by

part 1

ruling from his capital at Babylon. Promulgating the first written law code in human history, Hammurabi demonstrated his power by calling himself "King of the Four Quarters of the World." But the wealth of "the world" continued to attract outsiders intent on their own expansion, including the Hittites who used innovative militarized chariots to carve out their own substantial empire. By the fourteenth century BCE the Hittite Empire included much of Anatolia (modern Turkey), Syria, and Upper Mesopotamia.

After Hittite power declined, new invaders known as Assyrians used their sophisticated armies (also based on the devastating effectiveness of horse-drawn chariots) to invade the region and create the largest agrarian civilization thus far seen in human history. Southwest Asia thus offers the first striking example of the trend toward military and imperial expansion that characterizes much of the Era of Agrarian Civilizations. The first cities and states that had appeared in the Sumerian delta almost 2,000 years earlier now found themselves small parts of an enormous imperial structure that stretched from the Persian Gulf to the Mediterranean Sea. Between 1300 and 612 BCE the Assyrians were, along with the Egyptians, one of the two great powers of western Afro-Eurasia. The last great Assyrian king, Assurbanipal (668–627 BCE), expanded on Hammurabi's claim, and also noted the much larger size of his domain, by naming himself "King of the Universe"!

Egypt demonstrates a similar process during the second millennium BCE. Centralized rule and stability had been restored in 2040 BCE, and for the next four centuries powerful pharaohs focused on resource-driven state expansion by launching military campaigns to the south into the mineral-rich lands of Nubia. But between 1640 and 1550 the tables were turned as Egypt came under the rule of outsiders, whom the Egyptians named the Hyksos, or "foreign rulers." This gave the Nubians the opportunity to raid down river, so that the core Egyptian state was reduced to an enclave trapped between hostile Hyksos to the north and Nubians to the south. By approximately 1540 the Pharaoh Ahmose I (r. ca. 1550–1525) had driven the Hyksos from Egypt, and for the next 500 years pharaohs of renewed power ruled a wealthy, autonomous civilization. Egypt entered an age of imperial expansion as the pharaohs sought to increase their resources through war. Military expeditions were relaunched into Nubia; and under Tuthmosis III (r. 1479–1425), the Egyptian military conducted 17 separate campaigns up the Eastern Mediterranean coast. Eventually the pharaoh signed a treaty with the Hittites following a series of costly and inconclusive battles. These campaigns demonstrate the "zero-sum" expansionary policies practiced by elites throughout the era. Unable or unwilling to increase the resources available to the state through internal innovation, both Hittites and Egyptians sought land and wealth through military expansion and fought each other to a state of deadlock.

Eastern Mediterranean

Even as the conflict between Egyptians and Hittites was playing out, new states were appearing in the lands bordering the Mediterranean Sea. The name *Mediterranean* is derived from Latin and means "in the middle of the Earth." The Mediterranean Sea is connected by the Hellespont to the Black Sea in the east and by the Straits of Gibraltar to the Atlantic Ocean in the west. The coastline of the Mediterranean is almost 29,000 miles (46,400 kilometers) long, and it is on this extensive *littoral* (a zone along a coast where water and land meet) that a range of human communities eventually found themselves incorporated into new agrarian civilizations. Both Mesopotamian and Egyptian civilizations influenced these communities, which included Hebrews, Phoenicians, Minoans, and Mycenaeans.

Virtually all of our knowledge of ancient Hebrew history comes from the Old Testament of the Hebrew Bible, although much of this has yet to be substantiated by archaeologists. The Old Testament tells us that many Hebrews moved into the cities of Sumeria; that one branch migrated to Egypt in perhaps 1800 BCE; and 400 years later, under the leadership of Moses, their descendants left Egypt and migrated north to Palestine, on the southeastern shores of the Mediterranean. This group of Hebrews, now known as the Israelites, organized themselves into a loose confederation of a dozen tribes, which evolved politically into a monarchy. The Kingdom of Israel eventually fell to the Assyrians in 722 BCE, and tens of thousand of Israelites were deported and resettled throughout the Assyrian realm, the beginning of the Jewish **Diaspora** (Greek for "scattering"). For more than 2,000 years thereafter the region and its scattered people remained under the hegemony of a series of foreign powers. Although the Hebrews played a minor political role in the history of ancient Afro-Eurasia, their influence on religious thinking has been profound. Three of the world's most influential monotheistic religions—Judaism obviously, but also Christianity and Islam—were all heavily influenced by early Hebrew beliefs.

To the north of Israel, another group of migrants known as the Phoenicians settled on the shores of the Mediterranean around 3000 BCE, where they established a series of city-states that flourished because of Phoenician expertise at seagoing trade. Between roughly 1200 and 800 BCE, the Phoenicians dominated Mediterranean trade, establishing commercial colonies in numerous locations on the coasts and islands of the middle sea. This is an early example of a phenomenon we will see many times: a militarily weak state establishing a very large commercial "empire." As Phoenician fleets sailed across the Mediterranean and on to the Atlantic coasts of France, Spain, and Africa, and even the British Isles, they quickened the pace of commercial activity in the lands centered on the middle of the Earth and facilitated high levels of cultural exchange between all the great civilizations and smaller states of the region.

The Phoenician example foreshadows a significant historical development that flowed out of the Era of Agrarian Civilizations and into the early Modern era, namely the dynamism of smaller commercial states. The Phoenicians established a series of purely commercial city-states that were similar in nature to the ancient Greek *poleis,* the great trading cities of the Indian Ocean, and even the Italian

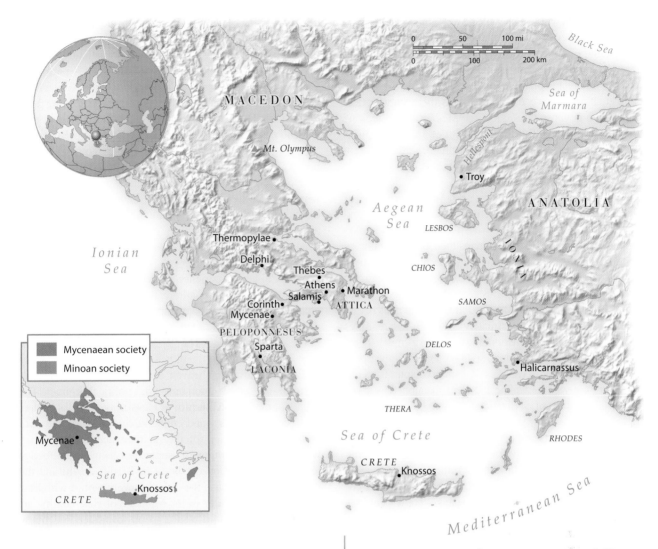

MACEDON

Mt. Olympus

Thermopylae

Delphi

Thebes
Athens
Salamis • Marathon
Corinth
Mycenae
ATTICA

PELOPONNESUS

Sparta

LACONIA

Ionian
Sea

Aegean
Sea

LESBOS

CHIOS

SAMOS

DELOS

THERA

Sea of Crete

CRETE
Knossos

Mediterranean Sea

Troy

ANATOLIA

IONIA

Hellespont

Sea of
Marmara

Black Sea

Halicarnassus

RHODES

0   50   100 mi
0   100   200 km

Mycenaean society
Minoan society

Mycenae

Sea of Crete

CRETE

Knossos

MAP 7.1 Eastern Mediterranean, ca. 1500 BCE.
Key regions and sites associated with the Minoan and
Mycenaean cultures.

city-states of the early Modern era. Because they were focused primarily on trade, commercial city-states were much more innovative than the great tributary empires. They also tended to engage more actively with transregional webs of exchange, because of their own limited internal resources and highly urbanized commercial populations. Eventually, as we will see in Chapter 10, these often geographically tiny states became politically and militarily powerful enough to challenge and sometimes defeat the vast but sluggish tributary civilizations.

At the same time that the Hebrews were active in Mesopotamia and Egypt, and that Phoenicians were constructing their commercial city-states along the coast of modern-day Lebanon, a complex new society emerged on the island of Crete, in the Eastern Mediterranean. Like the Phoenicians, the Minoans (2700–1450 BCE, named after their legendary founder King Minos) were active maritime traders, and because of its central location Crete became a major commercial center in regional trade networks. The Minoans copied Phoenician shipbuilding techniques and designs and sent their fleets all over the Eastern Mediterranean. The Minoans used the wealth generated by successful trade to build magnificent palace complexes such as at Knossos. But the Eastern Mediterranean is prone

to earthquakes and volcanic eruptions, which meant that after 1700 BCE plate tectonic movements and other geological processes destroyed many Minoan centers. Although they rebuilt, the wealth of the Minoans attracted too many raiders, and by 1400 BCE Crete was under the control of the Mycenaeans (Map 7.1).

Mycenaean society (ca. 1600–1100 BCE) was constructed on the mainland of the Greek peninsula by migrants who spoke Indo-European languages. They built farming communities dominated by great stone fortresses and copied writing and building techniques from the Minoans. The script of the Minoans (known as Linear A) has never been deciphered, but Mycenaean Linear B clay tablets have been deciphered in the thousands, providing invaluable sources for historians about affairs in the region between roughly 1500 and 1100 BCE. It was the Mycenaeans who attacked the nearby city of Troy, in a campaign later immortalized by the Greek poet Homer in the *Iliad*. After the war, the entire Eastern Mediterranean was subjected to violent invasions

part 1

by a mysterious wave of so-called Sea Peoples. These invasions were so devastating that Mycenaean, Eastern Mediterranean, and Egyptian Bronze Age cultures all but collapsed into what some historians call the terrible Dark Ages. Why were so many people suddenly on the move? Why was there such a widespread collapse? Was there some sort of Malthusian collapse throughout the Mediterranean region? We just don't know. But the new cultures and civilizations that emerged in the region were fundamentally different from their predecessors because of these events.

South Asia

Meanwhile in the region of modern-day Pakistan, at around the same time that Sargon was building his Akkadian Empire in Sumeria and the Minoans their commercial state centered on Crete, the Indus civilization constructed a large, well-organized, and sophisticated urban culture along the course of the Indus River. Indus civilization thrived for half a millennium between 2500 and 2000 BCE, and at its height covered an area of approximately 500,000 square miles (1.3 million square kilometers), meaning it was much larger in area than Mesopotamia and Egypt combined. But early in the second millennium BCE, as we saw in Chapter 6, its cities entered a period of decline and were abandoned by about 1700 BCE. The entire civilization had more or less collapsed by 1500 BCE.

The invaders who were originally blamed for the collapse of the Indus civilization were Indo-European-speaking nomads who began migrating into the region around 1500 BCE (that is, after the collapse of Indus cities). They called themselves the Aryans ("noble people"), and they represent one of many examples of the profound impact of pastoral nomads on ancient Eurasian history. This was not a purposeful invasion by any means, but a piecemeal movement into the agrarian communities of the Indus valley and northern India. Although essentially pastoral nomads when they arrived, the Aryans were also familiar with agriculture, and regular clashes took place between the migrants and the native peoples over land ownership. Like militarized nomads throughout world history, the Aryans utilized the horse as an effective part of their strategy and in particular used the horse-drawn chariot as a devastating war machine against the sedentary farming communities, which gradually lost control of the Indus valley between 1500 and 500 BCE in an era known to historians as the Vedic age.

The era name comes from an important collection of more than 1,000 hymns written by Aryan priests, known as the *Rig-Veda,* which provide valuable information about social and political life during the Vedic age. The Aryans feuded regularly among themselves and were never unified, instead forming hundreds of chiefdoms under the leadership of powerful rulers called *raja.* Aryan infiltration of the subcontinent continued throughout the first millennium BCE until most of India had been occupied. So rather than providing evidence of steady imperial expansion, by the mid-first millennium India was still a politically fragmented, decentralized region in which small kingdoms jostled for power and influence.

China

The same could not be said of China, where a succession of home-grown dynasties succeeded in dramatically expanding the power and size of the state during this period. In Chapters 5 and 6 we traced the story of ancient China from its Paleolithic origins through to the emergence of the powerful Shang Dynasty, which ruled a substantial part of central and eastern China from about 1600 to 1045 BCE. The Shang kings used their army to suppress other regional powers and to demand tribute and slaves from rival states. One of their most tenacious enemies was the Zhou state, which by the twelfth century BCE had captured the Shang capital. Accusing the Shang monarch of being a criminal obsessed with women, wine, and tyranny, the Zhou beheaded him and declared the start of their own Zhou Dynasty in 1045 BCE.

The Chinese experience provides striking evidence of continuously evolving administrative structures and increasing government power during the Era of Agrarian Civilizations, which facilitated a corresponding rapid increase in the size of the state. The Zhou validated their seizure of power by arguing that there was a parallel between affairs on Earth and affairs in heaven, and that heaven had the ability to bestow power upon terrestrial political regimes. The Zhou claimed this **Mandate of Heaven;** so long as leaders ruled conscientiously and ethically, and observed all rites and rituals necessary for the maintenance of order, they would continue to enjoy the support of heaven. Ineffective leadership would unsettle both the earthly realm and the cosmic, in which case the divine powers would withdraw their support. The idea of the Mandate of Heaven, first articulated by the Zhou, would go on to influence Chinese imperial politics for the next 3,000 years, until the abdication of the last emperor in 1911.

With a Zhou state that was much larger in area than the Shang, a decentralized administrative structure was put in place that allowed local leaders to rule their own kingdoms so long as they supported the Zhou with tribute and troops. For several centuries this system worked well, but eventually regional leaders amassed enough power to set up their own bureaucracies and military forces. As iron metallurgy was developed in China in the ninth century BCE, regional military forces became better armed and less inclined to support the Zhou. By the fifth century BCE all sense of unity had disappeared, and widespread conflict broke out between the regional kingdoms. As we will see, the violent Warring States era that followed (480–256 BCE) ended only when the most powerful of these states, the Qin, conquered their rivals and instituted their own dynasty in 221 BCE.

Second Cycle of Expansion and Contraction: ca. 500 BCE to ca. 500 CE

Eastern Mediterranean and Persia

As political order returned to the Eastern Mediterranean after centuries of unrest, new fortified settlements were constructed that evolved into fully fledged city-states. By 800 BCE, the **polis** (city-state) had become the heart of an emerging Greek culture in which commercial activity and political structures revived. The poleis became thriving urban centers administered by a range of different, types of government, including monarchy, aristocracy, and oligarchy; many also came under the control of ambitious individuals who ruled as tyrants. The history of each of these city-states, particularly Athens and Sparta, is characterized by evolving power relationships between nobles, peasants, and the emerging merchant and artisan class. The fact that these two powerful poleis were quite different, politically, militarily, and culturally, underlines the fact that the Greeks never constructed a unified agrarian civilization, but rather coexisted in a series of small, competing states that were as often at war with each other as they were with external civilizations like the Persians. Ultimately this disunity resulted in the virtual self-destruction of Greek culture in a bitterly contested civil war.

Under the leadership of the elected general Pericles (461–429 BCE) Athens was one of the most vibrant commercial and cultural centers in western Afro-Eurasia; earlier in the century (as we will see) it had played a leading role in defeating the invading armies of the Persian emperor, Darius. But this very success, along with accusations that Athens was building its own empire, caused resentment among the other Greek poleis. This led to the outbreak of the bitterly divisive Peloponnesian War (431–404 BCE) between Athens and its allies, and Sparta and its allies. Following nearly three decades of conflict, intrigue, and plague, the Spartans emerged as nominal "winners," but Greece was now so weakened and divided that it became easy prey for its northern neighbors the Macedonians.

While the Greeks never constructed a unified imperial civilization, they did practice impressive commercial expansion, partly through colonization. Between about 750 and 250 BCE, many of the Greek poleis founded colonies along the Mediterranean and Black sea coasts. These colonies built upon the trade networks established by the Phoenicians and Minoans and further unified the entire region. Transplanted Greek colonists also enhanced cultural and intellectual life, and Greek scholars in the Ionian colonies in particular (along the Aegean coast of modern-day Turkey) began systematically to investigate both the natural and metaphysical world. These same Ionian colonies brought the Greeks into direct conflict with the rapidly expanding power of western Eurasia, the Achaemenid Persians. Indeed, the histories of many of the regions thus far considered in this chapter—certainly Mesopotamia, Egypt, the Eastern Mediterranean and parts of South Asia—were brought together by the Persians, who late in the sixth century BCE constructed the largest, wealthiest, and most impressive agrarian civilization the world had seen.

The Iranian Plateau, located to the east of Mesopotamia, is a natural crossroads between western and central Eurasia through which numerous migrating peoples have passed, including hominines and Paleolithic humans moving out of Africa. It had also been home to an impressive early commercial state known today as the Oxus civilization, which was flourishing in the oases of the region by ca. 2000 BCE.

During the Bronze Age two migrating groups, the Medes and Persians, settled in the region and organized themselves into loose tribal confederations. Both Medes and Persians were highly militarized, and as the Babylonian and Assyrian Empires waned, the Persians in particular began to use their military prowess to construct their own imperial state.

Under the leadership of Cyrus (r. 558–530 BCE) the Medes were crushed. Cyrus then led his forces out of Iran on a series of expansionary campaigns to the east and west. By 539 BCE much of western Eurasia had been conquered, and the Achaemenid Empire (*Achaemenid* comes from the name of the semilegendary ninth century BCE founder of Cyrus's dynasty) stretched from Afghanistan to Turkey. Cyrus's son Cambyses (r. 530–522 BCE) added Egypt to the realm, and his successor Darius (r. 521–486 BCE) enlarged the empire in all directions until it included parts of India in the east and regions of southeastern Europe in the west. Controlling an area of some 3 million square miles (7.8 million square kilometers), or more than 10 percent of the land surface of the Earth, this was the largest agrarian civilization the world had seen.

The Achaemenids administered their huge, multicultural empire through achieving a fine balance between centralized and local administration. The kings claimed absolute power and ruled from royal capitals like Persepolis and Pasargadae with the advice and assistance of an army of bureaucrats, diplomats, and scribes. Imperial administration was further decentralized by the appointment of governors (called *satraps*) who presided over different and semiautonomous provinces (*satrapies*). No attempt was made to institute an imperial law code, and local laws remained in place at the regional and even village level. Yet to facilitate imperial unity the Achaemenid kings built a network of roads that stretched for almost 8,000 miles (12,800 kilometers), notably the impressive and well-equipped 1,600-mile- (2,560-kilometer-) long "Royal Road" that connected the western and eastern regions of the empire. Road construction on this scale was expensive, but the Persian elites were able to access vast tributes paid under threat of coercion by the various conquered states that made up the empire. Through the measures they adopted to deal with the central question of state viability, the Achaemenids learned to administer the largest empire ever seen, and at the same time established a model for subsequent Afro-Eurasian imperial governments.

Ultimately the Achaemenid elites overreached themselves by attempting to incorporate the sophisticated Greek colonies of the Ionian coast, which rebelled in 500 BCE. The Persians responded by launching an attack on the Greek peninsula, but a Persian army sent by Darius in 490 BCE was defeated on the plains of Marathon. Ten years later, Darius's successor Xerxes invaded Greece with probably the largest military force ever assembled to this point in world history, but the Spartans famously forestalled the Persians at Thermopylae, and the Athenians destroyed the Persian fleet at Salamis.

Despite combined Greek success against the Persians, the subsequent Peloponnesian War poisoned the hope of any further Greek unity, and within a century the demoralized Greeks had been conquered by their northern neighbors the Macedonians, under the inspired rule of King Phillip II (r. 359–336 BCE). When Philip was assassinated, leadership of the Macedonians, and de facto of the entire Greek world, fell to his 20-year-old son Alexander, who immediately set out on an audacious campaign to invade the Persian Empire. Alexander had inherited his father's skills of charismatic leadership and superb strategic thinking, and despite being vastly outnumbered the Macedonian–Greek forces routed the Persians in three separate battles. Alexander became the new "emperor" of Persia and then continued his march into Central Asia and as far as the Indus River before eventually returning to Babylon and an early death in 323 BCE, at age 33.

Alexander's empire was divided up among his generals, and from 275 BCE Greek culture spread, largely through commercial expansion rather than conquest, throughout much of western Eurasia during the so-called Hellenistic ("Greek-like") era. In the same way that Greek commercial activity and colonization had facilitated cultural integration in the Mediterranean and Black Sea basins, Greek traders, diplomats, and administrators facilitated exchange and integration from India to Europe. Greece came under the control of the Macedonian Antigonids, and despite Greek resentment at outside rule, commerce flourished. Egypt was transformed into the wealthy Ptolemaic Empire, and the city of Alexandria (founded by Alexander) became the great metropolis of the region, renowned for its commercial activity, multicultural tolerance, and intellectual synergy focused on the state-sponsored library.

Persia, Central Asia, and India

Central Asia was controlled, with difficulty, by the Seleucids, descendants of Alexander's general Seleucus. Greek colonists and merchants flooded the region, recreating transplanted Hellenistic society in regions like Afghanistan and Pakistan. The Greek language become so widespread that the Indian emperor Ashoka found it necessary to put up multilingual inscriptions that included the major Eastern Mediterranean languages of Greek and Aramaic. In the heart of the Seleucid realm was Bactria (Afghanistan), where a series of Hellenistic kings ruled independent Greco-Bactrian and Indo-Greek kingdoms from about 250 BCE until the arrival of militarized nomads a century later. Through these various regional polities, the vast empire of the Persians, now recreated as a looser Hellenistic commercial and cultural "civilization," acted as a spatial bridge between Europe and Asia, and a temporal bridge between the creation of the Achaemenid Empire and the arrival of the Romans (Map 7.2).

MAP 7.2 Central and West Eurasia, ca. third and fourth centuries BCE. Note the impressive size of the expansive Achaemenid Persian Empire, and of the Hellenistic Seleucid Empire that replaced it.

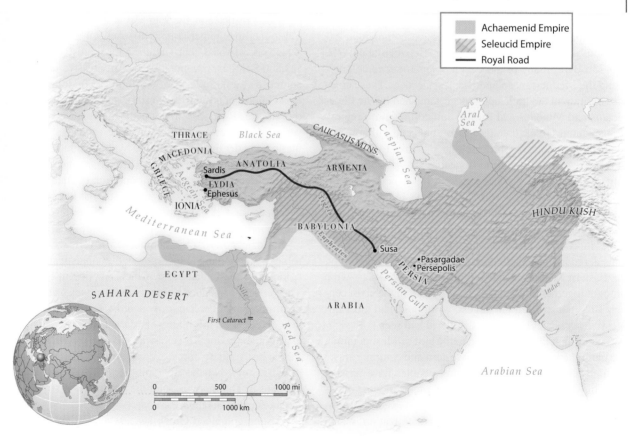

The defeat of the Achaemenids by Alexander, and the subsequent dismemberment of the Persian Empire by his successors, was not the end of Iranian ambitions, however. Although the Seleucids were able to hold on to the remnants of their diminishing realm until the arrival of the Romans in the region in 83 CE, a new power had emerged in Iran in the third century BCE that was determined to create its own empire. The Parthians, also descended from steppe nomadic peoples, had settled in eastern Iran, and in 238 BCE they revolted against the Seleucids. Under Mithridates I (r. 170–138 BCE?) the Parthians used their considerable military skill to build a substantial state that extended from the eastern edge of the Iranian plateau down into the flatlands of Mesopotamia. The Parthians modeled their administration on the Achaemenids, and, despite frequent periods of infighting, were able to maintain a stable empire for more than three centuries. Not only were the Parthians a formidable adversary of the Romans in the region, but they also helped facilitate high levels of cultural exchange across Afro-Eurasia during the first Silk Roads era, as we will see in Chapter 8.

In the third century CE the Parthians were replaced by another group of Persians, the Sasanians, who ruled their own significant empire for more than 400 years, from 224 to 651 CE. At its peak their imperial state stretched from the headwaters of the Tigris and Euphrates to Afghanistan. In the same way that the Achaemenids had functioned as a bridge between Europe and Central Asia, through their encouragement of trans-Eurasian trade and exchange, the Sasanians acted as a geographic bridge between China and the West, and a chronological bridge between the ancient civilizations and new Islamic empire that went on to control these vast arid lands. Although the Sasanians fell to the expanding world of Islam in the seventh century, the Persian legacy continued to influence the region through Muslim adoption of Persian models of government and administration. For more than 1,000 years during this Era of Agrarian Civilizations, through three distinct cycles of expansion and contraction, it was Persian peoples who, through their pursuit of resources, power, and effective models of administration, created some of the most formidable imperial structures of all.

India

The struggle between Persians and Greeks for control of Central Asia had far-reaching consequences for agrarian civilization in India. The Achaemenid king Darius conquered parts of northwestern India soon after 520 BCE and incorporated them into the Persian Empire. Two centuries later, Alexander crossed the Hindu Kush to campaign along the Indus valley, where he defeated a series of local rulers and in so doing created a power vacuum that facilitated the rise of a new dynasty that was able to unite most of India into a single imperial state for the first time.

Following the withdrawal of Alexander in 325, an ambitious local prince known as Chandragupta Maurya used a small but well-trained army to conquer several of the regional states of northern India. Chandragupta was fortunate to have the advice of a political adviser named Kautyala; and as the Mauryan Empire he created (321–185 BCE) expanded, effective administrative structures were put in place. Mauryan elites demonstrate that leaders were becoming more adept at the task of administering large agrarian civilizations—at its peak the empire covered an area of close to 2 million square miles (5 million square kilometers)—by using a mixture of tribute collection, centralized bureaucracy, regional governors, and powerful, mobile armies to maintain order and power.

Chandragupta's grandson Ashoka (r. 268–232 BCE) was one of the most successful rulers in the history of India. Ashoka maintained the expansionary dynamic of the Mauryan Empire, but after a particularly bloody war he became sickened by the conflict and converted to Buddhism. Ashoka then governed with the assistance of an efficient bureaucracy from a new Indian capital of Pataliputra. Like the Persians, Ashoka had an extensive road network constructed, which encouraged trade within the empire and also with surrounding states like Bactria and Persia. But following the death of Ashoka, the Mauryan Empire entered a period of economic decline, and by 185 BCE it had collapsed.

India remained fragmented for the next five centuries. In the north a series of nomadic invaders established their own substantial states, including the Indo-Scythian Kingdoms and the Kushan Empire. The Kushan Empire (ca. 45–225 CE), which flourished at the same time as Roman, Parthian, and Han Chinese civilizations, incorporated some 1.5 million square miles (3.8 million square kilometers) of Central Asia, including all of Afghanistan and Pakistan and much of northern India. As we will see in the next chapter, by controlling and effectively governing the crossroads of Eurasia, the Kushans facilitated extraordinary levels of trans-Afro-Eurasian trade during the first Silk Roads era.

Imperial rule and unification returned to India with the establishment of the Gupta Empire (ca. 320–414 CE). Founder Chandra Gupta (no relation to the Mauryan emperor) created a dynamic kingdom in the Ganges valley that was enlarged by his very able successors until it approached the territorial size of the Mauryans. The Mauryan city of Pataliputra was revived as the imperial capital, and stability returned to most of India north of the Deccan plateau. The highly centralized administration of the Mauryans was replaced with a looser form of regional government by the Guptas, who presided over a golden age for India politically, economically, and intellectually. Following new waves of nomadic invasion in the fifth century, however, particularly the White Huns, the Gupta realm slowly contracted and disappeared. A brief attempt to reunify the subcontinent was made by Prince Harsha (r. 606–648), but local rulers had amassed too much regional power to accede to a single, central authority. Following Harsha's death at the hands of an assassin, India reverted to a divided realm again before the arrival of Islam in the ninth century ushered in a new stage of commercial vitality, but also of political and religious tension.

Rome

At the same time Cyrus and the Achaemenids had been busy in Central Asia establishing the first Persian Empire, a small city-state in central Italy was driving out its foreign king and replacing monarchical government with a republic ruled by an aristocratic elite. At that moment, late in the sixth century BCE, Rome was no more distinguished than a score of other Latin, Etruscan, and Greek cities scattered about the Italian peninsula. The site had been settled by Indo-European-speaking migrants soon after 2000 BCE, who had established their village around a group of seven hills above the plains of Latium, on the banks of the Tiber River. The residents farmed and traded, using bronze tools by 1800 BCE and iron by 900 BCE. To the north of Rome were the Etruscans who controlled much of northern and central Italy from their fortified cities in Tuscany. To the south, Greek colonies flourished along the coast of the mainland and the island of Sicily. The Etruscans, wanting to control Rome because of its strategic location, ruled the city until the Romans evicted the last Etruscan king in 509 BCE. For the next 1,000 years, the fate of the city, country, and indeed much of western Afro-Eurasia remained firmly in the hands of the citizens of Rome.

The constitution adopted by the Romans in 509 BCE placed executive power in the hands of two officials, known as consuls, who were elected by a body made up of Roman citizens divided according to property and military classes. Decisions made by the consuls were ratified by the Senate, the real source of power in Republican Rome. Over the ensuing two centuries a struggle for a more equitable distribution of power was waged between plebeians, equestrians and the elite patricians. Begrudgingly, the latter were forced to give up their monopoly on power; by the third century BCE the plebeians had gained the right to elect their own officials (tribunes) who were able to veto ("I forbid") unfair consular decisions. Eventually the plebeian assembly was granted the right to pass laws binding on all Romans. By these various political compromises the power base was expanded and full-scale social war was averted for the moment, although the patricians clung to their remaining privileges more fiercely than ever.

In its foreign affairs, the Roman Republic responded to a series of external threats in a hard-nosed and practical manner that led, rapidly and perhaps unexpectedly, to Roman domination of the Mediterranean basin. Historians are divided on the question of whether Rome ever intended, at least in its early history, to create a large tributary empire or whether expansion was rather a result of responses to security threats. Rome was humiliated in 309 BCE by a party of marauding Gauls, a Celtic people from modern-day France, who occupied the city and were persuaded to leave only when they were paid a substantial ransom. Thereafter Rome rebuilt its military into a formidable force that waged successful wars against other Latin states and Greek colonies. The Romans did not impose harsh sanctions on defeated peoples, however, allowing conquered states to retain the right of self-government so long as they provided levies of troops and supported Roman foreign policy. This enlightened form of hegemony paid enormous dividends when the Republic faced its sternest challenge in a major struggle with Carthage.

By the year 270 BCE Rome's one remaining rival in the Central Mediterranean was the Phoenician colony of Carthage, which was probably wealthier than the Republic at that stage and certainly possessed a superior navy. Here was another case of two large regional powers—one agrarian the other commercial—intent upon enhancing their resources through the conquest of each other. The Mediterranean was simply too small to accommodate these two powers. In a series of three Punic Wars (264–146 BCE), the Romans eventually crushed the Carthaginians, but it was a hard-won victory. In the end it was Roman practicality (the determination to rapidly construct a navy larger that that of Carthage, for example); foreign policy (the allied city-states in Italy mostly remained loyal to Rome, even when it looked likely that the Republic might be defeated); and endurance (surviving the extraordinary 16-year-long campaign waged by Hannibal in Italy) that won the day. Following a subsequent series of smaller campaigns, by 133 BCE Rome was supreme in the Mediterranean and in control of a substantial tributary empire (Map 7.3).

To administer their expansive state the Romans adopted a provincial system similar to the Persian satrap model, with a governor selected from the senatorial class installed in each province. Many governors, however, as representatives of an elite deeply imbued with a philosophy that gave them the unquestioned "right" to extract tribute, took this as an opportunity for personal profit, and corruption became widespread. Senators also took over Italian farmlands abandoned during the Punic Wars and grew profitable crops like olive oil and wine, rather than necessary staples like grain. Unemployed peasants flocked to the city where they lived in squalid conditions, and the gap between rich and poor widened. In this atmosphere of discontent, Rome was preoccupied through much of the first century BCE with a series of civil wars between the personal armies of powerful men. When one of them, Julius Caesar, claimed the title of "Dictator for Life," the Republic was effectively dead; and after his assassination in 44 BCE, his adoptive son Octavian presided over the transition of the Roman state from republic to empire. Octavian was named Augustus ("Revered One") by a grateful Senate for ending the civil wars and restoring peace to the state.

Augustus's successors ruled as emperors, and by the end of the fourth century CE, some 140 different men, ranging from the brilliant to the insane, had claimed the title emperor of Rome. Roman expansion slowed but continued throughout the region during the first two centuries of the empire. When the Roman state attained its maximum extent during the second century, its government was administering the affairs of perhaps 130 million people and controlling some 2.5 million square miles (6.5 million square kilometers) of territory. The city of Rome, home to 1 million people, provided an extraordinary contrast of opulence and poverty.

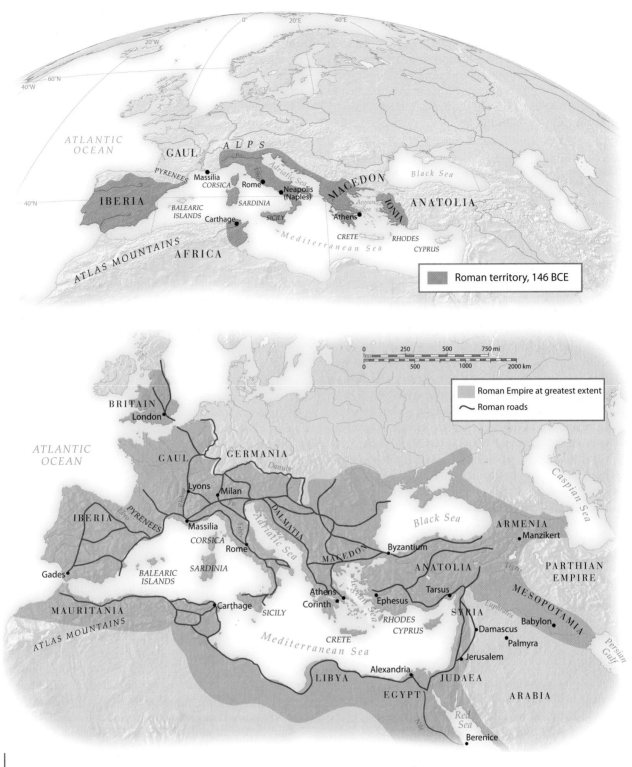

MAP 7.3 Rome. These maps show how the Roman state expanded between ca. 146 BCE and ca. 117 CE.

In common with most agrarian civilizations, Roman administrators also invested considerable resources into transport infrastructure to speed the movement of armies and aid communications. In total, Roman roads may have been more than 50,000 miles (80,000 kilometers) in length. As the contemporaneous Chinese dynasties had discovered, by linking all parts of the empire together effectively, by abolishing all internal trade tariffs and tolls, and by establishing common laws, the Romans were able to integrate enormous areas of Afro-Eurasia into a relatively homogeneous cultural entity. As we will see in the next chapter, through intensive trade along the Silk Roads during the first two centuries of the Common Era, something similar was achieved across much of the entire Afro-Eurasian world zone, as each of the contemporary agrarian civilizations became embedded into a functioning, semi-integrated exchange network that linked the planet's largest world zone.

By the beginning of the third century, however, the Roman Empire faced serious economic problems, and the trend toward expansion slowed. As the elites struggled to find solutions, Rome endured a half-century of near-anarchy during the *Crisis of the Third Century* (235–284 CE). More than 20 emperors ruled during this period, most of them dying a violent death. The capable Diocletian (r. 284–305) temporarily stemmed the crisis through effective government and sheer force of will, but his attempt to divide the empire into two more manageable halves, each ruled by a co-emperor failed. Constantine (r. 306–337 CE) made the decision to move the capital of the Empire to the city of Byzantium (renamed Constantinople), and to rule the entire structure from there.

Along with these internal economic and political problems, the Romans also faced dangerous external threats. From the early fourth century, westward migrations by restive Germanic tribes placed considerable strain on the northern borders of the empire. With the arrival of the semi-nomadic Huns from Central Asia in the mid-fifth century CE, the pressure became so intense that numerous German tribes poured across the border and resettled throughout much of the western half of the Roman Empire. Many regions of modern Europe reflect these German settlement patterns, including France (Franks) and England (Angles). In 476 CE a German general Odovocar (435–493) was anointed emperor of the western empire. For many classical historians, influenced by the eighteenth-century English historian Edward Gibbon, that date marks the moment that the Roman Empire "fell." Modern historians are unlikely to use a phrase like "the decline and fall of the Roman Empire." As they focus on cycles of expansion and contraction in human history, sharply episodic phrases like "decline and fall" or "the Dark Ages" have been replaced by phrases emphasizing the continuity of history, such as "the era of late antiquity."

| China |

Meanwhile in China, by the fifth century BCE all sense of unity had disappeared during the late Zhou Dynasty, and widespread conflict had broken out between regional kingdoms. The violent Warring States era that followed (480–256 BCE) ended only when the most powerful of these states, the Qin, conquered their rivals and instituted their own dynasty in 221 BCE.

It was during the troubled later Zhou period that three significant philosophies emerged, which would guide Chinese thought through to the twentieth century—Confucianism (which argues that education is the key to producing ethical leaders and thus good governance); Daoism (a spiritual approach focused on living in harmony with nature and the cosmos); and Legalism (which uses laws and strict—even brutal—punishments to create an orderly society). In an attempt to create a more ethical leadership class, a lower-level aristocrat from the State of Lu,

Kong Fuzi (known in the West as Confucius), attempted to redefine the criteria for status in society. He argued that a superior individual was not necessarily someone born into a superior class, but someone who had attained the rank of *junzu* (or "princeling") through pursuing high levels of intellectual and ethical cultivation. Men who had attained the rank of junzu would have the intellectual and ethical capacity to lead by example and restore order and harmony to Chinese society.

The appearance of Confucianism, Daoism, and Legalism in late Zhou China reminds us that the mid-first millennium BCE was a particularly rich age for philosophical thinking across Afro-Eurasia. Confucius, who lived from about 551 to 479 BCE, was a near contemporary to several other great thinkers. This intellectually fertile period was given the name the "Axial Age" by the modern German philosopher Karl Jaspers (1883–1969). As Jaspers pointed out, the Central Asian prophet Zoroaster, founder of the important pre-Islamic religion of Zoroastrianism, lived probably from 628 to 551 BCE; that in India the traditional dates for the life of Siddhartha Gautama, who became the Buddha, are 563 to 483 BCE; and in Classical Greece the philosopher Socrates was born around 10 years after Confucius's death, in a life that spanned from 469 to 399 BCE.

As Karl Jaspers described it, during the Axial Age "the spiritual foundations of humanity were laid down simultaneously and independently in China, India, Persia, Palestine, and Greece. And these are the foundations upon which humanity still subsists today."[5] The key features of the Axial Age identified by Jaspers were the relatively sudden appearance of intellectuals engaged in a similar search for human meaning; the near simultaneous emergence of new religious and philosophical elites; and the advent of itinerant (traveling) scholars who roamed from city to city as teachers and religious figures. This search for universal ethical and philosophical principles was not uniform in approach, however; for some it was associated with gods and religions, for others with rational thought.

Later historians have suggested that the more or less simultaneous emergence of these universal ideas was a clear reflection of the growing interconnectedness of agrarian civilizations and cultures during the period. Jaspers argued that these ideas were being articulated during a period characterized by a dramatically changing social environment (such as China during the later Zhou Dynasty). Like Siddhartha and the Greek philosophers, Confucius was most interested in defining the essential duties and obligations of correct living during a time of social and political upheaval, rather than in any spiritual or religious response. Confucius was not interested in offering spiritual stories about the origins of the Earth, or in devising some new religious faith for his contemporaries. Confucianism was a genuine philosophy, and was never intended to be a religion.

It was not Confucianism that ultimately succeeded in reuniting China, however. One of the "warring states," the powerful Qin from northwestern China, adopted the authoritarian ideology of Legalism, which attempted to achieve social cohesion through the application of strict laws and harsh, collective punishments. For Legalists, the foundations of a state's strength were the military and agrarian sectors, and they sought to channel as many individuals as possible into those occupations and away from socially "useless" professions like education, philosophy, or business. Using often brutal Legalist tactics, the Qin reunited China and paved the way for the long-lasting Han Dynasty that followed.

The Qin Dynasty (221–207 BCE) was short-lived but astonishingly successful. The Qin constructed a powerful army that systematically defeated rival states and brought unification and order to much of China. Adopting administrative policies similar to those of the Persians and Romans (an example of convergent political evolution), the first emperor, Qin Shi Huangdi (r. 221–210 BCE), established a centralized bureaucracy that replaced the regional nobility with provincial administrators. Like the Achaemenids and Romans he built roads throughout the kingdom to facilitate the movement of his armies; and he also connected a series of defensive walls in the north to construct the first Great Wall of China. Determined to crush all opposition, he disarmed regional armies, then used execution to blunt the criticism of Confucian intellectuals who opposed him. Intent on unifying the many peoples of China, the emperor standardized weights, laws, measures, coinage, and, perhaps most important, the Chinese writing script throughout the empire. Finally, he arranged for the construction of his own extraordinary tomb near modern Xian, in which an army of life-sized terracotta warriors was housed to defend the emperor in death (Figure 7.3).

After the first emperor's death in 210, the Qin was quickly replaced by the Han Dynasty (210 BCE–220 CE), which went on to be one of the most successful of all Chinese dynasties. Where the Qin may have controlled an area of around 1 million square miles (2.6 million square kilometers), the Han Empire at its peak expanded to some 2.5 million square miles (6.5 million square kilometers). The great emperor of the Early Han was Wudi (r. 141–87 BCE), who relied on a vast bureaucracy to govern the state. To ensure the supply of educated bureaucrats, Wudi established an imperial institute of higher learning in 124 BCE, and made Confucianism the core curriculum in an attempt to ensure a continuous supply of highly educated scholar-bureaucrats to administer the affairs of state. Wudi also expanded Chinese interests deep into Central Asia, Vietnam, and Korea. The emperor was even able to keep at bay the great nomadic confederation of the Xiongnu, whose predecessors had menaced Chinese sedentary states from the northern steppes for much of the first millennium BCE.

The Han Dynasty continued to dominate China during the first two centuries of the Common Era. By maintaining Chinese control in Central Asia, the Han ensured the continued operation of the lucrative Silk Roads. But problems of unequal land redistribution led to a series of uprisings by disgruntled peasants; and these, along with increasing factional division, ended the dynasty in 220 CE. Thereafter, China endured three and a half centuries of contraction, disorder, and shifting regional power relationships, including having the north completely overrun by nomads at precisely the same time Rome was experiencing something similar in western Eurasia.

Right across Afro-Eurasia then, the expansion of the size, power, and effectiveness of agrarian civilizations continued during this second cycle into the first millennium CE, before a period of contraction slowed the tendency toward growth for several centuries.

Third Cycle of Expansion and Contraction: ca. 500 CE to ca. 1000 CE

Rome and Byzantium Even as the western Roman Empire fragmented into a series of competitive regional kingdoms in the fifth and sixth centuries CE, the eastern half remained relatively stable and strong. Indeed the Byzantine Empire that emerged there lasted for another 1,000 years, and along with Tang China and the Dar al-Islam was one of the economic and cultural pillars of Afro-Eurasia during a renewed wave of expansion in the later first millennium CE. The early emperor Justinian (r. 527–565 CE) was responsible for much of Byzantium's success. He and his wife Theodora crushed an internal revolt, strengthened the defenses of Constantinople, published a complete codex of Roman law, and even attempted to reconquer parts of the western empire, ultimately without success. In the seventh and eighth centuries, Constantinople was able to withstand concerted sieges by the expanding forces of Islam, although large regions of the empire were lost to the Muslims. The core empire survived, however, and after defeating opponents in the eleventh and twelfth centuries, used its strategic position to increase its territories and grow wealthy through trade and

FIGURE 7.3 Terracotta warriors. These figures, from the monumental tomb of the first emperor of China, Qin Shi Huangdi, date from late third century BCE.

innovative manufacturing. This ensured Byzantium's continuing status as the dominant agrarian civilization of the Eastern Mediterranean until late in the Era of Agrarian Civilizations.

China After the collapse of the Han Dynasty in 220 CE, China endured three and a half centuries of contraction and disorder before reunification returned under the Sui. The short-lived Sui Dynasty (598–618 CE) restored order and paved the way for the success of the Tang, which established one of the most successful agrarian civilizations of all. The Sui undertook extensive infrastructure construction, including the construction of the Grand Canal, the largest hydrological project attempted to this point in world history.

The Tang Dynasty (618–907 CE) turned China into probably the wealthiest and most powerful state on Earth. The second emperor, Tang Taizong (r. 626–649), continued the work of improving China's transportation and communications infrastructure. Good roads, government-owned inns and postal stations, and an effective courier system united China as never before. A genuine attempt was made to redistribute land more equitably to the peasants by allotting fields according to fertility and the family's needs. Like the early Han, the Tang also attempted to ensure a steady supply of educated and ethical government officials by supporting an examination system based on knowledge of Confucianism. The Tang then used their armies and administrators to become an expansionist imperial state that at its peak controlled almost 4.5 million square miles (11.7 million square kilometers) of East and Central Asian territory (Map 7.4).

In contrast to most imperial administrations, the Tang government actively supported agricultural innovation, particularly in the south of the country, which became the economic hub of China. The Chinese

population increased as a result, and rapid urbanization followed. By the tenth century Tang China was the most urbanized agrarian civilization ever seen. Chang'an, the capital, home to 2 million residents, was the largest city on the planet. Craft innovation flourished in the workshops of these great cities, contributing to a surging market economy. Trade on the Silk Roads revived, and foreign merchants established a substantial presence in many Chinese cities. Virtually every known religion of Afro-Eurasia was practiced somewhere in the country. The vast, cosmopolitan, flourishing civilization dominated the eastern half of the Afro-Eurasian world zone at the same time that the western half was being influenced culturally and politically by the expanding realm of Islam. Tang collapse, a product of complacent rule by the later emperors, brought to an end this extraordinary chapter in the history of agrarian civilizations. But as we will see in Chapter 10, under their successors the Song Dynasty, China came close to an industrial revolution that, had it been sustained, might have radically altered the history of the modern world.

Islamic Civilization Similar to what the Achaemenid Persians achieved in the mid-first millennium BCE, late in the first millennium CE the histories of many of the regions discussed in this chapter became even more interconnected because of the expansion

MAP 7.4 China. After 350 years of disorder China was reunified under the Sui Dynasty; under their successors, the Tang, the Chinese state expanded to an enormous size.

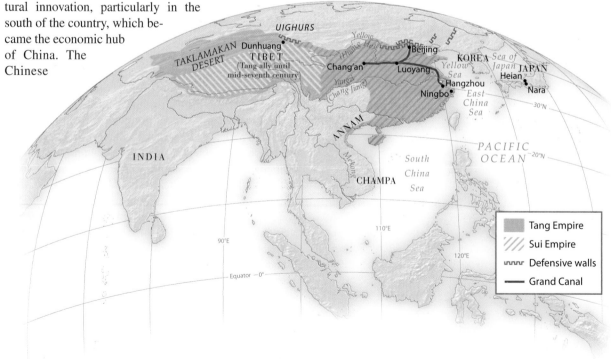

of Islamic civilization. The vast **Dar al-Islam** ("Abode of Islam") created by Muslim warriors and administrators was one of the most significant economic, intellectual, and cultural structures of the latter part of the first millennium CE; it dominated the western half of the Afro-Eurasian world zone the same way that the Tang dominated the eastern.

Both the Islamic faith and its early cultural practices were products of the environment and Bedouin traditions of the Arabian Peninsula. Into this arid world of merchants and pastoral nomads Muhammad ibn Abdullah was born about 570 CE. When he reached his late thirties Muhammad had a profound spiritual experience and became convinced that, rather than the host of deities worshiped by his fellow Bedouin, there was only one all-powerful God named Allah. Muhammad's spiritual beliefs soon took on political and social dimensions. As he described his new beliefs to friends and family, Muhammad attracted a substantial following. The increasing popularity of his preaching offended the polytheistic beliefs of the authorities in Mecca, and Muhammad and his followers were forced to flee to the city of Yathrib, which was renamed Medina, or "the city" (of the Prophet). This migration, or *hijira,* in 622 CE marks the official start of the Islamic calendar and also the moment that the spiritual visions experienced by Muhammad were transformed into a powerful religious, social, and political movement.

In Medina, Muhammad and his followers organized the Muslim community of the faithful, or *umma,* into a society within a society, with its own law code (*sharia*), social welfare system, educational institutions, and income. As the umma grew in size and confidence, Muslims aggressively sought converts and engaged in a *jihad,* or "struggle," to enlarge the size of their congregation and territories. This introduced a new prime mover for the territorial expansion of agrarian civilizations—a spiritual imperative. In 630 Muhammad led the now powerful umma back to Mecca, overthrowing and replacing the government there with their own theocratic administration. By the time of Muhammad's death in 632, a substantial part of Arabia was under Muslim control. Muhammad's capable successor Abu Bakr was elected *caliph* (or "deputy"). The caliph was head of state, military commander, chief judge, and chief religious leader, perhaps the quintessential example of the evolution and consolidation of secular, spiritual, and legal power during the Era of Agrarian Civilizations. Under Abu Bakr and his successors, the jihad continued and, after conquering the remaining non-Muslim tribes of Arabia, Muslim armies turned northward to confront aggressively the now complacent and somewhat stagnant Byzantine and Sasanian Empires.

The lightning-fast expansion of the Dar al-Islam was unprecedented, even during an era in which, as we have seen, many great empires grew rapidly to enormous size in their search for tribute, land and imperial glory. By 637, within a mere five years of Muhammad's death, Syria, Palestine, and all of Mesopotamia had fallen to Islam. During the decade of the 640s, much of North Africa was also incorporated into the Islamic realm. By the time the

Sasanian imperial heartland of Persia fell to the Muslims in 651, the Dar al-Islam stretched from the Mediterranean to Afghanistan. Islamic armies resumed the jihad early in the eighth century. Several Hindu kingdoms of northern India were conquered in 711; and Muslim hegemony in North Africa was extended to the Atlantic coast of Morocco, then across the Straits of Gibraltar and into Spain by 718. In an era characterized by substantial civilizations, the Islamic realm, covering more than 5 million square miles (13 million square kilometers), was simply the largest the world had seen (Map 7.5).

Islamic authorities now faced the same challenge that had been faced by Akkadians, Assyrians, Persians, Mauryans, Romans, and Han before them: how to effectively administer a vast, multicultural empire. Competing claims for leadership of the Islamic realm led to the emergence of bitterly opposed political factions. Eventually the caliphate was consolidated into two stable dynasties, those of the Umayyads (661–750 CE) and their successors the Abbasids (750–1258 CE). The Umayyads adopted a tightly centralized administrative structure, with Arab elites installed as governors of the newly conquered lands. Although the Arabs generally allowed people to follow their own religious beliefs, they placed enormous pressure on conquered peoples to convert by levying a special religious tax on non-Muslims. As resentment built throughout the realm, the Umayyad caliphs became increasingly aloof, eventually losing the support of all sectors of the realm until the Umayyad clan was violently annihilated.

The Abbasid caliphate then ruled the Dar al-Islam for the next 500 years, until it was destroyed by the Mongols in 1258. The Abbasids instituted a more cosmopolitan form of government in which power and administrative responsibilities were shared more equitably among Arabs, Persians, Egyptians, and Mesopotamians. In thinking of more effective ways to govern their vast realm, the Abbasids were influenced by Persia's long experience at imperial administration. Baghdad became the new capital of the Islamic world, and governors were appointed to administer the far-flung provinces. The Abbasids established centralized bureaucracies, minted coins, controlled taxes, ran the post office, and maintained a standing, professional army. With a steady flow of tributary revenue coming in from all over the Islamic world, Baghdad was beautified with magnificent buildings, mosques, and squares, and became one of the great commercial, financial, industrial, and intellectual cities of the world. The outstanding caliph Harun al-Rashid (r. 786–809 CE), who was a lavish patron of the arts, enjoyed diplomatic exchanges with leading European rulers and presided over a stable and immensely wealthy realm. The ninth-century Muslim historian Muhammad al Tabari claimed that when Harun al-Rashid died, the treasury at Baghdad contained 900 million dirhams, an immense fortune.

Although territorial expansion of the Dar al-Islam continued under Abbasid leadership, it did so less because of official Abbasid policy and more as a result of campaigns carried out by autonomous regional Muslim forces. An

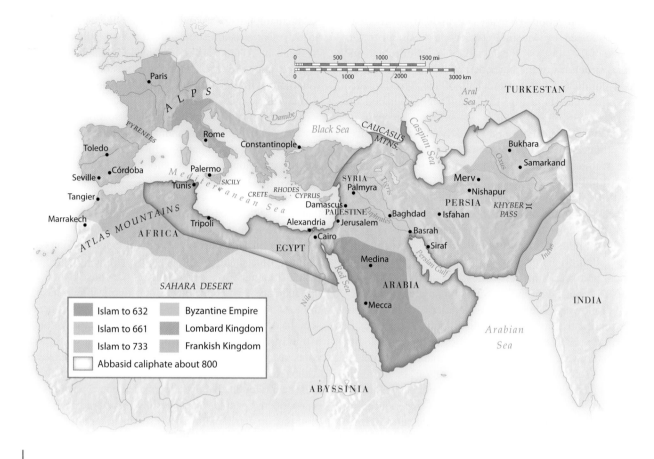

MAP 7.5 Central and western Afro-Eurasia. This map illustrates the extraordinary expansion of the realm of Islam in the seventh and eighth centuries.

Legend:
- Islam to 632
- Islam to 661
- Islam to 733
- Abbasid caliphate about 800
- Byzantine Empire
- Lombard Kingdom
- Frankish Kingdom

important battle was fought deep in Central Asia between Abbasid and Tang Chinese forces in 751. During the multi-day Battle of the Talas River, a large Muslim force struggled to overcome a much smaller Chinese army and its allies for control of the Syr Darya valley. Although Chinese forces were eventually overwhelmed, this confrontation marked the end of westward Tang expansion and opened up much of Central Asia to Muslim penetration, facilitating the continued expansion of the Islamic faith amongst the Turkic-speaking peoples of the region.

The reign of Harun al-Rashid marked the high point of the Abbasid Caliphate. Plagued by disagreements over succession and eventually by civil war, provincial governors began keeping tax revenues for themselves and building their own independent power bases throughout the Dar al-Islam. The Abbasid "throne" was taken over by Persian aristocracy in the tenth century, and by the mid-eleventh century real power had passed to the Saljuqs, militarized Turkish nomads who had converted to Islam and now occupied much of the caliphate. With the arrival of the Mongols in the thirteenth century, the Turks retreated to their new Anatolian homeland, and the Dar al-Islam became simply one part of the vast Mongol Empire, which as we will see in Chapter 10, at 10.35 million square miles (27 million square kilometers) was the largest contiguous empire that has existed in all of world history.

SUMMARY

In this chapter we traced the political evolution over 3,000 years of a new type of human community that we first introduced in Chapter 6—the agrarian civilization. We argued that the seemingly constant (on the long scale) expansion of agrarian civilizations was driven by the need to achieve growth through external conquest. The ruling elites of the majority of these civilizations were generally disinterested in commercial and agricultural innovation, which meant that they were forced to tackle the problem of growth through warfare. Growth was a zero-sum game that necessitated taking what others had produced, rather than trying to increase productivity within the state. This helps explain the almost constant warfare and attempts at expansion through conquest of one's neighbors that so characterizes the era. We explored the history of Afro-Eurasian agrarian civilizations in three distinct cycles of expansion and contraction: from roughly 3000 BCE to 500 BCE; 500 BCE to 500 CE; and 500 to 1000 CE. When agrarian civilizations first appeared in Southwest Asia and Northeast Africa 5,000 years ago, they accounted for only a tiny portion of the human family. By the end of the era, the overwhelming majority of the human population, and certainly the densest human communities, were housed somewhere within an agrarian civilization.

The growth of civilizations and the evolution of power within their administrative structures is only one part of the story, however. As these structures expanded they joined up with others to create larger networks or webs of interconnected civilizations. This gradual linking and interconnectedness ensured that the defining feature of the human species, our ability to exchange information and learn collectively, was given a powerful boost during the era. By engaging more and more peoples and their diverse lifeways and cultural practices in the Collective Learning process, agrarian civilizations dramatically enhanced the human capacity to innovate technologically, socially, politically, and spiritually. In the next chapter we will explore some of the cultural practices that evolved as a product of trans-Afro-Eurasian cultural exchange during the Era of Agrarian Civilizations, practices that sent human history spiraling along dramatic new pathways that led into the modern world.

CHAPTER QUESTIONS

1. What are some of the defining characteristics of agrarian civilizations?
2. Discuss some of the key motives or prime movers that drove expansion during the era.
3. How did the Persians create and govern the largest agrarian civilizations seen in world history to that point?

4. How did the Romans in western Afro-Eurasia, and the Han in eastern Eurasia, govern their enormous civilizations?
5. Why did attempts to create durable imperial structures in South Asia continuously fail?
6. What is the meaning of *jihad,* and how did it result in the creation of the enormous Dar al-Islam?

KEY TERMS

| Dar al-Islam | Era of Agrarian | Mandate of Heaven | Silk Roads |
| diaspora | Civilizations | polis | |

FURTHER READING

Andrea, Alfred J., and James H. Overfield. *The Human Record: Sources of Global History,* Vol. 1 to 1700, 4th ed. Boston, MA: Wadsworth, 2008.

Bentley, Jerry, and Herbert Zeigler. *Traditions and Encounters: A Global Perspective on the Past.* 5th ed. New York: McGraw-Hill, 2010.

Biraben, J. R. "Essai sur l'evolution du nombre des hommes." *Population* 34 (1979).

The Cambridge Ancient History. 14 Volumes, 2nd ed. Cambridge, UK: Cambridge University Press, 1970.

Fernandez-Armesto, Felipe. *The World: A History.* Upper Saddle River, NJ: Pearson Prentice Hall, 2007.

Jaspers, Karl. *The Way to Wisdom: An Introduction to Philosophy.* New Haven, CT: Yale University Press, 2003.

Mitchell, Stephen, trans. *Epic of Gilgamesh.* New York: Free Press, 2004.

Strayer, Robert. *Ways of the World: A Global History.* Boston: Bedford/St. Martin's Press, 2009.

Taagepera, Rein. "Size and Duration of Empires: Growth-Decline Curves, 3000 to 600 BC." *Social Science Research* 7 (1978):180–96.

ENDNOTES

1. Stephen Mitchell, trans., *Epic of Gilgamesh* (New York: Free Press, 2004), 198–99.
2. Alfred J. Andrea and James H. Overfield, *The Human Record: Sources of Global History,* vol. 1 to 1700, 4th ed. (Boston, MA: Wadsworth, 2008), 23–24.
3. J. R. Biraben, "Essai sur l'evolution du nombre des hommes," *Population* 34 (1979).
4. Rein Taagepera, "Size and Duration of Empires: Growth-Decline Curves, 3000 to 600 BC," *Social Science Research* 7 (1978):180–96.
5. Karl Jaspers, *The Way to Wisdom: An Introduction to Philosophy* (New Haven, CT: Yale University Press, 2003).

part 1

chapter 8

Afro-Eurasia during the Era of Agrarian Civilizations

Seeing the Big Picture

2000 BCE to 1000 CE

▶ How did the establishment of large-scale exchange networks enhance Collective Learning during the Era of Agrarian Civilizations?

▶ Why did increased population densities lead to steeper hierarchies based on wealth, power, and gender during the Era of Agrarian Civilizations?

▶ How fast was the pace of change and growth during the Era of Agrarian Civilizations?

173

In the previous chapter we introduced the Era of Agrarian Civilizations and considered the first of four major themes or patterns that characterize the era: the expansion and increasing size, power, and effectiveness of agrarian civilizations and their tribute-taking administrations through three large cycles of expansion and contraction.

In this chapter we will explore three additional overarching themes that help define the Afro-Eurasian world zone during the era: the establishment of significant networks of exchange between civilizations (notably via the Silk Roads and Indian Ocean); the increasing complexity of social and gender relationships within agrarian civilizations;

and the pace of change throughout the era. Although we argued in the previous chapter that the pace and scale of technological innovation during the Era of Agrarian Civilizations was sluggish compared to the explosive scales of the Modern era, there was still significant change. Major developments occurred in commercial activity, cultural exchange, philosophical thinking, and in social and gender relations, which make this period in human history hugely fascinating. These processes also laid the foundation for the eventual emergence of the modern world. In this chapter we will explore some of these developments as they occurred in the Afro-Eurasian world zone.

Second Trend: The Establishment of Significant Networks of Exchange among Agrarian Civilizations of Afro-Eurasia

Agrarian civilizations did not exist in isolation; as they grew and stretched their administrative boundaries, they joined up to form larger networks. Sometimes they joined up simply because their borders met and merged. Often they joined up in a looser sense; some of their people traded with, or traveled to, or borrowed ideas from, or fought with people from other regions of agrarian civilization. In fact, the very idea of distinct agrarian civilizations with rigid borders is misleading. Borders that can be identified on maps and guarded by frontier guards are, for the most part, modern inventions. The borders of agrarian civilizations were often large, vague regions within which the control of rulers fluctuated or dwindled away gradually or was contested by the claims of neighbors or local rulers.

Despite the complexity of these processes, the slow linking up of different regions of agrarian civilizations was an immensely important process because it ensured that Collective Learning reached further and embraced more people and greater diversity than ever before. Expanding exchange networks magnified the power of Collective Learning, intensifying our uniquely human capacity for finding new ways of relating to the natural world and to each other. By the end of the era, virtually every single human living within the vast Afro-Eurasian world zone was connected together within a vibrant web. This was true only within individual world zones, however. As we will see in the next chapter, significant developments also occurred during the era in the Americas, Australasia, and the Pacific. The four world zones were so isolated from each other during the Era of Agrarian Civilizations, however, that human populations in each remained utterly ignorant of events in the others.

Networks of Exchange and Collective Learning

As a result of the expansion in size and reach of Afro-Eurasian agrarian civilizations, opportunities for exchange of goods and ideas among different regions within each world zone increased. We might compare the great cities of the era with stars, because they dominated their surroundings in a similar way. They were the most powerful entities in their region; their "gravitational pull" affected large regions; towns and villages orbited around them like planets and moons; they energized the area around them; and they were constantly drawing in ideas, goods, innovations, and people. In this way, agrarian civilizations, and the great cities that were at the heart of many of them, directly stimulated exchanges and Collective Learning.

Eventually, particularly in the Afro-Eurasian world zone, all civilizations along with groups following different lifeways outside the civilizations found themselves linked together in a vast interconnected network. Not only were trade goods exchanged in these networks, but also social, religious, and philosophical ideas, languages, new technologies, and diseases. The most important exchange network that existed anywhere during the Era of Agrarian Civilizations is known today as the **Silk Roads,** but significant smaller exchange networks developed much earlier among many of the agrarian civilizations, and eventually major sea routes also emerged through the Indian Ocean. Because of these connections, some world historians argue that, from the moment they appeared, agrarian civilizations were embedded in a much larger geopolitical structure known as a *world-system.* A world-system is essentially a self-contained relationship between two or more societies.

Before the 1970s, most large-scale historians thought of the civilization as the basic unit for understanding history on the macro scale. This way of thinking was heavily influenced by the work of Oswald Spengler and Arnold Toynbee in the early twentieth century, who suggested that civilizations could somehow be studied as distinct, separate entities. There was less interest in the *relationship* among these apparently discreet entities. In the 1970s, Immanuel Wallerstein pioneered a theoretical framework for what he called the **world-systems theory.** Unlike earlier theories, Wallerstein's model shifts the focus to the interactions and connections among civilizations. Although it was only in the twentieth century that the entire world did actually become connected together, the term can be applied to many eras and regions in history where societies over large areas were engaged in some sort of relationship, be it through trade, war, or cultural exchange. A study of the Era of Agrarian Civilizations shows us that, virtually from the moment these new types of human communities appeared, they established relationships that led quickly to the emergence of very extensive "world-systems."

More recently John and William McNeill have argued for the reconceptualizing of networks of human interconnections into an entity that they call the "human web." From the beginning of human history, they suggest, humans have formed webs—both large and small, loose and rigid—and within these webs historians can discern patterns of interaction and exchange, and cooperation or competition, that have driven history relentlessly into modernity. From the "thin localized" webs of the Early Agrarian era, through the "denser, more interactive, metropolitan webs" of the great agrarian civilizations, through to the "electrified global web" of today, the McNeills, like world-systems theorists, argue that world historical analysis has to deal with these larger structures of connectivity. Our big history analysis of the Era of Agrarian Civilizations borrows from both world-systems theory and the idea of a single, evolving human web.

Trans-Civilizational Linkages through Warfare

The almost continuous warfare that characterizes the era was a powerful way of linking agrarian civilizations that were not too distant from each other. It was through warfare, for example, that the Romans found themselves masters of a large regional empire. Continuing conflict with states and peoples beyond the borders, including Germans and Parthians who were never actually incorporated into the empire, also brought these peripheral outsiders into the same, Roman-dominated world-system. As Islamic armies constructed a vast Dar al-Islam that stretched from the Pyrenees in Europe to the borders of the Tang Chinese Empire deep in Central Asia, they also brought diverse and peripheral groups like Frankish kingdoms, Byzantines, and Chinese into an enormous Afro-Eurasian-wide web. As significant as these military relationships were in establishing connections, however, the most effective and ultimately influential world-systems were built through trade.

Early Afro-Eurasian Trade Networks

From the very beginning of the Era of Agrarian Civilizations, trade, often conducted by relays of traders or intermediaries of different kinds (the "middle mediators"), was the most powerful form of linkage established among regions of agrarian civilization, particularly those that were more distant from each other. By the early second millennium BCE, Egyptian, Mesopotamian, and Indus civilizations were involved in commercial relationships. By the mid-second millennium BCE, the Eastern Mediterranean was a tightly integrated trade network. Phoenicians, Egyptians, Minoans, Mycenaeans, and a host of smaller cultures exchanged an extraordinary array of commercial goods.

An intriguing glimpse into this web has come to us through the discovery of a sunken trading ship, the Uluburun Shipwreck. The small ship sank off the southwestern coast of Turkey in the fourteenth century BCE while following its regular regional trading route connecting Phoenicia, southern Anatolia (Turkey), the Aegean Sea, and Egypt. In the ship's hold archaeologists discovered an eclectic cargo including ingots of copper and tin (which would later have been alloyed together to produce bronze weapons); cobalt-blue and turquoise glass; terebinthine resin (a cosmetic perfume ingredient); ebony logs from Egypt; elephant tusks, hippopotamus teeth, ostrich feathers, and tortoise shells; exotic fruits and spices; superb pottery from Cyprus; a gold scarab of the Egyptian Queen Nefertiti; and Mycenaean weapons. They also found a blank writing board on which inscriptions could be made with a stylus in wax, demonstrating the importance of written records (no doubt using the Phoenician alphabet) to commerce.

Significance of the Silk Roads

Although both small- and large-scale trade networks and relationships existed in myriad locations across Afro-Eurasia throughout the era, the most significant Afro-Eurasian exchange web was that of the Silk Roads. As we have seen, from the beginning of human history, the exchange of information and ideas among diverse peoples and cultures has been a prime mover in promoting change through Collective Learning. As the smaller exchanges of the early Era of Agrarian Civilizations began to expand, the enhanced Collective Learning that followed led to more and more significant changes in the material, artistic, social, and spiritual domains of human history. The most influential of these intensified exchange networks emerged around a trading hub located deep in Central Asia, along the Silk Roads, which crisscrossed much of Afro-Eurasia. The trans-civilizational contacts that occurred through this exchange resulted in the most significant Collective Learning so far experienced by humans.

Although some trade and migration had occurred along these routes for millennia, the first really important period of the Silk Roads was between roughly 50 BCE and 250 CE, when material and intellectual exchange took place between the Chinese, Indian, Kushan, Iranian, steppe-nomadic, and Mediterranean worlds. The demise of the western Roman and Han Chinese Empires early in the first millennium CE resulted in several centuries of less regular contact, but a second "Silk Roads era" subsequently operated for several centuries between ca. 600 and ca. 1000 CE, connecting China, India, Southeast Asia, the Dar al-Islam, and the Byzantine Empire into another vast web based on overland and maritime trade. The primary function of the Silk Roads during both periods was to facilitate trade. Not only material goods were carried along the Silk Roads, however, but intellectual, spiritual, cultural, biological and technological ideas as well. Arguably it is these less tangible exchanges that have been of greater significance to world history, as the following few examples might suggest.

An example of significant *intellectual* exchange facilitated by commercial activity occurred when Arab merchants began operating in India in the fifth century CE. As a product of what world historian Lynda Shaffer calls **southernization** (the movement of material and nonmaterial products from Africa and India into northern Eurasia), Arab merchants replaced Roman numerals with the more flexible Indian numbering system they encountered there. Indian numbers, and particularly the concept of zero which the Indians had invented, facilitated more rapid and complex calculations, and they eventually spread all over the world. Because the numbers came to the West via Arab merchants and scholars, they became known in Europe as Arabic numbers, although the Arabs called them Hindi numbers. This particular exchange was of profound importance to world history and helped facilitate the emergence of the modern economy.

Perhaps the most important *spiritual* consequence of material Silk Roads exchanges was the spread of religions across the world zone, particularly Mahayana Buddhism, which moved from India through Central Asia to China and East Asia. An associated *cultural* exchange that led to enhanced Collective Learning was the spread of artistic ideas and techniques, particularly the diffusion eastward of syncretistic sculptural styles that developed in the second century CE in the workshops of Gandhara (in Pakistan) and Mathura (in India), where the first ever representation of the Buddha was conceived. (The terms *syncretism* and *syncretistic* refer to the blending together of traits from various cultural traditions to create a new culture.) (See Figure 8.1.)

The major *biological* consequence of Silk Roads trade was the spread of disease and plague. Not only did the passing of disease bacteria along the Silk Roads by traders play a significant role in the depopulation and subsequent decline of both the Han and Roman Empires, but the exposure of millions of humans to these pathogens meant that antibodies spread extensively throughout the Afro-Eurasian world zone, and important immunities were built up within populations. These immunities proved incredibly significant in the premodern age, when Muslim, Chinese, and particularly European traders and explorers carried Afro-Eurasian diseases to the other world zones, with disastrous consequences for native populations. These four brief examples all support the claim that the Silk Roads and Indian Ocean networks profoundly affected the subsequent shape and direction of *all* human history.

FIGURE 8.1 Gandharan Buddha, ca. second century CE. Gandharan sculpture epitomizes the syncretistic cultural developments that occurred in Central Asia during the first Silk Roads era.

Origins of the Silk Roads

Commercial and cultural exchange on this scale became possible only after the small and fragmented river valley states of Afro-Eurasia had been consolidated into substantial agrarian civilizations, a process that was, as we saw in the previous chapter, largely the result of warfare. Continuing expansion by the major civilizations meant that, by the first Silk Roads era, just four imperial dynasties—those of the Roman, Parthian, Kushan, and Han Empires—controlled much of the Eurasian landmass, from the China Sea to Britain. The consolidation of these huge states meant that order and stability were established over a vast and previously fragmented geopolitical environment. Extensive internal road networks were constructed, great advances were made in metallurgy and transport technology, agricultural production was intensified, and coinage appeared for the first time. By the middle of the first century BCE, conditions in Afro-Eurasia were ripe for levels of material and cultural exchange—and Collective Learning—hitherto unknown.

Also critical in facilitating these exchanges were the pastoral nomads, who formed communities that lived primarily from the exploitation of domestic animals such as cattle, sheep, camels, or horses. The exact chronology of the origins and spread of pastoralism remains obscure, but certainly by the middle to late fourth millennium BCE the appearance of burial mounds scattered across the steppes of Inner Eurasia suggests that some communities that were dependent on herds or flocks of domestic animals had become seminomadic. Just how nomadic these various groups were remains unclear. There were probably many degrees of nomadism, ranging from groups that had no permanent settlements at all to communities like the Andronovo that were largely sedentary and lived in permanent settlements. The highly mobile, militarized pastoralism of Inner Eurasia, associated with the riding of horses by Scythians and Xiongnu, probably did not emerge until early in the first millennium BCE.

In Afro-Eurasia, by the time the first cities and states appeared, the technologies of the secondary products revolution (which we discussed in Chapter 6) had generated more productive ways of exploiting livestock, some of them so productive that they allowed entire communities to depend almost exclusively on their herds of animals. The more they did this, however, the more nomadic they had to be, so that they could graze their animals over large areas. The result was that there slowly developed, over several millennia, entire lifeways based mainly on pastoralism, capable of exploiting the arid lands that ran in a long horizontal belt from northwestern Africa through Southwest Asia and Central Asia to Mongolia.

By the middle of the first millennium BCE, a number of large pastoral nomadic communities emerged that had the military skills and technologies, and the endurance and mobility, to dominate their sedentary agrarian neighbors. Some of them, including the Scythians, Xiongnu, Yuezhi, and Wusun, established powerful statelike confederations that formed in the steppes between the agrarian civilizations (Map 8.1). These states do not count as agrarian civilizations because they lacked many of the crucial features of such communities, including major cities and large sedentary populations. But they demonstrated the ability

MAP 8.1 Nomadic and sedentary states of Inner Eurasia. This map shows some of the major nomadic confederations and agrarian civilizations of the region between ca. 200 and ca. 100 BCE.

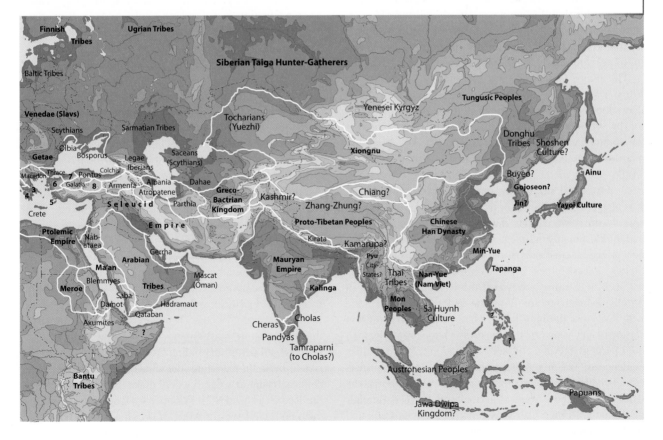

of pastoral nomads to prosper in the harsh and arid interior of Afro-Eurasia. Once such communities emerged, they facilitated the linking up of all the different lifeways and communities. Prior to the success of pastoralists in these more marginal zones, agrarian civilizations were considerably more isolated from each other. Ultimately it was the role of pastoralists as facilitators and protectors of trade and exchange that allowed the Silk Roads and other networks to flourish.

First Silk Roads Era

With these preconditions in place, it was the decision by the Han Chinese to begin to interact with their western neighbors and engage in long-distance commerce that turned small-scale regional trading activity into a great trans-Afro-Eurasian commercial network. The Han became involved after Emperor Wudi (141–87 BCE) dispatched envoy Zhang Qian on a diplomatic and exploratory mission into Central Asia. When Zhang returned after an epic journey of 12 years, he convinced the emperor that friendly relations could be established with many of the states of Central Asia because they were "hungry for Han goods." Those that weren't eager to trade could be subdued by force and compelled to join the Han trade and tributary network. Within a decade the Han had established a tributary relationship with 36 city-states of Central Asia, and mercantile traffic began to flow out of China along the ancient migration routes into Central Asia. As we saw in the previous chapter, half a century after the Han began to engage with their western neighbors, Augustus came to power in Rome following a century of civil war. This restored peace and stability to much of western Afro-Eurasia, leading to a sharp increase in the demand for luxury goods in Rome, particularly for spices and exotic textiles like silk.

The major Chinese export commodity in demand in Rome was silk, an elegant, translucent, sensual material that soon came to be regarded as the last word in fashion by wealthy patrician women. The Chinese, realizing the commercial value of their monopoly on silk, carefully guarded the secret of silk production, and border guards would search merchants to make sure they weren't carrying any actual silk worms out of the country. Han iron was also prized in Rome for its exceptional hardness. Fine spices were imported into the Roman Empire from Arabia and India, notably nutmeg, cloves, cardamom, and pepper, prized as condiments, but also as aphrodisiacs, anesthetics, and perfumes. Trade with China and Central Asia for such high-value goods cost the Romans a fortune. In 65 CE, Roman senator Pliny the Elder fumed that trade with Asia was draining the treasury of some 100 million sestertii every year. (A sestertius was a large bronze Roman coin.) Even if Pliny's figure is exaggerated, it provides evidence of the incredible scale of Silk Roads commercial exchanges. In return for their high-value exports, the Chinese imported a range of agricultural products (including grapes), Roman glassware, art objects from India and Egypt, and horses from the steppes.

FIGURE 8.2 Two-humped Bactrian camel. The bulk of Silk Roads trade goods was literally carried on the backs of these animals that are so perfectly adapted to the environments of Central Asia.

The major Silk Roads land routes stretched from the Han capital, Chang'an, deep into Central Asia by way of the Gansu corridor and Tarim basin. The animal that made Silk Roads trade possible in the eastern and central regions of Afro-Eurasia was the Bactrian camel. Native to the steppes of Central Asia, the two-humped Bactrian camel is a supreme example of superb evolutionary adaptation. To survive the harsh winters the camel grows a long, shaggy coat, which it sheds rapidly as the season warms up. The two humps on its back are composed of sustaining fat and its long eyelashes and sealable nostrils help keep out dust in the frequent sandstorms. The two broad toes on each of its feet have undivided soles and are able to spread widely as an adaptation to walking on sand. The bulk of overland Silk Roads trade was literally carried on the backs of these extraordinary animals (Figure 8.2).

In western Eurasia, the major land route departed from the great trading cities of Roman Syria such as Palmyra, crossed the Euphrates and Tigris Rivers, then climbed across the Iranian plateau toward Afghanistan (then known as Bactria). Significant information on the geography of the western part of the Silk Roads has come to us from a document produced around the year 1 CE—*Parthian Stations*—written by a Parthian Greek merchant Isodorus of Charax. Around the time *Parthian Stations* was being composed, the amount of trans-Afro-Eurasian trade taking place by sea was also increasing, particularly between Roman Egypt and the coast of India. The survival of an extraordinary first-century CE mariner's handbook, the *Periplus of the Erythrian Sea,* has given historians a detailed account of maritime commerce at that time. The *Periplus* shows us that sailors had discovered the geographic secrets of the monsoon "trade" winds. The winds blow reliably from the southwest in the summer, allowing heavily laden trade ships to sail across the Indian Ocean from the coast of Africa to India. In the winter the winds reverse, and the same ships carrying new cargo would make the return journey to the Red Sea (Map 8.2). Whether by land or by sea, however, no traders we are aware of ever made their way along the entire length of the Silk Roads during the first era of its

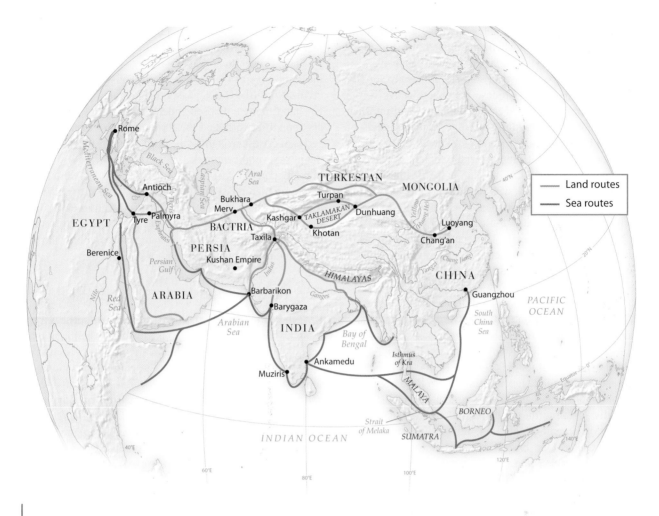

MAP 8.2 **The Silk Roads.** This maps shows land and maritime trade and exchange routes, ca. 100 CE.

operation. Instead, merchants from the major Eastern and Western civilizations took their goods so far, then passed them on to a series of middlemen, including traders who were operating deep within the Kushan Empire or in commercial ports throughout the Indian Ocean basin.

The Crossroads of Afro-Eurasia

At the heart of the Silk Roads network, straddling and influencing both the land and maritime routes, was the Kushan Empire (ca. 45–225 CE), one of the most important yet least known agrarian civilizations in world history. The Kushans were able to maintain relatively cordial relations with Romans, Parthians, Chinese, Indians, and the steppe nomads. They played such a crucial role in facilitating the extraordinary levels of cross-cultural exchange that characterize this first Silk Roads era that the period could justifiably be renamed the Kushan era. The Kushan monarchs were not only effective political and military rulers; they also demonstrated a remarkable appreciation of art and were patrons of innovative sculpture workshops within their empire. The output from these workshops reflects the sort of synthesis typical of the Collective Learning of the era.

The sculpture produced in the workshops of Gandhara and Mathura during the Kushan era was created by the combined talents of Central Asian, Indian, and (perhaps) Hellenistic Greek artists who placed themselves at the service of a resurgent Buddhist spirituality and created a whole new set of images for veneration. Until this moment the Buddha had never been depicted in human form, but had instead been represented by symbols including an umbrella or footprints in the sand. The first ever representation of the Buddha, which appeared in Gandhara (in modern-day Pakistan), was influenced by depictions of Greco-Roman deities. This physical representation then spread along the Silk Roads, penetrating south to Sri Lanka and east to China, Japan, Korea, and Southeast Asia.

An equally striking example of this cross-fertilization of ideas and traditions is the spread of Buddhist ideology along the great trade routes. Buddhism first emerged in northern India in the sixth century BCE. Eight hundred years later, according to ancient Chinese Buddhist documents, the Kushan king, Kanishka the Great (ca. 129–152 CE), convened an important meeting in Kashmir at which the decision was taken to rewrite the Buddhist scriptures in a more popular and accessible language. This helped facilitate the emergence and spread of **Mahayana** (or Great Vehicle) **Buddhism,** partly because the scriptures were now written in a language the common people could understand, and not one that could be read only by religious elites.

The well-traveled trade routes from India through the Kushan realm and into China facilitated the spread of Buddhist ideas that, because they offered the hope of salvation to all regardless of caste or status, was already popular with India's merchants. Chinese merchants active in the silk trade became attracted to the faith, too, and returned home to spread the Buddhist message. Chinese edicts of 65 and 70 CE specifically mention the spread of Buddhism and opposition to it from imperial scholars devoted to Confucianism. By 166 CE the Han emperor himself was sacrificing to the Buddha, and the Sutra on the "Perfection of the Gnosis" was translated into Chinese by 179 CE. By the late fourth century, a period of disunity in China, much of the population of northern China had adopted Buddhism, and by the sixth century much of southern China as well. The religion also found ready acceptance in Korea, Japan, Tibet, Mongolia, and Southeast Asia.

The Silk Roads also facilitated the spread of Christianity, Manichaeism, and later, Islam. Christian missionaries made good use of the superb Roman road and sea transportation networks. The Christian missionary, Paul of Tarsus, may have traveled some 8,000 miles (13,000 kilometers) along the roads and sea lanes of the eastern Roman Empire preaching to small Christian communities. Christianity eventually spread farther to the east along the Silk Roads, through Mesopotamia and Iran, into India, and eventually into China. One branch of Christianity, that of the Nestorians, became particularly strong throughout the central and eastern Silk Roads. The Central Asian religion of **Manichaeism** also benefited from the silk routes after it emerged in Mesopotamia in the third century CE. Its founder, Mani (216–272 CE,) was a fervent missionary who personally traveled extensively throughout the region and also dispatched disciples. Manichaeism was based on a cosmology in which the struggle between a good, spiritual world of light, and an evil, material world of darkness was continuously being waged throughout human history. Like Buddhism, Manichaeism was particularly attractive to merchants, and eventually most of the major Silk Roads trading cities contained Manichaean communities.

Decline of the First Silk Roads Era

During the third century of the Common Era, the Silk Roads fell gradually into disuse as both China and the Roman Empire withdrew from the trans-Afro-Eurasian web, part of the cycle of contraction we observed in the previous chapter. Ironically, Silk Roads trade itself was at least partly responsible for this disengagement, because it contributed to the spread of disastrous epidemic diseases. Smallpox, measles, and bubonic plagues devastated the populations at either end of the routes, where people had less resistance. Population estimates from the ancient world are always difficult, but the population of the Roman Empire may have fallen from 60 million to 45 million between the mid-first and mid-second centuries CE. As smallpox devastated the Mediterranean world late in the second century, populations declined again, to perhaps 40 million by

400 CE. In China, populations fell from perhaps 60 million in 200 CE to 45 million by 600 CE.

These huge demographic losses, which happened at the same time as the decline of previously stable agrarian civilizations (the Han Dynasty disintegrated in 220 CE, the Kushan Empire collapsed under a wave of Sasanian invaders soon afterward, and the Roman Empire experienced a series of crises throughout the third century) meant that, for the next several centuries, the prevailing political situation in many parts of Afro-Eurasia was not conducive to large-scale commercial exchange. However, with the creation of the Dar al-Islam in the eighth and ninth centuries CE, and the establishment of the Tang Dynasty in China at the same time, significant Silk Roads exchanges along both land and maritime routes revived.

Second Silk Roads Era

Both the Tang Dynasty (618–907 CE) and its successor the Song Dynasty (960–1279 CE) presided over a vibrant market economy in China, in which agricultural and manufacturing specialization, population growth, urbanization, and infrastructure development led to high levels of internal and external trade. New financial instruments (including printed paper money) were devised to facilitate large-scale mercantile activity. At the same time, Arab merchants, benefiting from the stable and prosperous Abbasid administration in Baghdad, began to engage with Chinese merchants in lucrative commercial enterprises. Large numbers of Muslim merchants actually moved to China where they joined communities of Byzantine, Indian, and Southeast Asian migrants in the great Chinese trading cities. As maritime trade gradually eclipsed overland trade in volume, merchants and sailors from all over Afro-Eurasia flocked to the great southern port cities of Guangzhou and Quanzhou.

The recent discovery of a sunken ninth-century CE Arab ship in the waters of Indonesia has provided historians with tangible evidence of both the intensely commercial nature of Chinese–Muslim trade and the significance of maritime routes in facilitating it. The dhow was filled with tens of thousands of carefully packaged Tang ceramic plates and bowls, along with many gold and silver objects. The Belitung Wreck demonstrates the existence of a mass production and export industry under the Tang, with most of the goods intended for the Arab market. There is something strikingly modern about this commercial relationship between the two great powers of Afro-Eurasia at the end of the first millennium of the Common Era.

Unlike the high-value artifacts discovered in the Uluburun Shipwreck, the Tang bowls discovered on the Belitung Wreck were functional and intended for the ninth-century equivalent of a "mass market." Their almost factory-like manufacture demonstrates the existence of a well-organized commercial infrastructure (Figure 8.3). The bowls required the use of cobalt for blue coloring, which was imported by the Chinese manufacturers in significant quantities from Iran. The firing date of the bowls was carefully noted in the ship's manifest. The cargo also included large quantities

FIGURE 8.3 Tang Dynasty Changsha bowls. These ninth-century Changsha bowls were manufactured in China during the Tang Dynasty for export to markets in the Islamic caliphates. They were discovered on the wreck of an Arab dhow off the island of Belitung in modern Indonesia.

of standardized inkpots, spice jars, and jugs, clearly export goods manufactured for specific markets. Decorative patterns painted or glazed on the various items—including Buddhist, Iranian, and Islamic motifs—show the particular market the goods were intended for. China and the Dar al-Islam were engaged in intense commercial exchanges during this second Silk Roads era, and Arab mariners undertaking lengthy seagoing voyages were maintaining this vibrant trans-Afro-Eurasian web late in the first millennium of the Common Era.

As with the first Silk Roads era, although the material exchanges were important and impressive, the cultural exchanges seem of even greater significance than the material exchanges. One enchanting example of this is the collection of stories in Arabic known as the *Thousand and One Nights*. Some scholars suggest that many of the stories were originally of Indian origin, and were spread into Persia by merchants plying the Indian Ocean trade networks. The original core of stories was probably quite small, but as they made their way into the Dar al-Islam many more stories from Persian and Arabic traditions were added until the *Thousand and One Nights* became one of the great syncretistic compilations of world literature.

Religious exchanges continued to occur along the Silk Roads during this second era. As we have seen, even before the Tang Dynasty came to power in China, many foreign religions had made their way into East Asia. With the advent of Islam in the seventh century and the establishment of substantial Muslim merchant communities in the centuries that followed, mosques also began to appear in many Chinese cities. Yet of all the foreign beliefs that were accepted in China, only Buddhism made substantial inroads against Confucianism. Between 600 and 1000 CE, hundreds if not thousands of Buddhist *stupas* (mounded buildings that housed the remains of the dead) and temples were constructed in China. With its promise of salvation, Buddhism seriously challenged Daoism and Confucianism for the hearts and minds of many Chinese, and in the end the syncretistic faith of Chan Buddhism (Zen Buddhism in Japan) emerged as a popular compromise.

The Silk Roads, both the land and maritime variants, are the quintessential example of the interconnectedness of civilizations during the Era of Agrarian Civilizations. Along these often difficult routes through some of the harshest country

on Earth traveled merchants and adventurers, diplomats and missionaries, each carrying their commodities and ideas enormous distances across the Afro-Eurasian world zone. Each category of exchange was important, and each helped drive the world inexorably on toward the next great revolution in human history—the modern revolution. For many the most significant consequence was the spread of religion, particularly Buddhism, which became one of the key ideological and spiritual beliefs of South and East Asia during the era. To this day Buddhism remains one of the great cultural bonds shared by millions of Asian people, one of the many legacies that the modern world owes to the Silk Roads. As a result of this interaction, despite the diversity of participants, the history of Afro-Eurasia has preserved a certain underlying unity, expressed in common technologies, artistic styles, cultures and religions, even disease and immunity patterns.

Third Trend: Evolving Social and Gender Complexity

A third large-scale trend that defines the Era of Agrarian Civilizations is the increasing complexity of social relations. In the same way that rising populations and the great diversity of lifeways created the most dynamic zone of Collective Learning seen in human history, the intensified scale of urbanization, population density, interdependence, and intercultural exchange led to dramatic changes in the way humans related to each other within and between societies. In this part of the chapter we will discuss some of the major social changes that occurred in Afro-Eurasia during the Era of Agrarian Civilizations.

In general we can observe that, as population densities increased after 2000 BCE, humans were forced to devise more complicated ways of living together. This means that one of the central themes of big history, the notion of increasing complexity at all scales, also occurred in social processes. Agrarian civilizations became characterized by steeper and more rigid hierarchies based on wealth, on the perceived status of different occupations and ethnicities, and on gender. By the end of the era, virtually every society on earth had become embedded within a rigidly hierarchical and patriarchal system. As cities and populations continued to grow throughout much of the era, social and gender trends first observed in Sumer intensified. Now we follow these trends across three millennia. Inevitably some of this analysis will seem to offer sweeping generalizations about these trends, and we have no doubt that the real-life experiences of men and women throughout the era were much more variable. What we can say is that the surviving evidence from the era clearly supports this trend of increasing complexity.

Trends in Social and Gender Relations between ca. 2000 and ca. 500 BCE

Mesopotamia and Egypt

In Mesopotamia, hierarchies of wealth and power appear to have steepened during the second millennium BCE. Babylonian, Hittite, and Assyrian societies were all structured hierarchically, with a semidivine king on the top, supported by a powerful landowning nobility that provided armed troops at the request of the king. Written laws appeared for the first time, perhaps in an attempt to address social tensions. The 282 case laws inscribed on a large stone slab by King Hammurabi offer an intriguing insight into social relations in the Babylonian state. Hammurabi claims that his laws are intended to "cause righteousness to prevail in the land" and "prevent the strong from plundering the weak," but the laws are ambiguous. While some appear to take an egalitarian approach by demanding, for example, "an eye for an eye" or a "broken bone for a broken bone," the punishments differ substantially depending on the wealth and status of those involved. The ambiguity might be partly resolved if we remember that this was still early in the Era of Agrarian Civilizations, when consensual power was in the process of evolving into full-scale coercive power. Hammurabi's laws illustrate the complex interplay of both these types of power. On the one hand, the ruler accepts that he has a duty in some sense to protect all citizens; yet in practice he is acutely aware that his power depends on giving much more protection and support to the elites that were the basis of his claim to power. Such tensions were played out over and over throughout the era.

Hammurabi's law code also suggests that adult men held both public and private power in the Babylonian state, and also that a gender double standard was already in place. Women could be drowned for adultery, but it was acceptable for married men to have sexual relations with concubines and slaves. Women were expected to cover their heads and bodies in public, a cultural practice that first emerged in Mesopotamia and was later adopted by other cultures, including Islam. Yet, as an example of how complicated gender relations were becoming, some laws offer definite protection for women. Men could be punished for making false accusations against women; rape of a virgin was punishable by death; and men were expected to provide sufficient food for their wives. Many women rose to positions of influence and even power in Mesopotamian society. Some joined priesthoods and managed large estates dedicated to particular gods and goddesses, while others became scribes and rose through the social ranks because of their talents. Many women also pursued professional careers as midwives, brewers, bakers, or shopkeepers.

Ancient Egyptian society also developed well-defined hierarchies, with peasants and slaves on the bottom providing all the agricultural labor, and a ruling elite on top. But with the entire Egyptian state under the control of a single, all-powerful ruler there was little room for a landowning nobility in Egypt, where priesthoods and scribal administrators formed the upper social strata, just below the pharaoh. Because many of these senior bureaucratic positions were open to individuals from different strata of society, it was theoretically possible for members of the middle class and even commoners to work their way into positions of high social status through their administrative talents.

Women in second-millennium BCE Egypt also appear to have had more opportunities than their Mesopotamian counterparts. They could manage, own, and sell private property, institute legal settlements before the courts, free slaves, and adopt children. If an Egyptian woman brought private property into a marriage, such property always remained her possession and would be returned to her as part of any divorce settlement. Egyptian girls generally married around the age of 14, and acknowledged their new status by leaving their father's house and entering that of their husband. Divorce could be instituted by either party for a range of reasons, and the affair was generally resolved privately without government interference. Not only did Egyptian women enjoy this unusual array of legal rights, they were also able, at various times, to rule the state as pharaohs. The best known female rulers are Hatshepsut (r. 1473–1458 BCE) and Cleopatra (69–30 BCE), who ruled as queen during the period of Roman control of Egypt. But we know of at least three other female rulers, one each in the Old, Middle, and New Kingdoms (Figure 8.4).

India

Archaeological evidence from the Indus civilization suggests that a social hierarchy was in place by the late third millennium, which may have gone on to influence the emergence of the Indian caste system 1,500 years later. The elites in Indus cities collected tribute from the lower classes; specialist artisans produced pottery and tools; and merchants controlled internal and interstate trade. Dwellings unearthed in the cities of Harappa and Mohenjo-Daro show differences in the lifestyles of rich and poor. Elites lived in large multistoried houses with up to a dozen rooms and several courtyards; the poor lived in crowded, one-room tenement structures. Yet in this sophisticated ancient society, all dwellings featured private bathrooms with showers and toilets that drained into a superbly engineered underground sewage system.

With the arrival of Aryan migrants in the mid-second millennium BCE, Indus social patterns blended with Aryan kinship-based structures, leading to the emergence of

FIGURE 8.4 Cleopatra. Queen Cleopatra of Egypt, last ruler of the Ptolemaic Dynasty, reigned between 69 and 30 BCE.

syncretistic Indian society. The *Rig-Veda* (a collection of hymns) describes the early Aryans as being organized into tribal societies headed by a warlord or raja. As the migrants spread out over much of India, these tribal structures evolved into more complex, interdependent political institutions, and social hierarchies became entrenched. By about 1000 BCE, a rigid class system was in place. Indians called this *varna* (from the Sanskrit word for "color"), but Portuguese traders and missionaries later translated this as the caste system. Priests of the Vedic religion made up the highest caste (*brahmans*); followed by secular rulers and warriors (*kshatriyas*); merchants, artisans, and commoners (*vaishyas*); and landless peasants and serfs (*shudras*). Later a fifth "untouchable" class was added, which included those members of society who performed the most menial tasks or who handled the bodies of dead animals. They were declared untouchable because their touch would defile another human. The varna system would go on to influence every aspect of Indian society from the Era of Agrarian Civilizations through to the modern age, but it is worth remembering that despite the apparent rigidity of formal cast rules, there has always been some flexibility in the real-life experiences of the Indian people.

The syncretistic foundations of Indian society had implications for gender relations, particularly the entrenchment of a three-generation patriarchal household in which women were expected to be subordinate to men. When a young woman married, she automatically left her father's household and entered that of her new father-in-law. The children in any marriage were considered by law to be the exclusive property of the father, never the mother. Women required a male protector at all times—her father, father-in-law, husband, brother, or even her son. According to religious laws, women were not able to inherit property and could not participate in Vedic religious rituals where their presence was thought to defile the process.

China

Social and gender hierarchies were also in place in China by the early second millennium BCE. From what we can tell about the Xia Dynasty, peasant farmers were under the control of ruling elites who had learned to use elaborate ritual to consolidate their position. Elites of the subsequent Shang Dynasty, particularly the kings, had enormous power based on the extraction of tributes, and they used this to coerce armies of peasant laborers to construct their cities, palaces, and tombs. At the head of the Shang social pyramid was the king, followed in descending order by the members of his family, a noble class, court officials, local aristocrats, commoners, and slaves. As in Egyptian society, with the increase in the size and complexity of the states, scribes and other administrators learned to use their skills to obtain enhanced position and status. Social mobility was thus theoretically possible, although denied to the peasant farmers who had few rights and lived and worked in primitive conditions but made up the vast majority of the population in China, as in all agrarian civilizations. The hereditary Shang Dynasty kings ensured their continuing occupation of the highest social strata by claiming to be the sole link between the Chinese people and a parallel spirit world (which was also headed by a single supreme entity, Di).

Our earliest written evidence concerning gender relations in China also comes from the Shang Dynasty. Of the 700 or so personal names recorded on Shang oracle bones, 170 of them are women's names. Elite women were supervising religious rituals, paying valuable tribute to court, and taking responsibility for the harvests. One group of oracle texts concerns the Lady Fu Hao, a woman of considerable power and influence at the court of Shang king Wu Ding. Two inscriptions describe the lady as a general in charge of troops on an important mission for the king. In 1976, Fu Hao's tomb was discovered (Figure 8.5). Her wealth and power was confirmed by the grave goods found with the body: 400 ritual bronze vessels, 600 carved jade ornaments, and 7,000 cowrie shells, which functioned as mediums of exchange during the Shang. Yet, as a further example of just how contradictory gender relations had apparently become, despite the lady's wealth and eminence, one of the oracle inscriptions concerning her confirms that she was unlucky in childbirth because she gave birth to a girl!

Eastern Mediterranean

As we saw in the previous chapter, complex societies appeared on the islands and coasts of the Mediterranean basin during the second millennium BCE. Archaeological evidence of Minoan society is ambiguous. Legend speaks of a founding king Minos, and archaeologist Arthur Evans based his

FIGURE 8.5 Tomb of Lady Fu Hao. The tomb of the wealthy and powerful Lady Fu Hao of the Shang Dynasty is one of few Shang graves discovered by archaeologists that had not been robbed.

reconstruction of the throne room at Knossos on the idea of a ruling priest-king. However, later scholars have questioned whether there was ever a single male king of the Minoans, and while fresco evidence seems to suggest that certain groups or even individuals might have occupied positions of leadership for specific tasks within society, there remains almost no evidence of powerful elites or hierarchies.

Elite Minoan women seem to have enjoyed extraordinary levels of freedom, if the colorful depictions of them in frescoes from Knossos are an indicator. Far from being confined to their homes, they are shown playing roles at least equal to those of men at public events like athletic games and religious festivals. Their elaborately patterned dresses, which were often open to the waist to reveal their breasts, and their beautifully curled and arranged long dark hair, suggests that these were women with the time, resources, and social freedom to follow high fashion. Indeed, the fact that both men and women are depicted participating equally in sports like bull jumping has led many historians to argue for gender equality, even for matrilineal inheritance, particularly in the absence of any evidence of a male warrior class on Crete.

Minoan religion may have been focused on female divinities; certainly women played the lead role as officials at religious ceremonies. The principal deity was a beautiful Mother Goddess, who was usually dressed in the most fashionable of clothing that sometimes includes a strapless fitted bodice (the first fitted garment known to history). (See Figure 8.6.) In the same way that Indus fertility divinities might have been the prototypes for subsequent Hindu goddesses, it is possible that the Minoan Mother Goddess was the inspiration for later goddesses of classical Greek religion, including Athena, Demeter, and Aphrodite.

There is less uncertainty about Mycenaean society, which was clearly organized into a hierarchical social system, with a king on top and a series of clearly defined sociopolitical groups below. The king of the Mycenaean city-state of Pylos, for example, who possessed large estates and may have been seen as semidivine, appointed individuals to powerful administrative positions and was supported by delegates and officials known as the *hequetai* ("followers"). Below the noble and administrative classes were workers employed in agriculture, and textile and metal production. Trade in material goods was a vital component of Mycenaean society, yet in all of the tablets thus far discovered there is no mention of a merchant class, suggesting that the elites used their monopoly control of this lucrative activity to strengthen further their wealth.

After they became aware of Minoan culture through trade and conquest, Mycenaean women adopted some elements of Minoan fashion, but also added their own decorative touches with cosmetics and jewelry. Mycenaean society was decidedly more patriarchal, however. Although elite women were given the responsibility of tending to the estates while the men were away at war, both upper- and lower-class females are often depicted performing a range of domestic tasks, including laundry, reaping and grinding grain, and bathing and anointing male warriors.

FIGURE 8.6 Minoan Mother Goddess. The beautiful Mother Goddess of the Minoan culture may have been the inspiration for later Greek goddesses like Athena and Aphrodite.

Trends in Social and Gender Relations between ca. 500 BCE and ca. 500 CE

India

The trend toward the increasing complexity of social and gender relations during the early millennia of the Era of Agrarian Civilizations intensified in the mid-first millennium BCE. The varna system in India powerfully influenced all aspects of Indian society through the late first millennium and beyond. Within each caste individuals married, socialized, and cared for fellow members, creating a strong sense of intracaste unity. Foreigners who arrived in India were automatically assigned a caste based on their occupation, which allowed them quickly to find a place in Indian society. Some social mobility was possible, if one changed occupations or married into greater or lesser social status, yet many members of the lower castes came to resent their diminished status. As Indian society became more urbanized in the period, merchants in particular began to reject their designated and subordinate place.

One of the reasons that Buddhism became so popular in India during this era is because, by arguing that the secret to a happy and fulfilled life did not lie exclusively in the hands of the brahmans and that men and women of all castes could obtain *nirvana* (or salvation), they offered a more inclusive and egalitarian notion of society. Because of this conception merchants, in particular, became prominent devotees of Buddhism and helped spread the belief along the Silk Roads into China. However, while the Mauryan emperor Ashoka strongly supported Buddhism, the later Gupta kings offered royal patronage for the more traditional religious practices, making regular land grants and even transferring ownership of the royal mines to the brahmans. Partly because of this, the religion that evolved into Hinduism eventually eclipsed Buddhism as the faith of the Indians, and the associated varna system was—and remains—profoundly embedded in Indian society.

Much of our evidence for gender relations in India during the period comes from the Laws of Manu (ca. 500 BCE). Many of these statutes are patriarchal, while others appear to offer women genuine protection. The laws recommending that widowed women follow the practice of suttee illustrates the lengths women were expected to go to demonstrate their utter dependence on men. Widows were encouraged to go willingly to their deaths by voluntarily jumping on the funeral pyre of their dead husbands, a practice Indian moralists recommended that widows of prominent men in particular follow, in the hope that their example would reinforce patriarchy more widely.

China

Rulers of the Zhou Dynasty in China attempted to redress some of the inequalities of Shang society. By making it possible for land to be purchased rather than just inherited, a middle class emerged to challenge the inherited status of the nobility. But the peasants were still excluded of course; they were tied to their villages as tenant farmers of the elites and generally worked plots so small that there was no chance of creating a surplus. Confucius attempted to redefine the criteria for status in society by arguing that a superior individual was not necessarily someone born into the nobility, but someone who had attained the rank of *junzu* ("princeling") through pursuing high levels of intellectual and ethical cultivation. On the one hand, Confucius appeared to be offering an argument in favor of the maintenance of a hierarchical society headed by an elite; but on the other it should be possible for any man to attain his elite position through superior education and higher moral standards.

Gender relations were complicated further during the later Zhou period when some philosophers began to advance the idea that the universe consisted of two primal opposing but complementary forces, the *yin* and the *yang*. This idea took on social ramifications once yang became associated with the sun and all things male, warm, and active, and yin with the moon and all things female, dark, and passive. This was a simplification of a more complex philosophy which argued that elements of both yin and yang existed in most forces of nature and that the two forces are idealized complements of each other, rather than opposites. Nonetheless, because the masculine yang was seen as active, and the feminine yin as passive and receptive, it was easy for subsequent Chinese thinkers to use this idea to argue that male domination of submissive women was in keeping with the natural laws of the cosmos.

Although women continued to play important roles in society during the Han Dynasty, the notion of an *ideal woman* emerged to further categorize and define female roles. Han emperors listened to often conflicting advice from male and (occasionally) female scholars at court. Emperor Wudi was assured by his Confucian advisers that the force of yang was superior to that of yin. The *Book of Rites,* originally compiled by Confucian scholars in the late Zhou era, but extensively reedited under the Han, stressed that young girls and boys should have different types of gender-specific training. Also published during the first century BCE was a series of 125 biographies of chaste, wise, and virtuous exemplary women from history, collected by Liu Xiang (77–6 BCE) to provide role models for women in the Han court.

The most important Han Dynasty text on gender relations was *Lessons for Women,* written by the only woman ever appointed to the position of official court historian, Ban Zhao (45–116 CE). Her education and scholarly abilities allowed her to overcome the restraints on women achieving high office, and Emperor He (89–105 CE) employed her as an instructor in history, astronomy, geometry, and writing. She also completed the great history of the early Han—the *Han Shu*—started by her dead brother Ban Gu. Her text, *Lessons for Women,* has been extraordinarily influential on Chinese and wider East Asian society for almost 2,000 years. Although the essay appears to strongly support patriarchy and female submission to men, it has been open to very different interpretations over the centuries.

Ban Zhao suggests that the ideal woman should have four qualifications: "womanly virtue; womanly words; womanly bearing; and womanly work." Women must be chaste and modest, avoid vulgar language, keep themselves and their clothing clean, avoid gossip, prepare wine and food, and devote themselves to sewing and weaving. But, in a direct challenge to the *Book of Rites,* Ban Zhao makes an explicit demand for equal education for girls and boys, based on the argument that the only way women will learn to behave in the appropriate manner is through education.

Classical Greece

Meanwhile in the Mediterranean region, tensions between nobles and commoners dominated several centuries of classical Greek history, as the prevailing social structure was constantly called into question. As the polis emerged as the most important political and social institution, control of the state was soon monopolized by groups of nobles. These aristocrats (the "best") or oligarchs (the "few") abolished the common assemblies and reduced the agricultural poor to the status of virtual debt slavery. Increasing trade and manufacturing in the poleis led to the emergence of a middle class, which shared with the commoners a bitter resentment of noble privilege. But it was not until the reforms of Cleisthenes in 508 and 502 BCE that the struggle for greater social and political equality achieved tangible results. Cleisthenes reduced the power of the nobles, created 10 new tribes, gave the popular assembly the right to pass laws, and set up a new democratic Council of 500, elected by lots. In so doing Athens established the most democratic government known to have existed within agrarian civilizations, and during the subsequent Golden Age, particularly under the rule of Pericles (469–421 BCE), even the poorest citizen in Athens had some say in government. These attempts to create a more egalitarian society were limited, however. Only male citizens could participate; women, resident aliens, and slaves had no votes whatsoever.

Notions of patriarchy also became entrenched throughout the classical Greek world. In principle at least, the household was ruled absolutely by the male head, who even had the power to decide whether newborn infants would be allowed to live or die. Elite women were often confined to their homes and were allowed to venture out in public only in the company of male chaperones. Many were forced to veil their faces. Women were forbidden by law from owning property, although middle- and lower-class women did run small businesses (like a shop) or act as priestesses in religious cults.

Women-only cults became an important outlet for Greek women, who were otherwise denied any public status. The cult of the grain goddess Demeter was for women only. Women gathered on hillsides all over Greece for several days each year, partaking in sacrifices and feasts in an attempt to ensure an abundant harvest. The dramatist Euripides, in *The Bacchae,* describes a women-only gathering to worship the god of wine, Dionysius (also known as Bacchus). When the women discover a peeping-tom watching their naked and frenetic revels, they tear him to pieces!

As far as we can tell from the evidence, Athenian and Spartan attitudes toward women demonstrate some interesting contrasts, and also remind historians why generalizations can be dangerous. In Athens, women had almost no chance to participate in public life and led lives of seclusion, locked in their homes, forbidden to speak to men outside the family.

FIGURE 8.7 Spartan woman. This bronze sculpture depicts a young Spartan female athlete stretching before a competition.

In Sparta, women participated in vigorous public exercise and sporting competitions (Figure 8.7). In Athens, women married at age 14 or 15; in Sparta, at 18. In Athens, women were forbidden from owning property; in Sparta many women owned property, and most managed their own households. In Sparta women were taught to read and write, definitely not the norm in Athens. Athenian men visited prostitutes without incurring disapproval (generally resident alien women not subject to the same social control as citizens), but female adultery was completely unacceptable. In Sparta, women had the right to take another husband if their first was away at war too long. Rather than exaggerate these differences, however, it is worth remembering that women in Sparta were still under the control of elite males; and tombstone inscriptions suggest that many married Athenians were genuinely happy and devoted to each other.

Rome

A long-running conflict for greater equality between different social groups also characterizes the history of the Roman Republic, further evidence of the complicated and tense nature of social relations during the era. After throwing out the last Etruscan king, Roman elites of the *patrician* (or "father") social strata kept firm control of power through the Senate. A popular assembly was retained, but its members were forced by their patrician masters to vote in accordance with their wishes. Even after the *Concilium Plebis* was given the right to pass laws binding on patricians in 287 BCE, the elites still managed to maintain their privileged position in society through their ownership of agricultural land, continuous self-enrichment through corrupt practices in the provinces, and their ability to "buy" the votes of plebian elected officials. The inability of the patricians to deal with massive unemployment, a huge population of urban poor, and the demands of an increasingly influential merchant class led ultimately to the collapse of the Republic and the emergence of the more autocratic political structure of the empire.

We have some statistics about the size of the Roman urban poor population in the mid-first century BCE. When Julius Caesar came to power he established colonies for military veterans outside Italy and also passed a law declaring that one-third of laborers on senatorial estates had to be free. This helped reduce the numbers of people receiving government-subsidized grain (the "dole") from 320,000 to 150,000, out of a total population of around 500,000. Before Caesar's laws, then, some 64 percent of the population of the city was poor enough to require government handouts to survive.

From the early days of the Republic, Roman families were also legally patriarchal; the eldest male ruled with all the rights of *pater familias*, literally "father of the family." Although the law of *pater familias* meant in theory that the father could arrange marriages, apportion duties, mete out punishment, practice infanticide, and even sell his family into slavery, in practice many *patrician* families in the Republic were more egalitarian. The wife often supervised domestic arrangements while her husband conducted his business and political affairs in public. But gender historians offer mostly critical interpretations of the patrician Roman family. They remind us that, regardless of their educational status, women were in effect confined to their homes, and all positions of status were reserved for men, who "allowed" their wives to manage the tedious affairs of the household because they were too busy with the affairs of state. Elite women often resented their confinement and lack of opportunity; the only genuinely prestigious public position in society available to them was to become a Vestal Virgin, one of the keepers of the sacred fire of Vesta.

Nonelite women in Rome had pressures of a different kind to deal with. Infant mortality rates of approximately 300 per every 1,000 live births meant that Roman women needed to give birth successfully to an average of five or six children to ensure continuing population growth. This stark statistic is at the heart of the condition of women everywhere during the Era of Agrarian Civilizations. Because a woman's primary role was the birthing and rearing of children and the provision of a steady stream of new workers, soldiers, and citizens, women of necessity were confined to the home for most of their lives.

As republic gave way to empire, some aspects of Roman society did change, although the gulf between top and bottom remained wide. The middle strata (the *equestrians*), which now included freed slaves who had managed to make a fortune in business, increasingly bought their way into positions of power and status. The wealthy of both the patrician and equestrian classes learned very well during the empire to control the *plebeians* and guard against rebellion by ensuring that there was always enough food for them to eat, and entertainment to divert them from egalitarian

FIGURE 8.8 Livia Drusilla Augusta (58 BCE–29 CE). This bust depicts the wife of the first emperor Augustus and the most powerful Roman woman of her time.

aspirations. The first-century CE satirist Juvenal expressed this new mechanism of social control beautifully but bitterly with the phrase *panem et circenses* ("bread and circuses")!

Elite women in Rome made some gains in the early empire, beginning with the administration of the first emperor Augustus, whose own formidable wife Livia Drusilla Augusta (58 BCE–29 CE) was the most powerful Roman woman of her time (Figure 8.8). But during the reign of Augustus Rome faced a demographic crisis, with serious population decline among the patricians. Although the real cause of this demographic decline was the century-long civil wars that preceded the Augustan Age, women were blamed because of their "fixation" on pleasure and adultery and their unwillingness to bear children. In this atmosphere of "women out of control," Augustus attempted to regulate the private lives of elite women through a series of moral laws and adultery court cases that unfortunately caught up several women from within his own family, including his daughter and granddaughter.

The closest thing to an outright gender war that occurred anywhere in Afro-Eurasia during the Era of Agrarian Civilizations erupted in Rome in 195 BCE, when elite women objected publicly to attempts in the Senate to retain the *Lex Oppia*. This law, which had been passed in 215 BCE in the aftermath of the disastrous loss to Hannibal at the Battle of Cannae, barred women from wearing gold or silver jewelry or expensive clothing and from driving about in public in chariots or expensive litters. Two decades later, upper-class women essentially revolted against attempts to retain the law; they poured into the forum and surrounding streets and blocked all access to the city. Although conservative senators like Cato the Elder were outraged that women should be congregating in public and insisted that it was men who should be deciding such matters, the law was abolished and women were triumphant!

Trends in Social and Gender Relations between ca. 500 and ca. 1000 CE

China During the last half of the first millennium CE, social relations continued to evolve in new agrarian civilizations that emerged to take the place of those that had entered cycles of contraction. As we saw in Chapter 7, after several centuries of disunity in East Asia, political stability returned to China in the seventh century under the Tang Dynasty. The Tang wrestled with the problems of social inequality and instituted an equal-field system in an attempt to more fairly distribute agricultural land. Land was now allocated according to the needs of individual families and villages, and for about a century the system succeeded in reducing the sort of concentration of land ownership in the hands of the aristocratic class that had so bedeviled the Han. The system fell apart early in the eighth century, however, as corruption and the gifts of large parcels of land to Buddhist monasteries took too much land out of the system and into the hands of special-interest groups. Nonetheless, the Tang were moderately successful in breaking the monopoly hold by the aristocracy on all positions of status within society. Tang government officials were selected from the ranks of candidates who had passed a series of rigorous exams, and this talented new class of scholar-bureaucrats created an elite civil service that was able to concentrate power in its hands for most of the next 1,300 years.

The Tang Dynasty also provides fascinating and often contradictory insights into the often contradictory nature of gender relations in China. Legal codes suggest that rigid patriarchy was enforced through severe punishments for women who were unfaithful or even disobedient. Women had almost no rights to divorce, possess property, or remarry. These laws paved the way for even harsher legal and societal attitudes toward women that appeared during the subsequent Song Dynasty, including the emergence of foot binding. Yet under the Tang, many women gained positions of great influence at court. Musical courtesans played an important role in court life, composing their own art songs and setting lyrics by famous male poets to music they composed. It was also during the Tang that the only woman ever to rule China, the extraordinary empress Wu Zetian, reigned as supreme leader for 20 years (685–705 CE). (See Figure 8.9.) Wu was no complacent or ineffectual "feminine" ruler. During her reign she further weakened the old aristocracy, supported Buddhism, worked to strengthen the civil service exam system, and even defeated the Korean kingdom in a military campaign. She also studied music and literature and sponsored the writing of biographies about famous women.

The Ballad of Mulan, composed in the century before the Tang came to power, offers a further intriguing glimpse into

FIGURE 8.9 Empress Wu Zetian. The empress was the only woman ever to rule China. She reigned as absolute leader for 20 years between 685 and 705 CE.

attitudes toward women during the era. The poem tells the story of a young woman, Mulan, who substitutes for her elderly father after he is conscripted into the army to fight militarized nomads in the north. Dressed as a man, the brave and competent Mulan campaigns for 12 years with her soldier comrades, who never suspect she is a woman. When the war is over, Mulan's prowess earns her a reward from the emperor himself. She then returns to her village, astonishes her colleagues by changing back into her woman's clothing, and returns to the role of dutiful Confucian daughter. The message here is decidedly mixed. On the one hand, here is a woman of extraordinary initiative, courage, and military prowess more than capable of mastering the world of men. On the other, having proven her ability (and fulfilled her filial duty to her father), all she desires to do is to return to the sort of role Ban Zhao had articulated in *Lessons for Women.* Ultimately, the ballad seems to imply that in the cut and thrust of life there is little significant character or skill difference between male and female:

> The male hare's legs have a nervous spring,
> The eye of the girl hare wanders.
> But when two hares run side by side,
> Who can tell if they are boy or girl?

India In India too, with the emergence of a fully developed Hindu religion in the first millennium CE, gender relations became more complicated. A range of formidable goddesses appeared who needed to be both worshiped and feared, including Parvati, the wife of Shiva; Lakshmi, the wife of Vishnu; Sarasvati, the Hindu muse; Durga, the warrior goddess; and Kali, who sprang from the brow of Durga. Collectively, these extraordinary deities represent several idealized faces of all women: tender mother to their families (or faithful followers), ferocious warriors against any who would threaten their families, the inspiration for great art and music, and the symbol of sexuality and eroticism.

Despite the power of these goddesses, however, at the same time that the Guptas were providing royal patronage for the Hindu religion, gender laws were becoming more patriarchal. Child marriage became common, with girls being betrothed by their families at the age of eight or nine and a formal marriage ceremony taking place when the girls reached puberty. This ensured that very young wives, children really, were explicitly placed under the control of older men and forced to devote themselves completely to the household rather than to public affairs.

Islamic Civilization

A final example of evolving social complexity during the Era of Agrarian Civilizations, and a further reminder of the difficulty of generalizing, comes from Islamic civilization. As we saw in the previous chapter, much of Afro-Eurasia, including many older agrarian civilizations, was incorporated into the vast Dar al-Islam that appeared in the first millennium of the Common Era. As Muslim Arabs began to expand their faith and their political control into regions of Afro-Eurasia with long histories of patriarchy, these ancient cultural practices influenced evolving Islamic attitudes. The sacred books of Islam also had much to say about the role and status of women in Islamic society, so that what emerged was a synthesis of core Islamic and borrowed ideas that continues to influence Islamic society to the present day.

Scholars have contradictory views on the status of women in Arabian Bedouin society before the emergence of Islam. Some argue for relative equality (and cite the example of the Prophet Muhammad's own wife, the successful merchant Khadijia, as an example); others suggest that Bedouin society was rigidly patriarchal (as the acceptance of female infanticide and unlimited polygyny suggests). The Qur'an offers a mixed view of the status of women under early Islam. Women are often portrayed as honorable companions, not property, and Muhammad was kind and respectful to his own wives. The Qur'an outlaws female infanticide and urges that the payment of dowries should be made to the wives, not to their husbands, allowing women the right to manage the wealth they had brought into the family. Marriage was also regarded as a contract in which the wives' consent was imperative. Because of these and other statements, some gender historians argue that Islamic law gave women considerable rights compared to those of many other contemporary societies. Other historians point to the explicitly patriarchal nature of Islamic law, which attempt to strictly regulate the sexual and social lives of women, and note that where women were permitted only one husband, men were allowed to take up to four wives.

As Islam move into the ancient Persian and Mesopotamian heartlands in the eighth century CE, Muslims under the subsequent caliphates adopted many of the cultural practices already in place there. The veiling of women had been a common practice in Mesopotamian society for millennia; and upper-class women had long been confined to their homes and permitted to move about in public only when veiled and in the company of male chaperones. Concerned about ensuring the genealogical purity of their offspring, Muslim men quickly adopted these practices and enshrined them in Islamic law.

Many elite women with access to high levels of education were able to play a semipublic role in the Moslem caliphates through the first and into the second millennia CE. Fatima al-Fihri founded the important institute of higher learning of al-Karaouine in 859 CE; and in Damascus, in the twelfth and thirteenth centuries, 26 mosques and madrasahs were funded by women through charitable trusts. Yet historians estimate that woman accounted for at best only 1 percent of scholars by the twelfth century, and their attendance at lectures was roundly criticized by conservatives. Middle- and lower-class women also found employment in the Dar al-Islam, which allowed them to play a greater public role in society. Some examples of this include women working as farmers, construction workers, nurses, brokers, and lenders; and the fact that the dying, spinning, and embroidery sectors of the textile industry were monopolized by women. Female nurses were also employed in many Muslim hospitals, and two women doctors are known to have served in the Almohad Caliphate in the twelfth century. But of course, female medical staff was needed only because men and women patients were strictly segregated.

These examples drawn from agrarian civilizations across Afro-Eurasia between roughly 2000 BCE and 1000 CE demonstrate the fascinating complexity of social and gender relationships during the Era of Agrarian Civilizations. Trends toward specialization, interdependence, and social hierarchies that we first observed in Uruk were intensified in the great cities and states of the era. Distinctions based on wealth, birth, occupation, and gender became more sharply defined, leading to the entrenchment of rigid structures in which elites used force and written law to exercise coercive power over lower members of society. This would remain the situation until well into the Modern era, when the appearance of various political ideologies based on egalitarian and feminist ideals led to major political and social revolutions throughout much of the world.

Fourth Trend: The Generally Slow Pace of Change and Growth

We have discussed several large-scale trends in the Era of Agrarian Civilizations: the expansion and increasing size, power, and effectiveness of agrarian civilizations and their administrations; the establishment of significant networks of exchange between them; and the increasing complexity of social and gender relations during the era. Now we will

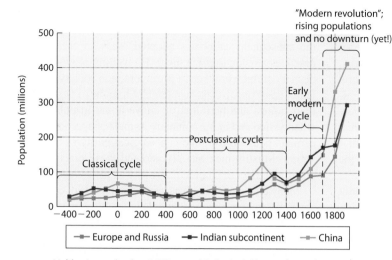

Malthusian cycles: last 2,300 years: (1) classical, (2) postclassical, (3) early modern, (4) modern revolution

briefly explore a fourth trend: the generally slow pace of change in the era, tied to rates of innovation, growth, and Malthusian cycles. As we saw in Chapter 6 when we first introduced the term, by *Malthusian cycles* we mean the slow pattern of rise and fall that we see in the histories of all agrarian civilizations (Figure 8.10). What was its source?

There is no doubt that, compared to the Early Agrarian era that preceded it, significant growth did occur during the Era of Agrarian Civilizations, and growth was even more rapid in comparison with the Paleolithic era. Populations grew five-fold across the era; there was considerable commercial and technological innovation, notably in coinage, mathematics, science, navigation, textiles, and military technology (such as chariots and stirrups); and important agricultural innovations appeared, including complex irrigation structures and new crops. Factors that encouraged growth and innovation during the era included population growth itself (which created a sort of positive feedback cyclical demand); some elements of government policy (e.g., road building, and the seeking out of distant goods); commerce in and between cities; and expanding trade networks within the Afro-Eurasian web, all of which encouraged higher levels of Collective Learning.

On the other hand, as we will see when we move into the chapters devoted to the Modern era, growth and innovation during the Era of Agrarian Civilizations were very slow by modern standards. Why would this be so? The answer is that there were significant barriers to growth during the era. The most important barriers included the prevailing trend toward slow growth itself, which discouraged innovation (why invest in innovation if you knew you'd have to wait 100 years for any return?) and encouraged governments instead to seek tributes through military expansion. A second important barrier to growth was the regular outbreak of disease in cities and towns, partly because cities were such unhealthy places, and partly because expanding exchange networks brought diseases from regions where people were immune to them, into regions where people lacked any immunity. The Black Death of the fourteenth century is the best known of these catastrophic diseases, but there are many other examples from earlier in the era.

The most significant barrier, however, was the militaristic, tribute-taking nature of most elites in premodern states. All the evidence suggests that, with some exceptions, ruling elites in agrarian civilizations were generally opposed to commercial and agricultural innovation because investing resources in raising productivity was generally seen as unreliable, unrewarding, and, as the returns would become apparent only sometime in the future, politically useless. In tribute-taking societies, getting wealthy was thought of primarily as a matter of taking resources from others. So most ruling elites who wanted to increase their resources tackled the problem of growth through warfare. Growth was seen as a zero-sum game that necessitated taking what others had produced, rather than trying to increase productivity within the state. This helps explain the almost constant warfare and attempts at expansion through the conquest of one's neighbors that so characterizes the era. And it explains why there was little incentive to invest in innovation—except, sometimes, where they affected military power. The result was that productivity could never keep up with population growth for long periods, and that explains why ultimately each boom ended in a crash as populations fell, cities emptied out, trade declined, building ceased, and civilization itself seemed to fall back. Malthusian cycles were a consequence of the slow rates of innovation in the Era of Agrarian Civilizations, and during this period we see them over and over again.

So far we have outlined the expansion of Afro-Eurasian agrarian civilizations that, when they first appeared in southwestern Asia and northeastern Africa 5,000 years ago, accounted for only a tiny portion of the human family. They rapidly spread until, by the end of the era, the overwhelming majority of the human population in that vast world zone, and certainly in the densest human communities, were housed somewhere within an agrarian civilization.

In the next chapter we will consider the history of the other three world zones during the same era—the Americas, Australasia, and the Pacific. We will describe the distinctive features of agrarian civilizations in these world zones and explain some of the major similarities and differences in their histories. Although the histories of the four different world zones shared many important features, the scale and chronologies of these histories differed in important ways before the zones were joined together in the last 500 years. And, as we will see, these differences of scale and timing had enormous significance for subsequent global history.

SUMMARY

This chapter, the middle one of a series of three on the Era of Agrarian Civilizations, concludes our consideration of the era as it unfolded across the Afro-Eurasian world zone between roughly 2000 BCE and 1000 CE. We focused on the significance of contacts and exchanges, in particular the Silk Roads exchange network, that took place among civilizations and also among these communities and the many traditional communities of foragers and pastoralists who survived alongside the major civilizations. We also examined the complex social and gender relationships that evolved within agrarian civilizations as a product of increased population densities, specialization, and interdependence, which led to more sharply defined hierarchies based on wealth, status, ethnicity, and gender.

CHAPTER QUESTIONS

1. What processes are historians describing when they use the terms *world-system* and *human web*?
2. What role did pastoral nomads play in facilitating the establishment of major networks of exchange across Afro-Eurasia?
3. How did China become involved in Silk Roads trade?
4. What were the most important material and non-material exchanges that took place?
5. Why did the Silk Roads fall into relative disuse late in the first millennium CE?
6. Why did the expansion of agrarian civilizations lead to more rigidly hierarchical social structures?
7. What do written laws of the era tell us about the lives of women and gender relations during the era?
8. What are Malthusian cycles and how do they help explain the generally slow pace of growth during the Era of Agrarian Civilizations?

KEY TERMS

Mahayana Buddhism   Silk Roads   southernization   world-systems theory
Manichaeism

FURTHER READING

Anderson, Bonnie S., and Judith P. Zinsser. *A History of Their Own: Women in Europe from Prehistory to the Present.* New York: Harper and Row, 1988.

Anthony, David W. *The Horse, the Wheel, and Language: How Bronze Age Riders from the Eurasian Steppes Shaped the Modern World.* Princeton and Oxford: Princeton University Press, 2007.

The Ballad of Mulan, Asia for Educators, Columbia University, **http://afe.easia.columbia.edu/ps/china/mulan.pdf**.

Benjamin, Craig. "Hungry for Han Goods? Zhang Qian and the Origins of the Silk Roads." In M. Gervers and G. Long, *Toronto Studies in Central and Inner Asia*, Vol. 8. Toronto: University of Toronto Press, 2007, 3–30.

Bentley, Jerry H., and Herbert F. Ziegler. *Traditions and Encounters: A Global Perspective on the Past.* 4th ed. New York: McGraw-Hill, 2008.

Brown, Chip. "The King Herself." *National Geographic,* April 2009, 88ff.

Christian, David. *A History of Russia, Central Asia, and Mongolia*, Vol. 1. Oxford: Blackwell, 2004.

Garnsey, Peter. *Famine and Food Supply in the Greco-Roman World.* Cambridge, UK: Cambridge University Press, 1988.

Juvenal. *Satires,* Ancient History Sourcebook. Translated by G. G. Ramsay. **www.fordham.edu/halsall/ancient/juv-sat1eng.html**.

Laws of Manu. Indian History Sourcebook. Translated by G. Buhler. **http://hinduism.about.com/library/weekly/extra/bl-lawsofmanu10.htm**.

McNeill, J. R., and William H. McNeill. *The Human Web.* New York: Norton, 2003.

Shaffer, Lynda. "Southernization." *Journal of World History* 5, no. 1 (1994):1–21.

Stearns, Peter N., Stephen S. Gosch, and Erwin P. Grieshaber. *Documents in World History*, Vol. 1, 4th ed. Upper Saddle River, NJ: Prentice Hall, 2006.

Toner, Jerry. *Popular Culture in Ancient Rome.* Cambridge, UK: Polity, 2009.

Wallerstein, Immanuel. "The Timespace of World-Systems Analysis: A Philosophical Essay." *Historical Geography* 23, nos. 1 and 2 (1995).

Weisner-Hanks, Merry E. *Gender in History: New Perspectives on the Past.* Oxford: Blackwell, 2001.

Worrall, Simon. "Made in China." *National Geographic,* June 2003, 112ff.

part 2

chapter 9

Other World Zones during the Era of Agrarian Civilizations

Seeing the Big Picture

ca. 1000 BCE to ca. 1000 CE

▶ In what ways were American agrarian civilizations distinctive?

▶ What were the most distinctive features of the histories of the Australasian and Pacific world zones?

▶ In what ways did the history of the smaller world zones differ from the history of the largest world zone, Afro-Eurasia?

▶ In what ways were the histories of all four zones similar despite the lack of contact between the world zones?

In Chapters 5 and 6 we introduced the idea of *world zones*. These were four large regions of the world whose histories evolved almost independently during the Paleolithic and Agrarian eras: the Afro-Eurasian zone, the Americas, the Australasian zone, and the Pacific. Within each zone, there was some contact between different human communities, so that ideas, people, techniques, religions, and even styles could diffuse over large areas and sometimes from one end to the other. However, between the zones there was hardly any contact at all (although, of course, there was at least some contact at the point when humans first migrated from one zone to the other). As Jared Diamond pointed out in *Guns, Germs, and Steel,* the almost complete absence of contact between the world zones set up a natural experiment. As historians looking back at the four zones, we can study how human history evolved in several different environments and ask how much historical change was due to environmental factors and how much due to qualities shared by all human societies.

The world zones differed in their geography, their size, their internal connections, their climates, their animals and plants. So the effect is almost as if humans had been planted on different planets, and we could watch how differently human history unfolded on each planet. This is why studying the different histories of the four world zones is a powerful way of finding out whether there are any long-term features of human history that are universal. On the one hand, we may ask such questions as: Are there large trends in the history of the Agrarian era that show up wherever humans have settled? Does the fundamental mechanism of Collective Learning generate similar types of innovations in different societies? Can we see the same trends toward more energy control, larger populations, denser communities, increasing networks of interconnection, and more social complexity? On the other hand, it is also obvious that our species has generated a colossal variety of different ways of living, worshiping, or communicating with each other because of our unique capacity to create and invent new ways of doing things. These features illustrate our remarkable creativity as a species, but they do not necessarily point to any other fundamental features of human history as a whole. So we can ask to what extent the history of different zones and regions has been driven by "contingent" factors such as the decisions and tastes of individuals, or the accidents of geography and cultural change.

The previous two chapters focused on the Era of Agrarian Civilizations within the oldest, the largest, and the most populous of the world zones, the Afro-Eurasian zone. Because of its size, age, and the sheer number of communities that occupied this world zone, Afro-Eurasia has played an exceptionally important role in human history. Indeed, in historical accounts what happened in the other world zones is often neglected or omitted. In this chapter we pan back and focus on the other three world zones, taking a satellite's view of history in the Era of Agrarian Civilizations to try to sort out how much of the history of Afro-Eurasia was distinctive to that world zone and how much was shared by humans in all world zones.

Most of our attention will be focused on the American world zone, which was the second largest and the second most populous of the world zones, though not the second oldest (that was the Australasian zone, first settled 50,000 to 60,000 years ago).

Agrarian Civilizations of the American Zone

In this section we will describe the development of chiefdoms and/or agrarian civilizations in four areas of the Americas—Mesoamerica, the Andes, Amazonia, and North America. Here humans developed their cultures quite independent of experiments in Afro-Eurasia, since the Pacific and Atlantic Oceans presented barriers not regularly breached until the early 1500s CE. In contrast to the Afro-Eurasian world zone, societies of the American zone built their cultures with only intermittent interactions among their major areas and without the large animals and iron-working techniques that were of such importance in Afro-Eurasia.

Agrarian Civilization in Mesoamerica

Mesoamerica, including Mexico and neighboring parts of Central America, contained great geographic diversity, ranging from steamy rain forests to cold, high plateaus. By the beginning of the Common Era (ca. 1 CE), Mesoamerica had at least one city of 50,000 and a common culture consisting of staple food crops (corn, beans, chili peppers, squash), market exchanges, monumental ceremonial centers, religions of similar deities, belief in a common cycle of creation and destruction, human sacrifice, a common ritual calendar of 260 days, and four different emerging hieroglyphic writing systems. During the first millennium CE, small city-states filled the region, warring with each other as elites sought dominance, as crops failed or succeeded, as droughts came and went. In other words, by this time we see emerging all the crucial elements of agrarian civilizations, despite the fact that there was no significant contact between the Americas and Afro-Eurasia.

In Chapter 6 we briefly described the Olmec culture (1500–300 BCE) in the Gulf of Mexico area. Here we will sketch civilizations that evolved among the Maya, in the city of Teotihuacan, and among the Toltecs, before presenting the group usually called the Aztecs in the Basin of Mexico.

The Yucatan Peninsula and Guatemala The earliest heirs to the Olmecs were the Maya, located to the east and the south over the Yucatan Peninsula and Guatemala, in an area the size of Colorado or Great Britain. Their climate was hot and humid, with marked wet and dry seasons, no large rivers, and poor, infertile soil. Ceremonial centers appeared in Maya territory as early as 2000 BCE, but their society reached its height about 250 to 900 CE (see Map 6.5, p. 143).

The Maya depended on corn, beans, squash, and peppers as their basic food crops. Recent research indicates that manioc root, or cassava, likely also played a significant role in their diet. They grew cacao, or chocolate beans, to trade as a luxury good so valuable that it often served as money. Other luxury goods were jade, gold, shells, and feathers, all easily portable and of dazzling beauty. In a difficult environment, agricultural success was won by the work of draining swamps, terracing hillsides, and constructing water management systems. By 750 CE the Maya were supporting a rapidly growing population; Tikal, their foremost city, had about 50,000 inhabitants, with another 50,000 in the surrounding countryside.

In the Maya creation story the ***Popol Vuh*** (the version that survives dates from the mid-sixteenth century of the Common Era, but reflects beliefs from much earlier), the gods fashion humans from corn and water, reflecting the role of agriculture in their lives. Some of their earliest stories tell of the gods shedding their own blood to provoke the first movement of the sun and the moon. The Maya apparently believed that the gods kept the world going only in exchange for sacrifices by humans, especially the shedding of their own blood, which was thought to prompt the gods to send rain. In a central ritual the king used a bone needle or spike to draw blood from his penis or hand, letting it spill onto bark paper, which was burned with tobacco and other hallucinogenic drugs. Breathing in the fumes induced visions in the king, often of a snake rising from the smoke,

FIGURE 9.1 Blood sacrifice. In this stone relief sculpture a Maya king holds a torch over a woman from the royal family. She is drawing a thorn-studded cord through a hole in her tongue to shed her blood in honor of the Maya gods.

as serpents were seen as mouthpieces of the ancestors. In an environment with dramatic seasonal variations, death, regeneration, and the control of chaos were major themes in the Maya worldview (Figure 9.1).

Maya intellectuals, probably shaman-priests, developed a base-20 mathematical system that included the concept of zero. The earliest known Maya inscription that includes zero dates to about 357 CE, but there are indications that the earlier Olmecs may have come up with the idea. (As in Chapter 8, scholars on the Indian subcontinent were developing the concept in the first centuries CE, with their first notation, a small circle, appearing in the ninth century.)

Maya priests achieved a remarkable understanding of the cycles of time. They plotted planetary cycles and predicted eclipses of the sun and the moon. They devised three kinds of calendars: one of 365 days based on Earth's journey around the sun; a second of 260 days possibly based on the orbit of Venus; and a third, called the Long Count, that went back to the beginning of time, arbitrarily set more than 3,000 years in the past. The Maya calculated the length of the solar year as 365.242 days, only about 17 seconds slower than the figure reached by modern astronomers.

FIGURE 9.2 The Maya calendar. The Maya calendar showing how the 260-day calendar (left) meshed with the 365-day calendar (right). The reappearance of the conjoined days every 52 years was seen as a time of great significance and danger and was attended by elaborate ceremonies.

The Maya date for any single day could be calculated using both the calendar of 365 days and the one of 260 days. It took 52 years for the two calendars to work through all possible combinations and return at the same time to their respective starting points (Figure 9.2).

The Maya developed the most elaborate and expressive system of writing in the Western Hemisphere, although four other Mesoamerican groups developed their own writing systems (epi-Olmec, Mixtec, Zapotec, and Aztec). Maya writing, as important to them as cuneiform was to early Mesopotamian elites, included administrative and astronomical records, genealogy, poetry, and history. The Maya carved inscriptions in stone and wrote on beaten tree bark and on deerskin vellum, washed in lime plaster and folded into accordion books. More than 15,000 carved inscriptions have survived, but only four books, solely about historical and calendrical matters, remain, as Spanish conquerors and missionaries destroyed all the books they found in the hope of undermining indigenous religious beliefs.

Maya writing uses both pictographs and phonetic or syllabic elements, but has no alphabetic elements. Deciphering it has taken a heroic scholarly effort, which began in the 1960s and succeeded fully in the 1990s. The symbols often consist of a central picture surrounded by complex prefixes and suffixes.

One common feature of Maya sites, probably inherited from the Olmecs, was a long, rectangular court with sloping sides. The Maya used these courts for playing a ball game in which players tried to put a heavy, hard rubber ball through a stone ring set high on the sidewall or onto a kind of end zone, without using their hands or feet. The rubber balls, up to a foot (0.3 meter) in diameter and up to 15 pounds (6.8 kilograms) in weight, were made by adding the juice of a morning glory plant to the sticky sap of the rubber tree. Europeans and North Americans didn't figure out how to make rubber until the mid-nineteenth century.

There is no evidence that women played the ball game; it consisted of either two men against each other or teams of two to four members each. Some courts had skull racks along their sides, suggesting an ominous reason for the game. Archaeologists believe there must have been a variety of occasions for the game—as a simple sport, as a competition on which to place bets, as a ritual at the conclusion of treaties, and sometimes as a forced competition between high-ranking captives, in which the loser faced immediate torture and execution. The heads of the losers may have been displayed on the rack, yet one more way to please the gods by shedding human blood.

Besides the ball game, the Maya had another surprising entertainment. For their children they created miniature clay jaguars with their legs connected by clay tubes on which they attached clay disks, or wheels. In other words, they made wheeled toys without translating that idea to wheeled vehicles for adults. Of course, without large domestic animals to pull them, wheeled carts would not have been much use. Yet the wheel could have been used as a potter's wheel or a water wheel to turn grinding stones, if there had been flowing rivers. There is no evidence that the Maya used the wheel for anything other than toys. Can you imagine Afro-Eurasian history without wheels?

The Maya also enjoyed smoking tobacco, which they used for recreation and for ritual. Detailed drawings of themselves and their gods smoking pipes have been found (Figure 9.3). Plant geneticists estimate that tobacco was first cultivated in the Peruvian–Ecuadoran Andes between 5000 and 3000 BCE. Tobacco served as a feature common to all American cultures except those in the Arctic; it was chewed, sniffed, eaten, drunk, smeared over bodies, used in eye drops and enemas, and smoked. It was blown over warriors' faces before battle, over fields before planting, and over women prior to sex; and it was offered to the gods. It played a central role in the training of shamans; if taken in large doses, tobacco causes hallucinations, trances, and near-death experiences, allowing the novice shaman to demonstrate his ability to overcome death.

The Maya organized their society in strict hierarchical fashion, with royalty and nobility at the top and 80 to 90 percent of the population as farmers beneath them. There is no evidence of slavery. Rulers had the responsibility to communicate with the gods and the dead, to build ceremonial centers, and to conduct warfare. Kings, who personified gods in rituals and erected homes for them to dwell in, often had menacing names such as Great Jaguar Paw, Storming Sky, and Jaguar Penis (i.e., progenitor of the Jaguar kings). The Maya considered the jaguar the most dangerous predator of the forest. In the absence of a suitable male heir, women could serve as regents or queens.

The Maya region consisted of 45 to 50 local city-states with no central authority. They were never politically unified, forming a civilization more like the city-states of Mesopotamia and Greece than the imperial structures of China or Rome. Like the civilizations of Afro-Eurasia, Maya civilization had monumental architecture. Each city-state had a center dominated by pyramid temples, palatial residences, spacious public plazas, and ball courts. Some centers flourished for less than a century; the whole region experienced political and demographic instability and marked cycles of prosperity and decline throughout Maya history.

Archaeologists from the 1940s through the 1960s portrayed the Maya as a uniquely peaceful civilization. However, the decipherment of the glyphs and the discovery of fortifications, deliberate destruction of cities, and mass burials have revealed what was really going on. Relinquishing their previous view, archaeologists now see warfare among the Maya, including the capture of opponents and human sacrifice, as a frequent activity. As increasing archaeological evidence has been uncovered, the Maya seem more and more like other well-documented ancient agrarian civilizations.

Maya civilization collapsed with a rapidity rare in world history. By about 760 CE many Maya populations in the southern half of the Yucatan Peninsula began to desert their cities; within a century and a half the traditions of almost a thousand years contracted and almost disappeared, except in the northern Yucatan where Chichen Itza continued to flourish from about 900 to 1250 CE. After that, until the Spanish arrived, the Yucatan was the scene of small warring chiefdoms, without written language but with taxes, trade, and pyramids, a sort of watered-down version of Maya civilization.

Archaeologists and historians have offered many possible scenarios for this rapid decline: erosion, deforestation, soil exhaustion, earthquakes, revolts, disease, and most recently, drought. An extended drought began about

FIGURE 9.3 A Maya prince smoking a cigar.
Seated on a jaguar skin, this prince is reaching toward a vision serpent whose head is emerging from a conch shell at his feet. This depiction seems to show the use of tobacco for personal relaxation and mediation. Other depictions show tobacco smoking having a ritual function in communicating with the deities.

840 CE, but the social and political decline occurred in the wetter lowlands, not in the drier northern plateau. Most scholars agree that several factors must have interplayed, especially overpopulation and a deteriorating agricultural landscape, to produce famine, disease, population movements, unrestrained warfare, and loss of confidence in rulers. This evidence suggests that what occurred was a classic Malthusian crisis, of the kind that occurred regularly in Afro-Eurasia during the Agrarian era. Whatever happened, the Maya decline illustrates the fragility of dense populations, whether centralized into large empires or decentralized into city-states.

The Basin of Mexico

The other area of Mesoamerica capable of supporting large populations lay in central Mexico, in the Basin of Mexico where, on a plateau about 7,000 feet (2,100 meters) above sea level, several large lakes were fed by water running down the surrounding mountains. Farming in the fertile volcanic soil there began about 1600 BCE, as crops were adapted to the high climate. By about 400 BCE the population of the basin had grown to about 80,000 people living in five or six different city-states (see Map 9.1).

Volcanoes surrounding the Basin of Mexico erupted between 350 and 250 BCE, possibly causing the rapid colonization of a significant city on a site 31 miles

(50 kilometers) northeast of modern Mexico City, a city called Teotihuacan (Tay-uh-tee-wah-KAHN). This city grew so rapidly that by the beginning of the Common Era it consisted of 50,000 to 60,000 people and reached almost 200,000 people by its apex about 500 CE. It was the largest urban complex in the Americas at the time and one of the six largest in the world.

No one knows how Teotihuacan was governed; murals and paintings suggest a theocracy, since its art emphasized deities rather than royalty. (A theocracy is government by priests claiming to rule with divine authority, as we saw in early Sumer.) From 300 to 600 CE Teotihuacan served as an influential city, complete with temples, palaces, marketplaces, and spacious public plazas, all dependent on an irrigation system and extensive trading links with other parts of Mesoamerica. Without any written records, we know little of Teotihuacan's social and political structure.

Teotihuacan also experienced a rapid "collapse" as a major power, sometime between 550 and 750 CE, when invaders burned the city and the population was reduced to a quarter of its former level. Nearly 1,000 years later the Aztecs gave the city the name by which we know it, Teotihuacan, or "city of the gods." They revered it as the sacred place where the world had been created, in keeping with a widespread Mesoamerican belief in a great mythical metropolis inhabited by prosperous people and ruled by

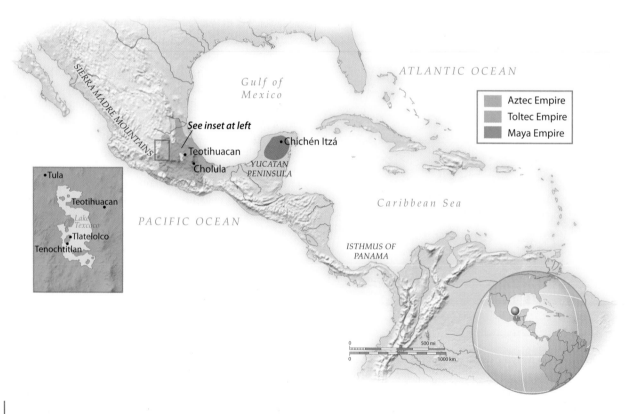

MAP 9.1 The Toltec and Aztec Empires, 950 to 1520 CE. Notice how much the Maya Empire has shrunk. How were Aztec rulers able to enforce tribute from their territories?

benevolent priests and kings, an ideal they wished to create in the real world.

Immediately after the fall of Teotihuacan, no state in the Basin of Mexico was strong enough to stop the fighting and restore order. Sometime after 700 CE the successor to Teotihuacan, the city of Tula was founded some 50 miles (80 kilometers) to the northwest of present-day Mexico City, at the confluence of two rivers. Tula had a cosmopolitan population who probably spoke **Nahuatl** (NA-wat-l), the language of the Aztecs to come. Tula, although never on a par with Teotihuacan, received tribute from several centers and possibly from the whole basin. About 1150 to 1200 CE Tula suffered some kind of violent collapse, indicated by burned buildings. It persisted as a small town subject to the Aztecs in the early sixteenth century.

Tula's importance resides mostly in its significance for the Aztecs, who considered it a legendary city of skilled artisans, whose ruler lived in a palace decorated with gold, silver, turquoise, and shells. Aztecs referred to Tula as Tollan and called its people Toltecs, believing that they worshiped a benign principal god named **Quetzalcoatl** (Ket-sahl-KO-tl), who required only the sacrifice of fruits and nuts. Under his protection, fields were always productive and cotton grew in colors. Aztecs believed that Tollan fell when an evil god was thought to have tricked Quetzalcoatl into fleeing eastward to the lands of the rising sun.

After the fall of Tula, a period of civil conflict and nomadic incursion ensued, until we come to the story of the people known as the **Aztecs.** Alexander Humboldt (1769–1859), a German naturalist and explorer, gave that name in the early nineteenth century to three allied city-states around Lake Texcoco. These groups shared a myth of a city, Aztlan, meaning "land of white herons," as their homeland. They had earlier called themselves "Azteca," until their tribal god, **Huitzilopochtli** (Wet-sei-lo-POK-tl-e), gave them the name "Mexica" as they began their journey to what is now central Mexico.

The Aztecs began as a small group of wanderers, semi-nomadic people from northern Mexico, without any land to call their own. Chased away by other groups, they established themselves in 1325 on a small, vacant island at the edge of Lake Texcoco. There, surrounded by several dozen small, warring city-states, they constructed their city and their military capacity. They served as mercenaries in a neighboring army until they could build up their own resources, calling themselves the Mexica-Tenochca and their city Tenochtitlan, "place of the cactus fruit." Within only a few generations these nomads achieved domination over a large agrarian civilization.

Since their island stood in marshy regions of the shallow lake at 7,000 feet (2,100 meters) altitude where cotton and cacao could not grow, the Mexica had to exploit an unusual situation. At least they had the advantages of plenty of water; fish, frogs, and waterfowl for food; and an easily defensible site.

To extend their agricultural land, the Mexica dredged fertile mud and plants from the bottom of the lake and built it into small floating plots of land known as *chinampas,* held together by planting willows all around. (See Chapter 5 for chinampa agriculture.) On these chinampas the Mexica could grow several crops a year of corn, beans, squash, peppers, tomatoes, amaranth, and chia (both types of grain). The seeds were germinated in seedbeds on reed rafts, which were pulled by canoes to replant the chinampas. The earliest dated chinampas are between 1150 and 1350 CE; they ringed the city of Tenochtitlan.

For domestic animals the Mexica had only dogs and turkeys, both of which they ate; they also consumed many kinds of insects and gathered in fine nets a blue-green spirulina algae from the surface of the lake, which they made into high-protein cakes. They had several natural hallucinogens and, like all ancient farmers, used fermentation to make alcohol of high-sugar plants; cactus was their principal source. (Today it is the source of *tequila.*)

In 1428 CE the Mexica formed the Triple Alliance with two other city-states around Lake Texcoco (Texcoco and Tlacopan) and set out to conquer their region, needing tribute to support their burgeoning population. Ninety-one years remained until the Spanish appeared, during which the Triple Alliance (the Aztecs) conquered some 400 small towns and cities and built up their population in the basin to at least 200,000 to 300,000, with some 3 to 10 million more in their extended empire.

The Aztecs exacted heavy tribute from their subject peoples—food crops and human-made goods including textiles, rabbit fur blankets, embroidered clothes, jewelry, obsidian knives, and rubber balls. Professional merchants called *pocteca* made extensive trading expeditions, both within their empire and beyond. Sometimes they traveled on their own private business; other times the ruling elites entrusted them with tribute goods to be exchanged for local goods, including luxury items such as jaguar skins, parrot feathers, translucent jade, emeralds, sea shells, vanilla beans, and cacao.

The Aztecs used the traditions and ideologies common to Mesoamerica—ball games, ritual blood-letting and human sacrifice, and belief in a cosmic cycle of creation and destruction. Out of these elements one ruler named Tlacaelel (1398–1480) created an ideology precisely fitted to support Tenochtitlan in its conquests. Tlacaelel, who served as the leader for internal affairs for more than 50 years, supervised the birth of the alliance and transformed the Aztecs into keepers of the cosmic order. The Aztecs had long believed that there had been four earlier historical periods, called suns, each of which had been destroyed, and that they were living in the fifth sun. They had long believed in Huitzilopochtli, god of war and human sacrifice, but Tlacaelel convinced them that Huitzilopochtli needed blood, the fluid of life energy, to keep the sun shining and prevent the destruction of the fifth world by earthquakes and famine. Since only human sacrifice could provide a copious source of blood, Tlacaelel taught the Aztecs that they had to conquer to obtain captives for the sacrifice. Later, whenever no war occurred, rulers of neighboring cities around Lake Texcoco would arrange a

FIGURE 9.4 Aztec sacrifice. This manuscript illustration shows a victim stretched over a sacrificial altar while a priest opens his chest, removes the still-beating heart, and offers it to Huitzilopochtli. Attendants at the bottom of the structure move the body of an earlier victim. How do you explain the extensive use of human sacrifice by the Aztecs?

"war of flowers," in which each side would bring young men to the prearranged battlefield to take prisoners needed for sacrifices.

Celibate priests carried out the sacrifices high on a pyramid by laying the victim over a curved stone, held down by someone at each limb, and by cutting open the chest with an obsidian blade. The priest reached into the chest and pulled out the still-beating heart, flinging it into a ceremonial basin, then rolling the body with blood still gushing down the pyramid steps. Some consumption of human flesh by the elites seems to have occurred sparingly and only during tightly controlled rituals. No one can accurately estimate how many people were sacrificed; human sacrifice had long been a part of Mesoamerican and many other world cultures, but it assumed a rare prominence in Tenochtitlan (Figure 9.4).

In the 1970s the anthropologist Michael Harner put forth the hypothesis that the scale of Aztec human sacrifice might lie in their need for protein, that perhaps eating human flesh was done not simply ritually but also to satisfy protein deficiencies. This hypothesis attracted much attention but is now out of favor; closer examinations of the Aztec food supply have shown no apparent protein insufficiency. However, cross-cultural studies of human sacrifice suggest that it correlates significantly with population pressure and warfare for land and resources; it seems not a direct function of food availability but of the stressful situation that density creates under conditions of scarcity and unreliability.

The Aztecs based their society on honoring warriors. A council of the 100 most successful warriors elected two leaders, one of external and one of internal affairs. The Aztecs worshiped two principal gods, Huitzilopochtli, the god of war, and Tlaloc, god of rain. Warriors, were promised an afterlife of accompanying the sun on its morning journey for four years; after which they would become hummingbirds sipping sweet nectar. (Women dying in childbirth were given equivalent status with warriors, promised to accompany the sun on its afternoon journey before becoming goddesses.) The Aztecs used no military garrisons or administrative apparatus to collect their tribute; fear of military reprisal kept the subject people in control. No standing army stood by, but rather all males were subject to immediate duty.

The basic unit of Aztec social life was the *capolli* (plural *capoltin*), meaning "big house," a group of families related by kinship or proximity over long periods. The elite members of the capolli provided land or occupations to the others, who gave service and/or tribute. The chief of the capolli was elected for life; there were about 20 capoltin in Tenochtitlan. Each capolli provided soldiers and military officers. Each also provided universal schooling for both sexes, sometime between 10 and 20 years of age, possibly the only people in the world to do this in the early sixteenth century. Commoner boys learned to be warriors; girls learned songs, dances, and household skills. At a third kind of school elite boys learned administration, ideology, and literacy.

The expansion of empire and creation of an agrarian civilization eventually brought order, explosive growth of markets, and flourishing intellectual life for the Aztec elites, but the cost was heavy. Social class distinctions became more rigid, with a large number of slaves (mostly people sold as children out of financial distress or captives); human sacrifice increased markedly; many thousands of people perished in a drought from 1450 to 1454; and military conscription hung over the lives of both elite and commoner men.

At the same time that Aztec culture supported warfare, priests and members of the nobility devoted themselves to poetry and philosophy. They thought that truth appears occasionally through "flower and song," their figure of speech for poetry, which they considered the highest art.

How do we know this much about the Aztecs? They had a system of writing, not as expressive as that of the

Maya, more like pictures with captions. Many inscriptions but only a few books remain, the rest destroyed by the Spanish. Much information comes to us from a 12-volume encyclopedia of Aztec life collected in four decades in the mid-sixteenth century by the Spanish Franciscan priest, Bernardino de Sahagun (1499–1590). Sahagun learned to speak Nahuatl fluently and interviewed many Aztecs to compile dictionaries, descriptions of customs, and collections of poetry and drama. His 12 volumes were first published in Mexico in 1829 and finally in the United States from 1950 to 1982, as the Florentine Codex, earning him the reputation as the first anthropologist, or the "father" of ethnography. Nahuatl is still a living language for hundreds of thousands people who live in Mexico, who interweave Aztec traits into modern Mexican culture; to English, Nahuatl has given the words *ocelot, coyote, tomato, chocolate,* and *tamale.*

After they destroyed Tenochtitlan in 1517, the Spanish built Mexico City on top of its remains. In 1978 electrical workers in Mexico City found an oval stone more than 10 feet (3 meters) in diameter and in excellent condition. This prompted the Mexican government to carry out excavations that uncovered a huge temple pyramid, called the Templo Mayor, which stood at the sacred center of the Aztec Empire. The excavations revealed new information about imperial rituals, tribute from distant lands, and Aztec cosmic symbolism. Carved on the uncovered stone was a decapitated and dismembered female goddess, Coyolxauhqui, sister of Huitzilopochtli, the war god, who cut her to pieces soon after he was born. Her blood is depicted as precious, symbolized by the jewels attached to it. A sacred song recorded soon after the Spanish conquest revealed how this stone represents a key element in the Aztec belief system.

The Aztec civilization in the Basin of Mexico offers a view into a developing agrarian civilization much closer to our time than the earlier ones of Mesopotamia, Egypt, the Indus valley, and China. Remarkable similarities between Aztec and earlier civilizations are present in, for instance, the similar innovations of irrigation, strict social hierarchy, divine kings, priests and elaborate religious rituals, coerced tribute, pyramids, scripts, warfare, and slavery. These innovations emerged as food supplies increased, population grew into denser communities, and more social complexity arose. Details do differ, but the overall pattern fits amazingly that of the general trends observed in Afro-Eurasia.

Agrarian Civilization in the Andes

History in South America is more difficult to uncover than in Mesoamerica because in South America people did not develop writing systems, at least not in the usual sense of script, and because the Spanish plundered the marvels of Inca civilization, as they did in Mesoamerica.

Pre-Inca History

To pick up from Chapter 6, the geography of the Andean region is simply unique in the world. Two high mountain ranges run parallel to each other, north and south, causing extreme rainfall on the eastern side from prevailing winds and cutting off rainfall from the western coast. The dry coast is habitable only because 50 or so small rivers flow down from the mountains. The mountains lie only about 60 miles (96 kilometers) from the coast, since they are being pushed up by the action of the tectonic plate at the bottom of the Pacific Ocean sliding eastward under the continental plate, which causes frequent earthquakes.

As described in Chapter 6, emerging states developed along the coast and the midlands of Peru, at least since about 2000 BCE. Anchovies from the sea, dried and ground into meal, provided sufficient protein and calories to sustain population growth, combined with some agricultural products from further inland, especially cotton for making nets. Many archaeologists call these "complex societies," with the characteristic traits of ceremonial centers, pyramids, specialized crafts, and irrigation. Yet earthquakes, floods, and torrential rains repeatedly destroyed these emerging states and prevented them from developing into larger states, or empires.

After the disappearance of Chavín de Huántar (900–300 BCE) and Mochica (300–700 CE), both in the midlands, other autonomous regional states filled the midlands and the highlands.

In the highlands two extended states held sway from about 650 to 1000 CE, with the Wari ruling in the north from a mountain city called Ayachuco and the Tiwanaku in the south from their capital on Lake Titicaca. Living at an altitude of 10,500 feet (3,200 meters), the Tiwanaku were limited to a staple of potatoes; they herded alpacas, llamas, and vicuna, all relatives of camels. At a lower altitude, the Wari were able to grow corn. About 1050 CE the climate became drier for centuries; as the economic stress undermined faith in religion and government, both states fragmented into small units.

Along the coast of what is now Peru, the Chimor state emerged in the tenth century CE, built by the Chimu, with their capital at Chan Chan, near modern Trujillo. They were able to build up their population between 50,000 and 100,000 before being subjugated by the Inca about 1470.

The Inca

The **Inca** began as a closed ethnic group, which may have come from an area near Lake Titicaca. About 1200 CE they settled at Cuzco, at an altitude of 13,000 feet (4,000 meters), with more than a dozen other ethnic groups living within a 62-mile (100-kilometer) radius of their city. With the population in the area rising significantly, constant warfare over land eventually made the inhabitants long for peace and orderly access to land, even if they had to exchange their labor to secure them (see Map 9.2).

Inca rulers married noble women of other groups to establish local coalitions. Once they secured their central area, the Inca launched a three-generation expansion by conquest, beginning in about 1438 with Pachacuti ("Earthshaker"), who ruled from 1438 to 1463; his grandson completed the expansion. Pachacuti retired from military affairs after some 25 years and stayed in Cuzco to

Caribbean Sea

ISTHMUS OF PANAMA

ATLANTIC OCEAN

Quito

Amazon

Chimu

Machu Picchu

Cuzco

Lake Titicaca

Tiahuanaco

PACIFIC OCEAN

ANDES MOUNTAINS

Atacama

Coquimpu

ATLANTIC OCEAN

Inca Empire

0   500   1000 mi
0   1000   2000 km

MAP 9.2 The Inca Empire, 1471–1532 CE.
This is the largest empire in pre-Columbian America. How did the Inca maintain control over such long distances?

which means "navel." They imposed their language, Runa Simi, called **Quechua** in Spanish, on their provinces for conducting business. In Runa Simi the word *Inca* would be romanized as "Inka," and the word *Cuzco* as "Qosqo." We are staying with the Spanish usage, but this may be changing as people around the world insist on using their own names—for example, Beijing rather than Peking, Rapa Nui rather than Easter Island, or Mount Denali instead of Mount McKinley. Quechua, or Runa Simi, is still spoken by millions of people from Ecuador to Chile and serves as the second official language of Peru.

In the Inca realm the emperor ruled as divine, the descendant of the creator god, Viracocha, and the son of the sun god, Inti. The emperor owned all the land, livestock, and property. He did not extract tribute from his people, but rather service (*mita*). Commoners of both sexes plowed, planted, and harvested government and religious lands, as well as land allocated to them. In addition, women were obliged to weave textiles, and men worked on building projects. The Inca people developed astonishing skills in weaving and built rock masonry without mortar. Some "chosen women" devoted their lives to weaving, while men built 18,600 to 24,800 miles (30,000 to 40,000 kilometers) of linked highway, not to mention temples and fortifications (Figure 9.5).

Some Inca roads were wide enough to accommodate eight Spanish horsemen. Inca runners carried information and goods; the emperor could have fresh fish from the coast 200 miles (320 kilometers) away in two days. Professional merchants like those in Eurasian civilizations did not arise, since government officials collected and distributed food and products.

From the work performed by commoners, the elites supported both themselves and their departed ones (as we will discuss in the following text). They also stored surpluses, which they distributed to widows and the poor in times of peace or to all in times of war or natural calamity. In addition, the governors felt obliged to hold elaborate feasts, complete with huge consumption of food and drink. This amounted to a kind of central planning, or vertical socialism, with the elites taking care of the commoners within a rigid hierarchy.

The Inca herded llama, alpaca, and vicuna for wool and transport. Their staple foods were corn, beans, potatoes, quinoa (keen-WA), and peppers. For meat they had dogs, ducks, and guinea pigs. They tended to store what little corn could be grown to feed armies, pilgrims, and royal

design the imperial government and build the city into a marvel fit for an emperor.

At its height the Inca Empire stretched some 2,500 miles (4,000 kilometers) along the edge of South America, including the coast and highlands, covering 32 degrees of latitude from modern Quito, Ecuador, to Santiago, Chile, the same degrees of latitude as from St. Petersburg to Cairo, or from Cairo to Nairobi. The largest native state ever to emerge in the Americas, the Inca Empire included 80 political provinces, each ethnically and linguistically different, with a total population of about 10 million people. In 1491 the Inca ruled the most impressive empire of their day in terms of encompassing environmental diversity and adaptability, in a world where Ming China was turning inward, the Ottoman Empire was cresting, the Great Zimbabwe and the Songhay were limited by geography, and the European maritime empires (Barcelona, Genoa, and Venice) were in decline.

The Inca grouped their provinces into four geographic territories, known as suyu. They called their realm Tawatinsuyu, "Four Parts Together," and symbolized this with four grand highways radiating out from the capital, Cuzco,

FIGURE 9.5 An Inca woman weaving. Notice the simplicity of the loom, which is attached to a tree, on which Inca women produced intricate woolen fabric.

FIGURE 9.6 Quipu, or knotted strings. The meaning of the strings depended on the type of knot, its position on its string, the color of the string, its position on the main cord, and the program of the main cord.

households, as well as to make the ritual beer for ceremonial occasions. They cultivated potatoes with much sophistication, developing hundreds of varieties and learning to freeze-dry them to store them for extended periods.

The Inca used no currency and had no forms of written language, as we generally understand that term. Rather, they developed a form of recording on *quipu*, or knotted strings (Figure 9.6). Becoming literate in quipu required four years of training; quipi have not been fully understood since this training ended. That quipu could record discourse, as well as numerical data, has been affirmed by several native writers of the sixteenth century. One of them, Guaman Pomo, who learned Spanish and wrote a 1,179-page letter to Philip III advising him to restore the good government of the Inca, wrote: "Since so much was known in the strings, I was hard put in the alphabet."[1]

Inca priests came from royal and elite families; apparently they led celibate and ascetic lives. The Inca worshiped both the sun, Inti, and the moon, Mama-quilla; male priests carried out the rituals in the Temple of the Sun, while women did in the Temple of the Moon. (Gold was considered sweat of the sun; silver, tears of the moon.) The Inca viewed their landscape as sacred and vibrant, with mountains the source of rainfall and water, to be propitiated with sacrifices of great value (goods and llamas) on mountain peaks. These sacrifices, on the most special occasions, included children of unusual purity and beauty, but these human sacrifices never came close to the scale of Aztec sacrifices.

In traditions that date from the earliest complex societies in the region (see Chapter 6), the Inca mummified the bodies of their deceased rulers and kept them in houses as if they were alive, served by their servants. The royal mummies retained their rights and their land; they were brought out to sit at high-level, decision-making councils, so that state policy could be deliberated in their presence.

In 1911 an archaeologist from Yale University, Hiram Bingham, found at a breathtaking site in the mountains of Peru the remains of an Inca masterwork. Known as Machu Picchu ("old peak"), scholars believe that it served as a vacation retreat for several generations of Inca rulers. At about 8,000 feet (2,400 meters), Machu Picchu was lower and warmer than Cuzco and provided a royal haven never detected by the Spanish.

Seen from a distance, Aztec and Inca civilizations can blur together, hard to distinguish from each other. Many similarities exist, but viewed up close striking differences come into view.

The Aztecs and the Inca shared a similar high-altitude environment, although the 7,000 feet (2,100 meters) of the Aztecs can be seen as quite different from the 13,000 feet (4,000 meters) of the Incas. They shared limited animal protein and dependence on one main crop, corn or potatoes. Culturally, the two groups shared basic technologies, without arches, wheels, axles, or iron. They shared cityscapes symbolic of the cosmic order, laid out geometrically and symmetrically. Both were large enough units to be considered empires; both practiced extensive

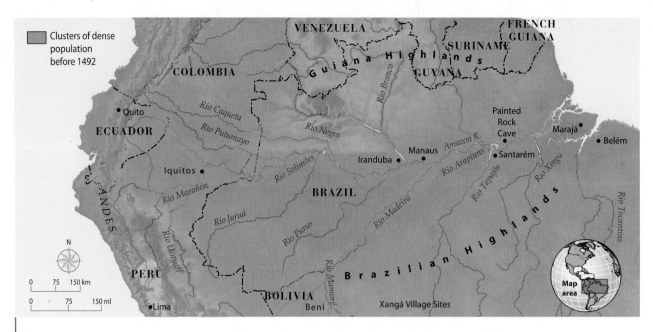

MAP 9.3 Amazonia, or Amazon River basin. The Amazon River drains a basin that constitutes 40 percent of South America; around the drainage basin Amazonia includes land from the Andes to the west, the Guiana Highlands to the north, and the Brazilian highlands to the south.

warfare and religious rites that included human sacrifice, although the scale of the Aztec practice far exceeded that of the Inca. Both had other features characteristic of agrarian civilization—monumental buildings, strict hierarchy of class, specialized work, and enforced tribute. Both were similar in many respects to Early Agrarian civilizations in Afro-Eurasia, and both appeared about the same time, in the fifteenth century.

The differences between Aztecs and Incas showed up in politics, religion, and art. The Aztecs chose their rulers by a vote of a council of warriors; the Inca king chose his successor. In Mexico political power was fragmented; a network of Aztec cities around Lake Texcoco shared power. There no standing armies garrisoned the tributary regions; the Aztecs seldom used enforced resettlement. The Inca exercised wider, direct central control; they laid waste to hostile towns and frequently used enforced resettlement. Aztecs put a god of war at the center of their pantheon; the Incas worshiped the sun and beneficent energy as their central god. The Aztecs drew and carved vivid, naturalistic designs and sculpture; the Inca tended to the abstract and unrealistic. These differences seem minor compared with the characteristics they shared.

Amazonia

The Amazon River is the world's largest river by volume; about 20 percent of all freshwater discharged into the world's oceans flows out its mouth. At its estuary, where it opens into the sea, the Amazon River is over 200 miles (320 kilometers) wide; oceangoing vessels can go two-thirds of the way up its length. Brazilian and Peruvian geographers

believe that it is slightly longer than the Nile, but no consensus has been reached on this; measurements vary every time they are made (Map 9.3).

The equator runs through the mouth of the Amazon River, and in the warm, tropical zone on either side of it about 400 inches (1,000 centimeters) of rain falls every year, more than 3 inches (7.6 centimeters) a day. It is estimated that in this rain forest live more than one-third of the world's species. Yet about a third of Amazonia is not rain forest, but savanna.

Archaeologists long ignored Amazonia. Any kind of evidence seemed difficult to locate there, given the dense vegetation, the scarcity of stone, the oscillation of the river channels, and the decaying properties of the hot, humid climate.

Since the 1970s, when archaeologists began to examine Amazonia, they have engaged in a continuing debate about whether Amazonia is inherently unable to support a dense sedentary population or whether its carrying capacity has been seriously underestimated. Recent research shows that greater cultural and ecological diversity existed in Amazonia than expected and that some parts may have been intensively used before European diseases drove the inhabitants back into hunter-gatherer villages. What seemed to visitors to be dense tropical jungles may well have been the remains of domesticated orchards.

As described in Chapter 5, manioc, sweet potatoes, and squash may have been domesticated in Amazonia by 5000 BCE. Early agricultural villages began by 2000 BCE, followed by extended societies and interregional interaction. Fish and other water creatures continued to provide the bulk of protein. Manioc root, sometimes called cassava, continued as a staple crop. A hefty root, it can be grown anywhere and can be roasted, fried, fermented, or ground. Even today in northeastern Brazil no meal is complete without crunchy toasted manioc flour sprinkled on top.

By the period 1000 to 1500 CE Amazonia had settlements that specialists agree can be called some form of "civilization." They had sophisticated technology, earthen mounds and enclosures, and a hierarchical society. Since Amazonian societies seem not to have been based on coerced tribute, we prefer to call them chiefdoms rather than agrarian civilizations.

The soil of Amazonia is famously poor in agricultural productivity, hence the argument referred to earlier that Amazonia might be inherently unable to support dense populations. Red-orange in color, the soil at the surface is eroded by heat and rain; nutrients are washed out, leaving the soil harshly acidic. Nutrients are stored in the fallen vegetation, from which they are reabsorbed by the efficient plant roots.

Yet sometime around 350 BCE Amazonians learned to create fertile soil by burning trees into charcoal, then mixing the charcoal pieces with excrement, fish and turtle bones, and vegetable waste to form *terra preta,* or black earth. This soil can still be identified; black earth sites, typically 5 to 15 acres (2.0 to 6.1 hectares), are found frequently throughout Amazonia. At Santarem the black earth extends 3 miles (4.8 kilometers) long and half a mile (0.8 kilometer) wide. The black earth indicates settlement, or at least settlement nearby, even if no artifacts are found. Was this long-term, small-scale settlement, or large-scale social formation? No one knows, but some archaeologists believe that 12 to 50 percent of the forests in Amazonia are ancient orchards of fruit and nut trees, the work of its former human inhabitants.

Agrarian Civilization in North America

Foraging lifeways persisted in substantial regions of North America from 3000 BCE through 1000 CE and up to the arrival of the Europeans. These areas included the Arctic and sub-Arctic, the Great Plains with its bison hunters, the Pacific Coast with its fishing communities, and the dry areas of the Southwest with nomads. Like their counterparts elsewhere, these people built societies on a small scale; wild food simply would not support dense populations (Map 9.4).

In other areas people became **semisedentary,** a term coined by Washington State University historian John E. Kicza. In these places people practiced agriculture and settled down into permanent or semipermanent villages. Their farming, however, proved less productive than in Mesoamerica or the Andes; they continued to supplement it with hunting and gathering, and they supported fewer people than fully sedentary societies. Two examples of these semisedentary people in North America are the Anasazi of present-day southwestern United States, now called the ancestral Pueblo, and the mound-building cultures of the eastern woodlands of present-day United States.

The Ancestral Pueblo People in the northern Southwest, in the Colorado plateau, acquired corn from Mesoamerica about 2000 to 1000 BCE. They had water control systems by 1000 BCE, yet it took some 2,000 years to provide enough food for permanent villages, which appeared about 600 to 800 CE, with expanding agriculture in the next 400 years. About 125 such sites have been found, the most dramatic at Chaco Canyon in the San Juan basin of northwestern New Mexico.

At Chaco Canyon five major pueblos have been found with large communal buildings four stories high, with thousands of rooms, dating between 860 and 1130 CE. The number of people at Chaco Canyon is speculative, anywhere from 2,000 to 10,000. Chaco was a center for the production of turquoise and perhaps a regional ceremonial center, with the buildings used as temples rather than residences; archaeologists have reached no agreement about this. Warfare occurred, and some cannibalism has been documented.

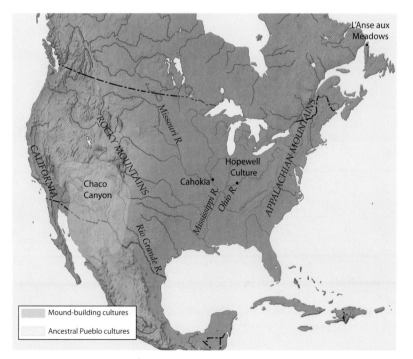

MAP 9.4 North America, 500 BCE to 1200 CE. The most intense exchange and communication occurred within the watershed of the Mississippi River.

L'Anse aux Meadows

Missouri R.

ROCKY MOUNTAINS

CALIFORNIA

Hopewell Culture

Cahokia

Chaco Canyon

Mississippi R.

Ohio R.

APPALACHIAN MOUNTAINS

Rio Grande R.

Mound-building cultures

Ancestral Pueblo cultures

People abandoned their settlement at Chaco Canyon by 1300 CE. Violent deaths on the Colorado plateau leading up to this date indicate significant competition among farming communities; apparently a severe drought from 1276 to 1299 sent people back to foraging, competing with outside foragers coming into their territory. From 1300 to 1500 CE the overall population of farmers in the Southwest dropped as much as 70 percent, showing the fragility of farming in dry areas.

Mound-Building Cultures The earliest mounds in the eastern woodlands of what is now the United States date to 2000 BCE, indicating that independent plant domestication and agriculture took place in this area. People supplemented their hunting and gathering with plants like sunflowers, sumpweed, goosefoot, maygrass, and a form of artichoke. Before corn-based agriculture arrived, the most elaborate and widespread culture was that of the Hopewell (200–400 CE), named after an early farmer in what is now southern Ohio near present-day Chillicothe, where one of the mounds was found. Hopewell mounds were the focus of elaborate burials; among the artifacts found are articles from as far away as 1,430 miles (2,290 kilometers), including mica from the Appalachians, volcanic glass (obsidian) from Yellowstone, conch shells and sharks' teeth from the Gulf of Mexico, and copper from the Great Lakes.

Significant individuals of both sexes, presumably from elite families, were buried in the most elaborate tombs.

Corn arrived in the eastern woodlands about 800 CE, with beans and squash introduced several generations later. Then larger populations could be supported; within 200 years chiefdoms became widespread. Chiefs in favorable ecological locations had the chance to extend their influences over those in less favorable areas. Much of the United States east of the Mississippi became a regional cultural complex, a network of ceremonial, cultural, and economic exchange.

The people of the woodlands built mounds to use as stages for ceremonies and rituals, as platforms for dwellings, and as burial sites. Most of their mounds have been destroyed by modern agriculture, road building, and real estate development; a few, like the Great Serpent Mound in southern Ohio, near Peebles, constructed about 1000 CE, remain.

The largest surviving mound is 1 of more than 100 at Cahokia, near East St. Louis, Illinois. The largest mound stood more than 100 feet (30 meters) high and covered an area of nearly 14 acres (5.7 hectares). The flat top of the mound held the houses of the rulers, the community buildings, structures for the bones of the ancestors of the elites, and a ritual space for occasional human sacrifice (Figure 9.7).

FIGURE 9.7 Cahokia. This artist's rendering of what Cahokia might have looked like at its height, about 900 to 1250 CE, is based on excavations.

Cahokia flourished about 900 to 1250 CE, with a population estimated anywhere between several thousand and forty thousand. A busy port town, Cahokia was located at the convergence of the Illinois and Missouri Rivers with the Mississippi, all formed from melting glaciers. Cahokians had to deal with frequent floods, but it was an earthquake at the beginning of the thirteenth century that razed the town; by 1350 CE few people were left.

Did Cahokia develop the structures of a state, or should it be classified as a chiefdom? Cahokia exemplifies the problems encountered in making this distinction. Larger than other mound-building societies, it has evidence for elite burial and monumental projects, both characteristics of states. Yet it is difficult to say whether it was structurally different from other contemporary sites or whether taxation and coercion were present. Indeed, the Americas are a reminder of how artificial it is to draw too sharp a line between more modest power systems such as chiefdoms and the huge systems we have described as agrarian civilizations.

North American Contact Contact between North America and other places was limited, but it did exist. A short-lived Viking colony was established in Newfoundland in 1000 CE. In addition, the cultivation of two crops spread northward from Mesoamerica and South America.

One was the Mesoamerican crop of corn, which spread slowly into southwestern North America, presumably carried by people traveling on land. The second crop, this time from South America, spread more rapidly into North America—tobacco.

First cultivated in the Peruvian–Ecuadoran Andes about 5000 to 3000 BCE, the use of tobacco spread northward prior to 2500 BCE, as indicated by simple pipes found in sites. By 1492 CE it had reached every corner of the North American continent, including the offshore islands and was used by nearly every tribe except those in the frozen tundra, even those like the Tlingit of Alaska and the Blackfoot and Crow on the plains who practiced no other form of agriculture. The Pueblo smoked through clay tubes. The mound-builders left in their burial sites an artistic repository of pipes carved from stone with exquisite renderings of birds, ducks, beavers, frogs, and human heads facing the smoker—was he communicating with the dead? (Many tribes restricted tobacco use to men.)

At its northeastern edge, North America reaches toward northern Europe. Iceland, east of Greenland, lies only a little more than 500 miles (800 kilometers) from the coast of Norway, at the same latitude, just south of the Arctic Circle. In Norway the Viking culture flourished and expanded from about 800 to 1070 CE. Fine shipbuilders, Viking traders reached all the way to Baghdad. Could they also have reached the mainland of North America? Historians asked this question for years.

In 1960 the answer came. The remains of a Viking settlement were found on the Newfoundland coast at L'Anse aux Meadows, where remnants of house walls were visible as raised areas in thick grass. Excavations revealed eight buildings that could shelter 70 to 90 people, dated about 1000 CE. The settlement apparently did not last long; when the Viking departed they left almost nothing, only iron nails to repair ships. Excavations showed that the iron smelting had occurred at L'Anse aux Meadows, the first iron smelting in North America.

This brief survey of North America has shown that no agrarian civilizations developed there, as they did in Mesoamerica and South America. The crops and animals available in the climatic conditions of North America did not support dense populations, with the increased stratification and coerced tribute that accompanies density. Contact with Mesoamerica and South American proved irregular and limited, and the one food crop that North Americans borrowed—corn—proved slow and difficult to engineer for the cooler climate. The other borrowed plant, tobacco, proved easy to grow and satisfying, but not sustaining.

Conclusion

Fifty years ago, historians tended to describe the Western Hemisphere before 1492 as two continents of wilderness, with scattered bands of foragers living unchanging lives, with only the beginnings of civilization emerging in two places, Mesoamerica and the Andes.

Today that view is much changed, as historians have realized that smallpox devastated American societies so rapidly that European explorers were finding only remnant societies of what had once been huge, and sometimes very complex societies. Now archaeologists and historians would say that the two continents held far more people than formerly thought and that at least two agrarian civilizations developed that were as complex and impressive as many earlier civilizations.

Let's take a quick imaginary plane flight over the Western Hemisphere in 1491. Starting at the mouth of the Amazon River, we would see the large city of Marajo on the island at its mouth. Further on we would see a city at Santarem, with a network of villages and orchards along the river. Over present-day Bolivia we could watch the Beni people building earthworks, until we crested the mountains to observe the awesome capital of the Incas at Cuzco, with immense stone highways extending in four directions, the Tawantinsuyu Empire, stretching north and south nearly 2,500 miles (4,000 kilometers).

In Mesoamerica we would fly over the Basin of Mexico where the Triple Alliance (Aztecs) extracted tribute from an empire somewhat smaller than the Inca and fought off their enemy empire, the Tarascans, in western Mexico. On the Yucatan Peninsula we would see Maya villages, in an area much smaller than at their florescence. Winging over North America, we would not find much remaining at Cahokia, already reduced by earthquake. We would notice a much less dense population than in Mesoamerica and South America, with many people still hunting and gathering, using cultivated crops as a supplement, except for the fully foraging hunters of the Great Plains and the Arctic peoples of the north.

In many of these regions people traveled and traded over wide areas. Sturdy canoes glided the rivers of eastern North America and the rivers of the Amazon basin. Along both coasts of Central America, the Maya used large dugout canoes holding 40 to 50 people. Caribbean people built ocean-going canoes, as did the Chincha along the Peruvian coast. Going by sea from Mexico to the Andes would certainly have been easier than walking across the high, rough terrain without any pack animals to carry loads. But since wooden boats leave little archaeological evidence, it is impossible to know how much traveling took place. Judging from the cultural exchange, only a loosely interacting network stretched from the North American Great Lakes and upper Mississippi to the Andes, not nearly the tight networks of exchange that developed in Afro-Eurasia and that supported long-term innovation.

Human society developed independently in the Americas, without any regular or lasting contact with other areas of the world until 1492—an independent experiment in agrarian civilizations to compare with those evolving in Afro-Eurasia. The comparison shows a convergence of general patterns, with similarities so basic that they bolster the conclusion that human cultural evolution has regularities wherever it occurs. The patterns include more social complexity, more hierarchy, and increasing control of resources.

Yet some key differences between the Americas and Afro-Eurasia stand out in the comparison. The power of the American states to extract tribute, to enforce coercion, and to maintain stability over time never reached that of the empire states in Afro-Eurasia. The size of the networks and exchanges, in distance covered and volume carried, never matched that of Afro-Eurasia. Finally, the population of the Americas, much contested, never reached anything like that of Afro-Eurasia. One recent estimate of worldwide population in 1000 CE put North America's share of world population at 0.8 percent, with South America's at 6 percent. The same source estimated Africa's share at 15 percent, with Eurasia's share at 77 percent. These are stark differences that must have mattered.

Why did people in the Americas create agrarian civilizations on a smaller scale than those in Afro-Eurasia? We can hypothesize based on the known evidence. Humans colonized the Americas later; they had less time to figure things out. They found no grasses with easily harvested seeds or large domesticable animals, whose absence made both plowing and pastoralism impossible. The change in latitude and climate north and south made sharing and trading more difficult than east–west exchanges, which involved little change in latitude. Perhaps Americans had a more challenging environment overall. These differences would matter significantly when the encounter between peoples of both hemispheres began to take place in 1492. But the rapid growth in the scale and size of agrarian civilizations in the centuries before the arrival of the Europeans suggests that eventually, agrarian civilizations would have flourished as they did in Afro-Eurasia, if their evolution had not been cut off by European conquest.

The Pacific and Australasian World Zones

In comparing the Afro-Eurasian and American world zones, it is striking that the general historical tendency toward large, and eventually more complex, social communities, appears in both. And in both world zones we see that social complexity leads to many similar phenomena, even if the timing may be somewhat different.

Is this a trend we can expect to find wherever there were human societies? At first sight, the history of the Pacific and Australasian zones may seem to contradict this conclusion. In neither region did there evolve large agrarian civilizations, so most of the trends explored in the preceding few chapters and in the section on the Americas do not appear here. Do the histories of these regions reflect utterly distinct historical trajectories? When examined more closely, it turns out that the appearance of profound differences is a bit misleading, as many of the same tendencies toward complexity that can be found in the Afro-Eurasian and American zones were also present in the other two zones, even if they did not progress as far. If we ignore the rather significant differences in the timing of long-term changes, and the huge number of specific cultural differences, we will see that in these zones, too, there was a familiar long-term trend toward increasing control of resources, larger populations, denser communities, expanding networks of exchange, and greater social complexity.

The Pacific World Zone

Colonizing the many small and not-so-small islands of the Pacific completed the process of global colonization that had begun in the Paleolithic era. The Pacific was colonized in two great pulses. The first occurred late in the Paleolithic era and can perhaps be thought of as part of the same pulse of migration as the colonization of **Sahul,** the unified ice age continent of Papua New Guinea, Tasmania, and Australia that made up the Australasian world zone. The islands of the Philippines and western Melanesia, including the Bismarck archipelago and the Solomons (sometimes described as "near Oceania"), were reached not long after the initial colonization of Australia, presumably through the use of similar seagoing skills. Modern humans had reached the Solomons by 40,000 years ago. But there exploration of the Pacific stalled for many millennia, presumably because traveling any further required navigational and seafaring skills that would not develop until after the Neolithic Revolution (see Map 9.5).

From about 3,500 years ago (mid-second millennium), a new pulse of migration took humans further into the Pacific, into "Remote Oceania." That pulse was driven by the

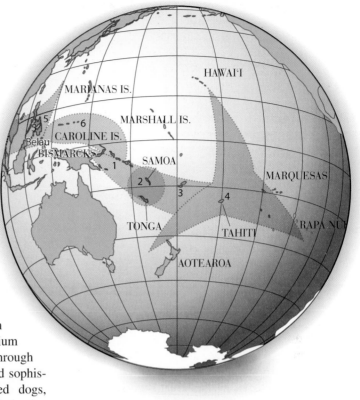

MAP 9.5 Migrations into the fourth world zone: the Pacific.
(1) from the Bismarcks to the mid-Pacific archipelagos of Fiji, Tonga, and Samoa; (2) the "homeland" of the Polynesians, now known as West Polynesia; (3) from West Polynesia to Central East Polynesia; (4) from Central East Polynesia to Hawai'i, Rapa Nui, Aotearoa; (5) from the Philippines to the western edge of Micronesia; (6) from the main migration sequence north to Micronesia and then west across the region.

emergence in Southeast Asia of seagoing cultures whose members spoke languages belonging to what modern linguists call the **Austronesian** language group. This seems to have originated in China and, more specifically, in Taiwan. From the middle of the second millennium BCE, we find evidence of extensive migrations through Southeast Asia by groups that used obsidian; had sophisticated fishing technologies; kept domesticated dogs, chickens, and pigs; and used rounded pots with distinctive patterns on them known to archaeologists as Lapita pottery. These are the key features of the **Lapita cultures.** By the mid-second millennium, evidence of these peoples can be found in Taiwan, in the Philippines, and in the Bismarcks. This migration over a large area of Southeast Asia was one of the most rapid migratory pulses we know of.

New migrations over the next few centuries took representatives of these cultures further into the Pacific, though they seem to have avoided densely settled Papua New Guinea, which may suggest that they were deliberately looking for easily colonizable, unoccupied islands. The parallels with Phoenician and Greek migrations at about the same time are striking, though the distances were far greater in the Pacific. Eventually the Lapita culture spread over almost 3,100 miles (5,000 kilometers). By 1,000 BCE we have evidence that bearers of the Lapita culture had reached Vanuatu, New Caledonia, and even Fiji, Samoa, and Tonga. Eastern Micronesia was probably colonized not from Asia but from Melanesia in the south, perhaps from the Solomons or maybe even from Fiji or Samoa. All these migrations, deep into the western Pacific, must reflect greatly improved technologies of navigation and sailing. These skills must have been of a very high order because there is evidence that obsidian was traded from Fiji to New Britain and Borneo, so we are probably not talking of single, one-way voyages of colonization. In particular, these migrants must have had triangular sails that enabled them to sail closer into the prevailing southeasterlies, because only if sailors could do that could they be assured of the possibility of a return journey. The crucial technological innovation may have been the evolution of single or double outriggers

to provide stability, an innovation that may date from as early as 2000 BCE (see Figure 9.8).

Polynesia, the rest of the Pacific world zone, seems to have been settled by migrants from Tonga and Samoa in the far east of Melanesia. Polynesia was finally settled between about 400 and 1200 CE. Most of these voyages, which covered much greater distances, were probably one-way trips. Melanesian migrants settled the Society Islands (so named by Captain Cook in honor of the Royal Society), which included Tahiti, then went on to settle Pitcairn and Easter Island to the east; to the north they settled the Hawaiian Islands; and eventually, somewhere between 1,000 and 1250 CE, they settled New Zealand in the far southwest. It is the wind patterns that explain why New Zealand was settled so late. If you come from the north, as Felipe Fernandez-Armesto points out, New Zealand is in a "navigational black hole," hard to find and reach because of the prevailing winds. These voyages depended on a rich navigational and technological lore built up over several millennia. Polynesian navigators could steer their vessels by the stars, by the winds, even by the feeling of the ocean swell. They also used an immense body of remembered geographic information that included mental maps covering thousands of miles of the Pacific.

Just as the existence of four different world zones sets up a natural historical experiment, so too does the settlement of Polynesia, for here colonizers encountered a huge range of different environments that were separate enough from each other so that local populations soon developed quite distinctive cultures. Particularly striking is the fact that adaptation sometimes led to cultural simplification rather than to

FIGURE 9.8 Polynesian ship. *Hōkūle'a* is a replica of a traditional Polynesian double-hulled voyaging canoe, which was built in 1975 by the Polynesian Voyaging Society. In 1976, *Hōkūle'a* traveled to Tahiti using traditional Polynesian navigational skills, in the first of 10 major voyages through the Pacific.

increasing social and technological complexity. The pottery that defined the Lapita cultures seems to vanish during the migrations beyond Samoa. This is a valuable reminder that "adaptation" does not always mean increasing complexity or increasing control of resources; and in some environments, survival over long periods may require simplification of both social and technological resources.

The history of New Zealand illustrates well the variety of evolutionary patterns that appeared in different regions. In much of the temperate South Island, settlers who arrived with farming technologies and crops adapted to tropical climates, reverted to foraging ways of living that survived until the arrival of Europeans. Chatham Island, east of New Zealand, provides an even more striking example of simplification. Here, migrants returned to foraging technologies in an environment in which the tropical crops of Polynesian farmers would not grow. They abandoned agriculture and gathered or hunted coastal resources, including seals, shellfish, and seabirds. Communities shrank in size, and organized warfare was unknown, which made the Chatham islanders easy prey to a huge

Maori invasion launched in 1835, an invasion described in graphic detail by Jared Diamond. The history of New Zealand's north island, where it was possible to grow tropical crops, was very different. Here, Polynesian settlers developed complex agrarian chiefdoms, with large populations, strict hierarchies, and organized warfare.

Similar contrasts appeared throughout Polynesia, with its unique combination of diverse environments and extreme isolation. On Easter Island, perhaps the most remote of all the Polynesian islands, there appeared small village communities that built the astonishing 30-ton (27.2-metric ton) stone statues (Ahu) for which the island is famous and developed a written script quite independently. At its height, the island's population may have reached 7,000 people, before eventually collapsing probably as a result of deforestation. Without timber, there was no fuel for heating or building or for the building of boats that could be used for fishing. After the collapse, the survivors reverted to crude forms of foraging. On the western islands of Hawai'i, which had high mountains and streams that could create rich soils, large populations made possible intensive irrigation farming that could produce up to 24 tons per acre (54 metric tons per hectare) of taro, as well as intensive breeding of pigs and of domesticated fish. Here, population densities were as high as 300 people per square mile (115 people per square kilometer), and chiefdoms or kingdoms emerged as large as those of Sumer's early city-states, ruling as many as 30,000 people, in contrast to the 5 people per square mile (2 people per square kilometer) of remote Chatham Island.

The Pacific world zone offers a peculiarly clear illustration of the many ways in which differences in environment shaped lifeways and social evolution.

The Australasian World Zone

As we have seen, during the last ice age low sea levels meant that Papua New Guinea, Australia, and Tasmania were linked as parts of a single continent, sometimes known as Sahul. Agriculture did emerge independently in one part of this continent, in the highlands of Papua New Guinea. But, partly because of the fragmented geography of the highlands and the fact that root crops could not be stored in large quantities, agriculture never seems to have generated political structures that reached beyond the scale of individual villages. Nevertheless, these societies were much more complex than those of the coastal regions of Papua New Guinea, generating rich artistic traditions and complex forms of warfare and ceremonies.

In Tasmania, in the far south of Australasia, there are many signs of a return to smaller, simpler social structures after rising sea levels severed connections with the mainland, leaving Tasmania's 4,000 or so inhabitants entirely isolated from other human communities. Some technologies that certainly existed earlier in the island's history, such as the use of needles and other bone tools, or the practice of fishing, seem to have vanished in the millennium or so before the arrival of Europeans. One cause may simply be that innovating, or even preserving new technologies, is harder within small, isolated populations because the synergy so necessary for Collective Learning is more limited. However, we should not necessarily think of these changes as signs of technological decline, for they may also have represented effective adaptations to climatic changes and to the realities of social isolation. For example, abandoning fishing and focusing, instead, on foodstuffs richer in fats, such as seals and seabirds, may have been a sensible ecological choice.

Although much bigger than Tasmania, the Australian mainland was also largely isolated from other human populations. And here, too, agriculture never developed, even though there seems to have been periodic contact between inhabitants of northern Queensland and parts of Papua New Guinea. (See the discussion of this issue in Chapter 5.) It is a reasonable presumption that here there were simply no regions where farming was clearly more beneficial than foraging. In general, Australian soils were poor and population densities low. The total population of the continent was probably no more than a few hundred thousand when Europeans arrived at the end of the eighteenth century, though there were certainly areas, particularly along the coasts, where populations were much denser than inland.

There is also the largely contingent fact that Australia, unlike Mesopotamia, did not evolve easily domesticatable plant species. The macadamia nut is the only indigenous plant to have been domesticated in modern times, although there were some potential domesticates, including types of yam and taro that were farmed in Papua New Guinea and gathered by Australians.

However, it is a mistake simply to think of Australia as a society stuck in a sort of Paleolithic time warp. One reason is that archaeological research has shown a long history of innovative adaptations to changes, including climate change. Rock art from 30,000 to 20,000 years ago shows us lifeways that would change profoundly later in response to climatic change. In Arnhem Land, for example, as rising sea levels transformed a once-dry region into a region of coastal swamps and lagoons, yams and marsupials begin to disappear from rock art, to be replaced by fish and turtles. This is when we also find the first art depicting what are now called rainbow serpents (see Chapter 1) but which probably depicted a form of pipefish.

Furthermore, there are many indications from the archaeology of the last few thousand years that there were regions of Australia—particularly those with more rainfall, in the southeastern and southwestern corners, or along much of the eastern coast—in which forms of intensification were occurring similar to those that preceded the emergence of agriculture in other parts of the world such as the fertile crescent. In Chapter 5, we described some of the remarkable forms that intensification would take in Australia, including the building of elaborate eel ponds in the Murray–Darling river system or the increasing use of seeds of wild millet. An increase in the number of archaeological sites suggests that population numbers may have doubled or tripled during the last two millennia before the arrival of Europeans. New types of tools also appeared, such as fishhooks made of shells, particularly in regions where fishing became more intensive. Furthermore, there is growing evidence of increasing interconnections over large areas. Narcotic drugs originating in southern Queensland turn up, along with stone axes from the Mount Isa range, in sites in South Australia. And the huge ochre mines of Wilgie Mia in western Australia produced so much ochre that their production seems to have been driven by the needs of interregional trade rather than by local demand. In Australia, then, it is tempting to think that if the region's history had played out for a few more centuries without European interference, we might have seen developments similar to those in Mesopotamia at the time of the first appearance of agriculture (Figure 9.9).

Conclusion: The Australasian and Pacific world zones

All in all, as Jared Diamond has argued eloquently, it is a mistake to ignore those regions of the world in which farming did not develop or to exaggerate the significance of differences in the pace at which agrarian civilizations evolved. We have much to learn about the trajectory of

FIGURE 9.9 Corroboree. Innovation was accelerating in Australia in recent millennia. One driver of innovation and Collective Learning was the periodic gatherings of local communities known as *corroborees,* because it was here that gifts, people, ideas, ceremonies, and dances from different groups could be exchanged and could spread from community to community.

human history in general from studying regions in which agriculture did *not* flourish. Studying the regions of independent evolution of agriculture tells us only half the story of agriculture and even of the evolution of agrarian civilizations. Systematic comparisons of the histories of the different world regions suggest that while population growth and intensification could be slowed significantly by environmental and geographic and social conditions that did not favor them, even many regions that did not develop agriculture independently were on evolutionary trajectories suggesting that they would eventually have stumbled on some form of agriculture, if these trends had not been disrupted by the arrival of European colonists.

These ideas suggest that the large trends described in the last few chapters were more or less universal, even if they proceeded at different speeds in different parts of the world and generated a great diversity of different cultural, artistic,

and religious styles. Everywhere we find innovation and technological and social change. Only in some regions did innovation stumble upon the mega-innovation of agriculture, which led eventually toward the next mega-innovation of agrarian civilizations. But if they had been given enough time, it seems likely that other regions, too, would eventually have developed their own forms of agriculture.

Having said that, it is also true that differences in the timing and geography of such processes really did matter. They affected the global distribution of populations and also of power and wealth. And they help, therefore, explain the geography of today's extremely lopsided distribution of the vast wealth now controlled by modern human populations.

Now we must turn to study the series of mega-innovations that created today's world, a world utterly different from that of the Era of Agrarian Civilizations.

SUMMARY

In this chapter we compared the three other world zones with the Afro-Eurasian zone in the era after 1000 BCE. In the American world zone we examined two agrarian civilizations, the Aztecs in Mesoamerica and the Inca in

South America, and found many similarities with earlier agrarian civilizations in Afro-Eurasia. Our survey of North America revealed that, while populations there were not dense enough to support agrarian civilization, corn and tobacco were cultivated and chiefdoms arose. In the Pacific and Australasian zones a wide range of lifeways emerged, depending on diverse local environments and the frequent isolation. No society reached the stage of agrarian civilization, and some did not develop agriculture, yet innovation and adaptation were always present. We conclude that the human capacity for Collective Learning and adaptation results in universal patterns of social evolution, while also depending on contingent factors of geography and local plants and animals.

CHAPTER QUESTIONS

1. Why is it helpful to compare four different world zones?
2. What seem to be universal trends in human history?
3. How were those trends affected by differences in the geography and ecology of the different world zones?
4. Compare Aztec and Inca agrarian civilizations.
5. What were the most distinctive features of the histories of the Pacific and Australasian world zones?

KEY TERMS

Austronesian (languages)	Inca	*Popol Vuh*	Sahul
Aztecs	Lapita culture	Quechua	semisedentary
Huitzilopochtli	Nahuatl	Quetzalcoatl	

FURTHER READING

Bellwood, Peter. *The First Farmers: The Origins of Agricultural Societies.* Oxford/Malden, MA: Blackwell, 2005.

Bellwood, Peter, and Peter Hiscock. "Australians and Austronesians." In Chris Scarre, ed., *The Human Past: World Prehistory and the Development of Human Societies.* London: Thames & Hudson, 2005, 264–305.

Brotherson, Gordon. *Book of the Fourth World: Reading the Native Americas Through Their Literature.* Cambridge, UK: Cambridge University Press, 1992.

D'Altroy, Terence N. *The Incas.* Malden, MA: Blackwell, 2002.

Davies, Nigel. *Human Sacrifice in History and Today.* New York: William Morrow, 1981.

Diamond, Jared. *Guns, Germs, and Steel: The Fates of Human Societies.* New York: Norton, 1997.

Fernandez-Armesto, Felipe. *Pathfinders: A Global History of Exploration.* New York: Norton, 2007.

Gately, Iain. *Tobacco: The Story of How Tobacco Seduced the World.* New York: Grove Press, 2001.

Gillmor, Frances. *Flute of the Smoking Mirror: A Portrait of Nezahualcoyotl, Poet-King of the Aztecs.* Salt Lake City: University of Utah Press, 1983.

Leon-Portilla, Miguel. *Fifteen Poets of the Aztec World.* Norman: University of Oklahoma Press, 1992.

Mann, Charles C. *1491: New Revelations of the Americas before Columbus.* New York: Knopf, 2006.

Marcus, Joyce. *Mesoamerican Writing Systems: Propaganda, Myth and History in Four Ancient Civilizations.* Princeton, NJ: Princeton University Press, 1992.

Milner, George R., and W. H. Wills. "Complex Societies of North America." In Chris Scarre, ed., *The Human Past: World Prehistory and the Development of Human Societies.* London: Thames & Hudson, 2005, 678–715.

Moseley, Michael E., and Michael J. Hechenberger. "From Village to Empire in South America." In Chris Scarre, ed., *The Human Past: World Prehistory and the Development of Human Societies.* London: Thames & Hudson, 2005, 640–77.

Scarre, Chris, ed. *The Human Past: World Prehistory and the Development of Human Societies.* London: Thames & Hudson, 2005.

Smith, Michael E. *The Aztecs.* 2nd ed. Malden, MA: Blackwell, 2003.

Webster, David, and Susan Toby Evans. "Mesoamerican Civilization." In Chris Scarre, ed., *The Human Past: World Prehistory and the Development of Human Societies.* London: Thames & Hudson, 2005, 594–639.

ENDNOTE

1. Quoted by Gordon Brotherson, *Book of the Fourth World: Reading the Native Americas Through Their Literature* (Cambridge, UK: Cambridge University Press, 1992), 81.

chapter 10

Toward the Modern Revolution

Seeing the Big Picture

1000 to 1700 CE

▶ What distinguishes today's world from all earlier eras of human history?

▶ In what ways did agrarian civilizations prepare the way for the "modern revolution"?

▶ What forces accelerated the pace of change in the last 1,000 years?

▶ Was the modern revolution inevitable given our capacity as a species for continual, sustained innovation through Collective Learning?

The Approach of the Modern Revolution

In this chapter, we will survey the era just before the eighth of our major thresholds. We call that threshold, with deliberate vagueness, the **modern revolution.**

In the wide-angle lens of big history, what stands out about the modern period is the sharp increase in human control over the resources of the biosphere that begins with the Industrial Revolution, described in the next chapter. We have already seen something similar in the agricultural revolution that began over 10,000 years ago. Suddenly, humans increased their control over the energy and resources of the biosphere. Increasing access to energy and resources allowed humans to form larger, more populous, more complex, and more diverse societies, societies that had new emergent properties that had never been seen before. The modern revolution was similar, except that this time everything happened much much faster and on a far larger scale (Figure 10.1).

A sudden increase in available resources meant societies could grow faster than ever before, they could produce more than ever before, and they could become much more complex. The results were transformative. In 2002, Paul Crutzen, a Nobel Prize–winning chemist, argued that early in the nineteenth century the planet entered a new geological epoch, the **Anthropocene.** By that he meant the era in which humans have become the dominant species on Earth. (We will discuss this idea in more detail in Chapter 12.)

Unwittingly, we have begun to change the chemistry of the atmosphere; the range, variety, and distribution of plant and animal species; and the nature of the water cycle and other fundamental geological processes such as erosion. These changes may transform the workings of the biosphere for centuries or even millennia, because many have long-term consequences and some, such as species extinctions, are irreversible. Never has a single species had such power before in the entire history of planet Earth, and it is not at all clear that we can control the forces of change we have unleashed.

In this chapter, we will look for the roots of the modern revolution in the period since 1000 CE. What prepared the way for the crossing of the eighth threshold? Why were different regions affected in different ways? And what did these changes have to do with Collective Learning?

The answer to the last question is simple: everything! The technologies and social structures that enabled humans to increase their control over resources arose from the ancient process of innovation through the sharing of information that is the most distinctive feature of human history. But why should the pace and synergy of Collective Learning have accelerated so sharply in the Modern era? And why did rates of change vary so greatly from region to region? These are the central questions asked in this chapter. To answer them we have to look more closely at some of the factors that can encourage or discourage Collective Learning and innovation.

Why Rates of Innovation Increased: Drivers of Innovation

We have already seen several factors that can affect the pace and power of innovation in different times and places. We call these factors **drivers of innovation.** In recent centuries, three powerful drivers of innovation have become more and more important, and as they have evolved they have worked together to generate powerful new synergies.

Driver 1: Increased Exchange Networks

Humans exchange goods and ideas through **exchange networks.** It is a reasonable assumption that more information will be exchanged and stored in a community of 1 million people than in a community of 100 people. Mathematically, this can be expressed by saying that, as the number of "nodes" (i.e., people) increases within a network, the number of possible links between the nodes (or exchanges between people) increases much faster (Figure 10.2). [For the mathematically inclined, if the number of nodes in a network is n, then the number of links $(l) = n * (n - 1)/2$.] So, as a general rule, we should expect rates of innovation (the generation of new ideas, whether religious, artistic, ethical, or technological) to be much faster in large than in small communities. That explains why, at large scales, population growth itself tends to encourage Collective Learning.

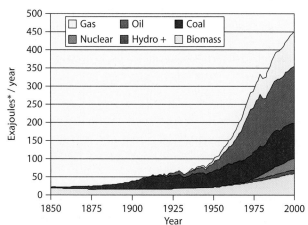

*Human energy consumption as measured in exajoules. A joule is the power required to produce one watt for one second; an exajoule is a million million million joules.

FIGURE 10.1 World energy consumption, 1850 to 2000 CE. In 1850, most of the energy used by humans still came from traditional sources: human and animal labor, water power, wind power, and the energy locked up in wood. By the year 2000, total human energy use had multiplied by many times and overwhelmingly that energy came from the three major forms of fossil fuels: coal, oil, and natural gas.

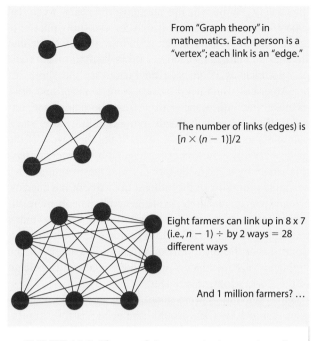

From "Graph theory" in mathematics. Each person is a "vertex"; each link is an "edge."

The number of links (edges) is $[n \times (n-1)]/2$

Eight farmers can link up in 8 x 7 (i.e., $n - 1$) ÷ by 2 ways = 28 different ways

And 1 million farmers? ...

FIGURE 10.2 The math is easy. As the number of people in a network grows, the potential synergy of Collective Learning within that network grows much faster. This can be demonstrated by a simple piece of mathematics from graph theory.

We also expect that greater diversity in the communities exchanging information should increase the likelihood of new ideas being generated within an exchange network. If everyone is a forager, people will probably talk mostly about what they already know. But if foragers meet agriculturalists, both sides may learn something entirely new. So we expect Collective Learning to work more powerfully in large and complex societies with diverse internal structures and extensive connections between regions with different resources, technologies, and cultures.

Cities (particularly trading cities) offer environments in which people from very different backgrounds can meet and exchange ideas and information as well as merchandise. Where many cities are connected over large areas, the possibilities for such exchanges are magnified. So, as a rule of thumb, we should expect more innovation in complex societies where goods, people, and ideas travel and are exchanged over large areas. In Afro-Eurasia, trading city-states often pooled information from across vast regions through networks such as the Silk Roads, which is one reason why, 1,000 years ago Central Asian cities such as Bukhara and Samarkand were major centers of world science and technology.

Driver 2: Improvements in Communications and Transportation

By **communications** we mean the technologies by which people exchange information and ideas; by **transportation** we mean the technologies by which people and goods are moved from place to place. Improving technologies of communications and transportation can increase the capacity of societies to store and spread information. By doing so, they can accelerate Collective Learning and encourage innovation.

Driver 3: Increased Incentives to Innovate

By **incentives to innovate** we mean those factors in societies that either encourage or discourage innovation. We should expect the power of Collective Learning to increase wherever we find direct incentives to innovate or seek out new information. Today, we take innovation for granted because we live in societies that actively encourage innovation through education, research, and by the use of many different kinds of incentives. So we can easily forget how hostile most earlier societies were to new ideas, new ways of doing things, new religions and technologies, and innovations in general. Conservatism has been the rule in most societies. Yet there have always been individuals who were incurably curious. And we can often identify structures and attitudes and interests that have encouraged the search for new knowledge and new ways of doing things.

For example, though governments and rulers were often suspicious of novelty, they usually had good reason to seek out new military technologies (such as chariots or guns) or to build roads for their soldiers and merchants or to seek new sources of wealth. In addition, some religious and philosophical traditions seem to have been more supportive of innovation than others. Classical Greece proved extremely innovative in philosophy; and the German sociologist Max Weber (1864–1920) famously argued that Protestantism was more supportive of entrepreneurial activity than Catholicism.

But perhaps the most powerful of all incentives to innovate was commerce: the existence of competitive markets for goods, services, and labor. It's not hard to see why commerce creates powerful incentives to innovate. If you are selling goods or services in a market where others are selling, too, and you cannot force people to buy your product, you will make a profit only if your product is better than that of your rivals. So competitive markets encourage innovation: new and cheaper ways of making clothes, or faster ways of building houses, or more effective cures, or better ways of storing cash or moving it from place to place. One of the fundamental axioms of modern economics is that competitive markets stimulate innovation, while **monopolies** (environments in which there is only one supplier of a commodity) stifle innovation because monopolists do not face competition. The more people there are engaged in market transactions on competitive markets, the more peasants selling grain or craft goods, the more merchants or farmers hiring laborers, the more financiers competing to sell loans at interest, the greater the likelihood of innovation. Not always, of course, and not all the time, but by and large we expect a more commercialized society to be one in which Collective Learning generates and spreads innovations more easily. On the other hand, monopolistic markets tend to discourage innovation because those who control the market have little incentive to improve or cheapen their product and every incentive to suppress new ideas that threaten their revenues.

Many societies of the Agrarian era had plenty of market activity. But most people were peasants who grew most of their own food and had limited contacts with markets. Besides, in agrarian civilizations governments often did not support merchants or competitive markets because they enjoyed monopolies over many of the resources and much of the labor of society. They were hostile to market activity because it could threaten the "tributes" they extracted through the use of legal or physical force. Elites in agrarian civilizations often despised those who did not have the right or power to exact tributes, including merchants. And that meant that they despised market activity in general and rarely supported it. That is why we have sometimes referred to agrarian civilizations as tribute-taking societies.

We will refer to societies in which elites and governments are highly supportive of commercial activity as **capitalist.** Today, most societies in the world can be described as capitalist in this sense because most resources, including taxes, are mobilized through market activity, through buying and selling, as individuals sell their goods or their labor to others, and governments encourage commercial activities because they expect to profit from them.

In summary, we have identified three key drivers of innovation that have become more and more important in the Modern era and can help us explain the dramatic increases in innovation in recent centuries:

1. The increasing size and variety of exchange networks.
2. The growing efficiency of systems of communications and transportation.
3. The expansion of commercial activity, competitive markets, and capitalism.

The World in 1000 CE

How important were these three drivers of innovation 1,000 years ago, toward the end of the Agrarian era? This question gives us a chance to review more generally how people lived, worked, traded, and exchanged information before the Modern era.

Driver 1: Exchange Networks

A thousand years ago, most exchange networks were still fragile and local. The world historian David Northrup has argued that for some purposes world history can be divided into just two periods: before and after 1000 CE. Before 1000 CE, human societies tended to get more and more disconnected and diverse; after 1000 CE they began to connect again, and to do so faster and faster.

David Northrup would be the first to admit that this is a highly simplified scheme, but there is much truth in it. In 1000 CE, the world really was a less connected place

than today. Above all, the major world zones were still separated from each other. It may be that individual voyagers had crossed the Atlantic before 1000 CE, or that Indonesian mariners sometimes made landfall on the coast of Australia, or Polynesian navigators on the shores of the Americas. But such contacts were too rare and brief to make much difference. Away from the main trade networks such as the Silk Roads, most people lived in small communities with few links to other regions. Most of the land surface of the Earth was occupied by foragers or pastoralists or by small-scale farmers, and these communities accounted for most of the cultural diversity of our species. Languages, for example, were generally much more diverse in regions of thin settlement. Today, when so many traditional languages have disappeared elsewhere, it is estimated that the once remote agricultural villages of the highlands of Papua New Guinea contain about 25 percent of the world's living languages.

However, things were about to change. John Man argues that in 1000 CE it would have been possible, in principle, for the first time in history for a message to circle the world. In his thought experiment, he imagines a message sent from a major city such as Baghdad, in the Islamic heartland of Afro-Eurasia. From Baghdad, the message could have traveled south along the Nile or on camel caravans through the Sahara, from where it could have been passed from community to community through villages of Bantu farmers and pastoralists to the Khoisan peoples of South Africa. The same message could also have traveled north through Byzantium to Russia, whose recently established Viking rulers could have passed it on to Scandinavia, where other Vikings could have carried it to the Viking colonies of Iceland and Greenland and then on to the recently established colony of Vinland in Newfoundland. Once in the Americas, locals could have taken the message south, to Mesoamerica, through the tropical forests of Central America to the Andes and perhaps as far as Tierra del Fuego in the far south. Or perhaps they could have carried the message north to Canada, where people of the Thule Inuit culture could have carried it west to Alaska and the Bering straits, from where there was an easy and familiar crossing to eastern Siberia. From eastern Siberia it could have traveled south to Japan, Korea, and China or westward through the steppes of Inner Eurasia. Or Chinese merchants might have carried it to Southeast Asia, where traders seeking sea cucumbers (*trepang*) along the northern coasts of Australia could have passed it to local communities that could have begun to spread it throughout Australia. The seafaring peoples of the Indonesian archipelago might conceivably have carried it to the islands of Melanesia and then, perhaps, to Polynesia where migrants might (just!) have carried it to newly settled lands such as Hawaii or New Zealand. Meanwhile, from China and India, the message could have returned either through the Inner Eurasian steppes or through Afghanistan and Iran to Baghdad.

Of course, none of this happened. But Man's point is that in 1000 CE, perhaps for the first time in human history it is just possible to imagine it happening. Here we have the shadowy beginnings of the millennium-long process of weaving new and larger exchange networks that would eventually reach across the entire world. Today, we call this process **globalization.**

Driver 2: Communications and Transportation Technologies

In part, the lack of connectedness of most agrarian civilizations arose from the inefficiency of traditional technologies of communications and transportation.

Writing was common only in the heartlands and cities of agrarian civilizations, in both Mesoamerica and Afro-Eurasia, and even there it was an elite skill, confined for the most part to scribes, officials, scholars, or monks and priests. Before the spread of paper, you had to write on papyrus (in Egypt) or on sheep or calfskins (parchment or vellum), neither of which was cheap, so manuscripts were treasured and copied many times, slowly and painstakingly, by hand. Often the materials on which they were written were used several times, as one message was scraped away and overlaid with another, producing the difficult-to-decipher documents known as palimpsests. The first printing, or mechanical copying, was developed in Korea, probably in the eighth or ninth centuries, using carefully carved wood blocks, though the Chinese had long been able to make multiple copies of documents using stone blocks. The first printing using movable type dates from eleventh-century Korea. Each word was carved on a single wooden block fixed in position in a printing frame using wax.

Books, whether written or printed, were precious stores of information. In Baghdad, in 900 CE there were about 100 booksellers. At that time, the Muslim world was perhaps the major clearinghouse for knowledge in the world, for it lay at the center of Eurasia's extensive exchange networks and here books, beginning with the holy Qur'an, were treated with exceptional respect. Early in the eleventh century, the library of Cairo is supposed to have contained 1.5 million books. Many used paper. This was a new medium that had been invented in China early in the first millennium, and had spread westward after the capture of Chinese papermakers during the battle of Talas in 751, the first time in which Arabic armies had fought armies from China.

But the Cairo library was unusual. One of the largest monastic libraries of medieval Europe, Germany's Reichenau, contained just 450 books, all written on parchment. Away from the agrarian heartlands, drums or hilltop beacons could carry very simple messages (DANGER! WAR! FIRE!) rapidly over large distances. But that was it! That was as good as communications systems could be.

As for travel and transportation, on land most people walked. If they were wealthier (or they were pastoralists) and lived in the Afro-Eurasian world zone, they might have ridden on horseback or in wagons or they might have been carried in litters. If they lived in arid and desert regions, they could travel in camel caravans, such as the caravans of 25,000 camels that took gold and slaves north across the Sahara from Timbuktu in the thirteenth and fourteenth

centuries. Caravans followed tracks, for roads were rare, and the best roads were built by the major empires for their soldiers. The Romans built a total of 50,000 miles (80,000 kilometers) of roadways over several centuries, and some were so well built that they survive to the present day. The best were cambered, to drain water, and for strength and durability they were built many feet thick using successive layers of sand, flat stones, gravel cemented in concrete, and cobblestones. Still, few people traveled faster than a quick walk, so it normally took three months to cover the 1,600 miles (2,560 kilometers) of the Persian Royal Road (referred to in Chapter 7) from Susa in modern Iran to Ephesus in modern Turkey. The ancient equivalent of the Internet, and the fastest possible way of getting information from place to place, was through post-horse systems. In the Persian Achaemenid Empire, relays of riders could travel the Persian Royal Road, changing horses every few miles, in just a week when necessary (or about 12 times as fast as travelers on foot). But most people didn't travel farther than the local market town, unless they were merchants, soldiers, pilgrims, or captured slaves.

The cheapest and often the fastest way of carrying people or goods was by water—along rivers or canals, along the coast, or on the open seas. A human porter (the main form of transportation in the Americas) could carry up to 50 pounds (22.5 kilograms) of goods over large distances, and a well-built medieval wagon drawn by well-fed and well-shod horses with shoulder-hugging collars could carry perhaps 2,100 pounds (950 kilograms) of goods. But the Arab dhows that sailed across the Indian Ocean using the monsoon winds could carry over 100 times as much cargo as a horse-drawn wagon in 1000 CE and 400 times as much by 1500 CE. The Chinese junks that the Muslim traveler, Ibn Battuta (fourteenth century) saw in India did even better; they could carry up to 2.2 million pounds (about 1 million kilograms), or 1,000 times as much as a horse-drawn wagon.

The fastest way to travel short distances over water was in ships powered by oars. Athenian triremes could briefly reach 13 mph (21 kph), but they were so expensive to build and run that they were normally used only in warfare (see Table 10.1).

Commercial ships used wind power or were hauled by teams of men (such as the famous "Volga boatmen" of Russia) or animals, along canals and rivers. Two thousand years ago, a Roman cargo ship with a favorable wind might take a week to travel from Sicily to Egypt; but the return voyage, against the wind, could take a month or two. In China, river transport was so reliable and cheap that under the Sui Dynasty (581–618 CE) a canal was built linking the Yangtze River in the south to the Yellow River in the north, to carry rice and other goods to the capital, Beijing. But until the twelfth century, when the first canal locks were invented, boats still had to be carried or hauled over land where river levels changed.

In general, in 1000 CE goods, people, and information traveled little further and no faster than they had 1,000 years earlier.

TABLE 10.1 Haulage Capacity by Land and by Sea

Form of Transportation	Approximate Weight Carried
Human porter, Andes	50 pounds (22.5 kilograms)
Llamas, Andes	70 pounds (32 kilograms)
Team of 30 llamas with 1 driver	2,100 pounds (950 kilograms)
Packhorse can carry 30% of its weight	300 pounds (140 kilograms)
With North Arabian saddle (invented ca. 500 BCE) camels	700 pounds (320 kilograms)
Roman horse-drawn wagon	700 pounds (320 kilograms)
Medieval horse-drawn wagon (after invention of padded, shoulder-hugging collar)	2,100 pounds (950 kilograms)
Indian dhows, 1000 CE	220,000 pounds (100,000 kilograms)
Indian dhows, 1500 CE	880,000 pounds (400,000 kilograms)
Large Chinese junks, 1500 CE	2,200,000 pounds (1,000,000 kilograms)

Driver 3: Incentives to Innovate

We have seen that in the Era of Agrarian Civilizations, innovation was painfully slow by modern standards.

Limits to Innovation in the Agrarian Era In the Agrarian era there were few incentives to innovate. Governments and aristocrats enjoyed monopolies over many of the resources in their societies, so they usually preferred traditional ways of doing things over new-fangled methods that were unlikely to work and might have unintended consequences. Merchants and craft workers were often equally conservative, and in a world without patent laws those who tried to innovate would often find their innovations copied instantly by others or suppressed by powerful craft guilds (as they were called in Europe). In such environments, it was rarely worth investing in new technologies.

Sometimes important inventions appeared, only to be ignored or left undeveloped. In Chapter 9, for example, we saw that the wheel was known in the Americas but used only for toys, probably because there were no large domestic animals that could haul wagons or carts. In China, the mixing of saltpeter (potassium nitrate) and sulfur with charcoal to make gunpowder was familiar by the year 1000 CE, but developing effective gunpowder weapons would take many centuries, and most of the innovations would take place in the constantly warring states at the western end of Eurasia.

The slow pace of technological change throughout the Agrarian era was itself a discouragement to innovation because it meant that investors were unlikely to reap any rewards in their own lifetimes. For entrepreneurs, it made more sense to use force and the law to protect monopoly rights over trade goods such as silks or precious stones than to seek ways of trading more efficiently. For governments, it usually made sense to grow your economy by seizing the wealth of neighboring states. In a society without research institutes and competitive corporations, warfare, though risky, was generally less risky than investing in uncertain technologies that might take decades or even centuries to yield a profit.

Peasant farming also discouraged innovation. Most food, fuel, and textiles came from small peasant farms that used traditional techniques and had little access to capital or new technologies. Most peasants lived in rural areas, away from the intellectual powerhouses of the cities. Their contacts with markets and new information were limited because they produced most of the food, fuel, and textiles they needed themselves. Finally, most peasants were taxed so heavily and so arbitrarily by governments or landlords that they had no incentive to improve their farming methods. Why produce more if you knew your landlord would confiscate any surplus? Rough estimates suggest that peasants often surrendered up to half of what they produced to rulers and landlords. The low productivity of peasant farmers, who made up most of the population and produced most of the wealth of agrarian civilizations, ensured that productivity in general remained low. Low productivity on farms also limited the size of towns and cities because, as a rule of thumb, it normally took about nine peasants to support one city dweller in much of the Agrarian era. This meant that cities could normally make up only about 10 percent of the population. In 1400, only about 10 percent of the world's populations lived in settlements of more than 5,000 people.

Limited supplies of energy also lowered productivity. Almost all the energy used by human societies came from sunlight recently captured by plants through photosynthesis. Sunlight grew the trees that supplied firewood or charcoal for fires and furnaces, as well as the crops that fed horses, oxen, and camels, and the humans who had domesticated them. Sunlight also drove the wind currents that powered sailing ships and the first windmills (introduced in Persia around 1000 CE). But the main way of mobilizing solar energy was by exploiting the energy of domestic animals (to draw plows and carts and to carry goods) and of humans, who, when captured as slaves, were often treated simply as stores of intelligent energy. This is why slavery was so important in so much of the premodern world; slaves were like highly versatile batteries. But this also meant that to generate a really large amount of energy you had to assemble a lot of people and animals in one place, and that was costly and difficult.

In a world whose energy came from recent photosynthesis, mobilizing resources was a political and administrative achievement rather than a matter of innovative technologies. The states that were most successful were those that could mobilize, transport, and feed the largest armies and build the most impressive monuments. This is another reason why, throughout the Agrarian era, growth generally meant not producing more or raising productivity, but seizing the wealth of neighboring states. Growth was seen as a zero-sum game in a world in which available resources seemed to be more or less fixed.

Commerce, Markets, and Innovation

However, there was at least one area of social life, even in agrarian civilizations, in which innovation was the key to success. That was where there existed competitive markets.

We have seen that the economies of the agrarian world were dominated by tribute taking and monopolies. But even the most powerful of empires had little control over goods produced beyond their borders. When Chinese emperor Han Wudi (156–87 BCE) wanted to secure the powerful "blood-sweating horses" of Ferghana in Central Asia, his initial impulse was to send an army. But that was so costly that eventually he realized he would have to trade silks for horses. And to do that he would have to employ merchants who had some knowledge of how to trade peacefully in competitive markets. But even in internal markets, there was sometimes room for competition, and where there was competition, efficiency mattered because, as a general rule, the traders or artisans who did their job best and most cheaply were most likely to find buyers for their goods and services.

Sometimes, usually at the edges of great empires and just beyond their reach, there emerged independent cities or states, such as the great city-states of the Phoenicians, whose elites specialized in handling international trade. Often, these cities were homes to interregional networks of traders bound together by ethnicity or family ties. In the first millennium CE, Armenian and Jewish merchants created huge networks that traded throughout Europe, the Mediterranean, and into Central Asia and India. As we saw in Chapter 8, in the late thirteenth century Muslim merchants in the Chinese city of Quanzhou provided Chinese potters from the great porcelain-manufacturing center of Jindezhen with Persian cobalt glazes so they could produce the famous white and blue porcelains that sold so well in the Muslim world. It was here, within trade networks in which brute force sometimes gave way to commercial finesse, that innovation was most likely.

Particularly important incentives to trade were innovations that made it easier to use and transfer cash over large distances. Before the appearance of coins, most trade had consisted of barter, which meant that both sides had to produce exactly the goods their counterparts wanted or there was no deal. The first coins officially stamped by the rulers that issued them, appeared in Anatolia in the middle of the first millennium BCE. By 1000 CE coins were in use throughout Eurasia. They made trade easier because they counted as general tokens of value. Where sufficient trust existed, merchants would sometimes sell goods in return for mere promises to pay, paper notes or "IOUs" on which the purchaser promised to pay by a certain date, often with an extra sum to compensate the seller for the delay. Such IOUs could often be bought and sold, which allowed money to be transferred over large distances. In 1024 CE, in response to shortages of bronze and silver coins, the Chinese Song Dynasty began to issue paper notes of its own, which were in effect government-backed IOUs, or promises to pay. These could be used universally, as long as customers were confident that the government would always honor the promises to pay that they represented. That was not always true, of course. But where such methods worked, they could cheapen the cost of exchanges and expand the reach of markets as well as the power of governments to raise taxes.

So, though markets existed throughout the Agrarian era, their influence was limited and rulers often discriminated against them, which is why during the Era of Agrarian Civilizations markets had a limited impact on innovation.

Slow Innovation and Malthusian Cycles

In general, then, we can say that in 1000 CE, as throughout the Agrarian era, incentives to introduce new ideas, methods, and technologies were much weaker than today. This was partly because the three drivers of innovation we have identified were less important than today. However, they were never entirely absent, and that explains why, throughout the Agrarian era, we have seen a slow trickle of innovations.

As we have discussed, the slow pace of innovation throughout the Agrarian era explains the pervasiveness of Malthusian cycles: long periods in which populations and production seemed to rise, only to be followed by sudden crashes. Often, Malthusian cycles began with innovations, such as the introduction of more productive strains of rice in southern China or improved horse collars in Europe that allowed horses to pull plows that cut deeper and turned tougher soils. As productivity-raising innovations spread, populations increased, which increased demand and encouraged economic activity, expanded the area being farmed, and increased supplies of human and animal energy. Such periods of growth normally stimulated commercial activity through exchange networks, and encouraged the growth of towns, building, and even artistic and literary activity.

But the booms always ended in a crash. Populations would grow faster than available resources; the land would be overused, leading to famines; towns would become more polluted, and eventually levels of health would begin to decline. Faced with declining resources, states would return to the familiar strategy of seizing resources from neighbors through war, and the brutality and devastation caused by warfare would reduce production in many areas and spread diseases and death. The source of the Malthusian cycles that dominated human history in the Agrarian era can be found in the slow rates of innovation throughout the era.

In the rest of this chapter, we will trace how, during two great Malthusian cycles, the three drivers of innovation we have identified began to increase in importance, first in the Afro-Eurasian world zone, and then throughout the world. The first Malthusian cycle, which we can call the *postclassical cycle,* began well before 1000 CE in Afro-Eurasia after the fall of the great classical empires. It lasted until the crash of the mid-fourteenth century associated with the devastating pandemic known as the Black Death. The second cycle, the early modern cycle, began in the fourteenth century and lasted almost until 1700.

The Postclassical Malthusian Cycle: Before 1350 CE

In the centuries before 1350, there was significant growth in many different areas, above all in the largest world zone, Afro-Eurasia. Innovation was not the only cause of expansion. Global climates were generally warmer between 800 CE and about 1200 CE, and in many regions, warmer climates meant more rainfall and increased production of foodstuffs and other agricultural products. This was particularly true in more marginal regions at the edges of the major civilizations. But new technologies also stimulated growth. For example, new crops appeared in the Islamic world, at the heart of the Eurasian world. Sorghum and cotton (originally from Africa) and citrus fruits (originally from Southeast Asia) spread widely, increasing output (sorghum often replaced millet because it was tougher and more productive), and expanding textile production.

During the long upswing of the postclassical Malthusian cycle, population growth stimulated urbanization and encouraged the cultivation of new lands, particularly in frontier regions such as eastern Europe and southern and western China. Farming expanded in Scandinavia, where population growth helped drive the astonishing migrations of the Vikings. With increasing rural prosperity, cities multiplied and grew in Europe, around the Mediterranean, in Africa south of the Sahara, in India, Southeast Asia, and China. This is the era of Angkor Wat in Cambodia, the Gothic cathedrals of Europe, and the Mali Empire of West Africa.

In China, growth was particularly marked in the south. In 750 CE, 60 percent of China's population lived in China's northern regions; by 1000 that percentage had fallen to 40 percent and China's center of gravity had shifted south. Populations increased in Africa south of the Sahara, rising from about 11 million to 22 million during the first millennium CE, as Bantu migrations spread iron metallurgy and the cultivation of bananas southward. In Europe north of the Mediterranean, and in Southeast Asia, population growth encouraged urbanization and the emergence of new regional states such as England and France. Finally, in the decades after 1200, the Mongols, from a base in the steppes north of China, created the largest land empire that had ever existed and eventually went on to conquer Iran and China.

In the Americas, there may have been renewed population growth both in Mesoamerica and the Andes as a result of warmer climates after 800 CE. As we saw in Chapter 9, new state systems emerged in Mesoamerica, first in the tenth century among the Toltecs. New state systems also appeared in the Andean region in Bolivia (near Lake Titicaca) and farther north, on the coast of Peru (the Chimor state from the tenth century).

During this long, and apparently global upswing all three of the drivers of innovation and Collective Learning described in the previous section seem to have become more influential.

Expanding Exchange Networks

Exchange networks expanded as a result of population growth, which encouraged the colonization of regions away from, or at the edge of, older regions of settlement.

In the centuries before 1000 CE the settlement of Polynesia was completed with the occupation of Hawaii and Easter Island, probably around 500 CE, and of New Zealand and nearby islands, probably in about 1000 CE. Although some of the most remote islands, including Easter Island, became disconnected from Polynesian exchange networks, exchanges continued between the islands dominated by the Lapita culture in the western Pacific. We know this because archaeologists have traced the movement of obsidian through trade routes extending over 2,800 miles (4,500 kilometers). The spread of sweet potatoes from South America to western Polynesia suggests that there must also have been some contact between South America and the islands of the eastern Pacific. Meanwhile, Hawaii reestablished contacts with Tahiti in the twelfth and thirteenth centuries.

In the Americas, the Toltec city of Tula exchanged goods over large areas of Mesoamerica, including the Maya city of Chichen Itza 930 miles (1,500 kilometers) to its south. The spread of Mesoamerican corn and influences (including the famous ball game) northward along the Mississippi River shows that there were at least intermittent exchanges between Mexico and lands far to the north in what is today the United States. In the Andes region, the great diversity of resources produced at different altitudes encouraged exchanges from the coastal regions, with their rich fishing resources, up into the highlands where corn, coca, and potatoes were grown and llamas and alpacas were herded. What is striking about the exchange networks of the Americas, though, is the absence of significant exchanges between the two major populated regions—the Andes and Mesoamerica.

In the North Atlantic, two ancient migratory currents converged in about 1000 CE to briefly link the world's largest world zones, the Americas and Afro-Eurasia. Warmer climates may help explain the migrations to Greenland of a whale- and seal-hunting people known today as the Thule Inuit. They traveled in kayaks or the much larger *umiaks*, which could carry up to 10 people along with their stores. Warmer climates and favorable ocean currents may help explain the success of Vikings in migrating from Scandinavia to Iceland by the 860s (where they had been preceded by Irish monks), and then, in the tenth century to Greenland and Newfoundland. Their Atlantic expeditions had limited consequences because they proved unprofitable. The Newfoundland colony could not be defended against local inhabitants; and by the fourteenth century, colder climates made Greenland more or less unfarmable.

Elsewhere, the Vikings were more successful. They raided Ireland, Britain, France, and the Mediterranean, first in search of booty and eventually in search of new lands to settle, creating Viking kingdoms from Normandy to Ireland and Sicily. To the east, Viking traders explored the river systems of Rus (today's Russia), trading honey, amber, furs, and other northern goods for the silver and craft products of Central Asia and Byzantium. We know this because Central Asian silver coins have turned up in large quantities in hoards that reach from Central Asia to Scandinavia. The activities of the Vikings were part of a larger pulse of expansion and colonization that shaped the history of all of Europe in this era. East European farmers colonized underpopulated lands to their east, and in the Netherlands land was reclaimed from the sea.

In Africa, trans-Saharan trade boomed. By 800 CE, Muslim merchants were traveling regularly across the Sahara in camel caravans. South of the Sahara they reached emerging states such as Ghana, between the Niger and Senegal Rivers, which Muslim writers first described in the eighth century as a "land of gold." Many goods were traded along these routes, including West African ivory and slaves, in return for horses, cotton, metal goods, and salt. But it was Ghana's gold that really stimulated trans-Saharan trade, both northward toward Morocco and eastward, through the steppes of the southern Sahara toward Cairo. West Africa was at the time the richest source of gold in the whole of western Eurasia. The rulers of Ghana converted to Islam, probably by 1000 CE. In the early thirteenth century, they were replaced by a new imperial system, the Mali Empire, founded by a warrior king known as Sundiata (1230–55). In 1324–25, emperor Musa (r. 1312–37) of Mali made a famous pilgrimage to Cairo, which brought so much gold that the Arabic historian al-Umari reported a sharp fall in the local price of gold.

Trade expanded in the Indian Ocean during the first millennium CE as navigators learned to make use of the region's monsoon winds (Map 10.1). Arabic traders were active along the eastern coast of Africa, where they established trading settlements and set up merchant colonies. Unwittingly, they

MAP 10.1 Indian Ocean trade networks, 600 to 1600 CE. The Indian Ocean sea routes and the land routes of the Silk Roads combined to make the Afro-Eurasian world zone by far the best connected of all the world zones.

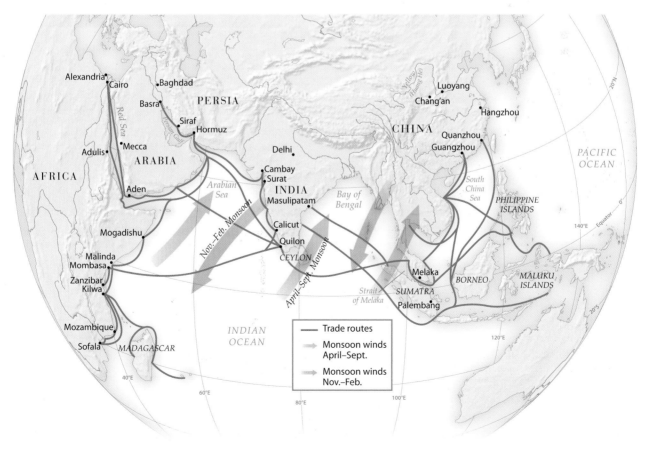

even began to create a new language, Swahili, which combined elements from Arabic, Persian, and Bantu languages. In the eighth century, Javanese ships began raiding the shores of Cambodia and Vietnam. There are depictions of some of these voyages in the remarkable temple of Borobudur in Java, which was built in the eighth and ninth centuries with profits from local trading systems. At about the same time, using the outrigger craft first developed in Southeast Asia and used for the great Polynesian migrations, migrants from the islands of modern Indonesia traveled right across the Indian Ocean to settle the island of Madagascar.

By the ninth century, Muslim traders were traveling regularly from the Persian Gulf to China and Korea, and a large Muslim trading colony was settled in Canton. The trading system of the Indian Ocean was dominated by small trading city-states dotted along the ocean shores from East Africa to the Middle East to India and Southeast Asia, rather than by great empires. Curiously, this meant that commercial competition in this region was genuine; rarely was it distorted by the activities of powerful rulers who could monopolize goods or trade routes.

These networks also helped spread Islam throughout much of the region. By doing so they began to create a common cultural zone within which traders could find similar financial and commercial practices (including long-range networks of credit), legal regulations, and forms of worship. The requirement to make the pilgrimage to Mecca encouraged travel and cultural exchange throughout the Muslim zone, and Arabic emerged as a common language for merchants throughout the Indian Ocean. This rich, variegated, and vibrant cultural world was described vividly in the literature of the time, including the *One Thousand and One Nights*. From around 1000 CE, Chinese merchants began to enter the trade at the eastern end as Song China, increasingly cut off from the land-based Silk Roads by its northern rivals, the Jurchen and the Xia-Xia, began to invest in trade through the Indian Ocean. Porcelain exports expanded because fragile porcelains could be transported more easily by sea than by land.

By 1000 CE, the Indian Ocean networks had begun to link the economies of China, India, Persia, Africa, and the Mediterranean into the world's richest and most active trading system.

There was also increased travel and trade along the Silk Roads (Map 10.2). This was a result of several factors, including the growing interest of local rulers that supplied protection and often (sometimes with the support

MAP 10.2 The Silk Roads. Exchanges through the Silk Roads and the Indian Ocean combined to make the Afro-Eurasian world zone by far the best connected of all the world zones.

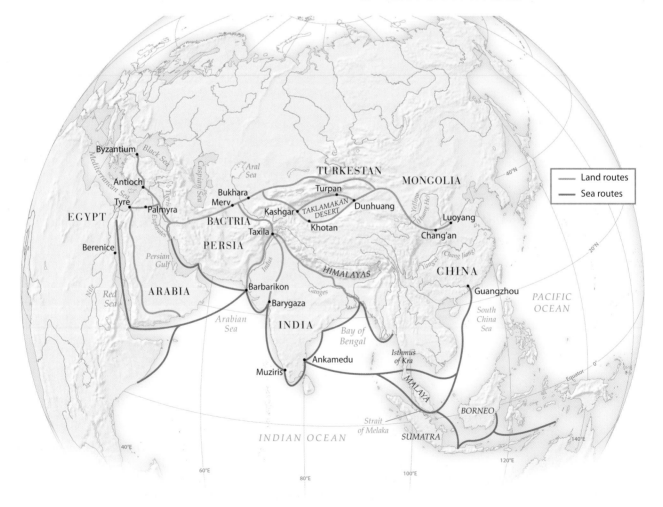

of religious charities) built caravanserais (roadside inns) where travelers could rest and resupply. Along the land routes of the Silk Roads, the Persian language established itself as the main language of commerce and trade. In the thirteenth century, the rulers of the Mongol Empire engaged in trade and protected trade routes all the way from China to the Mediterranean. As a result, more or less for the first time, merchants and travelers began to travel along the entire route from the Mediterranean to China and back again.

Best known of these trans-Eurasian travelers is the Italian merchant, Marco Polo, who left for China with his uncles in 1271, stayed for 17 years, and returned by sea through the Indian Ocean (Map 10.3). By the early fourteenth century, Italian publishers were printing handbooks for merchants planning on traveling to China, similar to the navigational guides that were already common for the Indian Ocean. We know of at least one comparable journey in the opposite direction, taken by a Turkic Nestorian Christian monk from north China, Rabban Sauma, in the late thirteenth century. Rabban Sauma would eventually visit Rome and Paris as an ambassador of the Mongol ruler of Persia, the Il-Khan.

Janet Abu-Lughod has shown that in the mid-thirteenth century, when the Mongol Empire was at its height, much of Afro-Eurasia was linked together by these vast and overlapping exchange networks (Map 10.4). By the thirteenth century all of Eurasia and large parts of Southeast Asia and Africa were joined within a series of linked exchange networks. This was the largest connected network of human societies on Earth and the largest that had ever existed.

Improvements in Communications and Transportation

The expansion of exchange networks was driven in part by improvements in communications and transportation technologies. The invention in China and eventual spread through the Muslim world of paper and papermaking cheapened the storage and dissemination of information. Wood block printing made it possible for Chinese governments to disseminate information on irrigation and agricultural improvements.

There were also important innovations in transportation. In China, canal locks were built for the first time in the twelfth century, improving transportation along China's extensive canal systems, which linked the economies of the south and the north. The compass made navigation easier away from land or under cloudy skies. Used in China from the eleventh century, by the thirteenth century the compass was in use throughout the Indian Ocean system and even in the Mediterranean, where it became possible for the first time to navigate with confidence away from the coasts. In the north, the Viking longboat could travel fast both at sea and along rivers, and when necessary it could be carried by portage from river to river. In China boat-building technologies also advanced with the construction of large junks equipped with stern-post rudders and watertight bulkheads.

Several innovations improved the importance of horses in farming regions. Fodder crops such as oats (in Europe) or alfalfa made it cheaper to feed horses. Improved horse collars that gripped the shoulders rather than the throat, allowing horses to pull much harder, were invented in China and spread through Europe from the end of the first millennium CE. They increased the value of horses both for plowing and (after the invention of improved wagons with brakes and front axles that could turn) in transportation. Nailed horseshoes were introduced in both China and Europe from the eleventh century, increasing the endurance of horses and widening the range of surfaces on which they could be used. Better feed and improved breeds increased the load horses could pull and reduced the cost of land transportation, which stimulated long-distance trade. In Roman times, transporting heavy goods 100 miles (160 kilometers) increased their cost by 100 percent; by the thirteenth century it increased costs by only 33 percent.

Increasing Markets and Commerce

Market activity increased in many parts of the world, in both urban centers and rural regions. In the Muslim lands, where commerce had always enjoyed higher status than in other agrarian civilizations, partly because the prophet Muhammad had himself been a merchant, governments were usually keen to support trade and benefited financially from it. By the tenth century CE, Cairo and Alexandria had become the major trading centers for goods traded between the Indian Ocean and the Mediterranean. In China, rulers of the Song Dynasty, after being expelled from northern China in 1125, came under the influence of the more commercialized southern regions and began to take more interest in commerce than most earlier dynasties, which had shared a traditional Confucian disdain for merchants (Map 10.5). To pay for conflicts with their northern rivals, the Manchurian Jurchen, the Song began to seek revenues from commerce, so they encouraged foreign trade by opening up new ports to foreign traders and by expanding the supply of money. Market activity began to reach deeper into the economy, encouraging specialization among peasant farmers and investment in improved farming and irrigation methods.

In Song China, the combination of state support for commercial activity and rapid economic growth and commercialization at many different levels of society led to remarkable innovation in the eleventh, twelfth, and thirteenth centuries. In the eleventh century, iron was produced in quantities that would not be exceeded anywhere in the world before the Industrial Revolution. Government factories mass-produced thousands of suits of armor. Copper production rose rapidly, and both the Song and the Jurchen began to use gunpowder in warfare. Paper money was issued in large quantities, and attempts were even made to mechanize the production of silk, anticipating innovations that would not really take off until the Industrial Revolution, over 700 years later.

In other parts of Afro-Eurasia, commercialization was more spontaneous, stimulated by rapid economic growth and the relative independence of merchants. The number and size of cities expanded in all the more densely settled

MAP 10.3 Travels across Afro-Eurasia. The Mongol Empire made it possible for almost the first time for individuals such as Marco Polo (thirteenth century) and Ibn Battuta (fourteenth century) to travel the entire length of Afro-Eurasia and helped bind the different parts of the Afro-Eurasian world zone closer together.

Mongol Empires

Marco Polo's travels

Ibn Battuta's travels

EUROPE

Moscow

Venice
Genoa

Black Sea

Constantinople

Baghdad

Mediterranean Sea

Jerusalem

Siraf

Cairo

Caspian Sea

Aral

Fez

SAHARA

Persian Gulf

Medina

Mecca

Red Sea

Timbuktu

MALI

AFRICA

Aden

Mogadishu

Malindi
Mombasa

Kilwa

ATLANTIC
OCEAN

MADAGASCAR

ASIA

Karakorum

Khanbaliq

Yellow (Huang He)

Yellow Sea

Sea of Japan

Yangzi

(Chang Jiang)

Hangzhou

East China Sea

Quanzhou

Guangzhou

Delhi

Indus

Ganges

INDIA

abian Sea

Bay of Bengal

PACIFIC OCEAN

Tropic of Cancer

CEYLON

South China Sea

ALDIVE IS.

Melaka

SUMATRA

Equator

JAVA

INDIAN OCEAN

Tropic of Capricorn

AUSTRALIA

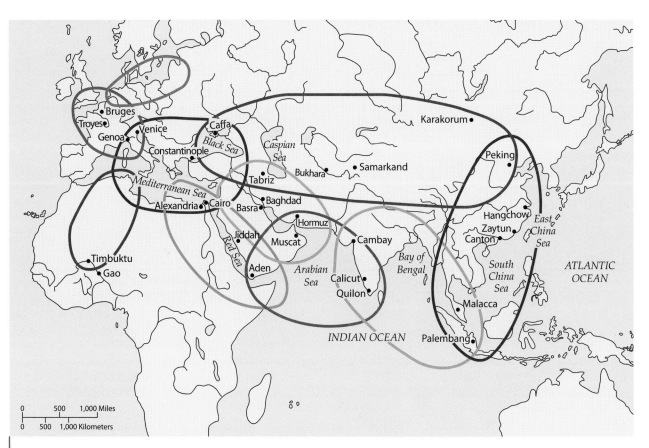

MAP 10.4 Janet Abu-Lughod's map of the thirteenth-century world-system. Each circuit represents a region of vigorous, interconnected trade networks. Note how networks in different parts of Afro-Eurasia seem to be coming into closer and closer contact with each other.

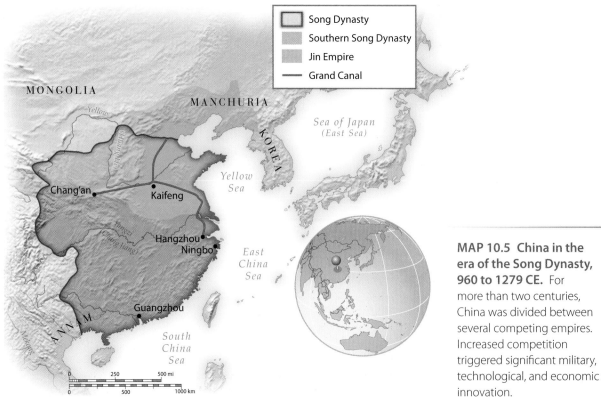

MAP 10.5 China in the era of the Song Dynasty, 960 to 1279 CE. For more than two centuries, China was divided between several competing empires. Increased competition triggered significant military, technological, and economic innovation.

Legend:
- Song Dynasty
- Southern Song Dynasty
- Jin Empire
- Grand Canal

regions of Eurasia. In 1400, the world's largest city was probably Nanjing, followed by Vijayanagar in southern India, then by Cairo and Paris. During the Song and Yuan Dynasties, China became the most highly urbanized region on Earth, with 9 of the 25 largest cities in the world in 1400. Particularly striking in the Mediterranean region and the Indian Ocean was the growing power of merchant city-states such as Venice and Genoa, whose commercial reach and military power enabled them to trade on almost equal terms with the great empires of the Muslim and Christian worlds. There is also growing evidence of peasants bringing goods to market or buying luxury goods in many parts of Afro-Eurasia. Peasants were often driven to markets by increasing taxes and, as populations grew, by land shortages that forced families to seek new sources of income by selling handicraft goods or by sending family members to seek wage labor in the towns.

The Fourteenth-Century Crisis

Sadly, as had happened so many times before, the long boom was followed by a crash. Climates began to cool in the fourteenth century CE, and famines became more common. The great European famines of 1315–17 may have killed off 15 percent of Europe's population. Most devastating of all, however, was the Black Death, a plague that spread from east to west across Eurasia's trade networks, beginning in the 1330s. In many regions the Black Death killed up to a third of the population. The exact nature of the Black Death is disputed today; it is no longer certain that it was the same as the modern bubonic plague. But whatever its source, it is clear that it spread rapidly through Eurasia for two main reasons. First, expanded exchange networks encouraged the circulation of diseases as well as goods, and they did so across entire continents and civilizations. Second, many regions of Eurasia lacked immunity to the plague. This was a sign of the limits of earlier exchange networks. In other words, the damage inflicted by the Black Death is itself powerful evidence that links between different parts of Eurasia were much more extensive and more important in this period than they had ever been before.

The Early Modern Malthusian Cycle: 1350 to 1700 CE

The Black Death left most of the more populous regions of Afro-Eurasia with fewer people, cities, towns, and villages; deserted farmlands; and shrunken economies. The reduction in farmlands was so sharp that William Ruddiman argues it led to a significant reduction in levels of atmospheric carbon dioxide as forests reappeared in what had once been flourishing frontier villages and began to absorb more carbon dioxide.

However, as had happened so many times before, growth resumed over the next century or two, starting a new Malthusian cycle that would last until the seventeenth

century. During the expansionary phase of this cycle, there would be important new developments in all three of the drivers of Collective Learning that we have identified: expanding trade networks, improved technologies of communications and transportation, and increased commercialization.

For the first time in human history, exchange networks would expand to embrace the entire world, forming the largest networks that had ever existed. Expanding exchange networks were energized by renewed population growth and by new technologies, including improved forms of transportation (particularly in deep-sea navigation) and communications (particularly printing). Finally, markets boomed as increasing competition between states and expanded commercial opportunities within the world's first global markets encouraged merchants and their overlords to seek new ways of making money. Commercialization was particularly striking in those societies most tightly integrated into the emerging global exchange networks.

Of the three crucial drivers of innovation, the most important in this era was the remarkable expansion of exchange networks. But this was so closely linked to changes in transportation technologies and increasing commercialization that we will not try in this section to treat the three drivers separately.

Creating the First Global Exchange Networks: Before 1500 CE

The period from 1350 to 1700 CE witnessed the most momentous expansion in exchange networks in the entire history of humanity. This is when humans became, for the first time, a truly global species, as societies in all the world zones were stitched into a single network of exchange, larger and more varied than any that had ever existed before.

Before 1500, renewed growth in the period after the Black Death stimulated trade and travel in many parts of the world (Map 10.6). Rulers and elites often played an active role in this process. For a brief period in the early fifteenth century, Chinese governments of the Ming Dynasty began sending out huge fleets of ships to show the flag and establish diplomatic relations with the countries of Southeast Asia, the Indian subcontinent, the Middle East, and East Africa. Beginning in 1405, Emperor Yongle (r. 1403–1424) launched seven overseas expeditions that ended only in 1433. They were led by a Muslim eunuch, Admiral Zheng He. His first fleet included 317 ships and 28,000 armed men. His flagship was one of the largest ships ever built, with four decks and a length of 400 feet (120 meters). (See Figure 10.3.)

The organizational, financial, and technological skills that made these expeditions possible would surely have allowed China to reach the Americas if there had been the incentive or the knowledge of deep-sea winds and currents needed to do so. But, with the rich markets of the Indian Ocean so close, few dangerous opponents (except in the north), and huge wealth within China itself, what incentive was there to brave dangerous and contrary winds by sending ships around Africa into the Atlantic or due east into

MAP 10.6 Chinese and European voyages of exploration, 1405 to 1498. In the fifteenth century, major voyages of exploration were launched from both ends of the Afro-Eurasian world zone. All were aimed at reaching the rich trade routes of the Indian Ocean. This map shows why it made sense for some European navigators to try to reach the Indian Ocean by sailing westward across the Atlantic, and it was those attempts that led Columbus to the Americas.

EUROPE

ice
me

SAHARA

AFRICA

ASIA

Yellow
(Huang He)
Yellow
Sea

Indus

Delhi

Persian
Gulf

Siraf

Mecca

Red Sea

Aden

Arabian
Sea

Calicut

CEYLON

MALDIVE IS.

Mogadishu

Mombasa

Kilwa

Sofala

MADAGASCAR

INDIAN OCEAN

Ganges

INDIA

Bay of
Bengal

MALAY
PENINSULA

Strait
Of Melaka

CHINA

Kangzi
(Chang Jiang)

Hangzhou

Nanjing

Quanzhou

Guangzhou

East
China
Sea

PACIFIC
OCEAN

South
China
Sea

Melaka

SUMATRA

JAVA

AUSTRALIA

on the brink of a threshold

Zheng He's ship
(c. 400 ft., or 120 m, long)

Columbus's *Nina*
(c. 85 ft., or 26 m, long)

FIGURE 10.3 Zheng He's treasure ship (400 feet or 120 meters) compared to Columbus's ship, the *Nina*. Between 1405 and 1433, the Chinese government sent out a series of naval expeditions through the Indian Ocean. They used some of the largest and most sophisticated ships ever built. The expeditions were commanded by a Muslim eunuch, Zheng He.

the apparently empty Pacific? How limited the incentives were became clear when, after Emperor Yongle's death, his successors, Emperors Hongxi and Xuande, abandoned the expeditions that had cost too much and diverted resources and attention from China's endangered northern frontiers. In truth, China had gained little of political, economic, or military value from them, so the decision made sense.

On large and small scales, similar forms of expansion could be found in many different parts of the world, including the Americas, where the mighty Aztec Empire was built mainly in the fifteenth century CE, at the same time as the far more extensive Inca Empire was being assembled in the Andean region. In Africa, the Mali Empire expanded its power and reach as it established trading relations with communities in the tropical lands of West Africa, but also with Morocco and Egypt. The great Muslim traveler, Ibn Battuta, would visit Mali between 1352 and 1354, after years of travel through the Islamic world, which took him to Mecca, to the Golden Horde and Central Asia, to India, and perhaps to China (see Map 10.3).

In the Mediterranean, the Ottoman Empire was founded in the late thirteenth century when a ruler known as Osman appeared in the complex political and military cauldron of Anatolia. In the decades after the Black Death, his successors, the Ottomans, seized parts of the Balkans and began

to build a highly disciplined army of "Janissaries": soldiers captured as children, mainly in the Christian Balkans, who had, as a result, no ties of loyalty to anyone but the Ottoman state. In 1453 the Ottomans would capture Constantinople; early in the sixteenth century they would conquer Egypt, Arabia, and much of Mesopotamia; and soon Ottoman fleets were patrolling the waters of the western Indian Ocean. This gave them monopoly control over the lucrative trades in spices from Southeast Asia. By the early sixteenth century, the Ottoman Empire dominated the Mediterranean world and had become one of the world's great powers.

Europe lay at the edge of the great trading networks of Afro-Eurasia, well away from the superpowers of China, India, and the Ottoman Empire. After the Black Death, Europe was a region of highly competitive medium-sized states whose rulers were often sufficiently cash-strapped to look benignly on commercial activities that might turn a profit. Markets and capitalism flourished in such an environment. In the Mediterranean, the most active traders were Italian city-states, above all Genoa and Venice. Merchants from both cities traded through the Middle East and in the Black Sea region and also in the growing markets of northern Europe, and their commercial wealth allowed them to pay for powerful armies and navies. After the rise of the Ottoman Empire, the Venetians managed to continue trading throughout the Eastern Mediterranean, but Genoese merchants were forced to look westward, toward western Europe and the Atlantic.

Several factors—including missionary zeal, knowledge of Mali gold, growing demand for fish in Europe, and the Ottoman blockade of Eastern Mediterranean trade routes to the Indian Ocean—encouraged western European rulers and entrepreneurs and their (often) Italian financiers to explore the waters of the Atlantic Ocean more energetically than ever before. The first small-scale forays into the Atlantic and down the coastline of Africa encouraged modest improvements in ship design (such as the use of triangular sails allowing navigation close to the wind), naval gunnery, and navigational technologies, mostly based on technologies borrowed from other regions. The result was the highly maneuverable Portuguese ships developed in the mid-fifteenth century and known as *caravels*.

By the 1340s, Portuguese navigators had landed on the Canary Islands, but in the fifteenth century, Castilian entrepreneurs seized the islands. In the Canaries, which had their own indigenous populations, they found modest commercial opportunities in slaving and the sale of local products such as dyes, as well as in fishing and supplying other ships plying the Atlantic shores. By the 1380s, Iberian and Majorcan navigators knew also of other Atlantic island groups, the Madeiras and the Azores. Discovery of the Azores shows that many navigators already understood that, though it was easy to travel southwest before the wind to the Canaries, the best way back to Spain, Portugal, or the Mediterranean was to head northward, deep into the Atlantic Ocean in search of westerly winds, and let them carry you back home.

From the 1420s, Portuguese navigators renewed their attempts to reach the source of West African gold to cut out Muslim intermediaries; and in the 1450s, a Genoese ship sponsored by Prince Henry of Portugal sailed up the Gambia and Senegal Rivers to the Mali Empire. As more ships followed, trading in gold, ivory, pepper, and sometimes slaves, gold caravans were diverted from the tortuous Sahara route to the West African coast, where Portuguese traders met them. In 1482 a Portuguese fort was established on the West African coast and soon much of Mali's trade was being diverted south, as Portuguese merchants traded textiles and weapons for gold, cotton, ivory, and slaves. Meanwhile, in the 1450s Portuguese settlers backed by Genoese investors began to set up sugar plantations on Madeira, which used slave labor and soon turned a healthy profit. Sugar plantations also appeared in the Canary Islands. These plantations provided models that would eventually be used in the far larger plantations of the Americas.

The modest success of these early commercial experiments explains why eventually European mariners learned how to navigate the wind patterns and currents of the Atlantic. In 1492, the Spanish rulers Ferdinand and Isabella backed an expedition that hoped to reach Asia's rich markets by sailing west, thereby getting around the Ottoman monopoly on access to the Indian Ocean. The expedition was headed by a Genoese sailor, Christopher Columbus. Columbus sailed via the Canaries, reached the Bahamas on October 12, 1492, and

then toured much of the Caribbean for the next few months. On his return, he claimed to have reached Asia.

Five years later, an English-backed expedition led by an Italian, Giovanni Caboto (known in English as John Cabot), sailed from Bristol to Newfoundland, a trip that would soon lead to the exploitation of the rich fisheries of the northeastern American coast. In 1498, a Portuguese expedition led by Vasco da Gama reached India and, though it had few goods that interested local merchants or rulers, it still brought back a profitable cargo, mainly of pepper and cinnamon. The cargo was profitable because Vasco da Gama had bypassed the commercial intermediaries of the Ottoman Empire and purchased his goods at very low prices; Indian pepper, for example, cost 1/20th of the price at which it was sold in Europe. The vast commercial possibilities of trade in the Indian Ocean that this voyage revealed caught the attention of the cash-strapped Portuguese government and of other potential investors.

In 1519, Portuguese navigator Ferdinand Magellan, serving the Spanish crown, sailed south of the Americas and crossed the Pacific. Magellan was killed in the Philippines in 1521, but his deputy, Juan Sebastian del Cano, returned to Seville in 1522 with just one of the original five ships and a tiny group of survivors, having completed the first known circumnavigation of the world. But it seems that del Cano and his shipmates were not quite the first humans to circumnavigate the world, for they had taken with them a Malay slave, Panglima Awang, who had acted as an interpreter before being returned home.[1] Just as Yuri Gagarin was the first human to circumnavigate the globe in space, Panglima Awang seems to have been the first human to circumnavigate it by sea.

Almost accidently, and with little understanding of the consequences of their actions, European mariners and their commercial and governmental backers, though situated at the very edge of Afro-Eurasia, had created the first global exchange networks in human history. Eventually, this would give European merchants and rulers access to huge potential profits. Above all, they found many new opportunities for global **arbitrage:** buying goods cheaply in one part of the world, and selling them at much higher prices somewhere else. Over the next few centuries these vastly expanded and remarkably diverse networks would create the first world economy. They would also place Europe and the Atlantic region at the center of the world's first global exchange networks, enriching Europe and making it the best-connected region on Earth.

After 1500 CE: An Emerging Global Exchange Network

By linking societies throughout the world into a single system, European navigators, backed by European governments, triggered a rearrangement of trade networks, of intellectual exchanges, of wealth and power, indeed of the entire geography of global exchange networks. The full significance of these changes would become apparent only several centuries later. As Karl Marx wrote in the nineteenth century in *The Communist Manifesto*: "World trade and the world market date from the sixteenth century, and from then on the modern history of Capital starts to unfold."

New Commercial Opportunities

European governments and merchants soon found new ways of exploiting their central position in the world's first global exchange networks.

In the world's richest trade system, that of the Indian Ocean, Europeans had few goods that interested local merchants. But they mostly encountered small- to medium-sized trading polities or city-states, and soon found that their gunpowder weapons could sometimes make up in force what their goods lacked in quality. Within a few decades, Portuguese fleets had built forts at crucial points in the networks of the Indian Ocean, such as at Kilwa on the coast of East Africa, or at Hormuz on the Persian Gulf, Goa (captured in 1510), and eventually at Malacca in the East Indies. From these strong points the Portuguese cut themselves a modest but valuable slice of the regional spice trade, because now they could bypass the Ottoman intermediaries who had monopolized control of trade from the Indian Ocean to the Mediterranean.

Early in the seventeenth century, the Dutch and then the English, using equally brutal tactics but with greater human and financial resources, began to oust the Portuguese from the Indian Ocean trade networks. The Dutch East India Company was the world's first great trading corporation, and it showed the many advantages of combining government support, military power, and commercial canniness. After overthrowing their Spanish overlords in the late sixteenth century, the Dutch would eventually displace the Portuguese in Southeast Asia and Indonesia, while the British would displace them in India. But until the eighteenth century, even these more aggressive colonial empires had only a limited impact on the trade networks of the Asian region.

In the Americas, European colonizers arrived not just as traders but also as conquerors. During the sixteenth and seventeenth centuries, the Spanish and Portuguese created huge American empires. In short and brutal campaigns, in which they often allied with the enemies of local empires such as the Aztecs, the Spanish seized the heartlands of the old American civilizations in Mesoamerica and the Andes region, while the Portuguese began to build new colonies in Brazil, where there were no large state structures to resist them.

Why they were able to conquer these lands with such apparent ease is one of the central questions of the era. The answers all have to do with the differences that had accumulated between the major world zones. The Spanish had a temporary military edge through their use of horses and gunpowder technology, though indigenous troops soon acquired both horses and guns. The Spanish had a political edge insofar as they operated under the brutal military and political rules of Europe's constantly warring states, and felt free from the moral constraints of the societies they were invading. Both Hernan Cortes in Mexico and Pisarro in Peru succeeded in part by capturing and massacring the leaders of their opponents, breaking all the diplomatic and moral rules of the societies they had entered. Finally, and perhaps most important of all, Europeans succeeded because they brought with them new diseases, to which the populations of the Americas lacked immunity. Both the Aztec and Inca Empires suffered terrible plagues during the wars of conquest, plagues brought unwittingly to the Americas by the Spanish.

From the seventeenth century, merchants and entrepreneurs from other European countries, above all Holland, France, and Britain, began to carve out empires of their own in the Caribbean and in North America.

Global Arbitrage

By the middle of the sixteenth century, Europeans, beginning with the Spaniards, had begun to realize that the real advantage of their new position at the center of global networks lay not just in exploiting particular parts of those networks, but in the arbitrage profits they could make by moving goods between the different world zones. They had begun to discover the huge commercial possibilities of the world's first global trading system.

Two vital elements in this emerging system of global arbitrage were Peruvian silver and China's rapidly expanding economy. In the fifteenth century, as Chinese populations grew and commerce increased, Chinese governments needed more silver for coinage. At first, they found the silver they needed in Japan. But by the sixteenth century, as populations grew, fed in part by the introduction of American crops such as corn, sweet potatoes, and peanuts, demand began to exceed supply. The Chinese government began to demand that taxes be paid in silver, the relative value of silver rose, and Japan could no longer satisfy Chinese demand.

Meanwhile, across the Pacific the Spanish, after their conquest of the Inca Empire, had discovered a mountain of silver in the 1540s at Potosi, in modern Bolivia. They had already found much gold and silver in both Mexico and Peru, but this was wealth on an entirely new scale. The Spanish began exploiting the mines of Potosi using the forced labor of the local population (by taking over the traditional Inca system of forced labor known as the *mita*), and then they began to use slave laborers from Africa. Potosi expanded rapidly, and by 1600 it was one of the biggest cities in the world. And here, at last, Europeans found a commodity that really was in high demand in the rich markets of East Asia.

Silver was carried to Mexico where much of it was minted into Spanish pesos. From Mexico some silver was transported across the Atlantic where the Spanish government spent it largely on military operations designed to control the vast empires of the Hapsburg monarchs, Charles V and Philip II. As a result, it flowed into the hands of Spain's North European bankers who used much of it to fund trade with the Indian Ocean, from where much of it ended up in China. Another portion of the silver from Potosi was carried across the Pacific in the Manila galleons, where it was traded for Chinese silks, porcelains, and other goods in Spanish-controlled Manila. That silver, too, mostly ended up in China. Indeed, according to some estimates, 75 percent of the silver mined in the Americas between 1500 and 1800 eventually reached China.

The high price of silver in China and its low price in the Americas (low because there was so much of it, and because it was extracted using slave labor under the most brutal of conditions) drove the world's first global system of exchange and allowed the creation of the world's first global financial network. Dominating that system was the world's first global currency, the Mexican peso. In the 1540s, silver was worth twice as much in China as in Europe, while Chinese silks and porcelains were far cheaper (and of much better quality) than the equivalent European products. Here were opportunities for superprofits generated by global arbitrage on a massive scale.

The Atlantic Trading System

In the Atlantic region, where before 1492 there had been no exchanges at all, an entirely new exchange network emerged in what would eventually become a new global trading hub.

This system also depended on finding goods that could be produced cheaply in one region and sold at high prices elsewhere. Sugar was the first in a series of commodities that began to drive highly profitable trading systems. Slave labor on plantations meant sugar could be produced cheaply, yet there was also huge demand for it in Europe and the Americas, where the only other sweetener was honey.

In the fifteenth century, sugar plantations had appeared in the Mediterranean islands of Cyprus, Crete, and Sicily before being introduced to the newly conquered islands of the eastern Atlantic. Worked by slaves, these early plantations provided brutal but effective models of how the Americas might be exploited. Columbus, whose father-in-law owned a sugar plantation in the Canaries, brought sugar to Santo Domingo on his second trip. By the middle of the sixteenth century, the Portuguese had established sugar plantations in Brazil worked by African slaves. Then Dutch, British, and French interlopers introduced sugar into the Caribbean islands early in the seventeenth century. Successful sugar plantations required large amounts of cheap labor as well as considerable investment in refining equipment. The emerging African slave trade soon began to supply the needed labor, particularly where, as in the Caribbean, indigenous populations had largely died out after the introduction of European diseases. European investors supplied most of the capital, African slave traders provided the labor, and European consumers provided the demand. After the sixteenth century, the plantation system would spread to other products including tobacco, and, in the eighteenth century, cotton.

The plantation system linked Africa, Europe, and the Americas within a single exchange network. African slave traders sold slaves to European traders in return for metal goods, weapons, textiles, wines, and other European goods. As the slave trade expanded, it reshaped societies throughout Africa, creating warlike slave-raiding regimes, often armed with European weapons. European traders carried slaves to the Americas. The plantation economies of the Americas, particularly those of the Caribbean, were so specialized that they had to import food and clothing from Europe or the agricultural colonies of North America, while sugar, their main product, went north to be distilled into rum or sold as a sweetener in the rapidly growing cities of Europe. In this way there emerged a highly profitable triangular system of trade between Europe, the coasts of Africa, and the English colonies in the Caribbean and North America (Map 10.7). Merchants and investors in England and New England, plantation owners in the Caribbean, and slave traders in western, central, and southern Africa all made huge profits. The main victims were the millions of Africans who were traded as cargo and whose cheap labor made the plantations so profitable.

Ecological and Cultural Impacts of Global Exchange Networks

The coming together of the old world zones transformed the world ecologically and culturally as well as commercially.

The Columbian Exchange

As goods, ideas, wealth, people, technologies, religions, animals, plants, and disease pathogens began to travel between the different world zones, the world began to be reconnected ecologically. Alfred Crosby has termed this global exchange of animals, plants, and pathogens the "Columbian exchange." As he points out, the last time the world had been linked like this was 200 million years before, when all the major continents had been joined within Pangaea.

Sheep, cattle, horses, pigs, and goats now reached the Americas for the first time (though horses had been present in the Americas in the Paleolithic era only to be wiped out soon after the arrival of the first humans). The results were transformative. In North America, indigenous communities that had subsisted from farming or foraging took to hunting from horseback, creating the horse-riding cultures of the Plains Indians. The horse also revolutionized transportation and agriculture in the Americas as draft animals became available for the first time, and plow agriculture began to displace the hoe agriculture of the past. Imported cattle, pigs, and sheep multiplied in the wild or on huge estates, often displacing native species and degrading grasslands not used to such aggressive grazers. By the seventeenth century, there were 7 to 10 million hooved animals grazing lands that had not known such animals for many millennia. New crops arrived as well, including wheat, rye, and sugar.

The spread of European domesticates helped colonizers, mostly of European origin, to build a whole series of "neo-Europes": societies whose agriculture, governments, culture, and lifeways were modeled on those of Europe. These new societies appeared first in the Americas, but eventually they would appear in Australasia and parts of the Pacific and Africa as well.

The ecological traffic also went in the opposite direction: The Americas exported indigenous crops such as corn,

on the brink of a threshold

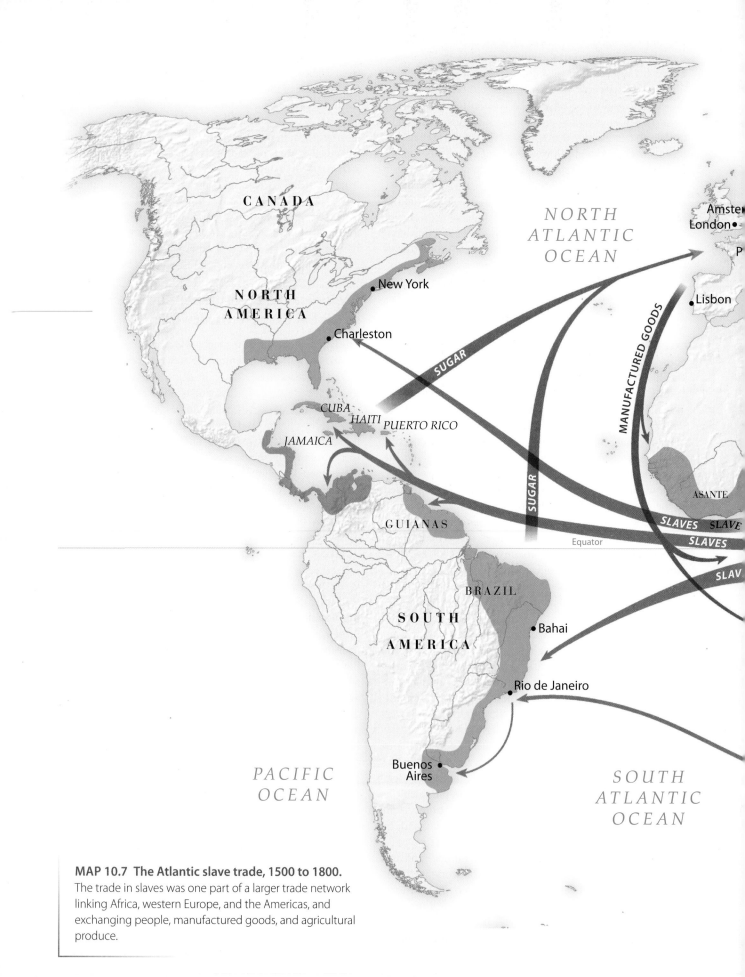

MAP 10.7 The Atlantic slave trade, 1500 to 1800.
The trade in slaves was one part of a larger trade network
linking Africa, western Europe, and the Americas, and
exchanging people, manufactured goods, and agricultural
produce.

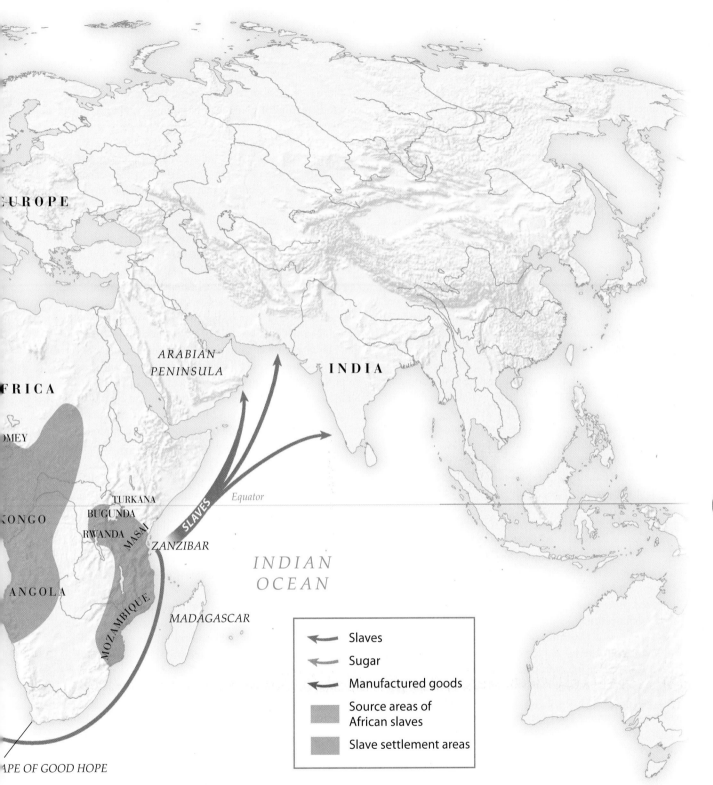

EUROPE

ARABIAN
PENINSULA

INDIA

AFRICA

OMEY

KONGO

TURKANA

BUGUNDA

RWANDA

MASAI

ZANZIBAR

SLAVES

Equator

ANGOLA

MOZAMBIQUE

MADAGASCAR

INDIAN
OCEAN

APE OF GOOD HOPE

←	Slaves
←	Sugar
←	Manufactured goods
▮	Source areas of African slaves
▮	Slave settlement areas

potatoes, tobacco, tomatoes, sweet potatoes, manioc, and squashes to Africa and Eurasia. Agrarian societies throughout the world gained access to a greater variety of crops that could be grown in those regions best suited for them. The result was a global agricultural revolution that would underpin population growth in the next two centuries. Stimulants such as coffee, tobacco, and sugar also became available to consumers throughout the world creating a diverse world of recreational drugs that had never existed before.

Diseases went global too, but here the traffic was mostly one-way. Just as diseases had once spread through the trade networks of Afro-Eurasia, decimating populations that lacked immunity to them, now they spread globally and the results were even more catastrophic. The main killers in the Americas were smallpox, measles, and typhus, diseases for which many European populations had developed some immunity. Their impact was devastating in all the smaller world zones, none of which had exchanged diseases and immunities on the scale of Afro-Eurasian societies. Predictably, the collapse was greatest where populations were densest and diseases could spread most rapidly. In the most populous regions of Mesoamerica some estimate that populations declined by 90 to 95 percent in the sixteenth century, and they fell by perhaps 70 percent in the Andes region. As populations fell, established social, political, and religious structures broke down, making it that much easier for the Spanish to create an empire modeled on their Iberian homelands, crops, and culture. The same story would be repeated many times over in the next few centuries. Afro-Eurasian diseases cleared spaces within which European colonizers could introduce their own crops, people, religions, governmental structures, and farming methods.

Cultural and Political Impacts: Toward Capitalism?

The emerging global exchange networks did not just transform Europe and the neo-Europes. Everywhere, the diffusion of crops, of gunpowder weapons, of new organizational methods, of improved agrarian techniques, of printing, and of commerce enhanced the power of governments. And as their power increased, governments did what they could to expand their populations and their revenues. Above all, they encouraged expansion, particularly into once marginal regions, to increase their populations, their wealth, their tax base, and ultimately their power in an increasingly competitive world arena. The expansion encouraged by governments meant an increase in human control of the land, forests, fishing grounds, lakes, and other species.

Perhaps the most spectacular example is the expansion of Muscovy. At the time of the Black Death, Muscovy was a Christian principality controlled by a Mongol state known today as the "Golden Horde." By 1700, Muscovy was the largest state in the world, controlling lands that reached from Poland in the east to the Pacific coasts of eastern Siberia. As Muscovy expanded, it encouraged peasant farmers and their masters to settle the forests and steppes that came under its control, and it also encouraged trade, above all in furs, a trade whose tentacles extended from Beijing through the forests of Siberia to the Eastern Mediterranean and western Europe and even into North America.

Everywhere, markets expanded in response to the many new opportunities created within the world's expanding trade networks. The tentacles of trade reached deep into Africa through the exchange of slaves for European manufactured goods, into the Americas through the fur trade and the creation of plantation economies, and into remote villages in Russia or Siberia or China, where government taxes forced peasants and even foragers to buy and sell locally produced goods. Expanding markets encouraged entrepreneurs to travel farther and farther in the search for furs (this was the engine that drove Russian expansion into Siberia and European expansion into much of North America), fish, whales, silver, sugar, or tobacco.

Such processes transformed environments throughout the world, leading to a sharp increase in human control of the biosphere. Colonizers settled and farmed lands never brought under the plow before, or hunted or fished on scales that threatened entire species, or moved species into environments they had never occupied before. Almost invariably, they did so with the backing of Afro-Eurasian governments and entrepreneurs keen to profit from new methods of mobilizing the resources of forests, steppes, rivers, and seas. As John Richards has shown, the two centuries after 1500 saw an increasingly frenetic exploitation of the resources of the biosphere in many different parts of the world. By applying old methods of exploitation in previously underexploited regions and with a new energy, humans as a species increased their control over the Earth's resources.

Strangely, information often traveled less well than commodities or people or diseases. Particularly in the old hub regions of Afro-Eurasia, the cultural impact of a unified world was limited for several centuries.

But in two areas the cultural impact of the first global exchanges was massive: in the Americas and in Europe. In the Americas, it was largely destructive, as cultural and political traditions were undermined and sometimes obliterated in the wake of disease and conquest. Traditional religious traditions were largely driven underground, though they would resurface in the form of an Americanized Catholicism shaped in distinctive ways by older American religious traditions.

Global exchange networks affected European societies mainly because Europe had became a sort of clearinghouse for information from all parts of the world. Because Europe lay at the center of these networks, it was there that flows of new information had their greatest impact. The discovery of the Americas, the sighting of new stars, and the discovery of peoples and cultures and religions and crops never known before and not mentioned in the Bible or in the works of classical authors created an intellectual earthquake that undermined trust in traditional knowledge. "New islands, new lands, new seas, new peoples; and, what is more, a new sky and new stars," wrote the Portuguese mathematician Pedro Nunes in 1537.[2] Among educated Europeans, growing skepticism toward traditional knowledge encouraged what were at first somewhat chaotic

FIGURE 10.4 Frontispiece of the *Great Instauration* by Francis Bacon. In his famous book, Bacon maintains that scientific discovery, like geographic discovery, depends on studying the world as it really is, not just what past scholars have said about the world. The quotation, from the book of Daniel in the Bible, reads: "Many shall pass to and fro, and knowledge shall increase."

attempts to assemble information in new ways that might provide firmer foundations for knowledge.

In the empiricism of the English scholar Francis Bacon (1561–1626), we find a sense that new knowledge gained through exploration and direct observation was the key to truth. Bacon saw the geographic discoveries of his time as a model of how science itself should proceed, not through the study of ancient texts, but rather by the exploration and careful study of the real world (Figure 10.4). In the philosophy of the French philosopher René Descartes (1596–1650), we find a sense of the importance of questioning established authorities so that knowledge could be reestablished on new and firmer foundations. Both the skepticism generated by new knowledge and the conviction that knowledge should be sought in exploration link the expanding intellectual horizons of Europe to what has traditionally been called the "scientific revolution" of the seventeenth century. Europe's position within the first global intellectual network may also explain a fundamental feature of that intellectual revolution: its universalism and its commitment to knowledge that was global in its reach and application and not bound by the traditions of any particular regional culture.

The World in 1700 CE

We have seen an increase in the importance of all three of the drivers of innovation described at the beginning of this chapter: exchange networks expanded, there were significant improvements in communications and transportation, and competitive markets became ever more important in much of the world. In principle, these changes should have led to sharp increases in innovation and profound global changes. Did they?

The Impact on Innovation

In fact, for a century or two the changes discussed in this chapter seemed to have surprisingly little impact on rates of technological innovation. Most of the innovations in shipping, gunnery, and navigation that European navigators used in the fifteenth and sixteenth century had been available for some time, and many, such as the triangular sail and the compass, had originated far from Europe and were widely used elsewhere. The Ottomans and the Mughals and the Russians had adapted gunpowder technologies equally successfully to other environments. The use of cannon was widespread throughout the Indian Ocean when the Portuguese arrived, and the galleys of the Mameluke and Ottoman fleets in the Indian Ocean carried cannon at their bows, though they could not match the coordinated cannon fire made possible by mounting cannon between the ribs and along the sides of Portuguese caravels.

Instead of revolutionary technological innovations, what we mainly see in this period is how expanding exchange networks allowed technologies and crops and organizational methods to spread more effectively from region to region, undergoing minor adaptations and adjustment as they did so. Joel Mokyr describes this as an "age of exposure effects, in which technological change primarily took the form of observing alien technologies and crops and transplanting them elsewhere."[3]

Perhaps the strongest claim for a real innovation concerns the European rediscovery of printing with metal movable type, by Johannes Gutenberg, in 1453. Printing with movable metal type was invented in Korea, and the oldest printed book using the technique is a Korean Buddhist text from 1377. But the technique flourished best in regions such as Europe with alphabetic scripts, where you needed only a small number of typefaces, so in Europe printing stimulated literacy and speeded up the circulation of information. By 1500 there were printing presses in 236 of Europe's towns, and 20 million books had been printed; a century later 10 times as many books had been printed. Printing began to turn Europe into a storehouse of global knowledge, as the Muslim world had once been a storehouse of knowledge within the Afro-Eurasian world zone. Printing would become a powerful driver of Collective Learning, first in Europe and then throughout the world.

Yet in this period we do not yet see a decisive increase in innovation. Global exchange networks allowed the spread and exploitation of technologies, crops, and business methods, many of which had been around for a long time in one part of the world or the other. In this way, the coming together of the different world zones in the sixteenth century accelerated technological diffusion. But the real explosion of new technologies would occur in the nineteenth century.

On the Brink of Change?

Sluggish innovation explains why, in 1700, much of the world still seemed very traditional. Most people were still peasants; most governments still thought of themselves in traditional terms and ruled in traditional ways; and energy sources had changed little since classical times. Nor had rates of innovation increased significantly.

In 1700, the fastest way of sending a message was still by courier; most bulk goods still traveled on horse- or ox-drawn wagons or by boat. Peasants were probably less self-sufficient than they had been 2,000 years earlier. They probably handled money more often, sold goods more frequently on local markets, or looked for wage work more often than in the past. But most still produced most of their own food and textiles. Markets were certainly increasing in scope and importance, but they did not dominate people's lives as they do today. The fact that most producers were peasants meant that cities and large towns, though multiplying everywhere, still contained a minority of the population, usually no more than 10 to 20 percent. We could have said much the same of the very earliest agrarian civilizations.

What had changed was the scale on which already existing ideas, goods, people, crops, and diseases were being exchanged and traded. This increase in the scale of exchanges and commerce prepared the way for a much more spectacular burst of innovation from the late eighteenth century. This was partly because, in region after region, societies were beginning to encounter resource limits: less land was available, wood and energy shortages became more common, furs became scarcer. By 1700, the world's forests, arable land, rivers, and seas were being exploited on an unprecedented scale, but still with largely traditional technologies. Expanding markets stimulated commerce in many different parts of the world and levels of commercialization increased, drawing more and more merchants, governments, and even peasants into market exchanges. As Adam Smith (1723–90) understood, larger markets encourage specialization and the efficiencies that go with it, a process that is peculiarly clear in the emerging plantation economies of the Atlantic.

We can also see in this period the beginning of a profound change in the global distribution of wealth and power. Before 1500, the societies of Eurasia's Atlantic Seaboard had been marginal, sitting at the edge of the vast exchange networks of the Afro-Eurasian zone. After 1500, societies of the Atlantic region suddenly found themselves at the center of the largest and most diverse trade networks that had ever existed. For two or three centuries, the volume and value of goods traveling on the newly discovered routes remained less impressive than the volume and value of goods traded through traditional networks, such as those reaching from the Mediterranean through the Indian Ocean to East Asia. But the intellectual and commercial benefits of Europe's position at the center of these networks would slowly increase, as European governments learned to exploit their central position within global trade networks, as the volume of global trade increased, and as European intellectuals grappled with the unprecedented torrent of new information that flowed through Europe's academies and universities and business offices.

Although in many ways the world of 1700 seemed very traditional, all the elements were gathering for an explosion of innovation in the next two centuries. The changes were perhaps easiest to see in the new Atlantic hub region.

In Europe, in a world of highly competitive, medium-sized states, the commercial, economic, and political impact of global exchange networks was obvious. Commerce got the attention of rulers, bankers, and governments. Arbitrage on global markets sustained the power of the Spanish empire in the sixteenth century and the power of its rival, the Dutch Republic, in the early seventeenth century. Here we see the roots of what would later be called capitalism. Commerce generated significant revenues for both governments and elites. Many nobles invested in trade, while governments found that as the markets for goods such as salt or liquor or textiles or sugar expanded, these commodities could yield huge revenues. By 1700, most of the revenues of the British government came from customs and excises of various kinds. That helps explain why British governments spent so much on supporting trade, by building a huge navy capable of protecting overseas empires and by founding the Bank of England to support investment in new commercial ventures.

In Britain and parts of western Europe the structure of society itself was changing rapidly as more and more people became dependent on markets and on wages. Modern analyses of the demographic studies of the pioneering English statistician Gregory King suggest that by the end of the seventeenth century, about half of England's rural population did not have enough land to support themselves. That meant they had to sell their labor, either in the countryside, working as rural laborers for large farmers, or by seeking wage work in the towns. King's figures suggest that toward the end of the seventeenth century over half of Britain's national income was generated from commerce, industrial production, or rents and services. If it really is true that highly commercialized societies are more likely to prove innovative than less commercialized societies, then this is an important omen of impending change. By the late seventeenth century, England and its great rival the Netherlands were both looking more and more "capitalistic." Not only did markets dominate their economies, but governments and elites were also deeply engaged in commercial activities of many different kinds.

The colossal extent and variety of exchange networks in this period, and the increasing importance of commerce, were perhaps the most important elements preparing the way for the remarkable burst of innovation that would begin in the eighteenth century during the Industrial Revolution.

SUMMARY

This chapter described how three key drivers of innovation—expanding trade networks, improved forms of communications and transportation, and increased commercialization—became increasingly important during two great Malthusian cycles. By 1700 CE, the world was linked within a single, global exchange network. Yet in many ways, the world remained quite traditional. The real breakthrough to modernity would occur in the eighteenth and nineteenth centuries; these changes are described in the next chapter.

CHAPTER QUESTIONS

1. Why did the three great drivers of growth—expanding exchange networks, improved communications and transportation technologies, and increasing commercialization—tend to encourage Collective Learning and innovation?
2. What was the most important consequence of the unification of the major world zones from the sixteenth century?
3. In what sense was the world beginning to run out of resources by the eighteenth century?
4. Why did the wealth and influence of European societies begin to increase after the creation of the first global markets in the sixteenth century?
5. Why is it still appropriate to describe most of the world as "traditional" in the early eighteenth century?
6. What signs were there in 1700 that the world was on the verge of fundamental transformations?

KEY TERMS

arbitrage	communications	globalization	monopoly
Anthropocene	drivers of innovation	incentives to innovate	transportation
capitalist societies	exchange networks	modern revolution	

FURTHER READING

Bentley, Jerry H., and Herbert F. Ziegler. *Traditions and Encounters: A Global Perspective on the Past.* 2 vols. 2nd ed. Boston: McGraw-Hill, 2003.

Clossey, Luke. "Merchants, Migrants, Missionaries, and Globalization in the Early-Modern Pacific." *Journal of Global History* 1 (2006):41–58.

Crosby, Alfred W. *The Columbian Exchange: Biological and Cultural Consequences of 1492.* Westport, CT: Greenwood Press, 1972.

Crosby, Alfred W. *Ecological Imperialism: The Biological Expansion of Europe, 900–1900.* Cambridge, UK: Cambridge University Press, 1986.

Fernandez-Armesto, Felipe. *Pathfinders: A Global History of Exploration.* New York: Norton, 2007.

Headrick, Daniel. *Technology: A World History.* Oxford, UK: Oxford University Press, 2009.

Man, John. *Atlas of the Year 1000.* Cambridge, MA: Harvard University Press, 1999.

Marks, Robert. *The Origins of the Modern World: A Global and Ecological Narrative from the Fifteenth to the Twenty-First Century.* 2nd ed. Lanham, MD: Rowman & Littlefield, 2007.

Northrup, David. "Globalization and the Great Convergence." *Journal of World History* 16, no. 3 (September 2005):249–67.

Pomeranz, Kenneth, and Steven Topik. *The World That Trade Created: Society, Culture, and the World Economy: 1400 to the Present.* 2nd ed. Armonk, ME: Sharpe, 2006.

Richards, John. *The Unending Frontier: An Environmental History of the Early Modern World.* Berkeley: University of California Press, 2003.

Ringrose, David. *Expansion and Global Interaction, 1200–1700.* New York: Longman, 2001.

Ruddiman, William. *Plows, Plagues, and Petroleum: How Humans Took Control of Climate.* Princeton, NJ: Princeton University Press, 2005.

Tignor, Robert, et al. *Worlds Together: Worlds Apart.* 2nd ed., Vol. 1. New York: Norton, 2008.

ENDNOTES

1. Luke Clossey, "Merchants, Migrants, Missionaries, and Globalization in the Early-Modern Pacific." *Journal of Global History* 1 (2006):58.
2. J. H. Elliott, *The Old World and the New 1492–1650* (Cambridge, UK: Cambridge University Press, 1970), 39–40.
3. Joel Mokyr, *The Lever of Riches: Technological Creativity and Economic Progress* (New York: Oxford University Press, 1990), 70.

chapter 11

Breakthrough to Modernity

Seeing the Big Picture

1700 to 1900 CE

▶ What was the Industrial Revolution, and why did it begin in Great Britain?

▶ How and where did it spread first?

▶ What consequences resulted from the Industrial Revolution? What did humanity gain and lose from it?

▶ In what ways does the Industrial Revolution seem to be a global, rather than a European, phenomenon?

By 1750 the preconditions for modernity were in place and there were increasing incentives to innovate, but the world was still overwhelmingly agricultural and traditional. What sparks were needed to ignite the modern revolution and push the world across a new threshold into modernity?

Those sparks—the efficient burning of coal and increasing innovation—occurred on a small island off the northwestern peninsula of Eurasia. The people of this island, with less than 1 percent of the world's population in 1700, pioneered the Industrial Revolution and rose, in less than 200 years, to dominate the world as no one group had ever done before. The Industrial Revolution, in consequence, transformed the world. Who could have predicted that? What more surprising story can one imagine?

Threshold 8: The Modern World/Anthropocene

We begin by asking: What is the Industrial Revolution, and why should it constitute the breakthrough to the modern world and the beginning of the Anthropocene?

Rationale for Threshold Eight

The **Industrial Revolution** may be defined as the multiple changes that followed upon the systematic application of fossil fuels in place of human and animal power to manufacturing, communications, and transportation. **Fossil fuels** are coal, crude oil, and natural gas, which contain stored solar energy from millions of years ago. Coal is made from fossilized trees living about 300 million years ago; crude oil results from fossilized one-celled plants and animals that lived in oceans between 10 and 600 million years ago; and natural gas is composed mostly of methane produced by fossilized organisms, usually found near crude oil.

The introduction of vast new sources of energy from fossil fuels resulted in a dramatic increase in innovation and in the productivity of industry (manufacturing, mining, and building), both of which changed social and economic organization. (See Figure 10.1, page 216.) Machines replaced hand tools; mass production in factories replaced cottage manufacture; fuel from burning fossils (first coal, then crude oil and natural gas in the twentieth century) replaced water wheels and animal and human energy, producing energy on a vastly greater scale. The visible signs of the new way of life were machines, factories, and smoke.

In Great Britain the Industrial Revolution began in the textile industry, as newly invented machines replaced hand spinning and weaving and as the coal-burning steam engine developed sufficiently to power mechanical looms. Later the revolution spread to iron and steel production, then to railroads and steamships. The main process took fewer than 100 years in Britain, from approximately 1780 to 1870.

The rationale for considering the Industrial Revolution as the eighth threshold lies in the swift transformation that it caused in human societies; they were fundamentally altered as they had not been since the breakthrough of agriculture 10,000 years earlier (the seventh threshold, also driven by a sudden increase in available energy and resources). The burning of coal and oil lies at the base of this transformation; it provided additional levels of energy never before available in human history (Threshold 8 Summary).

Threshold 8 Summary

THRESHOLD	INGREDIENTS ▶	STRUCTURE ▶	GOLDILOCKS CONDITIONS =	EMERGENT PROPERTIES
MODERN WORLD/ ANTHROPOCENE	Globalization; rapid acceleration in Collective Learning; innovation; use of fossil fuels.	Globally connected human communities with rapidly accelerating capacity to manipulate the biosphere.	Acceleration in Collective Learning at global scales.	Vast increase in human use of resources → entirely new lifeways, social relationships → first single species in the history of Earth capable of transforming the biosphere.

This extra energy broke the Malthusian cycle of population boom and bust. We have seen that before industrialization, people in various kinds of societies relied almost entirely on solar energy stored through photosynthesis in plants and trees. This meant that populations were limited by the land available and by its surface resources. The advent of industrialization temporarily overcame the Malthusian cycle on a global scale by making available the energy stored in fossil fuels. The world in 2012 extracted huge resources to support 7 billion people; in 1700 the traditional sources of energy could support a population of only 670 million. Thus, the Industrial Revolution has produced in just over 300 years enough food to support more than a 10-fold increase in world population.

Why Great Britain and Western Europe? The Global Context

Unlike the agricultural revolution, which began independently in at least seven different places, the Industrial Revolution began in only one place—Great Britain. Even though several other societies, particularly in the Atlantic region, were close to a similar breakthrough, industrial techniques spread so rapidly that there was no opportunity for separate industrial revolutions elsewhere. Historians and sociologists, after much discussion and argumentation, now mostly agree that a convergence of factors, both global and local, came together to produce that result.

To take off, the Industrial Revolution required at least some of these ingredients: large quantities of extra capital (money), lots of cheap labor, new markets for goods, new inventions, a new source of power, new raw materials, and an improved transportation system. In addition, changing social and ideological contexts played a significant role.

A rudimentary version of the first key invention of the Industrial Revolution, the steam engine, appeared in Turkey three centuries before it did in the West. Described in 1551 in a book by the Turkish engineer Taqi al-Din, this invention was used to power a spit that could roast a whole sheep at a rich man's banquet. This steam engine did not catch on in Turkey or anywhere else in the three great empires of the Islamic world (the Ottoman Empire, based in Turkey; the Safavid Empire in Persia; and the Moghul Empire in India). Islamic inventors worked for wealthy elites, who had all the consumer goods they wished, goods handcrafted by artisans. Social and ideological conditions offered little encouragement to entrepreneurs.

Why didn't the Industrial Revolution begin in China? For centuries China had been ahead in many technologies. It had even developed an iron and steel industry in the tenth century, supported by burning coal, but this industry died out by the fourteenth century. A Chinese monk, Su Sung, developed the first clock in 1094, but northern invaders destroyed it. As described in the last chapter, China's rulers made the decision in 1433 to abandon their trading expeditions abroad. Private merchants continued to trade in China, but without the support of their government. Yet still in the eighteenth century Chinese living standards, as measured by life expectancy or by the consumption of sugar or textiles, matched those of Europe.

Many geographic and cultural features have been suggested to explain why China did not take the lead in industrialization. A brief listing of a few of these hypotheses follows; the list can be expected to shift as more research is conducted:

- China had a faster population growth from 1300 to 1700 than did England, which reduced incentives for using machines and increased incentives for labor-intensive approaches.

- China had coal deposits, but they were located mainly in the north, while much economic activity had shifted to southern China.
- The Chinese state shaped the education of the elites and the beliefs of common people; an attitude of experimentation and questioning of authority did not develop widely.
- China focused on institutional and cultural stability; industrialization was seen as disruptive, promoting class differences and regional disparities contrary to Confucian values.
- China always had to contend with threatened or actual invasions, especially from nomadic peoples to the north.
- China did not lie on the new circuit of Atlantic exchange and trade, with its immense opportunities for growth.
- The world as a whole was much less interconnected in the twelfth century, so that Chinese inventions did not spread as fast as those developed in eighteenth-century Britain.

Great Britain and other western European nations such as France and the Netherlands benefited from two major decisions made by China. China's decision to withdraw from trade in the Indian Ocean offered the British East India Company, formed in 1600, and its Dutch and French counterparts the opportunity to enter the markets of Southeast Asia. In addition, Britain and other European nations gained from China's decision in the 1400s to use silver as the basis of its monetary system. After the Treaty of Utrecht (1713), Britain gained the right to sell slaves acquired in Africa to Spanish colonies in America, in exchange for some of the vast supplies of silver being mined in Potosi, Peru (now Bolivia), and at Zacatecas, Mexico. With this silver, which the Chinese needed to provide coinage in a booming economy, the British could buy Chinese tea, silk, and porcelain in large quantities.

Behind the silver, of course, lay the primary global card in Britain's fateful hand—the fact that, by winning the Seven Years' War in 1763 that involved the major European countries, Britain had displaced Spain, France, and the Netherlands, to become the hub of the new Atlantic world-system of trade. This brought Britain massive raw materials and provided consistent new markets. Besides silver, the Americas provided cheap food for industrial workers (fish, potatoes, and sugar), slave-produced cotton for the textile mills, and a market for everything the colonies would need—cradles, coffins, and clothing, including that for the slaves. British entrepreneurs accumulated capital from these ventures. In addition, the land in Britain's North American colonies provided products that Britain could not produce on its own. By 1830 Britain's former colonies in North America (now the United States) were producing so much cotton, sugar, and timber that Britain would have to have been twice as large to produce them. Historians Kenneth Pomeranz and Robert Marks call these American acres Britain's "ghost acres."

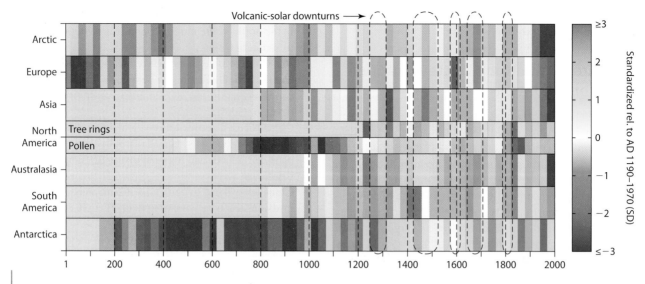

FIGURE 11.1 Regional temperature changes over 2,000 years. The chart shows temperature changes in different regions in 30-year periods over 2,000 years. Based on research by experts from 24 countries, the chart has many different types of sources, including evidence from glaciers, pollen, and tree rings, and is currently the most comprehensive account available. Outstanding features are (*a*) the warm temperatures of 2,000 years ago; (*b*) a long cooling period in the last 1,000 years, and (*c*) an abrupt rise in temperatures in the last century. (Some regions, including Africa, are not included because there is insufficient data.)

Another significant factor in pushing Great Britain into industrialization was the changing global climate. From about 1250 to 1900, often known as the **Little Ice Age (LIA),** temperatures cooled in many areas of the world (see Fig. 11.1). This seems to have been caused by widespread volcanic eruptions and lower levels of carbon dioxide and methane in the atmosphere. To keep warm people everywhere burned more wood. The British on their small island ran out of forests, which motivated them to figure out how to mine coal efficiently.[1]

Other possible explanations for why Britain became the first site of industrialization must be summarized even more briefly. For one thing, in the sixteenth century, Spain had failed to impose its empire on Europe, despite using vast sums of silver on war. Without a unified Europe, the system of competing states and markets continued, with Britain taking dominance by winning the Seven Years' War. Without a unified European government, neither the state nor religious institutions could dominate people's thinking. Religious toleration and attitudes of experimentation and challenge to authority (the Enlightenment) could prevail, encouraging innovations of many different kinds. Financial institutions also developed structures for mobilizing capital, as explained in Chapter 10 (see Table 11.1).

Economic historians stress the importance of coal and colonies as the primary explanation for Britain's dominance. Cultural historians stress the importance of particular skills, a parliamentary system that encouraged commerce, and freethinking. Important as each explanation may seem, all the forces for change interacted in complex ways, and

TABLE 11.1 Reasons for British Industrialization

- Shortage of wood that led to exploitation of coal.
- Coal deposits in useful places, hence cheap coal.
- Coastlines and rivers that made the transportation of coal and other goods relatively cheap.
- An island state's natural defense against invasion.
- Commercial-minded aristocracy; system of free enterprise.
- A government keen to support commercial projects, for example, by building up a huge navy and requiring that trade with colonies be in British ships.
- Monarchs who had limited power to impose their own will.
- Early abolition of serfdom (last ones freed in 1574).
- Limited guild system.
- Merchant fleet protected by powerful navy.
- Colonies in the Americas.
- Cheap cotton produced by slaves in North America.
- Innovation rewarded by prizes and profits, such as the prize for an accurate seaborne clock that allowed precise determination of longitude.
- Skilled instrument makers (best pocket watches in world).
- Interlocking roads and canals.
- Many valuable immigrants (Dutch, Jews, Huguenots).
- High wages: machines to replace wage earners paid off and created significant consumer demand for industrial products such as cotton.
- High literacy rates; middle-class culture.
- Mineral resources belonged to landowners, not to government.
- Dissenters (non–Church of England) banned from universities and government service, hence went into business.

all played out in a multicentered global arena, not just in Great Britain. Watch how the following account tries to integrate all the forces for change.

Social, Agricultural, and Industrial Revolution in Great Britain

This section will first describe the changes in social relations and agriculture that preceded the Industrial Revolution in Great Britain before presenting the revolution itself.

Changes in Social Relations

By the time the Industrial Revolution was complete in Britain in the mid-nineteenth century, the country had changed into a whole new kind of society—from an agrarian civilization into an industrial nation, from a tribute-taking society into a commercialized society. Some crucial changes began occurring before mechanical industrialization and prepared the way for it.

In the late seventeenth century Britain remained a traditional agrarian civilization, with agriculture as the most important sector of the economy and about half the population engaged in it (see Chapter 10, page 240). Most aristocrats thought of themselves as tribute-takers, entitled to the wealth produced by others on their land.

By the mid-eighteenth century this social arrangement had changed dramatically. Many people had moved to cities; London alone held 10 percent of Britain's population. Most peasants still on farms had become wage earners rather than tribute-payers; rather than farming their own land and paying dues to landlords, they worked on land now owned by others and earned wages. Most aristocrats had begun treating their estates as profit-making businesses, rather than as subsistence farms. At least half the income of the country came from industry, commerce, rents, and services. The British government drew most of its income from commerce, including customs; it protected commercial activities with its army and navy. Its position as the emerging hub of the new circuit of Atlantic exchange made this commerce possible. In short, by the mid-eighteenth century Britain had become one of the world's most commercial and capitalistic societies. The drivers of innovation mentioned in Chapter 10 could now play an increasingly important role in stimulating new forms of commerce and production and new innovations.

Changes in Agriculture

Commercial methods began to transform British agriculture in the eighteenth and nineteenth centuries, as agriculture shifted from largely self-sufficient manors to modern capitalistic farms producing specialized crops. Ownership of the land consolidated, as wealthy landowners, called "improving landlords," bought more land; many peasants were driven off their land, to become wage earners on larger estates or in cities.

Wealthy landowners in Parliament encouraged this development by passing hundreds of enclosure acts affecting several million acres. Traditionally, many individuals had used land in common. The enclosure acts gave landowners the right to increase their cropland by buying the land held in common. Many small farmers, who could not exist without their rights in the common lands, had to become wage earners.

Large landowners were more interested in selling their crops and less interested in producing just for their own consumption. They produced crops increasingly for the market, which meant producing them more efficiently and cheaply. As the wealthy landowners acquired larger farms, they were able to implement agricultural improvements that had been developed elsewhere, especially in France and Holland. For example, Viscount "Turnip" Townshend (1674–1738) experimented on his Norfolk estate with new crops from Holland—turnips and clover. By storing turnips, the viscount could feed his livestock through the winter, avoiding the customary slaughter at the onset of winter. Clover crops fixed nitrogen in the soil, improving fertility. Townshend worked out a four-year rotation for the same field—turnips, barley, clover, wheat—that rapidly became standard procedure on many estates. Many of these techniques had existed for a long time, but now more and more landlords began to introduce them as sales increased, creating more and more incentives to innovate.

Large landowners implemented other techniques that made a significant difference in agricultural output. Some figured out how to plant seeds in rows with a horse-drawn drilling machine instead of by sowing by hand. Some bred strains of sheep to double their weight and to produce appealing, fatty meat for the market. Fertilization, irrigation, and drainage all improved as large-scale landowners increasingly had both the capital and the incentive to invest in innovations.

With the application of these techniques, agricultural production in Britain soared. From 1700 to 1850 it increased 3.5 times, cheapening food supplies, which cheapened farm labor. The number of people employed in agriculture dropped from 61 percent to 29 percent of the population, releasing (or exiling) these people from farms to urban life and turning them into potential industrial workers and purchasers, thereby expanding both the labor supply and the market for consumer goods, as the new city workers had to buy what they formerly produced. Britain's population doubled from 1750 to 1800. The revolution in agriculture proved to be the other side of the coin of the Industrial Revolution, starting somewhat earlier and preparing the way.

Revolution in Industry

Concurrent developments in two areas—steam engines and cotton textiles—combined to produce the earliest signs of industrialization in Great Britain. Since **steam engines** burned coal, it was their use that launched human society over a threshold no longer limited by the annual flow of solar energy.

Coal is stored solar energy, laid down between 345 and 280 million years ago, during a period called the *Carboniferous,* meaning "carbon or coal bearing." Plants store energy from the sun. When they die, they decay; that is, oxygen from the air combines with their organic compounds to turn them back into carbon dioxide and water, as bacteria and fungi use the plant's other chemicals for their own growth. If plants fall into water, decay is prevented, since no oxygen is available. As the dead plants sink deeper, pressure from the weight of the materials above them compresses them gradually into peat, then into coal. Coal forms in areas where shorelines changed, where land and sea alternated over millions of years, and where trees grew up to 175 feet (53 meters) tall. During part of the era of coal formation, all the continents were squeezed together into one supercontinent, Pangaea; hence, coal deposits in the eastern United States formed as part of the same vein found in central England.

In the few places on Earth where coal came to the surface, people burned it. In China Marco Polo saw black stones burning, something he had never seen before. In Britain already in the sixteenth century people burned surface coal, for glassmaking, smithing, brewing, and brick and tile making, but it seemed too dirty and sooty to use for cooking and heating as long as wood was available.

Eventually whole forests were cut down, for building houses and ships, for fuel, and for charcoal to smelt iron, until Britain began running out of wood. By 1600 much of southern England had already been deforested to meet the demands of London for heating and cooking; by the end of the eighteenth century forests covered only 5 to 10 percent of Britain, and the government had to buy much of the timber for its navy from countries of the Baltic.

Increasing demand for energy drove some critical innovations. To save wood for lumber and charcoal, Britons substituted coal for heating and cooking. As miners depleted the veins of coal near the surface, they sank shafts deeper, until groundwater seeped in and flooded the shafts. Miners had to carry the water up in buckets, or hoist it up with horses working pumps. Something better was needed.

In 1698 Thomas Savery (ca. 1650–1715) patented a device that heated water by burning coal to produce steam, which was condensed to form a vacuum that worked a pump. (A French Huguenot refugee in Holland, Denis Papin, also developed such a device about the same time.) About a decade later Thomas Newcomen (1664–1729) designed the first real steam engine with a piston pushed by steam, but it was so inefficient that it proved useless, except in coal mines where fuel was almost free.

Meanwhile, factories began to develop, chiefly in the Midlands, the area in and around Birmingham. England's first factory, the Soho Manufactory, opened in 1755 less than 2 miles (3.2 kilometers) north of Birmingham; it included a metal-rolling mill run by water, with machines in workshops holding 400 workers, for working metals and alloys, stone and glass, enamel, and tortoise shells.

A Scottish instrument maker from the University of Glasgow, James Watt (1736–1819), configured the first steam engine that could be profitable away from coal mines. The idea of a steam engine with a separate condenser came to him on a walk in 1765, but it took until 1776 to build the first model. Watt knew capitalist entrepreneurs from Birmingham through his membership in the Lunar Society, a social club of inventors and provincial manufacturers that included two of Charles Darwin's grandfathers, Erasmus Darwin and Josiah Wedgwood. (The club met on the Monday night closest to the full moon, in order to have enough light to ride home by.) Watt moved to Birmingham and, supported by his friends there, developed at the Soho Manufactory a steam engine with a separate condenser, which replaced the inefficient Newcomen engines in pumping water from coal mines (Figure 11.2). Fifteen years later Watt adapted his engine to rotary

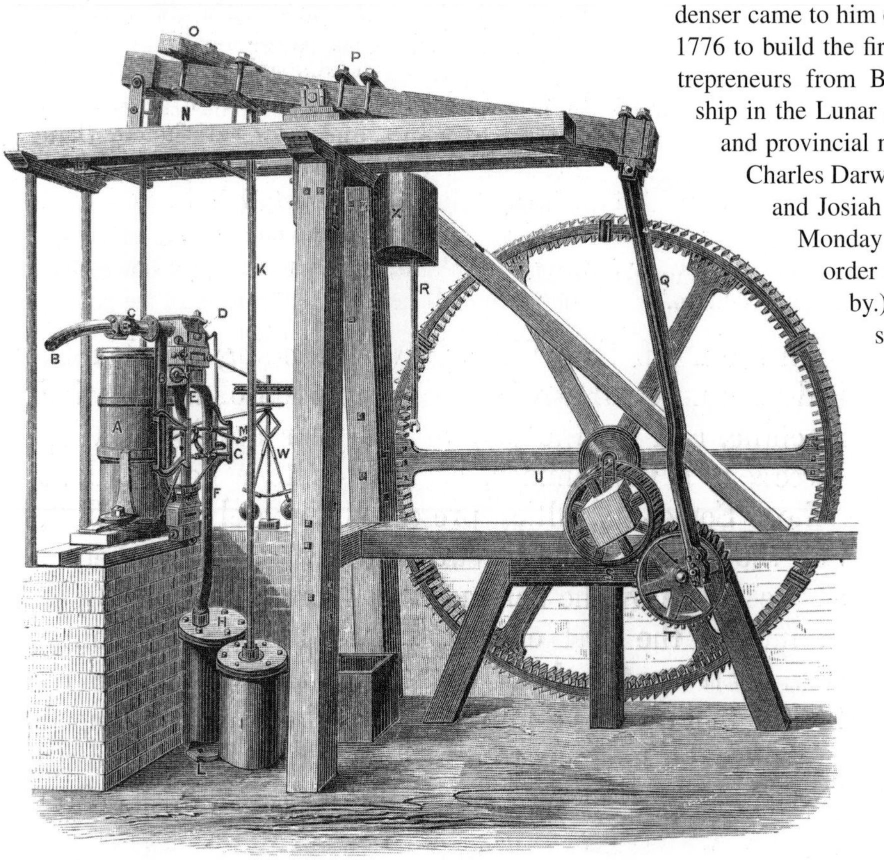

FIGURE 11.2 Watt's steam engine. Watt's machine contributed significantly to the rise of industrial power in England. It can be viewed today in the Science Museum in Birmingham.

motion, so that it could drive the wheels of industry. Watt became a wealthy man, bought three farms, and traveled widely in Europe.

Application of Steam

As Watt was developing the steam engine, others were trying to increase the production of cotton textiles. Plentiful raw cotton was being imported from the West Indies and the American colonies where it was grown by slave labor and demand was growing as the numbers of wage workers increased. The traditional system of production was for merchants to put it out to hand spinners and weavers in their cottages. In the early 1700s Parliament banned the importation of cheaper cotton textiles from India, which had increased the potential market in Britain for British textile producers. This encouraged innovation. In the mid-1700s British inventors came up with several kinds of machines that increased the speed of spinning and weaving. In 1793 Eli Whitney's cotton engine, shortened by Southerners in the United States to "cotton gin," appeared, making it possible to separate cotton seeds by machine. The final step followed in the 1790s and early 1800s: Watt's steam engine was attached to spinning and weaving machines.

Steam engines transformed the cotton textile industry; without them, cotton textiles could not have transformed the British economy. Between 1780 and 1800 the price of cotton textiles went down 80 percent, and they became available to the mass market. By 1850 the cotton industry in Britain used 10 times as much raw cotton as in 1800, ensuring that slavery on the cotton plantations of the southern United States continued to be profitable. Between 1820 and 1840 the tables turned between the British and the Indian cotton textile industries; British exports to India and Southeast Asia rose 1,500 percent. This marked a major change in industrial power, since even in the early eighteenth century India had produced perhaps 25 percent of all the world's manufactured textiles.

Steam engines encouraged the rapid growth of a new mode of production: the **factory system,** in which workers were brought together under supervision to work in factories where steam engines powered multiple machines. Used to working at home and at their own pace, people now had to appear somewhere else at a set time. Since many workers had no clock, employers had to send wakers to tap on windows in the dark morning hours (Figure 11.3).

In another wave of industrialization, the steam engine also transformed the iron and steel industry and transportation in Great Britain. Even before the Industrial Revolution, Britain had been a leading manufacturer and exporter of iron cannon, guns, and hardware. To smelt iron, charcoal was burned in small furnaces near forests for fuel and a river to power the bellows.

In the early eighteenth century Abraham Darby (1678–1717), not far from Birmingham, figured out how to smelt iron by burning coke instead of charcoal. Darby made coke by partially burning coal with limited oxygen, thus getting rid of impurities that affected the quality of iron. Britain's iron production increased 10-fold in the eighteenth century; iron began to appear in buildings and bridges. In the nineteenth century innovations continued and climaxed in 1856, when Henry Bessemer (1813–98) built a blast furnace that could produce steel cheaply, steel being harder and stronger than iron.

Watt's steam engine used too much coal to adapt well to transportation. After the patent for his steam engine expired in 1800, others designed high-pressure machines that used less fuel. Steam locomotives became regular sights in northern England by 1835, and regular steamship Atlantic voyages were occurring by 1840. British entrepreneurs laid about 13,000 miles (21,000 kilometers) of railroad between 1830 and 1870, carrying passengers, raw materials, and manufactured goods, providing cheap transportation that encouraged further industrialization. Steam engines were 10 times more efficient in 1900 than in 1800 and weighed a fifth as much per watt output. British coal production increased about four and a half times from 1830 to 1870.

In summary, coal applied to steam engines and iron production led to power spinning and weaving in factories and then to railroads and steamships, producing a noticeable revolution in British lifeways within 100 years. Simply stated, the Industrial Revolution consisted of coal-based steam power, improved machines, and factory organization. The innovations developed at a pace that may seem slow to us, but seemed without precedent to people of the time.

FIGURE 11.3 Women working in industry.
This engraving from 1835 shows women working at a textile factory. The shift to machine-based manufacturing often started in the textile industries, not only in Britain but also in the United States and Japan.

implemented by strong governments, or by both working together.

The first imitators were geographically or culturally close to Britain—Belgium, France, Prussia, and the United States—forming a second phase. By the 1880s a third phase had begun in Russia and Japan.

Western Europe

Great Britain tried to prevent the export of its industrial innovations. British law forbade the export of new technologies and the emigration of skilled workers. But other countries sent people to England to learn its secrets; they bribed entrepreneurs to set up factories, and they smuggled machinery out in rowboats.

Belgium was the first to industrialize after Britain. It had coal and iron deposits near each other; entrepreneurs used smuggled machinery to begin businesses in Belgium. In 1834 the government started a national railroad system.

In France, the Industrial Revolution proved slower than in the rest of Europe, but there industrialization proceeded with perhaps less disruption. France was hobbled by its relatively backward agricultural system, by its periodic revolutions and wars, and by its relative lack of coal deposits. France lost its only area rich in coal and iron, Alsace-Lorraine, to Germany after losing the Franco-Prussian War (1870–71). Yet France managed to open the world's first department store in Paris in the 1830s.

Capital to pay for new industries proved as important as new technologies. In Great Britain, the Bank of England, created at the end of the seventeenth century, had helped provide relatively cheap investment capital. As industrialization accelerated, large banks began to play an increasing role in industrialization. Five sons of a German Jewish banker, Mayer Amschel Rothschild (1744–1812), pioneered European finance in the nineteenth century. Each son established himself in an important city—one each in London, Paris, Frankfurt, Naples, and Vienna—and facilitated investments in his country. For example, when the French government decided in 1842 to build a national railroad system, the Rothschild banker in Paris negotiated investment of British capital in the French railroads, which were largely completed in the 1860s.

Germany did not exist as a nation until unification in 1871. Prior to unification, separate states imposed their own customs on goods until a customs union emerged in the 1830s. Full abolition of serfdom came late in the German states, not until the 1840s. As a result, in Germany

Increasing production in agriculture and industry reversed the Malthusian cycle. When the human population increased, it did not reach a dying-off point as Malthus had predicted in 1798 that it would. (Just when he figured out the pattern of the past, it changed, at least temporarily.) The standard of living also increased. The English population more than tripled from the 1740s to the 1860s, from 6 to 20 million. Yet at the same time British income per head doubled between 1780 and 1860. In 1700 one in six Britons lived in towns; by 1800 one in three did; by 1851 the majority lived in towns and cities; by 1899 London had become the world's largest city, with 6 million inhabitants. A new kind of world—modernity—had come into being on the small, damp island.

In 1851 London hosted the first world's fair to celebrate the country's achievements and to show off its technology. Queen Victoria, who ruled from 1837 to 1901, opened the "Great Exhibition of the Works of Industry of All Nations," which was held in the Crystal Palace, a marvel of structural engineering, constructed of iron and glass and covering 19 acres (7.7 hectares), including the trees of Hyde Park. By this time England led the world in textiles, metallurgy, mining, and machine building (Figure 11.4).

The Spread of the Industrial Revolution

Just as all *Homo sapiens* are descended from a common African ancestor, all industrial societies are descended from the common British predecessor, each one taking on its own distinctive features. Although the Industrial Revolution in Britain arose from a convergence of forces that no one could have planned, it could be replicated in other places either by energetic entrepreneurs or by plans

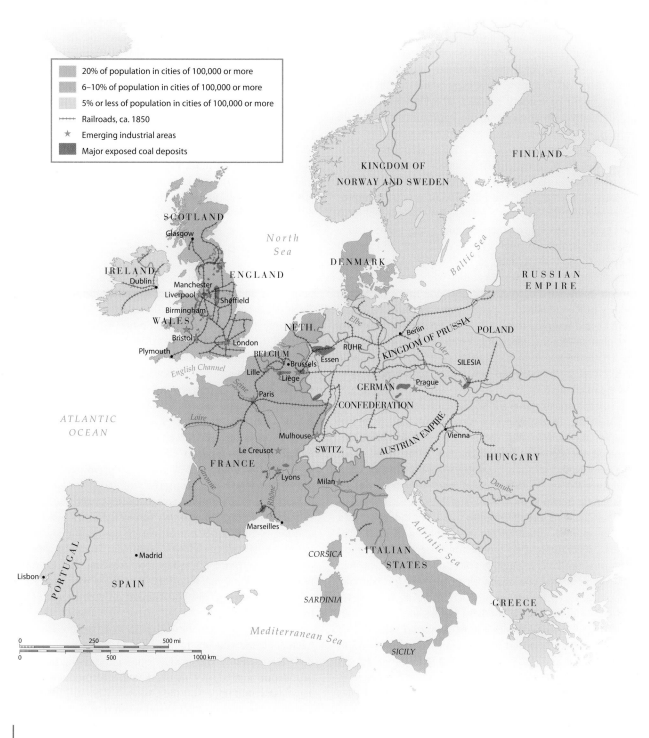

MAP 11.1 Industrial Europe, ca. 1850. By the mid-nineteenth century industry was emerging throughout the British Islands and central Europe.

the Industrial Revolution came a bit later than in France and focused on iron, steel, coal, and chemical industries. With considerable government involvement, railroads were built in the 1850s. Large firms, or cartels, controlled various sectors, a practice different than in Britain and France. Between 1830 and 1840, coal production in Germany doubled; between 1840 and 1870 it increased sevenfold (Map 11.1).

The United States

The newly proclaimed U.S. government enjoyed certain advantages unique in the world at the time. It, too, was an empire like Britain, since it had taken over huge expanses of land from native peoples whose populations had been severely reduced by the new diseases brought by Europeans. Because the cultures that the U.S. government supplanted were mostly those with little agriculture (unlike those displaced by Spain in Mesoamerica and Peru), no weight of agrarian civilization tradition slowed change, no traditional elite resisted. There were no titled nobility, no established churches, and no legal class distinctions. The colonists could start with a more or less clean slate. Technological change could be quickly adopted. The United States enjoyed relative isolation from the cauldron of European politics and war; opportunities for colonists abounded. The United States recapitulated the British model of industrialization but greatly enlarged the scope.

Industrialization began in the United States in the textile industry in the 1820s at the initiative of private entrepreneurs, not the national government. British secrets got to the United States via two men, Samuel Slater (1768–1835) and Francis Cabot Cowell (1775–1817). Slater left England to come to the United States in 1789 under sponsorship of a merchant and set up, from memory without written notes (which might have been confiscated), the first U.S. textile factory in Rhode Island. Cowell visited Britain from 1810 to 1812 and returned to establish the first power loom and first plant combining mechanical spinning and weaving. In the 1850s the textile industry received a boost when Isaac Singer (1811–75) built the first commercially successful sewing machine.

Railroad construction in the United States spanned the 1830s to the 1870s. The government provided grants of land for the rails to start the process; private companies financed the construction, sometimes using loans from European bankers. In large countries like the United States (and later Russia) railroads could have a huge impact by cheapening transportation.

The Civil War (1862–65), the first truly industrial war, greatly spurred industrialization of the northern United States, especially in arms production. After the war, American arms producers sought markets abroad. The war had other international consequences, producing, for example, a boom in Egyptian cotton production during the war (to replace the cotton of the southern states) and a bust afterward. Cuba increased its cotton and tobacco sales during the war and experienced a commercial depression afterward, leading to a revolt that contributed to the overthrow of the Spanish regime.

After the Civil War, industrialization in the United States grew explosively with little or no government regulation. In the 1870s Andrew Carnegie introduced the Bessemer process, which lowered the price of steel. In 1901 U.S. Steel Company had an annual budget three times that of the U.S. government. About one-third of the capital for this industrial development came from Britain, France, and Germany; the United States remained in international debt until World War I. A major depression occurred in Europe and the United States in the 1870s to 1890s, when growth in industrial output in the United States exceeded demand and triggered several bank failures. Yet by 1900 the United States had overtaken Great Britain in total output of manufactured goods, with the United States producing almost 24 percent of the world's output, compared to Britain's almost 19 percent.

By 1870, most of western Europe and the United States were well on the way to industrialization, with the exception of southern Italy, much of Spain, and the southern United States. No countries outside western Europe and the United States had yet embraced industrialization seriously. Aristocrats in Russia still preferred to import machinery and manufactured goods and to pay with grain and timber. Latin American landowners also preferred to trade, not to manufacture. Britain fought the Egyptians and forced them to lower their tariffs, putting their industries out of business. In India the only part of industrialization that flourished was the railroad. In China, restrictions imposed by Britain, plus the resistance of Chinese traditional elites, limited industrialization.

Japan and Russia

After 1870 the situation changed, when governments in both Japan and Russia decided to sponsor industrialization. Their decisions were not exactly voluntary. Russia had lost the Crimean War (1853–56) to France, Britain, and Turkey and had to face the fact that serfdom seemed incompatible with modern life. In Japan the American fleet had steamed into Tokyo Bay in 1853 with warships and guns to demand that Japan open its ports to trade with industrial countries. Lacking abundant raw materials, Japan had to figure out how to compete.

In Japan a brief civil war without massive destruction ended the old regime in 1868; a new era quickly began with the installation of a young emperor, the 15-year-old Meiji, who ruled from 1868 to 1912. Japan had no uniform currency and no national army; each feudal lord (*daimyo*) had his own military force (*samurai*), law codes, and tax system. After consolidating the regime and abolishing feudalism, the Meiji government launched a development plan to transform Japan by drawing on everything the modern West had to offer; since there were few capitalists to finance it, the government provided most of the finance.

Some feudal aristocrats adapted to become successful business leaders, a new industrial elite. Farmers got title to their land, plus fertilizer and equipment, and agricultural production soared. By mechanizing silk production, the Japanese could undersell the Chinese, who still made silk by hand. Workers in cities faced harsh repressions of their demonstrations; they did not secure the vote until 1920.

Poor in natural resources, especially oil, Japan early had expansionist tendencies. The Japanese defeated China in 1894 to 1895 over Taiwan and Korea and, testing themselves against an industrializing power, they defeated Russia in 1904 to 1905, expanding their influence in Korea and Manchuria, where they sought some of the raw materials that their nation lacked.

By 1900 Europe (including Russia) and the United States produced 85 percent of the world's industrial output, while Japan followed with 2.5 percent. (China produced just over 6 percent, reflecting its size rather than its level of industrialization, while India had fallen to less than

2 percent.) Yet Japan, using direct government policies and investments, was managing to industrialize faster than Russia or the West and without massive collective unrest. Japan also modernized its authoritarian monarchy sufficiently to retain it through early industrialization.

In Russia industrialization took a rockier road; its industrialization was associated with violent social and political revolution once it was underway. Profoundly rural and ruled by a traditional tributary autocracy, Russian had postponed into the nineteenth century the social and political developments of the modern world. The monarch, or tsar as he was called, ruled unchecked by anyone. Titled nobility dominated society; many were Westernized and spoke French better than Russian, although they had no formal political participation. Until 1861 most Russians were peasant serfs, bound to the estates of their masters and at their mercy, a condition approximating slavery.

After losing the Crimean War (1853–56), Tsar Alexander II freed 22 million private Russian serfs in 1861 and in 1866 another 25 million state-owned serfs. He undertook reforms moving toward industrialization, directed largely by the state in the absence of private entrepreneurs and beginning with a plan to develop the railways. The government created banks, hired foreign engineers, and put on tariffs to protect new industries. In 1892 the Ministry of Finance launched a massive railroad program linking Russia to Siberia and the Far East. By 1900 Russia's share of the world's manufacturing output reached 8.9 percent, above that of France, and the Russian Empire ranked fourth among the world's nations.

Yet the Russian Empire faced a basic contradiction: seeking to industrialize while preserving the dominance of the tsar and the nobility, who proved peculiarly inept. Immense tensions grew within the autocratic system, mainly because the Russian tsar, Nicholas II, failed to collaborate closely with industrial and commercial elites, unlike the Meiji emperor in Japan. At the end of the nineteenth century still only about 5 percent of Russia's total population were industrial workers, who often labored 13-hour days with no legal outlet for their grievances. After Russia lost its war with Japan in 1905, the country erupted into insurrection, including massive workers' strikes in Moscow and St. Petersburg. The regime of Tsar Nicolas II brutally suppressed the insurrection, but it was forced to make limited political reforms, on which it later reneged and which did not bring political stability. The result was that the government had to deal with the discontent not just of Russia's peasants and industrial workers, but also of large sections of the educated and commercial elites. Incompetent rule during World War I brought the crisis to a head. Revolutions in 1917 eventually brought the Communist Party to power. After a vicious civil war, the Communists, who created a disciplined and cohesive elite group, began to tackle the dilemma of how to industrialize backward Russia (see Chapter 12).

Looking back, we can see **three waves of industrialization.** The initial one began in Great Britain in the latter part of the eighteenth century. The second wave encompassed the spread of industrialization to Belgium, Switzerland, France, Germany, and the United States, beginning about 1820 to 1840 and lasting to the end of the century. The third wave began about 1870, with the spread of industrialization to Russia and Japan. The countries that were to become the powerhouse nations of the twentieth century all began to industrialize in the nineteenth century.

Political Revolution: The Rise of the Modern State

As industrialization proceeded and the resources available to governments increased, the nature of governments changed, as did the balance between consensual and coercive forms of power. The structures of agrarian civilizations gave way to new structures called nations, or **modern states.** Industrialists gained enough wealth and power to demand a voice in government, which depended on their services. Earlier, growing populations that required more central coordination changed chiefdoms into agrarian civilizations. This time the growing populations changed agrarian civilizations into modern states. The first states emerged to manage early cities; modern states emerged to manage the abundant wealth and growing power of industrial economies.

In modern states subjects were transformed into citizens as the power of the state reached more directly into the lives of its people. The organs of state power—standing armies, police, bureaucracy, clergy, and judicature—expanded powerfully. Modern states organized citizen armies with universal conscription instead of paying mercenaries. They increased taxation, regulated land use, controlled the supply of money and credit, and compelled parents to give up their children to be educated. To win the necessary loyalty, state leaders developed national ideologies that imagined national communities based on a common language and history.

In addition to regulations, modern states also provided services: infrastructure, protection, education, poor houses, and hospitals. They balanced regulations with services, always needing to retain the loyalty and support of their citizens. Both regulation and the provision of new services required enormous increases in the coercive power of the modern state over those of agrarian civilizations, while at the same time increasing their consensual power.

The First Modern State in France

Under Louis XVI and the Old Regime (*ancien régime*), France had no elected assembly, no central treasury, no central accounting or control over government revenues and expenses. By the 1780s, the government was close to bankruptcy.

France experienced a social and political revolution beginning in 1789 that rather abruptly eliminated the rights of the nobility (seigneurial rights), local privileges, municipal and guild monopolies, and provincial constitutions—the institutions most typical of traditional tribute-taking states. The French monarch was executed in 1793. Karl Marx, writing in 1871, called the French Revolution a "gigantic broom" that swept away governmental traditions to make way for the modern state to be erected under the National Assembly, then Napoleon and the First Empire.

After the French Revolution and the First Empire (1804 to 1814–15), the French state impinged more directly on the lives of its citizens, whether they wanted it or not. Through reorganization of public administration, the government had increased its capacity to mobilize people and resources. Although in many ways more democratic, the reformed state was also in many ways much more powerful than the monarchy it replaced, a paradox that would reappear in many different forms in most industrializing societies.

After Napoleon, France experienced many political regimes (restored Bourbon monarchs, then a "bourgeois" monarchy, a Second Republic, a Second Empire, a Third Republic), some of which tried to institute liberal parliamentary political controls. Yet the real power stayed in the state civil apparatus. In France, a unique combination existed, that of a centralized, professional bureaucracy together with a society dominated by some large and many small and medium owners of private property. French industrialization was marked by the peculiarities of the state's being a major force shaping it, while large numbers of peasants clung to their land, as France remained agrarian and industrialization proceeded gradually.

Distinctive in many ways, French government also illustrated many of the key features of modern government in general. Far-reaching central bureaucracy and representative assemblies seem the defining components of the modern state. Behind them lay a radical shift in the consciousness of Europeans, a new capacity for empathy that developed in the eighteenth century. Somehow, not yet clearly understood and the subject of much debate, many people developed an aversion to cruelties that in previous centuries they took for granted, such as slavery, torture, and extremely harsh criminal punishments. Somehow, many began to recognize in others the same feelings and sentiments as in themselves and to assert the existence of universal, equal, and natural human rights. These were proclaimed first by Thomas Jefferson and the American Congress in 1776 and again, more influentially, by the French Declaration of Rights of Man and Citizen in 1789. Five years later the French National Assembly abolished slavery in all French territory. Other countries at first abolished only their slave trade, the Danes in 1804, followed by Britain in 1807 and the United States in 1808. By 1842 the Atlantic slave trade was legally dead, although smuggling continued in the Atlantic and open slave trading continued on the eastern coast of Africa by Arabs and Egyptians.

The Modern State Elsewhere

France seems to most historians the first country to establish the modern state, partly because it did so with speed and decisiveness during the revolution. Elsewhere, the old regime gave way to the modern state in other ways.

England began its political revolution in the mid-seventeenth century, when civil war broke out in 1642, introducing a period of political instability that lasted for almost 50 years. England emerged with a parliament now consisting of traditional and capitalist landowners, who limited the monarch's power and used the government's power to further their business interests. Parliament had ties to local governments, which still controlled most local administration. Hence, England had a functioning representative assembly a century before France, but it acquired modern central administrative machinery more gradually over time.

The American Revolution occurred before that of France and helped promote the French one, as French soldiers returned from assisting the Americans filled with ideas of liberty and as French government support for American independence, motivated by hostility to its British rivals, brought France close to bankruptcy. Yet the American Revolution, driven by tensions of a colony in conflict with its distant imperial power, differed greatly from that of France, which was driven by sharp internal social conflicts. The Americans had no medieval arrangements to overturn, but they also had such low population density that central bureaucracy developed slowly.

Germany acquired a parliament (*Landtag*) in 1848, while the monarch remained. Otto von Bismarck (1815–98) succeeded in unifying the German states in 1871, in defiance of the elected representatives of the people. He manipulated public opinion to strengthen the power of the king, yet at the same time developed a modern administration. In trying to keep the loyalty of the working classes, even though he opposed the Social Democratic Party, he passed early social legislation in the mid-1880s, providing accident and disability insurance and old age pensions.

By 1914 the modern state had begun to reshape politics in most countries of the world. Even Afghanistan had instituted some type of census, and most had at least tried to impose direct income taxes instead of older assessments and land taxes. People expected something in return; for example, the idea of national primary and secondary education had taken root in many places, even if most agricultural workers could not afford to let their children attend on a regular basis.

The Emergence of Two Worlds—Developed and Developing

We have seen the Industrial Revolution begin in Great Britain and spread through much of western Europe, Russia, and Japan. What happened elsewhere? Industrialized powers proved economically, politically, and militarily powerful. So, during the nineteenth century most of the people in other parts of the world had to deal with the reality of the new power of industrialized societies—that is, with some kind of U.S., European, and Japanese **imperialism,** the term for the expansion of industrial powers and the conquest and colonization of African, Latin American, and Asian societies by the industrialized nations. In 1800 Europeans occupied or controlled 35 percent of the land surface of the world; by 1878 this figure had risen to 67 percent, and by 1914 to over 84 percent. If the European takeover of the Americas in the sixteenth and seventeenth centuries was the first wave of European conquest, the nineteenth century was the second wave.

Great Britain, as the first to industrialize, led the nineteenth-century conquests, ending the century with the largest noncontiguous empire known in world history. Britain exerted great influence over some areas, like China and the Ottoman Empire, without taking over direct rule. With other colonies, like India, Southeast Asia, and African countries, Britain assumed the costs and risks of direct control. The people confronted with the industrial and military power of Britain and other industrial nations reacted in various ways, not as mere passive victims or beneficiaries, but with their own agendas and styles of resistance or accommodation.

By the end of the nineteenth century the gap between the world's richest and poorest countries had widened enormously. In preindustrial times levels of wealth did not differ greatly from region to region, even if there were significant differences within each region between different classes. Some societies attained incomes three to four times that of other societies. After the Industrial Revolution, the gap between the richest and poorest regions of the world was on the order of 50:1. In particular, China and India, which had led the world's economic output in 1750, became, by 1900, among the least industrialized and poorest regions of the world. The rise of the West reversed, probably temporarily, what now seem to some historians to be long-standing historical trends that had concentrated much of the world's wealth in Asia.

In this section we will briefly review how countries became formal or informal colonies of Great Britain and other industrial nations, examine how Europeans viewed themselves in this process, and offer some possible explanations for the European conquests and for the growing gap between developed and developing countries.

Formal and Informal Colonies

India was politically unified in the mid-1500s, when the Mughals, an Islamized Turkic group, conquered most of it. When the Mughal Empire declined, India broke apart again in the mid-1700s. The British East India Company (EIC), formed in 1600, gained the right in 1765 to collect land taxes in Bengal, enough to raise an army, which by the mid-1800s had secured control of most of India, often

with the support of local traditional rulers. British colonial administrators allowed in cheaper British textiles, which then flooded the Indian market and destroyed much traditional Indian textile production. Instead of exporting finished goods, many Indians turned to farming and began to export the agricultural cash crops of indigo, sugar cane, cotton, and also poppies, from which opium was made. India became a prime example of American sociologist Immanuel Wallerstein's idea of world-systems, in which an industrialized nation forces other countries to become dependent on it, supplying it with raw materials cheaper than manufactured ones (see Chapter 8). "Free trade" became Britain's program, since in the 1830s it could outproduce any country in manufactured goods and could force others into raw material production. The British profit from Indian opium, sold mostly in China, became so great that the structure of world trade reversed; silver began flowing out of China into England after centuries of flowing in the opposite direction.

Between India and Europe lay the Ottoman Empire, centered in modern Turkey, which had originated after the Mongols destroyed Baghdad in 1258, ending the Abbasid caliphate, previously the dominant force in the Muslim world. (Two other Muslim empires arose from the remains: the Mughals in India and the Safavids in Persia.) As we saw in Chapter 10, after the Ottomans captured Constantinople in 1453, they were able to block European access to the Eastern Mediterranean, the Black Sea, and the trade circuits to China and the Indian Ocean. The Ottomans expanded around the Mediterranean Sea, including the whole southern coast from Egypt to Algeria. Their empire was an agrarian civilization, resting on productive agricultural economies that produced surpluses that rulers could tax; they ruled through a bureaucracy of officials posted throughout the realm, responsible to the emperor.

Gradually the Ottoman Empire weakened. Europeans had bypassed Constantinople by finding direct ocean routes to China, India, and Indonesia, and by the 1840s they were there arriving in steamboats. The central Ottoman state lost authority as provincial authorities and local warlords gained power. The French seized Algeria in the 1820s and completed the Suez Canal in 1869, which gave Europeans more rapid access to the markets of Asia. Britain gained control of the canal in the 1870s and occupied Egypt by 1882. In World War I the Ottoman Empire joined Germany and Austria-Hungary and was defeated, after which the victors—Great Britain, France, Russia, Serbia, and the United States—divided up its large Mediterranean empire.

In China, population grew rapidly, increasing more than fourfold from the mid-seventeenth to the mid-nineteenth centuries, as a result of increased agricultural production made possible by plants brought from the Americas—corn, sweet potatoes, potatoes, and peanuts. With no industrialization to soak up the extra workers, the Chinese developed more intensive agriculture to feed the expanding population. China already grew cotton and produced cotton clothing for its own people, while exporting silks, porcelain, and tea.

Great Britain had nothing to sell that the Chinese wanted—except silver, which China needed to remonetize its economy. By 1800 Britain was sending lots of silver to China; British textile workers and coal miners were spending 5 percent of their income on Chinese tea, bought with silver, which the British got by selling slaves they took from Africa to Spanish colonists in the Americas. After Britain abolished its slave trade, it had to cover its imports from China in some other way; it turned to selling the Chinese opium grown in India, despite the bans of the Chinese government. During the later part of Queen Victoria's rule, the British were running a massive smuggling operation; it played a crucial role in keeping the global economic system from crashing in the last quarter of the nineteenth century.

By the 1830s the British had built an all-iron gunboat, the *Nemesis,* designed for fighting and for running up Asian rivers from the sea. Using it, they forced China to open its ports to opium, by winning two so-called Opium Wars (1839–42, 1856–58). By the late 1800s about 10 percent of China's population were opium users of some regularity, with possibly 40 million actual addicts. (These are rough estimates.) By the turn of the century China was consuming 95 percent of the world's supply of opium.

Meanwhile, China's government weakened. Although its population had increased more than four times in less than 200 years, its bureaucracy had not expanded. A widespread peasant rebellion, called the Taiping Rebellion, provoked a terrible civil war that raged from 1850 to 1864, with a loss of almost 20 million lives. The international trade system suffered a bust from 1873 to 1896 (prices in Britain fell 40 percent), but, as mentioned, the opium trade probably kept the system from crashing. Another peasant uprising, the Boxer Rebellion, occurred in China from 1899 to 1901, and was put down by Western powers and Japan. China's imperial government collapsed in 1911.

By the early 1800s Americans were also involved in the opium trade, using sources grown in Turkey. According to historian Robert Marks, "Profits from the opium trade added to the endowments of prominent East Coast universities, padded the fortunes of the Peabody family in Boston (and hence the Peabody Museum) and the Roosevelt family in New York, and provided capital for Alexander Graham Bell's development of the telephone."[2]

Throughout the nineteenth century, Britain escaped major social unrest at home, in part by means of major migrations that helped populate settler colonies, or neo-Europes, in temperate climates around the world, notably in Canada, Australia, New Zealand, and South Africa. British emigration to the United States was part of these migrations; the United States became the top recipient of British investment, and the U.S. Midwest became the breadbasket of Europe. Since Britain favored these places with capital investment and favorable trade agreements, most British settlers prospered (Map 11.2).

One well-known British imperialist, Cecil Rhodes (1853–1902), believed that he was helping prevent civil war at home by providing new lands for British colonists. He dominated the diamond industry in South Africa and acquired for the British the land that became Zambia and Zimbabwe. After attending a meeting of unemployed workers in London, he wrote to a friend:

> In order to save the 40 million inhabitants of the United Kingdom from a murderous civil war, the colonial politicians must open up new areas to absorb the excess population and create new markets for the products of the mines and factories. . . . The British Empire is a matter of bread and butter. If you wish to avoid civil war, then you must be an imperialist.[3]

In Latin America, the Spanish and Portuguese colonies organized themselves into nations and achieved political independence from their European rulers between 1810 and 1825, with more extended struggle than had occurred in the United States. Economic independence, however, eluded the new South American nations, as their governments mostly failed to develop modern industries, with the result that most became dependent producers of raw materials with the support of European capital. In the 60 years or so after 1850, exports of Latin America boomed, increasing about 10-fold, with silver, copper, nitrates, guano (bird droppings for fertilizer), rubber, sisal, bananas, chocolate, coffee, and sugar leading the list. European and U.S. businesses invested large-scale capital in Latin America; by 1910 U.S. business interests controlled 90 percent of Mexican property and produced half of its oil.

In the nineteenth century, the United States and European nations acted to encourage worldwide free trade by gradually adopting a gold standard for monetary systems. Yet in 1873 the stock market in Vienna crashed, provoking a bust throughout Europe. Many industrialized nations sought to protect their industries and products by erecting tariffs, the opposite of free trade. They also began to compete with each other to take over colonies by direct rule, since the colonizers hoped they would have more privileged access to the markets and raw materials of colonized regions. A scramble for colonies in Africa took place, in which the European nations carved up the continent among themselves in the short period between 1880 and 1900.

The European scramble for Africa benefited from two significant innovations. The discovery of a way to prevent malaria by taking quinine, found in the bark of a tree native to South America, made it possible for Europeans to survive in sub-Saharan Africa. The other innovation was the invention by Hiram Maxim (1840–1916) of a reliable machine gun, called the Maxim gun. Maxim, an American who emigrated to Britain, unveiled his machine gun in the mid-1880s and sold it to other European nations by 1890. The British used it first in India and later in Africa where, in one 5-hour battle, the British lost 20 soldiers to the 11,000 Sudanese men they killed.

By 1900 Britain, France, Germany, and Belgium had divided up most of Africa among them, with Portugal hanging onto its seventeenth-century possession in Angola. Britain

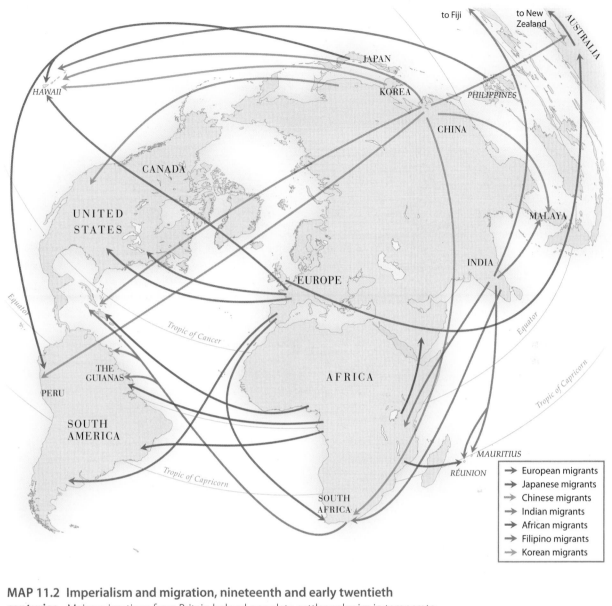

Legend:
→ European migrants
→ Japanese migrants
→ Chinese migrants
→ Indian migrants
→ African migrants
→ Filipino migrants
→ Korean migrants

MAP 11.2 Imperialism and migration, nineteenth and early twentieth centuries. Major migrations from Britain helped populate settler colonies in temperate climates around the world, notably in Canada, Australia, New Zealand, and South Africa.

alone controlled about 60 percent of Africa. Ethiopia was able to defeat Europe's weakest power, Italy, to remain the only independent country along with Liberia (Map 11.3).

With the carving up of Africa, Europe completed the division of the world into two camps—the industrial, developed world and the nonindustrial, developing world. The industrial process that enriched the nations of the Atlantic Seaboard ruined the economies of much of the rest of the world. The nonindustrial countries accounted for almost 75 percent of the world's output in 1750, but only 11 percent by 1900 (Table 11.2).

How much did parliaments in Europe initiate imperialism? Debates raged in ruling circles over the need for colonies and the costs of imperialism, while governments had many other preoccupations—social conflicts, military preparedness, and balanced budgets among them. Often

imperialists in the field, like Cecil Rhodes, simply acted, and parliaments later sanctioned their deeds.

The West's Comforting Ideas

As they increased their power and productivity at home and abroad, Europeans changed their perceptions of themselves dramatically. Weren't they unlocking the secrets of nature, while amassing unheard-of wealth and military power? Weren't they also doing what all past states had done by enhancing their own wealth at the expense of other regions? Using these criteria, they judged other peoples and cultures as inferior and took on the arrogance of believing themselves superior to all others. In many cases, this belief was added to their already existing belief in the superiority of their religion, Christianity.

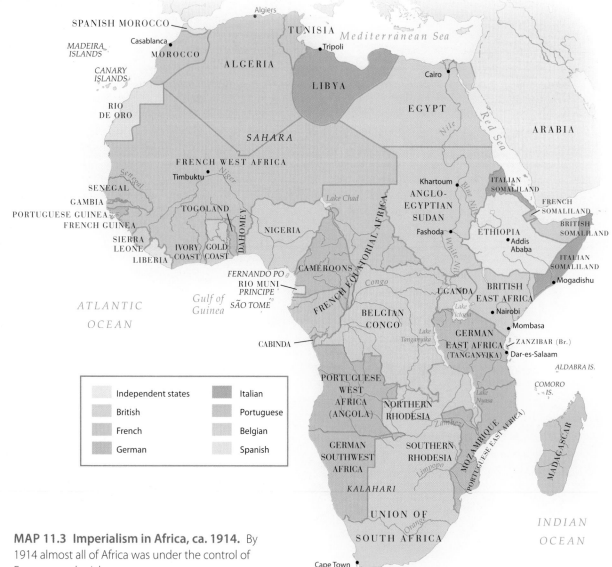

MAP 11.3 Imperialism in Africa, ca. 1914. By 1914 almost all of Africa was under the control of European colonial powers.

TABLE 11.2 Share of Total World Manufacturing Output (in Percentages)

	1750	1800	1860	1900
Europe as a Whole	**23.2%**	**28.1%**	**53.2%**	**62.0%**
United Kingdom	1.9	4.3	19.9	18.5
France	4.0	4.2	7.9	6.8
Germany	2.9	3.5	4.9	13.2
Russia	5.0	5.6	7.0	8.8
United States	**0.1**	**0.8**	**7.2**	**23.6**
Japan	**3.8**	**3.5**	**2.6**	**2.4**
Rest of the World	**73.0**	**67.7**	**36.6**	**11.0**
China	32.8	33.3	19.7	6.2
India/Pakistan	24.5	19.7	8.6	1.7

Source: Robert Strayer, *Ways of the World: A Brief Global History*, vol. 2 (Boston: Bedford/St. Martin's, 2009), 548.

Europeans began to express racist thinking in scientific terms. A Swede, Carl Linnaeus, who in 1735 made the basic classification of plants and animals, started racial classification. By the end of the eighteenth century, Johann Blumenbach at Göttingen, Germany, had named five races based on cranial measurements, claiming Caucasians as the original race with the others diverging from it. Later formulations assigned darker "races" as being closer to chimpanzees (who have light skin under their fur, remember?), with whites as the final, superior development. Scientists never agreed on the number of "races" and conceded in the mid-twentieth century that there is no scientific basis for this kind of classification. But for at least half a century many Europeans regarded racist thinking as both scientific and normal.

Many Europeans, forgetting how long the societies of Asia and the Mediterranean had dominated world history, viewed their race and their civilization as superior, and some felt a sense of responsibility to the "weaker races," a need to civilize "inferior races." Others applied the Darwinian idea of the "survival of the fittest" to society, and concluded that it was natural for Europeans to displace or to destroy backward peoples or "unfit races."

The hypothesis that individual people rise or fall in society depending on their personal strengths and weaknesses and that whole societies could be considered more or less fit came to be called social Darwinism in the twentieth century (see Chapter 12). When Darwin first proposed his theory of biological evolution, it was in the context of rapid industrial development in England and in Europe. Some individuals were rising rapidly, like Darwin's own maternal grandfather, Josiah Wedgwood, who rose from potter's apprentice to wealth on a scale previously unknown. In this context it was easy and comfortable for people to think of some individuals and some societies as being biologically more fit.

By now it must be clear that the colonial policies of European countries baldly contradicted their core values and their practices at home. While Britain and France became somewhat more democratic at home, with more male citizen participation, they ran their colonies, already at odds with their belief in national independence, as dictatorships. They did not encourage in their colonies the modernization they enjoyed at home, fearing that doing so would destabilize colonial rule. These blatant contradictions would help undermine the foundations of European colonial rule in the twentieth century.

Explaining Imperialism and the Two Worlds

As we look back on the big picture of European Industrial Revolution and international conquest, we seek explanations for this immense change in a mere two centuries of human life. The underlying factor seems to be the burning of coal on a new scale; when this extra source of energy, more than the sun provided each day, was attached to machinery, all else ensued. The extra energy of coal provided such an influx into human systems that a whirlpool emerged, a whirlpool of industrialization that changed the world.

Once coal is identified as the basic factor, we can see a cascade of consequent effects in the Modern era with all its new emergent properties. The productivity of industrialization created a need for new materials and agricultural products, just as it also created a need for new markets and new arenas for investment. Population growth proved so explosive in Europe that millions migrated to other areas of the world, avoiding rebellion or extreme repression at home and effectively exporting problems from the industrialized to the less developed world. Borders firmed up in Europe, and the modern state machinery of nations emerged, each competing for trade and colonies. This competition was driven by new racial self-conceptions and by the availability of powerful new technologies—quinine, railways, steam-driven gunboats, machine guns, and other machines.

Another factor shaped the imperialism of industrial nations—climate change in the late nineteenth century. Starting in the late 1870s, a series of three droughts occurred in the equatorial and subequatorial areas all around the globe. The monsoon rains did not come in India and eastern Africa, nor did rain fall in northwestern Brazil or northern China, for several years during each drought. Changes in the sea currents, called El Niño events, off western South America probably caused these changes in rainfall. The effects were magnified by the social and economic disruptions of industrial imperialism. Thirty to 60 million people died, and national production plunged in the areas mentioned, leaving the affected nations mired in underdevelopment.

Historians keep coming up with new hypotheses about the underlying causes of modern industrialization. A recent one is that of Daniel Smail, who proposes that underlying these developments is the desire of humans to alter their body chemistry to induce better moods. A fundamental aspect of modernity, according to Smail, lies in the increase of mood-altering practices picked up and accumulated from around the world—tobacco, tea, coffee, sugar, cacao, coca, opium, and cannabis. Certainly, after finding sea routes to the Americas and to the Indies, Europeans experienced an infusion of new "soft" drugs—tobacco, sugar, chocolate, tea, and coffee, which became mass-market commodities. For the first time in history, humans had available a wide range of mind-altering substances to choose from; before that, by and large, each society had had just one major substance of this type. Smail believes that even buying things, or shopping, induces neurotransmitters that reduce stress and that this desire to alter one's own chemistry lies at the heart of modern consumer society. Interpretations of history keep changing. What may seem eccentric today may become more widely accepted in the future.

Other Consequences of the Industrial Revolution

Whatever the other consequences of the Industrial Revolution, the world's total population rose faster than ever before in human history, from 610 million in 1700 to 1.6 billion in 1900, a threefold increase in just 200 years. Much of this astonishing rise was due to the increased nutritional value of diets enriched by the global exchange of plants and animals, and some was due to the sharing of immunities so that, in large parts of the world, diseases such as the bubonic plague became less damaging.

The Industrial Revolution is particularly difficult for historians to analyze clearly, since we are still in the midst of it and do not know yet what the outcome will be. We may be heading toward worldwide industrialization or toward the end of an unsustainable era. Without knowing the outcome, it is difficult to evaluate the effects. In two final sections we will survey some social, gender, and environmental effects of industrialization before the twentieth century, first in the industrial nations (Britain and most of northern Europe, the United States, Russia, and Japan), then in their colonies, the nonindustrial countries.

1899 London was the world's largest city, at over 6 million, having grown from 1 million in 1801. In England as a whole, 50 percent of the population was living in cities by 1850, in Germany the same level was reached by 1900, in the United States by 1920, and in Japan by 1930.

Not everyone in industrialized countries was affected by it in the same way. In Britain the class of aristocratic landowners declined relative to business entrepreneurs, manufacturers, and bankers, but in the mid-nineteenth century a few thousand families still owned half the cultivated land, most of which they leased to tenant farmers. The middle class benefited most from industrialization, with many middle-class men achieving the right to vote with the Reform Bill of 1832. The laboring classes suffered most and benefited least from industrialization, especially in the early phases before 1830, when they experienced smoky, crowded urban conditions, poor sanitation, inadequate water, severe monotony, and close supervision with fines for not working fast enough. No provisions were made for old age, and there was no plot of land to fall back on, once people had moved into cities (Figure 11.5).

These conditions in Britain are known best through the popular novels of Charles Dickens (1812–70), who portrayed the heart-wrenching social costs of industrialization in the individual characters he created in, for instance, *Oliver Twist* (1837–39), *A Christmas Carol* (1843), *David Copperfield* (1948–50), and *Hard Times* (1854). Dickens wrote from personal experience; at age 12, when his father was imprisoned for debt, Dickens briefly had to work as a child laborer pasting labels on boxes.

Some of those who suffered from industrialization resisted and protested. Employers tried to maximize the use of expensive machinery; some textile factories ran 16-hour days including Saturday. Between 1810 and 1820, in a series of riots starting in Nottingham, handworkers in England attacked and destroyed textile machinery. Called Luddites, they took their name from an imaginary leader, Ned Ludd, whose office supposedly existed in Sherwood Forest, from

Consequences in the Industrialized Nations

The previous descriptions of industrialization have emphasized its political and economic aspects—the money to be made, the rising power of capitalists and the middle class, contact and trading with new areas of the world. This section will focus on social and gender issues and the environmental consequences in the industrial countries.

Social Issues   The Industrial Revolution, wherever it occurred, caused epic transformations of social life. This transformation was marked by the appearance of factories instead of farms and fields, clocks instead of seasons, small families instead of large ones, change instead of stability. For the first time ever, wrenching social and technological change could be felt by many in a single lifetime.

One measure of industrialization is the percentage of the population living in cities. In the single decade between 1821 and 1831, factory centers in England, like Leeds, Birmingham, and Sheffield, grew by 40 percent. By whence the legendary Robin Hood had led attacks on the wealthy on behalf of the poor. Luddites wanted machinery to be outlawed, but they failed.

Many others opposed industrialization. Romantic poets in England, such as William Wordsworth and William Blake, saw the black smoke of factories as an evil attack on "green and pleasant" England. One Scottish capitalist, Robert Owen (1771–1858), ran his New Lanark textile mills with humane conditions like community buildings, an infant school, and a general store. Owen is considered a founder of Socialism and the cooperative movement.

The most long-lasting challenge to the new capitalist mode of production came not from riots, but from the pens of Karl Marx (1818–83) and his lifelong collaborator, Friedrich Engels (1820–95). Both men were German (Prussian). Marx was descended from two grandfathers who were rabbis and a father who converted to Protestantism to keep his job as a lawyer, while Engels's father was part owner of a textile factory in Manchester, England. Engels worked there as a young man, discovering for himself the horrors of factory conditions. In 1844, at age 24, he published *The Condition of the Working Class in England.* The same year Engels met Marx in Paris, and four years later the two of them published, on February 21, 1848, *The Communist Manifesto,* in which they threw out a new challenge to the capitalists of Europe:

> A specter is haunting Europe—the specter of communism. . . . The history of all hitherto existing society is the history of class struggles. . . . Our epoch . . . shows . . . this distinctive feature: it has simplified the class antagonisms. Society as a whole is more and more splitting into two great hostile camps, into two great classes directly facing each other: *bourgeoisie* [capitalist class] and *proletariat* [working class]. . . . What the bourgeoisie . . . produces, above all, is its own grave diggers. Its fall and the victory of the proletariat are equally inevitable.[4]

In this brief book Marx and Engels laid out their basic ideas. They believed that conflict between social classes drove the process of historical change and that society would never distribute its abundance to workers, because of the obstacles of private property, competition, and class hostility. This meant that the gap between rich and poor would continue growing until eventually there would be a revolution. Therefore, they concluded, capitalism was doomed to collapse, after which Communism would emerge, and under it the abundance produced by industrial technology would be shared by all, ending the historic conflict between the rich and the poor.

The day after *The Communist Manifesto* appeared, demonstrations and riots broke out in Paris. Two days later the French king, Louis Philippe, abdicated. The French wrote a new constitution, becoming a republic once again.

For a few months in 1848 it seemed that Marx and Engels's predictions were coming true. Revolts of working people toppled governments in the Italian states, the Hapsburg Empire, and Switzerland. Revolts threatened established order in Spain and Denmark and shook Ireland, Greece, and Britain. The underlying causes were varied and complex. Nationalism inspired the Germans and

Italians to seek political unification and the ethnic subjects of the Hapsburg Empire to seek autonomy. Liberal politicians demanded constitutions to limit monarchs and to liquidate feudal rights (thereby establishing modern states), suffrage reform, and, in France, guarantees for the right to work. Economic conditions were intensifying social misery—blight was ruining potato crops, the grain harvest of 1846 failed in western Europe, and the railroad-building boom of the early 1840s collapsed by 1847. Food prices and unemployment rose.

The "revolutions of 1848" were soundly defeated. Monarchical authority returned, as the middle class and owners felt threatened and supported suppression of the revolts, and as soldiers remained loyal to the tsar of Russia, to the Austrian Empire, and to the French Louis Napoleon Bonaparte, the nephew of Napoleon Bonaparte, who was elected but then declared himself Emperor Napoleon III. Monarchs compromised with property owners and commercial magnates, while some of the aims of the revolutionaries were accomplished after 20 or more years—the unification of Italy and Germany, the Third Republic in France. The ideas of Marx and Engels inspired political parties known as Social Democrats for years to come, and eventually they would inspire the Communist movements of the twentieth century.

Migration provided an escape hatch for some of Europe's poor. The steamship and the railroads enabled a great wave of European settlement to spread, mostly to the United States and Canada, to Argentina and Brazil, and to Australia and New Zealand (see Map 11.2). These migrations took some heat off home governments and strengthened neo-Europes around the globe. At the same time, these migrations had a disastrous effect on native peoples and animals in the areas where Europeans settled (see Environmental Issues, p. 263).

Meanwhile, governments in Europe enacted new political and social legislation, which eventually turned their governments into democracies and reduced some of the tensions that Marx had expected to cause revolution. Trade unions of workers became legal, labor laws began to control working conditions and wages, child labor laws came to prevent the abuse of young children, the right to vote (suffrage) gradually was extended, and, perhaps most important, public primary schooling became compulsory.

In the United States laws were gradually enacted to set minimum wages, limit child and women's labor, control hours of labor, regulate sanitation, and require compulsory primary education. These laws were passed at the state level, however, not at the national level, and varied greatly from state to state. Massachusetts passed the first compulsory school attendance laws in 1859.

In Russia and Japan, social legislation was very limited under absolutist monarchs. Russia had no parliament, or representative government, until after 1906; 60 percent of its people were serfs until 1861. The 13-hour day was common in factories there until 1897. Japan became an industrial power without altering its traditional oligarchic and absolutist political structure. Protests peaked in 1883 to 1884 with attacks on government offices, but repressive laws crushed the budding labor movement. Suffrage was extended and trade unions were permitted in Japan only after World War I.

Gender Issues To what extent did industrialization reduce gender inequality? There is no simple answer to this question, as there are many dimensions and forms to gender inequality, which vary in importance over time.

On farms and in artisan's shops, women had usually been subordinate to men, at least in theory, but often in practice relatively equal. As some women began to rise into the middle class with industrialization, they became cast as homemakers, separate from men, charged with creating at home a calm retreat from the cutthroat competition of capitalism. They became the center of morality and beneficence, plus the managers of consumption. Yet by the late nineteenth century some middle-class women were finding ways out of the isolated, rigid division of household work into teaching, clerical, and nursing professions. They, however, suffered a double work burden, with lower earnings and fewer promotions than men in similar positions.

Among the European working classes, many girls and young women worked in mills or as domestic servants. If they married, they left paid employment but often continued to earn by taking in boarders, doing laundry, or by sewing.

In Japan the results of early industrialization proved especially pernicious, experienced as they were as part of the massive rapid social transformation from samurai society to centralized, industrial nationhood. Many rural peasant families slid into poverty, forcing infanticides, sale of their daughters, and starvation. Many urban textile workers were young women from the countryside who endured terrible conditions until they were cast off as workers, often with terminal diseases.

Yet over time the overall standard of living under industrialization rose for both men and women as control of resources rose faster than increases in population. In Europe the early misery had been attenuated by the mid-nineteenth century. As children became expenses rather than assets, fertility declined, a benefit to women. As other countries industrialized, they underwent similar processes.

Environmental Issues As the capital of the industrial world, London exemplified its environmental impact. In the nineteenth century the area covered by greater London grew at three times the rate of the population. Workers commuted into work by three-horse omnibuses. Each horse dropped 3 to 4 tons (2.7 to 3.6 metric tons) of dung annually. The first railroad to be built underground began in 1859 to deal with this problem.

Sewerage in London flowed into the Thames River, but high tides brought it back, causing intolerable odors when tides went out, leaving the sewage in the mud. During the Great Stink of 1858 Parliament adjourned for a week. Fecal matter in the drinking water caused cholera epidemics in 1832, 1848, and 1865. By 1891 London had improved its sewers and water supply enough to escape another cholera epidemic that swept the continent.

In London each home had multiple fireplaces for heat, and by 1880 about 3.5 million fireplaces were burning coal, in addition to the smoke produced by factories. Smoky fog enveloped the city; one December the mortality rate reached 220 percent of normal rates. Rain deposited smoky air on trees and bushes, turning them black.

Consequences in the Colonized World

The industrialization that occurred in Europe, the United States, Russia, and Japan in the nineteenth century affected the rest of the world profoundly. The global system of the twentieth century began to be constructed in the nineteenth century by steamships, railroads, and telegraphs. Countries that did not industrialize became producers of raw materials for those that did.

Social Issues Since the industrial nations needed cheap raw materials, they prodded and sometimes forced their colonies to mine ores and to produce cash crops to sell, rather than raise their traditional mixed subsistence crops to eat. The desired ores included gold, silver, copper, tin, and diamonds; the desired cash crops included increased harvests of coffee, tea, and sugar, as well as cotton, cocoa, peanuts, palm oil, tropical fruits, rubber, and hemp. Raising these crops resulted in land redistribution, local famines, and the cutting of forests for new land to cultivate (see Environmental Issues, p.263). Huge plantations developed, financed by Europeans, where impoverished workers came from great distances and grew sugarcane, rubber, tea, tobacco, and hemp, suffering disease rates twice those of the colony itself.

As European nations took over colonies, directly or indirectly, violence was a prominent feature, both during the conquests and afterward. But cooperation also took place, as Europeans had to depend on local elites to act as intermediaries in carrying out government functions. Indian princes, African chiefs, and Muslim emirs found ways to retain their status and privileges, reinforcing traditional class structures.

With Europeans came their systems of values, through the work of government servants, missionaries, and volunteer services. Government and missionary schools provided some local people an opportunity for a Western education and access to better-paying jobs in government, mission organizations, and business firms. Both Roman Catholic and Protestant missionary work increased significantly in the nineteenth century. The campaigns in England for abolishing slavery initiated mission activity in West Africa and then throughout the British Empire. Roman Catholic missionary activity reemerged in France after 1815, with Catholic missions attempting to protect native people in the Amazon after 1850. By 1910 more than 10,000 missionaries had entered Africa alone.

Yet as Europeans sought to spur education in their colonies, they also constricted it by their racial fears. In East

Africa, Europeans regularly called African men "boys." They rarely permitted even highly educated Asians and Africans to enter the higher ranks of the colonial civil service. In places with much permanent white settlement, such as South Africa, Europeans set up systems of strict racial segregation, with separate "homelands," public facilities, and educational and residential areas. In India the British reinforced the traditional caste system, scorning as "non-Indian" the more egalitarian views of the new Indian elite educated in European schools.

Many colonial people chose not to cooperate with the colonizers, and sometimes open rebellions erupted. The most famous of these revolts were the Indian Rebellion of 1857 to 1858 and the two peasant revolts in China, the Taiping Uprising (1850–64) and the Boxer Rebellion (1899–1901) mentioned earlier.

The Indian Rebellion (called the Indian Mutiny by the British) began when the British introduced a new cartridge smeared with cow and pig fat as a lubricant. Cows were sacred to Hindus, and pigs were offensive to Muslims; both groups saw the innovation as an attempt to convert them to Christianity. Indian troops in Bengal mutinied to initiate the rebellion, which spread to other regions and social groups. British authorities crushed the rebellion and afterward took direct control of India, ending the rule of the British East India Company.

Migrations, which were broadly similar to the trans-Atlantic ones in size and timing, also took place across the nonindustrial world. From India and southern China, many people migrated to Southeast Asia, the Indian Ocean Rim, and the South Pacific. From Northeast Asia and Russia, many moved to Manchuria, Siberia, Central Asia, and Japan. Long-distance and transoceanic migration increased gradually from the 1820s, then increased dramatically in the last quarter of the nineteenth century, facilitated by the growth of railroads and steamships. Non-Europeans were as greatly involved as Europeans in the expansion and integration of the world economy (see Map 11.2).

Gender Issues

Contact between Europeans and their colonial subjects brought awareness of different gender standards and expectations, leading to increased tensions, modifications of standards, and/or resistance to modification. According to European—that is, Victorian—gender values, women should be in households headed by husbands, carrying out domestic obligations. This value made European males collaborators in male domination with many of their colonial subjects, but it also raised some complicated issues. Examples in India and in sub-Saharan Africa illustrate some of these complications.

In India, both Muslim and Hindu traditions permitted no divorce, no remarriage for women after the death of husbands, and no property ownership by women except in marriage. Europeans, with their ideal of domesticity, promoted remarriage after a husband's death. They got this written into the Remarriage Law of 1853, resistance to which contributed to the Indian Rebellion of 1857.

In sub-Saharan Africa, Europeans wanted women to stay at home and not engage in their traditional subsistence agricultural work. This was contradicted by the fact that many men left their homes to work in mines and on plantations, leaving women to assume more of the agricultural labor at home. In South Africa, some 40 to 50 percent of the able-bodied men were absent from rural areas, and women headed a majority of households.

African women coped with these trends in a variety of ways. They made closer relations with their family of origin; they formed self-help societies and found ways to sell food and cloth. Sometimes they could take advantage of schooling to escape rural patriarchy. African men responded by petitioning for laws to criminalize adultery and restrict women to their villages. Fearing Africans' high regard for sexuality, Europeans imposed European dress habits, which largely were rejected as not practical in African climates.

Environmental Issues

During the nineteenth century three global losses loomed large—the loss of forests, of animals, and of **indigenous peoples,** defined as native-born people without a well-defined state structure. Already by midcentury, in addition to local peoples' awareness of the local issues, some European scientists were aware that these were global problems needing state intervention.

The need of industrial nations for food and raw materials resulted in the removal of huge areas of forests and native ecosystems. Monocultures (the practice of growing a single crop over a wide area for a number of consecutive years) replaced them, like coffee and tea plantations in India; many of the monocultures were introduced species. In Brazil, for example, over 11,000 square miles (30,000 square kilometers) of forest were destroyed in the nineteenth century to grow coffee bushes. Changes to the soil made restoration impossible. The need for exports was so great that no voice was raised against this in Brazil until the 1930s, and no government policy response occurred until the 1970s.

An early critique of environmental degradation came already in the late eighteenth century out of the deforestation that took place on the islands of St. Helena in the South Atlantic and Mauritius in the Indian Ocean. On these islands French and English botanists could see the dramatic effects of deforestation and could begin early experiments in protecting forests and fish and controlling water pollution. Scottish scientists employed by the British East India Company made a report in 1852 on the probable effects of the destruction of tropical forests, including a whole planet threatened by deforestation, famine, extinctions, and climate change. These early conservationists, in their response to the conditions of colonial rule, were able to foresee quite precisely the environmental problems of today.

The loss of animals worldwide proved no less dramatic than the loss of trees. The fur-bearing mammals of the Russian steppes and the American prairies were all but exterminated from 1710 to 1914. The fish and whale stock of the southern oceans were massively reduced. The animals and birds of Africa and India and the Pacific Islands were decimated by habitat destruction and by hunting. In Africa, British hunters shot thousands of antelopes, elephants, giraffes, and rhinoceroes. At first the British supplied guns to native Africans to induce them to join the slaughter; later they tried to restrict the use of guns to themselves. In India, the British hunters shot tigers from high on elephants, restricting this type of hunting to themselves after 1857. Very few lions and tigers existed in India by the beginning of the twentieth century; by then, cheetahs had become extinct there.

Some action was taken. The British in India passed regulations in the 1870s for protecting elephants. The Foreign Office in London hosted in 1900 the first international conference on African wildlife, which resulted in ineffective agreements but set a precedent for more productive efforts in the twentieth century. In the United States a diplomat and philologist, George Perkins Marsh (1801–82), published a remarkable pioneering study in 1874, *Earth as Modified by Human Action,* which had appeared 10 years earlier as *Man and Nature.*

In addition to trees and animals, indigenous peoples suffered huge setbacks in the nineteenth century, as the massive expansion of settler populations penned them in. In the United States, European settlers were determined to move all Native American peoples to the west of the Mississippi River by means of the Indian Removal Act of 1830. This resulted in the 800-mile (1,300-kilometer) migration, known as the Trail of Tears, from the eastern woodlands to Oklahoma in 1838 and 1839. After this, white settlers encroached on trans-Mississippi land. The Sioux, Comanche, Pawnee, and Apache peoples resisted with firearms and equestrian skills and won some battles, but eventually the U.S. forces prevailed, using cannon and rapid-firing Gatling machine guns.

European migration to Australia and New Zealand devastated indigenous people, at first largely through diseases such as smallpox and measles. The aboriginal population of Australia fell from about 650,000 in 1800 to 90,000 in 1900; in New Zealand the Maori population fell from about 200,000 in 1800 to 45,000 a century later. By 1900 the British had displaced most indigenous Australians from their traditional lands and dispersed them throughout the continent. In New Zealand, wars continued from the mid- to late nineteenth century; by its end the British had forced many Maori into poor rural communities separated from European society.

In the next chapter the story of industrialization will continue, as the pace of growth and change accelerated throughout the world.

SUMMARY

The breakthrough to modernity, which in terms of the political economy manifested itself as industrial capitalism and the modern nation-state, began in Great Britain with the innovation of coal-burning steam engines powering textile machinery. The techniques of industrial capitalism spread to most of Europe and the United States, and to Japan and Russia, by 1900. With the economic transformation came the political transformation of increasing political participation and the reach of the state further into the lives of its citizens. The need for markets and raw materials, coupled with technological power, resulted in European colonization of much of the rest of the world, reducing other nations to dependencies and creating a steep gradient in wealth between the developed and developing nations of the world. Vast social, gender, and environmental consequences occurred in both industrialized and dependent areas. By 1900 the world's human population was increasing at its fastest rate in history, while the outcome of the Industrial Revolution, with its fateful decision to burn coal, remained to be seen.

CHAPTER QUESTIONS

1. Tell the story of how the Industrial Revolution unfolded in Great Britain.
2. Describe how and where the revolution spread.
3. How did monarchies become transformed into modern states? What is the difference?
4. Describe the consequences of the Industrial Revolution—economic, political, social, global, gender, and environmental. Evaluate these consequences.
5. What is the significance of threshold 8?
6. Tell your family history in the framework of the Industrial Revolution.

KEY TERMS

factory system	indigenous peoples	modern state	three waves of
fossil fuels	Industrial Revolution	steam engines	industrialization
imperialism	Little Ice Age (LIA)		

FURTHER READING

Allen, Robert C. *The British Industrial Revolution in Global Perspective.* Cambridge and New York: Cambridge University Press, 2009.

Ansary, Tamin. *Destiny Disrupted: A History of the World through Islamic Eyes.* New York: Public Affairs, 2009.

Bayly, C. A. *Birth of the Modern World, 1780–1914: Global Connections and Comparisons.* Malden, MA: Blackwell, 2004.

Bin Wong, Robert. *China Transformed: Historical Change and the Limits of European Experience.* Ithaca and London: Cornell University Press, 1997.

Cho, Ji-Hyung. "The Little Ice Age and the Coming of the Anthropocene." In Barry Rodrigue, Leonid Grinin, and Andrey Korotaev, eds., *From the Big Bang to Global Civilization: A Big History Anthology.* Berkeley: University of California Press, forthcoming.

Davis, Mike. *Late Victorian Holocausts: El Niño Famines and the Making of the Third World.* London: Verso, 2001.

Headrick, Daniel R. *The Tools of Empire: Technology and European Imperialism in the Nineteenth Century.* New York: Oxford University Press, 1981.

Hunt, Lynn. *Inventing Human Rights: A History.* New York: Norton, 2007.

Marks, Robert B. *The Origins of the Modern World: A Global and Ecological Narrative.* 2nd ed. Lanham, MD: Rowman & Littlefield, 2002.

McNeill, William H. *The Shape of European History.* New York: Oxford University Press, 1974.

Pomeranz, Kenneth. *The Great Divergence: Europe, China, and the Making of the Modern World Economy.* Princeton, NJ: Princeton University Press, 2000.

Ruddiman, William F. *Plows, Plagues, and Petroleum: How Humans Took Control of Climate.* Princeton and Oxford: Princeton University Press, 2005.

Smail, Daniel Lord. *On Deep History and the Brain.* Berkeley: University of California Press, 2008.

Strayer, Robert W. *Ways of the World: A Brief Global History,* 2 vols. Boston and New York: Bedford/St. Martin's, 2009.

Uglow, Jenny. *The Lunar Men: Five Friends Whose Curiosity Changed the World.* New York: Farrar, Straus and Giroux, 2002.

ENDNOTES

1. Ji-Hyung Cho, "The Little Ice Age and the Coming of the Anthropocene," in Barry Rodrigue, Leonid Grinin, and Andrey Korotaev, eds., *From the Big Bang to Global Civilization: A Big History Anthology* (Berkeley: University of California Press, forthcoming).

2. Robert B. Marks, *The Origins of the Modern World: A Global and Ecological Narrative*, 2nd ed. (Lanham, MD: Rowman & Littlefield, 2002):127–28.

3. Quoted by Robert W. Strayer, *Ways of the World: A Brief Global History,* vol. 2 (Boston and New York: Bedford/St. Martin's, 2009):562.

4. Quoted by Marks, 139, from Karl Marx and Friedrich Engels, *The Communist Manifesto* (New York: Washington Square Press, 1964), 57–59, 78–79.

crossing the eighth threshold

chapter 12

Globalization, Growth, and Sustainability

Seeing the Big Picture

1900 to 2010 CE

▶ How has industrialization transformed today's world?

▶ How did capitalism change in the twentieth century?

▶ What were the most important innovations in the twentieth century?

▶ Are we humans in control of the rapid changes occurring in our world?

▶ What are the main dangers and opportunities we face?

▶ Does the Anthropocene count as one of the most significant turning points in the history of our planet?

Introduction

Chapter 11 described the beginnings of the modern revolution during what is conventionally known as the Industrial Revolution. By 1900, the industrialized West was not only the wealthiest region of the world but also politically and militarily dominant. The world seemed split in two, with one part, mainly in the Atlantic region, benefiting from the increasing resources made available by new technologies and organizational methods, while much of the rest of the world experienced decline, loss of independence, loss of wealth, and cultural demoralization.

Within each region, too, the gap between rich and poor seemed to increase. In industrial societies such as Britain, conditions in the major industrial cities early in the nineteenth century were so appalling that they helped generate the new ideology of **socialism,** whose goal was to end the huge differentials of wealth between capitalists and proletarians by abolishing capitalism itself. (Most forms of modern socialism were inspired by **Marxism,** the ideology developed in the writings of Karl Marx [1818–83].) The modern revolution, like every major change in human history (and perhaps in big history as a whole), seemed to have both creative and destructive sides.

In the first half of the twentieth century, there was indeed a sort of breakdown, as industrializing societies used their increasing wealth and power to fight over markets, raw materials, and colonies. Global networks unraveled, world trade declined, and the pace of global economic growth slowed, while conflicts increased despite the awesome power of industrial weapons. These conflicts culminated in two world wars, the most destructive in world history, and helped create a profound division into two hostile worlds, those of capitalism and **Communism.** (Communist societies were hostile to capitalism and inspired by the socialist ideology of Karl Marx.) For 40 years, the world was divided by the **Cold War,** a competition between superpowers and their allies that kept threatening to turn into a "hot" war fought with **nuclear weapons.** Nuclear weapons had been developed during World War II. They unlocked the power lying in the heart of each atomic nucleus and were so powerful they had the potential to destroy much of the biosphere in just a few hours.

Then, in the second half of the century, global networks began to reweave themselves, and globalization and growth took off once more. Capitalism would prove more robust than most socialists had imagined. The major imperial powers abandoned their nineteenth-century empires and a new wave of industrialization spread the modern revolution more widely. Japan's rapid industrialization showed that growth was not a monopoly of the West; and eventually other Asian countries, both in the capitalist and the Communist worlds, would also undergo rapid industrial revolutions.

In 1991, the Soviet Union collapsed. This ended the Cold War and increased the pace of integration in a world now dominated by countries whose economies were commercial and capitalistic even if (like Vietnam or the People's Republic of China) they professed Communist ideologies. Capitalism seemed to have triumphed in most of the world. But new instabilities appeared, some caused by the boom and bust cycles of capitalism itself, others by the growing inequalities between different parts of the world, and others by deep-rooted cultural differences.

In the second part of the chapter we will look at some of the major technologies that drove growth during the twentieth century and helped create levels of material prosperity that would have been unthinkable only a century or two earlier.

In the third part of the chapter we will explore how societies and lifeways were transformed by increasing material wealth. How did rapid economic growth change the way most people lived?

In the final part of the chapter we will pan back and look at growth from the perspective of the biosphere as a whole. In the twentieth century, human impacts on the biosphere increased so fast that humans became the dominant force for change in the biosphere. The Anthropocene epoch marks the first time in 4 billion years that a single species has acquired the power to transform the biosphere. Are we really in charge of the colossal powers we have acquired? These questions point toward Chapter 13, where we ask questions about the future: where is it all going?

Part 1: Political and Military Changes

The political and military history of the twentieth century breaks into two major periods: first a period of intense military competition and slowing industrialization, and then a period of renewed globalization and growth.

Imperialism and Military Competition: 1900 to 1950

The first half of the twentieth century was dominated by global conflicts on an unprecedented scale.

What went wrong? Some of the paradoxes of this era make more sense if we remember that, throughout the Era of Agrarian Civilizations, most states had ruled primarily through the use or the threat of force, rather than through the economic levers of the market. Warfare seemed the main business of governments most of the time. It took a long time for rulers to realize that the direct, and often coercive, methods of government that had worked in the past did not work so well for modern capitalist societies. It took time for governments to learn that managing and encouraging growth in a capitalist society meant achieving a difficult balance between direct government intervention (to maintain infrastructure such as roads and railways, to protect the financial system, to protect new knowledge through patents, and to maintain law and order) and nonintervention (to avoid stifling the entrepreneurial competition that drove innovation in capitalist societies). Governments had to support market activity, but if they interfered too much, they could undermine the competitive forces that drove capitalism's astonishing technological creativity.

In the twentieth century we see a series of experiments as governments tried to find a new balance between intervention and nonintervention. Some governments tried to let market forces drive economic change, while, at the other extreme, some governments (mainly in the Communist world) tried to use the technologies and managerial methods of the Industrial Revolution to manage society more directly and sometimes more coercively than the great tribute-taking empires of the Era of Agrarian Civilizations.

Everywhere, though, the power and significance of governments increased. Governments became wealthier, and as they helped build the physical, financial, educational, and legal infrastructures needed by flourishing industrial economies, they reached deeper and deeper into the lives of those they ruled. Even in the United States, where many believed governments should minimize their economic role, the ratio between government expenditure and the total value of all goods and services (measured as **gross domestic product [GDP]**) rose from 8 percent in 1913 to 20 percent by 1938 and to 31 percent by 1973, before falling slightly to 30 percent in 1999. In Britain, the equivalent ratios were 13 percent in 1913, rising to 29 percent in 1938, and to 42 percent in 1973, before falling back to 40 percent in 1999. In Japan and Germany we see a fall after World War II, but then the ratio rises to 38 percent in Japan and 48 percent in Germany by 1999. In the Communist countries, the story is even more dramatic, for in some of these, including the Soviet Union, the government attempted to manage the entire economy so that by the late 1930s the ratio between government expenditure and GDP approached 100 percent. In other Communist countries, where a substantial private sector survived or reemerged (as in China), the ratio would have been high, but not as high as in Stalinist Russia.

| *The Wars of the Early Twentieth Century: World War I* |

By the beginning of the twentieth century, there was a growing tendency to view international relations as an arena of brutal, life-and-death competition. Voices in all the major industrial countries were arguing that each nation had to protect its own interests, if necessary by force. There was growing support for **protectionism,** for excluding potential rivals from valuable markets through tariffs or, if necessary, by force. Whereas Adam Smith had argued that free trade and rapid growth would benefit everyone by raising productivity and lowering costs, protectionists, like traditional rulers in the Agrarian era, continued to imagine a world of limited resources in which each state or nation had to seek out its own share of raw materials and markets or go under.

Typical of such attitudes were the remarks of the English parliamentarian Joseph Chamberlain in 1889:

> The Foreign Office and the Colonial Office are chiefly engaged in finding new markets and in defending old ones. The War Office and Admiralty are mostly occupied in preparations for the defense of these markets, and for the protection of our commerce.[1]

Radical socialists also argued that there were limits to growth. But they saw this as a hopeful sign that capitalism itself would eventually collapse as capitalists ran out of markets for the increasing amount of goods they were producing. In 1916, a year before leading the 1917 Bolshevik revolution, Vladimir Lenin (1870–1924) wrote a book called *Imperialism: The Highest State of Capitalism.* In it he borrowed from the ideas of an English economist, John Hobson, to argue that the world war that had begun in 1914 was caused by conflicts between the leading capitalist nations over shrinking markets. However, he argued, the real price of that conflict between capitalists was being paid not by the capitalists, but by working people and colonies throughout the world.

One consequence of increasing protectionism was a sharp decline in international trade. According to one influential estimate, the total value of world exports increased at an annual rate of about 3.4 percent between 1870 and 1913; then fell to 0.9 percent between 1913 and 1950; before rising again to 7.9 percent between 1950 and 1973 and 5.1 percent between 1973 and 1998. These figures capture well the difference in international integration between the two halves of the twentieth century. Declining international trade in the first half of the century was linked to declining growth rates in general. According to one estimate, global GDP per capita rose by 1.3 percent each year between 1870 and 1913, whereas in the period from 1913 to 1950 it rose at only 0.91 percent each year. Then, from 1950 to 1973 the rate rose once again to 2.93 percent per annum (Figures 12.1 and 12.2).

As protectionist thinking spread in the early twentieth century, governments in the major industrialized countries prepared for war. The major European powers locked themselves into a system of military alliances that pitted Russia, France, and Britain against the central European powers of Germany, Austria, and Turkey.

In the summer of 1914, after almost a century of relative peace in Europe, war broke out between the two alliance systems. Many expected the war to last just a few months; in fact, it lasted over four years, until November 1918. Europe's imperial reach ensured that the war would touch many different parts of the world. Japan, Britain and France seized German colonies in Africa, China, and the Pacific; troops from India, Africa, Australia, and New Zealand fought against Turkish troops in the Dardanelles, or on the western front. In 1917 the United States, the largest industrial economy in the world, entered the First World War with decisive results. Industrial technologies guaranteed the war would be peculiarly bloody. Improved medical

the anthropocene

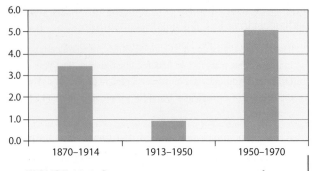

FIGURE 12.1 Percentage per annum growth rate of international trade, 1870 to 1970.

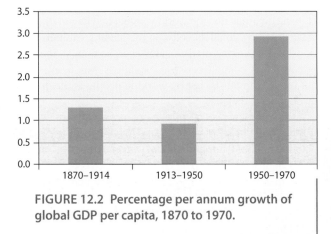

FIGURE 12.2 Percentage per annum growth of global GDP per capita, 1870 to 1970.

care kept soldiers in the front lines longer than ever before; machine guns slaughtered them in their thousands; and the German chemist Fritz Haber (1868–1934) discovered a way of synthesizing ammonia that made it possible to produce huge quantities of explosives. Haber also helped design the poison gases used to such terrible effect on the major battlefields of Europe.

The Interwar Years and World War II

The central European powers surrendered in 1918. But the bitterness generated by World War I ensured that the divisions that led to war would persist after it ended. Although the 1918 Treaty of Versailles created, in the League of Nations and related institutions, the first formal structures of world government, they were too weak to keep the peace. In the violently competitive spirit of the era, the victorious powers tried to secure their dominance by imposing a harsh peace on Germany and Austria and demanding the payment of massive war reparations. The harsh terms of the Versailles treaties undermined governments in both Germany and Austria/Hungary, destabilized their economies, and generated the anger that would eventually be mobilized by Fascist parties such as the German Nazis, with the goal of reversing the results of World War I. **Fascism** expressed the social Darwinian ideologies of the age of imperialism in peculiarly stark forms, portraying

international relations as a merciless battle between races and nations. In the 1930s, such attitudes sustained Adolph Hitler (1889–1945) and the Nazis in their drive for rearmament and expansionism. They would find their most extreme expression in the systematic murder by the Nazis of almost 6 million Jews during what is now known as the Holocaust.

As international trade declined and the defeated countries borrowed huge sums to pay reparations, the international financial system came under great strain. In 1929, a financial crash in the United States, whose banks had loaned much of the money used to maintain the system of reparations, led to economic breakdown in most of the capitalist world. This Great Depression reinforced the belief of many socialists that the capitalist system itself was doomed.

That belief was encouraged by the fact that in Russia, the world's largest country, the strains of World War I had brought down the traditional tsarist government and opened the way for a revolutionary seizure of power by Lenin's Bolshevik Party in October 1917. The Bolsheviks were determined to build the world's first socialist society, a society in which inequalities would be reduced and the working classes would collectively own and administer society's resources. Between 1917 and 1921, the Bolsheviks secured their power over most of the former Russian Empire during a bloody and destructive civil war that encouraged them and their opponents to continue seeing international relations as a matter of brutal and bloody competition.

The Bolshevik Party (renamed the Communist Party in 1918) proved that, if necessary, it was willing to use the coercive methods that had won the civil war in order to build a new type of society. But, unlike the Nazis, who saw the world as divided between competing races, the Communists saw a world divided between capitalist and socialist societies. They saw themselves as the leaders of the oppressed classes throughout the world, the workers and peasants. In their attempt to build a better society, they tried to build a modern industrial economy without the driver of capitalism, which they saw as the source of exploitation and inequality. Without competitive markets driving innovation and commerce, the government itself had to take over the complex task of administering resources. But to do this effectively it had to assume colossal power and it had to be willing to rule brutally when faced with opposition.

In 1929, the Communist Party confiscated the land of the peasantry and drove them into large collective farms. Doing so provoked massive resistance, disrupted agriculture, and caused terrible famines. In the 1930s, under new leader Joseph Stalin (1878–1953), the Communist Party imposed tough industrial discipline during the Five Year Plans, which helped it build a new, modern industrial sector. Many of the new technologies it used were borrowed from the capitalist West. To deal with opposition, the party created a huge empire of penal settlements and prison camps. The result of the Soviet industrialization drive was a strange hybrid society that combined the coercive and authoritarian governmental methods of tribute-taking states with the technologies of the twentieth century. Millions died in camps or during the purges that reached their peak in 1937, but something like a modern industrial society was built at the same time.

The global division between capitalist and Communist powers was paralleled by a division between imperialist and colonial societies. Colonial rule and the anti-imperial rhetoric of both the United States and the Soviet Union inspired anticolonial movements in Asia and Africa. The fact that even the victorious colonial powers, above all France and Britain, had been weakened by World War I gave such movements hope of eventually overthrowing their colonial masters. In some colonial countries there emerged inspirational national leaders such as the Indian politician Mahatma Gandhi (1869–1948).

In the Far East, Japan had industrialized rapidly in the late nineteenth and early twentieth centuries, but it had limited raw materials of its own. In the twentieth century it began to seek an empire that would enhance its power, prestige, and wealth. Japanese forces defeated China and conquered Taiwan in the Sino-Japanese War of 1894 and 1895. In 1904 and 1905 Japan defeated Russian armies in Manchuria, which Japanese nationalists regarded, along with Korea, as a natural region for Japanese colonial expansion. In 1910 Japan added Korea to its empire, and in 1931 it took over Manchuria, ruling it as the state of Manchukuo. In 1937, Japanese armies invaded China in a campaign of exceptional brutality. In 1940, after concluding a treaty of alliance with Germany and the Axis powers, Japan began to create an empire in Southeast Asia, in the pursuit of both prestige and raw materials such as oil and rubber that were vital to a modern army and the industries that supported it. By the end of 1942, Japanese armies had conquered French, Dutch, U.S., and British colonies in the Philippines, Southeast Asia, and Indonesia.

In a sense, World War II began with the Japanese conquest of Manchuria in 1931. War was reignited in Europe in September 1939, when France and Britain reluctantly declared war on Germany after Germany invaded Poland. The Second World War was even more global than the first. In June 1941 a 4-million-strong German army invaded the Soviet Union, and in December, the Japanese government led by General Hideki Tojo (1884–1948) tried to cripple its main rival in the Pacific region by bombing Pearl Harbor in Hawaii. This brought into the war the world's largest economic power, the United States.

World War II was fought in the Pacific and Southeast Asia as well as in Europe, North Africa, and the Soviet Union. Its bloody climax would be the dropping of the first atomic bomb on Hiroshima on August 6, 1945. The Soviet Union alone lost about 7 million soldiers and perhaps 20 million civilians. But it ended the war in control of much of eastern Europe, including half of Germany. Within five years, China, the most populous country in the world, would join the Communist bloc and the Soviet Union seemed stronger than ever. By 1950, the world was divided into three large regions, a capitalist bloc, a Communist bloc, and a large number of countries, many of them former colonies, that would try to maneuver between the two blocs.

Reintegration, Renewed Growth, and New Forms of Conflict: 1950 to 2010

Both the United States and the Soviet Union understood that economic growth—that is, the capacity to mobilize more resources than your rivals to build military power and raise standards of living—was the key to success in the modern world. Together, the United States, the Soviet Union, and their allies had outproduced the Axis powers, and that was the main reason they had won the war.

But what was the key to sustained economic growth in the twentieth century? Here, the two Cold War superpowers drew different conclusions, each seeing victory as proof of the virtues of their own system. The United States, which had suffered the least damage of all the major combatant powers during the two world wars, emerged as the most powerful and wealthiest of capitalist governments. Its government undertook to reform the global capitalist system to draw once again on the technological creativity generated by competitive markets and international trade to generate growth. Meanwhile, buoyed by victory in what they called the "Great Patriotic War," the leaders of the Soviet Union insisted that their system, which had largely eliminated market forces, would overtake the capitalist world in production, in living standards, and in political and military power.

The Capitalist World   The United States ended the war with its economic, political, and military power greatly enhanced. It had suffered fewer casualties (about 400,000, in contrast to the almost 27 million soldiers and civilians who died in the Soviet Union and the 7 to 8 millions who died in Germany), and less damage than the other major combatant powers. In 1950 its economy accounted for over one-quarter of global GDP. It was also determined not to repeat the mistakes made after World War I, which had virtually guaranteed a new world war. Instead, the United States bet on Adam Smith's central idea: that international trade could benefit everyone. Its government drew the conclusion that reigniting international trade and rebuilding the economies of other countries, including its former enemies, was the best way of sustaining growth for itself and the world as a whole. It also gambled on this being a strategy that would eventually expose the limitations of Communism and undermine the appeal of Communism's egalitarian ideology.

In 1944 a World Bank was created along with an International Monetary Fund to help establish a new and more stable capitalist financial order. A new world organization, the United Nations, was created on June 26, 1945, in San Francisco. Under the Marshall Plan, administered for President Harry Truman (1884–1972) by Secretary of State General George Marshall (1880–1959), the United States actively encouraged a revival of global trade by lending or

the anthropocene

granting many billions of dollars to rebuild the war-ruined economies of Europe and Japan.

By the late 1950s, the economies of western Europe, including West Germany, were booming, and the production of mass consumer goods such as washing machines, refrigerators, and cars began to create the sort of mass market that had already emerged in the United States earlier in the century. The Japanese economy flourished under pro-capitalist democratic governments. Forced demilitarization meant that Japan's military budget was tiny, so the Japanese invested, instead, in building a huge and productive civilian industrial sector. World trade took off. In 1913, exports of merchandise had accounted for about 8 percent of the total value of world trade; but by 1950 the level had fallen to about 5.5 percent. By 1973 exports accounted for an unprecedented 10.5 percent of global GDP, and by 1998 world trade would account for over 17 percent of global GDP.

Japan became one of the world's leading industrialist capitalist economies, but other East Asian nations followed a similar trajectory. Most spectacular was the growth of the "Asian tigers," South Korea, Taiwan, and Singapore. Between 1965 and 1989, the total share of global production coming from East Asia rose from 14 percent to 25 percent. In many other nations in the Muslim world, in Africa and in South America, new industries were established that created the promise of rapid economic growth, though in many of these countries growth was sabotaged as profits flowed into the hands of corrupt rulers or overseas creditors. Nevertheless, in the second half of the century even the world's poorest nations experienced some degree of industrialization. One of the most spectacular shifts in wealth was in the Persian Gulf, where the discovery of oil generated immense wealth in regions that had been colonized both by the Ottoman Empire and by Europe.

The End of Colonial Empires

Both the United States and the Soviet Union officially opposed imperialism, but for different reasons. In a sense, the United States was itself an imperial power. It had been built on the conquest of North America from its indigenous populations, and U.S. governments had acquired an empire of their own in the Philippines in the late nineteenth century. Nevertheless, the United States offered a powerful symbol of anticolonialism because it had been created in an anticolonial war of independence in the eighteenth century. The Soviet Union, too, could be viewed as an imperial empire; it incorporated the Russian Empire's former colonies in Central Asia, and, after the end of World War II, it supported puppet regimes in the countries of eastern Europe. But its rulers claimed to represent the exploited and oppressed including those oppressed by colonialism.

Meanwhile, the major imperialist powers—Britain, France, and Germany—had been weakened by war and lacked the resources and the will to maintain their colonies against growing resistance. Besides, imperialism no longer seemed legitimate in the postwar world, and it became harder and more costly to maintain as anti-imperialist movements emerged from Africa to India and Southeast Asia.

Defeat in war destroyed the colonial empires of Germany and Japan. In the decades after World War II, Britain and France and the other remaining colonial powers gave up their empires, often after long and bloody anticolonial wars. In China, the defeat of Japan ended direct foreign rule and resulted, after a civil war, in the eventual victory of the Communists, led by Mao Zedong (1893–1976) in 1949. In Algeria and Vietnam, France tried to restore its colonial authority. In Algeria, France conceded independence in 1960 only after a long and bloody anticolonial uprising. In Vietnam, socialist armies led by Ho Chi Minh (1890–1969) defeated the French in 1954 only to face a pro-capitalist state in the south that was backed by the United States. Not until 1975, after a long and costly guerilla war, would Vietnam be reunified under a Communist government. In Korea, similar divisions between a Communist north, supported by China and the Soviet Union, and a capitalist south, supported by the United States and its allies, led to a brutal civil war and eventually to a division into two rival countries, both of which survived into the early twenty-first century.

In 1947, Britain conceded independence to its colonies in the Indian subcontinent. The independence movement here was largely peaceful, partly because of the prominent role played by Mahatma Gandhi, who pioneered techniques of nonviolent protest. But independence led to the emergence of rival Hindu and Muslim states, India and Pakistan, which would fight three major wars over the next few decades. Britain gave up its African colonies, too, sometimes in the face of violent opposition. In 1963, Britain granted independence to Kenya, after a 10-year-long anticolonial war. Kenya's new ruler was Jomo Kenyatta (1893–1978), one of the leaders of the national resistance movement. In just 25 years, between 1945 and 1970, the breakup of empires had created over 70 new nations.

Newly independent nations soon faced new problems. Nations such as Nigeria had borders that had been determined by imperialist powers in the nineteenth century rather than by the customs and traditions of the people who lived within them. These borders often made little sense for newly independent nation-states. In Nigeria, maintaining unity between the Muslim populations in the north and the Christian or traditional populations of the south, and the many different tribal groupings of the country as a whole, proved extremely difficult; and between 1967 and 1970, the country descended into a civil war. A unified Nigeria survived, just. After the war massive revenues from offshore oil promised to provide the revenues for the building of a modern industrial society. But far too much oil wealth ended up in the hands of the corrupt or was used to service foreign debts, and Nigeria's unity remains fragile.

In many former colonies it appeared that the coercive rule of imperialism had been replaced by the subtler coercion of the market. Many newly independent states found themselves trying, against the odds, to survive in a highly commercialized capitalist world market, in which the leading industrialized nations seemed to hold all the cards. Colonial governments had rarely done much to develop the economies of their colonies in a balanced way, preferring, instead, to develop those forms of production most valuable for the home colony, such as rubber in Malaya, or coffee in Kenya, or palm oil in Nigeria. They often neglected crucial infrastructure, including education and health. Finding the expertise, the capital, the markets, and the policies needed for rapid but balanced industrialization proved an immense challenge to many newly independent countries.

The Communist World

To some newly independent countries, the Soviet Union offered a tempting alternative to the capitalist societies of the West. Had not Russia's debts made it a "semicolony" of the West, and had it not managed, through violent struggle, to escape the grip of the capitalist world and build a powerful modern economy against the odds? The Soviet Union encouraged such ideas by giving economic, technical, and sometimes military support to allies in the former colonial world, from Cuba to Nigeria to Egypt. In some cases, the results were indeed spectacular. In China, in North Korea, and in parts of eastern Europe the methods of the Soviet Union were used to build the foundations of modern industrial economies.

In the middle years of the twentieth century, Communism did indeed seem to many to offer a viable, and perhaps a more egalitarian, path to modernity than capitalism. By the mid-1950s the Soviet Union had largely recovered from the terrible devastation of the war years, and under a new leader, Nikita Khrushchev (1894–1971), it abandoned some of the more oppressive features of the Stalinist system and greatly reduced the prison camp population. Soviet armies seemed as powerful as those of the West; it boasted a modern educational system and a powerful industrial sector; and in the 1950s Soviet science would astonish the world by developing both fission and fusion bombs, and by sending the first satellite into space in 1957. On April 12, 1961, it sent the first human into space, an air force pilot named Yuri Gagarin. In the early 1960s, industrial growth was also raising the living standards of Soviet citizens as Khrushchev's government devoted more resources to consumer goods such as city apartments, washing machines, televisions, and refrigerators.

Industrial growth was also rapid in China and in parts of eastern Europe. For a time it seemed, as Khrushchev claimed, that the Communist system would "bury" the capitalist system by growing faster, generating more innovation, and raising the living standards of its citizens more rapidly. Former colonies watched the contest closely, and many accepted loans and technical help from both sides.

But during the 1970s, Soviet claims for the superiority of the Communist system began to look increasingly hollow. At stake was an issue of profound importance for understanding the modern world. Were the administrative and coercive methods of the pre-capitalist world perhaps capable of generating growth as successfully as the commercial methods of the capitalist world? Was this the deeper message of the Soviet command economy? Had the Soviet Union discovered new drivers of growth and innovation?

In the 1930s, Soviet industrial growth was exceptionally fast, and even in the period from 1950 to 1973 the Soviet economy was probably growing at about 3.4 percent per annum. But growth rates were slowing, and much growth was accounted for by the discovery of large amounts of oil and natural gas rather than by increasing productivity. Between 1973 and 1990 average growth rates fell to about 0.75 percent per annum, and eventually it became clear that even this growth rate was partly illusory. In the 1980s a new leader, Mikhail Gorbachev (1931–), would admit that by then growth was generated mainly by exports of oil and the sale of liquor. Living standards ceased to grow in the Soviet Union, and Soviet leaders and military planners realized that the Soviet Union was falling behind the capitalist West technologically and militarily.

The reasons for the slowing rates of growth in the Soviet Union were subtle but profound, and they tell us some important things about the nature of growth in the modern world. Part of the problem was that the Soviet command economy was not very good at stimulating Collective Learning and innovation. The Soviet command economy was ruled by a united and highly disciplined elite that was very good at mobilizing the huge human and economic resources of the largest country in the world for large projects such as rapid industrialization or war. What the system could not encourage was creative initiative from below, and Soviet economists were very much aware of the problem. We have seen in earlier chapters that tribute-taking political systems were never good at encouraging innovation. The reasons are fundamental: You can beat someone into digging a ditch, but you cannot beat someone into creative innovation. Modern industrial economies are just too complex to be run like armies. On the other hand, competitive markets provide powerful and efficient ways of adjusting prices and costs to reflect billions of individual decisions by millions of people. Planners simply cannot keep track of such complexity, and their attempts to do so ended up distorting prices and misallocating economic resources on a colossal scale.

Although aware of the need to raise productivity, Soviet governments felt they could not relax their grip on society without losing their own power, which was why they saw even literature and the arts as potential threats to the system. Indeed, they saw the electronic revolution and its products, including computers and photocopy machines, as threats because these new technologies allowed new ways of disseminating ideas and information that the state could not control.

By the 1980s it was clear that the system could survive only if it began to reintroduce competitive markets. A new generation of leaders that came to power in the mid-1980s understood that the Soviet economy and Soviet military

the anthropocene

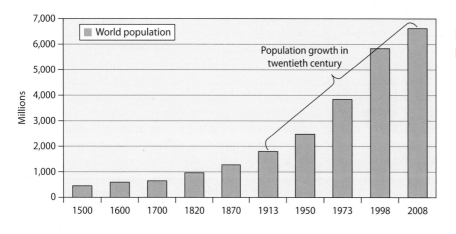

FIGURE 12.3 Growth in world population, 1500 to 2008.

power were in decline, and attempted to reduce the role of the government in economic, and even in political, activity. But their attempts to reform the system led to collapse, and in 1991, the Soviet Union fell apart, and its different constituent nations began to build new market-based societies. This proved a huge challenge because they lacked most of the legal, economic, and cultural infrastructure—the property laws, banking institutions, networks of credit, and entrepreneurial habits—that supported market activity in capitalist societies.

Chinese rulers seem to have managed a similar transition without a political collapse. After the death of Mao Zedong in 1976, his successor, Deng Xiaoping (1904–97), began to introduce market reforms in 1978. In some ways the transition to a market economy was easier in China partly because here capitalism had been eliminated for at most a generation, whereas in the Soviet Union it had vanished for almost three generations, long enough for most of the cultural and legal traditions of capitalism to vanish entirely. Market reforms led to rapid economic growth in China. Between 1973 and 1998 Chinese GDP per capita grew at the remarkable rate of 5.4 percent per annum.

The collapse of the Communist command economies highlighted the importance of competitive markets in the modern world, and the importance of finding the right balance of government authority and market freedom. As the experience of the Soviet command economy showed, excessive government control could stifle creative the entrepreneurial creativity that was the fundamental driver of innovation in the capitalist world. By the end of the century it seemed clear that, for better or worse, capitalist economies with competitive markets provided the structures best able to ensure sustained economic growth.

Part 2: Growth—More Humans Consuming More

Beneath the political, economic and military changes we have described so far, other and even more profound changes were taking place. Above all, industrialization and economic growth increased the ecological power of

human beings over the biosphere as a whole. One of the clearest measures of a species' ecological power is population growth, because populations can grow only if there are more resources to support them. In 1913 there were about 1.8 billion people on Earth; by 2008 there were about 6.7 billion people. In less than a century, world populations had multiplied by almost four times. It had taken almost 200,000 years for human populations to reach 1 billion; the 100 years of the twentieth century would add another 5 billion. Furthermore, most people were living longer, as average life expectancies doubled during the twentieth century, rising from about 31 years to 66 years. With populations four times as large and twice the life expectancy of a century before, this means that even if each individual had continued to consume resources at the same rate as in 1900, total consumption of resources would have risen by almost eight times (Figure 12.3).

But the average consumption of each individual was also rising, and rising spectacularly. Of course, we must remember that statistics like the following are full of inaccuracies, and they ignore important aspects of economic behavior, including most forms of domestic work and childrearing, as well as the impact of human activities on the environment. Nevertheless, they do provide a very rough measure of changes in human consumption of resources, for it is certain that increasing production requires more labor and more raw materials.

According to one of the more widely accepted statistical compilations, the total production of all countries (GDP, measured in billions of 1990 international dollars) increased from $2,700 billion in 1913 to $33,700 billion in 1998, an increase of almost 12 times. By 2008 global production had doubled again. If these statistics are not too misleading, they suggest that, as a species, in 2008 we were using almost 24 times the resources we used 100 years earlier. That represents an astonishing increase in human control of the Earth's energy and resources in just a single century (Figures 12.4 and 12.5).

Consumption increased because rates of innovation accelerated, particularly in the second half of the century. Innovation so widespread, so rapid, and so unexpected had never been seen before. Innovation transformed not just methods of production, but also how production was

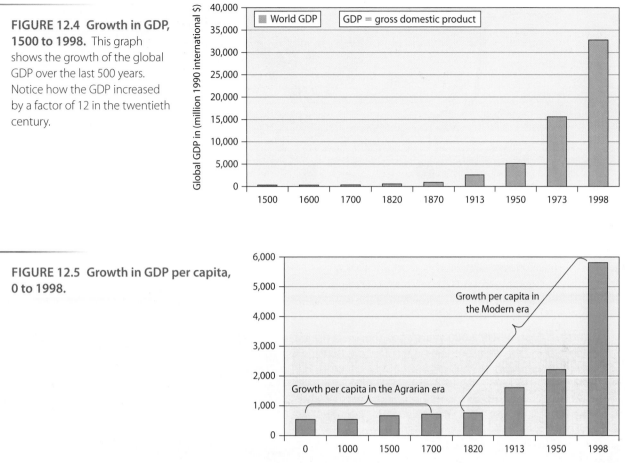

FIGURE 12.4 Growth in GDP, 1500 to 1998. This graph shows the growth of the global GDP over the last 500 years. Notice how the GDP increased by a factor of 12 in the twentieth century.

FIGURE 12.5 Growth in GDP per capita, 0 to 1998.

organized and financed and how goods were transported and advertised and bought and sold. It also generated entirely new products, services, and technologies, from plastics to the Internet and nuclear weapons. The description that follows is a short list of some of the new methods and technologies that increased our collective control over the resources of the biosphere. All these new technologies had the effect of cheapening production and therefore expanding markets, which encouraged investment in production and research, which further expanded markets in a powerful feedback cycle. Maps 12.1 through 12.4 summarize changes in regional wealth around the world over 2,000 years.

Food

Since 1900, food production has outpaced population growth. While the number of humans has increased by about three and a half times, total grain production increased by five times, from about 400 million tons (about 360 million metric tons) a year to 2,000 million tons (1,800 million metric tons). Meanwhile, the productivity of a given area of arable land increased by about three times. This remarkable increase in food production could *not* be achieved by tripling the amount of cultivated land because, unlike in previous centuries, there was little new land available. (The one major exception was the steppes of Eurasia,

which Soviet governments would bring under the plow in the 1950s during the so-called Virgin Lands program.) Most gains in productivity since 1900 have depended on new productivity-raising technologies.

Agriculture became an industrial activity, conducted on a huge scale, and dependent on massive investment and advanced science. Machines based on fossil fuels, first steam engines based on coal, then internal combustion engines based on gasoline, began to take over laborious tasks such as reaping and harvesting. The energy bonanza of the fossil fuels revolution also rejuvenated the ancient technology of irrigation. Fossil-fuel-powered earth-moving equipment reduced the cost of building dams and irrigation canals, while diesel pumps made it easier to draw water up from wells and aquifers. Between 1950 and 2000, the area of irrigated land increased from 230 million to 640 million acres (94 to 260 million hectares), and today irrigation accounts for about 64 percent of all water use. Fisheries, too, were exploited with increasing efficiency as more powerful engines, better navigational equipment, and larger nets made it possible for trawlers to effectively vacuum the seas. In the half-century after 1950, fish catches rose from 19 to 94 million tons (17 to 85 million metric tons). So good are we at catching fish that many fish species are now close to extinction.

The productivity of the land also increased. For millennia, renewing the fertility of the soil had meant taking

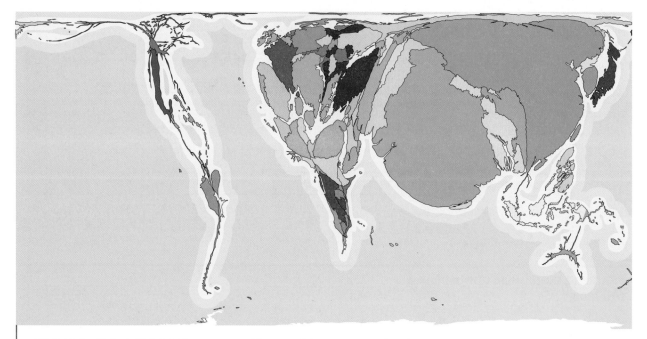

MAP 12.1 Global GDP 2,000 years ago. The size of the territory is related to estimates of the size of the economy of that territory. Note the superpowers of 2,000 years ago, India and China.

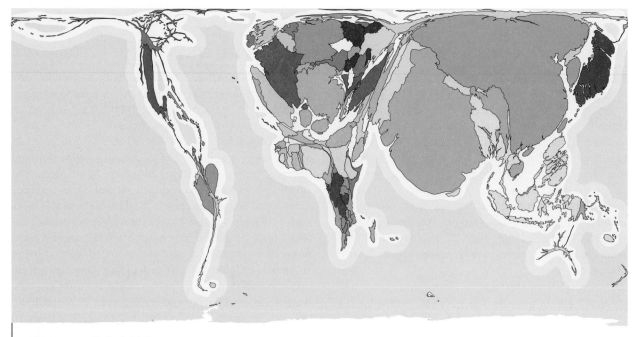

MAP 12.2 Global GDP 500 years ago. Notice that 500 years ago, East Asia still appears at the center of the world economy.

it temporarily out of cultivation (fallowing) or enriching it with animal or human wastes. But stores of natural fertilizers were limited, particularly in societies, such as those of the West that preferred not to use human wastes as fertilizer. By 1900 even the rich South American deposits of guano (the waste products of birds), discovered in the early nineteenth century, had largely been worked out. A major breakthrough came in 1909 when Fritz Haber showed how to synthesize ammonia industrially from atmospheric nitrogen and hydrogen, because ammonia could be used to create huge amounts

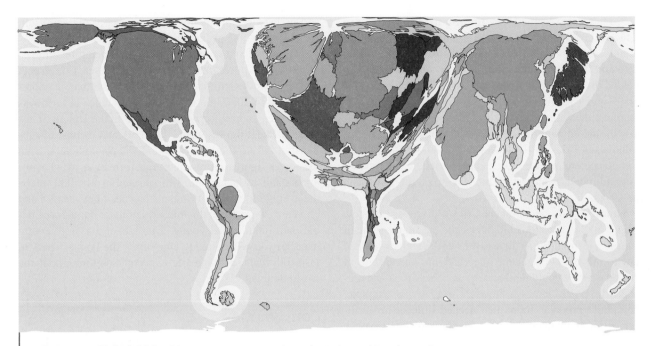

MAP 12.3 Global GDP 100 years ago. Notice how the Industrial Revolution has raised the wealth of Europe and North America and led to a sharp decline in the relative wealth of East Asia.

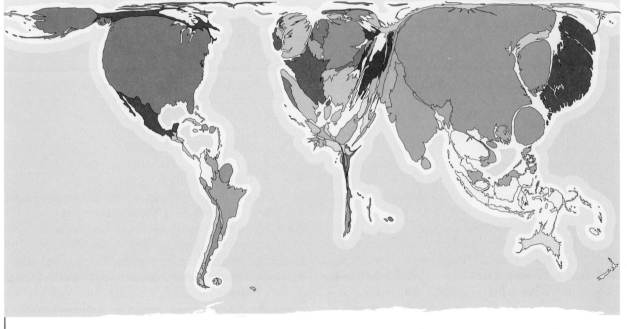

MAP 12.4 Global GDP today (2015, estimated). Notice the rapid reemergence of East Asia early in the twenty-first century.

of nitrates to fertilize the soil. John McNeill argues that Haber's invention may have done more than anything else to expand food supplies in the twentieth century, allowing perhaps 2 billion to eat who could not otherwise have been fed without a 30 percent increase in available croplands.[2]

Industrial chemists also raised agricultural productivity by creating chemicals to kill off pests, even though it eventually became clear that many, such as DDT, had harmful side effects as they worked their way into the soils and through the food chain into human bodies.

We have also learned how to raise the productivity of domestic crops and animals. Old-fashioned methods of artificial selection began to be applied more efficiently within large and well-funded research projects, such as those that yielded the new, more productive varieties of wheat of the 1960s green revolution. These strains responded well to liberal applications of fertilizer, and diverted more of their growth into edible products and less into roots and stems. In India and Pakistan alone, wheat production increased by over 50 percent in the 1960s; and in Mexico, wheat production multiplied by almost six times between the 1940s and the 1970s.

James Watson and Francis Crick's discovery of how DNA works in 1953 took biologists into the engine room of natural selection. From the early 1970s, scientists learned how to move bits of genetic material from one species to another so they could deliberately engineer crops and animals with useful genes from other species. For example, they could produce grains that needed little or no fertilizer or that contained natural protection against pests so that they needed few pesticides. Genetically modified grains were more productive, and some claimed that they were tastier than the species they displaced. In the United States, where the new technologies were embraced enthusiastically, 15 percent of corn, 30 percent of soybeans, and over 50 percent of cotton grown in 2000 were genetically modified.

Health and Longevity

Medical innovations, such as improved knowledge about the dangers of infection and the importance of cleanliness, had a dramatic impact on health, particularly for the very old and the very young.

Wastewater treatment and the supply of clean drinking water also had a colossal impact, but depended on well-funded local government agencies, so that even in 1980 only half of the world's population had access to treated water. New and improved medicines, such as aspirin or antibiotics, also reduced the suffering caused by disease. In 1928, Alexander Fleming (1881–1955) discovered that bacteria such as penicillin could be used to fight off infections, and after reliable methods of mass production were developed by Howard Florey (1898–1968) in the 1940s, antibiotics were widely used to protect the health of troops in World War II. Eventually, antibiotics would help improve the health of millions of humans as well as their animal domesticates. Yet we are also realizing that the war against disease is far from over, as evidence grows of how effectively disease-carrying organisms—ranging from the human immunodeficiency virus (HIV) responsible for acquired immunodeficiency syndrome (AIDS), to *Staphylococcus aureus* (golden staph)—can develop immunities to the chemical and biological weapons we use against them. Expensive high-tech medical procedures such as organ transplants or brain surgery have had a more limited impact on human health, though they hold out the hope that we will eventually engineer away many forms of disease

and perhaps remove many of the causes of old age itself, thereby extending average life spans by many decades.

More food and improved health and sanitation allowed more people to live healthier and longer lives. Life expectancies are still significantly higher in richer than in poorer countries. In 2000, the world life expectancy at birth was 65 for men and 69 for women, while in the United States the equivalent figures were 74 and 80, and in most of sub-Saharan Africa they were 46 and 47. Nevertheless, even the lower figures represent a transformation in what we understand by a human "life span." For 100,000 years, the average life span of humans has been between 25 and 35 years. In practice, this meant that huge numbers of babies and infants died young. That meant that if you were over 35, you were already enjoying a life bonus. Then, in just 100 years, average life expectancies throughout the world doubled.

Consumption

People are also consuming more than ever before. In the Agrarian era, most people were farmers, living close to subsistence. Only a tiny elite group, rarely accounting for more than 5 percent of the population, consumed luxury goods. Agricultural productivity was so low that it was rarely possible to support more than 5 to 10 percent of the population in nonfarm occupations. Today, as productivity rises, the relative size of the nonfarming population is increasing, and the production and consumption of goods has outstripped population growth. A new, global middle class is emerging that enjoys unprecedented wealth.

Electric cables and oil and gas pipes have brought the energy of the fossil fuels revolution into our homes as well as our factories, creating mechanical slaves such as washing machines that are more powerful, more docile, and usually more efficient than the human slaves of the Agrarian era. Electricity made it possible to distribute energy cheaply and in precisely calculable amounts to drive small machines from lightbulbs to phones to washing machines and computers. The key to making energy so transportable was Michael Faraday's (1791–1867) discovery in 1821 that if you moved a metal coil inside a magnetic field, you could generate an electric current. By the 1860s, powerful generators designed in Germany and Belgium and driven by steam engines or hydropower could produce huge electric currents. Alternating current, developed in the 1890s, made it easier and cheaper to distribute electricity over large distances. In 1889, Nicola Tesla (1856–1943) designed the first cheap electric motors, and in the early twentieth century, electric lights and machines began to transform the lives of consumers. In the Soviet Union, the Bolshevik government saw electrification as vital to the building of socialism. In the 1920s and 1930s electricity began to transform the life of ordinary consumers in the more industrialized societies. By the mid-1930s, almost 90 percent of Japanese households had access to electricity, almost 70 percent of households in the United States, and almost 50 percent in Britain.

Cheap oil and electricity could be used to run private cars, washing machines, heaters, coolers, air conditioners, televisions, and eventually computers. The internal combustion engine was more efficient than the steam engine because the fuel was burned directly inside the piston that drove the motor. The first gasoline-fueled internal combustion engine was built in 1883 by Karl Benz (1844–1929). But the first automobiles were expensive, handcrafted luxury goods. In 1913, Henry Ford (1863–1947) began to produce an assembly-line car that sold cheaply enough to bring cars within reach of the growing middle class. He cut costs by borrowing the techniques of producing interchangeable parts that had been pioneered in the manufacture of guns (interchangeable parts were identical so they could be mass-produced and did not need hand tooling); and combining it with the use of assembly lines, a manufacturing technique pioneered in the meat-packing industry.

An increasing number of goods that would once have seemed luxuries began to be produced so cheaply, and on such a scale that they could be purchased by a majority of consumers. The synthesis of new, cheap, raw materials such as plastics and synthetic rubber (pioneered in Germany, which lacked easy access to sources of natural rubber) also cut costs. Meanwhile, advertising encouraged those who could afford them to buy new consumer products, and banks provided loans to many who could not really afford such goods. As the market expanded, money and credit became cheaper. The result was a positive feedback cycle that is familiar to every economist: as more people bought once-expensive consumer goods, costs of production and of credit fell, so that even more could afford to buy them.

Transportation and Communications

Innovations in transportation and communications have always been crucial drivers of growth and innovation. Improved methods of transportation cheapened consumer goods by reducing the cost of moving them from producer to retailer to consumer.

The transportation revolution began in the nineteenth century with the introduction of railroads and steamships. From 1877 many steamships were refrigerated so they could carry fresh produce from one side of the world to the other. Steamships alone cut the cost of shipping freight across the Atlantic by almost 95 percent between 1815 and 1900, and railways cut the cost of land transportation even more dramatically. In the twentieth century, new forms of transportation included the private car and the truck. Both required networks of paved roads, which governments were willing to pay for because they understood how improved transportation could stimulate economic growth. Automobiles and trucks and buses made it easier than ever before to transport people and goods over short and medium distances. After World War II, commercial air transport began to speed up the transport of low-bulk goods such as mail. Since the 1950s, the introduction of containers—uniform-sized metal boxes that could be loaded and unloaded easily from trucks to trains to ships—has slashed the transportation costs of heavier goods.

In the twentieth century humans invented rockets that could carry them into space. Although the Soviet Union was the first society to launch a human into space, the United States was the first to land a human on another body in space: Neil Armstrong (1930–2012) landed on the moon on July 20, 1969. In a small way, humans had become an interplanetary species. Seeing photos of the Earth from space helped millions understand the smallness and fragility of our home planet.

Changes in the technologies of information exchange and storage proved even more important than changes in transportation. Before industrialization, information could move no faster than the individual humans who carried it. The information revolution began with the discovery in 1837 that electric charges could be used to carry information through wires. In the same year, Samuel Morse (1791–1872) created the code that would make telegraphy practical. In 1876, Alexander Graham Bell (1847–1922) patented the first telephone.

Long-distance communication took off when Guglielmo Marconi (1847–1922) showed how electric waves could be used to send messages through the air "wirelessly." Commercial shippers and navies were particularly interested in wireless technologies because they could not use forms of telegraphy that depended on fixed cables. In 1899 Marconi sent a radio message in Morse across the English Channel, and in 1901 he sent one across the Atlantic. By the middle of the next decade it was possible to transmit voices and music. The first commercial radio station, KDKA, was launched in Pittsburgh in 1920. Transmitting moving pictures wirelessly was a more complex challenge, and television did not take off until after World War II, though the mechanical projection of moving pictures through the cinema was a technology developed in the last years of the nineteenth century.

Communications would be transformed once more as a result of the computer revolution of the late twentieth century. Computer technology was pioneered during World War II to calculate the trajectories of rockets or to crack codes. But early computers depended on large and unreliable vacuum tubes and were huge, expensive, unreliable, and unwieldy. Like cars, computers began to transform society only when they became cheap enough for mass consumers. That was made possible by the invention of the transistor in 1947. The power of transistors began to increase exponentially, while their size and cost fell. The first computer for a mass market was produced in 1975 by a company called Altair: it cost US$400. In the 1980s, computers began to be linked in networks, magnifying their power many times over, and in 1989 Tim Berners-Lee (1955–) wrote the programs that would allow even amateurs to use the "Internet," the vast web of information being exchanged between the world's computers, large and small. Fiber-optic cables cheapened the cost of linking computers and reduced the cost of sending messages to almost zero. Information was becoming almost free. In 1930 it cost $300 to make a three-minute phone call from New York to London; by 1970 it cost $20; by 2007 it cost $0.3. But e-mail was virtually free. Collective Learning could now function with a speed and efficiency inconceivable even a century earlier.

Warfare and the Technology of Destruction

Innovation also increased the effectiveness and productivity of war machines. The internal combustion engine was adapted to tanks, and planes and rockets were adapted to drop bombs. Meanwhile, the power of explosives increased exponentially. In 1866, Alfred Nobel (1833–96) improved on traditional gunpowder-based explosives by creating dynamite, which was based on nitroglycerine.

Early in the twentieth century, Albert Einstein (1879–1955) showed in his *general theory of relativity* that it should be possible to transform matter into huge amounts of energy. During World War II, governments on both sides set scientists the challenge of creating weapons that could use the awesome power buried in the heart of atoms. The first fission weapon, based on the breakdown of uranium and developed by the U.S. government's Manhattan Project, was exploded at the Trinity test site in New Mexico in July 1945. J. Robert Oppenheimer (1904–67), the scientific director of the Manhattan Project, wrote that as he witnessed the first explosion, he thought of a line from the Hindu *Bhagavad Gita,* in which the god Vishnu declares: "Now I am become Death, the destroyer of worlds." Three weeks later an atomic bomb destroyed the Japanese city of Hiroshima, killing 80,000 people almost immediately; within a year, radiation and other injuries raised the death toll to almost 150,000.

In the 1950s, the United States and the Soviet Union both began producing even more powerful atomic weapons based on hydrogen fusion, the same energy-producing mechanism that fuels the sun. By the mid-1980s, the United States and the Soviet Union could deploy some 70,000 nuclear warheads, whose total explosive power was equal to about 3.7 tons (3.4 metric tons) of TNT for every human on the planet. Humans had acquired enough destructive power to inflict on themselves and the biosphere a level of destruction equivalent in its scale to the asteroid impact that had driven the dinosaurs to extinction 65 million years ago.

Behind all these increases in human control over resources were two fundamental changes: increased control of energy and increased control over innovation itself.

Energy

What really brought the fossil fuels revolution to individual consumers was the invention of generators (whether driven by coal-fired steam engines or water power) that could supply cheap electricity. The invention of the internal combustion engine allowed the mass consumption of

a second major form of fossil fuel: oil. Oil was easier to transport than coal, and the energy it contained was more concentrated. The first large stocks of oil were discovered in Titusville, Pennsylvania, in 1859. At first, it was used mainly in the form of kerosene, as fuel for lamps. But from early in the twentieth century, gasoline, produced from crude oil, would provide the power for internal combustion engines. Natural gas would complete the trio of major fossil fuels. Figure 10.1 illustrates both the vast increase in available energy in the twentieth century, and the relative proportions of different types of energy. The energy bonanza of the fossil fuels revolution, the energy equivalent of a gold rush, has been a fundamental driver of growth in the last 100 years. Indeed, energy became so abundant that humans began to treat it like a free good. In the twentieth century we became energy junkies.

The importance of other forms of energy would increase as it became apparent in the late twentieth century that it might be shortsighted to rely exclusively on fossil fuels. The energy locked up in atomic nuclei could be used in peace as well as war, but controlling that energy was not easy. The first civilian nuclear power station began operation in the Soviet Union in 1954. By the year 2000, about 400 nuclear reactors were in operation, producing almost 80 percent of all the electricity generated in France and almost 40 percent in South Korea and Japan. Nuclear power would have played a greater role if it had not been for several costly and dangerous accidents. Most destructive of all was the 1986 explosion of a reactor at Chernobyl in Ukraine, but the March 2011 accident at Fukushima in Japan, caused by the impact of a tsunami, was another reminder of the dangers of nuclear reactors. There is also uncertainty about how to dispose of the highly radioactive and long-lived by-products of nuclear reactors.

Meanwhile, there have been active attempts to develop alternative ways of generating energy, including solar power and wind power, but none is yet cheap or productive enough to compete commercially with fossil fuels. Besides, much commercial and political muscle has been devoted to protecting the substantial interests bound up with fossil fuels. Fusion power, if it could be controlled and handled safely, might solve many of these problems, but at present, practical fusion power generation still seems a long way off. The trouble is that we don't know how to tame the huge energies generated by fusion, the same process that powers up the sun. At present, the use of powerful magnetic fields seems the most promising solution, but the difficulties remain immense.

Making Innovation Systematic: Science and Research

Another important driver of innovation in the twentieth century has been the systematic encouragement of innovation itself. For the first time in human history, innovation has become a primary goal of human societies, supported by governments, businesses, and educational institutions.

The first modern scientific societies were founded in the seventeenth century: the Royal Society of London in 1660 and the Paris Academy of Sciences in 1666. Both received royal charters, a sign of growing official recognition of the importance of science.

In Britain, the Royal Observatory at Greenwich was founded to improve understanding of navigation, and in 1714 the British government offered a substantial prize for anyone who could find a clock accurate enough to determine longitude on long ocean voyages. The problem would not be solved until the 1760s, when John Harrison built a sufficiently reliable clock. It was first used by Captain Cook in his voyages to the Pacific. Government-sponsored scientific organizations soon appeared in Sweden, Prussia, Russia, and elsewhere. Such bodies created networks for the sharing of scientific research and journals in which scientific results could be published. The idea that science should serve the good of humankind was a commonplace of the eighteenth-century Enlightenment. But even in the first century of the Industrial Revolution, most of the major scientific and engineering breakthroughs were the work of enthusiastic individuals, sometimes, as in the case of James Watt, with the backing of wealthy entrepreneurs.

In the nineteenth century, science and technology began to work together more systematically. Science itself underwent fundamental changes as it became clear that deep ideas such as Darwin's theory of natural selection (first published in 1859), or James Clerk Maxwell's (1831–79) mathematical accounts of electromagnetic energy in the 1860s, or the development of thermodynamics showed the underlying unity of what had once seemed quite separate areas of science. Meanwhile, governments and large businesses began to see science as a powerful source of innovation, wealth, and power, and began to organize scientific research more systematically. Particularly in Germany, the sciences acquired a more important place within universities such as the University of Berlin, founded by Wilhelm von Humboldt in 1810. In 1826, Justus von Liebig (1803–73) created one of the first university chemistry laboratories, an activity that encouraged university scholars not just to teach but also to engage in innovative research. Later in the century, businesses began to set up their own laboratories. In 1874, the Bayer company set up one of the first commercial research laboratories in Germany, and two years later, at Menlo Park in New Jersey, Thomas Edison (1847–1931) set up his own research laboratories.

By the twentieth century it was clear that good science and technology were fundamental components of military, economic, and political power. Governments supported research into improved weapons and explosives; and the American government's Manhattan Project was in its time the largest state-organized research project ever known. At its height, the project employed over 40,000 people working in almost 40 different institutions on the task of creating atomic weapons. The Soviet government backed research on a similar scale and with equal urgency. Particularly in the more commercialized environments of the capitalist world, major government projects, though driven first and foremost by military goals, often had significant spinoffs into civilian technologies. Radar, the computer chip, computers, satellite technology, and many other elements of the electronic revolution were products of research driven initially by the military needs of governments.

Today, science is a major activity of all industrialized societies. According to one estimate, 80 to 90 percent of all the scientists who have ever lived are alive today. Early in the twenty-first century, the CERN (European Organization for Nuclear Research) Large Hadron Collider (which we last met in Chapter 1) provides a model of the sort of large-scale collaborative research that increasingly dominates research. Working together on Atlas, just one of CERN's particle detectors, are more than 1,900 scientists from 164 research institutes from 35 different countries. Perhaps most remarkable of all is the fact that CERN was designed for pure scientific research.

Part 3: The Impact of Growth and Industrialization on Lifeways and Societies

Growth and industrialization have transformed how people live. And, though millions remained trapped in poverty early in the twenty-first century, an astonishing number of people began to enjoy levels of material prosperity that could only have been dreamed about in any earlier epoch of human history.

The Decline of the Peasantry

In 1994, the great British historian Eric Hobsbawm (1917–2012) wrote: "the most dramatic and far-reaching social change of the second half of this century and the one which cuts us off for ever from the world of the past, is the death of the peasantry."[3]

Throughout the Agrarian era, most people were peasants and peasants produced most of society's resources. If you had been born in the Agrarian era, the odds are that you would have lived in a peasant household that fed its members from a small plot of land made available by overlords to whom your family paid tributes or rents in labor, kind, or cash. As late as 1800, perhaps 97 percent of all humans still lived in settlements of less than 20,000 people, and most were peasants. But this would soon change because everywhere, industrialization destroyed peasantries, as they were outcompeted by commercial farmers, forced to sell their land, and driven to take up wage labor either in the villages or in the rapidly growing industrial cities. The decisive shifts occurred in the twentieth century. By the middle of the twentieth century, only 75 percent of humans lived in settlements of less than 20,000 people, and by 2000, for the first time in human history, only half of humans lived in small communities. We had become an urban species. The peasant lifeways that had shaped the life experiences of most humans for most of the previous 10,000 years were vanishing.

For peasants driven off the land, often into impoverished, dangerous, unsanitary, and polluted environments in towns and cities, the change was destructive and brutal. Yet for increasing numbers of their children and grandchildren, the change would eventually raise material standards of living as the cities themselves became wealthier, as infrastructure spread, as clean water and electricity were installed, as health and education became more accessible, and as job opportunities multiplied. Gradually, towns, which had once been death traps for peasant migrants, began to provide more opportunities and better living conditions than rural areas.

Capitalism Evolving

To understand why living standards began to rise for an increasing number of people, it is helpful to think of the evolution of a new type of capitalism that we can call **consumer capitalism.** In the late nineteenth and early twentieth century, socialists such as Karl Marx argued that capitalism was doomed because it generated wealth by the increasingly brutal exploitation of wage earners or *proletarians.* Socialists argued that eventually fewer and fewer workers would have enough wealth to buy the increasing output of capitalist factories, and without sales there could be no profits, which would eventually bring the entire system crashing down. In addition, argued the socialists, the working class as a whole would become more revolutionary as its living and working conditions declined. Capitalism could never afford to make the workers rich.

The thinking behind such arguments was, in a sense, a hangover from the Agrarian era, like the thinking that encouraged European powers to compete violently for colonies, raw materials, and markets. Both groups assumed that available resources were so limited that different classes or nations would have to fight each other for what was available. Yet, as we have seen, the spectacular increases in productivity of the nineteenth and twentieth centuries began to undercut this traditional way of thinking, and to make a reality of Adam Smith's hope that eventually growth, driven by commercial competition, could benefit more and more people.

In the twentieth century, productivity rose faster than anyone could have dreamed. And as productivity increased, it turned out that it might be possible to spread wealth to larger and larger sections of the middle and working classes, while continuing to enrich capitalists and governments. In the United States, such changes were already underway by the early twentieth century. Goods that had once seemed luxuries, such as automobiles, could now be produced cheaply enough so that ordinary workers could purchase them, particularly if banks were willing to provide easy credit and wages were allowed to rise in response to union activity. Consumer capitalism was a type of capitalism so productive that it could afford to sell cheap goods to the wage workers who produced most of its wealth. As

working-class living standards improved, the market for consumer goods expanded while the alienation and hostility of the working classes was reduced, and so was the appeal of revolutionary socialist ideologies. Here was the formula that made it possible to combine sustained growth and political stability in the most advanced capitalist societies in the late twentieth century.

To support consumer capitalism, retail outlets, the advertising industry, and consumer credit, all of which had existed for many centuries, began offering their services to more and more people. The first advertising agency was created in the United States in the 1870s. The first department stores were established in Paris as early as the 1830s; by the 1850s they were already common in Russian cities, and by the 1890s they could be found in Tokyo's Ginza district and a decade later in Shanghai. Appealing at first to wealthy middle-class customers, by the twentieth century they were used by a much wider public. Consumer capitalism represented an ethical revolution because it celebrated consumption and extravagance, instead of encouraging restraint and thrift, the traditional virtues of peasant societies.

Demographic Changes

Families, the most intimate of human communities, were transformed as they adapted to modern urbanized industrial societies.

In most peasant societies it made sense for parents to produce as many children as possible, because children were the one productive asset over which peasants had some control. Children were valuable because they could be put to work on the farm from a young age. Yet rates of infant mortality were high in all peasant societies so that, to maximize the chances of having, say, three or four children, it was necessary for women to keep producing children as long as possible, in the almost certain knowledge that several would die young. As we have seen, the consequence of these rules was that in most societies throughout the Agrarian era, women spent most of their lives either bearing or rearing children. Rates of child mortality were high, and so were rates of fertility.

From the nineteenth century, improved sanitation, food production, and health care, as well as the global exchange of disease immunities, improved the survival chances of infants in the more industrialized societies. In many rural areas mortality rates fell and populations soared as more children survived to adulthood. Eventually, fertility rates—that is, the number of births—also began to fall. The reasons are complex. In industrial environments, children could contribute less to the household budget, particularly if they were forced into schools. As the costs of having children rose as well as their chances of survival, the incentive to overproduce children diminished.

New forms of birth control also helped lower fertility rates. Industrially produced rubber condoms began to be produced from the 1830s; and in the twentieth century, new contraceptives became available, including the contraceptive pill, first introduced in 1960. Increasingly, women could choose how many children they bore, and more and more women chose to have fewer children. Fertility rates began to fall from the late nineteenth century, beginning in the more industrialized and urbanized regions. Then they fell again, even more decisively and in much more of the world, in the late twentieth century. These changes, which are known as the **demographic transition,** created a new demographic world of low mortality and low fertility. Families had fewer children, and rates of population growth, which had peaked in the 1960s, began to slow until, by 2000, over 30 countries had zero population growth. Demographers predict that sometime in the twenty-first century global population growth will slow to zero, stabilizing at somewhere between 9 and 10 billion people. Then, perhaps, global populations may start to fall.

Human Rights and Increasing Living Standards

Reduced pressure to produce children, compulsory education, and a growing hostility to interpersonal violence transformed relations between men and women. Women found more opportunities to take up roles outside the family, either as wage earners or in professional roles previously dominated by men, in education, medicine, and even politics. Women gained voting rights in democracies beginning with New Zealand (1893) and Australia (1902), Finland (1906), Russia (1917), Britain (1918), and Germany and the United States (1919). By the end of the twentieth century, women could vote in most of the world's democracies and pseudo-democracies. The sharp divisions between the roles of men and women that had shaped lives in the Agrarian era began to break down, particularly in the more industrialized regions, though even there, women's wage rates remain below those for men early in the twenty-first century.

The long trends we have described will surely seem positive to most readers of this book. They increased welfare, wealth, and freedom for more and more people. But we must not exaggerate the successes. Today's huge populations mean, paradoxically, that more people live in dire poverty than ever before. In 2005, 3.1 billion people, or twice as many as the total population of the world 100 years earlier, lived on less than US$2.50 a day. The gap between rich and poor has also widened since the Industrial Revolution, particularly in the twentieth century. This was mainly because the rich got richer. In 1800, it has been estimated that the average income per person of the richest countries was 2 or 3 times that of the poorest countries; by 1900, it was 12 to 15 times as much; and in 2002 it was 50 to 60 times as much. In 2005, the richest 20 percent of the world's population accounted for 77 percent of all private consumption, while the poorest 20 percent accounted for just 1.5 percent.

But even here there is a good story to be told: The absolute numbers of people living in modest comfort, and the *proportion* of all humans living in modest comfort, are both greater than ever before. Regarded from the point of view of our own species, this is a great technological, organizational, and moral achievement. The changes of the twentieth century seemed to have done more than any earlier epoch to raise the living standards of people throughout the world.

Part 4: The Anthropocene and the Human Impact on the Biosphere—Is Growth Sustainable?

But how secure are these gains? The word *growth* reflects a human perspective: It means growth in the resources controlled by human beings for their own benefit. Yet from an ecological perspective the big story of the twentieth century is how one species suddenly began to dominate the energy and resources of the biosphere as a whole. What was "growth" for humans was experienced by many other species as a decline in available land, food, and habitat. Human activity also began to destabilize nonliving geological and meteorological systems, such as the movement of water and patterns of climate change or the ancient biochemical cycles of carbon and nitrogen.

Can humans keep extracting more and more resources from the biosphere? Or is growth beginning to threaten the ecological foundations on which modern societies depend?

It is not at all clear that humans are really in control of the immense power generated by our astonishing technological creativity. Perhaps the most terrifying expression of the dangerous power our species has acquired is the development of nuclear weapons. By 1986, there existed almost 70,000 nuclear warheads, mostly held in the arsenals of the United States and the Soviet Union. If ever used, these weapons could have inflicted terrible damage on the biosphere. And in the twentieth century human societies came perilously close to all-out nuclear war. In 1962, the Soviet government agreed to install nuclear weapons to protect its ally, Cuba, which had been ruled since 1959 by a socialist government under Fidel Castro (1926–). The U.S. president, John F. Kennedy (1917–63), ordered a blockade of Cuba to prevent the arrival of the nuclear weapons, and for a few days the world was on the brink of nuclear war. At the last minute, the Soviet government led by Nikita Khrushchev (1894–1971) backed down and ordered its ships to reverse course. Since then, there have been several other occasions when the superpowers approached the brink, sometimes through simple misunderstandings. And early in the twenty-first century the weapons are still there. In 2010, Russia and the United States still had hundreds of nuclear weapons on "hair-trigger alert," which means they could be launched in just 15 minutes. We have avoided nuclear war so far, but only just.

Other expressions of the growing ecological power of our species were less obvious. The artificial chemical synthesis of products useful for humans began in the nineteenth century. In the twentieth century 10 million new chemicals have been synthesized, and perhaps 150,000 have been produced and used commercially, from pesticides and fertilizers to artificial rubber, plastics, and synthetic textiles. In the 1980s, it was eventually realized that some of these chemicals, the so-called chlorofluorocarbons (CFCs), mainly used in aerosols, air conditioners, and refrigerators, were dispersing in the atmosphere and breaking down the thin layer of ozone (O_3) that protects the Earth's surface from dangerous ultraviolet emissions. Scientific evidence that a hole was appearing in the ozone layer eventually prompted international action, and in 1987, a United Nations–sponsored agreement generated a global effort to phase out the use of CFCs. Since then, global production of CFCs has fallen to almost zero, as substitutes have been found to replace them; and current evidence suggests that the hole in the ozone layer is no longer expanding. This is a story that demonstrates both the scale of the potential problems and the types of measures that may be needed to cope with them.

Human activities are also transforming the Earth's soils, and not just through farming. More powerful internal combustion engines have allowed miners and road builders and dam builders to move earth on a larger scale than the combined natural forces of erosion, glaciation, and mountain-building. Human use of water increased by 9 times in the twentieth century, and currently we are using the stores of water contained in aquifers at 10 times the rate at which they are being renewed. Within a few decades many of the world's great aquifers will dry up, including the Ogallala aquifer in the United States, which stretches from the Dakotas to Texas.

As we take more and more of the biosphere's resources, other species are feeling the pinch. Most damaging of all is increased human use and transformation of the habitats of other species, as humans pave land over for roads and cities, chop down forests, or plow land for farming. Estimates of rates of decline of **biodiversity** (the number of different species) are rough and ready. But in recent decades much research has been devoted to the problem. According to a 2010 assessment by the International Union for Conservation of Nature, current rates of extinction are about 1,000 times more rapid than they have been for most of the Earth's recent history. These rates are approaching those during the five episodes of most rapid loss of biodiversity in the last 600 million years. Of more than 47,000 species whose likelihood of extinction has been assessed so far, one-third, or over 17,000, are estimated to be in danger of extinction in the near future. Of about 5,500 mammal species, over 700 (13 percent), are estimated to be "critically endangered" or "endangered," while another 500 (9 percent) are "vulnerable" (Figure 12.6). In addition, about 70 percent of coral reefs, one of the most diverse environments on Earth, are currently threatened or already destroyed. Declining biodiversity is not just an aesthetic matter because many species play vital roles in the maintenance of the biosphere. Bees, for example, are vital for the pollination of food crops.

While stable climates have allowed agrarian civilizations to flourish for several millennia, we are now beginning to transform the atmosphere in ways that are likely to have a

FIGURE 12.6 Diminishing biodiversity. The silky sifaka is a lemur found only in northeastern Madagascar and is one of the rarest mammal species on Earth, with only a few hundred surviving in the wild and none in zoos. Hunting and destruction of their habitat make it unlikely that the species will survive in the wild.

profound impact on global climates and ocean levels in the next century. The critical change seems to be an increase in the atmospheric levels of greenhouse gases, such as carbon dioxide and methane. These gases absorb and retain the sun's heat and reduce the amount that is reflected back into space, so as they increase they tend to raise average global temperatures. The increased use of fossil fuels has meant pumping into the atmosphere in just a few decades carbon that was stored in fossil fuels over hundreds of millions of years. In the twentieth century alone, carbon dioxide emissions rose by 13 times.

Studies of long-term changes in the composition of the atmosphere suggest that since 1800 carbon dioxide has begun to rise beyond the range that was normal for some 800,000 years (see Figure 11.1 and Chapter 13). Between 1900 and 2000, the amount of carbon dioxide in the atmosphere rose from about 295 to almost 370 parts per million (ppm), taking carbon dioxide levels well beyond the levels typical of the last million years. Predicting the long-term impacts of such change is difficult, but there is a broad consensus among climate scientists that such levels ensure a long-term increase in average temperatures, which will lead to rising ocean levels (caused partly by the melting of glaciers in polar regions and partly by expanding warming oceans) and changing climates throughout the world.

Most worrisome of all is the knowledge, based on the study of climate histories over many millions of years, that climate change is not necessarily a smooth process. There are tipping points, moments of sudden rapid change, when positive feedback cycles can take over and change can occur with great rapidity, as it did at the end of the last ice age. For example, the melting of polar glaciers reduces areas of white that reflect sunlight, increasing the capacity of these regions to absorb sunlight and accelerating the melting of more ice. Similarly, the melting of tundra regions will release huge amounts of methane which, like carbon dioxide, is a potent greenhouse gas, so it will accelerate the warming process, which will accelerate the melting of the tundra, and so on.

Our power to change our environment seems to be increasing much faster than our understanding of the effects of these changes or our capacity to change our economies.

SUMMARY

The idea of the Anthropocene epoch provides a powerful way of thinking about the deeper meaning of the accelerating changes we have seen in the twentieth century. As we saw in Chapters 4 and 10, Dutch climate scientist Paul Crutzen argued that since 1800 we have entered a new geological epoch, the Anthropocene, in which our species has begun to dominate the biosphere. In 2008, a distinguished group of scientists argued that the International Commission on Stratigraphy (the body that formally decides on the dating of geological eras) should formally consider introducing this new period into the geological time scale. They argue that what distinguishes the Anthropocene from the preceding epoch, the Holocene, is the fact that humans have begun, without fully understanding what they are doing, to transform the chemistry of the atmosphere; the range, variety, and distribution of plant and animals species; the nature of the water cycle; and fundamental processes of erosion and sedimentation. We have become the first single species in almost 4 billion years that is powerful enough to transform the biosphere single-handedly.

It now seems likely that humans may be affecting what happens to between 25 and 40 percent of all the energy that enters the biosphere through photosynthesis. In other words, between a quarter and a half of the biosphere's entire energy budget is allocated according to the whims of one species. All of this means that the appearance of our species marks a threshold that is not just of interest to us, but is of fundamental significance in the history of our planet. John McNeill, in his environmental history of the twentieth century, has argued: "the human race, without intending anything of the sort, has undertaken a gigantic uncontrolled experiment on the earth. In time, I think, this will appear as the most important aspect of twentieth-century history, more so than World War II, the communist enterprise, the rise of mass literacy, the spread of democracy, or the growing emancipation of women."[4]

Pessimistic interpretations of these figures suggest that we may already have launched changes we can no longer control. James Lovelock has argued that it's already too late. Indeed, Lovelock has argued for years that we cannot regard the biosphere as a passive object: it is, rather, a complex, evolving superorganism that will react to the actions of humans in ways that may not always please us. It will, to put it anthropomorphically, defend itself against us if that is necessary.

If the pessimists are right, we are now in the middle of a sort of global traffic accident; events are moving too fast for governments and businesses and consumers to react appropriately to them and certainly too fast for the achievement of a global consensus about how to react. Does this mean that growth itself no longer sustainable? If so, does this mean that countries such as China and India, whose populations are beginning to enjoy the benefits of the modern revolution in increasing numbers, need to check the growth that is generating such benefits? Or should the countries that industrialized first, and that contributed most to these ecological problems, be the ones that pay the price, perhaps even by partial deindustrialization? Or will the world as a whole have to abandon the benefits of the modern revolution and return to the conditions of the Agrarian era in which available resources were so scarce that the most promising form of "growth" was warfare to secure the resources of your neighbors?

On the other hand, perhaps Collective Learning, the defining feature of our species, will allow humans to generate new technologies and new strategies for avoiding ecological disaster. Will genetic engineering allow us to produce bacteria that can turn coal directly into natural gas, or turn garbage into energy, or suck carbon dioxide from the atmosphere, or produce cheap energy in fusion reactors? Will nanotechnology create tiny machines that will prove more powerful, but much less costly to run, than the huge machines of the Industrial Revolution? Will politicians develop new forms of global collaboration to deal with these problems? Will there be a sort of "consumption transition,"

a slowing in consumption, that matches the demographic transition, which is slowing population growth?

Optimists point out that humans are now better informed and better equipped than ever to deal with the problems they face. Even 50 years ago, awareness of the urgency of environmental issues was minimal. Today, such awareness is global, and governments throughout the world know that global collaboration is necessary to solve them. The difficulties of such collaboration have not yet been overcome, but the awareness is there. If ever there was a species capable of solving some of the problems that we have created, it is the one species on Earth capable of Collective Learning, and capable, now, of sharing ideas and knowledge within a global community of over 7 billion individuals.

CHAPTER QUESTIONS

1. What do you regard as the single most important development in the history of the twentieth century? Why?
2. How did the human relationship to the biosphere change in the twentieth century?
3. What are the most interesting lessons to be learned from the prolonged twentieth-century contest between capitalism and Communism?
4. What were the most important changes in the nature of capitalism in the twentieth century?
5. What were the most important gains for human societies during the twentieth century, and what were the most important losses?
6. What were the most significant technological innovations of the twentieth century, and what were the most important changes in human lifeways?

KEY TERMS

biodiversity	consumer capitalism	gross domestic product (GDP)	nuclear weapons
Cold War	demographic transition	Marxism	protectionism
Communism	fascism		socialism

FURTHER READING

Berkshire Encyclopedia of World History. Edited by W. H. McNeill et al. 5 vols. Great Barrington, MA: Berkshire, 2004.

Bulliet, Richard, et al. *The Earth and Its Peoples: A Global History.* 2nd ed. Boston: Houghton Mifflin, 2003.

Christian, David. *Maps of Time: An Introduction to Big History.* Berkeley: University of California Press, 2004.

Crosby, Alfred W. *Children of the Sun: A History of Humanity's Unappeasable Appetite for Energy.* New York: Norton, 2006.

Crutzen, Paul. "The Geology of Mankind." *Nature* 415 (January 3, 2002):23.

Diamond, J. M. "Human Use of World Resources." *Nature* 6 (August 1987):479–80.

Ferguson, Niall. *Empire: The Rise and Demise of the British World Order and the Lessons for Global Power.* New York: Basic Books, 2004.

Headrick, Daniel. *Technology: A World History.* Oxford: Oxford University Press, 2009.

Hobsbawm, Eric. *Age of Extremes: The Short Twentieth Century: 1914–1991.* London: Little, Brown, 1994.

Maddison, Angus. *The World Economy: A Millennial Perspective.* Paris: OECD, 2001.

McNeill, John. *Something New under the Sun: An Environmental History of the Twentieth-Century World.* New York: Norton, 2000.

Tignor, Robert, et al. *Worlds Together: Worlds Apart.* 2nd ed., Vol. 2. New York: Norton, 2008.

ENDNOTES

1. Cited in Niall Ferguson, *Empire: The Rise and Demise of the British World Order and the Lessons for Global Power* (New York: Basic Books, 2004), 210.

2. John McNeill, *Something New under the Sun: An Environmental History of the Twentieth-Century World* (New York: Norton, 2000), 25.

3. Eric Hobsbawm, *Age of Extremes: The Short Twentieth Century: 1914–1991* (London: Little, Brown, 1994), 289.

4. McNeill, *Something New under the Sun,* 4.

the anthropocene

more thresholds?

chapter 13

The History of the Future

Seeing the Big Picture

From Now On . . .

▶ What can we expect in the next 100 years?

▶ How much can humans influence what happens in the next 100 years?

▶ What predictions are possible about the next few thousand years?

▶ Can we know anything about the future of our solar system or the history of the universe? If so, how?

The idea of a history of the future may seem a contradiction in terms. How can the future have a history? Is it legitimate to describe how the future might unfold? Traditionally, historians look at the past and do not speculate about the future.

Traditional historians may be among the few, however, who shy away from thinking about the future. Natural selection has built into humans and other animals the ability to predict; indeed memory itself evolved not just so we could remember the past, but rather to help us predict the future because for many animals (including our ancestors) survival depends on answering correctly questions like "Is there a leopard out there?" Stockbrokers, gamblers, astrologers, and those who bet on the horses all profit from their skills in predicting. Politicians must project the consequences of the policies they endorse: Will taxes on energy slow carbon dioxide emission, or will they stifle economic growth? Which is more important to the well-being of our grandchildren? People cannot avoid thinking about the future, since the decisions we make and the actions we take will affect the lives of our children, grandchildren, and our society as a whole.

Big history provides us with a wonderful perspective within which to think seriously about the future. Since we have looked at some very large trends over a vast period of 13.8 billion years, peering into the future seems natural and unavoidable, unless we are content to leave humanity simply hanging on a cliff. Furthermore, now is the first time in our history that the big history perspective has been available to us.

In this chapter we will divide the future into three parts. In the first part we will examine the near future, or the next 100 years, while in the last two parts we will consider the middle future (the next few thousand years), and then the remote future (the next billions of years). Trends are easiest to project into the near future; the middle future is too far away to see with any clarity; but strangely, astrophysicists can describe the remote future with some confidence, even though humans will not be around to experience it.

In considering any part of the future, we must proceed with extreme caution. The future really is difficult to predict; there are no sure bets. Even present reality is fuzzy, and the future is much more so. Quantum physics tells us that at the smallest level particles do not have a defined, determined position. At a larger scale, complexity theorists tell us the more turbulence there is in a system, the greater the role of contingency, or chance. Examples of predictions far off the mark are easy to find; here are a few:

In 1900, when cars were becoming more efficient and reliable, Edward W. Byrn thought that humans would never be able to get along without the horse. (He may be right yet!)

In 1952, some thought that electronic brains would soon decide who marries whom and marriages would be happier.

Herman Kahn predicted in 1976 that the twenty-first century would be a benign high-tech world with everyone living at the standard of Scarsdale, the suburb of New York City where he lived.

Predictions often fail to pan out, yet people who think carefully about the future are sometimes able to identify crucial features of it:

Svante Arrhenius, a Swedish chemist, observed in 1896 that CO_2 in the air acts as a blanket to keep Earth warm, and a few years later realized that burning fossil fuel was going to heat up the planet.

Rachel Carson published *Silent Spring* in 1962 to call attention to the damage done by pesticides.

Frances Moore Lappe published *Diet for a Small Planet* in 1971, showing there could be food for all if people ate less meat and more plants.

Lester R. Brown, a former tomato farmer in New Jersey, started World Watch in 1974 with a grant from Rockefeller Foundation, to monitor the growing human footprint, or impact on the environment.

The basic procedure for thinking responsibly about the future seems to be: start with existing trends and see if we can reasonably project them into the future. The trick, of course, is to analyze correctly the existing trends. That has been our goal in this book, and we now apply it to thinking about the near future.

Future 1: The Near Future

One of the patterns we have seen repeating in the Agrarian era of human history is the Malthusian crisis (see Chapters 6 and 10), in which the increase in population outruns food production, resulting in famine, warfare, and a reduction of population. An even larger pattern is that of increasing complexity, in which more energy flows through systems and a larger number of components are present. Will we face new Malthusian crises even in the Modern era? Will human society become even more complex and perhaps more vulnerable to breakdowns?

Early in the twenty-first century, many signs suggest we will face a major Malthusian crisis, as the fossil fuels that underlie our global civilization begin to run out. On a larger scale, Earth's climate may be changing rapidly enough that it can be said that humans have reached the end of some 10,000 years of relatively stable climate, suggesting we are on the verge of a period of much greater instability and rapid change.

At the same time, the impact of human activity on Earth is so great that, as we have seen in the previous chapter, some geologists argue that the Holocene epoch (some 10,000 years since the last ice age) has ended and the Anthropocene has begun.

To discuss the near future, we will first describe our present location on long-range scales; then we will survey the dark side and the positive side, before concluding with some key questions to be answered in the next 100 years.

The Present Situation

Many voices are currently marshaling evidence to argue that humans cannot continue with business as usual much longer, that the whole enterprise of industrialized society based on burning fossil fuels and committed to endless growth is no longer sustainable or projectable into any long-range future.

The reasons for this conclusion are complex, multidimensional, and interlocking. We will describe them in more detail in the section "Ominous Trends," but in short they are as follows. The human population is growing, albeit at reduced rates, and the food supply is increasingly insecure. Oil supplies will gradually diminish; some believe that peak production has already been reached. Rates of extinction for plants, animals, and other life are so high that some are calling this the Sixth Great Extinction. Human disruption to many ecosystems has increased beyond sustainability, while emissions of carbon dioxide from burning fossil fuels are contributing to a rapidly changing global climate.

The previous paragraph can be expressed by using the term **human footprint,** to mean the collective demands that humans make on our planet's regenerative capacity, sometimes called Earth's "carrying capacity." A study in 2002 by the U.S. National Academy of Sciences concluded that the human footprint probably first surpassed Earth's carrying capacity about 1980.

Many scientists have concluded that humans face a choice in the next several decades between going forward as usual to some kind of a global collapse or finding ways to avert collapse, either by dominating nature more completely or by setting limits to human material wants, or by a combination of both strategies.

A major contributor to the focus on collapse has been the U.S. physiologist Jared Diamond with the publication in 2005 of his popular book, *Collapse: How Societies Choose to Fail or Succeed.* In this book Diamond presents examples of societies that collapsed into warfare, disease, famine, and ecological breakdown (Greenland Norse, Anasazi, Rapa Nui [Easter Island], Classic Lowland Maya), together with examples of societies that avoided such calamities (Greenland Inuit, Inca, Tokugawa Japan). Some historians have questioned whether Diamond's judgments of successes and failures in the past can be substantiated (see McAnany and Yoffee's *Questioning Collapse*), but most are convinced that we do indeed face serious dangers.

There is no way to know just how likely some sort of global collapse is in the next 100 years. In the following two sections we will describe both the ominous trends that point in the direction of collapse and the positive trends that could avoid it.

Ominous Trends

After taking into account the exaggerations that newspapers print to sell their product and that nonprofit organizations make to appeal to their donors, we must still acknowledge that many trends are in reality dangerous and ominous. In this section we will summarize them in four groups: the growth of population, the limits of fossil fuels, the destabilization of climate, and the damage to ecosystems.

Growth of the Population

The human population has recently grown with unprecedented speed (see Chapter 12). Between 1950 and 1990 it doubled in just 40 years. The rate of growth has declined since 1990, so that the population is currently doubling about every 58 years (Figure 13.1). Never before in human history has the population doubled in the life span of a single individual, yet today everyone over 60 has experienced such a doubling.

Since no one knows what the population figures in the future will be, the United Nations makes a range of projections. In its most recent projection, its middle estimate sees world population reaching 8.9 billion by 2050. Its high estimate puts the population at 10.6 billion by 2050, its low estimate at 7.4 billion, which assumes that the world's people will quickly move to below-replacement levels of fertility (the number of children per couple).

If the fertility rate falls only to replacement level (or about 2.1 children per couple), the population will still grow for 70 years. This is due to the disproportionate number of children and young reproductive-age people in today's population, which is a result of recent population

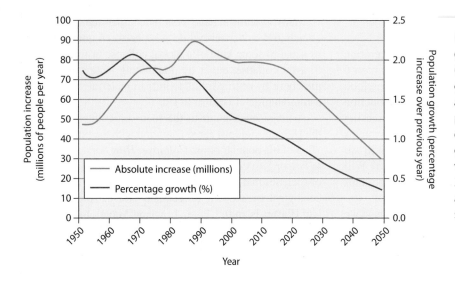

FIGURE 13.1 Global populations growth rate, 1950 to 2050 (estimated). The global population growth rate (the population increase as a percentage of the world's population) has slowed in recent decades in most countries. While it grew at about 2 percent in 1965, it was growing at about 1.2 percent in 2010. But the total number of people added each year was still about the same as in 1965!

growth. This is referred to as the "demographic bulge," or "population momentum."

Population projections differ widely by country. In one group of about 33 countries, including Spain, Japan, Russia, and Germany, populations are projected to remain stable or to shrink because of falling fertility rates. Another group of countries, including Lesotho and Swaziland, have declining population due to a rising death rate. Other countries, including China and the United States, have reduced fertility to replacement level, but their population is still expanding due to the demographic bulge just described. Still other countries, especially in Africa and other less developed areas, continue to increase their population rapidly, even though the rate of growth is decreasing. If downward trends continue, their population growth could slow to replacement level by 2050.

From 2000 to 2100, the placement of the world's population is expected to shift dramatically, as Europe's share declines from 12.0 to 5.9 percent, and as Africa's almost doubles, from 13.1 to 24.9 percent. North America will grow until 2050 from migration; after that the UN projects no further migration. By 2100 the UN projects a high estimate of 14 billion people, a middle one at 9 billion, and a low of 5.6 billion.

The absolute size of the world's population is one element in the human footprint; another is the impact that individuals make depending on their levels of consumption. Citizens of developed countries consume much more than do citizens of developing countries. If China reaches what the consumption levels were in the United States in 2005, the human impact on Earth will likely double. So levels of consumption are as important as the sheer numbers of humans in measuring our impact on the biosphere.

The Limited Supply of Fossil Fuels

This section could be called "The End of Cheap Oil," to put the matter bluntly. Has oil production already reached its height? No one knows. Optimists say not before 2020 at least. Pessimists say that production has probably already peaked. Oil will not completely run out; it will become more and more costly to extract, while demand for scarce supplies will drive the price upward.

As we saw in Chapter 11, oil was made sometime between many millions of years ago when melting glaciers flooded lowlands. Tiny marine life (coccoliths, diatoms, foraminifera) sank to the bottom, leaving sediment that pressure from rocks above and Earth's internal heat from below cooked into oil.

Major sources of oil formed only in certain regions of Earth. One-fourth of the world's oil is found in Saudi Arabia; the Middle East holds more than 60 percent of the world's remaining petroleum. The amount of oil pumped annually in the world has risen from about 100 million barrels a hundred years ago to about 20 billion barrels currently.

The price of oil is set by the market forces of supply and demand. The supply, however, is set by the governments of many different producing countries. In 1960 eleven countries formed a cartel (or group of competing firms that collaborate over shared interests), called the **Organization of the Petroleum Exporting Countries (OPEC),** to vie with the Soviet Union and the United States over control of the world's oil markets. Members of OPEC try to agree on levels of production; Saudi Arabia has so much spare capacity for producing cheap oil that it can affect oil prices by rapidly increasing or decreasing production. Three times in recent history oil production has dropped dramatically—during the Arab oil embargo in 1973 to 1974 in response to the Arab–Israeli war, during the Iranian revolution in 1979, and during the Persian Gulf War in 1991—each time causing a temporary economic recession in the United States and worldwide.

If we consider all fossil fuels (oil, coal, and natural gas), we find that by 2009 they accounted for 80 percent of all energy produced in the world, with **renewable energy** (all forms of energy that can come from easily renewable sources such as sunlight, wind power, or hydropower) at 12 percent and nuclear at 8 percent. The United States had about 4.5 percent of the world's population but used about 20 percent of the world's oil and produced more than half

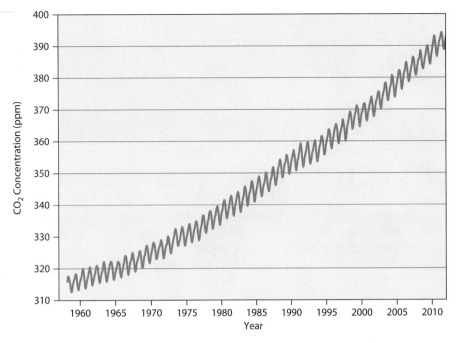

FIGURE 13.2 Atmospheric carbon dioxide, 1957 to 2010.
This graph, known as the Keeling curve, shows the concentration of carbon dioxide in the atmosphere as measured at the Mauna Loa Observatory in Hawaii. Charles David Keeling (1928–2005) worked at the Scripps Institute (University of California–San Diego). He was the first to make regular measurements of CO_2 concentrations and the first to bring its increase to the world's attention. In May 2013, CO_2 levels reached 400 ppm for the first time in 3 million years.

its electricity by burning coal. Japan and Germany, with no domestic oil, enacted energy-efficient policies that encouraged more economical use of energy, though even these societies consume some oil.

Fossil fuels not only produce our electricity and drive our cars, they also help feed the world's 7 billion people. Fossil fuels provide the energy used to create the fertilizers of modern agriculture. They pump groundwater and power tractors and the vehicles that move crops to kitchens. They are used to produce and distribute pesticides and herbicides. The time will come when the remaining fossil fuel will be too difficult to extract at a reasonable cost. For coal and gas, this will be further in the future than for oil. The longer people of the world wait to make the transition from fossil fuel to other forms of energy, the less peaceful and orderly, the more chaotic and violent, the transition must be. Weaning civilization from the fuels that currently sustain it without disrupting modern industrial civilization may prove as difficult as developing that civilization in the first place.

The Destabilized Climate

Carbon, the core element of life on Earth, has become in our time a threat to the relatively stable climates that sustained human societies over the last 10,000 years. How could that be?

Recent advances in climate study techniques—ice core sampling, long-term measurements of carbon dioxide (CO_2) in the atmosphere—have revealed that climate change has been a regular feature of history on the large scale and that, despite some fluctuations, the past 10,000 years have been a period of relative stability. Early in the twentieth century a few scientists foresaw that carbon dioxide emissions from burning fossil fuel could cause warmer climates. They welcomed the warming, as previous patterns suggested that the warm ten thousand years would be followed by another ice age. Contemporary researchers like William F. Ruddiman now believe that increases in carbon dioxide emissions, due to deforestation since farming began and to burning coal since industrialization, may have prevented a return to increased glaciation.

Since climate has often shifted on its own, humans have been reluctant to believe that they could be responsible for any of its current changes. By 1970, however, the annual increase of CO_2 since 1958 had been directly measured (Figure 13.2). Scientists began warning that human emissions of CO_2 into the atmosphere, leading to a greenhouse effect, were starting to contribute heavily to climate change. In 1988 the United Nations Environment Programme (UNEP) and the World Meteorological Organization (WMO) set up a body of the world's leading climate scientists, called the Intergovernmental Panel on Climate Change (IPCC), to monitor changes. Although global warming is now widely accepted by political and economic leaders, many citizens do not yet accept its reality.

To understand the **greenhouse effect,** think of entering a car parked in the sun, which is like a greenhouse insofar as the sun's energy gets in more easily than it gets out. Certain trace gases in Earth's atmosphere turn Earth into a greenhouse; they keep the sun's heat reaching Earth from reflecting back into space. Without these trace greenhouse gases (water vapor, CO_2, methane, ozone, CFCs, and others) in our atmosphere, the average temperature on Earth would be about 12 degrees Fahrenheit (minus 11 degrees Celsius), or significantly below freezing. This is so because the major constituents of Earth's atmosphere—nitrogen and oxygen—do not absorb the infrared heat radiation reflected back from the Earth.

Carbon dioxide is a tiny part of Earth's atmosphere now, only 0.04 percent of it, or 380 parts per million (ppm) per volume (the ratio of the number of CO_2 molecules to the total number of molecules of dry air). The level of CO_2 in

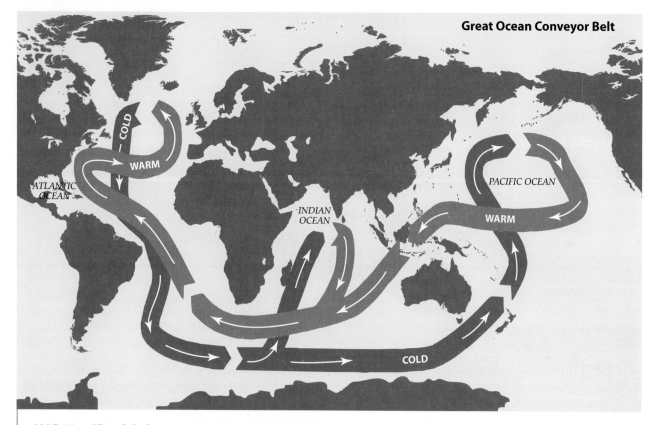

Great Ocean Conveyor Belt

MAP 13.1 The global water circulation. When ocean water freezes in the Arctic, it releases its salt into the remaining ocean water. Since saltwater is heavier than freshwater, it sinks, pulling northward the lighter, warm seawater from the tropics. This sets up a circulation pattern around the globe, often called a conveyor belt, that warms the Eastern Seaboard of the United States and the British Isles. If less water freezes in the Arctic, this conveyor belt could be disrupted.

the atmosphere has varied over Earth's history, from almost all CO_2 in primordial times to 190 ppm during Paleolithic times to 280 ppm at the beginning of the Industrial Revolution. The natural range over the last 800,000 years, as determined by ice core samples that contain bubbles that preserve tiny samples of prehistoric atmospheres, has been between 180 and 300 ppm. Measurements tell us that the average annual CO_2 level in 2011, at nearly 400 ppm, is higher than at any time in the previous 800,000 years and is likely higher than in the past 20 million years.

Earth's climate responds to increased greenhouse gases by warming, both on land and in the oceans. The oceans are the most reliable indicator of warming, as temperatures do not fluctuate there as much as on land. A report in 2009 by the National Oceanic and Atmospheric Administration (NOAA) advised that even if atmospheric carbon dioxide were suddenly to start declining, the oceans—which have slowed climate change by absorbing heat—would release that heat back into the atmosphere for at least another 1,000 years.

The factors regulating Earth's climate are far more complex than humans currently understand. Among them are ice sheets, which reflect the sun's rays directly back into space, and algae, which reduce CO_2 from the air but which grow less profusely as the climate warms. Water vapor increases warming, but cloud cover decreases it. When water freezes, it expels its salt into nearby waters, making them heavier, so they sink. As they sink they draw warmer water in to replace them, setting up a circulation pattern moving like a conveyor belt around the globe. This circulation includes the Gulf Stream, which warms Florida and northern Europe. Further warming could reconfigure the conveyer belt of currents, sharply cooling the coastal areas now warmed by the Gulf Stream, including much of western Europe (Map 13.1).

Global CO_2 emissions continue to rise, by an average annual increase of 2.7 percent in the last decade. (In 2011 China increased its emissions by 9 percent to 7.2 tons [6.5 metric tons] per capita, the European Union dropped 3 percent to 7.5 tons [6.8 metric tons] per capita, and the United States dropped 2 percent to 17.3 tons [15.7 metric tons] per capita.) Levels of CO_2 in the atmosphere are expected to reach 550 ppm by 2050. A concentration of 500 ppm was last seen some 30 million years ago. Climate scientists initially believed that stabilization at 550 or 450 ppm could keep the climate within the range to which life is adapted. Since 2008, however, with Arctic and glacial melting and ocean acidification increasing faster than expected, leading climate scientists now believe that CO_2 levels must drop back to **350 ppm** to ensure a climate safe for life as we know it.

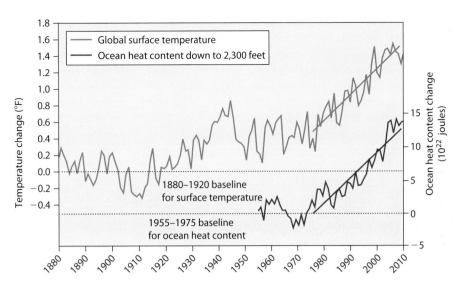

FIGURE 13.3 Global average surface temperature and ocean heat content. This graph shows global average surface temperature change on the left axis and change in ocean heat content on the right axis.

The global average temperature has risen 1 degree Fahrenheit (0.6 degree Celsius) since 1970 (see Figure 13.3). In its 2007 report the IPCC projected temperature rises of up to 11 degrees Fahrenheit (6 degrees Celsius) by 2100. Yet scientists warn that any rise over 3.6 degrees Fahrenheit (2 degrees Celsius) will make serious climate change inevitable. Some scientists believe that the IPCC tempers its predictions in order not to cause alarm and that the crisis is worse than is officially recognized.

The effects of rising temperatures are predicted to be pervasive, but to affect some regions more adversely than others. Higher temperatures are expected to produce more erratic weather, reduce crop yields, melt glaciers that feed rivers that provide irrigation, cause seas to rise, generate more destructive storms, increase flooding, intensify drought, cause more wildfires, enable tropical diseases to spread, acidify oceans, and alter ecosystems everywhere. Like an individual's fever, each degree that the Earth's temperature rises becomes more threatening to its current inhabitants. Sustaining existing living standards would be impossible in the rapidly changing environment produced by much higher temperatures.

Damaged Ecosystems While pumping heat-trapping gases into the atmosphere, humans are also damaging other parts of the ecosystems that sustain them. At the top of the list of **damaged ecosystems** are water and soil, the foundations on which human civilizations are built.

Groundwater is being depleted and contaminated worldwide. For example, 15 percent of India's food supply is produced by mining groundwater, while in the middle United States the water table has dropped more than 100 feet (30 meters) due to irrigation. Many regions will experience flooding in the coming years as glaciers melt, followed by extreme water scarcity once they have melted. On much of the world's cropland, topsoil is eroding much faster than can be regenerated by geologic processes. Examples are Haiti, Lesotho, Mongolia, and Ethiopia. Dust storms are increasing in China and parts of Africa. In Iowa the topsoil is about half as deep as when the first European settlers came; farmers have substituted fertilizer. People know how to avoid soil degradation by biological processes, but it costs more than using chemical fertilizer.

Next on the list of damaged ecosystems are oceans and fisheries. Oceans not only absorb the increasing heat, but CO_2 from the atmosphere dissolves in surface waters, making them less alkaline and more acidic. This acidity interferes with the formation of external skeletons and shells in many organisms from plankton and algae to coral and crabs, preventing them from removing massive amounts of carbon from the atmosphere–ocean system. Humans are changing the chemistry of oceans, which may be a bigger problem than global warming. Meanwhile, fisheries are beginning to collapse from overfishing as did, for example, the cod fishery off the coast of Newfoundland in Canada in the 1990s (Figure 13.4). Three-fourths of oceanic fisheries are being fished at or beyond capacity, or are recovering from overexploitation. Since 1996 the growth in the supply of seafood has come almost entirely from fish farms, on

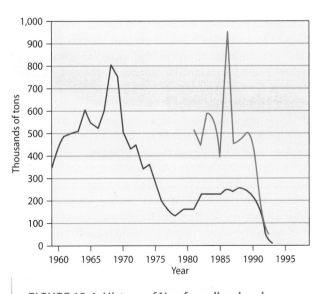

FIGURE 13.4 History of Newfoundland cod fishery. The annual harvest in thousands of tons is shown as a purple line; the size of the stock is shown as a red line.

which fish have to be fed grain and soybean meal, further intensifying pressures on land and water supplies.

Forests and loss of biodiversity through extinctions are two more areas of concern. Forests are being converted to ranches and farms at an astounding rate. About half the loss is regained in reforestation, but the net loss of 17 million acres (7 million hectares) a year threatens the Earth's remaining 9.9 billion acres (4 billion hectares) of forests. Up to half of all species on Earth face the threat of extinction in the twenty-first century. Extinction is a natural process, but the current speed is almost unprecedented. During the past 600 million years, there have been five major periods of rapid extinction (see Chapter 3); many experts believe that humans have started the sixth major extinction in Earth's history (see Chapter 12).

The human food supply is imperiled in many ways. Topsoil and water supply are threatened, as described earlier. We are literally eating oil, since our chemical fertilizers are made by combining nitrogen from the air with hydrogen from natural gas or oil. In 1985 about one-third of the energy contained in human food was derived from fossil energy; without this subsidy the food supply could have fed only about 2.5 billion instead of the actual 4.8 billion. Huge amounts of antibiotics, half of the total used in the United States, are fed to farm animals, a practice banned in many parts of Europe because it increases the rate at which bacteria mutate to become resistant to antibiotics. The world's expanding population has cut the grain land per person in half since 1950, to a mere quarter acre, threatening survival in subsistence communities. Nations like Libya, Saudi Arabia, South Korea, China, India, and Egypt are now buying or leasing land, together with its water, in other nations, to grow food for their own people. At the global level, we are running out of supplies of new land.

A further threat to ecosystems comes from the radiation emitted by testing and using nuclear bombs and from the radioactive materials left over from nuclear power plants. Looked at positively, one can say that humans have used "only" two nuclear bombs in war, and had only a few accidents at nuclear plants, the worst at Chernobyl, Ukraine, when a reactor exploded in 1986. Yet by the year 2000 more than 400 nuclear plants in 30 countries produced radioactive waste that they stored temporarily, hoping to find a safer solution. In 2010 the nations that chose to develop nuclear bombs had an estimated 23,000 nuclear weapons, down about 4,000 over the previous three years, and down significantly from 70,000 in 1986 (see Chapter 12). (Some nations have gotten rid of their nuclear weapons: South Africa, Ukraine, Belarus, and Kazakhstan. Others pursued nuclear weapons, but stopped, among them Brazil, Egypt, Libya, Switzerland, and Sweden.)

The level of consumption in industrialized nations has reached unprecedented proportions. The total volume of material entering the global market came to nearly 10 billion tons (9 billion metric tons) in 1995 alone, two and a half times more than in the early 1960s. Humans worldwide move 40 billion tons (36 billion metric tons) of earth each year, churning it up in mining and construction and eroding it by planting and clear-cutting. Only rivers, and possibly ants, rival humans with bulldozers for tonnage of earth moved.

A hidden problem in the way we do business lies in the fact that the market price of consumables does not include the cost of the loss and damage to ecosystems. The free market does not recognize these costs and does not allocate the price accordingly. For example, energy cost-accounting experts calculate the hidden costs of driving a car over its lifetime as $1,162 in health costs from pollution, $846 in damage to the environment, and $1,571 for protecting access to oil, for a total of an additional $3,579. The real costs of a hamburger have been estimated at $200.

In 2009, Lester R. Brown of Earth Policy Institute, a research organization based in Washington, DC, believed that humans were making demands on Earth's natural systems that exceeded by nearly 30 percent their sustainable yield capacity. In other words, humans are devouring their own life support system. This, he and others conclude, resembles a Ponzi scheme, a fraudulent operation that pays returns from the asset base itself, rather than from actual profits earned. (Charles Ponzi was an American who became notorious for his frauds beginning in 1920.) The scheme continues as long as there are sufficient new investors to pay the so-called returns to past investors; when there are not enough new investors, the scheme collapses. Humans are taking from the assets of ecosystems to pay themselves, stealing from descendants for whom the assets will not be there.

As the world's unprecedented economic growth puts increasing pressure on ecosystems, the potential for conflict over scarce resources increases. Ecological crises can reduce the quality of government because, as difficulties mount, some governments lose control of part or all of their territory and cannot collect taxes and ensure the basic security of their people. People's desperate situations impel them to renounce the legitimacy of their governments. Society devolves into civil wars, with local leaders competing for available power. To describe these situations, the term **failed state** entered public discourse in the 1990s. Examples of the top failed states in 2008 include Somalia, Zimbabwe, Sudan, Chad, Democratic Republic of the Congo, Iraq, and Afghanistan.

Failed states become havens for terrorist groups to recruit and train their members, places to grow drugs considered illegal elsewhere, and sources of infectious disease, as in Nigeria and Pakistan for polio, derailing efforts to eradicate it. Crime, instability, and disease increase for everyone when wealthy governments do not assist states at risk of failure. As Sarah O'Hara, a geographer at the University of Nottingham, said in 2002: "We talk about the developing world and the developed world, but this is the deteriorating world."[1]

Hopeful Trends

However, as we have seen throughout recent chapters, humans are an extraordinarily resourceful species, and Collective Learning is a remarkable problem-solving device.

Humans are learning at a staggering speed. Human awareness of what needs to be done has greatly increased in recent years, along with many pioneering actions and hopeful trends.

As described previously, one of the more hopeful trends has been the slowing of the population growth rate, with the rate going down faster than was projected a decade ago. The average world rate of population growth has declined from over 2 percent per year in the 1960s to 1.2 percent per year in 2005, with projections now of reaching peak population at anywhere between 8 and 12 billion. The possible reasons for this slowing growth rate include higher living standards and levels of education, especially for women; parents finding other forms of security than the support of their children; increased use of contraceptives; and in some places, higher death rates. Family planning has been a great success story; otherwise, population pressures would be much worse. Some believe that Earth's natural systems will not permit population growth past about 8 billion; it will be checked by rising mortality. Analysts point out that if there were any way to limit every human female to one child, the population would drop to 5.5 billion in 2050, 3.43 billion in 2075, and 1.6 billion in 2100, back where it was in 1900.

Other hopeful trends will be described under the headings of (a) stabilizing the climate, (b) restoring ecosystems, (c) reducing consumption and redesigning cities, (d) developing new forms of democracy, and (e) increasing global cooperation and communication.

Stabilizing the Climate

The climate is changing faster than any predictions made a decade ago. Climate change now is unavoidable; the only question is how much change there will be over the next 100 years. Most scientists believe that humans have only a decade or so in which to make the rapid reductions in CO_2 emissions that might prevent severe long-term warming. Rapid climate change has mobilized people to seek substitutes for fossil fuels, like solar and wind energy.

Conservation would seem an obvious response. Carefully designed incentives are a powerful way of encouraging conservation. Some countries have discouraged the use of fossil fuels by taxing gasoline and automobiles. The average gas tax in Europe is $4 per gallon, while in the United States it is $0.46 a gallon. Denmark levies a car tax of 180 percent the cost of the car; in Singapore the tax is three times the cost of the car; in Shanghai the registration fee averages $4,500 per car. During World War II the United States banned auto production for almost four years and rationed gasoline, tires, and fuel oil, a possible response not often mentioned.

Around the world researchers are racing to develop alternative sources of energy. Biofuels, made from plants, are hopeful possibilities, except that when made from corn or other edible plants they put fuel production in competition with food production. In Brazil biofuels that are made from sugar cane roughage already provide a mandatory 25 percent of auto fuel. Much research is underway to develop biofuels from other nonfood sources. Other promising trends in renewable energy are wind turbines for producing electricity, solar energy, and thermal energy (heat in Earth's upper 6 miles [9.6 kilometers] near volcanic activity).

Nuclear energy by fission plays a positive role because it does not contribute to global warming as fossil fuels do. In nuclear energy electricity is generated by bringing uranium fuel rods together to create an atomic chain reaction that produces heat, turning water into steam passed to turbines connected to dynamos that generate electricity. By 2012 nuclear plants provided about 12 percent of the world's electricity production, with 66 more plants under construction. But there are problems with nuclear energy. Mining, refining, and concentrating uranium use enormous amounts of energy and produce high levels of ground and air pollution. No long-term solution has been found for storing the radioactive waste, and accidents at plants have raised serious safety issues. In addition, serious security issues remain unsolved, namely how to prevent theft and black market sales of uranium and how to prevent its further refinement into material for bombs. Perhaps nuclear energy is best seen as a transition strategy to renewable forms of energy.

One of the greenhouse gases, ozone (O_3, i.e., oxygen molecules with three atoms of oxygen instead of the more normal two atoms) not only has helped warm Earth, but also has protected living organisms from damage from too much ultraviolet (UV) light. Remember from Chapter 3 that when the ozone layer built up sufficiently to prevent UV damage, about 600 million years ago, life proliferated on Earth.

In the 1980s scientific evidence had accumulated that a class of chemical compounds used in refrigerators and air conditioners, chlorofluorocarbons (CFCs), was causing damage to the ozone layer. International agreement to phase out CFCs could be reached when Dupont Chemical Company found other chemical compounds that could easily be substituted at about the same cost. This hopeful story shows that humans can collaborate globally to solve an environmental problem (see Chapter 12).

Those who believe in technological solutions are considering many possible ways of dealing with the consequences of fossil fuels. These include atmospheric engineering (spraying sulfur dioxide into the atmosphere to reflect solar radiation back to space), injecting CO_2 underground into empty aquifers, transforming coal into oil, and bioengineering fuel from bioengineered bacteria. Either by finding alternative sources of energy or new methods of mitigating the effects of burning fossil fuels, we may be able to limit the consequences of global warming.

Restoring Ecosystems

Humans have responded to their growing ecological footprint by beginning to watch and track it; for example, the Living Planet Index of the World Wildlife Fund for Nature tracks changes in forest, freshwater, and marine ecosystems. Lester R. Brown and his Earth Policy Institute present a plan each year for reducing the human footprint. These reports are accurate summaries of helpful trends; this section relies heavily on Brown's 2009 report, *Plan B 4.0: Mobilizing to Save Civilization.*

Restoring the environment begins with water and soil. "More crop per drop" is being achieved by using perforated rubber hoses for drip irrigation. Water is being recycled, while rainwater is being harvested in ponds and receptacles. Genetically modified crops that require less water can be developed. Desalination, a way of extracting freshwater from seawater, requires much energy; with wind or solar energy it might be possible on a large scale, but probably is economically feasible only near coasts and major energy sources. Soil is being conserved by drilling seeds into undisturbed soil, planting walls of trees, reducing herds of goats and sheep, and banning clear-cutting of forests.

The restoration of oceans and forests is underway using several approaches. Restoring oceans involves reducing CO_2 emissions; establishing marine reserves; eliminating fishery subsidies; reducing fertilizer, sewerage, and toxic chemical runoff; and banning the plastic bags that collect in ocean areas the size of Texas. Restoring forests requires limiting deforestation and planting new forests. Inspired by the work of **Wangari Maathai** (1940–2011), who founded the Green Belt Movement in Kenya, the United Nations Environment Programme (UNEP) sponsored the Billion Tree Campaign. By July 2009 it had 4.1 billion new trees in the ground, with 2.1 billion more pledged. Among the leaders of this initiative were Ethiopia, Turkey, Mexico, Kenya, Cuba, and Indonesia. At present, only about half the annual loss of forests is regained by reforestation. Also, planting trees sequesters carbon only as long as they live; when they die, their decay converts their carbon into CO_2, unless they are buried and fossilized or used in building, which delays the onset of decay.

Reducing the rate of species extinctions requires humans to share resources with other animals and plants. Preserves have been created; some 3 percent of Earth's land surface is now in parks and nature preserves. More corridors and preserves are needed—probably about 8 to 10 percent of the land surface, but they will be effective only with population and climate stabilization.

In the first decade of the twenty-first century, food production began to decline in some countries because of water shortages and soil erosion. Possible promising trends include genetic modifications to develop pesticide-producing and disease-resistant plants. Other unrealized production potential lies in double cropping, food subsidy policies, and local gardens. Yet no food output is possible without inputs; plants simply reorganize the chemicals available.

Reducing Consumption and Redesigning Cities

Strides have been made in many countries in reducing consumption by conserving energy and recycling materials. Compact fluorescent lamps (CFLs) use 75 percent less electricity than incandescent bulbs. They cost twice as much but last 10 times as long. Light-emitting diodes (LEDs) use 85 percent less energy and last 50 times as long. A worldwide switch to CFLs and LEDs would cut the portion of electricity used for lighting from 19 to 7 percent. Brazil has already replaced half of its bulbs; by 2009 Australia, Canada, and the EU had approved phasing out the sale of incandescent bulbs.

Efficiency has been increased with many household appliances, especially refrigerators. Large energy efficiencies have been achieved in green buildings, electrifying the transport system, and using smart grids to manage electricity.

Reducing the use of virgin raw materials by recycling is beginning to replace the throw-away economy. Steel and aluminum can be reused indefinitely. In the United States virtually all cars are recycled and household appliances are being recycled at about a 90 percent rate. There remains a huge potential for more recycling in construction. Advanced industrialized economies with a stable population, like Japan and Germany, could rely primarily on existing materials. Among the largest U.S. cities, recycling rates of public trash in 2009 varied from 34 percent in New York City, to 55 percent in Chicago, to 60 percent in Los Angeles, to 72 percent in San Francisco. In the country as a whole 33.4 percent of solid waste is recycled or composted, 12.6 percent is burned, and 54 percent goes to landfill, down from 89 percent in 1980.

Starting in 2008 more than half the world's population lived in cities, the largest of which was Greater Tokyo with 36 million people (more than Canada), followed by metropolitan New York City with 19 million (almost equal to Australia). Nineteen mega-cities each contain over 10 million people, many of them breathing unsafe air. Cities everywhere need to be redesigned for people rather than for cars. Successful examples are Curitiba, Brazil, which began restructuring its transport system in 1974, reducing car traffic by 30 percent in 20 years while the population doubled, or Amsterdam, where 40 percent of all trips in the city are by bicycle. The bicycle, on which Brown claims he can get 7 miles (11 kilometers) with the calories from one potato is returning as significant transportation—to Paris as a rental program, to police departments, to U.S. college and university campuses, where at least two universities give all first-year students a bike if they agree to leave their cars at home. Look for ratings of the world's top green cities; Reykjavik, Iceland, usually appears at number one (Figure 13.5).

Urban gardens are beginning to produce significant amounts of food. In Vancouver, British Columbia, Canada, 44 percent of residents produce some of their own food. In Shanghai half of its pork and poultry, 60 percent of its vegetables, and 90 percent of its milk and eggs come from the city and its immediate surrounds. Caracas, Venezuela, has 8,000 microgardens 1.2 square yards (1 square meter) each; each garden, continuously cropped, can produce annually 330 heads of lettuce, or 40 pounds (18 kilograms) of tomatoes, or 35 pounds (16 kilograms) of cabbage.

These examples suggest that many ways of reducing consumption and redesigning cities are being pioneered. Efficiency in appliances has increased, raw materials are

FIGURE 13.5 The world's top green city. In Reykjavik, Iceland, all heat and electricity come from renewable geothermal and hydropower sources. The transit system uses buses run on hydrogen. The city plans to be fossil fuel–free by 2050.

being recycled more often, bicycling and urban gardening are having significant effects, as people worldwide confront their ecological challenges.

| *Developing New Forms of Democracy* | The carboniferous Industrial Revolution transformed monarchies and empires into modern nation- |

states, with increasing governmental reach into the lives of their citizens and increasing participation of citizens in selecting their governments or representatives to their governments, usually called democracies. The last half of the twentieth century saw a significant global increase in democracies, as judged by the minimal standard of the regular occurrence of free, fair, and contested elections by an inclusive citizenry. In 1950 only 22 nations, with 14.3 percent of the world's population, qualified as democracies by this definition; by 2002, 121 of the world's 192 sovereign states, with 64.6 percent of the world's population, did.

The transition from fossil fuels to sustainability may provide an opening for new political forms. What might they be?

David Korten (1937–) provides one example in his book, *The Great Turning: From Empire to Earth Community* (2006). Korten, an economist who worked for 30 years in the international development establishment, is critical of corporate globalization. He frames the choice as between empire and earth community. He uses "empire" as a label for the 5,000-year era of hierarchical ordering of human relationships based on domination (what we have called in earlier chapters *tribute-taking societies*), while "earth community" refers to egalitarian, democratic ordering of human relationships based on partnership. He holds out **the great turning** as a possibility, not a prophecy, a choice to be made by people everywhere for stronger democracy, for active participatory citizenship, and for cooperation for mutual advantage. The other choice he describes as "the

great unraveling," consisting of collapsing environmental systems, violent competition for resources, human dieback, and ruthless local lords.

Examples of change toward more participatory democracy can be found. Benjamin Barber, professor of political science emeritus at Rutgers University, calls participatory democracy "strong democracy," to be built on the "thin" liberal democracy of the past 200 years. His agenda for strong democracy would include a national system of neighborhood assemblies, experiments in lay justice, and a program of universal citizen service (including a military option). Matt Leighninger, director of the Deliberative Democracy Consortium, tells stories of shared governance happening at local and regional levels. Vandana Shiva, former physicist and now environmental activist based in Delhi, has documented the action of women, small farmers, and small producers in India. They have shut down Coca-Cola plants for using up and polluting water, stopped corporate patenting of seeds and plants, and resisted privatization of water supplies. According to Shiva:

> The project of multinational corporate rule . . . threatens to annihilate the very conditions of life for large numbers of humans and other species. . . . Dictatorship is no longer partial. It engulfs entire economic, political and cultural lives in every society and every country. . . . We have just begun to tap our potential for transformation and liberation. This is not the end of history, but another beginning.[2]

Globally, more people now live in democratic governments than ever before, with the potential to develop stronger participation in decision making. The power of the people, with their accumulated Collective Learning directed toward finding solutions, may be expressed through new political forms.

| *Increasing Global Cooperation and Communication* | Strong international cooperation began after World War II with the establishment of the United Nations. Additional global scaf- |

folding was put in place at the end of the century; three UN environmental treaties came out of the Earth Summit in Rio de Janeiro in 1992, a Plan of Action emerged from the 1994 International Conference on Population and Development in Cairo, and a UN Millennium Declaration was signed in 2000 with eight specific goals. A climate summit in Copenhagen in 2009 proved less encouraging; no treaty regarding CO_2 emissions could be agreed on, although many countries proceeded with their own targets.

In addition to governments, increasing numbers of nongovernmental organizations (NGOs) are spending hundreds of billions of dollars on global issues, exploring what ideas can work effectively. A few examples include the Carter Center, founded by former U.S. president Jimmy Carter (1927–), devoted to social and economic development; Doctors Without Borders for delivering health care to the most impoverished areas; and Amnesty International for keeping human rights on the global agenda. Ashoka and the Skoll Foundation are supporting networks of social entrepreneurs for local change. The World Wildlife Fund and the Nature Conservancy are devoted to preserving biodiversity. Also playing a crucial role are the transformative philanthropists, like John D. Rockefeller, George Soros, David Packard, William Hewlett, Bill and Melinda Gates, and Warren Buffett. A new organization, the World Future Council, began in 2007 as an international lobby for future generations. Founded by the Swedish writer Jacob von Uexhuell, the World Future Council has offices in Hamburg, London, Brussels, Washington, DC, and Addis Ababa.

Global cooperation on all levels has intensified since the arrival in 1991 of the World Wide Web, created by Tim Berners-Lee, a mathematician working at CERN, a physics research center in Geneva, Switzerland. People worldwide now have access to 25 billion pages of knowledge on the web and can make international contact directly. Money is going digital; only 10 percent of the $4 trillion circulating in the United States is actually cash and coins. The growth of digitalization and worldwide computing is projected to continue.

These are hopeful signs of increasing global cooperation and the increasing power of Collective Learning, but looming questions continue to haunt our imaginations. Is there an inherent conflict between commercialism, based on economic growth, and sustainability? Will people mobilize the political will to change rapidly or wait until a crisis is upon us? Can economic incentives produce results through the marketplace, or will governments need to impose measures such as rationing? Will the rich assist the poor, or care only for themselves? What will the current massive shift of wealth from West (United States and Europe) to East (China and India) mean?

To prepare for the next 100 years, people everywhere can encourage positive trends and design or redesign their lives around the most promising current practices— conserving energy however possible, having fewer children, using more bicycles, and growing more gardens. However, personal lifestyle changes are not likely to be sufficient; citizens will need to be more engaged in political action for larger-scale changes. Getting a grip in a rapidly changing world requires clarity, creativity, compassion, and courage, as it always has. And the view of big history is a great way of seeing the issues clearly.

Humans share a common fate on a crowded planet; the human experiment in culture and Collective Learning has put much of our fate into our own hands. If there are solutions to our global challenges, surely interconnected humans will find them. The battle for the future of humanity has just begun. Whatever the next 100 years bring, it will be a surprise.

Beyond the Near Future

Thinking about the distant future is very different from thinking about the next 100 years. We can care about the near future because it will affect the lives of people we will know, including our children and grandchildren. We may also have some influence over it, so it is worth thinking hard about how we can use that influence. Finally, it seems (though we can't be sure) that it is close enough that our predictions shouldn't be too far off the mark.

Once we start to look much beyond the year 2100, things get tougher. Beyond about 100 years into the future it gets harder to care so much about what happens. Caring about the fate of one's grandchildren or even great-grandchildren is one thing; but it is harder to feel strongly about the fate of our great-great-great-grandchildren (and we doubt if they will care much about us). The subject becomes less personal and more abstract. It's also less clear whether our predictions matter much at these scales. Can we really influence how the world will be in 500 years' time, particularly given the remarkable pace of change today?

Besides, if it's hard to predict what the world will be like in 100 years as the pace of change accelerates, the possibilities multiply even faster the further away we get from the present, so our predictions are likely to get more and more fantastic. Particularly with Future 2 (the next few thousand years), it is hard to predict because we are still talking about extremely complex entities such as human societies.

But we will see that when we move on to Future 3, millions or billions of years from now, there is no point in talking about human societies, so we start talking about other things like the history of Earth or even the universe. As we return to simpler and slower processes such as those of plate tectonics or planetary evolution, or even the evolution of the whole universe, the possibilities begin to narrow again so that, curiously, our chances of making realistic predictions seem to increase once more. So we'll see that Future 2 is the most difficult of all futures to predict, while Future 3 permits more confident speculation.

Future 2: The Next Few Thousand Years

What will the world be like 500 years from now or 1,000 or 2,000 years from now? We have seen that human societies are among the most complex entities that we know about, and that is why making such predictions seems almost impossible. Future 2 is where our capacity to think about the future really breaks down.

We are left with some interesting guesses and lots of science fiction. There have been several "histories of the future" that make for fascinating reading. While none count as serious predictions they do suggest the range of futures that writers have imagined, and they range from the very bleak (dystopian) to the very hopeful (utopian).

In the first half of the twentieth century, George Orwell and Aldous Huxley wrote famous "dystopias," descriptions of exceptionally bleak futures. Orwell's *1984* described a totalitarian future in which global dictators ruled using crude propaganda, torture, and violence to protect their power. International politics was a matter of continuous war for no clear ethical goals, but merely with the aim of maintaining power for a privileged few.

Huxley's *Brave New World* described a world in which humans were hatched like battery chickens and kept happy on drugs, a world that in some ways seems closer today with our growing capacity to manipulate genes and to fertilize eggs in the lab. It is a curious dystopia because it represents many things that people aspire to, including freedom from pain, suffering, and the difficulties of ordinary life, yet it represents such a life as severely degraded in comparison with the complex, unpredictable but sometimes meaningful world of happiness and suffering inhabited by normal people today. Will our capacity to minimize pain end up creating a world that is emotionally, psychically, and intellectually impoverished, a world in which the very idea of freedom loses its meaning?

Walter Miller's science fiction novel, *Canticle for Leibowitz,* begins in a world that seems eerily like the European Dark Ages, a world that has patchy memories of past civilizations, most of whose technologies and skills have been lost. The novel moves forward several centuries in each section until you slowly realize that you are in a world that has lived through a nuclear war, the so-called flame deluge. What is happening is a repeat of the familiar story of modern world history, with a revival of cities, of commerce, and then, in the final chapters, of modern science. Eventually, scientists invent a nuclear weapon once more, and, sadly, it is used in a war that throws human societies back two millennia in time. And now you realize that what the novel is really describing is a world in which humans never progress beyond the discovery of nuclear weapons because, once discovered, nuclear weapons will be used. It is tempting to think that here we have a possible explanation for the fact that, despite several decades of looking for evidence of signals from alien civilizations through the Search for Extraterrestrial Intelligence (SETI), we have detected nothing. Is it possible that once species such as ours appear, with a capacity for Collective Learning, after a few hundred thousand years they will inevitably create technologies so powerful that they destroy themselves? This picture of an endless and unwinnable struggle with technology that can never move beyond a certain level is one of the bleakest of all future scenarios.

Similar, in a sense, are some of the ideas sketched out by James Lovelock in his work on Gaia. Lovelock has argued that all living things on Earth can be thought of as working together to form a huge superorganism. He calls that organism *Gaia,* a name suggested by his friend, the novelist William Golding, and borrowed from the name for the Greek goddess of the Earth. Lovelock argues that in some sense Gaia has managed to ensure that Earth remains habitable for living organisms. As science, the theory is controversial. But one of the most striking arguments Lovelock presents is that the surface of Earth has remained within the Goldilocks range, the range within which water is a liquid, despite the fact that the heat from the sun has increased steadily over 4.5 billion years. Something on the surface of the Earth, presumably some complex feedback system between the atmosphere and the biosphere, seems to be ensuring that, by alterations in the color and reflectivity

of Earth's surface and the composition of its atmosphere, our planet remains biofriendly because it remains within the narrow band of temperatures in which liquid water can fill the oceans. Is the vital feedback system geological (based perhaps on erosion and the burial of CO_2 in rocks, as many geologists would argue), or is it managed by Gaia, as Lovelock argues?

Lovelock goes on to argue that our own species is threatening to upset this ancient mechanism by hogging so many resources. Humans, he suggests, are beginning to behave like cancer cells, multiplying so fast that they are threatening to damage the larger organism of which they are a part. This leaves two possibilities, neither of which is attractive if you happen to be a human being. One is that humans will indeed kill off the biosphere (Gaia) of which they are a part and, like an excessively virulent virus, will kill themselves in the process. The second is that Gaia will find a way of healing itself by getting rid of the rogue organism, perhaps through the spread of terrible plagues or perhaps by simply waiting for humans to destroy themselves in a nuclear war.

Stableford and Langford's *The Third Millennium* and Warren Wagar's *History of the Future* both read like histories written in the distant future. Both imagine futures in which there will be major crises involving the use of nuclear weapons, from which humans will learn new ways of organizing societies and international relations. Wagar's novel, inspired by the work of H.G. Wells and published in 1989, imagines a future in which people successively try socialist, capitalist, and anarchist ways of organizing society. Technology is important in both books, but, like most futuristic writings, both are really exploring the political and moral problems of today's world.

Dystopias make for interesting reading, while utopias tend to be boring (humans often seem more interested in misery than happiness), so there are fewer genuinely utopian futuristic novels. The utopias tend to be found in the work of specialists in the future of technology who predict longer, healthier lives, and technologies that will supply endless, virtually free energy and resources. Many also discuss new forms of genetic engineering and **nanotechnologies** (technologies using tiny, bacteria-sized machines) that will remove many forms of physical suffering, ensure sustainable supplies of food and other resources, and repair much of the damage we have inflicted on the biosphere by creating entities such as plastic-eating bacteria. Some, such as Ray Kurzweill, imagine a future in which humans will merge with computers, becoming, effectively, immortal.

It may be useful to think of two main types of utopian futures. The first type foresees sustained growth into a remote future and the solution of many of today's ecological problems through technological fixes. The second group foresees a slowdown in growth and a future in which growth and increased consumption cease to provide the basic definitions of a good life. Instead, in these utopias, the future is imagined as a realm of well-being, but not necessarily of constant change or "growth." Such utopias assume a slowing in the rate of change and a humanity whose numbers may be far less than today and whose societies are content to maintain a good life without endlessly seeking more resources.

Migration to other planets may be a part of either dystopian or utopian futures. We are, after all, a migratory species, so cosmic migrations would seem to imitate the astonishing migrations that took Pacific navigators to places as remote as Rapa Nui, in voyages from which migrants must have known they would never return. Some of the technology is already available for the exploitation of minerals from asteroids or the creation of space stations on the moon or Mars or even hovering in space. One model for a space colony rotates slowly, creating a sort of gravity as it does so, and a rough equivalent of day and night for its various internal regions or "continents."

More ambitious are plans for the **terraforming** of planets such as Mars, to make them habitable for human beings and other earthly species. This was one of the many futuristic ideas of the novelist and scientist, Arthur C. Clarke. Terraforming might involve massive nuclear explosions to melt ice beneath the surface of Mars, in the hope of creating oceans and an atmosphere; the seeding of bacteria capable of surviving Martian conditions; and the placing in orbit of huge mirrors to reflect and concentrate the heat and light of the sun (Figure 13.6). These, of course, are massive engineering projects that would presumably take hundreds of years with no certainty of success!

Migrations outside our solar system are harder to imagine because the distances are so vast. In any scenario we can imagine at present, migrations to even the nearest stars would take generations of travel through outer space, with no possibilities of resupply or repairs if anything went wrong and no guarantee that habitable planets would be found at the other end. Of course, it is possible that much faster forms of travel will be invented, but at present we have no conception of how they might work. But if we allow ourselves to imagine a slow spreading of humans through the galaxy, superficially like the migrations of Pacific Islanders, we must remember that the distances and times will be so huge that isolated populations of humans will almost certainly evolve and change in different star systems. Eventually, our species will divide into numerous subspecies. Of course, just 30,000 years ago there existed several species of hominines on Earth, so such a scenario is not really so far-fetched.

That piece of speculation is a reminder that our species, like all others, evolves. Whether or not we start steering our evolution through genetic manipulation, we will change, and there will eventually come a point where it will no longer be clear (to an imaginary time traveler from today's world) whether our descendants count as humans or not. That will presumably mark the end of human history as we know it today.

Future 3: The Remote Future

Now we must turn from these speculations to the more remote future in which our kind of humans no longer exist. Once we start thinking about futures that are hundreds of millions or even billions of years in the future, we must return to the types of objects that evolve on large time scales: to planet Earth, to the galaxy, and to the universe as a whole. At these scales, most change is slower and simpler, and that means, curiously, that we can begin to predict with more confidence once again. Indeed, we can predict events in the very remote future with much more confidence than we can predict the history of the next few centuries.

Plate tectonics provides a good example. We know, roughly, the direction and speed of movement of the major tectonic plates, and we also know roughly how they have moved over the past few hundred million years, so we can make some reasonable predictions about what Earth will look like in 50 or 100 or perhaps even 200 million years' time. The Atlantic Ocean will widen and the Pacific Ocean will narrow, while Africa will crack and split along the great African Rift valley. According to one prediction, the Earth's continents will eventually regather around the North Pole to form a new supercontinent, *Amasia* (Map 13.2).

We can also say something about the future of Earth as a whole because of our knowledge of how stars like our sun evolve. In perhaps 3 to 4 billion years our sun will run out of fuel. It will shed its outer layers, while its core will collapse, then it will start burning helium, and it will expand once again, turning into a red giant and growing much larger than it is today. At that stage, the outer layers of the sun will reach the orbit of Earth and our

FIGURE 13.6 Terraforming Mars?
Could Mars be made inhabitable by artificial "global warming"? If so, the process would take hundreds of years.

MAP 13.2 Amasia. In
100 million years, the continents
of the Earth may join to form the
supercontinent of Amasia.

North Pole

planet will be folded into it. That will be the end of planet Earth and any organisms still living on it. Eventually, the sun will collapse one last time to form a dwarf star, which will slowly cool over a period much longer than the mere 9 billion years during which it will have been active. Our sun is not large enough to form a supernova.

At about the time our sun dies, our galaxy, the Milky Way, will collide with the neighboring Andromeda galaxy (Figure 13.7). The collision will be a polite affair. Few stars will come close to each other, but their gravitational pull will warp planetary systems and transform the overall shape of both galaxies, causing some local chaos. No humans will be there to observe the collision; but of course there may be millions of inhabited planets whose inhabitants will observe it; and it is just possible that some will be descendants of emigrants from our planet.

And what of the universe as a whole? Strangely, the universe evolves in ways that are much simpler than the evolution of human society. And this gives cosmologists confidence that they can say something reasonably sensible about its future.

As we have seen, big bang cosmology posits an expanding universe. But cosmologists have always been aware that there must be a tension between the forces that drive the universe apart and the fundamental force of gravity, which tends to pull everything together. In the long run, which force will win?

In the late twentieth century, cosmologists tried to answer this question by estimating the speed of expansion of the universe and the total gravitational pull of all the matter in the universe. The idea was that if there was enough matter in the universe, the force of gravity would slow the rate of expansion to a halt and eventually the universe would start to shrink, perhaps some 200 billion years into the future. The collapse would accelerate until the entire universe would be compressed once again into a tiny ball of intense energy/matter perhaps

400 billion years after the big bang. At that point the sheer pressure of the ball of matter might spring it apart again to create a new big bang and perhaps an entirely new universe with a new life cycle of its own. There is something intrinsically satisfying about such a story.

Unfortunately, most cosmologists now believe that this cyclical account of the universe's future is wrong. The reason is a curious discovery made in the late 1990s. Attempts to estimate the speed of expansion of the universe by looking at extremely distant supernovae showed that, over time, the rate of expansion of the universe seems not

more thresholds?

FIGURE 13.7 Collision! This is an artist's rendering of the Milky Way colliding with Andromeda.

TABLE 13.1 A Chronology for the Remote Future of the Universe

Time since Big Bang (Years)	Significant Events (Don't take the dates too seriously! There's a lot of guesswork here.)
10^{14}	Most stars are dead; the universe is dominated by cold objects, black dwarfs, neutron stars, dead planets/asteroids, and stellar black holes; surviving matter is isolated as the universe keeps expanding.
10^{20}	Many objects have drifted away from galaxies; those remaining have collapsed into galactic black holes.
10^{32}	Protons have largely decayed, leaving a universe of energy, leptons (particles like electrons), and black holes.
10^{66} to 10^{106}	Stellar and galactic black holes evaporate.
$10^{1,500}$	Through quantum "tunneling," remaining matter is transformed into iron.
$10^{10^{76}}$	Remaining matter is transformed into neutronic matter, then into black holes, which eventually evaporate.

Note: 10^{14} looks innocent enough until you remember that it does not mean 14×10 but 10 multiplied by itself 14 times, or 1,000,000,000,000,000. The number in the lowest line is even more humungous. It means 10 multiplied by itself 10 times (i.e., 100,000,000,000). Then take that number and multiply it by itself 76 times. To print that number would take up much of this book. That's why in the text we use the nonscientific term *gazillions*. What we really mean is lots and lots and lots . . . of years.

Source: Adapted from Nikos Prantzos, *Our Cosmic Future: Humanity's Fate in the Universe* (Cambridge, UK: Cambridge University Press, 2000), 263.

to be slowing but rather to be accelerating! This was the opposite of what most cosmologists had expected. Most explanations of this unexpected phenomenon have returned to an idea Einstein once posited: that there is a basic force that works in the opposite way to gravity, a force that tends to push things apart; and this, they argue, is a force that arises from space itself, so it tends to get more powerful as the universe expands. At about the time our sun and Earth were created, the force of expansion began to take over from the pull of gravity and the pace of expansion began to increase.

What does that mean for the future of the universe? One thing seems clear. In the very remote future, countless billions of billions of billions of years from now, the universe will start getting more and more boring (Table 13.1). The gaps between galaxies will increase so that observers will see fewer objects in the skies until eventually each galaxy will seem to be a self-contained universe of its own. Star formation will cease, and the number of stars will start diminishing until finally there will no longer be any stars at all. And no stars will surely mean no planets, no biospheres, and no living organisms. The universe will be dead once again, and any complex structures will be slowly broken down, beginning with living organisms, progressing to planets, and then eventually to stars. The Goldilocks conditions that made it possible to create planets and life will no longer exist. The universe will become a place inhabited by clouds of chemicals, including, perhaps, great lumps of iron. Where there are clumps of matter, they will either form black holes or eventually get gobbled up by black holes, which will graze on the slim pickings left in an increasingly empty universe. Eventually, gazillions of gazillions of years from now (*gazillions* is not a technical term, by the way, but we hope you know what we mean), even the black holes will leak energy and begin to evaporate. The universe will get simpler and simpler and bigger and bigger forever and ever and ever and . . .

Conclusion—The End of the Story: Humans in the Cosmos

Whether you find this conclusion satisfying or not, it is at present our best shot at describing the eventual fate of the universe. And in a way it is quite satisfying when we return from this bleak picture to think of the universe today. In the light of these predictions we can see that we live, not in an old universe (of course, 13.8 billion years may seem extremely old to us), but in the springtime of the universe, at a time when the universe had plenty of energy, plenty of gradients, and all that was needed to create complex things such as stars and planets and living organisms and even human beings. Today, the Goldilocks conditions exist for the creation of stars, planets, life, and human beings! We are products of the universe at a time when it had the dynamism needed to create the wondrous world that surrounds us.

SUMMARY

Future 1, the "near future," is hard to predict, but we cannot avoid trying to do so. We have to try to identify both ominous and hopeful trends and try to imagine how we can influence the trends we consider most hopeful. Future 2, the new few thousand years, seems much harder to predict, so it provides fertile ground for the imagination of science fiction writers. Future 3, the remote future, is in some ways simpler and slower-moving. So, curiously, we can predict with more confidence. Our sun will become a red giant, then collapse into a dwarf star; our galaxy will collide with the Andromeda galaxy. The universe will probably continue to get bigger and cooler and simpler forever. We have the good fortune to live in the springtime of the universe.

CHAPTER QUESTIONS

1. Describe some ominous trends and some hopeful ones.
2. As you assume life as an adult, what changes in your lifestyle are you considering to protect the environment?

3. How reliable are our ideas about the future of the solar system and the universe?
4. Do you have a sense that you may know the ending of the big history story?

KEY TERMS

damaged ecosystems

failed states

the great turning

greenhouse effect

groundwater

human footprint

nanotechnologies

Organization of the Petroleum Exporting Countries (OPEC)

renewable energy

terraforming

350 ppm

Wangari Maathai

FURTHER READING

Brown, Lester R. *Plan B 4.0: Mobilizing to Save Civilization.* New York and London: Norton, 2009.

Davidson, Eric A. *You Can't Eat GNP: Economics as If Ecology Mattered.* Cambridge, MA: Perseus, 2000.

Diamond, Jared. *Collapse: How Societies Choose to Fail or Succeed.* New York: Viking, 2005.

Huxley, Aldous. *Brave New World.* Originally published 1932.

Kaku, Michio. *Visions: How Science Will Revolutionize the Twenty-First Century.* Oxford, New York, and Melbourne: Oxford University Press, 1998.

Korten, David. *The Great Turning: From Empire to Earth Community.* San Francisco: Berrett-Koehler, 2006.

Kurzweill, Ray. *The Singularity Is Near: When Humans Transcend Biology.* New York: Penguin, 2006.

Lovelock, James. *The Vanishing Face of Gaia: A Final Warning.* New York: Basic Books, 2009.

McAnany, Patricia A., and Norman Yoffee. *Questioning Collapse: Human Resilience, Ecological Vulnerability, and the Aftermath of Empire.* Cambridge, UK: Cambridge University Press, 2010.

Miller, Walter M. *A Canticle for Leibowitz.* New York: Bantam, 1997. Originally published 1959.

Mueller, Richard A. *Physics for Future Presidents: The Science behind the Headlines.* New York and London: Norton, 2008.

Orwell, George. *1984.* Originally published 1949.

Prantzos, Nikos. *Our Cosmic Future: Humanity's Fate in the Universe.* Cambridge, UK: Cambridge University Press, 2000.

Roberts, Paul. *The End of Oil: On the Edge of a Perilous New World.* Boston: Houghton Mifflin, 2004.

Roston, Eric. *The Carbon Age: How Life's Core Element Has Become Civilization's Greatest Threat.* New York: Walker, 2008.

Sachs, Jeffrey D. *Common Wealth: Economics for a Crowded Planet.* New York: Penguin, 2008.

Shiva, Vandana. *Earth Democracy: Justice, Sustainability, and Peace.* Cambridge, MA: South End Press, 2005.

Smil, Vaclav. *Energy in World History.* Boulder, CO: Westview Press, 1994.

Stableford, Brian, and David Langford. *The Third Millennium: A History of the World, AD 2000–3000.* London: Sidgwick and Jackson, 1985.

Wagar, Warren. *A Short History of the Future.* 3rd ed. Chicago: University of Chicago Press, 1999.

ENDNOTES

1. Quoted in Lester R. Brown, *Plan B 4.0 Mobilizing to Save Civilization* (New York and London: Norton, 2009).

2. Vandana Shiva, *Earth Democracy: Justice, Sustainability, and Peace* (Cambridge, MA: South End Press, 2005), 185–86.

Glossary

A

absorption lines: when broken into different frequencies by a spectroscope, light from stars or galaxies often shows dark lines that indicate the presence of particular elements that have absorbed some of the light's energy. The presence of absorption lines can also be used to determine if light from distant objects has been shifted to the blue or red ends of the electromagnetic spectrum.

accretion: a process through which materials orbiting new stars grow in size through the collision and sticking together of particles, until eventually they form planetesimals and planets.

agrarian civilizations: large communities of hundreds of thousands or even millions of people, with cities and states together with their surrounding farmed countryside. Common features of agrarian civilizations include coerced tribute, specialized occupations, hierarchies, state religions, kings, armies, systems of writing and numbers, and monumental architecture.

agriculture: a way of exploiting the environment by increasing the productivity of those plant and animal species most beneficial for human beings. A form of symbiosis, it generally results, over time, in genetic changes in the "domesticated" species. Agriculture is vastly more productive than foraging technologies. Its appearance marks a revolutionary transformation in human history.

Anthropocene: a new epoch, not yet formally accepted by geologists, during which our species has become the dominant force for change in the biosphere. It was climatologist Paul Crutzen who first argued, in 2000, that we had entered a new geological epoch in the last 200 years, and that the Holocene epoch had effectively ended at about the time of the Industrial Revolution, about 200 years ago.

arbitrage: making profits by buying goods cheaply in regions where they were undervalued, and selling them at higher prices in regions where they were overvalued.

atmosphere: the gaseous mass or envelope surrounding and retained by a celestial body, especially the one surrounding Earth.

atomic matter: the types of matter from which atoms and stars and people are made; all forms of matter apart from dark matter.

Australopithecines: an early group of hominine species with brains about the size of those of chimpanzees; they flourished in Africa between 4 and 1 million years ago.

Austronesian (languages): a group of languages that probably originated in China before spreading through Southeast Asia and then east into the Pacific and west to Madagascar as a result of seaborne migrations that began almost 4,000 years ago. Today, Austronesian languages are spoken by nearly 400 million people.

Aztecs: a group of seminomadic people who settled in the Basin of Mexico on an island in Lake Texcoco about 1325 CE and created within a few generations an agrarian civilization that survived until the arrival of the Spanish in 1519 CE. Based on honoring warriors, the Aztec civilization had all the usual characteristics of an agrarian civilization, including writing.

B

big bang: the name, first used facetiously by the astronomer Fred Hoyle and now in general use, for the primal event from which the universe emerged according to *big bang cosmology*.

big bang cosmology: the modern understanding of the origin of the universe; first proposed in the 1930s, it became the central idea (paradigm) of modern cosmology from the 1960s.

big history: the attempt to construct a unified account of the past at all scales from those of human history to those of cosmology; the modern, scientific equivalent of traditional origin stories—what this course is about!

biodiversity: the number of different species in existence on Earth or in a particular region at a particular time.

black hole: a region in space of such high density that its gravitational pull does not allow even light to escape. Black holes can be formed by the collapse of large objects such as very large stars.

C

Cambrian explosion: during the Cambrian era (542–488 million years ago) many large fossils appeared, and animal life developed an astonishing diversity of structural forms. This was long thought to be the era in which life first appeared on Earth, though it is now known that single-celled organisms existed for several billion years before this.

capitalist societies: societies in which market exchanges were the main way of exchanging goods and resources, and in which elites and governments supported and encouraged commercial activity because their own wealth depended on flourishing commerce.

caste system: a system of social organization in which people are rigidly organized in hierarchical groups determined by heredity. The caste system in India began as color-coded, since the incoming Aryan people were much lighter-skinned than the native Dravidian people.

Cepheid variables: a type of star whose brightness varies in a regular rhythm; Polaris, the North Star, is an example. Henrietta Leavitt realized that their variations could tell you about their size and real brightness, and that meant it was possible to estimate their real distance. So Cepheid variables provided a powerful tool for measuring the distance to other stars and galaxies. It was the identification of Cepheid variables in nearby galaxies that first proved that the universe consists of more than one galaxy.

chemical differentiation: because of gravity, liquid blobs of heavy metals sank toward the center of the planet producing its dense iron core.

chinampa agriculture: a farming method that involves growing crops on human-made floating fields of timber and soil, and anchoring them in the middle of lakes; an invention of early Mesoamerican farmers.

city: a dense collection of tens of thousands of people, with specialized occupations and dependent on outside resources.

coercive power: power based on coercion, also described as power from above, or top-down power. It describes a process whereby leaders acquired the ability to control people and resources, if necessary, by force.

Cold War: a long period of hostility between capitalist and Communist societies in the second half of the twentieth century. As both sides had nuclear arms, the threat of a "hot" war never seemed too far away.

Collective Learning: the ability, unique to human beings, to share in great detail and precision what each individual learns through symbolic language, so that information can be preserved in the collective memory and accumulate from generation to generation. Collective Learning may be the source of the unique technological creativity of our species.

communications: the technologies by which people exchange information and ideas, from speech to writing to printing and the Internet.

Communism: an ideology committed to the building of anticapitalist societies and usually inspired by Marxism. For a time in the twentieth century, Communist societies in the Soviet Union, China, eastern Europe, and East and Southeast Asia included almost half the world's population.

complexity: entities with many precisely linked internal components, and novel emergent properties, whose survival depends on flows of free energy.

consensual power: power based on consent, also described as power from below, or bottom-up power. It describes a process whereby humans willingly gave up some personal and family autonomy and allowed leaders to gain control over their lives and resources.

consumer capitalism: the most recent phase in the history of capitalism, in which productivity levels are so high that profits can be realized only by selling goods to the wage workers who produce them. Consumer capitalism requires paying workers high enough wages so that they can purchase these goods, thus encouraging steadily rising average consumption levels. Consumer capitalism originated in the early twentieth century and is typical of the wealthiest capitalist countries today.

continental drift: the movement, formation, and reformation of continents.

convergent evolution: the acquisition of the same biological trait (e.g., eyes) in unrelated lineages.

cosmic background radiation (CBR): low-energy radiation pervading the entire universe, released about 380,000 years after the big bang, when the universe cooled sufficiently for neutral atoms to form so that energy and matter could separate. Its discovery, in 1964, persuaded most cosmologists to accept the big bang theory.

cosmology: an explanation of the history and evolution of the universe.

cuneiform: the world's first known system of writing, written with reeds on wet clay in Mesopotamia; the earliest texts that survive date from about 2100 BCE.

D

damaged ecosystems: humans are severely damaging, in many ways, many parts of the ecosystems that sustain them—water, soil, oceans, fisheries, forest, and biodiversity. These systems are threatened as well by nuclear radiation and high levels of human consumption.

Dar al-Islam: Arabic for "Abode of Islam." Created by Muslim warriors and administrators, this was one of the most significant economic, intellectual, and cultural structures of the latter part of the first millennium CE.

dark matter and **dark energy:** studies of the movements of stars and galaxies have shown that there must exist much more energy and/or matter than we can observe. At present, astronomers have no idea what either dark energy or dark matter consists of—one of the great mysteries of contemporary astronomy.

demographic transition: the decline of birthrates, which is slowing population growth throughout the world.

diaspora: Greek for "scattering"; used to describe the ancient dispersal of the Jews, and many other peoples.

DNA: deoxyribonucleic acid; the double-stranded molecule, present in all living cells, that contains the genetic information used to form and maintain the cell and pass that information to offspring cells.

domestication: genetic modification of species by humans to make them more docile, more productive, and more amenable to human control; a form of symbiosis, in which domesticated species benefit from human protection. Agriculture depends on the process of domestication, which applies not only to individual plant and animal species, but also to entire landscapes. In a desire to feed, protect, and propagate our species, humans have domesticated vast areas of the planet and entire ecosystems. Today, some 50 percent of the world's surface area has been domesticated to suit grazing and land cultivation, and more than half of the world's forests have been lost in that transformation.

Doppler effect: the apparent stretching out or contraction of wave lengths because of the relative movement of two bodies. The Doppler effect explains why an ambulance siren seems higher when the ambulance is traveling toward you than when it is moving away. It also explains why the light from distant galaxies is displaced toward the red end of the spectrum if they are moving away from us—crucial evidence for the idea that our universe is expanding.

drivers of innovation: key factors that tended to encourage innovation and Collective Learning. Among the most important drivers of innovation have been government activity, population growth, expanding exchange networks, improvements in technologies of communications and transportation, and the expansion of competitive markets and commercialization. These drivers were particularly powerful when they overlapped, creating powerful new synergies.

E

Early Agrarian era: roughly 7,000 years of human history, between about 10,000 and 3000 BCE—from the earliest evidence of agriculture to the appearance of the first cities and states.

emergent properties: properties of a complex entity that are not present within its component parts but emerge only when those parts are linked together in a particular configuration. An automobile has emergent properties that its parts lack when it is dismantled.

energy: consists of the various forces in the universe that can do work or make things happen. Physics currently identifies four main types of energy: gravity, the electromagnetic force, and (operating at the atomic level so we are rarely aware of them) the strong and weak forces. In addition, there exists a form of energy known as dark energy that we do not fully understand, though it seems to operate as a sort of antigravity. As Einstein showed, energy and matter are interchangeable at very high temperatures. See also *matter*.

Epic of Gilgamesh: the world's first written literature. The earliest texts that survive date from about 2100 BCE. The story of the superhero king Gilgamesh of Uruk portrays universal human concerns: urban versus Paleolithic life, grief over mortality, defiance of the gods, and environmental degradation.

Era of Agrarian Civilizations: this era lasted from ca. 3000 BCE to ca. 1000 CE. It can be defined as the era of human history in which agrarian civilizations were the largest, the most complex, and the most powerful of all human communities.

eukaryotes: cells more complex than prokaryotes, in which there are distinct "organelles" (such as "mitochondria") and in which the genetic material is protected within the nucleus; many single-celled organisms are eukaryotic, and so are all multicelled organisms. Lynn Margulis has shown that the first eukaryotes probably arose through a symbiotic merging of prokaryotic cells.

exchange networks: networks that link people, societies, and regions through exchanges of information, goods, and people. All forms of Collective Learning work through exchange networks.

extensification: a word that describes processes of innovation and growth that lead to more extensive settlement, without leading to increase in the size of individual human communities. Extensification was the characteristic form of growth in the Paleolithic era. See also its opposite, *intensification*.

F

factory system: an arrangement in which workers are brought together under supervision to work in factories where steam engines or other prime movers power multiple machines.

failed states: governments that lose control over part or all of their territory and cannot collect taxes or ensure the basic security of their citizens.

fascism: an ideology pioneered in Italy that saw the world as divided into conflicting racial groups; the dominant ideology of the German Nazi Party under Hitler.

fire-stick farming: not a form of farming, but a foraging strategy. Foragers regularly burn the land, to encourage new growth, and to attract grazers that can be hunted. Though a form of foraging, it also counts as a way of manipulating the environment to increase the productivity of resources useful to humans, so it can be regarded as a step toward farming.

foraging: technologies that depend on the use of natural resources more or less in their natural state; hunting and gathering. Foraging was the dominant type of technology during the Paleolithic era.

fossil fuels: coal, natural gas, and oil, which contain stored solar energy that was captured and buried hundreds of millions of years ago.

fossils: the mineralized remains of dead organisms; any hardened remains of plant or animal life preserved in rock formations.

fusion: stars are powered for most of their lives by the fusion of hydrogen nuclei into helium nuclei, as a result of which vast amounts of energy are released; source of the power of hydrogen bombs.

G

genus *Homo*: the group of hominine species that appeared in Africa between 3 and 2 million years ago that were more human-like than ape-like. It includes *H. habilis, H. rudolfensis,* and possibly *H. ergaster.* These species are characterized by use of simple tools, independence from trees, and rapid brain growth.

globalization: the expansion of exchange networks until they begin to reach across the entire world.

Goldilocks conditions: environments where conditions are just right for the emergence of more complexity—not too hot, not too cold, not too big, not too small, and so on.

the great turning: developing a stronger, active participatory democracy in which people defend their long-term interests, as proposed by David Korten, an economist critical of corporate globalization.

greenhouse effect: certain trace gases in the Earth's atmosphere keep the sun's heat that reaches Earth from reflecting back into space, thus warming up the climate on Earth, as in a greenhouse.

gross domestic product (GDP): a measurement used by economists for the market value of all goods and services produced by a country in a given period of time. Although a helpful approximate measure of total production, GDP ignores many important forms of economic activity—including unpaid household work and activities such as deforestation or carbon emissions.

groundwater: water stored underground in fractures of rock formations, or aquifers. Such stores take thousands of years to fill up, so current rates of groundwater use appear unsustainable.

H

Hadean eon: the geologic eon lasting from 4.5 to 3.8 billion years ago. It is named after the underworld of the ancient Greeks, the realm where departed spirits dwelt. Geologists refer to this earliest stage of our planet's history as the Hadean Earth because it was such a hot, "hellish" place.

half-life: the time taken for half the mass of a given radioactive element to decay into another element.

Hertzsprung–Russell (H–R) diagram: a diagram showing different phases in the life cycle of stars by graphing different features, such as their absolute brightness and their surface temperatures.

hieroglyphics: Egyptian writing, named in English from the Greek meaning "holy inscriptions," because Egyptians decorated their buildings with this writing. It used both pictographs and symbols representing sounds and ideas and was widely used until the fourth century CE, when Arabic superceded it.

Holocene epoch: the geological period since the end of the last ice age about 13,000 years ago up to the start of the Anthropocene epoch about 200 years ago (see also *Anthropocene*).

hominines: all species in the human line since it diverged from the common ancestor with chimpanzees; first appeared 8 to 5 million years ago. The only survivors of this line are *H. sapiens,* or modern humans.

***Homo erectus* or *Homo ergaster*:** hominine species that appeared in Africa almost 2 million years ago. Almost as tall as modern humans, their brains were larger than those of *H. habilis,* and they tamed fire, pair bonded, and made more complex stone tools. Some *H. erectus* migrated into Eurasia, reaching as far as China.

***Homo sapiens*:** the biological name for our species, modern humans, which seems to have appeared some time after about 200,000 years ago in Africa. In this text, we argue that the appearance of our species marks a new threshold as we are the first species in the history of the Earth that was capable of Collective Learning.

horticulture: a farming method that historically used the energy of humans, and traditional techniques and implements such as stone axes hafted onto wooden handles, for clearing the land; the foot plow and hoe for planting; bone or stone sickles hafted onto wooden handles for harvesting; and stones for grinding grain.

Huitzilopochtli: Aztec god of war, sun, and human sacrifice; patron god of the city of Tenochtitlan.

human footprint: the collective demands that humans make on our planet's regenerative capacity, sometimes called Earth's carrying capacity.

I

imperialism: the expansion of industrial powers and the conquest and colonization of African, Latin American, and Asian societies by the industrialized nations.

Inca: an ethnic group centered in Cuzco, Peru. In the fifteenth century they created a large agrarian civilization along the western edge of South America. Based on potatoes and quinoa, with llamas for wool and transport, this civilization was characterized by superior stone masonry work and weaving, and worship of a sun god. Unlike most agrarian civilizations, the Inca developed knotted strings (quipu) as recording devices instead of writing.

incentives to innovate: those factors in societies that either encourage or discourage innovation. They may include the opportunity to make profits or to rise high in the ranks of government, or to earn prestige or simply the chance to improve one's own life and the lives of others.

indigenous peoples: the prior inhabitants of a given region.

Industrial Revolution: the multiple changes that followed upon the systematic application of fossil fuels in place of human and animal power to manufacturing, communications, and transportation.

intensification: the type of growth or innovation characteristic of the Agrarian and Modern eras, in which innovation allows the support of more people from a given area, and therefore generates larger and denser human communities. See also its opposite, *extensification*.

isotopes: atoms of a given element that have varying numbers of neutrons in their nucleus, and therefore varying atomic weights. Carbon-dating techniques depend on measuring changes in the ratio of different isotopes of carbon, as carbon-14 (the only radioactive isotope of carbon) breaks down over time.

L

Lapita culture: a distinctive type of pottery with distinctive geometric marks that has been found from Papua New Guinea to Samoa, and is used by archaeologists to trace early migrations into the Pacific.

last universal common ancestor (LUCA): the most recent organism or populations of organisms from which all organisms now living on Earth descended, thought to date about 3.8 billion years ago.

life: three commonly accepted attributes of life are that it uses energy from the environment by eating or breathing or photosynthesizing (metabolism), it makes copies of itself (reproduction), and over many generations it can change characteristics to adapt to its changing environment (adaptation).

light-year: light is a form of electromagnetic energy; nothing can travel faster than light, which moves at about 186,000 miles per second (300,000 kilometers per second). A light-year is the distance light can travel in one year, about 6 trillion miles (9.6 trillion kilometers).

Little Ice Age (LIA): a period from about 1250 to 1900 when temperatures cooled in many regions of the world. This seems to have been caused by widespread volcanic eruptions and lower levels of carbon dioxide and methane in the atmosphere.

M

Mahayana Buddhism: the largest of the two major traditions or schools of Buddhism, Mahayana offers a path toward complete enlightenment. It is also known as the Great Vehicle.

Malthusian cycles: long cycles of economic, demographic, cultural, and even political expansion, generally followed by periods of crisis, warfare, and demographic, cultural, and political decline. These cycles, generally lasting several centuries, are apparent throughout the Era of Agrarian Civilizations and were probably generated by the fact that, though there was innovation (which generated the upward swings), rates of innovation could not keep pace with rates of population growth, which explains the eventual crashes. Named for Thomas Malthus (1766–1834), an English pastor and economist.

Mandate of Heaven: a Chinese belief that so long as leaders ruled conscientiously and ethically, and observed all rites and rituals necessary for the maintenance of order, they would continue to enjoy the support of heaven.

Manichaeism: an ancient Central Asian religion based on a cosmology in which the struggle between a good, spiritual world of light and an evil, material world of darkness was continuously being waged throughout human history.

Marxism: ideologies inspired by the writings of Karl Marx (1818–83). Marx argued that capitalism was the key feature of the modern world, but that capitalism created such profound inequality that it would eventually have to be abolished in a future socialist society.

matter: entities that have mass and can occupy space. As Einstein showed, matter and energy are interchangeable, according to the famous formula: E (energy) $= m$ (mass) $\times c$ (the speed of light)^2. Matter can, therefore, be regarded as a form of congealed energy; for much of the first second of the big bang, matter and energy were still interchangeable.

megafaunal extinction: the extinction of large animal species in the Paleolithic era, probably as a result of overhunting by humans. Megafaunal extinctions were particularly severe in lands newly colonized by humans in the Australasian and American world zones, which is why those regions had fewer large mammal species and therefore fewer potential animal domesticates.

Mesoamerica: a cultural area that encompassed central Mexico to Panama, all of Guatemala, Belize, and El Salvador and parts of Honduras, Costa Rica, and Nicaragua.

Milankovitch cycles: regular changes in three aspects of Earth's orbit around the sun, named for the Serbian astronomer who first described them, Milutin Milankovitch (1879–1958). One cycle concerns Earth's wobble on its axis, the direction its axis points; this changes about every 21,000 years. The second concerns the degree of tilt of Earth's axis; it changes from 22.1 to 24.5 degrees in a cycle of about 41,000 years. The third cycle is caused by changes in Earth's orbit around the sun, as it deviates from a perfect circle due to the gravitational pull of nearby planets. This varies about every 100,000 years and every 400,000 years.

modern revolution: a deliberately vague label for the revolutionary transformations that have created the modern world. The modern revolution ushered in the Modern era of human history.

modern state: a new structure of political power, also called *nation*, characterized by expanded power of state organs—standing armies, police, bureaucracy, clergy, and judicature. Modern states increased taxation, regulated land use, controlled the supply of money and credit, made education compulsory, and developed national ideologies based on a common language and history. They also provided services to retain the loyalty of their citizens, thereby increasing both their coercive and consensual power.

molecules: two or more atoms linked by different types of chemical bonds.

monopoly: a situation in which there is only one supplier of a commodity. According to economic theory, monopolies stifle innovation because monopolists have a captive market so they do not need to worry about improving the quality or reducing the price of their products.

monumental architecture: large structures, such as pyramids, temples, public spaces, or large statues, that seem to appear wherever powerful leaders emerge; a feature of all agrarian civilizations.

N

Nahuatl: the language spoken by Aztecs, still spoken by hundreds of thousands of people in Mexico. Words in English taken from Nahuatl include *ocelot, coyote, tomato, chocolate,* and *tamale.*

nanotechnologies: technologies that use tiny, molecule-sized machines.

natural selection: key idea in the modern understanding of how living organisms change, developed in the nineteenth century by Charles Darwin. Darwin argued that tiny, random variations in individuals may increase or decrease their chances of survival. Those whose chances are enhanced are more likely to pass on their genes to their offspring so that, eventually, more and more individuals in a population will inherit the successful variations. Over long periods of time such tiny changes lead to the emergence of new species—the central idea (paradigm) of modern biology.

Neandertal: a species of hominine very closely related to our own species, *H. sapiens.* The two lineages probably diverged at least 500,000 years ago; Neandertals went extinct 35,000 to 30,000 years ago. Genetic research shows that the DNA of people with Eurasian ancestry is 1 to 4 percent Neandertal.

Nubia: the area along the Nile River stretching from the first to the sixth cataract, encompassing what is today the northern part of Sudan. It has been called Nubia since the fourth century CE; earlier it was called Kush.

nuclear weapons: weapons based on either the fission of large atoms such as uranium or plutonium (like the bombs dropped on Hiroshima and Nagasaki in 1945), or on the fusion of hydrogen atoms. Such weapons are so powerful that, if used in large numbers, they could destroy much of the biosphere.

O

Organization of the Petroleum Exporting Countries (OPEC): a group of competing oil-producing countries that collaborate over shared interests. Such a group is called a cartel, with the aim of increasing individual members' profits by reducing competition.

origin stories: stories told in all societies about the origin of all things: of people, animals, landscapes, Earth, stars, and the universe as a whole. They provide a sort of road map to the history of everything.

ozone: a molecule consisting of three oxygen atoms, in contrast to the more common form consisting of just two atoms. A thin layer of ozone high in the atmosphere shields the Earth's surface from harmful forms of ultraviolet radiation. This layer took billions of years to

form. In the 1980s it was found that the use of chlorofluorocarbons (CFCs) was breaking up the ozone layer; international treaties have led to the banning of most production and use of CFCs.

P

Paleolithic era: the first age of distinctly human history, from the appearance of *H. sapiens* roughly 200,000 years ago, to the beginning of agriculture about 12,000 years ago. The Paleolithic is sometimes subdivided into the Middle Paleolithic (ca. 200,000 to 50,000 BP), and Upper Paleolithic (ca. 50,000 to 12,000 BP).

paleomagnetism: a science that uses magnetic minerals to study the history of Earth's magnetic field and the movement of tectonic plates.

Pangaea: the vast supercontinent formed more than 200 million years ago as plate tectonics joined most of the major continental plates together. It is probable that such supercontinents have formed periodically throughout Earth's history; the existence of a single huge landmass probably reduced biodiversity.

parallax: the change in the apparent relationship between two fixed objects caused by the movement of the observer. If you hold your finger up and move your head, your finger will appear to move against the background. Parallax measurements can be used to measure the distance to the nearest stars.

periodic table: a way of listing chemical elements in groups with common features; first constructed by the great Russian chemist Dmitri Mendeleev in 1869.

photosynthesis: the use of sunlight by plants or plantlike organisms to store energy. The first evidence of photosynthesis is from about 3.5 billion years ago. It is the source of most of the energy that drives life within the biosphere and the source of most atmospheric oxygen.

plasma: a state of matter in which protons and electrons are not bound together. This was the state of the entire universe before about 380,000 years after the big bang, and is the normal state inside stars.

plate tectonics: the central idea (paradigm) of modern Earth science since the 1960s, based on the notion that Earth's crust is broken into separate plates that are in constant motion, driven by heat from the Earth's interior.

polis: Greek for "city-state"; *poleis* (plural).

***Popol Vuh*:** a group of mythohistorical narratives from the Quiche Maya of Guatemala. The name translates literally as "Book of the People." This origin story has the gods creating humans from corn and water. Only one copy has survived, made by a Dominican friar in the mid-sixteenth century.

power: power relations in human societies can usefully be analyzed into two fundamental forms: power from below (*consensual* or bottom-up power) is power granted by followers to a leader to ensure the successful achievement of group tasks (such as the election of captains in sporting teams). Power from above (*coercive* or top-down power) is power that depends, in addition, on the ability of rulers to impose their will by force. In the history of human societies, power from below preceded power from above for the simple reason that, to pay for a body of retainers that could impose one's will by force, it was necessary already to have the ability to mobilize significant resources.

prokaryotes: simple, single-celled microorganisms in which the genetic material is not bound within a nucleus.

protectionism: the notion that the best way to protect the national economy was not through free trade but by creating trading zones from which rival nations were excluded, by tariffs or, if necessary, by force.

Q

Quechua: the Spanish name for the language spoken by the Inca, known by them as Runa Simi. Quechua is still spoken by millions from Ecuador to Chile and serves as the second official language of Peru.

Quetzalcoatl: a benign god of the Toltecs, who required only fruit and nuts as sacrifice; patron god of the Aztec priesthood and of learning and knowledge. The Aztecs believed that an evil god tricked Quetzalcoatl into fleeing eastward, with the promise of returning someday.

R

radioactivity: the breakdown of an unstable atom, such as uranium, through the spontaneous emission of subatomic particles.

radiometric dating: a technique used to date materials such as bones or rocks by measuring the rate of radioactive decay.

Rapa Nui: also known as Easter Island. This Pacific island owned by Chile was first settled by Polynesian navigators approximately 1,000 years ago and is remarkable for the presence of many large stone figures.

red giants: very large stars with relatively cool surfaces that have expanded at the end of their lives. Betelgeuse in the constellation of Orion is a red giant.

red shift: in the 1920s, Edwin Hubble observed that the light from many distant galaxies appeared to be shifted toward the red end of the spectrum. He interpreted this as the result of a Doppler effect, which implied the galaxies emitting such light were moving rapidly away from us—the first piece of evidence that our universe was expanding.

renewable energy: forms of energy that can come from easily renewable sources such as sunlight, wind power, or hydropower.

respiration (aerobic): the reverse process of photosynthesis. In respiration, oxygen (O_2) is ingested and used by the cell to digest carbohydrates, releasing energy used by the cell and giving off carbon dioxide (CO_2) and water as waste. Photosynthesis uses CO_2 and gives off O_2; respiration uses O_2 and gives off CO_2, the reverse of photosynthesis.

RNA: ribonucleic acid; similar to DNA, but a single strand with slightly different chemistry. This molecule carries out the instructions for protein synthesis specified by the DNA molecule. RNA may have formerly had the ability both to encode genetic information and to engage in metabolism, which may have played a crucial role in the early evolution of life on Earth.

S

Sahul: the name used for the ice age continent that included Australia, Papua New Guinea, and Tasmania. It broke up into its components as sea levels rose at the end of the last ice age.

science: the dominant form of knowledge in the modern world. Science began to flourish in the scientific revolution of the seventeenth century. Scientific knowledge is global in its reach and is based on the rigorous use of carefully tested evidence.

seafloor spreading: a process in which new ocean floor is created as molten material from the Earth's mantle rises in margins between plates or ridges and spreads out.

sedentism: living in one place for most of the year. Sedentism was rare in foraging societies but became widespread with the adoption of agriculture because agriculture made it possible to produce more resources from a given area and encouraged farmers to stay in one place to protect their crops.

semisedentary: a term used to describe people who practiced farming but needed to supplement their crops with hunting and gathering. Such people were not able to support as large a population as fully sedentary societies.

Silk Roads: a modern term referring to a network of trade and exchange routes through Central Asia that connected much of Afro-Eurasia during the Era of Agrarian Civilizations.

socialism: an ideology committed to building societies free of the extreme inequalities that seemed to be generated by capitalism.

southernization: a term coined in 1994 by world historian Lynda Shaffer to describe the movement of material and nonmaterial products from Africa and India north into Central, eastern, and western Eurasia.

spectroscope: an instrument that, like a prism, makes it possible to split light into different frequencies. Because different elements absorb light at different frequencies, spectroscopes can be used to determine the presence and amount of different elements in stars and galaxies, so they have provided a fundamental tool for studying the nature and evolution of stars.

state: a regionally organized society, capable when necessary of imposing its will by force, based on cities and their environments, and containing populations of tens of thousands and up to many millions of people.

state religion: religions adopted by rulers to achieve social cohesion and to legitimate their authority, often at the expense of local varieties of religion, which often flourished locally nonetheless.

steam engines: machines that burned coal to produce steam that performed mechanical work. James Watt configured the first profitable one at the time of the American Revolution. Their use launched human society over a threshold no longer limited by the annual flow of solar energy.

swidden agriculture: a form of agriculture in which woodlands are burned down, crops are planted in the ashy soil, and then, when the fertility of the newly cleared fields declines, new regions are cleared. Because it is a seminomadic lifeway, swidden agriculture is possible only in regions of low population density, such as the Amazon basin. Also known as *slash-and-burn agriculture*.

symbiosis: relations of interdependence between different species, such as those between humans and domesticated plants and animals, which offer benefits (of different degrees) to each species. Such relations are extremely common in the natural world.

symbolic language: a form of communication that is much more powerful than those used by all other animals because it can convey much more information much more precisely. Symbolic language is so powerful that it allows humans to share huge amounts of information so that information can accumulate from generation to generation. In other words, symbolic language makes Collective Learning possible, and Collective Learning seems to be the key to understanding the changeable and cumulative nature of human history.

T

taxonomy: a system of naming and classifying based on shared characteristics. Biologists use a taxonomy to arrange species into larger and larger groups that show their relationships to form a hierarchical classification. From most inclusive to least inclusive, the names used are domain, kingdom, phylum, class, order, family, genus, and species.

terraforming: making other planets habitable for humans through methods like melting the ice below the surface of Mars or seeding bacteria there.

theory of chemical evolution: the theory that slow changes in complex yet nonliving chemicals, operating in a similar manner to natural selection, led to the emergence of the first true living organisms.

350 ppm: the upper level of carbon dioxide in the atmosphere, as estimated by leading scientists, that can maintain a safe climate for human civilization as we know it.

three waves of industrialization: the initial wave began in Great Britain in the latter part of the eighteenth century. The second wave encompassed the spread of industrialization to Belgium, Switzerland, France, Germany, and the United States, beginning about 1820 to 1840 and lasting to the end of the century. The third wave began about 1870, with the spread of industrialization to Russia and Japan.

thresholds of increasing complexity: moments when something new and more complex appears. In this book we focus on eight major thresholds of increasing complexity.

transportation: the technologies by which people and goods are moved from place to place, whether they were carried by porters, or in horse-drawn wagons, or on boats or in planes and containers.

tribute: resources, which could include goods, labor, cash, or even people, controlled by the state or by officials or representatives of the state largely through the threat of coercion.

U

Uruk: the first of several cities that emerged in Sumer before 3000 BCE, probably the first city to emerge in the world.

W

Wangari Maathai: a Kenyan woman (1940–2011) who founded the Green Belt Movement to reforest her country.

warfare: a feature of life more organized and specialized in agrarian civilizations than formerly, especially characteristic under tribute-taking rulers, as they fought to extend their territory, resources, and tribute.

wave of advance model: the idea that population growth at the periphery of farming communities, in combination with local migration patterns, inevitably results in a population range expansion that moves outward in all environmentally suitable directions and advances at a steady rate.

world zones: four nonconnected geographic zones that emerged as sea levels rose at the end of the last ice age. The four world zones were (1) Afro-Eurasia (Africa and the Eurasian landmass, plus offshore islands like Britain and Japan); (2) the Americas (North, Central, and South America, plus offshore islands); (3) Australasia (Australia, the island of Papua New Guinea, plus neighboring islands); and (4) the island societies of the Pacific (New Zealand, Micronesia, Melanesia, and Hawaii).

world-systems theory: pioneered by Immanuel Wallerstein, world-systems theory explores large transnational networks of interaction through trade or other exchanges.

Credits

Photo Credits

Design Elements   Opening door for Threshold Summary tables:
© evirgen/Getty Images RF; **Stars behind door:** NASA/JPL-Caltech/
Harvard-Smithsonian CfA.

Front Matter   Pages i–iii: NASA; **xix** (*top*): © Photo by Daniel
Robbins; **xix** (*bottom*): © Photo by Pamela Benjamin.

Introduction   Opener: © SuperStock/Getty Images.

Chapter 1   Opener: NASA/CXC/PSU/L. Townsley, et al.;
1.1: © Amar Grover/Getty Images; **1.2:** © The Gallery Collection/
Corbis; **1.3:** © Mary Evans Picture Library/The Image Works;
1.4a: NASA and The Hubble Heritage Team (STScI/AURA);
1.4b: © Steve Cole/Getty Images RF; **1.6:** This item is reproduced
by permission of The Huntington Library, San Marino, California;
1.7: © 1987 CERN; **1.8:** © Roger Ressmeyer/Corbis; **1.9:** © Paul
Wootton/Science Source; **1.11:** © CSIRO, http://outreach.atnf.csiro.au;
1.11 (*inset*): The Hubble Heritage Team (STScI/AURA/NASA);
1.13: NASA, ESA, J. Hester and A. Loll (Arizona State University);
1.14b: © Dr. Mark J. Winter/Science Source.

Chapter 2   Opener: © Mark Garlick/Science Photo Library/Corbis
RF; **2.1:** NASA-STScI; **2.2:** © Photo courtesy of NASA/Corbis;
2.3: © Corbis; **2.4:** © BSIP/UIG/Getty Images; **2.5:** © Stocktrek
Images/Getty Images RF; **2.6:** NASA; **2.9:** C. Amante, and B. W.
Eakins, ETOPO1 1 Arc-Minute Global Relief Model: Procedures,
Data Sources and Analysis. NOAA Technical Memorandum NESDIS
NGDC-24, 19 pp, March 2009; **2.10:** © incamerastock/Alamy;
2.11: © Tom Bean/Corbis.

Chapter 3   Opener: © Science Photo Library RF/Getty Images;
3.4: © A. Barrington Brown/Science Source; **3.9:** © Ted Mead/Getty
Images.

Chapter 4   Opener: © akg-images/The Image Works; **4.3:** © Adam
Jones/Science Source; **4.4:** © Mauricio Anton/Science Source;
4.7: © Paul Almasy/Corbis; **4.8:** © The Natural History Museum/The
Image Works; **4.9:** © VC Ross/Age Fotostock; **4.10:** © Anne Musser;
4.11: © Peter Murray.

Chapter 5   Opener: © Klaus-Werner Friedric/Age Fotostock;
5.1: © Andrew McRobb/Dorling Kindersley; **5.2:** © Eric Carlson,
Illustrator; **5.3:** © Dario Lopez-Mills/AP Photo; **5.4:** © UIG via Getty
Images; **5.5:** © Gianni Dagli Orti/Corbis; **5.6:** © Namit Arora, shunya.
net; **5.7:** © Danita Delimont/Getty Images; **5.8:** © Lorenzo De Simone/
Age Fotostock; **5.9:** © Dorling Kindersley/Getty Images RF.

Chapter 6   Opener: © Jonathan Wright/Photoshot; **6.1:** © DEA
PICTURE LIBRARY/Getty Images; **6.2:** © bpk, Berlin/
Vorderasiatisches Museum, Staatliche Museen, Berlin, Germany/
Art Resource, NY; **6.3:** © The Trustees of the British Museum;
6.4: © Corbis; **6.5:** © Andrew Rakaczy/Science Source; **6.6:** © Rivi
from http://en.wikipedia.org/wiki/File:Ahu_Tongariki.jpg.

Chapter 7   Opener: © akg-images/Peter Connolly/The Image
Works; **7.1** (*left, right*): © Werner Forman/TopFoto/The Image Works;

7.2 (*left, right*): © The Trustees of the British Museum/Art Resource,
NY; **7.3:** © LatitudeStock - Mel Longhurst/Getty Images.

Chapter 8   Opener: © North Wind Picture Archives/Alamy;
8.1: © World History Archive/Alamy; **8.2:** © David Tipling/Getty
Images; **8.3:** Photographed by Wikipedia user Jacklee on 18 June 2011;
8.4: © DEA PICTURE LIBRARY/Getty Images; **8.5:** © Dr. Gary L.
Todd, Ph.D.; **8.6:** © Ashmolean Museum/Mary Evans/The Image Works;
8.7: © The Art Gallery Collection/Alamy; **8.8:** © DEA/S VANNINI/Age
Fotostock; **8.9:** © Time & Life Pictures/Getty Images.

Chapter 9   Opener: © Herbert Kawainui Kane/National Geographic/
Getty Images; **9.1:** Photo K2887 © Justin Kerr; **9.4:** Library of Congress
Prints and Photographs Division [LC-USZC4-743]; **9.5:** © The Royal
Library, Copenhagen, ms. GKS 2232 4°, p. 217; **9.6:** Neg. #3614(2).
Courtesy Department of Library Services, American Museum of Natural
History. Photo by Perkins/Becket; **9.7:** © William R. Iseminger/Cahokia
Mounds State Historic Site; **9.8:** © Jason Patterson. Photo of Hōkūle'a
taken on August 8, 2012 ™Polynesian Voyaging Society; **9.9:** © Dixson
Galleries, State Library of New South Wales/The Bridgeman Art Library.

Chapter 10   Opener: © INTERFOTO/Age Fotostock; **10.3:** © Jan
Adkins; **10.4:** © Universal Images Group/Getty Images.

Chapter 11   Opener: © The Granger Collection, New York;
11.2: © Universal History Archive/Getty Images; **11.3:** © Bettmann/
Corbis; **11.4:** © London Metropolitan Archives, City of London/The
Bridgeman Art Library; **11.5:** © Stapleton Collection/Corbis.

Chapter 12   Opener: © Henglein and Steets/Getty Images RF;
12.6: © Jeff Gibbs.

Chapter 13   Opener: © Dennis Hallinan/Alamy; **13.5:** © L. Toshio
Kishiyama/Getty Images RF; **13.6:** © David A. Hardy/Science Source;
13.7: NASA, ESA, Z. Levay and R. van der Marel (STScI), T. Hallas,
and A. Mellinger.

Text Credits

Chapter 7   p. 154: Excerpt (11 lines) from "The Epic of Gilgamesh."
Reprinted with the permission of Free Press, a division of Simon &
Schuster, Inc., from GILGAMESH: A New English Version by Stephen
Mitchell. Copyright © 2004 by Stephen Mitchell. All rights reserved.

Chapter 8   p. 188: "Mulan." Excerpt (4 lines) from THE FLOWER-
ING PLUM AND THE PALACE LADY: INTERPRETATIONS OF
CHINESE POETRY, by Han H. Frankel (New Haven: Yale University
Press, 1976), p. 72. © 1976 Yale University Press. Reproduced with the
permission of the publisher. All rights reserved.

Chapter 13   Fig. 13.1: Data from UN Population Division (2007).
Used in Eric A. Davidson, *You Can't Eat GDP* (Cambridge, MA:
Perseus, 2000), p. 163. **Fig. 13.2:** Scripps CO_2 Program. Used in Eric
Roston, *The Carbon Age: How Life's Core Element Has Become
Civilization's Greatest Threat* (New York: Walker, 2008), 176. Updated
at www.scrippsco2.ucsd.edu. **Fig. 13.6:** From the cover of Arthur
C. Clark's *The Snows of Olympus,* published in 1995.

Index

Mahayana Buddhism, 179
Malaria, 256
Malaya, 273
Mali Empire, 147, 223, 232, 233
Malthus, Thomas, 59, 136
Malthusian cycles, 136, 190
    early modern cycle: 1350 to 1700 CE,
        229–239
    fossil fuel and industrialization overcoming,
        244–245
    Maya decline and, 198
    postclassical Malthusian cycle: before 1350
        CE, 222–229
    prediction of future crisis, 291
    slow innovation and, 221–222
Mammals
    evolution of, 74–76
    in history of life on Earth, 74–76
Man, John, 218
Manchuria, 271
Mandate of Heaven, 160
Manhattan Project, 280, 281
Mani, 180
Manichaeism, Silk Roads and spread of, 180
Mantle, Earth's, 43–44
Manu, Laws of, 185
Maori, 264
Mao Zedong, 272, 274
Marconi, Guglielmo, 279
Marco Polo, 225, 226–227, 248
Margulis, 63
Margulis, Lynn, 63, 71
Mariana Islands, 51
Marianas Trench, 51
Markets. *See* Commerce/Commercialization
Marks, Robert, 245, 256
Mars, 40
    atmosphere of, 45
    relative size of, 40, 41
    space probes of, 35–36
    terraforming, 302
    water on, 68
Marsh, George Perkins, 264
Marshall, George, 271
Marshall Plan, 271
Martin, Paul S., 99
Marx, Karl, 233–234, 254, 261, 268, 282
Marxism, 268
Mathematics
    first abstract numbers, 135
    Indian numbering system, 176
    Maya and, 195
Matrilocality, 84
Matter
    at beginning of universe, 19
    defined, 19
Matthews, D. H., 48, 49
Mauryan Empire, 163
Maxim, Hiram, 256
Maxim gun, 256
Maxwell, James Clerk, 281
Maya Empire, 195–198
    ball game and entertainment, 196–197
    calendars, 195–196
    creation story, 195
    organization and collapse of, 197–198
    writing system, 196
McBrearty, Sally, 92
McNeill, John, 175, 277

McNeill, William, 175
Measles, 180, 238, 264
Mecca, 169, 224
Medes, 161
Medicine, improvements in, during
    Anthropocene, 278
Medina, 169
Mehrgarh, 115
Meiji, 252
Mellaart, James, 119
Men. *See also* Gender/Gender relations
    hierarchy of power with women, 130
    social trends during Era of Agrarian
        Civilizations
        China, 183, 185–186, 188
        Eastern Mediterranean, 183–184
        Greece, classical, 186
        India, 182–183, 185, 188–189
        Islamic civilization, 189
        Mesopotamia and Egypt, 182
        Rome, 186–188
Mendel, Gregor, 62
Mendeleev, Dmitrii, 25, 26
Menes, 128, 137, 138
Meroe, 137, 138
Meroetic language, 138
Mesoamerica
    agrarian civilizations in, 194–201
    Aztecs, 199–201
    Basin of Mexico, 198–201
    defined, 143
    early societies in, 143–144
    Maya Empire, 195–198
    Olmecs, 144
    postclassical Malthusian cycle and, 222
    spread of diseases in Columbian exchange,
        238
    Teotihuacan, 198–199
    Toltecs, 199
    Tula, 199
Mesopotamia, 131. *See also* Sumer
    defining, 130, 131
    expansion and contraction during Era of
        Agrarian Civilizations, 157–158
    overview of characteristics and geography
        of, 131
    pottery and metallurgy, 130
    social and gender relations during Era of
        Agrarian Civilizations, 182
    state religion, 132
    terminology about region, 131
    Uruk, first city, 131–136
    warfare in, 135–136
Mesosphere, 43
Metallic bonds, 30
Meteorites
    composition of, 44
    origin of life and, 64
Mexica-Tenochca, 199
Mexico City, 201
Mezherich, 96
Mid-Atlantic Range, 48, 49
Middle class, in classical Greece, 186
Middle Paleolithic, 90
Migration
    Industrial Revolution and imperialism,
        256–257, 261, 263
    into Pacific world zone, 208–209
    during Paleolithic era, 95

Mikhail Gorbachev, 273
Milankovitch, Milutin, 83
Milankovitch cycles, 83
Military. *See also* Warfare
    armies as defining feature of agrarian
        civilization, 154
    in Era of Agrarian Civilizations and slow
        growth, 190
    imperialism and military competition: 1900
        to 1950, 268–271
    Qin Dynasty, 167
    trans-civilizational linkages through
        warfare, 175
Milk, as secondary product, 129
Milky Way, 16, 303
Miller, Stanley, 65
Miller, Walter, 301
Ming Dynasty, exploration voyages of,
    229–232
Minoans
    expansion/contraction during Era of Agrarian
        Civilizations, 159
    social and gender relations during Era of
        Agrarian Civilizations, 183–184
Mithridates I, 163
Mitochondria, 70
Modern global society, as type of
    community, 152
Modern revolution
    approach to
        drivers of innovation, 216–218
        early modern Malthusian cycle: 1350 to
            1700 CE, 229–239
        postclassical Malthusian cycle: before
            1350 CE, 222–229
        world in 1000 CE, 218–222
        world in 1700 CE, 239–240
    energy consumption in, 216
    Industrial Revolution
        consequences of, 259–264
        imperialism and emergence of developed/
            developing worlds, 254–259
        racism and social Darwinism, 257–259
        reasons for, 244–247
        rise of modern state, 253–254
        social, agricultural, and Industrial
            Revolution in Great Britain, 247–250
        spread of, 250–253
    overview, 216
Modern state
    defined, 253
    first, in France, 253–254
Mohenjo-Daro, 140, 182
Mokyr, Joel, 239
Molecules, 29–30
Monera, 57
Monetary Fund, 271
Money, 180
    coins and paper money, 221
    Mexican peso, 234
Mongol Empire, travel and trade during, 225,
    226–227, 226–228
Monopolies, as discouraging innovation, 217,
    220
Monsoon winds, 223–224
Monumental architecture, 132
Moon (Earth's)
    formation of, 39
    surface of, 39–40

tides and, 40
tilt of Earth and, 40
Moons, formation of, 39–40
Moore, Frances, 290
Morse, Samuel, 279
Moses, 158
Mother Goddess (Minoan), 184
Mound-building cultures, 206–207
Mountains, plate tectonics and, 51
Mount Wilson observatory, 17
Mughal Empire, 255
Muhammad al Tabari, 169
Muhammad ibn Abdullah, 168
Multicelled organisms, in history of life on
    Earth, 71–72
Multiregional hypothesis, 90
Mummies, 144
Musa, 223
Muscovy, 238
Muslims. *See also* Islam/Islamic civilization
    books and Cairo library, 219
    commercial trade with China during Second
        Silk Roads era, 180
    increase in commerce during postclassical
        Malthusian cycle, 225
    traders routes and spread of Islam, 223–224
Mycenaean society, expansion/contraction
        during Era of Agrarian Civilizations,
        159–160

N

Nagasaki, 23
Nahuatl, 199, 201
Nammu, 132
Nanjing, 229
Nanotechnologies, 301
Napoleon, Louis, 261
Napoleon Bonaparte, 254, 261
Naqada, 137
Naram-sin, 135
Narmer, 128, 137
Narmer Palette, 154, 155
NASA, 41–42
National Assembly, 254
National Oceanic and Atmospheric
        Administration (NOAA), 294
Native Americans, 264
Natufian people, 109–110, 118
Natural gas, 280
    defined, 244
Natural selection
    background to, 58
    central tenets of Darwin's theory, 59
    defined, 59
    DNA and, 62
    evidence of, 60–62
    fossil evidence, 60
    Galapagos Islands research, 58–59
    geographic distribution, 60
    homologies, 60–61
    intermediate form, 60
    mammalian eye and, 72
    sexual reproduction and, 71
Nature Conservancy, 300
Nazis, 270
Neandertals, 81
    compared to modern humans, 90–91
    evolution from *H. erectus,* 87
    physical traits of, 91

Nebulae, 34
Nemet-Nejat, Karen, 136
Neon, 26
Neptune, 34
Nestorians, 180
Neutral mutations, 82
Neutron capture, 28, 29
Neutrons
    atoms and, 25
    big bang and, 19
Newcomen, Thomas, 248
Newton, Isaac, 26
    gravity and, 15, 22
New York City, 298
New Zealand, 209, 210
Nicholas II, Russian tsar, 253
Nigeria, 272, 273, 296
Nile River valley, Egypt and Nubia, 136–139
Ninsun, 134
Nippur, 135
Nirvana, 185
Nishida, Toshisada, 82
Nitrogen, in common proteins of life, 65
Nobel, Alfred, 280
Noble gases, 26
Nongovernmental organizations (NGOs),
        299–300
North America
    agrarian civilizations in, 205–208
    Ancestral Pueblo, 205–206
    corn and tobacco spread to, 207
    mound-building cultures, 206–207
Northrup, David, 218
Nubia, 136–137, 158
Nuclear energy, 280, 296, 297
Nuclear weapons, 268, 283, 296
Nucleic acids, first cells and, 67
Nucleotides, 66
    chemical evolution and, 64–65
Nucleus, 65
Numbers
    first abstract numbers, 135
    Indian numbering system, 176
Nunes, Pedro, 238

O

Obsidian, 119
Oceans
    as damaged ecosystem, 295–296
    global average surface temperature and heat
        content, 295
    global water circulation, 294
    plate tectonics and, 50–51
    restoring ecosystems and, 298
    seafloor spreading, 48
Octavian, 164
Odovocar, 166
Ohalo II, 106
O'Hara, Sarah, 296
Oil, crude, 280
    defined, 244
    limited supply of, 292–293
    in Nigeria, 272
    rise of consumption and, 278–279
Old Testament, 158
Olduwan tools, 86
Olmec society, 144
Oparin, Alexander, 64
Opium, 255, 256

Opium Wars, 256
Oppenheimer, J. Robert, 280
Oracle bones, 142, 183
Orbiting telescopes, 35
Organelles, 70
Organization of the Petroleum Exporting
        Countries (OPEC), 292
Origin of Species, The (Darwin), 59, 60, 61
Origin stories, 4
    traditional, 12–14
Orion Cloud, 37–38
Orkney, 116
Ortelius, Abraham, 46
Orwell, George, 300
Osman, 232
Ottoman Empire, 232–233, 255
Outer core, 43
Outgassing, 45
Out of Africa hypothesis, 90–92
Owen, Robert, 261
Oxus civilization, 161
Oxus culture, 142
Oxygen
    in common proteins of life, 65
    importance of photosynthesis, 69
Oympus Mons, 36
Ozone, 284, 297
    formation of, in history of life, 71

P

Pachacuti, 201–202
Pacific world zone
    adoption of agriculture, 105, 112, 114
    defined, 143
    early societies in, 147
    during Era of Agrarian Civilizations,
        208–211
    migration into, 208–209
Packard, David, 300
Pair bonding, 86, 87
Pakistan, 296
    end of colonial rule, 272
Palaces, first, in Uruk, 129
Paleoarchaelogy, evidence of human evolution,
        81
Paleoclimatic evidence, 46
Paleolithic era, 93–100
    climatic changes during, 93–95
    definition of, 93
    extensification, 95
    global migration of humans, 95
    impact on planet, 98–100
        fire-stick farming, 99
        megafaunal extinctions, 99–100
    lifeways during, 95–98
        foraging, 95–96
        gender relations, 97
        living in small groups, 97
        religious beliefs, 97–98
        standard of living, 96–97
    Middle, 90
    population during, 95–96, 98–99, 113
    Revolution of the Upper Paleolithic, 91–92
    significance of, 93
    timeline of, 93
    Upper, 90
Paleomagnetism, 48
Pangaea, 47, 73, 248
Pangenesis, 62

Panglima Awang, 233
Panspermia, 64
Paper, 219
    invention and spread of, 225
Papin, Denis, 248
Papua New Guinea, 211, 218
Papyrus, 138
Parallax, 15–16
Parent isotope, 36
Paris, 229
Paris Academy of Sciences, 281
Parthians, 163
Parthian Stations, 178
Parvati, 189
Pasargadae, 161
Pasteur, Louis, 64
Pastoralist societies, 152, 153
    pastoral nomads and origins of Silk Roads, 177–178
Pataliputra, 163
Pater familias, 187
Paterson, Clair, 3
Patriarchy
    in Classical Greece, 186
    Islamic civilization, 189
    Roman Republic, 187
    Tang Dynasty, 188
Patrician class, 187
Patrilocality, 84
Paul of Tarsus, 180
Pearl Harbor, 271
Peasants, 218, 220, 240
    decline of, 281–282
Peloponnesian War, 161–162
Penicillin, 278
Penzias, Arno, 20
Pericles, 161, 186
Periodic table, 25
Periods (geological), 44
Periplus of the Erythrian Sea, 178
Persepolis, 161
Persian language, 225
Persian Royal Road, 219
Persia/Persians
    Abbasid Caliphate, 169–170
    Achaemenid Empire, 161–162, 163
    defeat by Alexander, 162
    early organization of, 161
    expansion and contraction during Era of Agrarian Civilizations, 161–163
    Parthians, 163
    Peloponnesian War, 161–162
    Royal Road, 161, 162
    Sasanians, 163
    Seleucid Empire, 163
Peso, Mexican, 234
Pharaohs, 137
Phase changes, 19
Philip II, Hapsburg monarch, 234
Philippines, 272
Phillip II, King (Macedon), 162
Phoenicians
    as commercial state, 158–159
    expansion and contraction during Era of Agrarian Civilizations, 158–159
Phosphorus, in common proteins of life, 65
Photosynthesis
    formation of Earth's atmosphere, 45
    in history of life on Earth, 69–70

importance of, 69
process of, 69
Pictographs, 135, 138, 142
Pikaia, 72
Pili, 66
Pinker, Steven, 89
Pisarro, 234
Plagues, Black Death, 229
Planck satellite, 3
Planetesimals, 39
Planets
    accretion and formation of, 39
    criteria for, 40
    exoplanets, 41–42
    formation of, 39
    gravitational instability model of, 39
    relative size comparison of, 40, 41
    search for other, 41–42
    of solar system today, 40–41
Plantations, Atlantic slave trade, 235–237
Plant kingdom, 57
Plants
    Columbian exchange, 235, 238
    decline of biodiversity, 284
    domestication of, 105, 108–109, 111
    fire-stick farming, 99
    life moves to land, 72–73
Plasma, big bang and, 19
Plasma membrane, 66
Plate tectonic
    Amasia, 302, 303
    as core paradigm, 52
Plate tectonics, 3, 48–52
    continental drift and, 46–48
    major plates, 49–50
    paleomagnetism, 48
    plate boundaries, 50–52
    plate velocities, 50
    seafloor spreading, 48
Plebeians, 187
Pliny the Elder, 178
Plow, 129
Pluto, downgrade to dwarf planet status, 40
Polis, 160–161
Polynesia, 209–210, 222
Polynesian societies, 123
Pomeranz, Kenneth, 245
Ponzi, Charles, 296
Ponzi scheme, 296
Popol Vuh, 195
Population
    agricultural revolution and increases in, 104–105, 109, 110
    Black Death and, 229
    cities emerge and increase in, 130
    current slowing of growth rate, 297
    density by lifeway, 104–105
    during Early Agrarian era, 113
    epidemic diseases, and decline in during Silk Roads era, 180
    expansion and contraction cycles of agrarian civilizations, 156–157
    for foraging vs. farming communities, 95
    growth during Anthropocene, 274, 291–292
    growth during postclassical Malthusian cycle, 222
    increase in England during Industrial Revolution, 250

increasing density and social changes during Era of Agrarian Civilizations, 181–182
    Industrial Revolution changes to support increased population, 244–245
    Malthusian cycles, 136
    during Paleolithic era, 95–96, 98–99, 113
    projections for the future, 291–292
    rise of, and Industrial Revolution, 259
Porcelain, 224
Portugal
    colonization in Africa, 256–258
    commercial networks, 234
    exploration and commercialization by, 233
Postclassical Malthusian cycle: before 1350 CE
    communication and transportation improvements, 225
    exchange networks expansion, 222–225
    fourteenth-century crisis, 229
    market and commerce expansion, 225–229
Potassium, radiometric dating and, 37
Potosi, 234, 245
Pottery, emergence of cities and, 129–130
Poverty
    number of people living in, 283
    in Roman Republic, 187
    widening gap between rich and poor, 283
Power. See also Wealth and power
    bottom-up power, 121
    burial site as evidence power structures, 121, 122–123
    coercive, 119, 121
    consensual, 119, 121–123
    defined, 120–121
    in Early Agrarian era, 122–123
    explanations of appearance of, 121–122
    gift giving, 121
    top-down power, 121
    women and men hierarchy, 130
Primatology, 81–82
Primeval atom, 18
Printing
    expansion of exchange networks and, 225, 229
    first, in Korea, 219
    printing press, 239
Productivity
    increased agricultural, and cities emergence, 129
    increases in, during Anthropocene, 282
Prokaryote cell
    compared to eukaryote cell, 70
    emergence of, in history of life on Earth, 69
    structure of, 65–66
Protectionism, 269–270
Protestant Reformation, 14
Protists, 57
Protons
    atoms and, 25
    big bang and, 19–20
    elements and, 26
Protosun, 38
Proxima Centauri, 16
Ptolemy of Alexandria, 14–15
Punic Wars, 164
Pygmies, 146
Pylos, 184
Pyramids
    Egypt, 137–138
    Olmecs, 144

Watson, James, 62, 278
Watt, James, 248–249, 281
Wave of advance model, 114
Waves, seismic, 44
Weak nuclear forces, 19
Wealth and power. *See also* Power
  burial sites in Early Agrarian era,
    115, 116
  gap between richest and poorest countries,
    255, 257, 268
  Industrial Revolution and changes in Great
    Britain, 247
  Mesopotamia during Era of Agrarian
    Civilizations, 182
  widening gap between rich and poor, 283
Weapons
  Maxim gun, 256
  nuclear weapons, 280, 283
  of WWI, 269–270
Wedgwood, Josiah, 248, 259
Wegener, Alfred, 46–47
Weiner, Jonathan, 61–62
Wells, H. G., 3, 301
Wheat, domestication of, 108
Wheel, Maya, 196–197
White dwarfs, 27, 28
White Huns, 163
White Temple, 131–132
Whitney, Eli, 249
Wilkinson Microwave Anisotropy Probe
    (WMAP) satellite, 22
Wilson, Alan, 3
Wilson, E. O., 63
Wilson, J. Tuzo, 49
Wilson, Robert, 20
Wind, stellar wind, 38–39
Wind power, 280
Wolf, Eric, 128
Women. *See also* Gender/Gender relations
  decrease in fertility rates, 282–283
  hierarchy of power with men, 130
  ideal woman in Han Dynasty, 185–186
  Industrial Revolution and, 262, 263

social trends during Era of Agrarian
    Civilizations
  China, 183, 185–186, 188
  Eastern Mediterranean, 183–184
  Greece, classical, 186
  India, 182–183, 185, 188–189
  Islamic civilization, 189
  Mesopotamia and Egypt, 182
  Rome, 186–188
  voting rights for, 283
  work of
    characteristics of, 129
    secondary product revolution and, 129
Wool, 134
  as secondary product, 129
Wordsworth, William, 261
Work
  factory system and, 249
  Uruk, list of standard professions, 133
  of women and secondary product
    revolution, 129
World Bank, 271
World Future Council, 300
World Meteorological Organization
    (WMO), 293
World-systems, 174–175
World-systems theory, 175
World War I, 269–270
World War II, 270–271
World Watch, 290
World Wide Web, 300
World Wildlife Fund, 300
World zones
  absence of contact between, 194
  defined, 143
  timing of agricultural revolution, 105, 112
Wrangham, Richard, 87
Writing
  Aztecs, 201
  Collective Learning and invention of, 135
  cuneiform, 134
  as defining feature of agrarian
    civilization, 154

earliest writing in Uruk, 134–135
  in Egypt, 138
  hieroglyphics, 138
  from Indus valley, 139
  Maya, 196
  oracle bones, 142
  paper, 219
  pictographs, 135, 138, 142
  printing, 219
  Shang Dynasty, 142
  world in 1000 CE, 219
Wudi, Emperor, 167, 178, 185, 221
Wu Ding, 142
Wusun, 177
Wu Zetian, Empress, 188

X

Xenon, 26
Xerxes, 161
Xia Dynasty, 141, 183
Xia-Xia, 224
Xiongnu, 177
Xuande, Emperor, 232

Y

Yangshao culture, 115
Yangtze River valley, 143
Yanomami, 111–112, 113
Yin, 142
Yin and yang, 185
Yongle, Emperor, 229, 232
Younger Dryas, 94, 107, 111, 130
Yucatan Peninsula, 195–198
Yuezhi, 177

Z

Zhang Qian, 178
Zheng He, 229–232
Zhou Dynasty, 141, 142, 160, 166
  social and gender relations, 185
Ziggurat of Ur, 132
Zimbabwe, 296
Zoroaster, 166